# STRATEGIC MANAGEMENT IN THE ASIAN CONTEXT

A Casebook in Business Policy and Strategy

# STRATEGIC MANAGEMENT IN THE ASIAN CONTEXT

A Casebook in Business Policy and Strategy

**Luis Ma. R. Calingo**
*California State University, Fresno*
*Formerly of Nanyang Technological University, Singapore*

JOHN WILEY & SONS
Singapore, New York, Chichester, Brisbane, Toronto

*Other Wiley Editorial Offices*

John Wiley & Sons, Inc. 605 Third Avenue,
New York, NY 10158-0012, USA

Jacaranda Wiley Ltd, G.P.O.Box 859, Brisbane,
Queensland 401, Australia

John Wiley & Sons (Canada) Ltd, 22 Worcester Road
Rexdale, Ontario M9W1L1, Canada

John Wiley & Sons Ltd, Baffins Lane, Chichester,
West Sussex PO19 1UD, England

***Cataloging-in-Publication Data:***

Calingo, Luis Ma. R.,
Strategic Management in The Asian Context:
A Casebook in Business Policy and Strategy /
p. cm.
Includes Biliographical Reference
ISBN: 0-471-19003-9
1. Strategic Planning — Asia — Case Studies
2. Management — Asia — Case Studies
3. Strategic Planning — Pacific Area — Case Studies
4. Management — Pacific Area — Case Studies I. Title
HD30. 28. C345 1996
658. 4'12'095 — dc 20 95-52959
CIP

Printed in the Republic of Singapore

10 9 8 7 6 5 4 3 2 1

*Dedication*

*To Gem, Ashley, Alexa, and Arienne —*
*For their love and support throughout these years.*

# Preface

"Because wisdom can't be told."
— *Charles I Gragg*

The case method is one of the most effective means of management education. It is widely used in business schools throughout the world, and its use is based upon the belief that tackling real business problems is the best way to develop practicing managers. Real problems are often complex and messy, yet very interesting. The case method requires the student to be an active participant in a situation closely resembling the real thing. It is a way of gaining a great deal of experience in a short amount of time. It is also a way to learn about how certain businesses operate and how managers manage.

Given the managerial orientation of strategic management as a discipline, the case method has been the cornerstone of strategic management pedagogy since the field's inception. Although there is a proliferation of strategic management teaching materials in the United States and the United Kingdom, there is a dearth of cases specifically dealing with Asia-Pacific companies. While it may be cogently argued that the analytical tools and techniques of strategic management are transferable across cultures, case materials do not enjoy the same transferability. Under these conditions, it would be pedagogically inappropriate to use the time-tested cases from classic strategic management casebooks published in the United States or the United Kingdom. This situation is, indeed, unfortunate, given the increasing importance of the Asia-Pacific Region as a center of world commerce.

*Strategic Management in the Asian Context: A Casebook in Business Policy and Strategy* is the product of many years of efforts aimed at developing a variety of strategic situations that are meaningful to Asian business students. This preface seeks to acquaint both the student and the professor with the objectives, special features, cases, and instructional aids associated with this book.

## Objectives

This casebook deals with the management of the organization as a total enterprise and, in particular, the fundamental strategic issues that provide the framework and direction for the overall operation of the firm. It is structured on the generally recognized objectives of the strategic management course. The strategic management course, also referred to as "Business Policy," "General Management" or "Corporate Planning and Strategy," is usually designed to provide the student with a capstone opportunity to integrate into a unified body of knowledge the concepts, principles, skills, tools, and techniques learned separately in other, more specialized business courses.

The strategic management course develops in the student a general management point of view which forces the student to explicitly think about the business enterprise as a complex system in a total environment. The general management point of view is useful not only to general managers, chief executive officers or managing directors, but also to any business professional who needs to sharpen his awareness and understanding of his individual contribution to the total enterprise.

A second objective is to acquaint the student with the concepts of strategy — its content, formulation, and implementation — and the translation of these concepts into practice. The formal study of strategic management enables the student to see how an organization can become a master, rather than a captive, of the unique circumstances it faces — deliberately pursuing objectives and formulating strategies, rather than being shaped by luck and external forces.

## Special Features

*Strategic Management in the Asian Context* is intended primarily for use in strategic management courses for advanced undergraduate students and final-year MBA students. It is designed for the professor who demands an extraordinarily high degree of flexibility in the teaching of strategic management. In contrast to currently available textbooks that commit the students and the professor to a single framework of strategic management, this casebook allows the professor the opportunity to specify a course pedagogy that best reflects the specific needs and capabilities of both the students and the professor.

This casebook may be used in conjunction with a variety of pedagogical approaches, such as computer simulations and experiential exercises. It may also be used in combination with any conceptual material of the professor's choice: a traditional textbook, a compendium of journal articles related to strategic management, a collection of readings on real-life organizations such as those that appear in each issue of *Asian Business*, or the professor's own lecture notes and case studies. The book contains some conceptual material for those who desire to be guided by the author's own perspectives on strategic management case analysis. If greater conceptual depth is warranted, this book may be used with the paperback text *Developing Business Strategies*, Third Edition (1992) by David Aaker or with other texts or books of readings at either the undergraduate or graduate level. Clearly, there are other approaches to analyzing a case, and the professor should use any method with which he or she feels most comfortable.

The following are some of the special features of this book:

1. The book contains 27 comprehensive cases on actual organizations in the Asia-Pacific region. Contributed by scholars mainly from the Asia-Pacific region, these cases were selected on the basis of the following criteria: (a) breadth and depth of financial data presented, (b) scope of issues raised, (c) variety of industries and countries represented, (d) clarity and conciseness of writing, and (e) variety of well-known companies represented.
2. Most of the cases are current. Only one case was written before 1985 — The Jim Thompson Thai Silk Company, Ltd case. This case is accompanied by a sample student case analysis, which presents just one way of analyzing the case.
3. The 27 cases presented in this book are followed by an appendix chapter that explains the case method, suggests an approach to case analysis and presentation, reviews financial analysis techniques for strategic management case analysis, summarizes pertinent economic and news information, and presents tips for conducting strategic management research using the Internet.

## The Cases

*Strategic Management in the Asian Context* contains 27 current, comprehensive cases of actual Asia-Pacific business organizations and industries undergoing strategic change. Students will recognize many of the names of the companies, although some of these companies may be new to them. Five cases are time-tested cases which have already been published in either management textbooks or Asia-Pacific business publications. The other 22 cases are completely new. This provides a balance of some of the most popular Asia-Pacific cases already published and the most current cases available today.

The organizations described in these cases vary in size from the small, local Noel Gifts International Ltd (Case 4) to the large First Philippine Holdings Corporation (Case 3). Some of them, such as La Tondeña Distillers Inc (Case 21), are units of even larger conglomerates, like San Miguel's Expansion into Southeast Asia (Case 1). Others, like Purba-Paschim Trading Company (Case 25) and DCM-Toyota Ltd (India) (Case 26), are examples of companies that have actively pursued international market development strategies. A few, however, are like Gateway Technology Singapore (Case 14) and P T Sepatu Bata (A) (Case 23), which must face the unique challenges of localization in their host countries. Panyu Security Gate Company (Guangdong, China) (Case 15), Nan Feng Household Appliance Company (Case 16), and SIFCO Industries, Inc (China) (Case 24) are examples of cases highlighting business activities in the People's Republic of China, the fastest-growing economy in Asia.

Complete notes on The Asia-Pacific Airline Industry (Case 5) provide background information for the Singapore Airlines: Comparative Case Studies of the British and Singaporean National Airlines (Case 6), and Malaysia Airlines and Its Media Image in the Visit Malaysia Year (Case 7). The Shangri-La Hotel Ltd (Case 9) case may be used as a basis for strategic comparison with The Deluxe Hotels in the Philippines in 1989 (Case 8). The Johan Cement Bhd and Utara Cement Sdn Bhd (Case 10) case highlights the strategic issues facing competitors in a vital industry of a tiger economy.

The cases in this book cover a wide range of process-related issues that are of concern to general managers. Rayalaseema Biscuits Company, Kurnool (Case 17) presents the typical problems experienced by organizations on the transition from the entrepreneurial stage to professional management. Ben Santos (Case 19) and Corporate Planning at Metro, Inc (Case 20) deal with the introduction of organized strategic planning processes. The British Banking Corporation (Case 22) case presents the outputs of an organized strategic planning process.

Each case documents the real problems faced by a real organization. These cases enable the student to narrow the gap between the "ivory tower" theories of academia and actual business practices in the real world. The high quality of these cases is proven by the fact that they have been tested in many different situations, ranging from groups of young students without any firsthand business experience to groups composed solely of seasoned corporate executives. The casewriters' collective experience has been that these very different groups of students were able to learn from these cases effectively.

The 27 cases in this book demand a familiarity with, a working knowledge of, and competence in the application of concepts, tools, and techniques, and points of view of the various functional areas of an enterprise: production, marketing, finance, human resources, procurement, and technology. These cases also require a basic understanding of accounting, economics, organizational behavior, and quantitative methods. In analyzing these cases, the student is not likely to learn more about any of the basic functional areas of business. However, working with these cases will enable him or her to learn more about the relationships among the various functional areas and their reference disciplines.

## The Use of Disguised Cases

To the fullest extent possible, the real names of individuals, organizations and places portrayed in the cases are used in this casebook. However, there are many reasons why this was not always possible. Sometimes, the people in the organization who have cooperated in writing the case perceive some issues to be private and certain comments they made to be unflattering. Often, the organization's management is sensitive to having the names of organizations and employees in print. In these situations, the casewriter used a light disguise wherein all the remaining data in the case are real. In other instances, organizations are sensitive to disclosing financial data in a case and want such data disguised. In these cases, the casewriter applied a factor to the data, although maintaining important relationships in the data. The organizations described in these cases have cooperated with the casewriters so that students may benefit from their experience; therefore, the casewriters have honored all requests for disguise.

Each case will have an indication as to whether or not it has been disguised. Although students may prefer that all cases are presented in undisguised form, the fact that they are disguised should not be a critical issue. The main point is that notwithstanding the disguise, the student is able to identify the issues and analyze the problems in the cases.

## Learning Aids

**Appendices.** The appendices at the end of the book are designed to increase the student's ability to analyze strategic situations. Appendix A introduces the student to the case method in strategic management and provides extensive guidance on how to prepare a written case analysis and an oral case presentation. Appendix B translates the conceptual material into a Strategic Management Audit which the student can use in analyzing the cases in this book. Appendix C reviews the financial analysis techniques which are useful in analyzing strategic management cases. Appendix D contains Asia-Pacific economic data and news highlights from 1985 to 1995, the period covered by the cases. Appendix E presents tips for conducting strategic management research using the Internet.

**Instructor's manual.** A comprehensive Instructor's Manual has been carefully developed to accompany this book. The Instructor's Manual features teaching notes for each of the 27 cases. A standardized format is provided for each case note:

(a) suggestions for using the case,
(b) case objectives,
(c) case assignment questions,
(d) case description/overview, and
(e) case analysis.

Most of the teaching notes contain one or more of the following supplemental information:

(a) suggestions for readings that can be used with the case,
(b) copies of student papers prepared on the case,
(c) comments on the case by third party observers,
(d) outcome information describing what actually occurred after the case was written, and
(e) follow-up versions of the case that can be duplicated for use in class.

I feel confident that this consistent format will greatly facilitate the instructor's critical task of preparing for each case and leading the discussions.

The Instructor's Manual also includes the following supplemental teaching aids:

(a) a list of texts and other materials (e.g., periodicals, games, films) that can be used with this book,
(b) suggestions regarding the sequencing of cases contained in the book, including a list of cases that can be used for written reports and examinations,
(c) sample course outlines using cases in the book.

# Acknowledgments

Many persons contributed to this book. First and foremost is the intellectual debt I owe to several researchers, practicing managers, and writers who have contributed to the advancement of strategic management as an academic discipline.

I am particularly indebted to the following talented case researchers who generously contributed cases to this book:

Lindsay Alley, Chemical Bank
Bienvenido M Aragon, University of the Philippines
Achara Chandrachai, Chulalongkorn University
Chang Young-Chul, National University of Singapore
Chen Zhen Xiong, Zhongshang University, China
Donald J Lecraw, University of Western Ontario
Reuben T Mondejar, City University of Hong Kong
S Raghunath, Lal Bahadur Shastri Academy of Administration, India
Alan G Robinson, University of Massachusetts at Amherst
Rafael A Rodriguez, University of the Philippines
Dean Schroeder, Valparaiso University
Sharifah Mariam Syed Mansour, Malaysian Institute of Management
Madhav S Shriram, DCM Shriram Industries, Inc.
Hafiz G A Siddiqi, North South University, Bangladesh
Douglas Sikorski, National University of Singapore

Siti Maimon Kamso Wan Rafaei, Universiti Malaysia Sabah
Thomas Stanley, Guardian Industries
Uthai Tanlamai, Chulalongkorn University
Liming Zhao, University of Alabama

Thanks go to my past students who tried out some of the cases originally written for this book and provided insightful comments and suggestions that have greatly improved their pedagogical value. I would also like to thank the managers of the organizations examined in the cases for providing the time, assistance and information, often at the risk of embarrassment, in the service of others' learning.

Because I have been affiliated with three academic institutions while I was writing this book, I have three groups of colleagues to thank. I am grateful to President John D Welty and Provost Alexander Gonzalez, both of California State University, Fresno, who gave me in 1993 the opportunity to take a long-term leave of absence for professional development, thereby making this work, among others, possible. The dynamic growth and stimulating environment at the Nanyang Business School in Singapore, under the leadership of Dean Tan Teck Meng, has also contributed greatly to the development of this book. The University of the Philippines has graciously provided me over the years a second home for the writing of Philippine cases, and I very much appreciate having Dean Rafael A Rodriguez as an enabler and a friend.

I am indebted to Professor Stanley Gordon Redding, at the University of Hong Kong, for his review which resulted in valuable contributions to improving the content of this book. I am also indebted to Bradford Wiley, Stephen Smith, Henry Leung, and Selvi Kannan, all of John Wiley & Sons, for guiding my efforts during the various stages of the evolution of this book from concept to a completed manuscript. Special thanks are due to my copy editor, Edith R Borbon, for the special interest she took in this project.

I am especially indebted to my wife Gem and our daughters Ashley, Alexa, and Arienne, to whom this book is dedicated. I simply could not have done this work without their patience, faithful support, and love.

As you use this book, your comments and recommendations for improving the book will be most welcome, as well as your calling my attention to specific errors. Please write to me at The Sid Craig School of Business, California State University at Fresno, 5245 North Backer Avenue, Fresno, California 93740-0007, USA.

**Luis Ma. R. Calingo**
Singapore, June 1996

# About the Author

**Luis Ma. R. Calingo, PhD**, has been Professor of Business Policy and Strategy at California State University, Fresno (CSUF), USA, since 1983. He received his BS in Industrial Engineering and Master of Urban and Regional Planning from the University of the Philippines, as well as his MBA and PhD in Business Administration from the University of Pittsburgh.

At CSUF, Professor Calingo held various administrative positions culminating in an appointment as the Dean of the Sid Craig School of Business. He received the California State University's Meritorious Performance and Professional Promise Awards in 1985, 1987, and 1989 for excellence in teaching, research, and service. He has published journal articles and delivered numerous conference presentations in Asia, North America, and Europe. He has also reviewed manuscripts for the Academy of Management, the Decision Sciences Institute, and the International Trade and Finance Association, as well as served on the Editorial Boards of the *Journal of Managerial Issues* and the *Asia Pacific Journal of Quality Management*.

Professor Calingo held visiting appointments at the College of Business Administration, University of the Philippines as a Fellow of the United Nations Development Programme. He was also Senior Lecturer at the Nanyang Technological University in Singapore and a Visiting Scholar at the Universiti Kebangsaan Malaysia.

# Contents

# PART ONE

## Strategic Management

# Understanding Strategic Management

"Cheshire Puss," Alice began, "Would you please tell me which way I ought to go from here?"
"That depends on where you want to get to," said the cat.
— *Lewis Carroll*

## The Need for a Strategic Management Course

In 1959, a Ford Foundation-sponsored comprehensive study of American business education, conducted by Professors Robert Aaron Gordon and James E Howell, cogently argued for the need to have an integrating course in every business curriculum:

> The capstone of the core curriculum should be a course in "business policy," which will give the students an opportunity to pull together what they have learned in the separate business fields and utilize this knowledge in the analysis of complex business problems.
>
> The business policy course can offer the student something he will find nowhere else in the curriculum: consideration of business problems which are not prejudged as being marketing problems, finance problems, etc; emphasis on the development of skill in identifying, analyzing, and solving problems in a situation which is as close as the classroom can ever be to the real business world; opportunity to consider problems which draw on a wide range of substantive areas in business; opportunity to consider the external, non-market implications of problems at the same time that internal decisions must be made; and situations which enable the student to exercise qualities of judgment and of mind which were not explicitly called for in any prior course. Questions of social responsibility and of personal attitudes can be brought in as a regular aspect of this kind of problem-solving practice.[1]

[1] Robert Aaron Gordon and James Edwin Howell, *Higher Education for Business* (New York: Columbia University Press, 1959): 206–207.

Another major study of business education, sponsored by the Carnegie Foundation and conducted by Professor Frank C Pierson, supported the adoption of a course in every business curriculum which emphasizes "the role of management in coordinating internal operations and in adapting to change in the external environment" and which "serves as a focus for the student's entire studies."[2] In this study, Professor George Leland Bach, then Dean of the Graduate School of Industrial Administration at Carnegie-Mellon University, stressed the need for a course which provided "a more advanced, integrating approach to a wide variety of business policy and administrative problems, mainly at the upper management level. Stress would be on integrated use of *both* the analytical tools from the three major foundation areas *and* knowledge from the various functional fields of business, in making company-wide policy decisions and getting these decisions carried out effectively."[3]

Since the publication of the two studies, capstone courses in business policy have increasingly been offered in educational programs — at the undergraduate level, at the graduate level, and in executive development programs for practicing managers. This has now reached a point where business students are required to study "Business Policy," "Strategic Management," or a similarly entitled integrative course at the end of their business curriculum. This capstone course is now usually required in most business degree programs throughout the world.

## The Need for a Conceptual Framework

Initially, Business Policy was thought of as a capstone course, not as a field of study or an academic discipline with a substance of its own. The intent was to accomplish the integration of finance, marketing, production, and other business functional areas by simply considering these diverse topics simultaneously. The landmark study by Professors Gordon and Howell perpetuated this view by stating:

> Without the responsibility of having to transmit some specific body of knowledge, the business policy course can concentrate on integrating what already has been acquired and on developing further the student's skill in using that knowledge. The course can range over the entire curriculum and beyond.[4]

Over time, Business Policy has evolved into a legitimate academic discipline — Strategic Management — with a body of knowledge of its own. This is evident in the number of professional associations (e.g., Strategic Management Society), scholarly journals (e.g., *Strategic Management Review*), and trade publications (e.g., *Journal of Business Strategy* and *Planning Review*) devoted to business policy/strategic management.

The thrusts of the theoretical developments in strategic management have been the *content* of effective organizational strategies and the *process* of formulating and implementing organizational strategies. What emerges is a definition of the multiple, simultaneous roles played by the general manager: architect of organizational purpose (articulating strategy), chief strategist (formulating strategy), and organization builder and leader

---

[2] Frank C Pierson, *The Education of American Businessmen* (New York: McGraw-Hill, 1959): 257.
[3] Frank C Pierson, *The Education of American Businessmen* (New York: McGraw-Hill, 1959): 333.
[4] Robert Aaron Gordon and James Edwin Howell, *Higher Education for Business* (New York: Columbia University Press, 1959): 207.

(implementing strategy). Although these general management roles are integrally related and cannot be separated, they will be discussed individually for pedagogical reasons.

Flowing from a synthesis of the strategic management literature, the remainder of this essay attempts to present the author's perspectives on the concept of organizational strategy, the process of formulating strategies, and the process of implementing strategies. You may wish to be guided by these perspectives in analyzing the various cases in this book.

## The Concept of Organizational Strategy

The word *strategy* has its roots in military science and literally means "the act of the general," having been derived from the Greek word *strategos*, "a general leading an army." Indeed, the Greek verb *stratego* means to "plan the destruction of one's enemies through effective use of resources."[5] The military use of the strategy concept has remained prominent throughout history and has been discussed by such writers as Sun Zi (*The Art of War*), Miyamoto Musashi (*The Book of Five Rings*), and Kautilya (*Arthasastra*). As used in business contexts, the meaning of strategy includes the character and purpose of the organization as a total enterprise. Professor Kenneth R Andrews' seminal book on corporate strategy contains the following definition:

> Corporate strategy is the pattern of decisions in a company that determines and reveals its objectives, purposes, or goals; produces the principal policies and plans for achieving those goals, and defines the range of business the company is to pursue; the kind of economic and human organization it is or intends to be; and the nature of the economic and noneconomic contribution it intends to make to its shareholders, employees, customers, and communities.[6]

It therefore follows that every organization, whether it performs formal strategic planning or not, has a strategy. The strategy can be determined from the plans or statements of top management. Given that strategies may have gradually evolved over time, strategies can also be deduced from the organization's actual actions and behaviors in the marketplace.

To illustrate the complex nature of strategies, a student examining a Business Policy case on the Matsushita Electric Industrial Company deduced the following summary statement of Matsushita's strategy at a time when Matsushita was pondering how it would position itself to maintain its Japanese dominance and compete in emerging growth areas:

> Matsushita Electric Industrial Company produces and distributes a wide variety of electric and electronic products, primarily communication and industrial equipment, video equipment, and home appliances, in both Japan and 32 other countries. Aiming to be a low-cost, integrated manufacturer, it purchases about 80 percent of all components from subsidiaries. Its focus on research and development, rather than product leadership, is to analyze competing products and, through investments in production engineering, figure out how to do the job better. It aims to finance its growth through the use of debt, participation in the world's stock markets, and its "Venture Capital Fund" administered from the company's 60 percent of profits. In the pursuit of its 250-Year

---

[5] Jeffrey Bracker, "The Historical Development of the Strategic Management Concept," *Academy of Management Review* 5 (April 1980): 219–224.

[6] Kenneth R Andrews, *The Concept of Corporate Strategy*, 3rd ed. (Homewood, Ill.: Richard D Irwin, 1987): 13.

> Plan to eliminate poverty, its stated mission is to contribute to the well-being of mankind by providing reasonably priced products and services in sufficient quantities to achieve peace, happiness, and prosperity for all.[7]

Although it may be argued that this summary statement was not clearly set in the mind of Konosuke Matsushita, it is consistent with Japan's pattern of past strategic decisions — at least as reported in the case. Although in many ways incomplete (no mention is made of specific organizational goals and objectives), this statement does give rise to the question of whether Matsushita can sustain its "fast second" technological strategy at a time when product life cycles are growing even shorter.

In operational terms, the strategy of an organization consists of three major components: how the organization defines its business, how the organization defines its competitive posture, and how the organization defines its concept of itself.[8]

### Concept of Business

The organization faces some fundamental choices in terms of how it will define its business. Professor Derek Abell proposed that these choices can be categorized into four dimensions of a business definition: customer functions, customer segments, degree of vertical integration, and technology.[9]

What *customer functions* does the organization provide? These strategic choices deal with the breadth of the organization's product/service offerings, the way its product or service is positioned, and whether the product/service definition is narrow or broad (representing a generic customer need). What *customer segments* does the organization serve? Who are the target market segments and how is the market segmented? What is the organization's *degree of vertical integration*? In which stages of the value-added chain — the sequence of stages from raw materials to finished products — does the company operate? With what *technology* does the company perform its customer functions? Considering that several different technologies may serve the same function or satisfy the same customer needs, the technology-strategic choices involve decisions on the particular combination of technologies in which the company will participate and the technological posture the organization will adopt (e.g., "first to market," "second to market," cost minimization, or market segmentation).[10]

### Concept of Competition

How the organization defines its competitive posture — its competitive strategy — hinges on the question of how the company competes within the boundaries of its business definition. A fundamental strategic choice involves the *weapons* (e.g., differentiation, cost leadership, focus) which the organization employs to secure a sustainable competitive advan-

---

[7] James Brian Quinn, "Matsushita Electric Industrial Company 1994," in Henry Mintzberg and James Brian Quinn, *The Strategy Process: Concepts, Contexts, Cases*, 3rd ed. (Upper Saddle River, NJ: Prentice-Hall, 1996): 457–468.

[8] Hugo E R Uyterhoeven, Robert W Ackerman and John W Rosenblum, *Strategy and Organization: Text and cases in General Management*, rev ed. (Homewood, Ill.: Richard D Irwin, 1977: 13.

[9] Derek F Abell, *Defining the Business: The Starting Point of Strategic Planning* (Englewood Cliffs, NJ: Prentice-Hall, 1980).

[10] Modesto A Maidique and Peter Patch, *Corporate Strategy and Technology Policy*, Case No. 0-679-033 (Harvard Business School, 1978, revised 1980).

tage in the marketplace.[11] A related issue is the organization's *intended competitive position* in terms of market share, general image and other key success factors in the industry (e.g., industry leader, challenger, follower, or nicher).

### Company Self-concept

How the organization defines its self-concept is often relegated to statements of company mission or corporate creed. However, the fundamental choices in this area often shape how the organization defines its business and its competitive posture. To begin with, what are the company's *performance goals and objectives*? What are the stated and unstated goals of the organization? What incentive and reward systems are in place? In what areas has the company starred or succeeded as a competitor? In most instances, the organization's business definition, competitive posture, and performance goals are a reflection of the prevailing *corporate mentality and culture*. The organization's philosophy, top management style, risk-taking behavior, and orientation toward its public are just a few of those other internal factors that may influence strategic choices.

### Formulating Organizational Strategy

The process of formulating organizational strategy involves several steps. While most general managers would probably concede that the strategy formulation process could be carried out only by an examination of both the external environment and the organization, there have lately been conflicting views on the sequence in which these external and internal analyses are carried out. The current model subscribes to the market-structure view of competitive advantage, which emphasizes market-attractiveness analysis as the starting point.[12] The model depicted in Figure 1 is an eclectic representation of the foremost thought in the market-structure view of the strategy formulation literature.

### Profile of Current Strategy

In formulating organizational strategy, it is often useful to begin with a thorough understanding of the organization's *current strategy*. This task involves determining how the organization has defined its business, its competitive posture, and its self-concept. Given that the organization may have made its strategy explicit or deductible from actual behaviors, this task is a feasible exercise both for the organization and for its competitors.

### Environmental Analysis

The organization operates in an environment that is replete with *opportunities* which must be exploited, as well as *threats* which must be overcome, by strategic action. An opportunity is an environmental trend or event that could result in a significant upward change in sales and profit patterns, given the appropriate strategic response. A threat is a trend or event that will result, in the absence of a strategic response, in a significant downward departure

[11]Michael E Porter, *Competitive Strategy: Techniques for Analyzing Industries and Competitors* (New York: The Free Press, 1980): 34–46.

[12]For a discussion of the alternative resource-based view, see *Competence-Based Competition*, eds Gary Hamel and Aimé Heene (Chichester, England: John Wiley & Sons, 1994).

FIGURE 1

**MODEL OF THE STRATEGIC MANAGEMENT PROCESS**

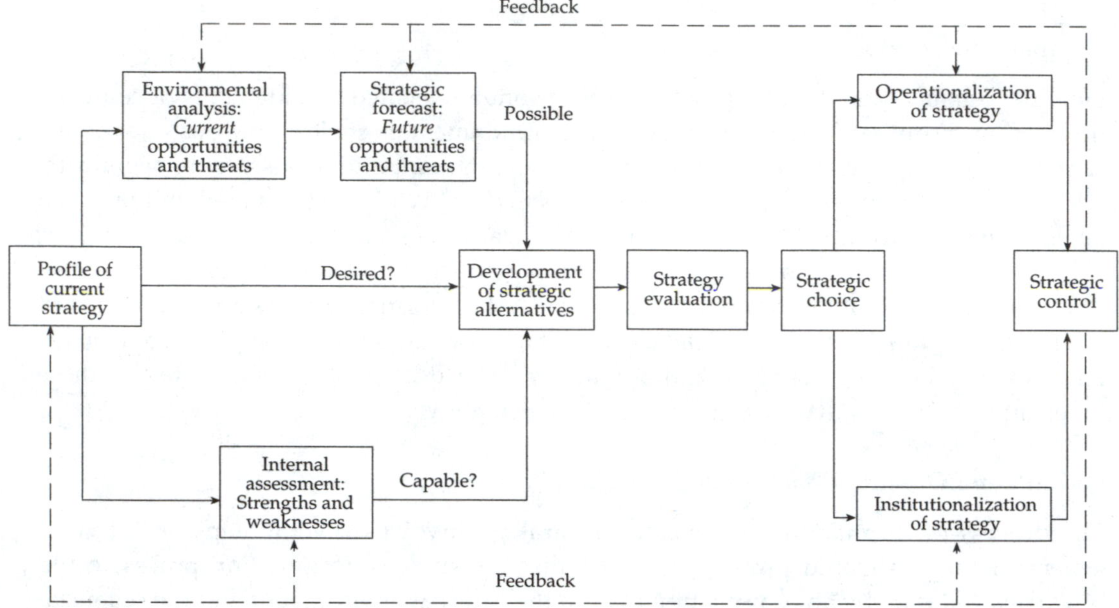


from current sales and profit patterns. It is, therefore, important to systematically identify the environmental opportunities and threats which the organization faces.

Normally, analysis of the environment will focus on social, economic, political, and technological factors of the macroenvironment, as well as the competitive factors in the task environment. Although there are competing explanations of the phenomenal success of the East Asian newly industrializing economies (NIEs), these NIEs share common characteristics. These are more rapid output and productivity growth in agriculture; higher rates of growth of manufactured exports; earlier and steeper declines in fertility; higher growth rates of physical capital, supported by higher rates of domestic savings; higher initial levels and growth rates of human capital; and generally higher rates of productivity growth.[13] Asian business firms would expectedly view any changes in these macroenvironmental characteristics with great interest as these changes would ultimately give rise to business opportunities and threats.

### Strategic Forecast

In the previous task of identifying environmental factors, the general manager has described *current* conditions. However, it is necessary to predict future environmental conditions because of the long-term nature of an organization's strategy. The general manager must determine what is going to happen to the changes and trends identified in

[13]World Bank, *The East Asian Economic Miracle: Economic Growth and Public Policy* (New York: Oxford University Press, 1993): 27.

the environmental analysis in order to determine *future* threats and opportunities. It is necessary for the general manager to *predict*, not simply project; the past cannot often be relied on as the sole predictor of the future! It will be necessary to determine, for example, whether a change occurring in the industry or the macroenvironment is simply a "random fluctuation," a "cyclical decline," or a "major structural change."

Nowhere is this uncertainty more pronounced than in the East Asian NIEs, which were the economic success stories of the 1970s and 1980s. They now face a more hostile global competitive environment as their competitiveness in labor-intensive and traded-goods manufacturing industries is being undermined by China, Indonesia, Malaysia, the Philippines, and Thailand. With the emergence of new competitors, the rise of trading blocs, and the shrinkage of export surpluses, questions are currently being raised as to whether the NIEs will be able to sustain past rates of growth as they approach the 21st century.[14] Because these new realities create problems that fall beyond the inherent limits of econometric forecasting models, the use of judgmental forecasting models such as the Delphi method and multiple scenario analysis is expected to rise in popularity among business strategists in the Asia-Pacific region.[15]

### Internal Assessment

The fourth step of the strategy formulation process involves an internal assessment. Before the organization can respond to the opportunities and threats in its environment, the general manager must take inventory of the organization's resources, capabilities, and internal constraints. The internal assessment seeks to address this need by identifying the organization's *strengths and weaknesses* and comparing them against the competition. More importantly, the general manager needs to determine the organization's *competitive advantages* from among its strengths and *key vulnerabilities* from among its weaknesses.

The focus of the analysis is identifying strengths and weaknesses in different internal dimensions: operational, financial, and managerial. Diagnosing strengths and weaknesses requires disaggregating the organization into its component activities. The "value chain" concept (see Figure 2) developed by Professor Michael E Porter is a viable framework for disaggregating the organization's activities in a strategically significant way.[16]

### Development of Strategic Alternatives

The fifth step builds upon the strategic forecast and the internal assessment. After developing a sense of the opportunities and threats in the environment and the organization's strengths and weaknesses, the general manager must identify what strategic options are available to the organization. The identification of viable strategic alternatives, using all pertinent information from the previous external and internal analyses, is the creative (i.e., nonprogrammable) step in strategy formulation.

---

[14]Gordon L Clark, "The End of an Era: Asian NIEs in the Global Economy," *Growth & Change* 25 (Fall 1994): 487–508.

[15]Kau Ah Keng, Yeong Wee Yong, and Daleen Richmond, *A Delphi Study of Future Lifestyles and Consumption Patterns in Singapore* (Singapore: National University of Singapore, Centre for Business Research & Development, 1993); Nicholas C Georgantzas and William Acar, *Scenario-Driven Planning: Learning to Manage Strategic Uncertainty* (Westport, CT: Quorum Books, 1995).

[16]Michael E Porter, *Competitive Advantage: Creating and Sustaining Superior Performance* (New York: Free Press, 1985): 33–61.

FIGURE 2

**THE GENERIC VALUE CHAIN**

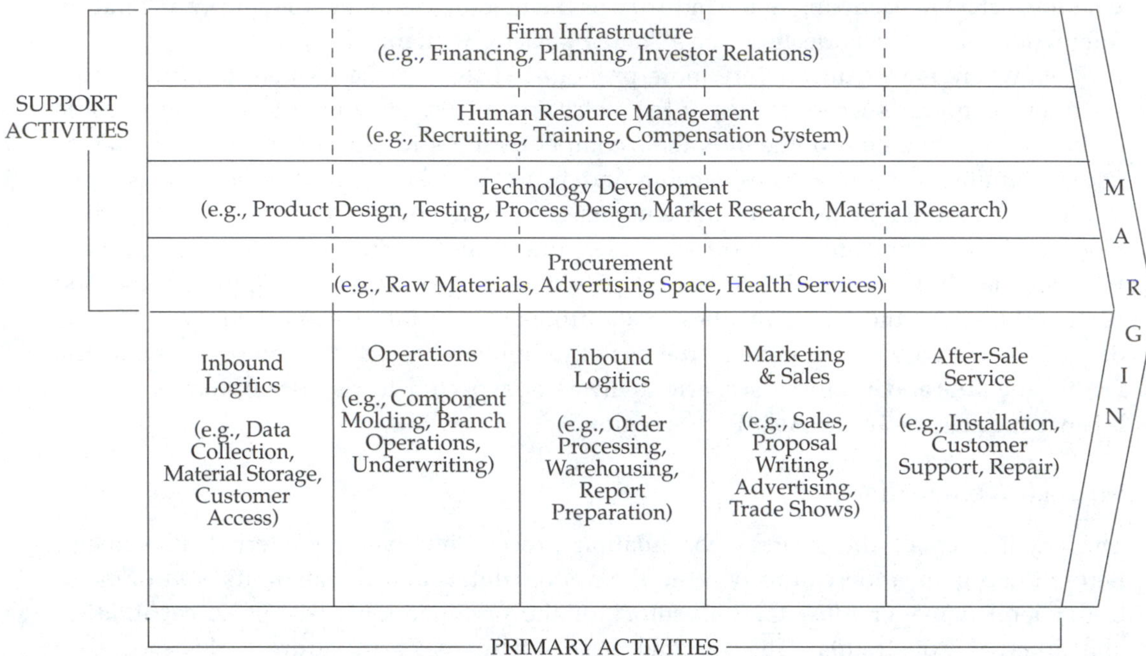


Source: Michael E Porter, "Global Strategy: Winning in the World-Wide Marketplace," in The Portable MBA in Strategy, eds Liam Fahey and Robert M Randall (New York: John Wiley & Sons, 1994): 111. Copyright © 1994 by John Wiley & Sons, Inc.

In general, a viable strategy is one where the organization is able to *exploit environmental opportunities* and/or *ward off the threats* it faces by *employing its strengths* and *overcoming its weaknesses* in order to *achieve its performance goals and objectives*. Further, a good set of strategic options include strategic alternatives that are both mutually exclusive and collectively exhaustive.

The Threats-Opportunities-Weaknesses-Strengths (TOWS) Matrix is one of many strategy matching tools which can aid the general manager in developing strategic alternatives.[17] Figure 3 illustrates how the TOWS Matrix may be applied to generate strategic alternatives for NIKE, Inc, a leader in the world athletic-leisure apparel industry with an extensive presence in Asia. Alternatively, the general manager can benefit from an understanding of generic strategy options that can then be tailored to fit the situation.[18] Whichever approach the general manager takes in developing strategic alternatives, he or she relates what the organization is *able* to do with respect to its resources to what is *possible* in its external environment.

[17]Heinz Weihrich, "The Tows Matrix — A Tool for Situational Analysis," *Long Range Planning* 15 (April 1982): 54–66.
[18]Henry Mintzberg, "Generic Strategies: Toward a Comprehensive Framework," in *Advances in Strategic Management*, ed Robert Lamb and Paul Shrivastava, vol 5 (Greenwich, Conn.: JAI Press, 1988): 1–67.

FIGURE 3

**APPLICATION OF THE TOWS MATRIX TO NIKE, INC**

| INTERNAL FACTORS<br><br>EXTERNAL FACTORS | **STRENGTHS** | **WEAKNESSES** |
|---|---|---|
| | 1. Brand loyalty<br>2. Marketing prowess: effective advertising and promotion<br>3. Technological leadership in product development<br>4. Low-cost, high-quality manufacturing ("hollow corporation")<br>5. Profitable; above-average profit margins<br>6. Strategic funds of $124 million available<br>7. Phil Knight's future-oriented, entrepreneurial leadership style gets things done quickly | 1. Limited borrowing capacity due to above-average leverage<br>2. Financially unable to achieve 30% annual growth objective<br>3. Loose management style contributes to inadequate communication and is inappropriate to a large company.<br>4. Inadequate controls due to lack of formal management systems<br>5. Product line too diverse |
| **OPPORTUNITIES**<br>1. Increase in U.S. market demand due to favorable social trends (e.g., fitness) and events (e.g., 1984 Olympics)<br>2. Introduce lower-priced product line<br>3. Introduce new products for the more affluent, status- and fashion-conscious customer<br>4. Introduce new, specialized products (e.g., footwear for soccer and other sports) or new uses<br>5. Growth in overseas markets | **S.O. STRATEGIC OPTIONS**<br>*How can NIKE utilize its strengths to exploit the opportunities it faces?*<br>1. More extensive R & D to further development of new product lines, such as footwear for specialized groups ($S_1S_3O_3O_4$)<br>2. Pursue market development to target senior citizens, women and international markets ($S_2S_6O_1O_5$) | **W.O. STRATEGIC OPTIONS**<br>*How can NIKE overcome its weaknesses in order to exploit its opportunities?*<br>1. Prune product line and concentrate on more profitable offerings ($W_2W_5O_3O_4$)<br>2. Reorganize management structure to enable more centralized direction ($W_3O_3O_4O_5$) |
| **THREATS**<br>1. Increase in U.S. competition due to maturing market<br>2. Potential rise in price competition due to increased customers' price-sensitivity<br>3. Potential growth of generics and private labels due to customers' price-sensitivity<br>4. Societal trends from sporty wear to fashion wear<br>5. Entry of new competitors | **S.T. STRATEGIC OPTIONS**<br>*How can NIKE utilize its strengths to ward off the threats it faces?*<br>1. Continue innovativeness in R & D to reduce cycle time for new product development ($S_3T_1T_4T_5$)<br>2. Institute a competitive pricing policy ($S_4T_2T_3$) | **W.T. STRATEGIC OPTIONS**<br>*How can NIKE overcome its weaknesses in order to ward off threats?*<br>1. Prune product line ($W_2W_5T_1$)<br>2. Institute improved management control systems to keep up with unwieldy product line ($W_2W_5T_1$) |

Source: Based on the author's analysis of "Phil Knight: CEO at NIKE (1983)," Harvard Business School Case # 390-038, 1990.

### Strategy Evaluation

The subsequent step of the strategy formulation process entails an evaluation of strategic alternatives. The existing strategy and various strategic alternatives are evaluated to determine which of them represents the "best" match between the organization and its environment, in light of company objectives management values/preferences. Minimum tests of each alternative strategy are suitability, validity, consistency, feasibility, vulnerability, and potential rewards.[19]

### Strategic Choice

Following the evaluation of their organizations' strategic alternatives, general managers move to the final step: they make their *strategic choice*. This involves either reaffirming the current strategy or crafting a new strategy. The outcome of this step is a restatement of how the organization defines its business, its competitive posture, and its self-concept.

The strategy formulation process therefore moves from the generation of a profile of the organization's current strategy to the execution of environmental analysis, strategic forecast and internal assessment, followed by the development of strategic alternatives. These strategic alternatives are, in turn, put to evaluative tests before a strategic choice is made. This strategic choice step sets the stage for the strategy implementation functions of general managers.

### Implementing Organizational Strategy

Although an important task of general managers, strategy formulation alone cannot guarantee success. The chosen strategy must be translated into carefully implemented actions. Before strategic thought ("planning the work") can be translated into organizational action ("working the plan"), the organization must clarify the strategy it intends to implement. The strategy implementation process can be conceived as consisting of three activities: assessing the organization's capability for strategy implementation, creating an action plan, and installing strategic controls. Figure 4 presents a model for diagnosing strategy implementation problems.

### Assessing the Organization's Capability for Strategy Implementation[20]

**Functional fits.** The organization must operationalize the strategy through the implementation of functional strategies that translate the organizational strategy into carefully implemented action. *Functional fits* refer to the adoption and execution of functional strategies that are consistent with the strategic objectives of a business. It is essential that all functional areas adopt strategies and operational plans that reinforce the organization's overall strategy.

Applying Porter's Value Chain analysis (Figure 2), the organization's activities can be grouped into six major areas for functional strategies: financial strategy, human

---

[19]George S Day, *Strategic Market Planning: The Pursuit of Competitive Advantage* (St Paul, MN: West Publishing Co, 1984): 151–180. See George S Day, "Evaluating Strategic Alternatives," in *The Portable MBA in Strategy*, eds Liam Fahey and Robert M Randall (New York: John Wiley & Sons, 1994): 297–317 for a more recent discussion of these strategy evaluation criteria.

[20]The discussion in this section is based on Richard G Hamermesh, "A Note on Implementing Strategy," Harvard Business School Case # 9-383-015, July 1983.

FIGURE 4

**DIAGNOSTIC MODEL FOR STRATEGY IMPLEMENTATION**

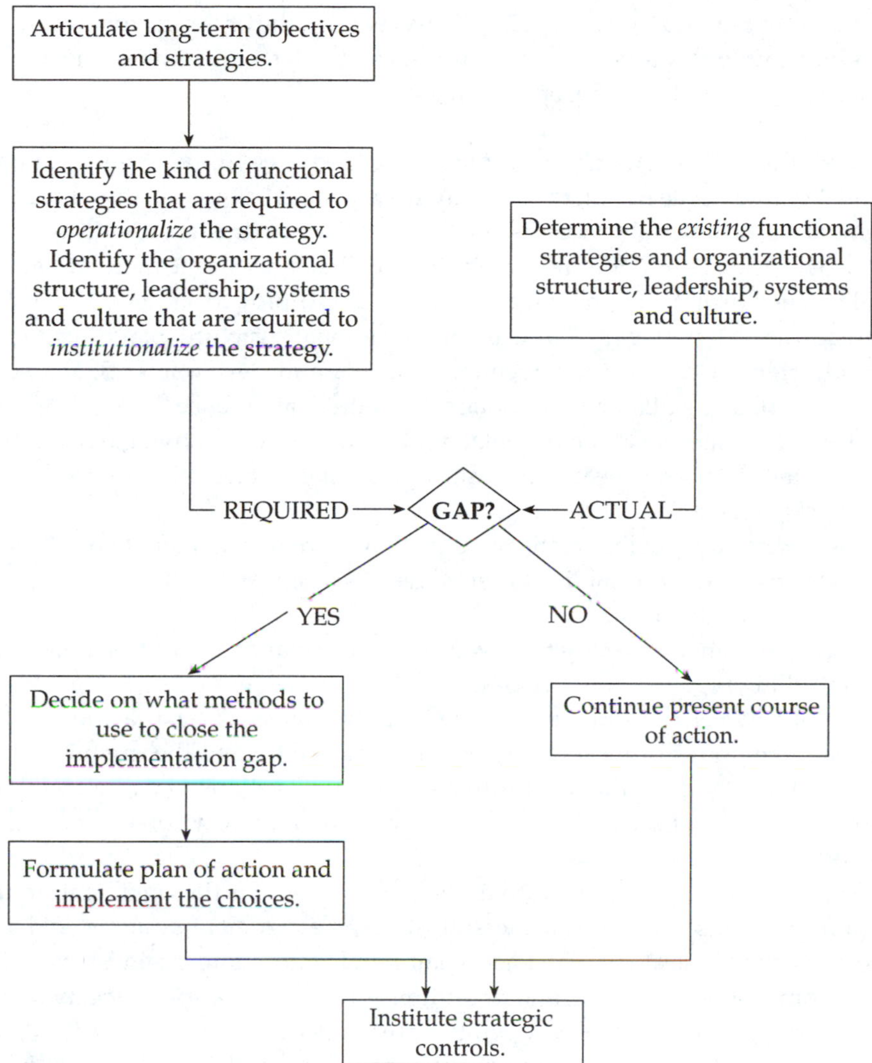


resources strategy, technology strategy, procurement strategy, manufacturing strategy, and marketing strategy. The key to achieving functional fits is to ensure that the strategic decisions made in each functional area are consistent with the organization's chosen strategy.

*Hoshin kanri* (policy deployment) is an increasingly popular methodology to effect this vertical consistency among organizational strategy, functional-area strategies, and operational plans.[21] First documented by Bridgestone Tire Corporation in a 1965 study of

---

[21]Yoji Akao, *Hoshin Kanri: Policy Deployment for Successful TQM*, trans. Glenn H Mazur and Japan Business Consultants, Ltd (Cambridge, MA: Productivity Press, 1991); Bruce M Sheridan, *Policy Deployment: The TQM Approach to Long-Range Planning* (Milwaukee, WI: ASQC Quality Press, 1993). On-line information on hoshin kanri is available through the World Wide Web at URL *http://mijuno.larc.nasa.gov/dfc/hp.html* or *http://www.tqe.com/hoshin.html*.

Deming Prize winners, hoshin kanri has been the strategic planning process implemented by several Deming Prize winners (e.g., Yokogawa Hewlett-Packard) and leading American companies (e.g., Procter & Gamble). Hoshin kanri is a system of forms and rules that communicate company strategy and policy to everyone in the organization. It also encourages individual employees to analyze situations, create plans for improvements, conduct performance checks, and take appropriate action.

**Administrative fits.** To be effectively implemented, a strategy must be institutionalized, that is, it must permeate the organization's day-to-day life. The organization must develop and implement organizational processes and systems that are consistent with and reinforce the strategy. The McKinsey 7-S Framework (Figure 5) suggests that there are at least six managerial levers which the top management team can employ to successfully institutionalize the organization's strategy.[22] These are organizational structure, planning and control systems, leadership style, staff (management selection and development), shared values (corporate culture), and skills (synonymous with "core competence").

These six components can be organized into four administrative elements that provide fundamental, long-term means for institutionalizing strategy:

1. The organization's *structure.*
2. The *leadership* provided by the organization's top management team. This encompasses the need to establish an effective *style,* as well as the necessary *staff* and *skills* to execute the strategy.
3. The organization's *systems* for rewarding performance, as well as monitoring and controlling organizational action.
4. The fit between the strategy and the organization's *culture,* the *shared values* that create the norms of individual behavior and the tone of the organization. Since this element will be the most difficult to change, actions must be taken to make the implementation of the strategy more compatible with the organization's culture.

The key to achieving administrative fits is to ensure that the organization designs, adopts, and implements structures, leadership styles, management systems, and a culture that support the chosen strategy. The East Asian mindset to doing business includes such principles as compromise, patience, and deception as a means to a strategic advantage, and avoiding strong emotions.[23] Clearly, operational success in the Asia-Pacific region will require the adoption of attitudes and organizational behaviors that are likely to differ from traditional Western practices.

**Diagnostic model.** Having understood the objectives of functional and administrative fits, the following diagnostic questions are helpful in evaluating the capability of the organization to implement its strategy:

1. **Functional fits.** What functional strategies and policies must the organization establish in order to best implement the strategy? *[IDEAL]* What functional strategies and policies is the organization actually pursuing? *[ACTUAL]*
2. **Administrative fits.** What type of organizational structure, leadership, systems,

---

[22]Robert H Waterman, Jr, "The Seven Elements of Strategic Fit," *Journal of Business Strategy* 2:3 (Winter 1982): 69–73.
[23]Rosalie L Tung, "Strategic Management Thought in East Asia," *Organizational Dynamics* 22 (Spring 1994): 55–65.

FIGURE 5

**THE McKINSEY 7-S FRAMEWORK**

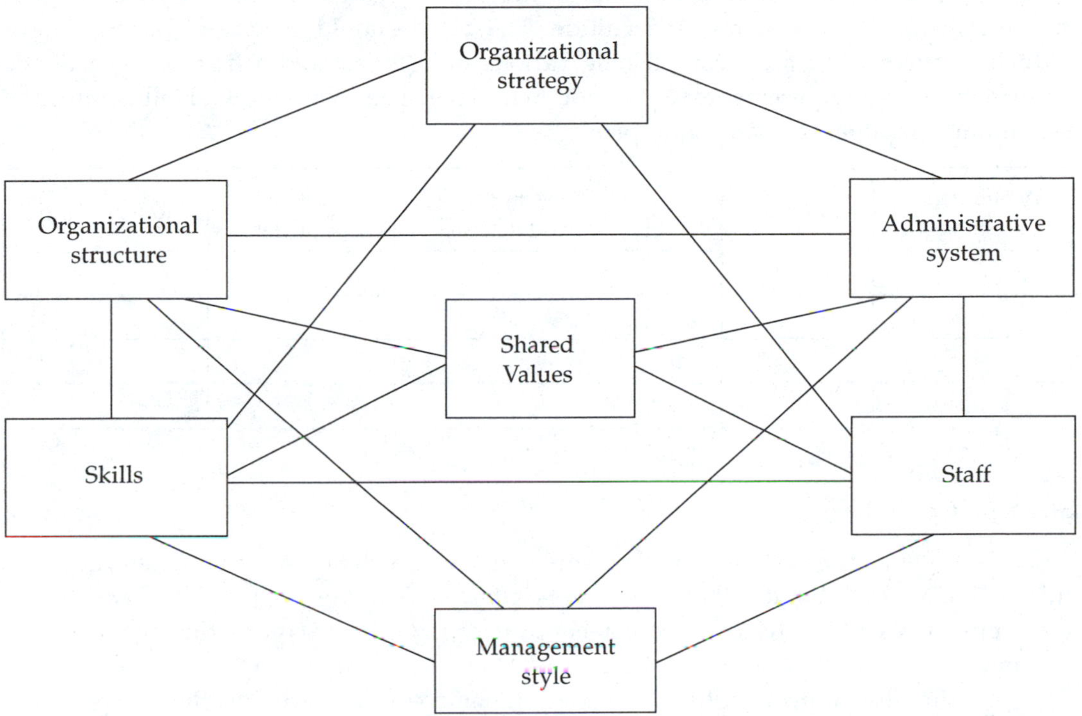


Source: Adapted from Thomas J Peters and Robert H. Waterman, Jr, *In Search of Excellence*, (New York: Harper & Row, 1982): 10.

and culture must the organization establish in order to best implement the strategy? *[IDEAL]* What type of structure, leadership, systems, and culture are actually in place? *[ACTUAL]*

**Plan of Action: Closing the Implementation Gaps**

The organization needs to create a plan for closing the gaps between the ideal and actual sets of functional strategies/policies, organizational structure, leadership, management systems, and culture. The top management team must be sensitive to the interaction between the changes necessary to implement the new strategy and the compatibility or "fit" between those changes and the organization's culture. There are four generic approaches for closing strategy implementation gaps:[24]

1. Ignore the culture.
2. Manage around the current culture by changing the implementation plan.
3. Attempt to change the culture to fit the strategy. This is an extremely difficult task to accomplish, requiring a lengthy process and significant resources.

[24]Howard Schwartz and Stanley M Davis, "Matching Corporate Culture and Business Strategy," *Organizational Dynamics* 10:1 (Summer 1981): 30-48.

4. Change the strategy to fit the culture, perhaps by reducing performance expectations.

The action plans should encompass necessary changes in functional strategies, structure, leadership, systems, and culture. The plans should specify responsible individuals, a time frame for accomplishing various milestones, and a first estimate of the strategic resource requirements (e.g., labor, materials). The following table illustrates the minimum components of an action plan:

| *Action Plan/ Program* | *Priority* | *Cost* | *Manpower Requirements* | *Scheduled Completion* | *Responsibility* |
|---|---|---|---|---|---|
| | | | | | |
| | | | | | |
| | | | | | |
| | | | | | |

**Strategic Control**

Since the organization's strategy will be implemented in a changing environment, successful implementation requires that execution be controlled and evaluated. There are at least four approaches which the top management team can employ to control the organization's strategy:[25]

1. **Premise control.** Check systematically and continuously whether the premises (i.e., assumptions or predictions about environmental and industry factors) on which the strategy is based are still valid.
2. **Implementation control.** Assess whether the overall strategy should be changed in light of the results associated with the incremental actions to implement the overall strategy.
3. **Strategic surveillance.** Monitor a wide range of events inside and outside the organization that are likely to affect the course of its strategy.
4. **Special alert control.** Conduct a thorough, often rapid, reconsideration of the organization's strategy in light of a sudden, unexpected event.

## Application to Cases

By now you have an idea of strategy and the strategic management process. In the cases which follow, you will have repeated opportunities to consider the contributions that the concept of organizational strategy would have made to these organizations. The cases will also permit you to explore the dynamic interplay between the organization and its environment in a wide range of different industries, markets, and countries. Adopting the general management point of view will force you to focus your energies on the relationships between the organization and its environment.

[25]Georg Schreyogg and Horst Steinmann, "Strategic Control: A New Perspective," *Academy of Management Review* 12:1 (1987): 91–103. See also Michael Goold, *Strategic Control: Establishing Milestones for Long-Term Performance* (Reading, MA: Addison-Wesley Pub. Co, 1993).

If you have little or no prior exposure to case preparation and discussion, I advise you to read Appendix A for an introduction to the case method. As you attempt to apply the concepts of strategic management to the analysis of the cases in this book, try to keep in mind the following questions:

1. What is the strategy of this organization?
2. In light of (a) the economic characteristics of its industry and the predicted developments in its environment, (b) its internal strengths and weaknesses, and (c) the personal values of the top management team, is the strategy appropriate?
3. What changes in organizational strategy will you recommend to the general manager?
4. What changes in functional strategies and policies must the organization implement in order to best operationalize the recommended strategy?
5. What changes in organizational structure, leadership, systems, and culture must the organization implement in order to best institutionalize the recommended strategy?
6. What recommendations for strategic control might appropriately be made to the general manager?

The Strategic Management Audit in Appendix B will guide you in applying the abovementioned questions to the cases. After analyzing these cases, you will have a better understanding of the general management roles of architect of organizational purpose (articulating strategy), chief strategist (formulating strategy), and organization builder and leader (implementing strategy).

# The Jim Thompson Thai Silk Company, Ltd*

In June 1979, Mr William Booth, Managing Director of the Jim Thompson Thai Silk Company, Ltd (TSC), Thailand's largest retailer and exporter of native silks, could look back on the previous six years with considerable satisfaction. Since assuming managing directorship in March 1973 the company's sales and profits had more than doubled (see Exhibits 1, 2, and 3 for historical financial information). The company had also successfully entered two additional phases of the silk business, fabric-printing and garment-making, during this period and was on the verge of yet another major backward integration move, this time into weaving. These developments and the significant increase in demand for the company's products so far in 1979 led Mr Booth to look forward to a continued healthy rate of growth for the firm.

This case provides a brief description of the Thai silk industry, details the founding and early development of TSC, and describes major developments at the company since Mr Booth's assumption of the managing directorship in 1973.

## Thailand

Thailand's 47 million population is made up of three major ethnic groups. Native Thais, approximately 80 percent of the total, constitute the largest. They are descendants of the

---

* This case was prepared by Professor Robert A Pitts, Gettysburg College, Pennsylvania, while serving as Professor of Business Policy at IMEDE Management Development Institute, Lausanne, Switzerland, on leave from Pennsylvania State University. It is designed to serve as the basis for class discussion rather than to illustrate either effective or ineffective handling of an administrative situation. 

groups which had migrated into the Southeast Asian peninsula from southern China during the 12th, 13th, and 14th centuries pushing before them the Khmers, ancestors of the present-day Cambodians, who had previously ruled the region. A second group, approximately 15 percent of the total, are native-born first or second generation Chinese. A third, located in the extreme south of the country, are of Malay stock. (Exhibit 4 is a map of Thailand.) In general, Thais dominate agricultural activity and government administration while the Chinese handle manufacturing and commerce.

Thailand is the only Southeast Asian country never to have been colonized by Europeans. Though still officially a kingdom, it had been ruled in recent decades by a series of relatively benign military dictatorships.

Economically speaking, Thailand is moderately prosperous by Southeast Asian standards. Its 1978 annual per capita income of US$380 (7,600 baht) was well below Singapore's $2,580, the highest for the region, yet comfortably above Indonesia's $280, the region's lowest.[1] The bulk of the Thai population (in excess of 85%) is still engaged in agriculture, primarily of rice. Bangkok, however, the nation's capital and only city, is a large (1979 population was in excess of 3 million), rapidly growing, and relatively modern metropolis.

## Thai Silk Industry

The production of Thai silk involves a number of stages. The earliest silk fiber production was carried out by approximately 500,000 individual peasant families primarily in the economically depressed northeastern portion of the country. Several hundred family firms located in the larger provincial towns and in Bangkok undertook intermediate stages — dyeing, spinning, and weaving. Final stages — printing, converting, and retailing — were dominated by fewer than 100 enterprises located in Bangkok.

### Fiber Production (Sericulture)

Most Thai silk producers use the polyvoltine variety of silk worm. This is a very hardy species compared to the bivoltine worm used by all other major silk-producing countries. It is also relatively easy to rear. However, its yield is low and its fiber is of soft, coarse, uneven texture with low tensile strength. This latter characteristic makes it unsuitable for warp yarn (the thread that runs end-to-end throughout the length of woven fabric) because it breaks easily during weaving. The former endows it with a very pleasing glow, however, making it a highly valued material for weft yarn (the thread which runs across the warp during weaving).

A silk worm's chief diet is mulberry leaves. The cultivation of mulberry trees, the picking of their leaves, and the feeding and care of silk worms are highly labor-intensive activities, which in Thailand are carried out mostly by women and children as a supplementary family income source. The half million or so families engaged in these activities in Thailand in 1978 produced about 700 metric tons of raw silk fiber. Only a portion of this amount (462 tons) entered commercial channels, however, the remainder being used by growers for their own consumption. Market price of this commercially

[1] The international exchange rate of BHT 20 = US$1 has remained unchanged for more than two decades.

available silk varied considerably by grade and time of year. Average price per kilogram during 1978 was 380 baht.

The 462 tons entering commercial channels had been used in the proportions shown in Table 1 to supply the three major segments of the industry in 1978. The 189 tons used to supply the tourist and export segment — the one in which TSC is active — was supplemented by 83 tons of imported material, mostly warp yarn (see Table 2). Principal warp yarn suppliers in recent years had been China, Korea, Japan, and Brazil.

TABLE 1

**Commercial Thai Silk Industry**

| *Market* | *Looms* | *Requirements of Raw Silk (tons)* | *Fabric Production (million yds)* | *Value of Fabric Produced (million baht)* |
|---|---|---|---|---|
| Domestic: Village | 150,000 | 234 | 1.8 | 90 |
| Domestic: Towns and Bangkok | 1,000 | 39 | 0.3 | 21 |
| Tourist & Export | 1,800 | 189 | 2.0 | 240 |
| Total | 152,800 | 462 | 4.1 | 351 |

TABLE 2

**Raw Silk Production for Tourist and Export Markets (in tons)**

| *Material* | *Commercial Requirements* | *Supplied by* | |
|---|---|---|---|
| | | *Local Sources* | *Imports* |
| Warp | 68 | 28 | 40 |
| Weft | 204 | 161 | 43 |
| Total | 272 | 189 | 83 |

Output of the Thai sericulture industry had expanded significantly since 1971 (see Table 3). This expansion was insufficient to keep up with burgeoning demand, however, as the following article appearing in the December 31, 1978 issue of the *Bangkok Post* suggests:

> Surprisingly, the fortune of Thai silk ebbs and flows not so much with overseas or domestic demand but rather with the supply of raw materials. The main headache is the shortage of silk yarn, particularly in the hot season (January-May) when sericulture is practically abandoned due to the lack of mulberry leaves to feed silk worms.

Faced with this situation, leading retailers, including TSC, established up-country buying offices over the years to secure supplies for their weavers.

TABLE 3

**Thai Sericulture**

| Year | Number of Households (000's) | Area Under Mulberry (Rai* in 000's) | Silk Production (tons) |
|---|---|---|---|
| 1971 | 398 | 234 | 443 |
| 1972 | 381 | 233 | 498 |
| 1973 | 458 | 265 | 571 |
| 1974 | 432 | 323 | 706 |
| 1975 | 455 | 335 | 637 |
| 1976 | 457 | NA | 650 |
| 1977 | 460 | NA | 690 |
| 1978 | 500 | NA | 700 |

*One rai = 1,659.3 square meters.

Source: From article, entitled "Yarn Supply Causes Problems," in *Bangkok Post*, December 31, 1978 supplement.

### Weaving

Weaving houses in Thailand purchased raw silk, cleansed and dyed it, spun it into thread, and wove the thread into fabric. All activities tended to be hand operations utilizing traditional methods.

There were 314 weaving establishments in 1978 producing for the tourist and export markets. They were concentrated in three locations — Bangkok, Korat, and Khonkaen. As Table 4 indicates, most establishments had fewer than 5 looms. Their total output in 1978 was approximately 2 million yards of fabric.

TABLE 4

**Weaving Establishments in Thailand Producing for the Tourist and Export Market**

| Number of Looms | Number of Establishments | | |
|---|---|---|---|
| | Bangkok | Korat | Khonkaen |
| 1–4 | 20 | 100 | 100 |
| 10 | 20 | 10 | 2 |
| 20 | 10 | 20 | 3 |
| 30 | 10 | 10 | 2 |
| 50 | 2 | 4 | 1 |
| Total | 62 | 144 | 108 |

### Finishing and Converting

Much Thai silk moved directly from weavers into retail channels to be sold as fabric. However, a portion was "finished" (e.g., printed with a design) and/or "converted" (e.g., made into a pillow case, garment, window drape, etc) before reaching retail. There were seven finishing establishments in the country, all located in Bangkok. The largest of these was a 51-percent-owned joint venture of TSC, which contained 16 hand painting tables compared to only 10 for its next largest competitor and was the only finisher in the country specializing in silk to own an automatic printing machine.

There was only one garment-maker in Thailand devoted primarily to the conversion of Thai silk. It too was a TSC joint venture (38.7-percent-owned). It was located immediately adjacent to TSC's retail store in Bangkok.

### Retailing

As Table 5 indicates, the 1,453,839 tourists visiting Thailand in 1978 spent a total of about 8 billion baht in the country. These expenditures were allocated as follows: food and lodging (50 percent), shopping (26 percent), sightseeing (17 percent), and other (7 percent). Approximately 200 million baht went toward the purchase of Thai silk. Most of these purchases were made from about 30 Bangkok retailers. The largest of these was TSC. The next largest did less than one-third of TSC's volume.

TABLE 5

**Thai Tourism**

| *Year* | *Hotel Rooms in Bangkok* | *Number of Tourists Visiting Thailand* | *Average Length of Stay (days)* | *Total Revenue from Tourism (million baht)* |
|---|---|---|---|---|
| 1960 | 959 | 81,340 | 3.0 | 196 |
| 1965 | 2,469 | 225,025 | 4.8 | 506 |
| 1970 | 8,763 | 628,671 | 4.8 | 2,175 |
| 1973 | 9,746 | 1,037,737 | 4.7 | 3,457 |
| 1976 | 10,485 | 1,098,442 | 5.1 | 3,990 |
| 1978 | 11,376 | 1,453,839 | 4.8 | 8,000 |

### Exporting

Approximately 100 million baht worth of Thai silk products were exported in 1978. TSC dominated this segment as well. It made up 30 percent of all fabric exports and 50 percent of all higher-value product exports in 1978.

## The Jim Thompson Thai Silk Company, Ltd

### Early History

The company was founded as the Thai Silk Company in 1951 by Mr James Thompson, an American who had been attached to the United States Army Intelligence Corps in Thailand during the latter part of the Second World War. A member of a prominent Delaware family and a graduate of Princeton University, Mr Thompson determined to make a career in Thailand following the cessation of hostilities. The original capital for his company was 500,000 baht supplied by himself (20 percent), two other Americans (21.2 percent), and 29 Thai weavers and silk traders (58.8 percent).

The company's mission was to provide a market for Thai silk fabric. A retail location was secured in the heart of Bangkok's tourist district and local weavers were invited to place their products on consignment. Under this arrangement, TSC did not assume ownership of the merchandise but simply acted as sales agent for weavers. Over time, this policy evolved to one in which TSC took ownership of all merchandise sold.

During the early years of the company, Mr Thompson devoted considerable effort to assisting indigenous workers improve their methods. For example, he worked closely with weavers to improve yarn color combinations. He persuaded European dye manufacturers to send technical agents to Thailand to help weavers upgrade dyeing techniques. Mr Thompson was also largely responsible for the adoption in Thailand of the flying shuttle (a mechanism for mechanically carrying the weft thread back and forth during weaving). Perhaps most important, he was an early experimenter in the printing of designs on silk fabric. His superb sense of color quickly made printed fabric a major TSC seller.

With increasing tourism throughout the 1950s and 1960s and the buildup of US troops in Southeast Asia in connection with the Vietnam War, TSC flourished. By 1967 sales and profits had reached 31.5 million and 3.0 million baht, respectively. Then a strange event occurred. During a 1967 Easter holiday in a Malaysian jungle resort (Cameron Highlands), Mr Thompson mysteriously disappeared and was never seen again. Mr Sheffield, an American who had been Assistant Manager under Mr Thompson for 10 years, took charge and directed the company's affairs until 1973 when he suddenly died. It was on the evening of Mr Sheffield's death that Mr William Booth, an American who had joined TSC in 1964 following a term of military duty in Vietnam, telephoned to the U.S. to seek guidance from Mr Henry Thompson, nephew of Mr James Thompson and heir to his interest in the company. Mr Henry Thompson suggested that Mr Booth take over the managing directorship of the firm, and Mr Booth accepted.

**Developments Since 1973**

The company's activities had evolved considerably since 1973. For example, the proportion of higher-value silk items sold at retail had increased significantly — from 25 percent of retail sales in 1973 to 57 percent in 1978. Big-selling higher-value categories in 1978 had been pillow cases (25 percent of sales), garments (23 percent) and neckties (9 percent). A breakdown of 1978 sales by major product and market segment is shown in Table 6. Table 7 summarizes the results of a 1975 survey of TSC retail customers.

TABLE 6

**Jim Thompson Thai Silk Company**
**1978 Sales by Category**
**(Percent)**

| | *Local* | | | | |
|---|---|---|---|---|---|
| *Category* | *Retail* | *Wholesale* | *Export Agents* | *Mail Order* | *Total* |
| Silk Fabric | 21.0 | 4.0 | 12.2 | 2.8 | 40.0 |
| Cotton Fabric | 0.6 | 0.2 | 2.3 | 0.9 | 4.0 |
| Ready to Wear | 20.6 | 1.7 | 1.6 | 1.2 | 25.1 |
| Sundries | 16.4 | 0.1 | 11.9 | 2.3 | 30.7 |
| | 58.6 | 6.0 | 28.0 | 7.2 | 99.8 |
| Total | 64.6 | | 35.2 | | 99.8 |

Note: The above percentages apply to 1978 finished goods of 111.6 million baht.

TABLE 7

**Jim Thompson Thai Silk Company**
**Customer Profile**
**(Percent)**

| *Attribute* | *Category* | *Percentage* |
|---|---|---|
| Nationality | Thai residents | 5 |
| | Other residents | 18 |
| | Tourists | 77 |
| Gender | Men | 31 |
| | Women | 52 |
| | Couples | 15 |
| Age | Under 25 | 2 |
| | 25–39 | 62 |
| | 40 or over | 35 |

Source: 1975 questionnaire survey of 852 TSC retail customers.

The company had made two major backward integration moves since 1973, both through joint ventures. The first, in 1974, had taken the company into garment-making through the establishment of Silco Garments Company (Silco). TSC, with a 38.7 percent common stock interest, was Silco's major shareholder. The remaining shares were held by TSC shareholders and Silco employees.

A second backward integration step involved the establishment in 1978 of Thai Painters and Finishers Company Limited (TP&F). TP&F was established to purchase the assets of Chumpan Industries, the firm which had traditionally supplied TSC's printing needs. Shares of the new company were held as follows: TSC (51 percent), Chumpan Industries (24 percent), a large German manufacturer of textile printing machines (15 percent), and Silco (10 percent). Additional information on both ventures is included in Exhibit 5.

**Proposed New Weaving Mill**

On top of these changes an important new development was currently under consideration. It involved a proposed 51-percent-owned weaving joint venture, the Thai Silk Handweaving Co, Ltd (TSHC). The plant was to be located at Pakthongchai in Korat Province, about 100 miles northeast of Bangkok. It would initially contain 120 hand looms of the traditional variety with capacity to supply about 20 percent of TSC's fabric needs. Current plans called for an increase in the number of looms to 600 over a 6-year period. TSC's share of initial capitalization would amount to 2.4 million baht.

Company personnel put forth a variety of reasons in favor of the weaving venture. Mr Booth, for example, felt that it would strengthen the company's position in the export market:

> The weaving mill will enable us for the first time to directly control quality and delivery. Both are becoming increasingly important as we attempt to expand export sales where our materials are used primarily for interior decorating. These customers must have consistency over large quantities of fabric and also over time as they reorder. They also need punctual delivery since

> they can't afford to tie up their customers' investments in new buildings simply because interior decorating materials have not arrived. With our present set-up, we just can't provide the necessary assurances.

Mr Henry Thompson emphasized quite a different reason. He saw the new venture as a source of information, knowledge, and expertise.

> At present we know very little about the economics of weaving. Nor have we been very successful in getting our weavers to improve their manufacturing methods. By operating our own mill we will generate valuable cost data on this activity and can experiment with improved procedures and methods.

Other reasons favoring the new project, supplied to the casewriter by company management, are detailed in Exhibit 6. The views of TSC's chairman on this and other recent developments included in the company's 1978 Annual Report are reproduced in Exhibit 7.

As Mr Booth tried to reach a final decision on the project, he wondered whether there were drawbacks to the project which had perhaps not been fully explored. For example, what risks did the project entail? And what alternate, perhaps better, uses for the 2.4 million baht required by the project were open to the company?

EXHIBIT 1

**JIM THOMPSON THAI SILK COMPANY, LTD**
**Historical Financial Summary**
(millions of baht)

| | *1978* | *1977* | *1976* | *1975* | *1974* | *1973* |
|---|---|---|---|---|---|---|
| **Balance Sheet** | | | | | | |
| Fixed assets | 10.9 | 8.5 | 9.1 | 9.7 | 9.9 | 9.7 |
| Investment in associated companies | 8.5 | 0.3 | 0.3 | – | – | – |
| Other investment | – | – | 0.2 | 12.2 | –6.1 | |
| Net current assets | 38.3 | 33.0 | 26.6 | 14.3 | 15.5 | 15.8 |
| Long-term liabilities | – | – | – | – | 0.8 | – |
| Shareholders' equity | 57.8 | 41.7 | 36.1 | 36.1 | 30.5 | 25.5 |
| **Earnings Statement** | | | | | | |
| Revenues | 135.5 | 92.6 | 76.4 | 57.5 | 52.3 | 56.9 |
| Income after tax | 16.9 | 8.6 | 7.1 | 6.2 | 5.5 | 6.2 |
| Dividends | 2.0 | 3.0 | 5.0 | 1.5 | 0.6 | 1.0 |
| Earnings per share (baht) | 3,376 | 1,720 | 1,426 | 1,249 | 1,093 | NMF |
| **Number of Employees** | 101 | 98 | 98 | 90 | 89 | 90 |
| **Common Shares** | 5,000 | 5,000 | 5,000 | 5,000 | 5,000 | 500 |

Source: Annual Reports.

EXHIBIT 2

## JIM THOMPSON THAI SILK COMPANY, LTD

### Income Statement
### For the Years Ended December 31, 1977, and 1978

(millions of baht)

| | 1978 | 1977 |
|---|---|---|
| **Revenues** | | |
| Sales: Finished goods | 111.6 | 77.5 |
| Raw silk | 17.7 | 11.2 |
| Miscellaneous | 0.9 | 0.4 |
| Rental & services | 0.6 | 0.4 |
| Other income | 4.7 | 2.8 |
| Total Revenues | 135.5 | 92.2 |
| **Expenses** | | |
| CGS: Finished goods | 70.2 | 51.4 |
| Raw silk | 16.9 | 10.9 |
| Miscellaneous | 0.8 | 0.3 |
| Cost of occupancy & rental | 2.1 | 1.7 |
| Selling & administrative expenses | 19.0 | 14.3 |
| Interest expense | 0.4 | 0.1 |
| Income tax | 9.2 | 4.9 |
| Total Expenses | 118.6 | 83.6 |
| Net Income | 16.9 | 8.6 |
| NetT Income per Share (baht) | 3,376.14 | 1,720.22 |

Source: Annual Reports.

EXHIBIT 3

## JIM THOMPSON THAI SILK COMPANY, LTD

### Balance Sheet
### As of December 31, 1977, and 1979
(millions of baht)

| | *1979* | *1977* |
|---|---|---|
| **Assets** | | |
| Current Assets | | |
| Cash | 1.8 | 0.7 |
| Short-term borrowings | 1.8 | 10.9 |
| Accounts receivable (Net) | 15.6 | 10.9 |
| Inventories | 40.2 | 24.9 |
| Other | 1.3 | 0.8 |
| Total Current Assets | 60.8 | 48.2 |
| Investments & loans to associated companies | 8.5 | 0.3 |
| Property, plant, & equipment | 10.9 | 8.5 |
| Total Assets | 80.3 | 57.0 |
| **Liabilities & Shareholders' Equity** | | |
| Current Liabilities | | |
| Bank | 7.3 | 4.5 |
| Accounts payable | 4.0 | 2.6 |
| Accrued income tax | 9.2 | 4.9 |
| Proposed dividend accrued | 0 | 1.5 |
| Other | 2.0 | 1.7 |
| Total Current Liabilities | 22.5 | 15.2 |
| Shareholders' Equity | | |
| Share capital (5,000 shares) | 0.5 | 0.5 |
| Retained earnings | 57.3 | 41.2 |
| Total Shareholders' Equity | 57.8 | 41.7 |
| Total Liabilities & Shareholders' Equity | 80.3 | 57.9 |

Source: Annual Reports.

EXHIBIT 4

**JIM THOMPSON THAI SILK COMPANY, LTD**
**Map of Thailand and Neighboring Countries**

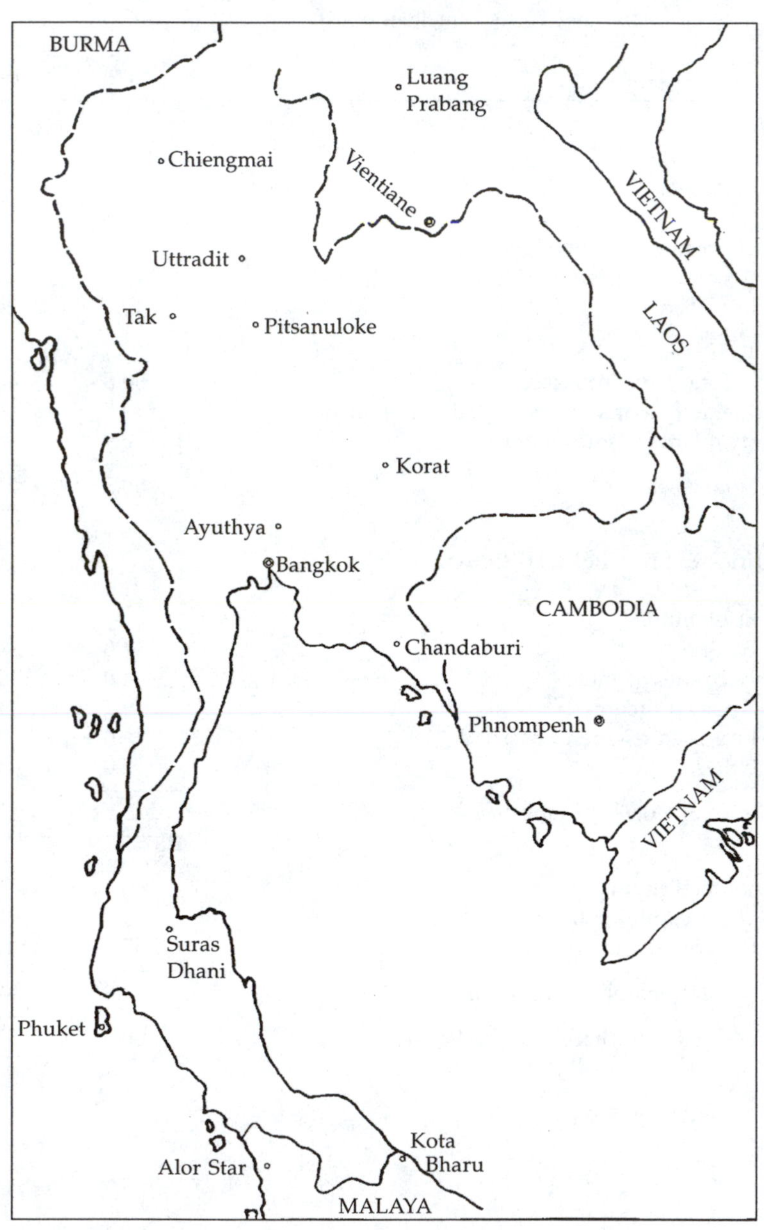

EXHIBIT 5

**JIM THOMPSON THAI SILK COMPANY, LTD**
**Joint Ventures**
(millions of baht)

| | | | | *TSC Investment* | | *Recent Annual* | | | |
|---|---|---|---|---|---|---|---|---|---|
| *Activity* | *Company Name* | *Date Founded* | *TSC Ownership* | *Through 6/79* | *Add'l Required in 1979* | *Sales* | *Pretax Profits* | *Employees* | *% of Sales to TSC* |
| Garment | Silco | 8/74 | 38.7% | 0.6 | 0.6 | 10.3 | 2.7 | 170 | 55%* |
| Printing | TP&F | 6/78 | 51% | 7.7 | 5.0 | 14.3** | 1.2** | 110 | 54% |
| Weaving | TSHC | In planning stage | Proposed 51% | — | 2.6 | — | — | — | — |

*Non-TSC sales were all export.
** Eleven-month figures (September 1978–July 1979).

Source: TSC management.

EXHIBIT 6

## JIM THOMPSON THAI SILK COMPANY, LTD.
## Rationale for Establishing New Joint Venture in Weaving

1. There are only a few large and reliable weaving houses manufacturing for TSC and owners are aging. These owners could discontinue at any day and find no one to succeed their expertise, seriously hurting the production quality and system for the TSC.
2. TSC is pressured all the time for quality products while the weavers aim profit at a lower cost; often, weavers delay and stop weaving.
3. Through the years of development and expansion, TSC has subsidized weavers for almost every new project related to expansion, raw materials, and technology. TSC's supply of raw silk, dyestuffs, equipments, etc, amounted to more than the weavers' money. These were given on credit terms at cost, as if TSC were doing its own production.
4. Weaving in processes was conducted at weavers' own decision, at the same time TSC weaving inspections were held. At some points, TSC was directing weavers' production; however, weavers did not properly follow given instructions.
5. Due to the nature of handicraft production of raw silk and weaving, often weavers would misrepresent products with subgrade material or engage in negligence. Expansion was always met with low-quality work because what a weaver could do was limited by her own capability, time, and money. And sometimes it was too difficult for a weaver to analyze what she did wrong. Often, an error happened and we used to admit that TSC and weavers were heading at different directions with regard to quality, delivery, profit, supervision, and investment.
6. Weavers always press TSC to accept low-quality work resulting from their error or negligence because they do not weave for others.
7. Whenever labor costs or costs of raw materials got higher, weavers would lower quality to keep their profit; conditions seriously hurled TSC's goodwill.
8. Weaving house owners did not and could not recruit new workers.
9. There are forty weaving houses scattered around Bangkok and Pakthongchai, each needing almost everyday supervision from TSC with respect to raw silk, dyeing, and weaving. This involved more men from TSC to supervise these details at these 40 weaving houses. The same job can be done in one factory with only one man supervising. In addition to our time and energy extended to weaver supervision, not all weavers followed our instructions and so far we have not been able to drive the weavers away from their old weaving behaviors. These conflicts cost money.
10. Due to the high overhead and poor knowledge, many weavers hesitated and strongly delayed new instructions or introductions. Some improvements took over a year to develop into practice. These delays cost money.
11. Through the years of conducting weaving inspections, techniques of pregrading raw silk, degumming and dyeing, loom-state weaving inspection remains a crucial job for TSC inspectors. Weavers need to be convinced to follow proper improvement methods. Weavers always want physical demonstrations at TSC's expense and manage to misrepresent products with inferior material and quality.
12. A standard production of weaving needs a huge inventory of raw silk to support a linear production system with absolute careful technical supervision arrangement and coordination of each step of work. No weaver can afford a huge inventory of raw silk; neither can TSC extend any welfare for the workers.
13. Raw silk qualities remain part of the dispute between TSC and weavers; weavers would not spend time and energy to use first-grade raw silk because it involved more wastage and negligence. Seventy percent of the total supply of first-grade raw silk comes from the farm.
14. Weavers do not care about tensile strength or fabric abrasion, partially because they are not involved in the end consumption.

Source: Material sent to case writer by TSC Production Manager Mr Surindr.

EXHIBIT 7

## JIM THOMPSON THAI SILK COMPANY, LTD
## Chairman's Statement

On behalf of your directors, I have the pleasure of presenting the trading report and the accounts of the company for the business year ended 31st December 1978.

For the Thai Silk Company, 1978 was a year of continued growth and expansion with revenues totaling Baht 135.5 million. Profits have reached a record level in 1978 but shareholders as well as employees should recognize that in order to safeguard the future, the company made sizable investments during 1978 and must continue to do so throughout 1979 using these hard-earned profits. This is not a time to distribute profits earned but a time to invest for the future.

### Retail Sale (Baht 73.7 Million)

Political stability has resulted in increased tourism, which accounts for the excellent results in our retail sales. We can see that local sales have increased by 52.5 percent or Baht 25.4 million over 1977.

### Export Sales (Baht 37.9 Million)

Again this year exports were given priority and as a result the company was able to take advantage of the improved world economy resulting in a 34.9 percent or Baht 9.8 million increase in export sales over 1977.

### Raw Materials

The supply of quality raw Thai silk to our weavers has become of primary importance to the company. In 1978 we were able to increase our production and sales to a record high because of adequate raw silk supplies. To further expand our raw silk sources a buying station was established at Khonkaen in the Northeast. Operations began in May 1978 and the increased amounts of raw silk purchased from the farmers and dealers is most satisfactory. In 1979 additional buying stations are scheduled to be established in other silk areas up-country.

### Outlook for 1979

There are good prospects for further improvement in both retail and export sales if increased amounts of raw Thai silk can be purchased and woven.

Development of new supply sources for Thai raw silk must be given the highest priority. A new Raw Materials Purchasing Department under the management of Khun Surindr Supaswasdebhandhu will be established with the primary objective of developing raw silk sources in new areas and encouraging increased production in the areas presently used.

### Investments

A total of over Baht 11 million was invested in new ventures designed to strengthen the Company.

Thai Printers and Finishers Company Limited (TPFC, 51 percent shareholding). TPFC represents a merger of Chupan Printers and Thai Silk forming a new company which continues our silk- and cotton-printing activities. The registered capital is Baht 25 million. Capital investment in 1978 for Thai Silk amounted to Baht 7.65 million. Additional capital is scheduled to be paid in during 1979 of approximately Baht 5 million.

Silco Garments Company Limited (38.7 percent shareholding). To meet the financial requirement of rapid sales growth the capital of this company was increased from Baht 500,000 to Baht 2 million in 1978. Thai Silk share of this capital increase amounted to Baht 580,500.

Thai Silk Handweaving Company Limited (51 percent shareholding). In order to meet our needs for increased quantities of high-quality handwoven silks, the company has planned to establish a handweaving factory in Pak Thong Chai, Korat Province during the year of 1979. Thai Silk will hold 51 percent of the shares, which will call for an investment in 1979 of not less than Baht 2.55 million.

Diners' Club (Thailand) Ltd, (5 percent shareholding). This also had another remarkable year. We received a dividend of Baht 70,000 (Baht 10,000 higher than 1977), which is considered satisfactory for an investment of Baht 100,000.

**Land and Buildings**

In January 1978 two shophouses were purchased, costing a total of Baht 2 million. The shophouses are located directly behind the Jim Thompson Office Building and adjoin the present property. The company will use the additional space for the selection and distribution of raw silk to weavers and storage of other raw materials, dye stuff, and supplies that are unsuitable for storage in the office building. This would also enable us to release additional rental space in the office building.

**Appropriation of Profit**

The statements of income shows net earnings of Baht 26,041,783.89 before tax, and Baht 16,660,685.22 after tax.

Your Board of Directors recommends the following appropriation of profit.

| | | |
|---|---|---|
| Retained earnings brought forward | Baht | 37,987,807.84 |
| Net income for the year | | 16,880,685.22 |
| Total retained earnings | | 53,968,493.06 |
| | | |
| Proposed Appropriation: | | |
| Cash dividend on share capital | | 500,000.00 |
| Directors' fees | | — |
| Contingency reserve | | 1,315,799.59 |
| Balance carried forward | | 52,152,693.47 |
| | Baht | 53,968,493.06 |

**Thai Silk Co Employees**

The number of employees increased by 3 persons from 98 to 101.

**Directorate**

In accordance with Article I of the Company's Article and Article 1153 of the Civil & Commercial Code, Mr William M Booth, Mr Chitr Jotikasathira, and Mr James I Bastable retire by rotation.

**Auditor**

Mr Toemsakdi Krishnamra, of Jaiyos & Co, Chartered Accounts, the retiring auditor, offers himself for reappointment.

In conclusion, I wish to express my appreciation to all staff members for their continued efforts and endeavor in helping to make 1978 the most successful year for the Company.

On behalf of the Board of Directors,

Mme Puen Asasonggram
Chairman

Source: 1978 Annual Report.

# The Jim Thompson Thai Silk Company, Ltd

## Sample Student Case Analysis

The Jim Thompson Thai Silk Company, Ltd (TSC) was formed by an American expatriate in Bangkok shortly after World War II to retail indigenous silk fabric. TSC devoted its early efforts in assisting local suppliers improve dyeing and weaving methods. More recent initiatives have involved the establishment of manufacturing joint ventures to finish and convert purchased fabric. By 1979, TSC was Thailand's largest retailer and exporter of silk fabric.

TSC management's attention has turned to the question of whether to establish a weaving mill. This question is of strategic importance to TSC should results of the decision be either a success or a failure. The following is an analysis of the situation faced by TSC's management. It first identifies and evaluates Mr Thompson's original strategy. It then evaluates the strategic changes which have taken place since Mr Booth assumed general managership of the company in 1973. Finally, it identifies and evaluates possible future changes in the company's policies, including the proposed new weaving mill joint venture.

### TSC's Original Strategy

The major policies constituting Mr Thompson's initial strategy for TSC were the following:

1. Retail sales (*not* manufacturing)
2. Silk fabric
3. Emphasis on quality enhancements through improvements in dyeing, weaving, printing, and general design
4. Consignment sales (TSC did not take ownership of fabric to be sold).

These policies meet quite well the key requirement of an effective strategy — which is to achieve an effective match between opportunity and capability. The opportunity presented to Mr Thompson was defined by several elements: local silk industry talent, low wages, and a growing market fueled by expanding tourism. However, to satisfy this market, several elements were missing before Mr Thompson's arrival: design expertise, sophisticated retailing skills, and dyeing technology. These were precisely the capabilities which Mr Thompson brought to the indigenous industry. When combined with the existing skills of the local Thai, they produce a formidable capability for exploiting tourist demand for quality silk products.

TSC had several other early policies. One was Mr Thompson's policy of not taking possession of merchandise to be sold. This approach served two purposes. First, it limited TSC's financial commitment and risk. Second, it presented a leverage in encouraging weavers to improve their manufacturing methods. Students may also want to discuss the virtues of Mr Thompson's taking only a minority equity position in his company.

This approach limited Mr Thompson's potential return from the venture. However, by the same token, it reduced his personal financial investment. Perhaps most importantly, it made TSC a locally owned, not a foreign-owned, company, with the many political benefits which accrue from that status in a developing country.

## Strategic Changes Since 1973

Mr Booth oversaw a number of important changes in TSC's operation since assuming the general manager position in 1973.

1. **Discontinuation of consignment sales.** With increasing financial strength and market presence, TSC no longer needed to rely on consignment sales as a source of financing and influence over weavers.
2. **Institution of up-country buying stations.** A natural solution to the increasing problem of securing adequate supplies of raw silk for TSC's weavers.
3. **Backward integration into manufacturing.** By moving into finishing and converting, TSC became a manufacturer in addition to a retailer. These moves have provided the company with higher margin merchandise compared to fabric. However, they have also increased the company's financial risk (it now has investments in brick and mortar) and imposed new skill requirements on TSC personnel. TSC has carefully hedged these risks by undertaking these activities as joint ventures with experienced parties.
4. **Increase in export sales.** The company has experienced a large increase in export sales in recent years. This shift is probably desirable from a profit margin standpoint. However, export sales have imposed difficult new requirements on TSC's operation, especially in terms of color consistency and delivery. These requirements are difficult for TSC's current highly fragmented weavers to meet. A chief motivation behind the proposed new weaving mill is the development of a manufacturing capability which can effectively meet these new requirements. Exhibit 1 visually portrays these changes in TSC's activities.

## Problem Statement

It would appear at first glance that TSC's problem or decision in this case is one of determining whether to establish the proposed new weaving mill given the risks and opportunities associated with this move. In a larger sense, however, the proposed weaving mill is only a decision element within TSC's grand strategy for increased profits. TSC could follow a number of routes toward the accomplishment of these ends; the establishment of a weaving mill is merely the implementation of a grand strategy of vertical integration.

Exhibit 2 lists 11 grand strategies recommended in the strategic management literature. The problem in this case is which grand strategy to pick, given TSC's resource and resource acquisition position, that is, which is the strategy most likely to accomplish the profit criteria TSC has established for itself. Once the grand strategy has been chosen, TSC must then outline the components of the grand strategy so that it can be implemented in a timely and correct fashion. In the final analysis, the establishment of the weaving mill may or may not be included as part of this grand strategy.

## Alternative Strategies

By mid-1979, TSC had become the clear market share leader in retailing, exporting, finishing, and converting Thai silk. The question now is, where does TSC go from here? The "correct" strategy for any organization is a function of the salient characteristics of the organization and its environment. A grand strategy cluster analysis, which considers these factors, will be employed to prioritize the alternative grand strategies that could be used by TSC.

As shown in Exhibit 3, grand strategy cluster analysis requires the classification of TSC's (1) markets as experiencing rapid or slow growth and (2) relative strength of a competitive position. Based on our previous analysis, TSC's markets have been growing rapidly, and TSC possesses a relatively strong competitive position. TSC finds itself in cell I, which indicates the employment of grand strategies of concentration (market penetration, market development, and product development) and vertical integration, or concentric diversification, in order of their level of decreasing attractiveness.

TSC can remain as it is. It can integrate backward into weaving, as currently under consideration, or even as far back as sericulture. It can explore new geographical markets, perhaps even by opening retail outlets in other countries. Finally, it can apply the Jim Thompson approach of providing a quality retail outlet to other Thai products such as jewelry, brassware, and rattan furniture. Each possible new direction must be assessed in terms of both the magnitude of the opportunity it presents and TSC's ability to exploit that opportunity. Exhibit 4 outlines the advantages and disadvantages associated with each alternative.

## Solution Choice

Depending on the time frame allowed by TSC's management, TSC should establish the weaving mill and expand geographically by opening retail outlets in other countries. A grand strategy of concentration, although costing very little to implement, would not provide TSC the outlet it needs for its cash flow. If the management takes a longer-term point of view, it should expand overseas — after thoroughly researching market potential in alternative countries. The establishment of the weaving mill not only reduces raw material costs and increases capacity but also increases flexibility in cloth design, which could boost the company's retail operations.

TSC's management should also seek to develop its ability to add product variants, continually improve quality, and attract and maintain a motivated and loyal work force, since these are the strategic imperatives of a market leader operating in the growth stage of its industry's life cycle.

EXHIBIT 1

**STAGES IN TSC'S VALUE CHAIN**

| *TSC's Contemplated Weaving Venture* | | | | *TSC's Retail Activity* | |
|---|---|---|---|---|---|
| *Sericulture* | *Dyeing* | *Spinning* | *Weaving* | *Finishing* | *Converting* |
| Rawfiber | Dyed fiber | Dyed yarn | Fabric | Printed fabric | Garments, pillows, drapes |

EXHIBIT 2

**GRAND STRATEGIES**

1. Concentration
2. Horizontal integration
3. Vertical integration
4. Joint venture
5. Concentric diversification
6. Conglomerate diversification
7. Retrenchment/turnaround
8. Divestiture
9. Liquidation

Note: The grand strategy of concentration encompasses market penetration, market development, and product development.

Source: C Roland Christensen, Norman A Berg, and Malcolm S Salter, *Policy Formulation and Administration* (Homewood, Il: Richard D Irwin, 1976): 16–18.

## EXHIBIT 3

## MODEL OF GRAND STRATEGY CLUSTERS

| | Competitive Position | |
|---|---|---|
| *Market Growth* | *Strong* | *Weak* |
| RAPID | 1. Concentration<br>2. Vertical integration<br>3. Concentric diversification<br>I | 1. Reformulation of concentration<br>2. Horizontal integration<br>3. Divestiture<br>4. Liquidation<br>II |
| SLOW | III<br>1. Concentric diversification<br>2. Conglomerate diversification<br>3. Joint ventures | IV<br>1. Turnaround or retrenchment<br>2. Concentric diversification<br>3. Conglomerate diversification<br>4. Divestiture<br>5. Liquidation |

Note: Grand strategies are listed in probable decreasing order of attractiveness.

## EXHIBIT 4

## EVALUATION OF STRATEGIC ALTERNATIVES
## Open to TSC in 1979

| *Alternative* | *Advantages* | *Disadvantages* |
|---|---|---|
| Status quo (market penetration) | • Involves no major new risk. | • Provides no outlet for cash flow.<br>• Not very exciting to manage. |
| Backward integration into weaving mill | • May improve consistency and delivery.<br>• TSC has sufficient funds. | • Impact on morale of current TSC weavers of new skills.<br>• Requires development of new skills.<br>• Increases TSC's exposure to the risk of a drop in demand and a shortage of raw materials. |
| Backward integration into sericulture | • Helps to protect existing business from shortage of raw materials.<br>• TSC can bring technology to end of the industry. | • TSC lacks skills currently.<br>• Low profit potential. |
| Expansion to other markets | • Stays close to existing skill base in silk. | • Thai silk may not have retail appeal elsewhere. |
| Introduction of other products | • The proven Jim Thomson strategy: Upgrade a local industry. | • Requires new product skills.<br>• Other products are not as high value (expensive) as silk. |

# PART TWO

## Cases

SECTION ONE

# The Concept and Significance of Strategy

| *Case Number* | *Case (Country)* | *Nature of Situation* | *Complexity* |
|---|---|---|---|
| 1 | San Miguel's Expansion into Southeast Asia (Philippines) | Product/market identification | Medium |
| 2 | Daewoo Electronics Co Ltd (Korea) | Globalization | Medium |
| 3 | First Philippine Holding Corporation (Philippines) | Portfolio planning | High |
| 4 | Noel Gifts International Ltd | Planned growth | Low |

| Products/ Services | Sector | Financial Data | US$ Sales (000) | Industry Conditions |
|---|---|---|---|---|
| 'ood & beverage, .griculture, and ›ackaging | Manufacturing, agriculture | No | 1,164,315 | Declining Growth |
| :lectric and electronic quipment, and omputers | Manufacturing | No | 2,4790,891 | Growth |
| Iolding office | Public utilities, manufacturing, construction, financial services, and wholesale trade | Yes | 28,774 | Growth |
| Jonstore retailers | Retail trade | Yes | 7,935 | Growth |

# San Miguel's Expansion into Southeast Asia* 1

The San Miguel Corporation (SMC) is a Philippine-based food and beverage conglomerate headquartered in Manila. The company's flagship product, San Miguel Pale Pilsen Beer, has been the driving force behind the 103-year-old firm's rise to dominance as Southeast Asia's largest beer maker. Since 1986, San Miguel has successfully fought to extend its reach outside its traditional home markets of the Philippines and Hong Kong. The company's actions have changed the face of the brewing industry in the region and provided the Philippines with a national champion. SMC's dynamic leader, Andres Soriano III, has committed himself to preparing the company for increased competition within the region and additional opportunities in the liberalizing Southeast Asian markets. His preparations have been driven by a formal plan of internationalization described by SMC in 1989.

The purpose of this case is to analyze San Miguel's expansion strategy thus far. This analysis is made in the context of the strengths that SMC has established in its home markets through an extensive modernization and decentralization program. The goal of this case is to paint a picture of SMC's internationalization effort and, acting as an art critic, rationalize the brush strokes. In addition, the issues regarding SMC's next move in the region are discussed.

---

* Reprinted from Lindsay Alley and Thomas Stanley, "San Miguel's Expansion into Southeast Asia," *Journal of Asian Business*, 9:3 (Summer 1993): 71–92. 

## The San Miguel Corporation

San Miguel's rounding marked the beginning of the brewing industry in Asia. In 1890, Don Enrique Maria Barretto de Ycaza established La Fabrica de Cerveza de San Miguel in the Philippines, the first brewery in Southeast Asia. With assistance from a German brew master, the company's beer gained recognition as a premium quality beverage and was exported to Hong Kong and China as early as 1913.

The first few decades of operations saw rapid growth and limited vertical integration into yeast production and cold storage facilities. San Miguel's brewing operations were halted from 1942 through 1946 due to the Japanese occupation, but growth resumed after the end of World War II. The company continued to consolidate its leading position in the Philippines, and in 1948 purchased a major Hong Kong brewery and began production of San Miguel in the colony. During the postwar period, vertical integration efforts continued with the construction of a power plant, a liquid carbon dioxide plant, glass bottle manufacturing facilities, and a carton plant. Throughout the second half of the century the company's flagship beer brand consistently garnered recognition in international competitions.

The Soriano family has been connected to San Miguel since the first year of the company's founding. Andres Soriano, his son, and his grandson have run San Miguel for most of the company's history. Today, Andres Soriano III holds the reins of San Miguel. Very much a Philippine institution, San Miguel is viewed by Filipinos as a national champion with a reputation for "honesty and good corporate citizenship" (**Asian Business**, November 1992: 30).

For many years, San Miguel's activities concentrated primarily on beer production and marketing. Today, however, San Miguel is well-diversified, with beer accounting for only 50 percent of total company revenues. The gradual expansion into non-beer activities was grounded in the core beer business. San Miguel's *Bulletin* states that, "Beer was the heart of San Miguel's business . . . and the soul from which emanated all its other businesses" ("The First 100 Years, Another 100 Years." **San Miguel Beer Bulletin**, 16: 5 August–September 1990: 2). Usually, the entry into non-beer industries stemmed from earlier vertical integration moves. For example, the company's barley growing business led to other agri-business ventures, and San Miguel's years of experience with ice plants and refrigeration led to the development of frozen and dairy-based food products. Today, San Miguel operates in three main industry segments:

**Beverages.** This segment comprises the company's beer brewing, soft drinks, distilled alcohol drinks, and bottled water operations. Major products include: San Miguel Pale Pilsen Beer, Red Horse Beer, Coca-Cola, and Royal brand soft drinks. In the Philippines, San Miguel operates four breweries, including its state-of-the-art San Fernando brewery.

**Food and Agribusiness.** This segment includes integrated poultry and livestock raising and processing operations, ice cream production and marketing, fruit drinks, dairy products, and frozen shrimp production. Major products include Magnolia brand processed foods and Monterey Farms processed meat products. San Miguel has a strategic alliance in the Philippines with Campofrio, a Spanish food processing company.

**Packaging.** Packaging operations include the production and marketing of glass containers, plastic crates, laminated pouches, and paperboard boxes and cartons. San Miguel has a joint venture in the Philippines with the Yamamura Glass Company of Japan, employing state-of-the-art glass manufacturing technology.

The relative contribution of each segment to San Miguel Corporation's overall sales is shown graphically in Figure 1. Through vertical integration in these three industry segments, San Miguel has developed expertise in other areas of business: microwave communications, warehousing and trucking operations, and power generation (**Asian Business**, November 1992: 30).

San Miguel has the reputation of being a tough, if not ruthless, competitor. Through acquisition, intimidation, superior products, and sheer size, San Miguel has maintained decades of dominance in its core businesses in the Philippines. In one case, San Miguel forced a competitor out of business by smashing its rival's bottles (**Asiaweek**, April 7, 1993: 48). Only one large brewer, the well-financed Asia Brewery, competes with SMC in the Philippines; but since 1978 it has captured only 10 percent of the market. The aggressiveness of SMC and lack of competition at home have resulted in the company commanding 90 percent of the beer market in the Philippines and 60 percent of the beer market in Hong Kong.

In the non-beer beverage market, San Miguel again plays a dominant role. Through its 70-percent-owned joint venture with Coca-Cola, San Miguel holds 76 percent of the domestic soft drink market. The joint venture is Coca-Cola's sixth largest operation worldwide, with 1992 revenues of US$3,543 million. The company's Magnolia subsidiary commands 80 percent of the country's frozen dessert market and is the country's thirtieth largest firm. The company's processed foods subsidiary, San Miguel Foods Inc (SMFI), is one of the country's twenty-five largest companies (**Asian Business**, November 1992: 36).

San Miguel's dominance in the Philippines has been brought about in large part by its size, superior products, and state-of-the-art technology. It should be noted, however, that until recently, San Miguel's central beer business has been virtually immune from outside competition by imported beer. This protection has allowed San Miguel to attain its near-monopoly in beer and use its size and accumulated capital to dominate selected

FIGURE 1

**RELATIVE CONTRIBUTION OF SAN MIGUEL'S INDUSTRY Segments to Overall Sales**

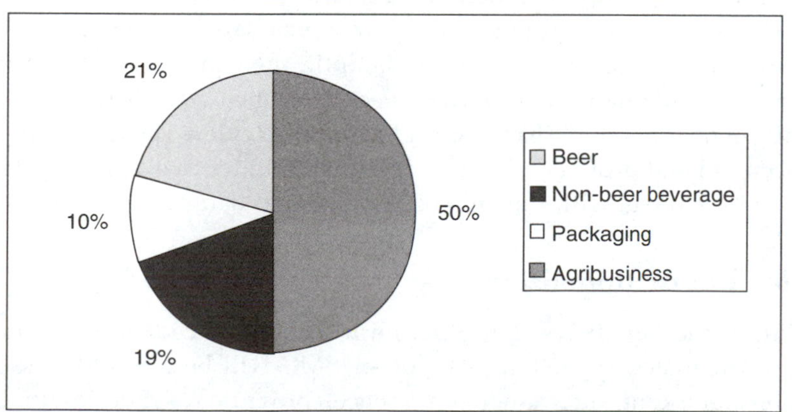

FIGURE 2

**SAN MIGUEL'S ANNUAL REVENUE AND PROFIT**
**For the Period 1982–1991**
(billions of pesos)

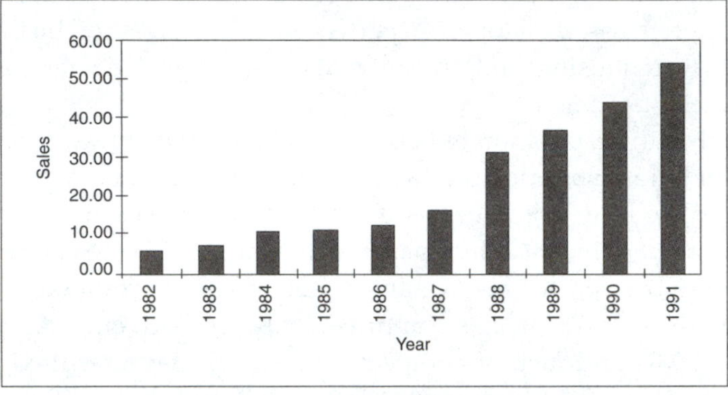


Growth in Sales

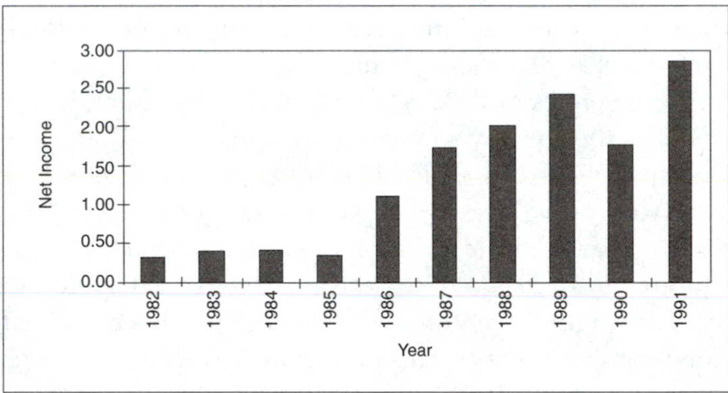


Growth in Net Income

non-beer markets. As a result, San Miguel has become the largest employer in the country, with over 36,000 employees. Company revenues represent 4 percent of the Philippine GDP, and taxes paid by San Miguel account for 7 percent of government tax receipts.

San Miguel has a tradition of successful financial performance and stability. A glimpse at SMC's revenue and profit growth (see Figure 2, **San Miguel Annual Report**, 1991: 38–39) clearly shows the success of Andres Soriano III, the company's chairman since 1986. These impressive results in recent years have been "snatched . . . from the jaws of a recession-battered Philippine economy" (**Far Eastern Economic Review [FEER]**, April 23, 1992: 52). It is these accumulated profits and SMC's financial stability that have enabled the firm to invest in foreign markets with the help of international banks.

## Impetus for Internationalization

It was not until the late 1980s that SMC formally announced its plans for expansion. Management articulated its vision as follows: "SMC will be a world-class organization with a more significant international presence, providing synergies to the domestic market" (San Miguel Corporation, **Visions**: 3). Their formal plan consisted of a three-pronged approach that can be likened to three legs on a stool: modernization, decentralization, and internationalization. Each leg serves an equally important role in developing San Miguel into a world-class company. Most of SMC's modernization and decentralization efforts have been completed through a significant overhaul of its operations in the Philippines and are described in greater detail below.

In light of San Miguel's long-standing dominance in its core Philippine and Hong Kong beer markets, one might expect that the company would be content to merely preserve its current position. Three factors, however, militate for increased activities in overseas markets: limitations in the domestic market, a changing competitive environment within the region, and the benefits that would accrue from international operations.

After decades of steady growth in the Philippines and Hong Kong, San Miguel in the mid-1980s found itself the victim of its own success. As the dominant player in both markets, it was becoming increasingly difficult to increase sales or market share; the company was left "with gradually diminishing room for domestic growth" (San Miguel Corporation, **Visions**: 2). Also limiting the potential for growth in these markets was the fact that beer consumption in the home markets of the Philippines and Hong Kong was already quite high compared to other markets in the region (see Table 1).

The company's reliance on the Philippine market also created genuine risks. The Philippine economy is highly cyclical and extremely sensitive to swings in world commodity prices and oil prices. As a result, the company's performance has been closely linked to the highly volatile Philippine economy. Internationalization would help insulate San Miguel from this exposure.

The threat of intensified competition in the Asia-Pacific region is another reason for San Miguel to internationalize. Several factors point to a changing competitive environment in Southeast Asia: the entry of large foreign beer-makers, increased regional competition of local brewers, and the expansion of Asia-Pacific Breweries.

TABLE 1

**Annual Beer Consumption in Asian Regional Markets**

| *Location* | *Liters per Capita* |
|---|---|
| Australia | 80 |
| Japan | 54 |
| Taiwan | 40 |
| South Korea | 35 |
| Philippines | 24 |
| Singapore | 22 |
| Hong Kong | 20 |
| China (Guangzhou) | 12 |
| Thailand | 4 |
| Malaysia | 4 |
| Vietnam | 4 |
| India | 1 |
| Indonesia | 0.5 |

Source: *Asian Business*, 2, November 1992: 29–36.

As the beer markets of Europe, the United States, and Japan stagnate or contract, large breweries are increasingly turning to Asia for expansion, including Anheuser-Busch and Miller of the United States, Kirin of Japan, and BSN of France: all more than twice as large as San Miguel. Internationalization would enable San Miguel to "know how to fight" and avoid being "trampled underfoot by those Goliaths" (San Miguel Corporation, **Visions**: 4).

Regional brewers are a threat as tariffs in the region slowly decline. While this clearly presents opportunities for San Miguel, it also puts the company's Philippine and Hong Kong profit sanctuaries at risk. By moving aggressively into other regional markets, San Miguel can deny other regional brewers their own profit sanctuary and hamper their ability to fight San Miguel in the Philippines or Hong Kong. Most regional brewers have confined their operations to their home markets which they, like San Miguel, dominate due to protective tariffs and lack of domestic competitors. For example, in Taiwan, the government alcohol monopoly's "Taiwan Beer" dominates the market; and in Thailand, two local brewers control the entire Thai beer market. In China there are no large national brewers, but over eight hundred regional brewers compete in their own local markets to dominate the beer industry. Not only will these regional brewers fight tenaciously to maintain their market share, but they may also seek to launch export drives of their own beer into other regional markets, including the Philippines.

Headquartered in Singapore, Asia Pacific Breweries (APB) is the only other Asian brewer with a significant regional presence. A joint venture between Fraser & Neave Brewery and Heineken Brewery (Netherlands), APB has access to world-class brewing technology and has extensive experience in marketing and production outside its home market of Singapore. APB produces in Malaysia, Vietnam, Shanghai, and Papua New Guinea, and exports its Tiger and Anchor beers throughout the Asia-Pacific region. In 1991, APB's annual sales were US$850 million.

While APB and San Miguel currently compete only in their export markets, Heineken's plan to make APB "the fastest-growing brewer in this part of the world [Asia]" (**The Straits Times**, February 21, 1993: 4) will lead to an increase in head-to-head competition. As the two brewers begin to compete more directly, APB could attempt to attack San Miguel's home territory. Again, internationalization would help thwart APB's ability to mount such an attack, as well as reduce San Miguel's dependence on its two home markets.

By moving into foreign markets, San Miguel could realize several important benefits. Internationalization would give San Miguel greater access to technology in brewing and other non-beer business segments. As competition intensifies in the brewing industry, technology will become increasingly important as a source of competitive cost advantage. The ability to transfer technology across national boundaries will increase SMC's access to incremental improvements in technology.

Expanding overseas would give San Miguel the advantages of scale economies in terms of production facilities, raw material prices, and research and development, especially as beer products become increasingly homogeneous. Without world-class technology and the economies of scale gained from internationalization, San Miguel would be extremely vulnerable to attacks by low-cost producers such as Anheuser-Busch. In addition, locations overseas will put SMC's brands closer to the consumer market, providing for faster reaction to changes in consumer tastes.

## Modernization and Internationalization

In 1988, SMC initiated a five-year, $1 billion investment program with the intention of accomplishing three primary goals: to boost the operating efficiency of SMC's existing plants in the Philippines, to revamp the SMC management structure through a major decentralization effort, and to lay a solid foundation in the Philippines for expansion overseas (**Asian Business**, November, 1992: 29). The investment program ended in December of 1992, rewarding SMC with extremely efficient, high-productivity manufacturing facilities. This program represents two of the legs of San Miguel's overall expansion strategy.

The primary theme of the investment program was an effort by management to instill quality into every aspect of operations. A program of total quality management within the organization has provided San Miguel with a competitive advantage over regional producers that do not have extensive quality management in place. The quality emphasis worked successfully for the modernization program; several of SMC's plants in the Philippines boast awards for quality and efficiency of production.

A walk through San Miguel's largest brewery, San Fernando, provides some clues as to the results of SMC's investment in technology. "Inside the plant, intelligent bottling lines equipped with computerized sensors have recently been installed. Sophisticated process-control equipment monitors the production flow" (**Asian Business**, November, 1992: 29). Engineers at the San Fernando plant frequently meet together in quality circles on the factory floor to suggest ways to improve production processes and increase quality. In addition, beer salesmen are being equipped with hand-held computers to expedite the ordering and delivery process, and non-beer factories are installing state-of-the-art equipment for the production of SMC products. For example, SMC's new glass-making facility features the latest in high-tech Japanese glass-making technology, making the facility one of the most efficient in Southeast Asia. In total, the investment plan covered the development of twenty-two new high-tech factories, putting San Miguel's operations on par with those of any Western multinational (**Asian Business**, November, 1992: 29).

In addition to completing an overhaul of its existing facilities, SMC reorganized its management and reporting structure during the five-year investment program. SMC's rapid growth has forced the firm to decentralize its reporting structure in order to provide the separate operating divisions more autonomy to react to changing environments. The firm's eighteen non-beer businesses are in the process of being spun off into separate operating companies. The largest spin-offs include the Magnolia division, San Miguel Foods Inc (SMFI), and San Miguel Properties Philippines Inc (SMPPI), which includes all of SMC's real estate holdings. Soriano has considered listing the firm's larger spin-offs on the Philippine Stock Exchange. This would allow each separate company additional access to capital and give investors the opportunity to concentrate their money on less-diversified assets.

The increased autonomy has resulted in more responsibility for division managers and has accomplished the task of keeping the day-to-day operations of the company distant from the problems in headquarters regarding control of the firm. Each division manager has been given responsibility for dealing with local politics, negotiating with labor unions, building a productive work force, and expanding existing product lines.

The additional responsibilities have forced SMC to develop an extensive system of checks and balances for all its managers. A rotation program for senior managers provides management with experience in several operating divisions and across many product lines. SMC has also improved the channels of communication by requiring each division to publish monthly newsletters. Because of the increased responsibility given to division managers and the improvements made in communication, Soriano was able to trim headquarters down to a lean staff of only 1,000 employees.

A further advantage of SMC's decentralization process is the firm's ability to recognize unprofitable product lines and "fat" management divisions. SMC recently pulled out of the coffee planting and fruit puree manufacturing businesses and has announced layoffs numbering in the thousands. Each incremental move toward decentralization provides SMC's separate operating divisions with more flexibility to expand overseas and enter into joint ventures at home.

In addition to investments in technology and efforts to decentralize management, SMC reorganized and diversified its product lines at home in order to increase the number of opportunities for investment in international markets and reduce the company's dependence on beer. Throughout the 1980s, SMC consolidated its beer division and expanded other product lines. Poultry hatcheries and breeder farms were built in 1982, an ice cream plant in 1983, a shrimp cold storage and freezer plant in 1984, and a hog and cattle plant in 1988. In addition, several joint ventures were initiated where SMC believed its distribution and marketing systems would provide foreign companies access to the Philippine consumer market. For example, in 1981 SMC's soft drink division was spun off into a partnership with the Coca-Cola Company. This joint venture holds over 70 percent of the soft drink market in the Philippines and is Coke's sixth largest worldwide operation. SMC also entered into a joint venture with the New Zealand Dairy Board. Joint venture agreements and additional production facilities successfully expanded SMC's non-beer product lines and decreased the company's reliance on beer to 50 percent of revenues.

The primary advantage of undergoing a modernization program as extensive as the one completed by SMC is the transferability of these efforts across national boundaries. SMC did not spend US$1 billion merely to better serve its existing customer base in the Philippines. The investment program was undertaken with the knowledge that SMC must embody world-class manufacturing and management to compete on an international level. Perfecting operations at home was a first step in the move toward internationalization. In addition, SMC's decentralization efforts have established a strong core of managers who are able to enter new markets and react to potential problems without the constant aid of headquarters.

## San Miguel's International Expansion

The strategy San Miguel has employed to internationalize can be broken down into four steps (see Figure 3). The first step of the expansion program was put into motion in the early 1980s; the second and third steps were emphasized from the late 1980s to the present; and the fourth step is just under way in certain areas. This four-step process represents the third part of SMC's expansion strategy described above.

The purpose of the first step (i.e., prepare domestically) of the expansion strategy was to make San Miguel a world-class company within the Philippines. This aim was

FIGURE 3

**SAN MIGUEL'S STRATEGY FOR INTERNATIONAL EXPANSION**

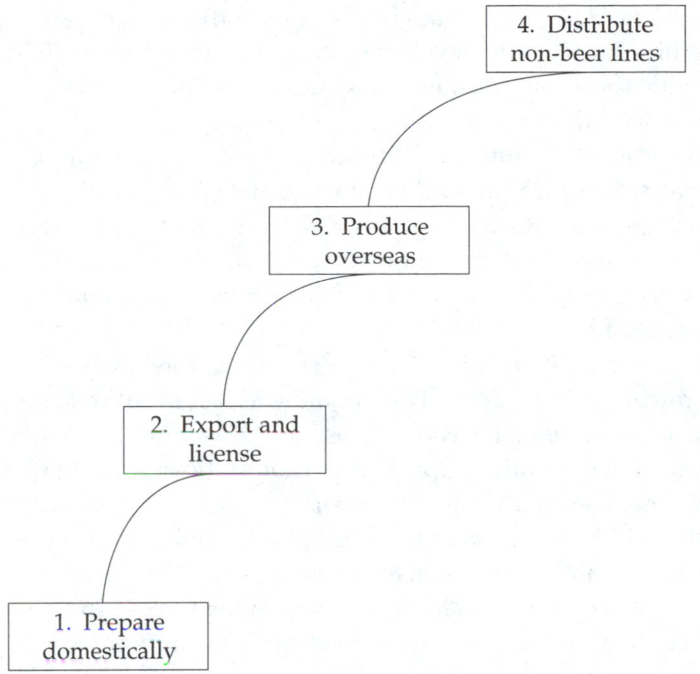


accomplished by consolidation in the Philippines of the company's primary markets. The bulk of this stage of the strategic plan, however, was the five-year, US$1 billion modernization and decentralization program that was launched in 1987. By developing world-class competence and resources and creating a broad product portfolio in its protected home market, San Miguel set the stage for expansion outside the Philippines.

The second stage of San Miguel's expansion plan was initiated concurrently with the first step. The company had exported its beer since 1913; in the late 1980s, there was a conscious effort to increase exports. From 1985 to 1989 alone, beer exports increased 150 percent ("SMC Expanding Exports of Beer." **Business World**, January 26, 1989: 20). The goal of this export drive was to establish brand recognition in target markets for San Miguel beer. In addition, the strong export presence allowed SMC to become increasingly familiar with local consumer preferences, business conditions, distribution systems, and regulations.

By 1993, San Miguel was widely available in every major market in Asia and was also exported to the United States, Australia, and the Middle East. Once an export market was firmly established, San Miguel entered distribution agreements in promising markets to further consolidate its market position. By the early 1990s, San Miguel had distribution agreements in Thailand, the United States, Malaysia, Australia, Sri Lanka, and Taiwan.

Where suitable opportunities have permitted, San Miguel has entered licensing agreements with local brewers to brew San Miguel beer locally. By 1993, licensees brewed San Miguel in Thailand, Nepal (with exports to Sikkim and Bhutan), and Papua New Guinea. Prior to its purchase of PT Delta Djakarta in 1992, San Miguel also had a licensee in Indonesia.

Although San Miguel has had overseas production in Hong Kong since 1948, it was not until 1991 that the third step, or the company's expansion strategy, began in earnest. In looking at where to locate production, San Miguel had to consider two important factors: whether the target market is large enough to support efficient large-scale production and the overall stage of infrastructure development of the target market. To date, San Miguel has elected to produce in "growth" countries while continuing to develop emerging markets through stage two activities.

In 1991 San Miguel acquired a 70-percent share in Guangdong's largest brewer, Guangzhou Brewery, for US$5 million. Prior to acquiring the facility in Southern China, San Miguel had exported into the region from Hong Kong for fifteen years, with its brands selling at a 50-percent premium over local brews. Currently, 10 percent of Guangzhou Brewery's output is devoted to San Miguel; the remainder is used for the brewery's original brands.

The move has made San Miguel the best-selling foreign beer in China and the largest foreign brewer in Guangdong. This is quite a feat for the company considering the presence of brewing operations for Pabst, Holstein, Miller, and Becks in the same region. San Miguel Guangzhou currently supplies 33 percent of the market in Guangdong, which is the fastest-growing beer market in the country.

San Miguel had brewed its beer in Indonesia through a licensee for over a decade when, in late 1992, the company announced its purchase of 49 percent of P T Delta Djakarta from the troubled Mantrust Group. The US$35 million deal gave San Miguel an immediate 40 percent market share of the Indonesian beer market through Delta Djakarta's Anker brand beer and Carlsberg (produced through a licensing agreement). P T Delta Djakarta's distribution is handled by another Mantrust unit, P T Borsumij Wehry Indonesia.

The final step of San Miguel's expansion strategy is to use the resources the company had established in overseas markets to introduce its non-beer businesses and products. Having established production, distribution, and marketing capability in a target market through its flagship beer lines, San Miguel can then push its ice cream, meat processing, or snack food products through the same channels. This process of leveraging its resources within a market is similar to its pattern of expansion in the Philippines during the 1980s. It is this characteristic of San Miguel that sets it apart from its other competitors in Asia, who have only limited non-beer product lines. Through this strategy, San Miguel can spread its overhead across more products and enjoy additional benefits such as marketing tie-ins.

### Strategic Analysis

SMC has divided up the countries of Southeast Asia into two categories depending on their stage of development as it applies to SMC's operations: "emerging" countries and "growth" countries. Growth countries are defined as "those where economic and technological infrastructure to support rapid and sustainable development are already in place and consumer activity is high." Examples of growth countries include Indonesia, Thailand, and Malaysia. Emerging countries are defined as containing "business opportunities that are becoming more promising as these countries begin to stabilize and build the infrastructure needed to sustain growth." Examples include Vietnam, Indochina and Cambodia (San Miguel Corporation, **Visions**: 3). Thus far, SMC has followed a "wait-and-see" investment strategy in its domestic market; the firm never enters a new market without analyzing the mistakes of its competitors. This strategy has proved successful in the Philippines where SMC can use its muscle to drive out small competitors. However, SMC realizes that the "wait-and-see" attitude could prove costly if used to drive its expansion strategy. This strategy, to date, is more aggressive than San Miguel's investment strategy at home.

This section provides an analysis of the factors that led SMC to make the expansion choices outlined in the previous section. In particular this section analyzes why SMC chose Southeast Asia as a starting ground for expansion and why the investments in southern China and Indonesia make good long-term sense.

SMC's decision to initiate its expansion strategy in Southeast Asia may appear to make sense because of the proximity of the region. However, there are three additional factors that influenced SMC's decision to invest in this part of the world:

1. the potential growth of the beverage industry in the region,
2. SMC's relative familiarity with the different cultures, traditions, and governments of Southeast Asia, and
3. SMC's experience distributing its product lines in difficult operating environments.

For the past several years, Southeast Asia has been the fastest-growing region in the world. Its country GDPs are growing from 7 to 12 percent per year. Growth in per capita income has provided Southeast Asians with many luxuries previously unaffordable to the region. As the quality of living improves, customers will increase their spending on entertainment and other luxuries of life. This includes their consumption of beer, wine, and spirits. Figure 4 presents consumption levels of beer versus per capita GDP for all the countries within the region. Obvious from the result is the strong relationship between the two factors. Considering the potential for GDP growth in countries like China, Malaysia, Indonesia, and Vietnam, it is easy to see why this region is attractive to the beer industry, and in particular, to San Miguel. The region becomes particularly

FIGURE 4

**CONSUMPTION LEVELS OF BEER COMPARED TO PER CAPITA GDP**
**for Southeast Asian Countries**

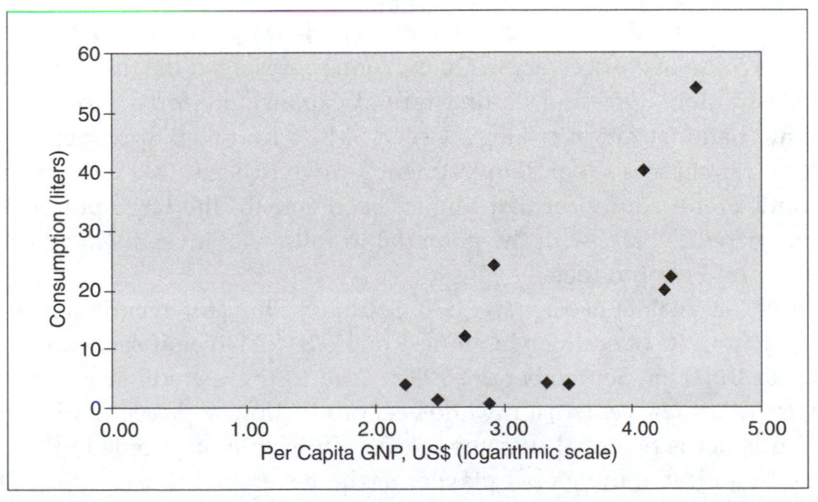

attractive when one considers the flat or declining growth of beer consumption in the United States, Germany, and Japan, the three largest beer markets in the world.

Due to the abundance of ethnic groups resulting in different traditions and preferences within Southeast Asia, an expansion strategy into this region of the world is a difficult move for any major multinational firm. To succeed at marketing consumer products in Southeast Asia, a multinational must understand the differences that exist in each market. In addition, multinationals must succeed at developing strong relationships with local governments. These governments often play an integral role in the business practices and investment strategies in their country. In many Southeast Asian countries, competition has been slow to develop because diplomacy and trade issues have significantly delayed investment by United States and German beer-makers; this is especially true in China, Vietnam, and other parts of Indochina.

SMC's century-old presence in the region has provided the firm with a significant advantage over its competitors in its ability to react to the different markets and cultures within Southeast Asia. Licensing and distribution facilities have penetrated every market in the region, giving SMC marketing experience that few other beer-makers command. In addition, SMC's presence in Hong Kong has resulted in significant business ties, with overseas Chinese operating in that part of the region. SMC's chairman, Soriano, sums it up best, "we picked an area we are comfortable with, where we can get along with the local culture" (**Asian Business**, November 1992: 2).

SMC's ability to deliver its products without compromising freshness or quality in a sometimes hostile environment in the Philippines has provided the firm with experience that will prove to be invaluable during its expansion into the rest of Southeast Asia. SMC has mastered ways of getting around the Philippines' poor infrastructure, enabling it to service and distribute its products to the hard-to-reach locations within the country. For example, SMC owns its own microwave communication network in order to prevent the firm from becoming a prisoner of the Philippines' inefficient phone system. In addition, SMC maintains its own fleet of trucks in order to provide timely delivery of products instead of depending on unreliable distribution services. The weak infrastructure and the "difficult-to-reach places" found in the Philippines are problems that exist in most Southeast Asian countries. SMC's experience in establishing distribution systems that minimize these problems has provided the firm with an advantage over other multinational beer-makers who are used to a more stable and efficient operating environment.

SMC's purchase of the brewery in Guangzhou represented the firm's first production expansion abroad since 1969 and its first formal expansion efforts into China under its announced internationalization strategy. Given SMC's four-step approach to expansion, the Guangzhou purchase is a logical investment for two reasons: (a) export presence in the region has built brand equity for San Miguel beer, and (b) the large potential customer base in China provides SMC with the potential to follow its investment in beer with the distribution of non-beer products.

San Miguel has maintained a presence in Southern China for over fifteen years through imports of beer from its operations in Hong Kong ("SMC Diversification, Foreign Moves Bared." **Manila Bulletin**, September 26, 1990). Due to the incredible growth of China's economy over the last few years, a foray into beer production made economic sense because of the magnitude of the potential customer base, over 55 million people in the Guangdong region alone. In addition, the global players in the beverage industry did not have any significant presence in China, leaving the traditionally fragmented market to local producers. The decision to purchase a large local brewery gave SMC a two- or three-year jump over the company's other option of setting up a brewery on a greenfield site. This may prove significant as regional competition intensifies.

The beer market in Southern China is not SMC's only incentive for entering the region. By the end of 1993, SMC hopes to begin the fourth step in its expansion strategy into China: the use of beer as a stepping stone for its other products. The size and potential growth of China's customer base makes the market particularly attractive to SMC's other product lines. SMC's operations in Guangdong have proceeded smoothly for the last two years, providing a strong distribution and marketing presence in the region. If SMC is able to successfully introduce its non-beer products into Guangdong, expansion into the rest of China could occur on a company-wide, full-product basis. SMC is developing the necessary contacts and is seeking partners in China as a means of investing in distribution systems in the Guangdong region. These joint ventures will be formed with the intention of using the distribution systems as a base from which to move into Northern China once that market becomes attractive ("San Miguel to Follow Familiar Trail in Mainland." **South China Morning Post**, September 10, 1992: 3).

SMC plans to invest heavily in China over the next several years. The company expects to open as many as seven plants over the next ten years, with investments split among the regions of Guangdong, Shanghai, and Beijing (**Hong Kong Standard**, May 15, 1991). Because of the cost of building a greenfield investment (US$100 million), SMC plans to continue its strategy of acquiring efficient, well-managed, local producers.

SMC's recent purchase of a large local Indonesian brewery continued the company's expansion efforts into the region. The choice of Indonesia as the next country to expand in is a good choice for two reasons: the investment continues what Baring Securities terms a "strategy of encirclement of San Miguel's primary competition in the region, and the size of the Indonesian market makes expansion into non-beer products very attractive for SMC (**Asian Wall Street Journal [AWSJ]**, September 10, 1992: 3).

As mentioned previously, SMC's largest regional competitor in Southeast Asia is Asia-Pacific Brewery. Until 1991, APB had limited its production facilities to Malaysia and Singapore, and competed in other markets with San Miguel primarily through exports. SMC's purchase of the Delta Djakarta brewery puts the company in a direct battle with APB because of its proximity to the competitor's Malaysian and Singapore operations. The *Asian Wall Street Journal* states that the acquisition preempts any opportunity APB had of becoming the primary beer-maker in Indonesia. In addition, San Miguel's investment into Indonesia acts as a long-term strategy to contain APB to their home markets until beer policy is liberalized and SMC is able to adequately compete in Malaysia and Singapore. As markets outside of Malaysia and Singapore deregulate direct foreign investment policy, SMC should continue to move quickly to develop joint ventures with local firms for the production of San Miguel beer.

Similar to the consumer market in China, Indonesia's size provides an excellent opportunity for SMC to expand into non-beer businesses once they have established a marketing and distribution presence in the country. In fact, Indonesia's beer market is severely limited due to a Muslim population of close to 90 percent. The size of the country (fourth largest population in the world) and Indonesia's growth in GDP makes the beer market attractive to any beer-maker, but SMC expects that its food division and Magnolia ice cream brand will have an opportunity to exploit the advantages of an established distribution and marketing system and sell to a much larger customer base (**AWSJ**, September 10, 1992: 3).

No one believes San Miguel will sit still with its latest Indonesian acquisition. Vietnam and Thailand continue to dominate rumors about locations for SMC's next acquisitions. In fact, to continue its aggressive expansion strategy, the company has begun talks with the government of Vietnam to build a brewing facility in Hanoi. SMC believes that from its vantage point in Vietnam, the company can begin an expansion into the rest of Indochina in the near future (**Manila Chronicle**, July 22, 1992: 9). If the facility in Hanoi is approved, it would represent SMC's first brewery in Indochina and its first foray into an emerging country. Vietnam law requires that all foreign investment take the form of a joint venture but the attractiveness of the SMC investment and the lack of an efficient local producer has resulted in the Vietnamese government itself stepping in to take the other side of the venture.

Vietnam's per capita beer consumption is relatively high, given its low per capita GDP. In addition, the country is considered one of San Miguel's "emerging" markets, with high growth rates expected in the future. San Miguel has enjoyed strong export sales into the country for several years but has yet to set up production there. In 1991 the company appeared close to a US$100 million joint venture investment agreement with the Vietnamese government, and in mid-1992, was negotiating a production deal with a brewery in Hanoi. One development that may have put San Miguel's Vietnam plans on hold was APB's aggressive entry into Vietnam. In 1992, APB purchased a 60-percent share of Vietnam's largest brewery in Ho Chi Minh City, and will begin production in late 1993 (**Asia Pacific Brewery Annual Report**, 1991: 15). Still, in late 1992, San Miguel officials were predicting that the company will be in Vietnam "in a couple of years" (**AWSJ**, September 10, 1992: 3).

In addition to investment discussions in Vietnam, SMC has made news in Thailand by agreeing to license its brands to a Thai brewery. The move in Thailand came shortly after a meeting with Philippine President Ramos and Thai Prime Minister Chuan Leekpai. Both leaders agreed to double the trade between the two countries to take advantage of the many years of friendship between Thailand and the Philippines ("SMC Eyes Thailand for Beer." **Daily Globe**, December 23, 1992: 11). Currently, there are only two local breweries in Thailand producing three brands of beer. Increased access to the Thai market through licensing and eventually by San Miguel production facilities will continue SMC's strategy of encirclement and should provide the Philippine brewer with an advantage over Thailand's much smaller, local competitors. The maturity of Thailand's consumer market (growth country) and the stability of its political environment may make the investment a more attractive option than the one in Vietnam.

San Miguel has captured a sliver of the Thai market through exports. The company entered into a distribution agreement in 1989 with a local company and in early 1993 reportedly entered into an agreement with Thai Phalit Sura to brew San Miguel in Thailand under license, although the Thai company had no prior brewing experience ("Thai Firm to Brew San Miguel Beer — Report." **Philippine Star**, January 6, 1993: 18). At the end of 1992, San Miguel Chairman Soriano had discussions with the Thai Life Group about building a brewery in Bangkok, a move that would be "vital to SMC's plans to expand beer exports to neighboring Vietnam" (**Business Times**, December 29, 1992). San Miguel may, therefore, choose to first concentrate on building a production facility in Thailand before entering Vietnam. The Thai facility could efficiently export to Vietnam and other Indochinese countries until the Vietnamese market and infrastructure have matured. This would be consistent with SMC's strategy of investing in "growth countries" suitable for production. Vietnam is still an "emerging" country better suited to the second step of expansion — export, distribution, and licensing.

## Potential Roadblocks to Success

The preceding sections have argued that San Miguel has followed a sound plan for internationalization and has developed the necessary strengths and resources to successfully expand into the region. As San Miguel faces the future, however, it must negotiate four critical problems. Two problems come from outside the company: legislation proposed by the Ramos administration and possible strategic moves by San Miguel's competitors in the beer industry. Two other threats to SMC's success come from within the company: the ongoing struggle for control of the firm and the increasing complexity of coordinating its actions in a variety of businesses and markets.

A significant threat to San Miguel's continued expansion strategy is the government's intention to break up domestic monopolies. San Miguel and the national telephone company, PLDT, are frequently mentioned as possible targets for government action. Fidel Ramos' administration wants to do away with "undue concentration of power in the hands of a few, suppression of competition, and control over markets" and "unreasonable market power" (**Asiaweek**, April 7, 1993: 48). The anti-trust bill proposed by Ramos could stop San Miguel from lowering prices to undercut the competition and stop the company from requiring its beer channels to carry its soft drink products. San Miguel has argued vehemently against the legislation, stating that it would harm "entrepreneurs who seek to benefit customers, regardless of the reasonableness of their prices" (**Asiaweek**, April 7, 1993: 48). There has also been speculation that the government will focus its efforts on unpopular, inefficient monopolies rather than breaking up a well-regarded national champion such as San Miguel.

As discussed previously, San Miguel has long had the Philippine beer market to itself. As competition heats up, San Miguel may find itself on the other end of the stick, defending its home market from attacks by competitors. The 1.5 billion liter Philippine market is significant. In terms of annual volume, it is larger than the Indonesian, Vietnam, Hong Kong, Malaysian, Thai, and Singapore beer markets combined. A competitor, such as APB, may wish to attack San Miguel at home to deny it the luxury of its own profit sanctuary. San Miguel may also face increasing competition from Asia Brewery, its only domestic rival, run by the deep-pocketed investor Lucio Tan. Certainly the proposed "trust-busting" legislation would increase the competitive threat to San Miguel's Philippine stronghold by domestic or foreign rivals. In recent years, San Miguel faced a similar onslaught in Hong Kong and has watched its market share and profits fall dramatically.

In its international ventures, San Miguel must also contend with competitive reactions from local beer producers and host governments. San Miguel is trying to take market share away from producers who have dominated their own local markets for decades. In countries such as Thailand or Taiwan, local beers have a strong national identity, similar to San Miguel's reputation at home. San Miguel may find it difficult to attract sufficient numbers of local beer consumers to a "foreign" brand, despite a positive image and low-cost producer status. Moreover, it can be expected that local beer producers will react fiercely to protect their sales.

In addition, host governments may cause difficulties for San Miguel in response to pressure from domestic brewers. By restricting ownership, distribution, or repatriation of profits, a host government could hamper San Miguel's efforts. While the company can try to minimize these risks by establishing good contacts, gaining understanding of the operating environment prior to full-scale entry, and finding large local partners or acquisition targets, it is nonetheless vulnerable to retaliatory action from the governments of the countries into which it plans to expand.

Despite stellar performance in his seven years at the helm, San Miguel Chairman Andres Soriano III may lose control of the company his father and grandfather helped create. In a battle that has been fought in the courts for several years, Soriano and Eduardo "Danding" Cojuangco have been jockeying for the right to control the company. Cojuangco served as San Miguel's Chairman from 1983 to 1986; the Sorianos had owned 25 percent of San Miguel in the 1970s but decided to divest from the Philippines in the early 1980s, at which time Cojuangco gained a controlling interest in the firm. Cojuangco fled the country with Ferdinand Marcos in 1986, however, and the government sequestered his shares. Since then, Cojuangco has returned to the Philippines and is now fighting to regain his shares. If and when he succeeds, the Sorianos, now holding under two percent of the firm, could be ousted. This public struggle for control of the firm has lasted several years and is still unresolved. The conventional wisdom holds that Cojuangco would not kill the "golden goose" if he regains control but there is some degree of fear that Cojuangco (also known as "Pacman" from his penchant for gobbling up companies) may tamper with San Miguel's proven recipe for success.

Another challenge facing San Miguel is whether it can organizationally keep up with the tremendous operational and geographical expansion it is planning. San Miguel has historically been rooted in the Philippine market; even today it receives only 13 percent (**Asian Business**, November 1992: 31) of its revenues from outside the Philippines. The company's ambitious expansion program will put new pressure on its organizational structure.

Currently, the company is able to coordinate international strategy from its corporate headquarters. As San Miguel continues to expand into new countries and introduce additional product lines in China, Indonesia, and elsewhere, it will find it increasingly difficult to coordinate the various movements of its decentralized parts. San Miguel's expansion has relied on careful central planning and a step-by-step entry into new markets. There is a significant danger that the decentralization of this planning process may blunt one of San Miguel's most potent competitive advantages, its superior size. A key challenge facing the company, therefore, is how to continue to be both large and nimble as it strengthens its positions overseas.

## Implications of San Miguel's Success

There are lessons to be learned any time a company is successful in its efforts to internationalize its operations. The example of San Miguel's expansion into Southeast Asia is no exception. There are three groups of companies that may benefit from analyzing the strategic moves made by SMC over the past several years: Western beer-makers, local beer-makers in Southeast Asia, and Southeast Asian multinationals.

Western beer-makers should take a close look at San Miguel before attempting to enter the region with any significant force. The Philippine conglomerate should no longer be considered a clumsy domestic beer-maker protected by tariff barriers. An extensive modernization program at home and successful expansion investments in the region have solidified San Miguel's dominance in Southeast Asia. Any moves by Western multinationals will undoubtedly be countered swiftly by a healthy, experienced, and determined San Miguel. SMC's superior location, marketing skills, distribution experience, and knowledge of the region will result in a formidable competitor for any Western brewer that plans to enter or expand in the region.

SMC's expansion efforts produce a significant threat to all local breweries in Southeast Asia, particularly in Thailand, South Korea, and Taiwan, where demand for beer is high and local producers are protected by government restrictions and regulation. SMC's support of the Asian Free Trade Agreement lends credence to the belief that the company will quickly move into high-growth markets that are pried open by regional trade agreements. Throughout Southeast Asia, local beer producers have been accustomed to limited competition at home and have long thrived on high margins and stable growth. No longer can these local producers expect to be protected by their governments.

These producers will have to do one of the following:

1. Enter into a strategic alliance or joint venture with a foreign partner.
2. Invest heavily in modernization programs to level the production playing field.
3. Define a niche market in their country and build a customer base in that market.

SMC's world-class operations and its superior size and experience put the Philippine multinational at a significant advantage over most of its Southeast Asian competitors.

The final group of companies that can use the San Miguel case as a learning experience are other large Southeast Asian manufacturers. San Miguel's corporate strategy since 1986 has been formed in reaction to a situation in which many other large Southeast Asian companies find themselves. SMC used its strength in the Philippines and revenues from its market protection to invest heavily in improvements at home. At the same time, SMC increased its export presence to all countries in the region to build brand equity for San Miguel beer. The success of SMC's expansion strategy rests on the company's ability to exploit its advantages at home and use the accumulated capital from its profit sanctuary to invest in operations overseas. These investments are followed by a transfer of SMC's state-of-the-art technology from its modernized Philippine facilities. Many Southeast Asian manufacturers have the ability to exploit the same advantages possessed by SMC throughout the 1980s. The ability of these firms to capitalize on the advantages offered in their home markets will add to their potential to expand and compete within the region.

## References

*Asian Business*, 2, November 1992: 29–36.
*Asian Wall Street Journal [AWSJ]*. September 10, 1992: 3.
*Asia Pacific Brewery Annual Report*. 1991.

*Asiaweek*. April 7, 1993: 48–49.

*Business Times*. December 29, 1992.

*Far Eastern Economic Review [FEER]*, April 23, 1992: 52.

*Hong Kong Standard*. May 15, 1991.

*Manila Chronicle*. July 22, 1992: 9.

San Miguel Corporation. *San Miguel Annual Report*. 1991.

San Miguel Corporation. "The First 100 Years, Another 100 Years." *San Miguel Beer Bulletin* 16:5 (August–September 1990).

San Miguel Corporation. *Visions*. no date: 2–4.

"San Mig to Follow Familiar Trail in Mainland." *South China Morning Post*. September 10, 1992: 3.

"SMC Diversification, Foreign Moves Bared." *Manila Bulletin*. September 26, 1990.

"SMC Expanding Exports of Beer." *Business World*. January 26, 1989: 20.

"SMC Eyes Thailand for Beer." *Daily Globe*. December 23, 1992: 11.

*Straits Times*. February 21, 1993: 4.

"Thai Firm to Brew San Miguel Beer — Report." *Philippine Star*. January 6, 1993: 18.

# Daewoo Electronics Co Ltd* 2

## Introduction

Daewoo Electronics Co Ltd was initially established as an apparel-maker under the name of National Apparel Co in 1972. The company changed its name to Daewoo Electronics (*Daewoo* means "great universe" in Korean) and its line of business to electronic and electric products in 1974. Since then, it has grown into an outstanding international manufacturer and supplier of quality electronics products. This was made possible through the company's dedication to creating a more competitive position through its corporate activities.

In 1983, the company was publicly listed with a paid-up capital of 40 billion won and acquired the home appliance division of the Taihan Electric Wire Co. In 1984, Daewoo Electronics added computers to its product line. In 1985, the company constructed its first color television sets for export to the Middle East and formed a joint venture with General Electric of the United States. In 1988, it constructed two plants in France and Northern Ireland to produce electronic ranges and videocassette recorders (VCRs), respectively. In 1991, it commenced production at its plants in Myanmar and Mexico.

By 1994, Daewoo Electronics was the third largest manufacturer of electronics products in Korea, controlling about 17 percent of the domestic electronics market. It

---

* This case was prepared by Professor Chang Young-Chul of the National University of Singapore to serve as a basis for class discussion rather than to illustrate effective or ineffective handling of an administrative situation. 

had the largest number of retail outlets and sales service centers in the nation. Its business activities were grouped into four major product divisions: (a) electronics, (b) electric products, (c) audio equipment, and (d) computers and other products including pianos.

Sales for the financial year ending December 31, 1993 reached about 2,000 billion won. This strong performance was attributed to the recovery of exports and the growing demand for its large-size color television sets, pianos, and computers in the domestic market. In 1994, the company was making efforts to: (a) diversify its overseas markets to Eastern Europe and the Commonwealth of Independent States, (b) expand production at its overseas plants, and (c) export under its own brand. It also sought to improve its profit margin by producing higher value-added products and implementing cost-effective operations at its overseas plants. At the same time, the company's progressive corporate philosophy, with its emphasis on innovation and growth, provided the boost for Daewoo to become an international leader in electronics for the coming century.

Daewoo spearheads advanced product technology today. Through intensive research and development (R&D), it has been able to provide a continuous flow of new and exciting ideas to meet consumer demands. It has also worked toward the integrated application of such high-tech areas as new material, robotic lasers, and bioengineering.

During the early 1990s, the company shifted its strategic focus to improving productivity and overall efficiency, rather than the simple pursuit of sales maximization. At the same time, by upgrading product quality and production technology as well as through improving organizational structure, the company has positioned itself to become a world-class electronics manufacturer.

All these efforts reflect Daewoo's relentless quest to continually adapt to the ever-changing globally competitive environment and to poise itself for continued success in the electronics industry. With the world fast becoming a global village, competition has taken a new dimension. To succeed, all players must take into account both domestic and international competition or face the prospect of failure.

## The Electronics Industry: Problems and Challenges

A brief review of the problems and challenges facing the electronics industry is necessary for a better understanding of the highly competitive business environment in which Daewoo Electronics operates. These issues provide the background in discussing strategies that the company has devised or must formulate in order to deal with them.

### Limited Access to Foreign Technology

The industry began facing more difficulty in accessing advanced foreign technology. By 1994, Korea was closer to the technological frontier than ever before. However with the country's poor record of intellectual property rights protection, foreign companies became increasingly wary about transferring advanced technology to Korean companies. In addition, they were apprehensive of the possible "boomerang effect" — when the Koreans compete in their markets with lower-priced products manufactured using the very technology they had transferred to them.

### Dependency on Imported Components

The business has depended largely on Japanese industry for component parts, making Korea vulnerable to foreign exchange fluctuations. Whenever the Japanese yen appreciated, Korean manufacturers would face higher components cost, leading to lower profits. As a result, the Japanese component suppliers have a higher bargaining position vis-à-vis Korean companies.

In addition, as more of the advances in electronics products occur at the component level, the Japanese definitely have a competitive edge over the Koreans, who are technologically less advanced in areas like VCR. The Japanese manufacturers are constantly improving the servomotor mechanism that controls the motion of the tape. By 1994, the Japanese were experimenting with how to integrate the start-up and winding-down of the servomotor into an integrated logic component. Korean manufacturers expected that this component would become available to them as well in due course. Effectively, this means that in terms of technology, the Koreans would never be able to surpass the Japanese unless they were able to integrate state-of-the-art consumer electronics technology into the silicon themselves.

### Rising Labor Cost

A large part of the Korean electronics industry's success could be attributed to its competitive advantage in productive low-cost labor. Until the early 1990s, the government had regulated wages in private firms by keeping them low (about 20 percent of that of American workers) using the "Growth First, Distribution Later" policy. Before 1987, the government had also acted against labor movements to suppress demands for wage increases. However, this practice stopped as part of the political reform process. By 1994, labor negotiations were left to the management and its employees. This resulted in rising labor costs as labor unions demanded better working environment and wages. As a result Korean industry no longer enjoyed a price edge over the Southeast Asian countries, which employed relatively cheap labor. These countries have since become threats for Korean electronics firms.

### Reliance on Assembly-type Strategy

The past assembly-type structure, which depended heavily on cheap labor and imported raw materials and parts for growth, was no longer a practical way for the industry to grow. The real problem was that the industry did not have enough strength to absorb even a small production cost hike. In such simple assembly-type operations, original equipment manufacturer (OEM) suppliers tended to squeeze most of their profits out of labor cost by keeping production costs low, and not through technological breakthroughs. As a result, Korean electronics firms whose bulk of business came from OEM contracts were unable to overcome deterioration in their cost advantage.

The Korean electronics industry's early addiction to OEM business actually limited the degree to which they could develop their technological base and expand their overseas marketing network. They were successful in acquiring and absorbing assembly technologies, but much less so in acquiring innovative design and component technologies. They were also successful in exporting on an OEM basis, but less so with their investments in marketing efforts such as distribution channels and own brand names.

### Weak Infrastructure of Suppliers and Support Industries

There remains certain weaknesses in the infrastructure of suppliers and support industries in Korea. Small and medium-size enterprises (SMEs) especially lag behind their *chaebol* (conglomerate) customers in terms of their technologies. Few, if any, local suppliers have been able to meet the precise specification of electronics firms.

### Protectionism

Korean electronics companies have been criticized for dumping in the E.C. and U.S. markets, leading to anticipated tighter import regulations and bans on Korean-made products. Further, Japan has long been criticized by its trading partners for protectionism in its domestic market. This raised the world's sensitivity to governmental support of its own industries. Pressure for protectionism in Korea's major export markets such as the United States may very well intensify Korea's success in developing its electronics industry and becoming the "second Japan."

### Brain Drain

The number of technologically capable Koreans who opt to live abroad has remained high. Many of these second-generation Koreans are inaccessible to Korean companies. Korean industry faces the challenge of not having enough talented manpower to begin with, while at the same time not being able to hold on to the few good ones it has produced.

### Retraining

As the industry upgrades technologically, employment opportunities for the semi-skilled are being rendered superfluous by automation. The government may consider retraining programs to enable existing workers to upgrade their skills and hence their productivity.

### Manufacturing Productivity

Korean industry still lags behind Japanese industry in such areas as productivity enhancement, quality control, and inventory management. In the area of productivity, the Japanese cost reduction philosophy was quite impressive — the Japanese had weathered a 50-percent cut in the value of the dollar in just over two years (1985–1987). In addition, the Japanese had shifted their design and manufacturing capabilities drastically to serve the need for computerized products. This whole concept of flexible manufacturing was a significant challenge to the Koreans, who are still behind the Japanese in this area. The establishment of such continual self-improvement efforts took the Japanese a long time to master. This means that the Koreans also have to invest much time and effort to improve in these areas.

### Government Deregulation

As the Korean government opened up its domestic markets, the electronics firms were expected to face more foreign competition domestically. The hands-off policy of the government, for example, in enacting the Fair Trade Act, meant less governmental support and incentives in the future. In addition, financing considerations also became a major issue. The deregulation of the financial system meant that the cost of funds would have been more expensive or difficult to access in the future. This could have upset the industry's push into more skill- and technology-intensive sectors.

In a nutshell, Daewoo Electronics faced new challenges and problems that require a new way of doing business. There was a need to develop strategies and to use its resources in order to cope with them and to continue its remarkable record of growth.

## Management Philosophy and Values

### Daewoo Spirit

Daewoo's managerial philosophy is based on three elements composed of what is called "The Daewoo Spirit."

| | |
|---|---|
| **Creativity**: | Wise and constructive approach to always seek the new. |
| **Challenge**: | The determination to be creative and pioneering in achieving goals and challenging possibilities for tomorrow. |
| **Sacrifice**: | The courage to make personal sacrifices for the greater good and future generations. |

A clear understanding of Daewoo Electronics is difficult without first understanding Kim Woo-Choong, the founder and chairman of the Daewoo Group. In 1994, Mr Kim was still the group's first-generation leader and was known for working year-round, round the clock, and not having taken a vacation for the past 20 years. His vision to make Daewoo Group companies leaders in their respective fields has been the prime motivation behind Daewoo's remarkable growth. Kim's philosophy of business was, naturally, implemented in all the managerial practices of its subsidiary companies, and Daewoo Electronics was no exception.

### Culture and Human Resource Management

Mr Kim established his business through hard work and accurate judgement. Therefore, he expects his employees to make themselves at least as busy as him. At Daewoo, new employees must make themselves at least as busy as the chairman. New employees are neither told what to do nor spoon-fed; they must find out what to do and how to do it on their own because job specifications are not clearly defined.

The value for innovation and creativity that are emphasized at Daewoo sprang from Mr Kim's belief that "with no action, nothing can be accomplished." He personifies the "Daewoo man" as an ambitious, young entrepreneur with creative ideas and a willingness to sacrifice himself in order to achieve the organizational goals. To compensate for such sacrifices, Daewoo offers many fringe benefits, such as all-expenses paid, three-day trips for employees to celebrate their wedding anniversaries, in addition to salary and regular bonuses.

Due to Daewoo's relatively short history, there is little nepotism to hinder the flow of young energy and ambition in the corporation. Daewoo is often thought of as a paradise for young and aggressive people. Hence, professional management, which is practiced extensively in the group, is a key characteristic that differentiates it from other *chaebols*, which are more family-run.

### Managerial Autonomy

Although the Daewoo Group has managed to attract and retain motivated personnel, there is still a lack of coordination within the ranks. An in-house survey on Daewoo's corporate culture, showed that Daewoo employees were becoming increasingly conservative. Despite the emphasis on innovation and creativity, there was a feeling within Daewoo that the actions of its employees were not living up to such thinking. Chairman Kim acknowledged this weakness in the group and initiated a management movement to place more responsibility and discretion at the subsidiary levels.

In response to the changing domestic and international environment, Mr Kim stressed in his 1992 New Year's address that the importance of greater independence in each subsidiary's operations lies within the group. It became imperative for each company to establish its own managerial responsibility system. This meant that Daewoo Electronics would be given greater autonomy and responsibility for its strategy formulation and performance.

Although Daewoo Electronics' business plan would be tailored to the opportunities and challenges peculiar to the electronics industry, there were several underlying strategies reflecting the overall direction of the group. This point was important because Daewoo Electronics had to coordinate its strategy with the group's corporate strategy.

## Changes in Strategy, Structure, and Culture

In view of the anticipated intensification of international competition, Chairman Kim outlined three broad strategies for 1993 and beyond.

First, the group would accelerate its efforts for greater managerial autonomy. Efforts would also be made to actualize autonomy throughout the levels of the organization. This would require the strengthening of independent sales strategies, independent finances and labor, and even independent manpower training and corporate image.

Second, the group would reaffirm its sense of mission for the Korean economy. It would be conscious that the results of its efforts reflect on the nation's economic development. Thus, the group would continue to promote large-scale overseas investment to create a second wing for the company.

Third, the group would give absolute priority to its clients and markets by institutionalizing a more marketing-oriented mind-set in their employees.

This broad strategic direction laid down by Chairman Kim had a profound influence at its subsidiary levels. The President of Daewoo Electronics, Bae Soon-Hoon, echoed the same strategic thinking.

### Strategy for Daewoo Electronics

Bae Soon-Hoon has been responsible for managing Daewoo Electronics since 1992. Before joining Daewoo, he was a professor at the Massachusetts Institute of Technology and Stanford University. Since becoming president of Daewoo Electronics, he has placed special emphasis on improving the quality of the company in all areas.

One difficult challenge Mr Bae has faced is in improving the brand reputation and quality image of Daewoo's electronics products, or the general image of "Made in Korea" products. His "can-do" attitude has not stopped the company in its efforts to achieve world-class quality products. Specifically, he believes that if his employees are confident and proud of being in Daewoo and their respective jobs, they will also be able to overcome any challenges.

**New production introductions.** The company has successfully launched several new quality and innovative products. For example, the air-bubble washing machine and "Impact" color, both employing technologies developed by the company and requiring little after-sales service, were well-received by consumers. In fact, the air-bubble washing machine achieved a doubling in sales despite a 20-percent contraction in demand for washing machines as a whole. The company has also developed a "3s" VCR with easy programming facility, a vacuum cleaner which operates at a low noise level, and an environmentally friendly non-CFC refrigerator.

Overall, these new product innovations contributed to the company's 10-percent increase in total sales with improved profitability. These results can be regarded as successful when compared not only to the domestic competitors, but also to world-class companies such as Sony and Matsushita, both of which have suffered flat or limited growth in these product areas.

**"Tankism" for quality differentiation.** To combat the more competitive export markets, Daewoo Electronics has declared "tankism" for quality differentiation. The objective of the campaign has been to produce durable (just like a tank), zero-defect, user-friendly products. This has to be achieved not by foreign brand imitation, but through indigenously developed technology. Tankism is the expression of a strong desire to transform Daewoo Electronics into a world-class quality company.

To achieve a high degree of product reliability, the company aims to lower the defect rate below one percent of total production and seeks to provide customer satisfaction in terms of product quality, marketing, and after-sales service. Domestically, the company will devote its energy both to improving productivity and to accelerating the implementation of cost-reduction programs.

**New organizational structure.** Another important strategic change was the establishment of a new management system based on self-imposed responsibility. This involved restructuring the organization into small business units organized by product line. The new structural change gave flexibility and ability to the company to adjust rapidly to changing market conditions. As a result, the company became well-positioned to speedily respond to even small changes in customers' needs.

**Overseas markets.** At the same time, Daewoo Electronics devoted considerable resources to expanding its overseas investment and to setting up new plants in low-cost countries. This new international expansion has enabled the company to achieve a high level of competitiveness by lowering production cost in export markets, and, in order to cope with rising trade barriers, by localizing production in each marketplace.

In line with the liberalization of the domestic electronics market by the government, Daewoo Electronics had to face up to the challenge posed by international manufacturers selling in a highly competitive but small domestic market. At the same time, competition was becoming more intense in the global market due to the following: (a) increased competition in overseas markets due to the recession in the EC and the US, which were Korea's biggest export markets, (b) protectionism of domestic markets by developed countries, and (c) increasing competitiveness of manufacturers in developing countries.

Despite such domestic and international economic conditions, the company still believes that future growth lies in overseas market. Hence it has continued to make overseas investments, set up manufacturing plants, and extend its sales network in foreign markets.

## Daewoo Electronics' Corporate Strategy for the 1990s

Management philosophy and various changes which occurred in the Daewoo Group had implications for the strategic orientations of Daewoo Electronics. Key issues facing the company included: (a) technology acquisition and R&D, (b) quality and productivity improvement, (c) globalization, (d) business-government relations, and (e) managerial independence.

### Technology Acquisition and R&D

In the past, a key aspect of Daewoo Electronics' technology strategy development was the acquisition and absorption of foreign production technology, especially for assembly-type operations, together with the managerial skills necessary to operate foreign production equipment. This involved acquiring foreign machinery and equipment and importing the basic components and other raw materials for assembly by productive low-cost labor, especially female workers.

Electronics technology was acquired by Daewoo Electronics through a mixture of technology licensing and OEM agreements, as well as through direct investment by foreign companies in joint ventures. The company's own research activities expedited the further absorption of technology as the company assimilated the technological know-how transferred to them through such arrangements. Hence, the company followed the technology adoption process typical in Korea, that is, implementation, assimilation, and improvement.

Although Daewoo Electronics had grown rapidly in the past through assembly-type strategy, it could no longer ensure its future success. As the industry developed further, foreign companies were no longer willing to transfer their technologies to them because of the possible "boomerang effect." In their struggle to remain competitive, Korean electronics firms began developing their own sophisticated production processes and product designs in order to cope with the challenges of higher labor costs, more complex market demands, and shorter product life cycles. It was only by investing in the development of their own R&D that they could leapfrog their competitors.

Thus, because of the changing market conditions, Daewoo Electronics had to shift its focus from an investment-type assembly strategy to a more innovation-intensive strategy. This new strategic paradigm called for the company to develop new and innovative products, reduce cost, and come up with more efficient processes.

Since the 1990s, Daewoo Electronics has been firmly committed to its R&D efforts under the new leadership of Bae. In 1992, for example, R&D expenditure amounted to US$136.1 million, or 6.2 percent, of total sales — more than twice the level of 1991. This expenditure covered a number of product areas including refrigerators, TV sets, VCRs, and laser disc players. Notable success has been recorded in the fields of high-definition and wide-screen TV, as well as ozone-friendly refrigerator and zoom-lens camcorders. Approximately 1,330 engineers work in seven research centers — five in Korea, one in Tokyo, and one in the Silicon Valley, U.S.A.

The company is committed to maintaining its emphasis on R&D and is expected to spend eight percent of sales on R&D by 1995, bringing it in line with other world-class electronics companies. The company's R&D programs want to secure Daewoo Electronics's position in the electronics industry.

**Declaration of "Daewoo Technology."** The rationale for the 1993 Daewoo Technology Declaration was the realization that technology is the greatest weapon to guard against the new economic war. It represented Daewoo's vision of developing some of the world's finest technologies and most outstanding products. The Daewoo declaration by the Daewoo Group encompassed three key strategies for developing its technical capability in the future.

The first goal set out to expand Daewoo's core technology. Daewoo would concentrate capital and manpower in areas where Korea lagged behind other advanced nations. Secondly, Daewoo would develop and utilize a highly efficient and systematic technology network centering around the group's own Institute for Advanced Engineering (IAE). The IAE would assume responsibility for the development of its core technology. Thirdly, Daewoo would develop an integrated technical and managerial system for better coordination and control in production, marketing, and R&D. Additionally, incentive programs would be used to promote responsibility for continual improvement. For example, Daewoo would give public recognition in newsletters and the media to those who contributed to successful commercial ideas.

**Specialization.** Daewoo Electronics also realized that the key to international success would be greater specialization in areas where it is well established and the identification of market niches in order to leverage its competitive position. This ensured that the company's R&D resources would not be spread too thinly across too many projects and thus enhance the chances of success in projects undertaken.

Daewoo planned to concentrate its technology development efforts in areas which demanded high royalties and which were difficult to acquire from abroad. The main R&D center had focused research on its new materials, new technology, and new product development in videocassette recorders, digital hi-fi VCRs, S-VHS VCRs, 8mm VHS-full camcorders; in television, LCD TV, HDTV, and teletext-related products; in audio systems, hi-fi components, CDPs, DATs, HA systems; laptop PCs, workstations, and a variety of other high-technology products.

Another area was the application of the latest ergonomics in the design of compact, attractive, and fully functional products. A good example was the introduction in 1990 of washing machines with fuzzy logic emphasizing "human-touch" electronics.

**Joint R&D arrangement.** The company operated R&D facilities in Tokyo and the Silicon Valley. Through these facilities, it was able to absorb the latest in foreign technical advances and knowledge, while at the same time carry joint research programs with local institutions. The company also enjoyed excellent relations with foreign multinational corporation partners, such as Toshiba, to jointly develop new and innovative consumer products. It also promoted industrial, academic, and research collaboration in Korea. In cooperation with Ajou University, it offered advanced degrees in areas related to the electronics industry. The program at Ajou University represented the first of such collaborative efforts among the industrial, academic, and research institutions in Korea.

### Quality and Productivity Improvement

As has been reiterated time and again, Daewoo Electronics faced the problem of overcoming its weak brand image. Traditionally, most Korean companies, including Daewoo Electronics, competed in low-cost, low-price segments because of Korea's competitive advantage in labor cost. This low-cost strategy remained viable as long as firms were able to sustain their cost advantages. However, rapidly increasing factor input costs and wages eroded the nation's cost advantage.

Until recently, many Korean electronics firms found themselves facing competition from the Japanese, who produce high-end quality products, and the Taiwanese and Hongkongers, who produce in the low-cost, low-price segments. No longer would Korean companies remain in this "stuck-in-between" position if they wanted to survive. Thus, the strategic direction chosen by Daewoo Electronics was to move into high-end quality products, competing head-on with the Japanese players.

To ingrain this concept of quality into the mind-set of its employees, the company began educating each and every one of them to "think quality." It launched a company-wide Total Quality Control (TQC) program that governed virtually every aspect of operations from market survey to planning, production, sales, to after-sales service. Regular QC training sessions were also held at all employee levels.

The aim of such TQM efforts was to make employees of Daewoo Electronics realize that their individual work effort would be ultimately reflected in the quality of Daewoo's products and that failure to improve quality would result in lost business, reflecting badly on the pride of the country. To improve productivity, Daewoo Electronics implemented several streamlining measures. It strived to remain lean in its operation by cutting down additional staff and installing more automated production processes. In addition, through the efforts of QCs, employees were encouraged to constantly seek new and better ways of doing things, that is, continuous improvement in process and product designs.

Daewoo reinforced this quality and productivity culture through its commitment to people and human capital development. The company belief is that every person has potential and works toward motivating and developing them to the fullest. The company actively sought to build up the depth and quality of its employees' managerial and technical capabilities by recruiting the right people with the right talents. The company also instilled a spirit of "being in the family" to make employees feel that they are a vital part of the organization.

### Globalization

The reasons for Daewoo Electronics globalizing its activities can be summarized as follows: (a) development of new markets, (d) access to lower-cost factor inputs, (c) acquisition of foreign technology, and (d) the overcoming of trade barriers.

However, these apparent reasons for its globalization efforts may not be as important as in the past if we analyze the circumstances faced by Daewoo Electronics during its founding years. Several decisions to globalize appeared to have been, in fact, forced upon Daewoo Electronics by circumstances, rather than being the outcome of a rational step-by-step strategy formulation. They are actually the direct response to the prevailing international business environment and policies of the Korean government.

Daewoo became a global company as a by-product of the role it has played as an OEM supplier to both Japanese and US companies. Hence, as these companies globalized, Daewoo's products became exposed to the wider international market.

In addition, the Korean government's export-led growth strategy in the 1970s and 1980s, with the incentives it provided, has induced many chaebols including Daewoo Electronics to follow the outward-looking strategy.

In the early days, Daewoo Electronics' main goal was to build up export volumes as fast as possible in order to receive greater governmental incentives. OEM, or subcontract production, was seen as the best way to achieve this end, even if margins were lower and control over product development was lesser. In fact, once the decision for export-led growth was taken by the government, Daewoo Electronics had no choice. With a limited technology base, negligible brand recognition overseas, and no international marketing presence, Daewoo had few alternatives. Thus, Daewoo Electronics' heavy dependence on OEM agreements to provide both process and product technologies and access to overseas markets. The strategy of relying on assembly-type production and OEM arrangement enabled Daewoo to overcome the handicapped position of a late entrant to the industry.

The rationale given above might have served as the impetus for Daewoo Electronics to go global in the past. However, the company started facing a completely new set of challenges and problems, both domestically and internationally. It has become a strategic imperative for the company to globalize in order to survive in this dynamic environment.

Chairman Kim has always been on the move all around the world in an effort to seek overseas opportunities. In fact, he has been branded the most traveled businessman in Korea.

The following are among the action plans adopted by Daewoo Electronics in its quest to become a world leader in the electronics industry.

**Overseas operation.** To meet the rising demand for the company's products while simultaneously reducing its costs, Daewoo Electronics expanded its overseas production facilities. By 1994, the company manufactured overseas at five plants in four countries, in addition to four domestic production plants. This overseas expansion continued with new plants being established in France, Uzbekistan, and Vietnam.

Daewoo's strategy of international expansion of production facilities enabled the company to achieve a high level of competitiveness in its export markets and to cope with rising trade barriers by localizing production in each market. In addition, cost advantages accrued to the company in terms of lower labor, material, and facility costs were substantial.

The company also saw the possibility that the "two Koreas" could cooperate to make internationally competitive products by combining the South's capital and technology with the North's cost-competitive labor in the near future.

**Sales subsidiaries and marketing development.** Sales subsidiaries have increased in number and expanded in size to promote the sale of Daewoo Electronics branded products.

Existing subsidiaries in the U.S., France, Spain, and Germany would be complemented by new operations in Moscow, St Petersburg, and Mexico in the near future. The aim is to establish a global distribution network in order to provide a fuller line of service to its business partners and customers.

**OEM supplying.** Given that the bulk of Daewoo Electronics' business traditionally came from OEM agreements, it is unlikely that these agreements would be discontinued in the future, although the focus has shifted to developing Daewoo Electronics' own brand name. Daewoo Electronics is also known for its skillful use of foreign brand names to penetrate overseas markets. OEM arrangements are still viable business because the company benefits from the technology transfer inherent in such arrangements.

In 1994, Daewoo solidified its relationship with its traditional OEM partners such as SONY and NEC of Japan. Sales were also expected to increase as a number of American retailers such as Walmart and K-Mart were included in such arrangements.

**Marketing.** One of the challenges faced by Daewoo Electronics is how to build up a good brand name and how to create consumer loyalty to its products. Although OEM agreements are beneficial in some ways, they offer several limitations to the company's future growth. The demand for OEM supplies is highly uncertain as it depends on its customers' orders, which may be irregular. This dependency could become problematic if and when these customers cut back on their orders in times of difficulty or make their orders through other OEM suppliers who offer better terms and conditions. Thus, the bargaining power of Daewoo Electronics is relatively low compared to that of OEM customers. In addition, it is difficult to carry out planning because an accurate demand forecast is almost impossible.

The main problem with OEM arrangements is that Daewoo is unable to establish for itself a brand and quality image in the minds of its end-consumers. This means that Daewoo Electronics, without an established brand name, would be unable to create consumer loyalty and charge a price premium.

To overcome this major weakness, Company President Bae stressed the importance of marketing Daewoo's products internationally under its own brand name. Several aggressive marketing programs were then put in place. The company started to market its own brand in all parts of the world from the beginning of the 1990s.

In the domestic market, the company launched a new advertising campaign, with a theme based on the rapid progress of its globalization efforts, to inform the public of the group's numerous international accomplishments. The aim was to create a brand image that Daewoo Electronics is a potential world leader in quality electronics.

Daewoo Electronics emphasized both quality and brand image in each and every new product introduced in its domestic and international markets. For example, the introduction of Daewoo's brand "Import" series of color TV and the popular air-bubble washing machine series "POWER" resulted in Daewoo's capture of 28 percent of the domestic market.

To institutionalize the company's commitment to quality improvement, a managerial program, TANK, was implemented. The program aimed to produce products which are as sturdy as tanks but are simple to operate and offer total quality and reliability. Through its intensive market research efforts, the company learned that consumers actually wanted a functional product with more durability and reliability, rather than complicated features that are often not used. This signified a move of the company to become more customer-oriented in its product designs.

To communicate this heightened commitment to customer satisfaction, a series of advertising campaigns were put in place. The campaigns generated a new image for the company's products, an image which was well-received by the Korean public. President Bae himself appeared in a TV commercial to explain the TANK concept and assure consumers of Daewoo's quality and reliability. Consumer surveys identified this Daewoo commercial as the country's most popular TV ad in 1993.

In its international efforts to promote its brand name, the company entered into brand contracts with firms in Italy, Spain, France, and Iran. In the very near future, it is expected that there will be a massive Daewoo Electronics presence in the Southeast Asia region, especially in Singapore and Malaysia.

Another important strategic move to get closer to and establish better rapport with its consumers was by setting up a global network of after-sales service centers. This allows the company to respond faster to customers' feedback and changing needs.

**Business-government relations.** The amazing growth of Daewoo Electronics has partly been due to the development of high-tech industries, including electronics, based on imported foreign technologies. Crucially, the electronics industry grew in the past 20 years by more than two-thousand-fold.

The success of the industry is largely attributed to the national economic plans and the determined execution of such national policies by government agencies. Of particular interest to Daewoo was the passage of the Electronic Industry Promotion Law in 1969, which made the electronics industry a strategic one and resulted in a boost in exports. The government's commitment to develop this industry has been the impetus for its phenomenal growth.

The Korean government has closely guided the electronics industry because of its strategic importance to the country's overall economic development. The electronics industry was made a strategic industry in consideration of its export potential, prospects for domestic demand, employment creation in the manufacturing sector, advancement for the nation as a whole, reduction on raw material dependency, the potential addition of a high amount of value, a reduction in trade friction, and an achievment of other beneficial side effects.

Comparing the development of Daewoo Electronics with the strategic direction of the Korean government as laid down in the series of five-year plans, we can see a close partnership between the company and the government. In particular, Daewoo Electronics has benefited from the many incentives and support provided by the growth-minded government. Since its establishment in the early 1970s coinciding with the rapid takeoff of the Korean economy, Daewoo Electronics has grown to its present size as a result of support given by the government.

The systems of governmental incentives can be categorized into two types:

1. Those granting duty-free and unrestricted access to imported intermediate inputs needed for export production.
2. Those granting automatic access to bank loans for working capital requirements associated with exports and R&D activities.

Daewoo Electronics was highly successful in its exporting activities in the 1970s and 1980s even though it was a relative newcomer. This enabled the company to receive preferential access to loans at subsidized interest rates for export activities, as well as for the expansion of facilities and the acquisition of foreign technology. It also received exemption from taxes on exports and the imports of components and equipment used for export products. Daewoo also benefited greatly from the protected domestic market against foreign competitors, which allowed it to grow and become a major player in the industry despite its late entry.

The government's emphasis on electronics export provided many incentives which Daewoo Electronics could capitalize on. For example, the company was able to get low interest rates for its capital borrowing and loans without mortgages. This kind of "partnership" allowed the government and Daewoo Electronics to mutually benefit from each other. This was also reflected in Mr Kim's support for the government's economic policies. The chairman always stressed the importance of the group's sense of mission for national economic development. This indicated his consciousness that the group's performance reflects on the economic well-being of the nation. Hence, there has always been a special relationship between Daewoo Electronics and the government.

This trend of government support for the electronics industry, particularly for the large chaebols, is not expected to continue in the future. As early as the 1980s, the government had begun to liberalize its economy by cutting down on support given to the chaebols and by allowing more foreign competition in the domestic market. In addition, the recently launched Seventh Five-Year Plan called for the implementation of far-reaching tax, financial, monetary, and administrative reforms that would significantly reduce the government's role in the economy. The government's gradual abolishment of the systems of incentives was a direct response to the over-concentration of economic power in the chaebols. It aimed to reduce the widening gap between the chaebols and SMEs and to rectify the seemingly "unfair" resource allocations.

Hence, large chaebols can no longer rely on the past systems of incentives. Nevertheless, Daewoo Electronics, just like the other chaebols, has accumulated much technical and manpower resources from the high growth periods of the 1970s and 1980s. This may equip the company with the technical and managerial resource capability to progress. However, the company's financial weakness in terms of its high debt-to-equity position might limit the growth of the company. The group's outstanding debt of 13,850 billion won at the end of 1991 surpassed revenues for that year. The average debt-equity ratio of 308 percent was well within the normal range for its affiliates. Of greater concern was the large portion of high-interest debt from domestic short-term finance companies, accounting for about two trillion of some 8 trillion won in local loans as of the end of 1991. Another two trillion won worth of corporate bonds are nearing maturity, raising the short-term share to about one-third of total Group debt. This makes the Daewoo Group one of the highest debt-ridden companies in Korea.

The challenge for Daewoo Electronics is how to leverage its technical and managerial resources amidst its financial constraint in order to secure a dominant global position in the future. For example, the Group may have to tap into cheaper sources of funds outside Korea in order to sustain its long-term growth strategy. Nevertheless, the economic policies of the government can still exert a heavy influence on the corporate planning of the chaebols.

## Conclusion

The rapid growth of Daewoo Electronics in the past is a result of many interlocking factors. It was established during the booming Korean economy of the 1970s, "free-riding" on the economic wave to export aggressively to international markets. Coupled with the aggressive industrial policy of the Korean government to promote the electronics industry, the company enjoyed tremendous institutional support and incentives given by the government for export-oriented companies.

In addition, the company grew rapidly because it adopted a cost-leadership strategy based on an assembly-type operation that capitalized on low-cost labor, economies of scale, and a highly motivated and educated labor force. This assembly-type strategy dovetailed neatly with the environmental conditions prevailing then. Another key success factor was the vision and determination of its entrepreneur founder to make Daewoo Electronics a major world player.

Daewoo Electronics has been reasonably successful in adopting strategies that make use of its strengths in the past decades. However, the strategies that served well in the past are not likely to be equally effective in the future. The new competitive environment calls for Daewoo Electronics to seek out new strategic directions.

The lessons learned by Daewoo Electronics during its rapid growth stage on competitive strategy and global competition augmented by a strong leadership of its founding chairman are invaluable for the company to craft out a "sure-fire" global strategy as it marches into the 21st century.

# First Philippine Holdings Corporation* 3

Tomas Santos, an MBA student, was browsing through the 1984 annual reports that his university library had recently received. He was leafing through the report of the First Philippine Holdings Corporation when his attention was struck by the final paragraph of the report to the stockholders, which read:

> The severity of conditions facing business in the past 18 months leads us to talk in terms of survival, for survive we must if we are to continue to develop and prosper. To do so it is imperative that we achieve in the coming fiscal year two conditions: A significant reduction, if not total elimination, of all corporate debt; and, the rapid and successful development of our new business thrust into engineering-related services in the overseas markets.

Santos was surprised for two reasons. First, he was not very familiar with First Philippine Holdings Corporation but he knew that its diverse business interests had been largely the result of an active policy of diversification. The move to consolidate resources into a narrower business thrust was therefore somewhat surprising. Second, he had learned in his finance courses that judicious use of leverage had the effect of improving return on stockholders' equity and the value of the firm. In this light, he wondered whether the move of First Philippine Holdings Corporation's management was too drastic. He decided to read further the annual report to gain more insight into the decision.

---

*This case was written by Professor Bienvenido M Aragon, College of Business Administration, University of the Philippines. This case was prepared to serve as a basis for class discussion rather than to illustrate either effective or ineffective handling of an administrative situation. 

## Company Background

First Philippine Holdings Corporation (FPHC) is a holding company with equity investments in fifteen companies engaged in the following lines of business. FPHC regarded these as its six "core" businesses:

1. Energy resource development
2. Electrical manufacturing
3. General construction
4. International contracting (construction, maintenance, etc)
5. Financial services
6. Trading and commercial services

Eight of the fifteen companies were fully owned subsidiaries and only in three companies did FPHC take a minority position. (Exhibit 1 presents a financial profile of firms in the FPHC group; Exhibit 2 presents in greater detail the activities of each of the companies, their recent performance, and future prospects. FPHC sees itself as ". . . a leading catalytic, innovative conglomerate developing resources and adapting technologies revolving around its core businesses . . .")

First Philippine Holdings Corporation traces its beginnings to the incorporation of Meralco Securities Corporation in June 1961 for the purpose of acquiring the Manila Electric Company (MERALCO) from General Public Utilities Corporation, one of the largest public utility holding companies in the United States. The following years saw MERALCO Securities diversifying into industrial activities supportive of MERALCO operations. First Philippine Industrial, Philippine Electric Corporation, and Philippine Petroleum Corporation were among the corporations formed in this diversification thrust.

In February 1978 Meralco Securities sold its interest in Meralco to the Meralco Foundation, Inc in accordance with a program to "mutualize" Meralco ownership rights to its customers. Following the sale Meralco Securities effected a corporate restructuring to combine nonutility interests into a new cohesive, dynamic group with an identity distinct from Meralco. Meralco Securities thus adopted the new name of First Philippine Holdings Corporation. The ensuing years were again a period of diversification, of efforts to shift the business base from an almost total reliance on income generated from the sale of Meralco toward a diversified multiproduct, multi-market conglomerate.[1]

First Philippine Holdings Corporation was headed in 1985 by Board of Directors Chairman Cesar Zalamea, Chairman of the Development Bank of the Philippines, and President and Chief Executive Officer Eduardo Regala. Among its directors were the presidents of the Philippine National Bank, the Consolidated Bank and Trust Company, the International Corporate Bank, and Meralco.

[1] Aggregate Meralco derived revenue fell to PHP109 million in 1981 from PHP159 million in 1980. This reduction is best explained by the manner in which settlement of the sale was structured. The block of common and preferred shares sold in 1978 was valued at an aggregated PHP873 million, payable in semi-annual installments stretching through 1991, with interest at 10 percent per annum, payable quarterly.

Additionally, an effective upward adjustment of PHP217 million was made, representing net income of Meralco for the period July 1, 1976 to June 10, 1977, prior to the sale; such amount is to be paid as "dividend adjustment."

In 1980, the remaining PHP26.5 million of this dividend adjustment was taken into revenues; the 1981 Meralco derived revenue total therefore, reflects an anticipated scaling down in the level of Meralco receipts. Moreover, with the installment receivable progressively reduced by the half-yearly receipt of installment payments, interest earned on the remaining balance of the receivable has similarly declined.

## 1984 Performance

In 1984 revenues fell by 25 percent from PHP213 million to PHP159 million.[2] Net income fell by an even larger amount, dropping from PHP39 million in 1983 to a loss of PHP47 million in 1984; on a per-share basis this meant a fall from an earnings per share of PHP0.88 to a loss per share of PHP1.75. This was the first time since 1975 that the company incurred a loss (see Exhibit 3 for the financial highlights and Exhibit 4 for the financial statements).

No cash dividends were paid on common stock in 1984 compared to PHP1.20 per share paid in 1983. However, dividends on preferred stock were maintained at the 1983 level.

Management attributed the poor performance to "abnormally severe business conditions." More specifically management meant:

1. Recessionary conditions that have prevailed since the decade begun.
2. Severe and sudden curtailment of credit from domestic and foreign sources.
3. Devaluation of the peso from PHP11:US$1 to over PHP18:US$1 with rates exceeding PHP20:US$1 in the "black market."
4. Escalating interest rates reaching close to 50 percent at times.
5. High rates of inflation.
6. Shortage in raw materials and commodities, especially those with substantial imported components.
7. Increasing unemployment.
8. Highly unstable political and economic environment.

Management, in its report to stockholders, pointed out that the company was particularly vulnerable to changes in the financial debts. Rising interest rates and tight credit strained liquidity and FPHC's ability to meet financial charges. Financial charges in 1984 amounted to PHP183 million, or 89 percent of total expenses and an increase of 42 percent over the previous year. Foreign debts exposed the firm to significant translation losses every time the peso depreciated.

However management also pointed out that during this extremely difficult period, the firm was able to service its debts on a current basis. Loan repayments of PHP103 million were made, although this was more than offset by a foreign exchange adjustment of PHP103 million on foreign currency borrowings due to two devaluations of the peso and a new debt of PHP22 million. Interest payments of PHP180 million were made during the same period. As a result, the overall level of debt was also kept essentially stable at PHP735 million as of June 30, 1984, compared to PHP703 million one year earlier. This was not achieved without the adoption of some rather severe measures on the part of the company, among which were:

1. The formation of corporate debt management group responsible for minimizing group exposure to foreign exchange and interest movements and for ensuring the servicing of debt on a current basis. The corporate debt management group was also tasked with formulating appropriate policy and strategy for corporate debt.

[2] In 1985, the exchange rate between the Philippine peso and the U.S. dollar was US$1.00 = PHP18.067.

2. Full divestment of interests in Shell Gas Philippines and the Philippine Commercial International Bank (PCI Bank) to generate cash. The sale of the firm's 22 percent interest in PCI Bank, while generating cash, resulted in a loss of PHP65.8 million. This resulted in a substantial reduction of the firm's full recognition as income of the balance of its gain on the sale of Meralco shares amounting to PHP231.4 million. There was a partial divestment of interests in Philippine Petroleum Corporation.
   Divestment was undertaken when the firm could no longer rely on traditional subsidiary cash flows or external credit sources to generate working capital for current needs, much less reduce the total level of debt.
3. Restructuring of foreign currency obligations was done in March 1984 through a "switching arrangement" involving the Central Bank of the Philippines and the Development Bank of the Philippines (DBP). This arrangement allowed FPHC to substitute for its $30 million outstanding term loan to a syndicate of foreign banks a PHP434 million loan from the DBP on the same repayment schedule as the original dollar loan. This restructuring eliminated foreign currency exposure and vulnerability of foreign exchange losses with the continued depreciation of the peso.[3]

It was against this backdrop and management's belief that there would be no appreciable improvement in business conditions in the near future, that major shifts in corporate strategy and debt policy were imperative — not for growth, but simply for solvency and survival.

## The Debt Management Program

The proposed debt management program was carried over from the measures taken in fiscal year 1984. It aimed at the total elimination of all corporate debt during the fiscal year 1984–1985. This program entailed the following:

1. An "offset" or, at least, matching of the PHP434 million loan to DBP with the Meralco Foundation installment payments. As of June 30, 1984, PHP428 million was still due from Meralco Foundation.
2. Raising PHP300 million through complete divestment of interests in Philippine Petroleum Corporation and the sale of the FPHC Center building in Makati.
3. Restructuring of current payment terms with existing creditors pending the completion of both the DBP and divestment programs.

## The New Business Thrust

The new business thrust sought to re-focus group efforts away from a diversified, domestic orientation built around the six core businesses towards concentration in engineering (and related) services primarily for overseas markets. It marked a move from asset and capital-intensive businesses into services, a move that complements highly the debt management program.

[3] Refer to Note 5 in the Notes to Financial Statements for details of the various long-term debt.

It also marked a move away from heavy dependence on domestic markets into international markets. The changing conditions and uncertain prospects in the domestic market, the increasing attractiveness of overseas markets and foreign exchange earnings, and the firm's strengths and capabilities in engineering and related services made this a natural move. It was also recognized that constraints on financial resources and liquidity also dictate this shift. As the report to stockholders noted:

> Most important, the new business thrust is financially appropriate: the projects envisioned require minimal capital commitment, produce immediate and sustainable cash flows, are highly bankable in the international market, and provide a currency hedge against a possibly weakening peso.

In line with the thrust on engineering services FPHC saw its target markets and product offerings as:

| *Markets* | *Products* |
|---|---|
| 1. Power generation | 1. Feasibility, design, and engineering studies |
| 2. Power transmission and distribution | 2. Operations and maintenance |
| 3. Heat, ventilation, and air conditioning | 3. Installation and commissioning |
| 4. Selected commercial and industrial projects | 4. Construction |
| | 5. Specialized services |

These products would be offered under any of the following terms depending on which was appropriate: manpower supply, supervised manpower, lump sum labor, lump sum labor and equipment, and turnkey arrangements. Where necessary, technology would be sourced from outside.

Geographically the target markets were Saudi Arabia and the ASEAN countries. The company felt that it was familiar with these markets and had established contacts that gave it a competitive edge. To date, the firm had booked orders totaling $97 million involving a wide range of projects in the Middle East, Indonesia, Sabah, Brunei, and Western Samoa. Working closely with Japanese contractors, the firm was also pursuing projects in Nigeria, Malaysia, and Bangladesh.

The report to shareholders ended on this optimistic note: "We are confident that the new business thrust is not only the right thing for us to do at this time, but that we can do it well and profitably."

EXHIBIT 1

## FIRST PHILIPPINE HOLDINGS CORPORATION
### Review of Investments
### 1983 and 1984

(in million pesos)

| | *Year of Initial Inv'ment* | *1984 Percentage Ownership* | *Total Assets* | | *Stockholder's Equity* | | *Gross Revenue* | | *Net Income* | |
|---|---|---|---|---|---|---|---|---|---|---|
| | | | *1984* | *1983* | *1984* | *1983* | *1984* | *1983* | *1984* | *1983* |
| ENERGY RESOURCE DEVELOPMENT | | | | | | | | | | |
| Philippine Petroleum Corporation | 1969 | 40.73 | 1,830.1 | 1,453.2 | 748.1 | 577.7 | 2,346.2 | 1,666.2 | 63.7 | 9.8 |
| First Philippines Industrial Corporation | 1967 | 60.00 | 515.1 | 376.1 | 487.3 | 345.2 | 55.7 | 54.5 | 9.6 | 2.0 |
| Pilipinas Shell Petroleum Corporation | 1975 | 25.00 | 4,645.6 | 2,749.9 | 900.3 | 944.4 | 9,332.9 | 7,581.5 | (10.7) | 28.5 |
| ELECTRICAL MANUFACTURING | | | | | | | | | | |
| Philippine Electric Corporation | 1969 | 51.53 | 492.4 | 2,749.9 | 111.8 | 91.7 | 117.3 | 212.4 | (25.9) | 1.4 |
| GENERAL CONSTRUCTION | | | | | | | | | | |
| Engineering & Construction Corp of Asia | 1969 | 100.00 | 123.2 | 166.3 | 66.3 | 103.1 | 57.9 | 108.1 | (38.6) | 1.1 |
| Pacific Engineering Company, Inc | 1978 | 100.00 | 78.9 | 101.6 | 11.6 | 27.0 | 30.4 | 151.3 | (14.6) | 6.5 |
| INTERNATIONAL | | | | | | | | | | |
| First Holdings International, Inc | 1982 | 100.00 | 702.4 | 235.7 | 43.8 | 9.4 | 390.7 | 54.0 | 14.2 | (0.2) |

EXHIBIT 1 (cont'd)

## FIRST PHILIPPINE HOLDINGS CORPORATION
### Review of Investments
### 1983 and 1984

(in million pesos)

| | Year of Initial Inv'ment | 1984 Percentage Ownership | Total Assets | | Stockholder's Equity | | Gross Revenue | | Net Income | |
|---|---|---|---|---|---|---|---|---|---|---|
| | | | *1984* | *1983* | *1984* | *1983* | *1984* | *1983* | *1984* | *1983* |
| FINANCIAL SERVICES | | | | | | | | | | |
| First Philippine Capital Corporation | 1978 | 100.00 | 83.4 | 127.7 | 66.9 | 60.2 | 23.3 | 44.7 | 6.7 | 2.2 |
| The CHARGEKard Corporation | 1976 | 100.00 | 60.9 | 101.4 | 5.8 | 11.2 | 15.7 | 30.2 | (17.4) | 1.1 |
| First Philippine Leasing & Equipment Corporation | 1976 | 100.00 | 25.3 | 32.0 | 10.1 | 8.8 | 6.8 | 8.6 | 1.3 | 2.4 |
| Ventures in Industry and Business Enterprises, Inc | 1977 | 22.35 | 8.1 | 8.5 | 7.8 | 8.5 | 0.7 | 0.8 | (0.7) | (1.2) |
| TRADING & COMMERCIAL SERVICES | | | | | | | | | | |
| Warner Barnes & Company, Inc | 1980 | 98.00 | 179.2 | 211.8 | (16.4) | 43.6 | 107.9 | 231.7 | (60.0) | 1.6 |
| First Philippine Trading Corporation | 1977 | 100.00 | 43.2 | 35.0 | 0.2 | 8.2 | 59.4 | 31.2 | (7.9) | (1.3) |
| First Philippine Realty & Development Corporation | 1976 | 100.00 | 1.0 | 4.0 | 0.9 | 1.0 | — | 0.3 | (0.1) | — |
| Tabangao Realty, Inc | 1981 | 60.00 | 16.3 | 17.0 | 6.2 | 6.8 | 2.7 | 2.7 | 1.2 | 1.0 |
| | | | 8,805.0 | 8370.1 | 2,450.7 | 2,246.8 | 12,547.6 | 10,178.2 | (79.2) | 54.9 |

*Source: Based on financial statements as of December 31, 1983 and 1982.

EXHIBIT 2

## FIRST PHILIPPINE HOLDINGS CORPORATION
## Corporate Review

### PHILIPPINE PETROLEUM CORPORATION

Philippine Petroleum Corporation's (PPC) performance during the year remained profitable and encouraging despite the difficult economic climate.

Although domestic sales of its principal product, lubrication oil basestock, was slightly below the preceding year's level, exported lube oil and sales of secondary basestocks and other products improved substantially as PPC pushed import substitutes such as base oils for rubber extender and technical white oil applications.

Total sales was PHP2.3 billion, an increase of 41 percent over the preceding year's sales revenue of PHP1.7 billion. Because of energy-saving projects to ride out projected sales volume declines and cost escalations, PPC realized a net profit of PHP63.7 million, a 28-percent improvement over the previous year's net income of PHP49.8 million.

### FIRST PHILIPPINES INDUSTRIAL CORPORATION

First Philippine Industrial Corporation (FPIC) still provided the most reliable and efficient means of transporting petroleum products through the country's only pipeline system. FPIC transported a total of 23.4 million barrels of white and black oil products, a decrease of 9 percent compared to last year's level. This decrease is traceable to the cut in the government's budget for oil imports.

Gross revenues rose to PHP55.7 million, 2 per cent higher than last year's PHP54.5 million. Net income, however, dropped to PHP9.6 million as total expenses increased by 15 per cent.

Because of anticipated lower volumes and higher costs of operating and maintaining the pipeline system, efficiency improvements, cost reduction, plus a serious study on offering operation and maintenance services to commercial and industrial establishments are the major thrusts.

### PILIPINAS SHELL PETROLEUM CORPORATION

Gross revenues of Pilipinas Shell Petroleum Corporation (PSPC) during the year amounted to PHP9.3 billion, of which PHP2.6 billion represented duties, taxes, and other levies collected on behalf of the government.

A major expense component was the imposition of a 65-percent surtax on inventory gains arising from four unique events: the price adjustment of July 1, 1983, the increase in duties by another 2 percent, the dismantling of the Consumer Price Equalization Fund CPEF), and the two-stage devaluation of the peso. This resulted in a net loss of PHP10.7 million for the year.

### VENTURES IN INDUSTRY & BUSINESS ENTERPRISES, INC

Ventures in Industry and Business Enterprises, Inc (VIBES) continued to focus its thrust on management assistance. However, operations suffered due to the tightness in the financial markets and the prohibitive costs of money, which in turn adversely affected the operations of the company's clients.

VIBES ended fiscal year 1984 with a net loss of PHP0.7 million. Total revenues of PHP0.7 million came from investments in equities, bond dealership, and interest from temporary placements.

### FIRST HOLDINGS INTERNATIONAL, INC

First Holdings International, Inc (FHI) commenced the fiscal year with an order book of approximately US$85 million involving eighteen contractual undertakings. Principal activities consisted of the construction of power transmission and distribution systems; electro-mechanical installation work; heat, ventilation, and air-conditioning (HVAC) system installation; and hospital construction, operation and maintenance, principally in the Kingdom of Saudi Arabia and Iraq.

Completions during the year totaled US$32 million and involved an average site manpower base of 2,000 individuals.

The Hail "B" Electrification Project, a turnkey undertaking for the Electricity Corporation of Saudi Arabia, represented FHI's single largest undertaking at a gross value of US$59.8 million. Construction work commenced in April 1983, was substantially on schedule as of 1984–1985, and was expected to be fully turned over by May 1985.

A decline in construction in the Middle East, precipitated by currently depressed oil prices and liftings, has resulted in fewer opportunities for installation and construction subcontracts for FHI. The current regime for tight credit for Philippine borrowers has also dictated a more prudent attitude toward contractual undertakings, with preference shifting from turnkey scoping to less exposure intensive participation.

FHI's response has been a shift toward higher-skilled operation and maintenance activities, principally for power transmission and distribution grids as well as for various categories of process plants. In addition, non-destructive testing and inspection services have been packaged for a wide range of preventive maintenance applications.

At fiscal year-end, FHI reported a net income of PHP15.7 million on gross revenues of PHP448.2 million. Its 1985 order book stood at approximately US$40 million.

**FIRST PHILIPPINE LEASING AND EQUIPMENT CORPORATION**

First Philippine Leasing and Equipment Corporation (FPLEC) also suffered declines brought about by the soaring interest rates. It restricted the company's ability to continually extend loans and other credit facilities. Although target markets still existed, the interest rates that FPLEC could charge reached prohibitive levels.

Rather than book new loans, which would place heavy burdens on prospective borrowers, the company focused on minimizing and/or totally liquidating borrowings, upgrading internal efficiencies, and reducing operating expenses. As a result, FPLEC was able to totally repay a term loan from collections and simultaneously was successful in restructuring the remaining loans.

For fiscal year 1984, FPLEC realized gross revenues of PHP6.8 million and a net income of PHP1.3 million.

**FIRST PHILIPPINE TRADING CORPORATION**

First Philippine Trading Corporation (FPTC) ended fiscal year 1984 with sales revenues of PHP59.4 million, 9 percent higher than last year's figure. However, FPTC incurred a net loss of PHP7.9 million during the year as the cost of raw materials and operations rose. Soaring interest rates and financial charges further negated positive sales revenues.

**PHILIPPINE ELECTRIC CORPORATION**

For fiscal year 1984, Philippine Electric Corporation (PHILEC) consolidated its domestic core businesses and increased its marketing activities for overseas projects.

A six-month long labor strike, coupled with government restrictions on raw materials importations impaired PHILEC's ability to deliver products and services to its major customers. Soaring interest rates, abnormal financial markets and collection difficulties substantially affected the company's funds sourcing. As a result, sales decreased from PHP212 million in fiscal year 1983 to PHP117 million in fiscal year 1984. The company also registered a loss of PHP26 million this year.

Activities were concentrated on transformer manufacturing and on the Service Technology Center, both profit and growth areas in the domestic markets. In Saudi Arabia, PHILEC's marketing activities resulted in new and ongoing contracts within the year.

**PACIFIC ENGINEERING COMPANY, INC**

Despite a sound head start, Pacific Engineering Company, Inc, (PACIFIC) suffered a revenue drop of 80 percent to PHP30 million, which also meant a loss of PHP15 million.

Despite the quick shift of marketing strategies from major plant expansions and turnkey projects to plant repairs, maintenance, and rehabilitation, PACIFIC could still not cope with the economic crisis.

The company undertook cost-reduction programs and continues to focus on projects involving the repair, maintenance, and rehabilitation of existing plants, as well as small components fabrication.

## FIRST PHILIPPINE CAPITAL CORPORATION

First Philippine Capital Corporation (FPCC), the Group's investment house, maintained its profitability in fiscal year 1984 despite difficulties in the business environment. Gross profits were posted at PHP23.3 million, with net income reaching PHP6.7 million. Total assets as of June 30, 1984 stood at PHP83.4 million on an equity base of PHP66.9 million. Return on assets remained healthy at 6.4 percent while return on equity decreased to 10.6 percent.

FPCC looked forward to the coming fiscal year with cautious optimism and with faith in its ability to overcome the trying times ahead.

## WARNER BARNES & COMPANY, INC

Warner Barnes & Company, Inc (WB) underwent another difficult year. A series of devaluations and import restrictions, together with spiraling interest rates and financial charges, resulted in a net loss of PHP60 million for the year.

Trading of product lines with thin margins, limited demands, and a heavy dependence on debt and/or unreliable sourcing were discontinued. Operating expenses were reduced consistent with the shrinkage of available business and the poor domestic business climate.

Warner Barnes' major thrusts for the coming fiscal year were debt restructuring and discontinuance of unprofitable businesses while developing and expanding viable ones (including possible joint ventures) and cost reduction.

## ENGINEERING & CONSTRUCTION CORPORATION OF ASIA

Fiscal year 1984 started with Engineering and Construction Corporation of Asia (Ecco-Asia) continuing work on seven major projects. But late in 1983, because of the economic crisis, three projects were suspended and three others were terminated. Only the Palimpinon geothermal project remained. Aggressive marketing yielded only two new projects for the period. Consequently, revenues declined to PHP57 million, a 46-percent decrease from last year's PHP108 million. This yielded a deficit of PHP39 million for the year.

Merger plans with Pacific Engineering Company, Inc were temporarily shelved while corporate and staff functions of both companies were streamlined and combined to provide better support and ease overhead burdens. Operations were sustained at merely framework levels, cost-cutting measures implemented, and marketing redirected to smaller government projects and the private industry sector; these were the thrusts for 1985.

## THE CHARGEKARD CORPORATION

The CHARGEKARD Corporation suffered reversals following a series of political and economic events which took place during the year.

Its merchant base was streamlined to maintain only those establishments that provided respectable yields and adequate billing volumes. Only 800 establishments were re-affiliated compared to 1,700 the year before. The cardholder base was also cut to only 17,500 "quality and maintenance-free" cardholders, as against 27,600 the previous year.

Billings were reduced to a more manageable level of PHP132.1 million, a 55-percent drop from last year's billings of PHP290.7 million. Despite the lower volume, the average yield from billings improved from 6.9 percent the previous year to 7.3 percent in fiscal year 1984. Total net collections for the year amounted to PHP167.7 million. CHARGEKARD suffered a net loss of PHP17.4 million.

**FIRST PHILIPPINE REALTY & DEVELOPMENT CORPORATION**

In fiscal year 1983–1984, First Philippine Realty and Development Corporation (FPRDC) sold an industrial site to one of the group companies. Accordingly, the underlying lease contract over that property was terminated and FPRDC did not realize revenues during the year. Its balance sheet as of June 30, 1984 showed total assets of PHP988,332; retained earnings stood at PHP51,522.

**TABANGAO REALTY, INC**

On its third year of operations, Tabangao Realty, Inc generated revenues amounting to PHP2.7 million, a net income of PHP1.2 million, and declared PHP0.36/share cash dividends to its stockholders of record as of October 31, 1983. On September 15, 1983, the Board of Investments approved the company's request to engage in expanded and related activities.

EXHIBIT 3

**FIRST PHILIPPINE HOLDINGS CORPORATION**
**Financial Review**
**For the Period 1979–1984**
(in million pesos)

| | *1979* | *1980* | *1981* | *1982* | *1983* | *1984* |
|---|---|---|---|---|---|---|
| Revenues | P 225.9 | 260.1 | 206.3 | 185.6 | 212.8 | 159.4 |
| Financial Charges | 51.6 | 44.8 | 81.0 | 125.8 | 128.9 | 183.0 |
| Net Income | 150.7 | 168.7 | 61.2 | 24.2 | 38.6 | (46.9) |
| Total Assets | 1,583.8 | 1,710.7 | 1,715.4 | 1,917.9 | 2,118.1 | 2,010.56 |
| Investment in stocks | 652.6 | 841.5 | 889.7 | 1,028 | 1,156.5 | 1,134.5 |
| Stockholders' Equity | 722.4 | 958.3 | 915.2 | 994 | 972.4 | 1,104.0 |
| Debt/Equity | .65 | .42 | .55 | .67 | .79 | .82 |
| Current Ratio | 3.05 | 3.27 | 1.36 | .95 | 1.28 | 1.20 |
| Earnings per Share | 4.90 | 5.49 | 1.88 | .70 | .88 | (1.75) |
| Book Value per Share | 26.63 | 29.44 | 28.12 | 28.94 | 28.26 | 32.31 |
| Cash Dividends per Share | 1.20 | 1.20 | 3.20 | 1.20 | 1.20 | — |
| Number of Common Shares | ———— 32,549.028 ———— | | | | | |
| Number of Shareholders | 12,603 | 12,860 | 13,114 | NA | NA | NA |

NA means not available.

Source: First Philippine Holdings Corporation Annual Reports.

EXHIBIT 4

## FIRST PHILIPPINE HOLDINGS CORPORATION
## CONSOLIDATED FINANCIAL STATEMENTS

### Balance Sheets
### June 30, 1984 and 1983

| | *1984* | *1983* |
|---|---|---|
| ASSETS | | |
| Current Assets | | |
| Cash | P 6,625,711 | P 27,058,257 |
| Short-term cash investments including interest of P6,180,836; P723,811 in 1983 | 49,850,158 | 89,709,810 |
| Accrued interest on installment receivable (Note 3)* | 3,448,728 | 3,937,856 |
| Due from subsidiaries & affiliates (Note 2)* | 114,310,516 | 53,004,652 |
| Current maturities on installment receivable (Note 3)* | 60,719,318 | 60,719,318 |
| Other current assets (Note 6)* | 147,043,771 | 130,171,009 |
| Total Current Assets | 381,998,202 | 364,600,902 |
| Installment Receivable – MERALCO Foundation, Inc. (Note 3)* | 367,398,689 | 428,118,006 |
| Investment in stocks of subsidiaries & affiliates (Notes 1, 4, 5 & 6)* | 1,134,542,639 | 1,156,486,966 |
| Property and Equipment, less Accumulated Depreciation of P8,400,771; P5,855,185 in 1983 (Notes 1 and 5) | 80,277,927 | 83,611,954 |
| Other assets (Note 6)* | 46,345,772 | 85,264,837 |
| Total Assets | P2,010,563,229 | P2,118,082,665 |
| LIABILITIES AND STOCKHOLDERS' EQUITY | | |
| Current Liabilities | | |
| Short-term borrowings | 194,976,448 | 118,448,956 |
| Dividends Payable (Note 8)* | — | 9,764,708 |
| Accrued interest & others (Note 6)* | 40,627,726 | 60,278,899 |
| Current maturities on long-term debt (Notes and 5)* | 82,855,769 | 65,405,900 |
| Total Current Liabilities | 318,459,943 | 283,898,463 |

*See Notes to Financial Statements.

EXHIBIT 4 (cont'd)

## FIRST PHILIPPINE HOLDINGS CORPORATION
## CONSOLIDATED FINANCIAL STATEMENTS

### Balance Sheets
### June 30, 1984 and 1983

| | *1984* | *1983* |
|---|---|---|
| Long-term debt, less current maturities shown under Current Liabilities (Notes 1 and 5)* | 457,360,188 | 288,726,700 |
| Unrealized Gain on Installment Sale of Investment in Stocks & Other Payables | 130,737,071 | 373,020,158 |
| STOCKHOLDERS' EQUITY | | |
| Common Stock | | |
| Authorized – 31,500,000 Class A shares at P10 par value Issued & outstanding – 28,787,356 shares | 287,873,560 | 287,878,560 |
| Authorized – 13,500,000 Class B shares at P10 per value Issued & outstanding – 3,761,672 shares | 37,616,720 | 37,616,720 |
| Preferred Shares (Notes 7 & 8)* | | |
| Authorized – 10,000,000 Class A shares at P10 par value Issued & outstanding – 3,657,542 shares (net of subscription receivable of P15,455) | 36,559,050 | 36,559,965 |
| Authorized – 10,000,000 Class B shares at P10 par value Issued & outstanding – 1,589,105 shares | 15,891,050 | 15,891,050 |
| Capital in excess of par value | 19,502 | 19,502 |
| | 377,960,797 | 377,960,797 |
| Retained earnings (Notes 4 and 8)* | 310,130,918 | 366,987,817 |
| Shares in subsidiaries' surplus arising from revaluation of property, plant & equipment (Note 1)* | 415, 914,312 | 227,488,730 |
| | 1,104,006,027 | 972,437,344 |
| Total Liabilities and Stockholders' Equity | P2,010,563,229 | P2,118,082,665 |

*See Notes to Financial Statements.

## STATEMENTS OF INCOME AND RETAINED EARNINGS
**Years Ended June 30, 1984 and 1983**

| | *1984* | *1983* |
|---|---|---|
| REVENUES | | |
| Shares in subsidiaries and affiliates' (losses) earnings (Notes 1 and 4)* | P(54,463,955) | P125,542,366 |
| Gain on sale of shares of stocks (Note 3)* | 165,569,411 | 30,260,980 |
| Interest & other income (Note 3)* | 48,296,240 | 56,962,607 |
| | 159,401,696 | 212,765,953 |
| EXPENSES | | |
| Financial charges | 183,007,834 | 128,929,926 |
| General & administrative | 12,415,483 | 16,347,631 |
| Net foreign exchange loss (Notes 1 and 5)* | 1,999,803 | 5,263,432 |
| | 206,290,418 | 174,216,457 |
| NET (LOSS) INCOME FOR THE YEAR (P1.75) per share; P0.88 in 1983 (Note 1)* | (46,888,722) | 38,549,496 |
| RETAINED EARNINGS, Beginning | 366,987,817 | 377,465,331 |
| DIVIDENDS DECLARED | | |
| Preferred (Note 8)* | (9,968,177) | (9,968,176) |
| Common | — | (39,058,834) |
| | (9,968,177) | (49,027,010) |
| | 357,019,640 | 328,438,321 |
| RETAINED EARNINGS, Ending | P310,130,918 | P366,987,817 |

*See Notes to Financial Statements.

## STATEMENT OF CHANGES IN FINANCIAL POSITION
### Years Ended June 30, 1984 and 1983

| | 1984 | 1983 |
|---|---|---|
| WORKING CAPITAL WAS PROVIDED FROM | | |
| Funds provided by operations — | | |
| Net (loss) income for the year | P (46,888,722) | P 38,549,496 |
| Charges (credits) to income not requiring outlay of working capital depreciation & amortization | 4,542,722 | 4,100,330 |
| Provision for foreign exchange losses | — | 82,478,000 |
| Provision for deferred tax benefit | 20,615,745 | (28,867,300) |
| Gain on disposal of shares of stocks | (165,569,411) | (29,971,132) |
| Share in subsidiaries' & affiliates' losses | 54,463,955 | (125,542,366) |
| | (132,835,711) | (59,252,972) |
| Collection of installment receivable | 60,719,317 | (60,719,316) |
| Disposal of shares of stocks & property | 110,109,191 | 83,131 |
| Disposal of other assets | 648,323 | — |
| Borrowings from local bank & financial institutions | — | 121,596,266 |
| Cash dividends from subsidiaries & affiliates | 19,948,983 | 52,585,698 |
| Payment received on overseas contract, net | 46,143,893 | 106,176,407 |
| Subscription on preferred shares | — | 67,962 |
| | 104,733,996 | 281,976,808 |
| WORKING CAPITAL WAS APPLIED TO | | |
| Additions to investment in shares of stocks | 51,215,657 | 67,025,326 |
| Additions to property & equipment | 258,375 | 1,137,176 |
| Additions to other assets | 29,089,455 | 2,700,390 |
| Payments of long-term debt net | 13,916,643 | 80,769,012 |
| Transfer of current portion of long-term debt | 17,449,869 | (15,863,112) |
| Dividends paid | 9,968,177 | 49,027,010 |
| | 121,898,176 | 184,795,802 |
| (DECREASE) INCREASE IN WORKING CAPITAL | P 17,164,180 | P 97,181,006 |

## STATEMENT OF CHANGES IN FINANCIAL POSITION (cont'd)
## Years Ended June 30, 1984 and 1983

| | *1984* | *1983* |
|---|---|---|
| CHANGES IN COMPONENTS OF WORKING CAPITAL | | |
| Increase (Decrease) in Current Assets | | |
| Cash | (P 20,432,546) | P 15,992,800 |
| Short-term cash investment | (39,859,652) | (32,869,405) |
| Accrued interest on installment receivable (Note 3)* | (489,128) | (489,128) |
| Due from subsidiaries & affiliates (Note 2)* | 61,305,864 | (24,276,347) |
| Other current assets (Note 6)* | 16,872,762 | 109,955,181 |
| | 17,397,300 | 68,313,101 |
| Increase (Decrease) in Current Liabilities | | |
| Short-term borrowings | 46,527,492 | (30,130,972) |
| Dividends payable (Note 8)* | (9,764,708) | — |
| Accrued interest and others | (19,651,173) | 17,126,179 |
| Current maturities on long-term debt (Notes 1 and 5)* | 17,449,869 | (15,863,112) |
| | 34,561,480 | 28,867,905 |
| (DECREASE) INCREASE IN WORKING CAPITAL | P 17,164,180 | P97,181,006 |

*See Notes to Financial Statements.

# NOTES TO FINANCIAL STATEMENTS
## June 30, 1984

### NOTE 1: SIGNIFICANT ACCOUNTING POLICIES

**Investment in Stock.** Investment in stocks of subsidiaries and affiliates representing 20-percent interest or more were recorded on the basis of equity method of accounting. Share in earnings or losses was computed based on reported net income or loss plus depreciation on appraisal increment charged to operations, if any.

**Depreciation and Capitalization.** Property and equipment were stated at cost. Maintenance and minor replacements were charged to expense as incurred while betterments and major improvements were capitalized. Property and equipment were depreciated by the straight-line method.

**Foreign Exchange Adjustments.** Foreign exchange transactions were recorded at current rates while balances at year-end were stated based on the then prevailing exchange rates. The resulting gain or loss was recognized as a deferred item and amortized over the remaining life of the loan.

**Income Tax.** The Company recognizes income tax expense based on the deferred income tax method, where income tax was provided on income and expense items with timing differences for financial and income tax reporting purposes.

**Loss Per Common Share.** Loss per common share was computed by dividing the net loss for the year after deducting the dividends on preferred shares over the weighted average of shares of stock outstanding during the year.

### NOTE 2: DUE FROM SUBSIDIARIES AND AFFILIATES

Due from subsidiaries and affiliates consists of cash advances for bridge financing, working capital requirements, and other operational needs.

### NOTE 3: INSTALLMENT RECEIVABLE – MERALCO FOUNDATION, INC

Installment receivable consists of the amount due from Meralco Foundation Inc (MFI) in connection with its purchase of the Company's holdings in Manila Electric Company (MERALCO) under a Stock Purchase Agreement dated October 21, 1977. This amount was payable in twenty-three (23) semi-annual installments in pre-determined percentages starting September 1, 1980 plus 10-percent interest payable quarterly starting March 1, 1978.

### NOTE 4: INVESTMENT IN STOCKS OF SUBSIDIARIES AND AFFILIATES, SHARE IN SUBSIDIARIES' AND AFFILIATES' EARNINGS AND RETAINED EARNINGS

The details of the investment in stocks, retained earnings, and net income for the year as adjusted from cost to equity method are presented below:

| | *Investment in Stocks* | *Retained Earnings* | *Net Income (Loss) for the Year* |
|---|---|---|---|
| At Cost | 554,141,277 | 125,545,460 | 76,736,495 |
| Share in subsidiaries' & affiliates' earnings (loss) | | | |
| Current year | (54,463,955) | (54,463,955) | (54,463,955) |
| Prior years | 238,899,988 | 258,998,396 | (49,212,279) |
| Share in subsidiaries revaluation surplus | 415,914,312 | | |
| Dividends received during the year | (19,948,983) | (19,948,983) | (19,948,983) |
| At Equity | 1,134,542,639 | 310,130,918 | 46,888,722 |

**NOTE 5: LONG-TERM DEBT**

Long-term debt, as of June 30, 1984, consisted of the following:

| | *Year of Final Installment* | *Interest Rate* | *Outstanding Balance* |
|---|---|---|---|
| 1. Long-term loan from the Development Bank of the Philippines (DBP) | 1991 | 21% | 434,000,000 |
| 2. Syndicated 5-year loan from local bank & financial institutions | 1987 | 25% | 100,000,000 |
| 3. Term loans from local banks | Various | Various | 6,215,957 |
| Total | | | 540,215,957 |
| Current Portion | | | (82,855,769) |
| | | | 457,360,188 |

The long-term loan from DBP, in which proceeds were used to prepay the foreign currency loan from APCO, was secured by a third party pledge executed by Meralco Foundation, Inc covering 9,591,318 unpaid Manila Electric Company (MECO) common shares and assignment of the receivables from Meralco Foundation, Inc (MFI) arising from the sale of MECO shares by FPRC to MFI. These shares were acquired by MFI from the Company in accordance with the terms of the Stock Purchase Agreement and the Memorandum of Closing referred to in Note 3. The Supplemental Agreement with MFI authorized the Company to use the unpaid MERALCO shares to collateralize the Company's obligations.

The credit agreements covering the foregoing indebtedness contained restrictions affecting the activities of the Company, among which were lending money and granting bonuses to its officers and stockholders, incurring new long-term debt, declaring cash dividends on common stocks, extending advances and loans in favor of other firms and entering into mergers or consolidations with any other company. These activities were allowed provided there was no event of default and the required debt to equity ratio was met. Undertaking of any of the above activities without DBP's prior approval shall either cause the loan to become due and demandable or trigger the exercise of the voting rights assigned to it by the borrower-firm or cause the foreclosure of the underlying collaterals.

The PHP100 million 5-year loan syndicated by local financial institutions bears interest at 21 percent per annum during the first 24 months and thereafter at a spread over Manila Reference Rate (MRR) or 21 percent, whichever is higher; it was payable at the rate of PHP4.8 million starting on the 24th month after drawdown and every three months thereafter up to the 57th month. The balance of PHP42.3 million was payable in full on the 60th month. This loan was collateralized by a real estate mortgage and a pledge of shares of stocks.

The term loans from local banks were secured by a real estate mortgage and pledge of shares of stock.

**NOTE 6: OTHER PAYABLES**

The Company, together with certain subsidiaries, was a party to a long-term turnkey subcontract in the Middle East for the installation of electrical transmission lines in Hail, Saudi Arabia. Under the contract, the Company received 20 percent of the total sub-contract price amounting to SR222.1 million as down payment subject to amortization against progress billings rendered by the subsidiary to the contractee in accordance with certain schedules. The down payment was released to the above subsidiary for the operating requirements of the project. This is reflected in the balance sheet as other payables and other current assets.

The Company pledged shares of stocks with carrying value of PHP307.5 million as collaterals to a financial institution that provided counter-guaranty support for the guarantee requirements of the aforementioned Middle East Project. Based on the agreement, partial releases of these shares of stocks were to be made as progress billings were collected from the project.

### NOTE 7: PREFERRED STOCK

The preferred shares were cumulative and non-participating as to dividends and were non-voting. They were redeemable at the end of the five years from issue date or, at the option of the Company, upon 60 days notice at the end of the first year from issue date and every year thereafter, in whole or in part and in multiples of PHP5.0 million to be determined by lottery and upon payment of a premium in accordance with the following schedules:

| *Redemption (From Issue Date)* | *Premium (Based on Par of Shares Redeemed)* |
|---|---|
| End of First Year | 1.00% |
| End of Second Year | .75% |
| End of Third Year | .50% |
| End of Fourth Year | .25% |
| End of Fifth Year | none |

The shares were further subjected to early redemption under such other conditions as the Board of Directors of the Company shall determine.

### NOTE 8: DIVIDENDS ON PREFERRED SHARES

Dividends on preferred shares declared out of the Company's earned surplus amounted to PHP0.95 per preferred share.

### NOTE 9: RETIREMENT PLAN AND PENSION FUND

The Company had a non-contributory pension plan for retirement, death, and disability benefits covering substantially all of its employees. Pension cost for the period amounted to PHP1,190,348 consisting of normal cost of PHP1,157,553 and past service liability amortization of PHP32,795. The unfunded past service liability as of June 30, 1984 was PHP927,082. This was funded and amortized over a period of twenty-eight (28) years.

The foregoing pension costs were determined on the basis of computations made by an independent actuarian.

### NOTE 10: CONTINGENT LIABILITIES

The Company had issued guarantees in connection with certain obligations of its subsidiaries in the amount of PHP522 million as of June 30, 1984, of which PHP425 million was related to the project referred to in Note 6.

# Noel Gifts International Ltd* 4

In April 1993, Alfred S H Wong, Managing Director of Noel Gifts International Ltd (Noel), Singapore's largest hampers, gift, and floral company, looked back on the past ten years with considerable jubilation. From its humble beginnings in August 1983, the company grew eightfold (see Exhibits 1 to 4 for historical financial information). In April 1993, Noel was the undisputed market leader in its industry in Singapore and was listed on the Stock Exchange of Singapore Dealing and Automated Quotation System (SESDAQ). The company had also expanded its portfolio and begun franchising its intellectual rights, trade name, and goodwill to Malaysia, Indonesia, and Thailand. These developments led Alfred Wong to look forward to a continued rosy financial picture for the company.

This case provides a brief description of the gift marketing industry, Noel's history and current operating performance, and the future prospects Noel faces. It also outlines the challenges Noel faces as it seeks to set new technological trends in the industry and to embark on a new corporate identity to strengthen the company's status as a leading force in the business of designing, producing, and marketing creative gift packages.

* This case was prepared by Professor Luis Ma. R. Calingo on the basis of a student report submitted by Frankie Chia Yeow Tiong, Ho Bee Tat, Catherine Mah Siok Hean, Tan Juat Swee, and Tan Hock Seng (MBA, Nanyang Technological University). It is designed to serve as a basis for class discussion rather than to illustrate either effective or ineffective handling of an administrative situation.

## Company History

The company was incorporated as Noel Hampers & Gifts Pte Ltd in Singapore on August 17, 1983. Its business activities encompassed the design, marketing, and distribution of floral arrangements, gifts, and hampers. The company also later operated as a master franchisor of these business activities using the full business format franchise approach.

### The Founding Siblings

The company's founder, Mr Alfred Wong, had been Noel's Managing Director since its inception. He pioneered and had since directed the group of companies on its growth path. With seventeen years of experience in the hampers, floral, and gifts business, he was responsible for the strategic planning, overseas franchising, and financial management at Noel. In 1991, the Entrepreneurial Development Centre (ENDEC) at Nanyang Technological University awarded Mr Wong that year's ENDEC Entrepreneurship Excellence Award in recognition of his entrepreneurial spirit and achievements in building a successful gift company from scratch. His persistent determination to succeed has been the main driving force behind the growth of the company.

Mrs Ivy Tan, Alfred Wong's sister, had served as Noel's Deputy Managing Director. As cofounder, she assisted Wong in overseeing the management of Noel Gifts International Ltd, as well as the business operations of its related companies. Mrs Tan spearheaded Noel's marketing efforts, including product design, merchandising, and advertising and promotions both for domestic and overseas markets. Her creative support helped Noel grow from a family business to its current position as the biggest and most thriving gift company in Southeast Asia.

### Early History

In the 1970s, gift hampers were a drab, unfashionable affair. Dull to look at and unexciting to unwrap, hampers did not have any frills at that time. In those days, hampers were generally plain and functional. They were packed and sold at provision shops and supermarkets with low-quality standards. Given that there was little or no advertising and promotion of gift hampers, no focus was given to hampers as a strategic business. However, hampers were sometimes featured in limited advertisements together with other household goods and food items. It was common to find in gift hampers dented and rusty cans of food, in addition to spoiled goods, which could not otherwise be sold on the shelves. Hampers were largely sold on a "cash-and-carry" basis.

Frustrated with the low quality and poor appearance of commercially available hampers, Mr Wong started to pack his own hampers. He prepared, packed, and delivered quality festive food and liquor hampers for the valued customers of Noel Group, his thriving construction business.[1] Mr Wong was very meticulous about the quality and presentation of the hampers. The recipients were so impressed by the hampers that they, in turn, asked if he would pack hampers for their own customers. Over time, more and more of Wong's early business associates asked if he could prepare hampers for them to give to their own valued customers. Mr Wong then realized that there was a demand for

[1] Mr Alfred Wong graduated with a Civil Engineering certificate from Singapore Polytechnic.

high-quality, creatively designed, and attractively packed hampers. He thus established a business in 1976 to capitalize on these opportunities by offering creative and better packed hampers.

Alfred Wong saw the long-term potential of his new business venture and was determined to satisfy customers' basic demand for quality hampers. Quality goods, therefore, became an important element of Noel's business. Noel's entry into the market transformed hampers into creative items containing quality goods which were attractively packed, often featuring fashionable concepts or themes. Mr Wong transformed hampers into attractive items, which were even lovelier to unwrap. He recognized the commercial potential presented by the gift-giving tradition of the different ethnic groups — Malay, Indian, Chinese, expatriates — in Singapore. Little did he know that hampers would prove so popular and that his mere sideline business would grow into a major business.

**Developments Since 1983**

To cope with the expansion of the hamper business, Noel Hampers & Gifts Pte Ltd (Noel) was founded in 1983 and became the flagship subsidiary of the Noel Group. Noel's business was driven by aggressive marketing and its ability to offer quality products, reliable service, and convenience. In 1988, Noel became the first company in Singapore's direct gift marketing industry to provide its customers with money-back guarantees on the freshness of the products and on-time delivery. In 1992, one of Noel's competitors introduced written money-back guarantees, but only with respect to freshness.

Noel changed the nature of the trade and was the first specialty gift company to introduce a total marketing approach which included media advertising and promotion, marketing through a telephone sales force, direct-selling through traveling salespersons, and distribution of brochures. Noel's telemarketers and customer service departments provided the necessary support in disseminating information and making recommendations on gift ideas. Noel turned the once passive gift hamper market into a service-oriented business. Emphasis was placed on high standards of customer service by offering customers the convenience of telephone and facsimile ordering, payment through credit or charge cards, and door-to-door delivery. Noel thus built a reputation for offering the convenience of shopping at home or in the office through catalogs.

Until the early 1980s, there were no known specialist gift hamper businesses offering the convenience of telephone ordering and delivery services. Noel's present competitors, Belvedere Florists and Gifts Pte Ltd, D & P Hampers Pte Ltd, and Tiffany Hampers and Gifts Pte Ltd, offered only the convenience of telephone and facsimile ordering and door-to-door delivery services after they were incorporated in 1984. Noel was thus the first specialized gift hamper company to make delivery a standard service available to all its customers.

Mr Alfred Wong realized that gift hampers were mainly festive gifts. To thrive during those periods of major festivities, the company started a complementary business — a floral arrangement service — which was later expanded to include an extensive range of gift ideas available to its customers. This diversification effort had contributed to a steadier business for the company between festive seasons. Later, in 1991, a reorganization was implemented to segregate the hamper business from the flowers and gifts business.

In the 1980s, Noel recruited professionals to help run the company's operations. Since the mid-1980s, the company has engaged specialist consultants including the Singapore National Productivity Board to sharpen its competitive edge, improve its internal systems, and upgrade the skills of its employees. Two other consultants also helped to enhance the company's public image and improve its internal systems. These consultants also provided strategic planning advice to the company.

As a natural extension to Noel Gifts's creative business, IKA Design Pte Ltd was established in 1984. From product concept and advertising to final product presentation upon delivery, the policy had always been to maintain the Group's image of creativity. IKA Design specialized in direct response advertising and was responsible for many successful campaigns for several multinational clients. These included cardmember solicitation campaigns for American Express and specialty product campaigns for Polaroid.

In January 1993, Mr Alfred Wong, Mrs Ivy Tan, and Mr James Wong formed Heritage Collections Pte Ltd (HCPL) to specialize in watches, jewelry, and collectors' items. HCPL sold these exclusive gifts by direct mail, primarily through credit card companies. HCPL has its own research and development department, which generates new products and concepts on an ongoing basis and has established a name for itself internationally in Southeast Asia, Canada, and the United States as a design company that creates and markets innovative products.

In February 1993, Noel and HCPL entered into a management agreement under which Noel would provide HCPL management and technical assistance in the form of specialized knowledge, expertise, experience, and know-how pertaining to the administration and financial operations of HCPL's business. Consultants from Noel would review, evaluate, and advise HCPL in key areas of management. These areas included personnel, financial operations, stock and billing management, budget and planning, new products, ventures and developments, market selection and market strategy, and key investment decisions. For these services, HCPL would pay Noel a management fee on a fixed-fee basis (about $42,500 in 1993) and Noel was able to purchase products from HCPL for its hampers and gifts at the same prices offered to HCPL employees.

The diversification, recruitment of professionals, and assistance from specialist consultants all helped the company to maintain its position as a leader in the direct gifts marketing industry as measured by its substantial sales growth. With the expertise and experience that it had accumulated over the years in Singapore, Noel was well-positioned to apply its expertise for international expansion in the 1990s. In August 1991, the company secured its first overseas franchise in Kuala Lumpur, Malaysia; in December 1992, it appointed its second franchisee in Jakarta, Indonesia.

## The Direct Gift Marketing Industry in Singapore

The direct gift marketing industry is unique in that direct gift marketers do not have retail outlets. Instead, product offerings are made mainly through catalogs, media advertising and promotion, marketing through a telephone sales force, and direct selling through traveling salespersons.

Revenue generation in the hamper and gifts business depended mainly on festive seasons, which traditionally peaked during the Christmas and Chinese New Year seasons. The number of major Asian ethnic groups in Singapore has given rise to a cosmopolitan society characterized by numerous festivals throughout the year: Chinese New Year,

Valentine's Day, and Hari Raya Puasa during the first half of the year, and Deepavali and Christmas during the second half of the year. Marketers usually try to diversify their business into gift-related areas in order to maintain steady sales for the companies between festive periods.

There is a tradition for business executives to present gifts at the time a service is rendered. In the United States, for instance, these year-round thank-you's accounted for about 40 percent of the occasions on which business gifts were given in the United States.[2] Although this potential market opportunity also existed in Singapore, gift marketers must recognize the Chinese custom that gifts are given only if there is a good reason for offering them.

Gifts and hampers are easy to imitate and are highly substitutable. Further, there are no regulatory barriers to entry in the direct-gift-marketing industry. Although industry players are vulnerable to competitive pressures, Noel believes that established gift marketers who have a reputation for quality and reliability would benefit from repeat orders. The nature of gift-giving is such that, normally, the final product is not available for personal inspection prior to purchase.

**Competition**

The direct-gift-marketing industry is characterized by a large number of retail florists, each with a relatively small market share. In 1993, there were about 20 hamper businesses and hundreds of retail florists operating in Singapore. Noel's main competitors were Belvedere Florists and Gifts Pte Ltd, D & P Hampers & Florists Pte Ltd, and Tiffany Hampers & Gifts Pte Ltd. Although there are no publicly available sales data on these companies, the combined sales of these three main competitors are estimated to be approximately equal to Noel's sales. Market surveys commissioned by Noel indicated that Noel had a 40-percent market share of the hampers market and a 10-percent share of the flowers and gifts market.

Competition in the hamper business is relatively fierce, especially with the entry of supermarkets and a large number of independent operators who are generally active only during the two major festive seasons (i.e., Christmas and Chinese New Year) and offer delivery services on gift hampers. The overheads of these operators are kept low by investing little money on product design and quality control. They compete on pricing and cater mainly to the budget-conscious segment of the gift hamper market and are therefore active in market segments that Noel did not actively serve.

**Customers**

A very large majority (about 75 percent) of Noel's customers consist of corporations, including both multinational corporations and local enterprises. A recent survey conducted by Noel revealed that a majority of these corporate buyers are women, mainly secretaries, clerks, and receptionists. A sizable portion of customers are also repeat customers. According to market research commissioned by Noel, the key considerations of customers are fuss-free ordering, wide product range, attractive packaging, fresh products, and reliable delivery at affordable prices. Armed with this knowledge, Noel sought to emphasize providing

[2] Kathleen O'Neill, "Firms Say Thank You with Business Gifts," *Public Relations Journal*, 47:9 (September 1991): 28.

"value for money" to its customers in terms of creative product design, quality goods, and prompt delivery and competitive pricing.

Business customers have long been recognized as a major growth segment in Singapore's gift marketing industry. Business gifts express appreciation, develop and nurture new clients, or create prospective clients' awareness of a company and its offerings. This customer segment was, however, vulnerable to corporate cost-cutting during bad economic times. The long-term growth of the business gifts market also depended on corporations' continuing ability to deduct business gifts as a business expense on their income tax returns. Before the cost of a gift could be deducted as a business expense, tax laws normally require that it be given in a business setting and proven to be ordinary, necessary, and reasonable in amount. In this respect, tax laws in Singapore are not as stringent as those in the United States where a US$25 (S$40) limitation per business gift has been in effect.[3]

Very limited data is available on the gift-giving behaviors of Singapore businesses. However, there are several facts about the US business-gift market which might be relevant to a newly industrialized economy like Singapore. Approximately US$3.5 billion was spent on business gifts in the United States in 1990, according to *Business & Incentives* magazine.[4] The most popular gifts ranged from pen sets to sportswear to electronics. Business gifts were most often given to major clients, employees, and prospective clients. Most business-gift buyers preferred to give items that were customized, bearing the company's name, logo, or slogan. These corporate gifts are designed to help increase a client's audience and awareness through their targetability and creative impact. Most American companies usually spent around US$25, since gifts costing up to this amount are tax-deductible. The food industry was the leader in business-gift spending, according to the survey.

The expected growth of the industry in Singapore depends on the number of individual and corporate customers. Customer figures, in turn, hinge on population growth as well as future economic growth. Although Singapore's population grew by only an annual average of 1.09 percent from 1985 to 1990 (compared to East Asia's average of 1.31 percent), the pronatalist population policies recently adopted by the government would likely result in more rapid population growth.[5] A potentially more important contributor to industry growth is the increasing affluence of Singaporeans and their preference for convenience. As a result of these factors, rapid growth of the direct-gift-marketing industry is expected to continue.

**Suppliers**

The industry has a network of about 200 suppliers. These suppliers provide liquor, flowers, fruits, toys, canned goods, confectionery, jewelry, ornaments, and electronic goods. Because the suppliers are a relatively fragmented group, gift marketers enjoy considerable economic leverage. Of the 200 suppliers, 125 were Noel's regular suppliers. Only two suppliers accounted for more than five percent of the company's sales for the last three years: Jardine Otard Wines and Spirits Pte Ltd and Colloquiums Advertising.

[3] Jim Donohoo, "Tax Deductions from Business Gifts," *Business Forum*, 15:4 (Winter 1991): 47.
[4] Kathleen O'Neill, "Firms Say Thank You with Business Gifts," *Public Relations Journal*, 47:9 (September 1991): 28, 30.
[5] Warwick Neville, "The Dynamics of Population Ageing Into the Twenty-First Century: ASEAN and Selected Countries of Pacific Asia," *ASEAN Economic Bulletin*, 9:1 (July 1992): 5–7.

Noel worked closely with its suppliers in order to achieve quality standards for its supplies. With the help of Noel's team of designers and merchandisers, suppliers were able to improve their packaging, product mix, and design to meet the needs of Noel's customers.

## Noel's Current Operations

### Marketing

Noel adopted a total marketing approach, encompassing market research, merchandising, advertising and promotions, service support, and quality assurance. Merchandise was selected based on market research in consumer demand, while advertising and promotion programs were geared toward creating the desired buyer awareness. Noel maintained a sales force trained in providing service support, accepting orders, and resolving customer complaints.

Market research was carried out on a regular basis to incorporate market feedback and the latest consumer trends into its products and services. Its offerings were designed to suit different occasions which ranged from office decorations to special occasions like inaugurations, birth, death, and sickness or festivities such as Christmas, Chinese New Year, Deepavali, Valentine's Day, Mother's Day, Father's Day, and the Moon Cake Festival. Noel appointed two market survey firms and commissioned four market studies from 1991 to 1993. It also maintained in-house resources to perform market studies and surveys. To support the company's operations, Noel's in-house product design team create about 500 new designs every year. Noel engaged external design firms and advertising agents to solicit wider design ideas and market experience.

Marketing was conducted through media advertising and promotion, telephone sales force, direct-selling through traveling salespersons, and brochures. Noel accepted orders through the telephone, facsimile, mail, or through sales representatives. Customers can either specify a custom design or choose from a wide range of available designs. Orders were then delivered according to customer specifications. The company offered a special 98-minute express delivery of flowers and gifts to any point in Singapore. This express service was available for a $13 surcharge and came along with a 100-percent discount for late delivery.

### Operations Management

Noel conducted in-house quality inspections on supplies and had back-to-back guarantees with several suppliers. Noel worked with design firms and consultants in creating attractive and appealing designs. Its quality checks helped to ensure that defects were kept to a minimum. The "Just In Time" (JIT) concept was introduced with the assistance of the National Productivity Board to reduce wastage from high inventory levels, to study work processes with the aim of achieving an organized workplace layout conducive to smooth operations, and to adopt efficient work practices. Noel kept a pool of transport contractors, its own delivery vans, and sufficient personnel to ensure timely delivery.

In 1993, Noel was the only company in the direct gift marketing industry in Singapore to provide written money-back guarantees on both freshness and on-time delivery. If hampers were delivered late, a 50-percent refund of the price was given. Since the commencement of this quality guarantee, the claims recorded by Noel against such guarantees have been negligible.

### Human Resource Development

Noel has a comprehensive and regular staff training program which consists of in-house and external courses in the areas of customer service, marketing, information systems and technology, creativity, management, and first-line supervision. Noel recognized that human resource development has been vital to the company's drive toward excellent service. For the fiscal year ended June 30, 1992, Noel invested 2.3 percent of staff payroll on staff training, slightly higher than the national average of two percent. The company is committed to the continuous upgrading of its employees' skills, improving customer service and productivity, and achieving cost savings. Noel's employees are not unionized, and Noel enjoys good staff-management relations.

### Financial Performance

Over a five-year period from 1988 to 1992, the hamper business grew from a yearly revenue of $5,373,000 to $8,950,000 (see Exhibit 5). This corresponded to an annual compounded growth rate of 13 percent, about twice the 6 to 8 percent annual growth of Singapore's gross national product. This tremendous growth was partly from the increased demand for gift hampers from both individual and corporate customers. Sales of gift hampers had historically been subject to seasonal demand, mainly during Christmas and Chinese New Year.

For the same financial period, net sales for the flower and gift product lines increased from $1,189,000 to $3,891,000, amounting to an annual compounded growth rate of 35 percent. Noel attributed this growth to aggressive advertising and promotions, as well as the constant introduction of new product designs. Sales from flowers and gifts were non-seasonal and occurred throughout the year from a diverse customer base.

Noel's franchising business activity began in August 1991 but started generating franchise fees and royalties (continuing management service fees) of $168,000 only in 1992.

Profits from the hamper product line grew from $314,000 in 1988 to $897,000 in 1992, corresponding to a 28-percent annual growth rate. The floral and gifts business moved from a loss of $575,000 in 1988 to a profit of $351,000 in 1992, reflecting an annual growth rate of 86 percent from 1989 to 1992. Franchising activity started with a loss of $104,000 in 1991 due to development costs and turned in a profit of $85,000 the following year.

Overall, Noel's sales grew at an annual rate of 18 percent, while its profits grew by an average of 43 percent each year. This financial performance contributed to Noel's success in being listed on the Stock Exchange of Singapore Dealing and Automated Quotation System (SESDAQ). The Singapore Government launched SESDAQ in 1987 to enable small- and medium-size Singapore companies with good growth prospects to raise funds for expansion. In early 1993, there were only some 20 companies listed on SESDAQ, about a tenth of the number of companies listed on the main board of the Stock Exchange of Singapore.

## Franchising

Although franchising has been a way of life in the West, it is still a foreign notion to most Asians. Noel is the first Singapore-based hamper, floral, and gift company to expand overseas through franchising. According to T S Tan, Managing Director of Franchise Development Services Pte Ltd in Singapore:

Franchising allows international expansion by using the investment of franchisees. For small and medium-size businesses, instead of using their own money to expand, people overseas pay the company to set up business in their country. However, franchising is not a "get rich quick" scheme. It is for those who want lower risks and moderate returns.

## Noel's Franchise Program

A separate division of Noel Gifts provided full business format franchising. As distinguished from "license-type" transactions in the full-business-format concept, "a person develops a complete system for the setting up and licensing of a business under an identified brand which may be a trademark, service mark, or trade name and licenses (or franchises) others to trade utilizing the particular system and the branding associated with it."[6] Noel's full business format franchise program offered the franchisee a range of services which included training, proven operating systems, ongoing technical and marketing support, sourcing opportunities, and the use of Noel's intellectual property, service marks, and trade name. The franchisee could choose to be a master franchisee, in which case it was appointed to manage the market on a national scale or an area franchisee, where coverage is limited to a specific city or region in a country. Master franchisees are allowed to subfranchise into towns and districts in the country, provided they adhere to Noel's rules on sublicensing and use the standard area franchise agreement.

The franchise program is attractive for two reasons. The initial benefits relate to the reduction of startup costs through the transfer of expertise in the first twelve months of operations, while the continuing benefits are those associated with the provision of materials, intellectual property, support services, bulk-purchasing opportunities, and access to improvements due to Noel's continuing research and development activities.

## The Franchisees

In marketing its franchise, Noel obtained the assistance of the Market Development Assistance Scheme (Franchising Marketing Program) administered by the Singapore Trade Development Board. With that grant, Noel successfully concluded its first franchise agreement in August 1991 with a Malaysian franchisee to operate in the Klang Valley states of Selangor, Negri Sembilan, and West Pahang. Noel Hampers and Gifts (KL) Sdn Bhd was incorporated in Kuala Lumpur to undertake these activities. To demonstrate its commitment to its first franchise, Noel agreed to invest in the equity share capital of Noel Kuala Lumpur to the extent of 19.9 percent. One of Noel Kuala Lumpur's shareholders had an option to purchase 5 percent of Noel's stake at par value as part of a negotiated agreement when he assumed the position of Managing Director of Noel Kuala Lumpur.

In December 1992, Noel appointed a second franchisee in Indonesia. The franchise was awarded to Exacty Sukamdani Sryantoro as promoter of PT Sahid Noel Mitra Sejati in Jakarta. The Indonesian franchisee was associated with the Sahid Group of Indonesia and was scheduled to begin operations in March 1993.

Noel has plans to expand its franchise network within the Asia-Pacific region — it plans to focus in particular on Johore Bahru (Malaysia), Taiwan, and the Philippines. Of

[6] Martin Mendelsohn, *The Guide to Franchising*, 5th ed. (London: Cassell, 1992): 3.

these three countries, Malaysia and the Philippines are expected to grow most rapidly during the period 1990–2010, with annual average long-term growth rates of 1.6 and 2.0 percent, respectively.[7] On top of these demographic factors, economic growth in Southeast Asia for the period 1993–1994 was expected to range from a low of 4.0 percent (Philippines) to a high of 9.0 percent (Thailand).[8]

Exhibit 6 briefly describes the climate for franchising in the East Asian countries of potential interest to Noel.

**Benefits to Franchisees**

In its survey of retail businesses conducted over a 10-year period, the US Commerce and Trade Board found that a franchised business had a success rate of 91 percent, while a non-franchised business had a much lower success rate of 10 percent. For a new entrant to the floral, gifts, and hampers business, participating in a franchise offered a shorter learning curve compared to starting a business from scratch. Noel's 18 years of valuable experience in the direct-gift-marketing business was compiled into a franchise program which could be transferred to potential franchisees within a short time.

Franchisees could also learn from and adopt Noel's proven operating systems in sales, administration, accounting, electronic data processing, and operations. They would receive training supported by a comprehensive set of manuals covering these aspects to aid them in running the business. They would also receive startup training in Singapore.

Franchisees have the right to use Noel's service mark and trade name, and, hence ride on the reputation that Noel has established in Singapore, Malaysia, Indonesia, and other countries. Franchisees are licensed to use Noel's intellectual properties, namely Noel's creative floral, gift and hamper designs, concepts, and quality specifications and standards. They have access to Noel's marketing expertise, including advertising and promotional materials produced by Noel, and proven market concepts and strategies developed by Noel. They can also source for products from Noel's suppliers at special bulk purchase rates, thereby benefiting from cost savings.

Franchisees receive substantial ongoing support from Noel. Noel's representatives make regular visits to the franchisees for the purpose of business review and market development. In addition, Noel provides technical and marketing support on a continuing basis by mail, telephone, and manual updates, together with follow-up training in Singapore.

The costs to the franchisee for these benefits are twofold. These included an initial lump-sum franchise fee for the franchisee to operate in a specific geographic area. In the case of the Indonesian franchisee, the initial lump-sum area franchise fee is $400,000 (in Singapore currency), net of all taxes. Secondly, a franchisee is required to pay a management fee and a royalty based on the franchisee's monthly sales for the duration of the franchise agreement.

The franchisee is also bound to adhere to Noel's specifications and standards on business operations. Noel's business concept is based on a production-cum-office facility

[7]*The Economist Book of Vital World Statistics* (London: The Economist Books, 1990): 16.
[8]*South East Asia Monitor*, May 1993: 458–467.

of 300 to 400 square meters in size, with good communication facilities and highly developed selling, operating, and administrative systems. Delivery services are envisaged for a radius of 30 to 50 kilometers from the operating base. Although the staff strength for each franchise outlet would depend on projected sales, the ideal size during the initial stage is from 20 to 25 — a mix of marketing, sales, operations, accounts, and administrative staff.

As the master franchisor, Noel provided start-up and ongoing training, prepared support and operating manuals, developed advertising and promotional concepts, nominated suppliers, and contested any infringement of trademarks.

### Vulnerability

Certain external environmental factors could affect Noel's hampers and gifts sales growth. Global events, particularly changes in the economic and political conditions in East Asian countries, could pose grave uncertainties in business outlook and slow down the growth of the direct gift marketing industry. The Singapore Government planned to introduce in April 1994 a 3-percent Goods and Services Tax (GST), and businesses in Singapore had been speculating about GST's adverse impact on consumer spending by Singaporeans. A reduction in the tax-deductibility of business gifts, although unlikely in the short term, could also slow down industry growth. However, the adverse impact of these factors might be mitigated by the Asian tradition of gift-giving.

The transfer of expertise by Noel to the franchisee also poses a potential competitive threat. Even though this has been addressed by "non-compete" clauses in the franchise agreements, there is always a possibility that trade espionage could create new potential competitors in foreign markets. Noel's overseas franchisees are also susceptible to the environmental factors described earlier. Cash flows from franchise arrangements are therefore influenced by the same economic and political risks.

## A View Toward the Future

The Wong siblings believe that the future holds great promise for Noel. They intend to further develop the company's people, enhance its operations, and strengthen and market its products regionally. Noel has embarked on a new corporate identity to strengthen its status as a leading force in the business of designing, producing, and marketing creative packages. The Wongs think that floral arrangements, gifts, and franchising should be the key thrusts of Noel's future growth.

In Singapore, the Noel Group has plans to focus its market efforts in the floral arrangement and gift market because Singapore presents good growth opportunities in these areas. As Singaporeans have become more affluent, giving flowers and gifts on special occasions has risen in popularity among individual and corporate customers.

Apart from the domestic market, Noel has also looked internationally for growth. Franchising offers an opportunity for internal expansion without unduly stretching its resources and capital when compared with establishing a branch or subsidiary overseas. Franchising has also enabled Noel to capitalize on the expertise it developed over the years and provide a sustainable revenue stream over the life of the franchise. The company plans to expand its international franchising program.

Within the next two years, Noel intends to expand its current market coverage to other countries in the Asia-Pacific region, such as Hong Kong, Taiwan, and Thailand. Extensive market surveys have since been conducted on the commercial potential in these markets. These studies showed that in these countries, there were no prominent specialist direct gift marketers. The company has started negotiating with interested parties in these countries. The company's long-term plans are to extend its franchising activities to other parts of the world.

Noel's directors believe that synergies exist between the company's domestic business and its overseas franchise operations. The invaluable feedback received from the overseas franchisees on Noel's offerings are used to further improve the company's current mix of products and services. Noel's international network of franchisees could refer the company to sources of creative products in overseas markets, hence resulting in greater cost efficiency. Franchise operations have also helped the company become more focused on staffing because expertise is required in training the staff of overseas franchisees. These synergies would further develop Noel's domestic operations and help its franchise operations grow to become one of the core business activities of the company.

As the Wong siblings pondered on the future directions of Noel Gifts International Ltd, Mr Wong wondered whether there were drawbacks to international franchising which perhaps have not been explored. He recognizes that while Noel might be a household name in Singapore, it might be practically unknown overseas. Mr Wong, in evaluating the franchising business, remarked: "We had to go around seeking consultants in each country to tell them about our products. And they were usually not keen initially."

EXHIBIT 1

**NOEL GIFTS INTERNATIONAL LTD**
**Income Statement**
**For the Year Ended June 30, 1992**
(Singapore dollars in thousands, except per share)

| | *Amount* | | *Percent* | |
|---|---|---|---|---|
| Net sales | | $13,009 | | 100.0 |
| Cost and expenses: | | | | |
| Cost of goods and services; selling, general, & administrative expenses | $11,434 | | 87.9 | |
| Depreciation | 300 | | 2.3 | |
| Interest | 61 | 11,795 | 0.5 | 90.7 |
| Operating profit | | 1,214 | | 9.3 |
| Net rental income[1] | | 107 | | 0.8 |
| Other income[2] | | 12 | | 0.1 |
| Earnings before taxes | | 1,333 | | 10.1 |
| Income taxes | | 482 | | 3.7 |
| Net income after tax | | $851 | | 6.4 |
| Net earnings per share (cents)[3] | | 2.43 | | |

Notes:
1. Rental income arose from the leasing out of part of Noel Building. The tenants renting space from the company in April 1993 were Heritage Collections Pte Ltd, Yunan Interior Pte Ltd, and Deo Silver Pte Ltd.
2. The company billed its related companies for the occasional use of its computer system and other resources.
3. Based on the pre-flotation share capital of 35 million shares after adjusting for the bonus issue and the share split.

Source: Company records.

EXHIBIT 2

## NOEL GIFTS INTERNATIONAL LTD
### Balance Sheet
### As of June 30, 1992
(in Singapore dollars)

| | | |
|---|---|---|
| ASSETS | | |
| Current assets | | |
| Cash | | $26,000 |
| Accounts receivable | $524,000 | |
| Less: Allowance for bad debts | (167,000) | 357,000 |
| Inventory | 224,000 | |
| Less: Provision for stock obsolescence | (63,000) | 161,000 |
| Other receivables, deposits & prepayments | | 59,000 |
| Total current assets | | 603,000 |
| Fixed assets | | |
| Land, building, improvements, vehicles, & equipment | | 6,877,000 |
| Less Accumulated depreciation | | (699,000) |
| Total fixed assets | | 6,178,000 |
| Investment | | 31,000 |
| Total Assets | | $6,812,000 |
| LIABILITIES AND NET WORTH | | |
| Current liabilities | | |
| Bank overdraft, secured | | $232,000 |
| Accounts payable | | 407,000 |
| Income tax payable | | 488,000 |
| Dividend payable | | 50,000 |
| Other creditors and accruals | | 527,000 |
| Lease purchase obligations, current portion | | 48,000 |
| Total current liabilities | | 1,752,000 |
| Long-term liabilities | | |
| Deferred tax | | 53,000 |
| Lease purchase obligation, long-term portion | | 18,000 |
| Total long-term liabilities | | 71,000 |
| Capital stock | | 1,000,000 |
| Retained earnings | | 1,489,000 |
| Revaluation reserve | | 2,500,000 |
| Total Liabilities & Net Worth | | $6,812,000 |

EXHIBIT 3

## NOEL GIFTS INTERNATIONAL LTD
## Condensed Income Statements
## Years Ended June 30, 1988–1992

(Singapore dollars in thousands, except per share)

| *Item* | *1988* | *1989* | *1990* | *1991* | *1992* | *Six Months Ended 12/31/92 (Unaudited)*[1] |
|---|---|---|---|---|---|---|
| Net sales | $6,562 | $7,601 | $9,103 | $10,325 | $13,009 | $5,858 |
| Cost of goods & services; selling, administrative & general expenses; other costs & expenses | 6,422 | 7,254 | 8,581 | 9,795 | 11,795 | 5,310 |
| Operating profit | 140 | 347 | 549 | 530 | 1,214 | 548 |
| Net rental income[2] | 0 | 0 | 65 | 170 | 107 | 58 |
| Other income[3] | 117 | 186 | 35 | 2 | 12 | (12) |
| Earnings before taxes | 257 | 533 | 649 | 702 | 1,333 | 594 |
| Income tax | (85) | (172) | (266) | (254) | (482) | (196) |
| Net income after tax and before extraordinary items | 172 | 361 | 383 | 448 | 851 | 398 |
| Extraordinary item[4] | 0 | 0 | 0 | 237 | 0 | 0 |
| Net income | 172 | 361 | 383 | 685 | 851 | 398 |
| Net earnings per share (cents)[5] | 0.49 | 1.03 | 1.09 | 1.28 | 2.43 | 1.14 |

Notes:
1. Annualizing the six months' unaudited results of the company would not give an accurate reflection of the full-year performance of the company because major festivals such as Chinese New Year, Valentine's Day, and Hari Raya Puasa occur between the months of January and June. The company's performance in the second half of the financial year had been typically stronger than that in the first half.
2. From FY 1990, rental income arose from the lease of part of Noel Building. The tenants renting space from the company in April 1993 were Heritage Collections Pte Ltd, Yunan Interior Pte Ltd, and Deo Silver Pte Ltd.
3. Up to FY 1989, other income arose principally because the company billed its related companies for the use of its staff and computer system. During FY 1990, these affiliates employed their own staff, resulting in substantial decline in other income. From FY 1991 to FY 1992, the occasional use of Noel's resources by its related companies accounted for the small balances in other income during this period.
4. The extraordinary item in FY 1991 represents the excess provision relating to a claim by a supplier which was written back to the income statement in FY 1991 after the claim was settled in May 1991.
5. Based on the pre-flotation share capital of 35 million shares after adjusting for the bonus issue and the share split.

Source: Company records.

EXHIBIT 4

**NOEL GIFTS INTERNATIONAL LTD**
**Condensed Balance Sheets**
**Years Ended June 30, 1988–1992**
(Singapore dollars in thousands, except per share)

| *Assets* | *1988* | *1989* | *1990* | *1991* | *1992* |
|---|---|---|---|---|---|
| Current assets | 1,905 | 2,546 | 373 | 541 | 603 |
| Fixed assets[1] | 211 | 131 | 3,917 | 3,740 | 6,178 |
| Investments | | | | | 31 |
| Total assets | 2,116 | 2,677 | 4,290 | 4,281 | 6,812 |
| Current liabilities[2] | 1,577 | 1,778 | 2,925 | 2,366 | 1,752 |
| Noncurrent liabilities | 9 | 8 | 91 | 56 | 71 |
| Total liabilities | 1,586 | 1,786 | 3,016 | 2,422 | 1,823 |
| Issued share capital | 170 | 330 | 410 | 410 | 1,000 |
| Revaluation reserve | | | | | 2,500 |
| Retained earnings | 360 | 561 | 864 | 1,449 | 1,489 |
| Total liabilities and net worth | 2,116 | 2,677 | 4,290 | 4,281 | 6,812 |
| Net tangible assets per share ($)[3] | 0.01 | 0.03 | 0.04 | 0.05 | 0.14 |

Notes:
1. Fixed assets increased from $131,000 in FY 1989 to $3.92 million in FY 1990 because of the purchase of the company's properties at 50 Playfair Road, Singapore. The subsequent appreciation of the properties is reflected in the increase in fixed assets value from $3.7 million in FY 1991 to $6.18 million in FY 1992 when the properties were revalued based on their open market values.
2. Net current liabilities (current liabilities less current assets) in FY 1990 amounted to $2.6 million due largely to a drawdown on an overdraft facility to pay for the purchase of its current properties, higher creditors, provision for taxation, accruals for directors' remuneration, promotional activities, one-time accruals for building renovation, provisions for gratuity payments, and payment of legal fees. Net current liabilities fell to $1.8 million in FY 1991 because of the absence of the one-time accruals in FY 1990 and the reduction in trade creditors and overdraft balances. The subsequent decline of net current liabilities to $1.1 million in FY 1992 is attributed to the repayment of a short-term advance during the year.
3. Based on the pre-flotation share capital of 35,000,000 shares after adjusting for the bonus issue and the share split.

Source: Company records.

EXHIBIT 5

## NOEL GIFTS INTERNATIONAL LTD
## Operating Results by Core Product
## Years Ended June 30, 1988–1992

(Singapore dollars in thousands)

| *Net Sales by Product* | *1988* | *1989* | *1990* | *1991* | *1992* |
|---|---|---|---|---|---|
| Hampers | 5,373 | 6,179 | 7,376 | 7,571 | 8,950 |
| Flowers and gifts | 1,189 | 1,422 | 1,754 | 2,754 | 3,891 |
| Franchising | | | | | 168 |
| Total | 6,562 | 7,601 | 9,130 | 10,325 | 13,009 |
| Profit by Product[1] | | | | | |
| Hampers | 314 | 481 | 569 | 676 | 897 |
| Flowers & gifts | (57) | 52 | 80 | 130 | 351 |
| Franchising | | | | (104) | 85 |
| Total | 257 | 533 | 649 | 702 | 1,333 |
| Net Profit Margin by Product | | | | | |
| Hampers | 5.8% | 7.8% | 7.7% | 8.9% | 10.0% |
| Flowers & gifts | 0.0% | 3.7% | 4.6% | 4.7% | 9.0% |
| Franchising | | | | | 50.6% |
| Average | 3.9% | 7.0% | 7.1% | 6.8% | 10.2% |

Note: 1. The profit figures for FY 1988 to FY 1991 are estimates. The company began to maintain separate cost allocations for hampers and flowers and gifts after FY 1991, when it became apparent that flowers and gifts will become another core activity of the company.

Source: Company records.

EXHIBIT 6

**NOEL GIFTS INTERNATIONAL LTD**
**The Franchising Climate in East Asia**

| *Country* | *Annual Population Growth Rate, 1990–2010* | *Regulations* | *Status of Franchising* | *Taxes* | *Recent Developments* |
|---|---|---|---|---|---|
| China | 11.0% | Foreign investment; exchange controls. | Joint ventures, with the Chinese government acting as the local franchisee. | 33% profit tax on joint ventures; 10% withholding tax on royalties and dividends payable to the franchisor. | China has only recently opened its doors to foreign businesses. |
| Hong Kong | 0.7% | Limit on the repatriation of royalties, while dividends can be paid back to franchisors. | Generally freely open to foreign franchisors; no trade barriers. | 16.5% profit tax on foreign subsidiary or joint venture; 1.65% withholding tax on royalties. | Food Service business and hotel franchisors are finding lucrative markets. |
| Japan | 0.3% | New regulatory climate conducive to franchising. | Franchising accounts for 4% of total retail sales. | 55% profit tax on joint venture or subsidiary; 10% withholding tax on dividends and royalties payable to the franchisor. | As the strongest advocate of franchising in East Asia, Japan recently underwent major changes in foreign investment regulations. |
| Philippines | 2.0% | Exchange controls; foreign investment. | Joint ventures; agreements limited to 5 years. | 35% profit tax; 20% dividend tax; 25% royalty tax; 1–2% expatriation of royalties. | |

EXHIBIT 6 (cont'd)

## NOEL GIFTS INTERNATIONAL LTD
## The Franchising Climate in East Asia

| *Country* | *Annual Population Growth Rate, 1990–2010* | *Regulations* | *Status of Franchising* | *Taxes* | *Recent Developments* |
|---|---|---|---|---|---|
| South Korea | 0.8% | Foreign investment; exchange controls. | Franchising not encouraged; joint ventures possible if local franchisees hold 50%; held by large conglomerates. | 40% profit tax on joint ventures; 10.75% withholding tax on royalties and dividends payable to franchisor. | In the process of recogzing international trademarks, patents, tradenames, and intellectual property. |
| Taiwan | 1.4% | Strict exchange control and foreign investment regulation. | Franchising through a wholly-owned subsidiary not usually granted; joint venture agreements; few agreements extend beyond 5 years. | 35% profit tax on joint ventures; 35% tax on dividends; 20% tax on royalties. | Recently opened a Patent & Trademark consulting center. |
| Thailand | 1.3% | Exchange controls; foreign investment. | Joint ventures; franchising with majority foreign ownership — not approved. | 20% dividend tax; 25% royalty tax; 40% profit tax. | |

Sources: *The Economist Book of Vital World Statistics* (London: The Economist Books, 1990): 16; Peng S Chan and Robert T Justis, "Franchise Management in East Asia," *Academy of Management Executive*, 4:2 (1990): 81–83.

SECTION TWO

# Strategy Formulation

| *Case Number* | *Case (Country)* | *Nature of Situation* | *Complexity* |
|---|---|---|---|
| 5 | The Asia-Pacific Airline Industry | Structural analysis | High |
| 6 | Singapore Airlines: Comparative Case Studies of the British and Singaporean National Airlines (Singapore) | Maintain growth rate | Medium |
| 7 | Malaysia Airlines and Its Media Image in the Visit Malaysia Year (Malaysia) | Crisis | Low |
| 8 | The Deluxe Hotels in the Philippines in 1989 (Philippines) | Increasing competition | High |
| 9 | Shangri-La Hotel Ltd (Singapore) | Maintain market share | Medium |
| 10 | Johan Cement Bhd and Utara Cement Sdn Bhd (Malaysia) | Increasing competition | Medium |
| 11 | Uraco Holdings Limited (Singapore, Malaysia) | Increasing competition | Low |
| 12 | Cycle & Carriage Ltd (Singapore, Malaysia) | Increasing competition | Medium |

| Products/ Services | Sector | Financial Data | US$ Sales (000) | Industry Conditions |
|---|---|---|---|---|
| transportation | Transportation | No | — | Mature |
| transportation | Transportation | Yes | 3,519,128 | Late growth |
| transportation | Transportation | Yes | 1,386,014 | Late growth |
| ging | Services | No | — | Growth |
| ging | Services | Yes | 74,336 | Growth |
| nent | Manufacturing | Yes | 95,460 | Growth |
| ricated metal ducts | Manufacturing | Yes | 57,005 | Growth |
| omotive dealers, estate developers, food stores | Retail trade, real estate and construction | Yes | 1,175,327 | Growth |

# The Asia-Pacific Airline Industry* 5

## Overview of the Aviation Industry

### The Beginnings

It was on December 17, 1903, that the Wright brothers left the ground from the sand dunes of Kitty Hawk, North Carolina in the world's first controlled powered flight. At that moment of takeoff, they ushered in what had proven to be the greatest period in the history of aviation — the inception of the "Golden Age of Aviation."

Until the outbreak of World War I, however, the airplane was regarded by most authorities, both technical and business, of potential use only for sporting or military purposes. When war broke out in 1914, the emphasis placed on the developments and improvements in both aircraft design and manufacture accelerated the progress in aviation. For the first time, organized research, coupled with strong government support, was centered on aircraft and engine design. With this intense attention, the airplane grew in power and speed.

---

*This case is based on a student report prepared by Cindy Leong Su Yen, Lim Huey Tyug, and Tan Siew Wan (Nanyang Technological University, Singapore) under the supervision of Professor Luis Ma. R. Calingo. The case was developed wholly from published sources and was written to serve as a basis for classroom discussion rather than to illustrate effective or ineffective handling of an administrative situation.

## The Development of the Commercial Airline Industry

In 1918, the U.S. Post Office Department began the world's first regular permanent civilian airmail service and the year 1919 marked the start of commercial air transportation. Heavy air traffic was first seen in the U.S. and Europe. Countries around the world from the Middle East, the Asia-Pacific region, and Latin America eventually jumped onto the band wagon and gradually initiated their own air services.

Despite the fact that the U.S. aviation network was superior to Europe's in many aspects, U.S. airlines initially did not offer scheduled passenger service. Although ground facilities were limited, harsh climatic conditions existed, and trimotors were low-performance, European countries were still eager to establish air links with their overseas territories. This interest led to the opening of trunk routes, which finally grew into the present global system uniting remote corners of the globe.

It was only in 1934 when the enormous growth of passenger service made airlines realize that their future did not depend on airmail contracts but on the development of passenger traffic. Air transport development, which might have taken a generation, was telescoped into a wartime period of a few intense years. This turn of events was made possible with technological innovations which improved by leaps and bounds, bringing in the jet age. Proof of the potential of air passenger transport came with a study conducted in 1953 which revealed that the airplane had become the prime mover of travelers. With this came the realization that airlines were no longer selling mere transport, but tailoring air travel services to individuals' needs.

With the increase in the number of airlines, associations that regulated the aviation industry came into force. The rationale for regulation was rooted in the economic and physical characteristics of the air transport industry. A regulatory framework was put in place in order to monitor aviation safety, regulate the airline economy, preserve service levels to communities, and prevent competition in the industry by setting fares that allowed airlines to cover their costs and earn a fair return on their investment. The better known associations in the international scene were the Civil Aeronautics Board (CAB), International Civil Aviation Organization (ICAO), and International Air Transport Association (IATA). In the late 1970s, the CAB began to ease its control over airline fares and routes to encourage greater competition and better services, culminating in the passage of the U.S. Deregulation Act in 1978.

## Deregulation in U.S. and Its Global Effects

The Deregulation Act of 1978 had far-reaching consequences in the airline industry. With deregulation, airlines were able to increase their route mileage, reduce fares, and operate in a more competitive fashion. Changes in the industry were massive, chaotic, and rapid. Fares were reduced sharply, schedules increased, and the industry strove to become a mass transit air system, without a master plan.

The advent of price competition had so greatly eroded revenue that even the larger companies were in precarious financial positions. Eventually, the airlines which survived and triumphed in the competitive battle ground would not necessarily be the largest. Rather, the survivors tended to be the most innovative and capable of addressing the problems of fuel waste resulting from excess capacity, while simultaneously raising load factors to maintain their competitiveness in the new environment. The U.S. had entered the era of mass air transport.

From an international perspective, deregulation in the U.S. in 1978 had a deleterious effect on the world's routes for travel. Passengers became far more cost-oriented than they had been in the past, and the airlines were forced to be more cost-conscious as well. Competition was stiff, with excess capacity and lower yields. Airplanes were maturing and new airplanes were economical to operate but extremely expensive to buy. The margin between debt and rate of return was narrow, therefore making funds difficult to obtain. A number of international airlines found themselves engaged in no-win marketing battles for limited passengers in an environment marked by overcapacity and declining demand. Airlines in the Asia-Pacific region were, however, shielded to a certain extent from the devastating effects by virtue of the cost advantage that they enjoyed through lower wage structures.

It is improbable that the air transportation industry would ever take again the simple shape it once had. The industry had been undergoing turbulent times. Many experts predicted that it would experience increased operational problems and a period of some questionable safety incidents, thereby seriously impinging upon industry profitability and resulting in many airline mergers and acquisitions.

## The International Passenger Airline Industry

### Major Characteristics

The airline industry is a service industry and its product offering has an extremely limited shelf life. It expires upon the plane's takeoff and seats left unsold cannot be recovered or stored away as inventory. The offer of a seat is open only at a certain time, making the product highly perishable.

Another distinguishing feature is the degree and extent of government regulation. Entry and access into international markets are strictly controlled by the host countries. Governments often specify the routing for each particular flight, the number of flights to be operated each week, and the type of aircraft that can be used. The cities where passengers can be picked up are all precisely defined in bilateral or multilateral agreements worked out between governments.

### International Regulation of Air Transport

Access to international markets had been regulated since the Chicago Convention of 1944 by bilateral air services agreements between governments. Bilateral agreements, negotiated between two countries, permitted airlines of these countries to offer service between the two countries and set the conditions under which the airlines would operate and compete. Some agreements delineated the routes that might be operated and the amount and frequency of service, and provided for regulation of prices by the governments. Once signed, an agreement would remain in effect until it expired or, if it was renounced by a signatory, for a year after the renunciation while the two countries attempt to renegotiate.

Bilateral agreements are based on the principle that nations have sovereignty over their airspace. This sovereignty had been defined by nine "Freedoms of the Air" that outline possible aviation rights between countries:

1. The first and second freedoms establish the right of an airline to overfly and, if needed, stop in another country for technical reasons, such as refueling or allowing a crew to rest.

2. The third and fourth freedoms establish the right of an airline to pick up and discharge passengers between its home country and another country.
3. The fifth freedom confers the right of an airline to carry passengers or cargo between two foreign nations on flights beginning or ending in its homeland.
4. The sixth freedom establishes the right of an airline to carry passengers or cargo between two foreign countries by way of its homeland, while the seventh freedom is an airline's right to carry passengers or cargo between two foreign countries without stopping in its homeland.
5. Additional aviation rights, sometimes referred to as the eighth and ninth freedoms, allow an airline to provide air service within a foreign country. The so-called eighth freedom, also known as "fill-up", or "consecutive" cabotage, allows a foreign airline to pick up and discharge passengers or cargo on the domestic segment of an international flight originating in the airline's home country, such as a Manila–San Francisco–New York flight. On the other hand, "full" cabotage, which is independent of international service, allows a foreign airline to pick up and discharge domestic passengers or cargo. Sometimes referred to as the ninth freedom, full cabotage would allow an Asia-Pacific airline, for example, to operate shuttle service between San Francisco and Los Angeles.

### Airline Operations

**Fuel costs.** Since jet fuel accounted for about 25 percent of an airline's total operating costs, increases in fuel prices posed a definite threat to the operating profits of the airline industry.[1] An airline industry analyst estimated that, in the U.S. alone, for each $0.01 per-liter decrease in the price of fuel, the airline industry would save an aggregate of approximately $380 million in fuel.[2] Three things happened as a result of escalating fuel costs: the major international airlines were forced to phase out older gas-guzzling jets sooner than they anticipated, thus leading to a premature antiquating of existing fleets;[3] the phasing out of the older jets made relatively cheap aircraft available to the new competing airlines; further, the major carriers were committed to incurring substantial debts to acquire more fuel-efficient aircraft.

**General operating costs.** Flying operations of an aircraft require the maintenance of the aircraft and crew. Airline and traffic servicing also require ground personnel expenses, and cost outlays arise from the handling of passengers on the ground and the landing and monitoring of flights. In the United States, labor costs accounted for 35 to 40 percent of all expenses in the airline industry.[4] Maintenance expenses include direct charges such as the cost of labor and material used in the repair and upkeep of aircraft and ground equipment; they also include indirect costs from the general overhead of the maintenance and overhaul facilities, periodic inspection of aircraft and ground equipment for compliance with safety standards, and the administration of the operation itself.

---

[1]Craig A Schmutzer, "The Economy," *Fortune*, November 26, 1984: 82.
[2]Craig A Schmutzer, "An Analysis of the Airline Industry," *The Journal of Commercial Bank Lending*, 66 (February 1984): 22.
[3]Craig A Schmutzer, "An Analysis of the Airline Industry," *The Journal of Commercial Bank Lending*, 66 (February 1984): 22.
[4]David Woolley, "Airlines Climb Out of the Red," *Interavia*, October 1984: 1036.

Passenger service expenses include cabin attendants' salaries and the cost of food, beverages, and in-flight entertainment. Promotion and sales costs cover the outlays made for advertising agency commissions, computer reservations, schedule printing, and so on. General and administration expenses in large part covered the activities carried out at the corporate headquarters and the various city stations that plan and direct the company's operations. Finally, depreciation and amortization expenses relate primarily to the charges associated with the aging of a carrier's tangible and intangible assets.

**Economies of scale.** Airlines must achieve a large volume of output in order to lower the costs per unit of each seat departure. In order to achieve economies of scale, airlines utilize the principle of specialization. Workers are employed fulltime on the particular operations for which they have special skills and thus become very proficient at the specific tasks assigned to them.

The established carriers can also utilize the latest technology available, bringing about economies of scale. Small airlines are often not able to utilize the most efficient and productive equipment because of the massive capital investment required. Bigger airlines also purchase larger supplies of both aircraft and spare parts, thus giving them better bargaining power to negotiate for more favorable terms. Even in financing, such airlines are usually in better positions to source for financial support in their capital investments. Economies of scale can also be reaped in marketing activities and advertising where the cost is more spread out.

**The industry's performance.** During the early 1990s, the international airline industry suffered the worst crisis in its history, with estimates from IATA pointing to a loss of around US$9 billion for its member airlines between 1990 and 1992.[5] Only a handful around the world were operating profitably. Several had collapsed, a number of airlines had filed for bankruptcy, and more than a few survived only because of cash injections made by their government shareholders.

### Market Segments

The passenger market can generally be broken up into two main segments, business travelers and discretionary travelers. Business travelers choose airline travel regardless of the state of the economy. Discretionary travelers (leisure travelers), however, are extremely sensitive to the state of the economy.

Discretionary travelers could be traveling for a variety of reasons, such as going on vacation, visiting relatives, furthering studies, or seeking medical attention abroad. Business travelers are different from the leisure traveler in a number of respects, and this has implications for the pricing policy and type of services offered by airlines. Generally, business travelers require a high degree of service in terms of schedule reliability, flight frequency, in-flight comfort, and flexibility of travel arrangements for which they, or more accurately their companies, are willing to pay. Leisure travelers, on the other hand, have greater flexibility in terms of travel times and choice of destinations. Because they have to

---

[5] N Cockerell, "Is Bigger Better?" *Business Traveller,* March 1993: 22.

pay for their own fare, they are more price-conscious. However, quality of service and reliability are key factors as well when leisure travelers evaluate airlines.

International air travel, traditionally dominated by business travelers, has seen the significant growth of the leisure market with the moderation of air travel costs. Specifically, traveling for pleasure (tourism) and, to a smaller extent, traveling for personal reasons (rather than business) made up two-thirds to three-quarters of all world travel by volume by 1993. Studies have shown that the business segment was much smaller in numbers than the pleasure traveler segment, although the business segment generated a larger portion of profits.[6]

### Global Trends and Strategic Issues

**Towards privatization of airlines.** In statistical terms, 50 percent of the world's airlines were privately owned, 35 percent were state-owned, and 15 percent were partially privatized by 1992. Private carriers account for 53 percent of the world operating revenues, compared to 30 percent earned by partially privatized carriers and 17 percent earned by state-owned carriers.[7] With the increasing challenges in the dynamic world of the airline industry, more airlines in the future are likely to be privately owned rather than state-controlled. There would be a shift from a state-owned, heavily protected industry to a more commercially oriented one and private shareholders would instill greater commercial discipline to compete more effectively. Recent examples include British Airways, Airlanka, Japan Air Lines (JAL), and Qantas Airways.

**Towards strategic alliances.** There has been increasing talk in the airline industry over the past few years about globalization, cross-border mergers, and mega-carriers. This trend has intensified with the growing recognition that the industry could support only so many airlines. There is a whole spectrum of different degrees of alliance which can be made between airlines, including low-profile alliances where joint services operate on certain routes in order to maximize capacity. Take the example of Japan Air Lines' European network. It signed an agreement with KLM to operate joint services between Amsterdam and the two points using its own flight designator. Passengers would fly Tokyo–Amsterdam with JAL — a route that operated very profitably — and then switch to a KLM aircraft for the final leg.[8] The trend towards alliances between airlines also led to the sharing of airport lounges and related facilities for passengers.

Airlines often enter into marketing alliances as well. For example, reservations systems of the All Nippon Airways, Cathay Pacific Airways, China Airlines, DragonAir, Malaysian Airline System, Philippine Airlines, Royal Brunei Airlines and Singapore Airlines were melded through a computer reservations system (CRS) pioneered by Abacus, thereby allowing the matching of a passenger's requirement with airlines' schedules and reservations.[9] Finally, there are the high-level alliances such as full-blown mergers which involve buyouts or some form of equity swaps, as in the case of Singapore Airlines and

---

[6] M Samuel, "Travel and Tourism Needs: Opportunities for SIA," *Outlook*, August 1992: 4.
[7] M Samuel, "Airlines of the Future," *Outlook*, October 1992: 1, 3.
[8] N Cockerell, "Is Bigger Better?" *Business Traveller*, March 1993: 22.
[9] Singapore Airlines, *SIA Annual Report: 1992/93*: 23.

Delta Airlines. Such alliances improve efficiency by cutting duplication and costs, thereby increasing economies of scale in purchasing and enhancing marketing power.

Whatever form they take, operating partnerships have been seen by airlines as a vital means of ensuring their future financial health and even survival in a highly competitive world. This is particularly true with the trend of privatization, making it more important than ever that airlines stand on their own two feet. While the confusing ownership structure of airlines is already starting to make it difficult for travelers to choose between airlines according to their traditional national identities, joint flight operations are viewed positively by both passengers and airlines alike. Mergers and commercial alliances offer an excellent opportunity of helping airlines strengthen their international presence, giving them a greater chance of remaining among the select survivors with improved efficiency. A plethora of commercial agreements were reached during the early 1990s, ranging from agreements on marketing cooperation to agreements on the full integration of services on specific routes. Commercial agreements, are likely to become more common as liberalization increases and traditional boundaries collapse through free-trade agreements.

In some situations, these marketing alliances also serve to limit competition. Take the case of the CRSs. Because each airline must, as a practical matter, have its flights listed on each CRS in order to market its flights successfully, each airline must pay the booking fees charged by the other airlines that own the CRSs. The lack of effective competition in the CRS industry has allowed the dominant CRSs to each receive substantial revenues in excess of the costs of the service provided (including a reasonable profit) from other airlines in the industry, most of which are financially weaker.

**Shrinking of corporate travel expenses.** Air travel expenses have been moderated over the years with technological advances but still constitute a big-ticket item for buyers, accounting for 12 percent of consumer spending, the largest expenditure item after food.[10] The global trend of the tightening of corporate budgets in traveling expenses has been putting downward pressure on the traditionally lucrative source of revenue from corporate travelers. The number of executives traveling in first class or business class, which accounted for about 60 percent of airline profit, dropped by 6 percent in 1992 over 1991.[11]

### Passenger Traffic Forecasts

**The global picture.** A recent study conducted by IATA revealed that the total number of international scheduled passengers is expected to be 43 percent higher in 1996 than in 1991. The average annual rate of growth for the period between 1991 and 1996 was forecasted to be 7.4 percent as shown in Exhibit 1.

The most significant growth forecast for this 5-year period would take place to or/and from and within Eastern or/and Central Europe. The opening of new services between these regions and the rest of the world would stimulate traffic. However, in absolute terms, the traffic is expected to remain relatively small.

[10] M Samuel, "Travel and Tourism Needs: Opportunities for SIA," *Outlook*, August 1992: 4.
[11] M Levin, "The High Cost of Going Cheap," *Asian Business*, January 1993: 50.

Exhibit 2 shows that traffic in the Asia-Pacific region has and will continue to show high growth rates, making the highest contribution in absolute terms to the world's traffic growth. It has been forecasted to grow by 8.2 percent during the period 1991 to 1995. By the year 2010, total international scheduled passenger traffic to, from, and within the Asia-Pacific region will represent 51.1 percent of the world total. Exhibit 3 illustrates the passenger traffic of each major Asia-Pacific airline during the first six months of 1992.

**The Asia-Pacific Region.** The Asia-Pacific region contains over 50 percent of the world's population and extends over half the circumference of the globe. This region includes 34 countries, as well as territories of Australia, France, New Zealand, Portugal, the United Kingdom, and the United States.

IATA predicted that the Asia-Pacific region's share of international scheduled travel will increase from 31.2 percent in 1990 to 39 percent by the year 2000. This translates into an increase of 420 percent to 380 million from a mere 90 million, implying that the Asia-Pacific region's share would increase from less than one-third to more than half of the total market in 20 years' time.[12] These are measures of the degree to which the world's economic center of gravity would shift decisively toward Asia in the years to come. There are a few main reasons that can account for this high growth in the Asia-Pacific region:[13]

1. Fast-growing economies projected in the region (mostly via export-oriented manufacturing industries)
2. Intensification of trade (in particular among the Asian countries)
3. Continuing air transport liberalization
4. Low traffic base at present for countries with large travel potential (in particular China, Malaysia, Vietnam)
5. Increase in disposable incomes
6. Growing importance of ethnic ties among countries

With such promising prospects of growth, it can be foreseen that the Asia-Pacific region will become the battleground where only the fittest of airlines would survive. The Asia-Pacific region has been characterized by many airlines in various forms ranging from the large, longer-range, mostly scheduled passenger carriers to feeder carriers that could reach parts of Asia that the major carriers find unprofitable. Although the commercial aviation market consists of both international and domestic flights, this case study focuses on international airlines in order to portray a more comprehensive picture of the airline industry in the Asia-Pacific. We will now focus on examining the competitive environment that airlines in the Asia-Pacific region operate in, as well as the strategies that they employed.

### The Competitive Environment of Airlines in the Asia-Pacific

The airline industry in the Asia-Pacific region has been a subject of great interest to airline economists worldwide because the Asian way of seeking competitive advantage is a radical departure from the American and European way of seeking such an advantage. This might have something to do with the traditionally high standards of in-flight services

---

[12] P J Jeanniot, "Growth is Still the Game," *Asia Travel Trade*, May 1993: 44.

[13] International Airline Transportation Association, *Asia Pacific Passenger Traffic Forecast: Travel Demand, 1985-2010*, 1985: 6.

offered by Asian carriers. Part of the reason is that airlines do not really compete heavily on price within the Asia-Pacific region. Cost leadership strategies are practically nonexistent in the Asia-Pacific region, with most airlines adopting a differentiation approach.

Airlines in the Asia-Pacific have reached the stage where their best strategy is to make the most of the opportunities which the region offers, that is, to give all Asian carriers a broader base from which to compete with developed mega-carriers. The experience in Asia shows that competition and liberal access results in a more efficient and service-oriented Asian market which is fast expanding and becoming increasingly competitive. The competition has been fueled in part by the ambitions of Asian airlines. Clearly, the fact that six of the world's ten most profitable airlines are Asian carriers boosted confidence and expansion plans.[14]

The Asian experience has also shown that competition should embellish profitability and not dull it, and that airlines should welcome and not avoid competition. Asian carriers and governments, therefore, saw it in their best interests to achieve a fair and open multilateral regulatory regime for international aviation. However, in calling for liberalization, many Asian governments have tended to focus on relations with distant countries, while aviation relations within the region have remained unnecessarily restrictive.

### Competition Among Existing Airlines

The massive potential of the Asia-Pacific region has not gone unnoticed in the international airline scene. Asian carriers are starting to face their first major market share battles with Amercian and European carriers.

**Airline marketing.** Airlines, especially those servicing international routes, bear a striking resemblance to each other in terms of what they have to offer to the consumer. The ultimate goal of airlines in order to achieve product differentiation is the drive that shapes the degree of rivalry in the industry. The basic product, a seat on board a plane, remains unalterable but what the airlines can do is to produce a unique version of the total product. For passengers contemplating the prospect of being locked in for up to 16 hours at a time, the differences are to be found at the margins: speed of check-in, size of cocktail, or even the state of the lavatories. Most carriers worked at achieving the perception of product improvement and tried to defend their market share through marketing innovations, pricing, and promotion of in-flight amenities. Essentially, the marketing strategy for an airline would be to provide a level of service to the customer so that the airline's seats could be fully utilized. Besides offering newspapers, magazines, and headsets on board, a few airlines even provide international phone services. Exhibit 4 compares some of the amenities offered by various airlines.

Passengers traveling on Asian carriers have come to expect glamorous and gracious cabin crews, good food, and comfortable seats. Technological and management advances have brought more airlines across the threshold of what was regarded as acceptable quality, forcing more carriers to differentiate their services. Royal Brunei Airlines, which in 1992 began operating long-haul services through Bangkok and Singapore to Frankfurt and

[14] Singapore Airlines, *Outlook*, March 1992: 42.

London, has gone to great expense to install gold-covered seat-belt buckles and arm rests. Although a relative newcomer to intercontinental operations, Royal Brunei Airlines has already managed to established a niche identity, largely by name association with the Sultan of Brunei, reportedly the world's wealthiest individual.[15] This has helped it to pursue a high-yield, low-volume approach on services to Europe, with generous seat pitch and luxuriously appointed interiors.

**Frequent Flyer Programs.** Frequent flyer programs (FFPs) were a very commonplace feature during the 1980s and still are in the 1990s. With these FFPs, airlines awarded passengers with free tickets or upgrade when they have traveled a certain mileage with the airlines. Until as late as 1991, regular travelers in the region received little more than upgrades and gifts in return for their loyalty, but passengers have been receiving an expanding array of FFPs and other travel incentives. Business travelers often chose an airline on the basis of FFPs, which generally favored the larger airlines in each market.[16]

Coupled with the worldwide recession, Asian carriers succumbed to the need to use FFPs as a marketing tool and began to offer plans similar to those which have been offered in the U.S. and Europe for many years. Qantas has upset other Asia-Pacific carriers by applying its FFP to its entire network, rather than restricting it to the U.S.-Australia market. To make matters worse, Qantas followed the U.S. carriers' example by making it available to people in other countries as well as in Australia. The plan, in theory, was aimed at the first-class and business-class flyers; however, it was available to all passengers for a fee. The activity in the Australasian market has forced other Asia-Pacific carriers to launch their own plans or hastily draw up plans for a launch.

Cathay Pacific Airways, Singapore Airlines, and Malaysian Airline System launched Asia's first frequent flyer program, with benefits weighted toward the first-class and business-class clients. Called "Passages," the joint venture was to be operated by Asia Frequent Flyer Pte Ltd in Singapore and was patterned after the FFPs in the U.S. and Europe. British Airways and Swissair were scheduled to become "partners" as of September 1993, further enhancing the program.

For all their fanciful names, FFPs are merely a disguised form of discount in an attempt to avoid price wars. Instead of knocking off 15 percent of airfares, FFPs spread the disguised discounts over a number of flights, thereby locking passengers into using one airline if they want to claim the free travel or hotel stay. It could thus be foreseen that FFPs would claim their rightful role in airline marketing programs, particularly in their bid to gain or defend market share.

**Technology as a competitive tool.** Airline reservations are undergoing a revolution. At the center of the turmoil is the computer reservation system (CRS), where improvements have made these systems quicker and more efficient in simplifying the procedure of flight allocations. This system is also able to predict uneven demands in flight movements and allows for changes in work shifts during busy and slack periods, thereby increasing responsiveness and cutting costs.

---

[15] J Bailey, "Fueling the Feel Good Factor," *Executive Travel*, September 1992: 105.

[16] Kenneth M Mead, "Airline Competition: Strategies for Addressing Financial and Competitive Problems in the Airline Industry," Testimony before the US House of Representatives, February 18, 1993 (GAO/T-RCED-93-11).

Major breakthroughs in aircraft technology improving both safety and fuel efficiency are expected to be introduced by the mid-1990s to benefit both airlines and their passengers. These include systems to detect flight deviation and wind shear, which would prevent collisions. The benefits of a younger fleet are twofold — commercial and operational. The airline passenger typically prefers flying in new and modern aircraft, incorporating the latest in passenger comfort, safety features, and facilities that enhance the flying experience. Newer technology also means better on-time performance, which was viewed as one of the top priorities by airlines such as Singapore Airlines and Thai Airways International. See Exhibit 5 for a comparison of on-time performance data for the major Asia-Pacific carriers.

**Threat of New Entrants**

The stakes are, indeed, high if one were to consider starting up an airline; the huge capital requirements alone would serve as a barrier to many an aspiring airline entrepreneur. The airline industry needs approximately $1 in capital to generate $1 in revenue.[17] This is particularly true if one expected to take on the major carriers; however, even in the case of smaller commuter airlines, the startup costs can run into millions. The level of technical expertise also poses a barrier: qualified pilots, skilled technicians, computer programmers, and hundreds of specialized managerial personnel are required to staff an efficiently operating air carrier. Additional barriers arise from airline operating and marketing practices, which make it more difficult for some airlines to compete by limiting access to airports and by limiting the ability of new airlines on a route to market their services. A U.S. government study found that fares were 5 to 9 percent higher on routes when two or more of these barriers to competition were present.[18]

By 2010, according to IATA estimates, 398 million international passengers would travel to and/or from and within the Asia-Pacific region, compared with 390 million in the rest of the world.[19] The potential lucrativeness has thus kept the industry buoyant with the entry of many new regional and international airlines (such as Thailand's Silk Air, Malaysia's Air Asia, and Hong Kong's Dragon Air) despite the extensive barriers to entry. Travelers stand to benefit from the entry of these new airlines. Studies by U.S. economists found that a 1-percent increase in competitors on a route led to a 0.12-percent decrease in fares.[20] There are obvious efficiencies to be achieved in synergy. For example, SIA works closely with its SilkAir subsidiary on scheduling, with the smaller carrier's passengers transferring to or from SIA's trunk or long-haul flights.[21] Likewise, ever since Hong Kong brought in DragonAir, the latter has become an essential partner for the larger carrier.

As far as passengers are concerned, these mother-daughter airline relationships tend to boost confidence when it comes to flying with lesser- known carriers. Originally intended to complement the international carriers, some have become intent on making a

---

[17] Craig A Schmutzer, "An Analysis of the Airline Industry," *The Journal of Commercial Bank Lending*, 66 (February 1984): 25.

[18] U.S. General Accounting Office, *Airline Competition: Effects of Airline Market Concentration and Barriers to Entry on Airfares*, April 26, 1991 (GAO/RCED-91-101).

[19] Brent Hannon, "Boarding Time for the Asian Airliner," *Asia, Inc*, June 1995: 27–32.

[20] Steven Morrison, "Airline Competition and Consumer Protection Panel," in U.S. General Accounting Office, *Meeting the Aviation Challenge of the 1990s*, July 1991 (GAO/RCED-91-152): 78–81.

[21] R Blumm, "Little Airlines That Could," *Business Traveller*, June 1992: 25.

mark on their own, with destinations ranging from fifteen minutes apart and others plying international routes. Myanmar's new international airline will also be ready to take off by the end of 1993 and four more new carriers are expected to be launched in China, Thailand, and Vietnam in the near future. The emergence of secondary airlines such as Japan's JAS, Korea's Asiana, and Taiwan's EVA Air reflect the region's traffic growth potential, while domestic airlines such as Indonesia's Air Sempati are all set to spread their airlines overseas.

Korean Air Lines, China Airlines, and Japan Air Lines have all lost their traditional long-haul monopolies to these young, aggressive, and privately owned competitors. Japan's All Nippon Airways has also been forced to overhaul its in-flight services to keep pace with competitors' offerings. Similarly, the Philippines' new international carrier, All-Asia Airline (AAA), launched in April 1993 by a group of Filipino businessmen, is set to give Philippines Airlines, the national carrier, a healthy dose of competition — something which the national airline is not accustomed to.[22]

Therefore, the threat of new entrants in the Asia-Pacific airline industry is very real and the chances for the continued survival of new entrants is very good. It is unclear how the industry would ultimately be shaped but what might develop is a two-tier system under which the major airlines control heavily traveled international and national routes, while smaller carriers carve out their own regional niches and feed the broader systems.

**Existence of Substitutes**

The traditional substitutes to air travel were few: automobiles, buses, trains, and ocean liners. These modes of transportation had not been viable for most business travelers. However, technological advances have led to new types of competitive substitutes.

**Video conferencing.** With the telecommunications multinationals offering everything from global data services to real-time video conferencing, the days of business travel appear to be numbered. Telephone conferencing already had its brief moment as the technology most likely to make business travel obsolete. In the early 1990s, a decade from the 21st century, video conferencing — combining voice and pictures — looked set to have far greater repercussions on business travel. By 1993, companies could buy video conferencing systems for as little as US$18,500, though the electronics technology behind top-quality video conferencing was still in its infancy. Industry experts predicted that by 1996 video conferencing would be as widely used as facsimile machines and would have greatly revolutionalized the way business is done.[23]

Although multinationals had in fact used video conferencing since the early 1980s, it was only in the 1990s that new technology cut costs enough to bring it within the reach of smaller companies. However, drawbacks such as the lack of personal touch and the inability to pick up visual cues from the on-screen faces were likely to restrict video conferencing for technical discussions, contractual support, servicing ongoing contracts, and meetings with fixed schedules.

[22]B Jaleco, "AAA is No Pal," *Asia Travel Trade*, August 1993: 34.
[23]M Rouen, "Beam Me Up, Boss," *Business Traveller*, August 1993: 18.

**Improved surface transportation.** Technology has also brought about the improvement of other surface transportation which satisfy the basic need of transport. However, it is still a poor substitute for business travels in which time is a crucial element, especially for long hauls. On the other hand, there have been an increasing number of luxury passenger ocean liners being launched, reflecting the growing popularity of tour cruises as an alternative to tours with air packages.

### Airline Passengers

The customers of the airline industry consist of discretionary travelers and business travelers. Discretionary travelers have a reasonable amount of latitude regarding flight times and connections. As such, they most certainly want to shop around for the cheapest fare. Whereas service was occasionally a selling point to discretionary travelers, price has been the key to this customer segment.

Business travelers, on the other hand, do not appear to be as price-sensitive as discretionary travelers. Business travelers tend to make reservations based more on convenience of flight times and connections. Service is also important to business travelers, especially those who fly frequently and who are likely to remember where and when they received good or bad service. Because business travel is relatively fixed price, airlines court the business traveler through FFPs, which offer everything from free flights to discounts on rental cars and lodging. Through these FFPs, airlines seek to develop brand loyalty and keep the business traveler flying their airline, irrespective of the fare.

Compared to their American counterparts, Asia-Pacific carriers have been much more prudent in tailoring their capacity to match the region's traffic growth and to meet business and leisure demand. Thus far, Asia-Pacific carriers have been spared from the precipitous plunge into the vicious cycle of price wars. Nevertheless, drops in load factors have been recorded throughout the region because of increased competition and the lower-than-expected traffic growth (see Exhibit 6). The fact that carriers were expanding their capacity in anticipation of the Asia-Pacific travel boom adds to their difficulty in sustaining their traditionally high load factors.

Industry surveys found that, while the amount varies widely, travel was eating up a rapidly increasing percentage of corporate budgets. More than half of businessmen surveyed in a report by travel industry consultancy Reed Travel Group made 20 or more business trips a year; more than one-third made 30 or more.[24] As corporate belt-tightening cuts travel budgets, more executives are finding themselves in the rear of the plane. While the difference between a full-fare economy class ticket and one in business class was relatively small, moving up to first class boosts traveling costs considerably. That helps to explain the growing popularity of business class, which was introduced in the 1970s. With business class offering improved service, companies were switching back.

Competition for the high-yield corporate travelers is so strong today that many Asia-Pacific carriers actively solicit clients rather than sit back and wait for bookings done through travel agents. Asia-Pacific carriers are going to new heights to beat boredom in the sky, and they are going to great lengths to ensure that no details would be overlooked when it came to coddling the most sought-after species — the business travelers. The

---

[24] M Levin, "The High Cost of Going Cheap," *Asian Business*, January 1993: 48.

challenge of keeping passengers amused and allowing them to remain in touch with their terrestrial lives is another key marketing battle. Airlines are jumping into the bandwagon to enhance satellite communication with modern gadgets, installing better cabin entertainment system with individual TV screens, and providing better cabin services. All these major overhauls pointed to a massive capital investment for the reconfiguring of aircraft.

However, their efforts are not unwarranted. Airline passengers have become more sophisticated, with a much greater variety of airlines to choose from to suit their individual preferences. In most cases, there are little switching costs involved and, with the generally increased purchasing power of clients, airlines have to go all out to earn the loyalty of their passenger.

### Other Key Players in the Industry

**Travel agents.** The threat of travel agents to the airline industry has been more significant than at first glance might seem evident. There is no way to eliminate their function and few ways to minimize their potentially adverse effect on the success of an airline. Airlines generally pay a 10-percent commission to agents who book passengers on their flights — if the passengers would have flown some other airline even without the travel agent's assistance. Further, travel agent commission overrides, bonus commissions paid by individual airlines to travel agents to encourage booking on a particular airline, are also substantial and tend to restrict competition. Most major international airlines offer additional bonuses of 2 to 6 percent of ticket prices to travel agents who throw a large proportion of business their way. Commission overrides and other travel agent incentives have been encouraging agents to divert traffic to the airline offering the best incentives, usually the largest in the market, when the passenger's needs could be met by the services of more than one airline.

**Aircraft manufacturers.** Carriers worldwide are cancelling orders and delaying retirement of older planes. New aircraft orders for 1991 have fallen to the level of the early 1980s, making 1991 the third consecutive year of declining orders. More and more carriers are requesting postponement of deliveries but due to the long lead time between orders and deliveries, it was 2 to 3 years after the recession began that manufacturers felt the effects. That, in turn, led to aircraft manufacturers to continue the substantial cuts in production and deliveries. Even if airline traffic did pick up, the overhang caused by a full 10 percent of the world's fleet in storage would dampen new orders for future years. In addition, projected low stable jet-fuel prices would force newer fuel-efficient jets to compete for sales, resulting in a large supply of used aircraft being offered at bargain prices.[25]

In the meantime, Asia-Pacific carriers will continue to have high bargaining power over the airline suppliers as they take delivery of new aircraft (particularly wide bodies, for which they will be the world's leading customers) at an ever-increasing rate. In 1994, the region's carriers already enjoyed very high bargaining power, accounting for about one-quarter of the current global order backlog for jetliners of about 2,700 aircraft.[26]

---

[25] D Knibb, "Design for the Future," *Airline Business*, December 1992: 57.

[26] B Jaleco, "Special Report," *Asian Aviation*, April 1993: 36.

**Financial institutions.** Thus far, Asia-Pacific carriers have been able to find the required financing for their orders of aircraft. Although many airlines still favor tax-driven lease structures due to their financial benefits, the equity markets have been becoming increasingly tight. Due to a drying up of Japanese equity and debt markets toward the end of 1990, the use of Japanese leveraged leases has been limited to major carriers for deliveries of smaller jet aircraft types. Foreign sales corporation leases continue to be used in relatively small numbers but these are generally available only to major airlines with good credit ratings. Such limitations have led airlines to look to other sources of financing, such as export credits and bonds.[27]

**Other suppliers.** Except for the suppliers of jet fuel, the other suppliers to the airline industry have not been a major threat. As a group, these other suppliers — aircraft manufacturers, tire manufacturers, caterers or tire retreaders — have been at the mercy of the airline industry. If the economy was good, people flew, airlines remained in business, and the suppliers prospered. Except for fuel, it was a buyer's market.

### Other Critical Issues Facing Asia-Pacific Airlines

**Strategic independence.** While continued recession puts the squeeze on the airline industry, the pressure for globalization would increase only in the "deregulated" skies of the U.S. and Europe. On the other side of the world, however, Asia-Pacific carriers seem to have avoided the trend with the exception of SIA, which has committed to an equity swap in its global partnership with Delta and Swissair. Other Asian airlines have kept any alliances they have with their counterparts much more low-key.

Most Asian airlines already have normal commercial arrangements with other airlines and believe that they could still go for market niches without having to merge and become a mega-carrier. In the Asia-Pacific region where the industry is enjoying high growth, low staff costs, and relatively less rigid regulation, Asian carriers can actually develop with greater flexibility on their own.

**Bilateral conflict.** Asia-Pacific carriers, traditionally an independent lot, have initiated joint action for the first time to protest against what they regard as outdated and lopsided bilateral air traffic rights with the United States. While American carriers fly from a total of 21 gateways into Asia, Asia-Pacific carriers could reach the U.S. from only nine cities.[28] There has been increasing recognition that defensive, bilateral bloc negotiations are no longer the way to go. The path to a more open and competitive aviation market lies with government moving directly to push for fair and open global access.

Aviation analysts predicted that the rapid growth in Asia-Pacific air traffic will produce more clashes with the U.S. as regional Asia-Pacific carriers become more assertive. Asia-Pacific carriers have been urged to form regional groups to combat increasingly competitive challenges from emerging U.S. and European mega-carriers. It is also predicted that the aviation interests of Asian nations will converge as they face concerted onslaught

[27] C Tyler, "Finance Keeps Flowing for Asian Airlines," *Aerospace*, January 1993: 22.
[28] Mecham, "Asian Airlines Protest US Bilateral Edge," Aviation and Space Technology, June 1993: 31.

by U.S. carriers with the high probability of a sustained period of bilateral conflict in the Pacific Rim for the next few years.[29]

**Forward and backward integration.** The region's air traffic is growing at such a rapid rate that many airlines are scrambling to build new hangars and workshops fast enough to keep pace with their fleet expansion programs. Some airlines, such as Korean Air Lines, have been backward-integrated to the extent of manufacturing their own aircraft. Such a move offers them self-sufficiency and better quality control over the aircraft, as well as the opportunity for profit generation.

Tapping into the potential lucrativeness of the tourism industry, forward integration has also taken place in the industry with airlines such as SIA taking a step toward the ultimate discretionary traveler through its subsidiary, Tradewinds Tour and Travel. By having Tradewinds offer a complete tour package by bundling meals, accommodations, and touring activities, SIA is not only able to guarantee a demand for its flights but also to gain an edge over competitors. SIA has also ventured into the hotel sector — the investment was not large enough to divert the airline from its core business of flying aircraft and selling seats but enough to fulfil its aim of ensuring steady room supply and competitive rates in Singapore, again a move to keep the flight demand in this region buoyant.[30]

**Congestions at key hubs.** Asian hubs, with a concentration of flights during limited periods of the day, will play a more active role in the future than they did in the past. With the trend toward hubbing at key airports in the region, creating large volumes of transfer traffic would only exacerbate peaking problems. By 1993, there were already congestion problems at key hubs, including runway and apron constraints, customs and immigration shortcomings, terminal overcapacity, and environmental limitations.

The situation would only get worse as airlines add more flights to cope with travel demand. Traffic forecasts indicate that new facilities under construction or planned for these airports will become congested as soon as they become operational. There is, therefore, an urgent need for governments of the region to discuss these problems at high levels. Failure to provide adequate infrastructure in Asia can have detrimental effects on the entire airline industry.

## Performance of Asia-Pacific Carriers

### Cost Structures

Asian carriers have traditionally enjoyed the advantage of having a lower cost structure, but annual traffic growth figures of 8 percent or more in the Asia-Pacific region tended to mask the fact that there were cost pressures. According to figures compiled by the Orient Airlines Association (OAA), whose members include major Asia-Pacific carriers, airlines' unit costs rose by 15.5 percent from 1988 to 1992. Labor costs rose to account for 33.2 percent of total airline costs, while sales and marketing costs also increased by 23 to 24 percent from 1988 to 1992. Infrastructure costs, both in terms of landing and route

[29] H C Chan, *Asia Travel Trade*, August 1993: 9–10.

[30] H B Tan, "SIA, the Hotelier," *PATA Travel News*, April 1993: 26.

charges and the funding of new airports, also have a differential impact given the variety of infrastructure development in the region.[31]

The Asia-Pacific airline community has cost structures more diverse than any other region because each airline faces unique differences in factors such as wage rates, inflation rates, and foreign exchange rates. Nevertheless, it is still possible to divide Asia-Pacific carriers into four broad categories, reflecting current cost and developing levels.[32]

### High Cost

Japan Air Lines, All Nippon Airways, and Japan Air System face the highest cost structures in the world and were the most seriously affected. Net profits at All Nippon Airways fell by 41.5 percent to US$57.4 million in the six months to September 30, 1992. Japan Air Lines suffered an even poorer performance, sliding to a mere US$36 million net loss over the same period. High domestic wage rates and rental prices have been blamed for pushing JAL's unit costs to around 30 percent higher than SIA's. In a bid to control costs, the two major airlines are seeking to develop low-cost subsidiaries by employing more non-Japanese cabin crew and to relocate labor-intensive activities to the region's lower cost economies.

### Medium Cost, Developed

Singapore Airlines, Cathay Pacific Airways, and Qantas Airways are efficient long-haul operators with a strong brand image and were able to weather the increasingly difficult operating conditions. Qantas management was stung by an US$85 million operating loss in 1991 but recorded a remarkable turnaround of US$172 million profit during the period from January to June 1992 after implementing extensive cost-cutting, including the retrenchment of 3,500 employees.

Cathay Pacific Airways, battling against a double-digit inflation rate in Hong Kong, had taken steps to improve the productivity of its reservations and ground handling services and planned to control labor by clamping down on wage increases among Hong Kong-based staff. There were also plans to relocate part of Cathay Pacific's accounts section to Guangdong, China in order to control both rental and staff costs. SIA, which recorded a 14.8 percent drop in its group pretax profit to US$56.3 million in the fiscal year 1992–1993, was also planning to relocate some of its accounting functions to Bombay, India.

### Medium Cost, Developing

Malaysian Airline System (MAS), Korean Air Lines, Thai Airways International, and China Airlines, together with Asiana and EVA Air, are airlines which are enjoying high growth rates and therefore show little urgency for curbing expansion in the face of rising costs — MAS and Asiana saw an increase in their net profits from US$288 million and US$407 million in 1992, respectively. The strong traffic growth triggered off by new markets such as China has allowed the carriers to push down unit costs by default. Nevertheless, MAS

[31] P Needham, "Asia Taxed by Growth," *Airlines Business*, February 1993: 30–33.
[32] P Needham, "Asia Taxed by Growth," *Airlines Business*, February 1993: 31.

already has plans in the pipeline to replace its expatriate flight crew and engineering staff with Malaysian employees before the year 2000.

### Low Cost, Developing

Garuda Indonesia, Philippine Airlines, and the larger airlines from the People's Republic of China are enjoying high growth rates from buoyant domestic economies so there was virtually no reason to implement cost-cutting programs. In fact, their low-cost structures have the potential to allow them to establish a stronger international presence and become serious threats when management expertise catches up with natural resources in these countries.

The potential problems in controlling costs for the Asia-Pacific carriers are slight compared to those faced by U.S. and European airlines. However, the higher-cost carriers could be expected to lead from the front in accepting that the region is not exempt from global cost pressures. While the effects of rising costs could no longer be masked, buoyant growth in the region has maintained a relatively healthy profit and loss sheet for Asian airlines thus far. Exhibit 7 reports the financial performance of 10 major airlines in the Asia-Pacific region. At the time of this case, the two major Japanese carriers (ANA and JAL) were the only airlines in the region which had to cut their international networks in the face of stagnant markets, rising costs and competition, but more and more carriers would start facing a critical decision — whether to keep expanding or to slow down and consolidate their position.

## Future Outlook

The outlook for the Asia-Pacific airline industry has been bright and unblemished. Interestingly, there are variations in financial performance ranging from SIA's outstanding performance as a top international airline to Garuda Indonesia, whose continued existence hinges heavily on government subsidies. Accordingly, SIA has often been viewed as a worthy model for emerging, as well as less successful, airlines in the Asia-Pacific region.

There appears to be three main determinants of prosperity in the industry, namely: economic growth, traffic growth, and yield. Since economic growth is outside the arena of control of the airlines, the airlines' main strategic emphasis has been to focus on maintaining and, where possible, increasing traffic and yield.

### The Key to Yield Maximisation

In the past, many airlines have focused on business travel because it was easier to sell to people who already wanted or had to fly. However, this did not mean that high-yield, quality travel necessarily produced a profit for the airlines. If high fares were mated to high costs, which high-quality travel required, then a carrier could end up no further ahead. If their future strategy was to concentrate a greater proportion of their effort on attracting lower yield leisure travel (a growing segment), airlines must then control costs tightly in order to do so profitably.

With the cost advantage traditionally enjoyed by Asia-Pacific carriers being gradually eroded, potential problems in controlling costs loom in the near future. Since fuel and maintenance costs accounted for approximately half of the airlines' operating costs, these two areas should be under close monitoring. Bearing in mind that the aviation business is in the service industry, there is a significant positive correlation between airline yield and staff productivity. Staff productivity is, in turn, determined by effective training programs, attractive incentives, and a strong commitment to the airlines's goals. Human resource management is a crucial component affecting the performance of the airlines and therefore warrants management's attention.

**The Key to Traffic Growth**

While most Asia-Pacific carriers have shunned away from mergers, strategic alliances might actually be a guarantee to market access and development of competencies, especially with the existing political constraints and capital shortages. High-cost airline operators might want to create worldwide alliances with an eye to saving money and not just buying market share. Alliances not only are an inexpensive way of servicing a wider market, but also a way of easing cultural sensitivity and countering the lack of knowledge of local business practices.

With the prevalent congestion problems faced by major airports in Hong Kong and Tokyo, the increase in traffic would only aggravate the problem further. The respective governments are expected to be responsible for developing and expanding the infrastructure to keep pace with growth. In addition, the governments are also expected to negotiate for more liberal exchange of air traffic rights.

Enhancing service offerings will continue to be a means to attracting passengers. Airlines have begun investing in the latest and most sophisticated in-cabin and on-going technologies. However, in view of the massive capital investment involved, the benefits have to outweigh cost requirements. The list of innovations and marketing gimmicks is almost limitless. We underscore the growing awareness of the need for a marketing-oriented strategy and the increasing importance of the marketing function in the structure of airlines.

In conclusion, the strategies to be employed by Asia-Pacific airlines in the 21st century would reflect a response to environmental forces, a concern with operational efficiency, and political realities. The particular strategy which an airline will eventually adopt shall depend on a variety of factors.

EXHIBIT 1

## THE AIRLINE INDUSTRY IN THE ASIA-PACIFIC REGION, 1994
### Passenger Traffic Forecast: 1991–1996
(in millions)

| *Year* | *Passengers* |
|---|---|
| 1991 | 262.5 |
| 1992 | 289.8 |
| 1993 | 309.8 |
| 1994 | 330.2 |
| 1995 | 352.4 |
| 1996 | 376.0 |

Source: IATA, *Asia Pacific Passenger Traffic Forecast: Travel Demand, 1985–2010.*

EXHIBIT 2

## THE AIRLINE INDUSTRY IN THE ASIA-PACIFIC REGION, 1994
### Regional Traffic Growth Patterns
### For the Period 1991–1996

| *Region* | *5-Year Growth Rate* |
|---|---|
| Eastern Europe | 12.6% |
| Northeast Asia | 9.8% |
| Southeast Asia | 9.0% |
| Atlantic South America | 7.6% |
| Pacific South America | 7.5% |
| Australia and New Zealand | 7.2% |
| United States and Canada | 7.2% |
| Western Europe | 6.9% |
| Caribbean | 6.8% |
| Indian subcontinent | 6.6% |
| Middle East | 6.6% |
| Northeast Africa | 6.2% |
| Northwest Africa | 6.2% |
| Central America | 6.1% |
| East Africa | 5.2% |
| Southern Africa | 5.1% |
| West Africa | 4.7% |

Source: IATA, *Asia Pacific Passenger Traffic Forecast: Travel Demand, 1985–2010.*

EXHIBIT 3

## THE AIRLINE INDUSTRY IN THE ASIA-PACIFIC REGION, 1994

**Major Asia Pacific Airlines' Traffic**

(in thousand passenger-kilometers)

| *Airlines* | *January* | *February* | *March* | *April* | *May* | *June* |
|---|---|---|---|---|---|---|
| Air India | 808,297 | 644,586 | 276,718 | — | — | — |
| Airlanka | 426,229 | 349,535 | 326,908 | 284,939 | 261,276 | 249,907 |
| All Nippon Airways | 860,336 | 739,344 | 928,901 | 690,221 | — | — |
| Cathay Pacific Airways | 2,120,189 | 1,906,619 | 2,176,526 | 2,442,816 | 2,368,164 | 2,321,485 |
| China Airlines | 1,277,222 | 1,073,796 | 1,123,131 | 1,203,749 | 1,163,857 | — |
| Japan Air Lines | 3,598,356 | 2,963,328 | 3,175,112 | — | — | — |
| Japan Air System | 69 | 73 | 78 | — | — | — |
| Korean Air Lines | 2,138,312 | 1,756,107 | 1,874,817 | 1,887,005 | 2,124,092 | — |
| Malaysian Airline System | 1,514,248 | 1,217,941 | 1,366,336 | 1,307,480 | 1,325,436 | — |
| Philippine Airlines | 1,062,621 | 869,417 | 938,260 | 1,026,165 | 1,021,454 | — |
| Qantas Airways | 3,271,719 | 2,712,604 | 3,049,269 | 2,853,067 | 2,851,800 | — |
| Royal Brunei Airlines | 107,078 | 90,417 | 90,417 | — | — | — |
| Singapore Airlines | 3,409,300 | 2,876,100 | 3,306,300 | 3,289,300 | 3,261,300 | — |
| Thai Airways International | 2,052,334 | 1,739,725 | 1,830,539 | 1,932,710 | 1,664,866 | — |

Source: *Asian Aviation*, June 1993 and August 1993.

EXHIBIT 4

**THE AIRLINE INDUSTRY IN THE ASIA-PACIFIC REGION, 1994**
**Amenities Offered by the Airlines**

| *Airlines* | *Phone* | *Fax* | *Individual TV screens* |
|---|---|---|---|
| Air India | — | — | — |
| Air New Zealand | — | — | — |
| All Nippon Airways | Yes | — | Yes |
| Cathay Pacific Airways | — | — | — |
| China Airlines | — | — | Yes |
| Garuda Indonesia | — | — | 1 |
| Japan Air Lines | 1 | 1 | 2 |
| Pakistan International Airlines | — | — | — |
| Philippine Airlines | — | — | — |
| Qantas Airways | — | 1 | 1 |
| Singapore Airlines | Yes | 1 | Yes |
| Thai Airways International | — | — | — |

Notes: 1 = To be installed or being tested in 1993–1994.
2 = Available in certain planes only.

Source: "Sky-High Work and Play," *Business Traveler*, February 1993.

EXHIBIT 5

## THE AIRLINE INDUSTRY IN THE ASIA-PACIFIC REGION, 1994
**Airlines' On-Time Departure/Arrival Performance**

(in percentage)

| | *1987* | | *1988* | | *1989* | | *1990* | | *1991* | | *1992* | |
|---|---|---|---|---|---|---|---|---|---|---|---|---|
| *Airline* | *Dep* | *Arr* | *Dep* | *Arr* | *Dep* | *Arr* | *Dep* | *Arr* | *Dep* | *Arr* | *Dep* | *Arr* |
| Air India | 92 | — | 90 | — | 87 | — | 85 | — | — | — | — | — |
| Air New Zealand | 74 | 75 | 74 | 70 | 72 | 71 | 74 | 72 | — | — | — | — |
| Garuda Indonesia | 73 | — | 79 | — | 80 | — | 83 | — | — | — | — | — |
| Japan Air Lines | 94.0 | 89.8 | 95.6 | 89.3 | 93.7 | 88.7 | 94.6 | 90.7 | 95.4 | 88.9 | 94.6 | 91.3 |
| Korean Air Lines | 88.7 | 75.3 | 86.7 | 72.4 | 87.6 | 74.3 | 91.5 | 79.7 | 95.0 | 83.5 | 96.1 | 84.0 |
| Malaysian Airline System | 92 | — | 88 | — | 83 | — | 88 | — | — | — | — | — |
| Singapore Airlines | 80 | 77 | 76 | 72 | 94 | — | 95.5 | — | 96 | — | 96 | — |
| Thai Airways | — | — | — | — | — | — | — | — | — | — | 81 | — |

Source: *Business Traveler*, February 1993.

EXHIBIT 6

## THE AIRLINE INDUSTRY IN THE ASIA-PACIFIC REGION, 1994
### Major Airlines's Passenger Load Factor
(in percent)

| *Airlines* | *Average in 1992* | *Average Since January 1993* |
|---|---|---|
| Air India | N.A. | 63.0 |
| Airlanka | 68.3 | 67.0 |
| All Nippon Airways | 69.7 | 61.6 |
| Cathay Pacific Airways | 73.7 | 67.8 |
| China Airlines | 76.8 | 75.6 |
| Japan Air Lines | 70.0 | 65.3 |
| Japan Air System | 72.1 | 75.9 |
| Korean Air Lines | 66.6 | 65.5 |
| Malaysian Airline System | 67.9 | 65.4 |
| Philippine Airlines | N.A. | 75.0 |
| Qantas Airways | 66.3 | 67.9 |
| Royal Brunei Airlines | 49.5 | 49.7 |
| Singapore Airlines | 71.7 | 69.9 |
| Thai Airways International | 62.0 | 66.3 |

Source: *Asian Aviation*, December 1992/January 1993 and August 1993.

EXHIBIT 7

## THE AIRLINE INDUSTRY IN THE ASIA-PACIFIC REGION, 1994
### Profitability of Airlines
(in millions of currency)

| *Airlines* | *1991* | *1992* | *1991/92* | *1992/93* |
|---|---|---|---|---|
| Nippon Airways | — | — | US$21.25 | US$66.65 |
| Cathay Pacific Airways | HK$2,950 | HK$3,008 | — | — |
| China Airlines | TW$154 | TW$144 | — | — |
| Japan Air Lines | — | — | — | (¥40,000)[a] |
| Korean Air Lines | US$20 | US$1.5 | — | — |
| Malaysian Airline System | — | — | RM$112.9 | RM$145.6 |
| Philippine Airlines | — | US$55 | — | — |
| Qantas Airways | (US$85) | US$172[b] | — | — |
| Singapore Airlines | — | — | S$929.8 | S$851.5 |
| Thai Airways International | — | — | Bht3,068 | — |

Notes: a = All losses are donated in brackets.
b = Interim profit for the period January 1–June 30, 1992.

Source: Respective Airlines' annual reports.

# Singapore Airlines: Comparative Case Studies of the British and Singaporean National Airlines* 6

These two cases depict an interesting contrast between the Singapore and British government administrations as to the direct and indirect roles they play in their respective national airline companies. The cases provide, in a sense, a cross-cultural analysis of state-owned, or public enterprise (PE), systems. Although both companies were outstanding performers as PEs, it is contended here that the Singapore PE was operating out of a more favorable political economic environment than its British counterpart. British Airways resembled the classic case observed in the literature — inhibited by government interference, politicization, confusion of long-term plans, and so forth. Singapore Airlines' (SIA) history manifests these classic afflictions much less, and the government's proactive role even seemed to provide a competitive advantage.

This joint study of two national airlines focuses on the period of government ownership in each case, that is, up to privatization of the companies by the late 1980s. A brief epilogue is added to cover the postprivatization experience, providing a sense of continuity of enterprise behavior and performance. There was not much change at Singapore Airlines, where the government anyway still held a controlling interest, but British Airways was exercising a newfound autonomy.

---

* This case was prepared by Douglas Sikorski, National University of Singapore, to serve as a basis for class discussion rather than to illustrate either effective or ineffective handling of an administrative situation. 

A comparative evaluation is contained in a separate section. The composite study constitutes a comparison of two state enterprise systems, as represented by one state-owned enterprise from each.

Although the cases have up-to-date information, the coverage is essentially historical and as such reflects behavior norms that may be changing in the 1990s. Certainly the British have modified their approach to national enterprise somewhat, but the best antidote for the "British disease" — for what is still today a turbulent political economic environment — was, and is, privatisation.

## Singapore Airlines (SIA)

SIA has a remarkable history of success and transformation from colonial enterprise formed in 1947, to national flagbearer in 1972, to partially privatised company by the end of 1985. The company has always been, and still is in the 1990s, widely acclaimed as the Republic of Singapore's premier enterprise.

### Management Performance and Objectives

Throughout its history SIA was one of the most consistently profitable among world airlines (see Exhibit 1). A British poll conducted by the journal *Executive Travel* announced in London on September 24, 1986 that SIA had displaced British Airways as "the world's number one airline."

Stated corporate objectives until 1981 reflected normal business purposes but also included two goals: "to be a flag carrier of Singapore" and "to promote the growth of the republic's economy and tourist trade." The company's formal objectives were revised at a two-day "Management Roundtable" commencing November 29, 1981 when these two goals were dropped to project a more commercial image. Just after "privatization" in December 1985, the Chairman's New Year 1986 message added a new goal: ". . . profit. It is not that profit has been a dirty word in SIA before. But it has never been elevated into an all-consuming, burning objective. All we wanted was to generate enough cash to enable us to regenerate our fleet and to continually train and develop our staff. Now, we have to respect the views of the investing public . . ."

### Group Investments and Financing

The SIA Group's most important investment was in the development of Singapore's ultramodern airport at Changi, contributing about one-third to the S$1.5 billion cost of Phase 1, which opened July 1981. Also, SIA invested in the largest computer installation in Singapore at Changi.

Singapore Airlines has made extensive acquisitions of new aircraft. For example, a 1978 purchase was a world record for that decade in money terms, and a 1981 purchase was again half as large. In its advertising campaigns beginning April 1982, it boasted "the most modern fleet in all the world." To finance fleet acquisitions, management tapped internally generated funds for a large part of the payments, but incurred some additional debt and also issued shares, SIA's equity financing from inception to privatization.

Initial debt consisted primarily of bank loans, with development fund loans from the government for "development" programs. SIA floated a bond in German marks in January 1976, and after 1978 relied on market financing only. From 1978 to 1979 group borrowings from international and local banks totaled two-thirds of a billion US$. The Singapore government guaranteed the United States Export-Import (EXIM) Bank loans because that was an EXIM Bank requirement. SIA also revealed that its government had guaranteed certain bond issues but had charged a service fee that raised the effective interest rate to what "any private corporation with an excellent credit rating" would pay.

SIA had been accused of unfair (subsidized) practices by foreign competitors. For example, in 1981 three American carriers, Pan Am, Northwest Orient, and Flying Tiger filed a complaint with the United States Civil Aeronautics Board (CAB) that SIA was subsidized by the government and engaged in below-cost pricing. Headlines in the local Straits Times newspaper on October 21 of that year read, "SIA comes under attack in the US", but the next day featured "SIA fights back", as its chairman and deputy chairman both adamantly denied all charges, inviting the American airlines' auditors to visit Singapore (at their own expense) and inspect SIA's books. The CAB was withholding approval of SIA's application for more routes and flights due to objections filed by the three airlines. Pan Am was arguing, "during a period of recession, foreign carriers like SIA can expand operations in search of increased market share, confident in the fact that they can anticipate government support." Northwest supplemented this argument by alleging subsidy, which "allows SIA to mount a scale of operation that a free capital market would never support", going on to say that "political considerations, not market conditions and prospects, determine the scale of SIA's competitive efforts". On June 4, 1983 the CAB's decision was reported in SIA's favour.

SIA was owned entirely by Temasek Holdings (until privatization), except for a small minority held by employees. Temasek was Singapore's largest corporation, wholly owned by the government and part of the Ministry of Finance portfolio. Although Temasek generally did not interfere in the decisions of SIA or its other subsidiaries, decisions concerning shareholder matters were monitored. The means of control was primarily through the appointment of company directors. There were also periodic reviews of past performance and future plans of selected companies, through meetings and reports. Equity capital or shareholder loans were provided where required for development of approved projects.

**Labor Relations**

The SIA Airline Pilots Association (SIAPA) "work-to-rule" protest, held from October 13 to November 26, 1980 to press for better pay and fringes, prompted the direct intervention of Prime Minister Lee Kuan Yew. The industrial action included flight delays, a high rate of sick leave, and other measures, prompting verbal censure from both the Chairman and Deputy Chairman of the National Trades Union Congress (NTUC). The Prime Minister had a 65-minute meeting with SIAPA officials and publicly suggested that he was ready if necessary to suspend operations. After the Prime Minister's own conference with SIAPA he appointed Devan Nair, an SIA director, soon to become President of the Republic of Singapore, to review personnel practices at SIA.

The other unions which were represented at SIA were the Airline Executive Staff Union (AESU) and the Singapore Air Transport Workers' Union (SATU), which was replaced by the Singapore Airline Staff Union (SIASU). These unions were NTUC affiliates. SIAPA, as a branch of the International Airline Pilots' Association, was independent of any Singapore affiliations; and local union officials were largely expatriate. Several months after the "SIAPA incident" SIAPA was deregistered by the Labor Ministry, and in 1982 the Airline Pilot Association of Singapore (Alpa-S) was formed to take its place.

For SIA, as was the case for Singapore companies in general, collective bargaining had not been the elaborate process it was for companies in most Western countries because pay increments generally could be derived directly from guidelines issued annually by the National Wages Council (NWC). The NWC, a tripartite body formed by the government with representations from the public sector, labor (the NTUC), and management (designated employers' associations) recommended specific pay increments applicable nationwide. During the 1980s, the government extricated itself from participation in the NWC deliberations and delegated responsibility to the NTUC and employers' associations. Subsequently the NWC itself declined to issue anything more than general policy guidelines for 1986 and urged each company to conduct its own pay talks. On May 20, 1986 SIA, in announcing its offer to the unions, became one of the first companies in Singapore to move toward the "flexible wage system" being promoted by the NWC. Negotiations continued without strong polemics, and settlements were reached with both unions.

Union leaders repeatedly stressed that their self-interest coincided with the company's well-being, which was the message the government had been instilling in Singaporeans for many years. Underlining the unions' interest in the company's profitability, SIASU had purchased 30,000 shares of SIA's privatization issue.

Throughout SIA's history no man-days were ever lost due to labor disputes.

**Overt Government Participation**

There were other instances, besides the "SIAPA incident", where the government intervened in SIA or on its behalf. Lee Kuan Yew's personal role in SIA's destiny was apparent twice in 1982. In August he announced agreement at prime ministerial level for a cooperative arrangement between SIA and Malaysia's national carrier MAS for a joint shuttle service between Singapore and Kuala Lumpur; in September a similar agreement was reached for direct flights between Singapore and some internal Indonesian points, including Bali. Bali was a lucrative stop exclusively served by Garuda, the Indonesian flag carrier, since 1979 when the Indonesian government suspended access by foreign airlines.

Another noteworthy example was the Prime Minister's 2-week trip to China in September 1985. Although the central objective was a "package of specific business", no businessmen were included in his party in order to keep the visit at strictly government-level. Discussions between Mr Lee and then Chinese Prime Minister Zhao Ziyang included many areas of mutual business interest involving banking services, oil refining, and others. One of Mr Lee's suggestions to Mr Zhao was direct airline flights to provincial capitals.

Ngiam Tong Dow, a top official in the prime minister's office who was also an SIA director, was with the prime minister's entourage. He was responsible for identifying the most promising proposals and coordinating feasibility studies and reconnaissance by interested businesses.

**Outlook**

On December 18, 1985 SIA obtained its long-awaited listing in the Stock Exchange of Singapore with a flotation of 100 million shares. However, the effect of privatization on SIA was less dramatic than it was for a nationalized industry in Britain. After privatization the board of directors of SIA was still government-appointed because Temasek's proportional ownership in SIA was reduced only to 63 percent. In March 1987 a government-appointed advisory group, the Public Sector Divestment Committee, recommended a further reduction of the government's shareholding, in stages, to 30 percent, and in June 1987 Temasek reduced its holding to 56 percent. However, even a minority interest of 30 percent could still be enough to maintain control. In contrast, the privatization of British Airways in 1987 constituted total divestment by the British government of its shareholding.

## British Airways (BA)

### Origins and Objectives

British Airways Plc evolved from British Airways Board (BAB) on April 1, 1984. BAB was a nationalized industry formed on April 1, 1972 from British European Airways (BEA) and British Overseas Airways Corporation (BOAC), both wholly government-owned statutory corporations.

BOAC's origins could be traced to Aircraft Transport and Travel Limited. On August 25, 1919 it commenced operations as the world's first daily international scheduled air service. The pioneer company joined forces with other privately owned air operators in 1924 to form Imperial Airways. This company, the only one of British air transport operators, enjoyed government subsidies. It was nationalized, along with its main competitor, to form BOAC in 1939.

In his final report (1972–1973), BOAC's chairman said:

> With the return of peace there came a flurry of White Papers each advocating its own pattern of change. The final decision, in 1946, was to divide the world between . . . nationalised corporations, BEA to have Europe . . . and BOAC the rest of the world . . . BOAC created a European division whose aircraft and staff were hived off later to become BEA . . . During its postwar career BOAC has had three main guiding principles: cooperation with Commonwealth airlines, support for the British aircraft manufacturing industry and the development of low-fare transportation . . .

BAB came into being with the appointment of a chairman and a board by the Secretary of State for Trade and Industry. By July 1972 the Board had decided on an organizational structure and the recommendations were accepted by the Secretary of State. The first corporate plan was submitted to the Department of Trade and Industry in December 1972. The Board sent its second report on organization to the government on January 22, 1973, which concerned a common trading identity under the brand name "British Airways." The government's approval was thus always required for major internal actions.

### Management Performance

BA was a company of renowned excellence. The brokers advising on BA's planned privatization, Phillips & Drew, purported that BA carried the most passengers on scheduled international services. From 1983 to 1984, BA became the world's most profitable airline. In its technology and facilities, BA had been a world leader throughout its history. BA marketed its expertise worldwide, including a provision of technology transfer to Singapore Airlines cited in the 1984–1985 annual report.

All nationalized industries were required to agree with the government on performance targets, such as return on assets, external financing limit, labor productivity, and unit cost reduction.

None of the board members were appointed from the civil service. During the period 1971 to 1981 BA had a succession of four chairman.

**Financing**[1]

The company's financial resources, financial performance and goals, and financial reporting were under the direct control of the government. For example, annual reports devoted several pages to "current cost accounts", required by act of Parliament.

The five-year investment program was reviewed by the Department of Trade before being incorporated into HM Treasury's expenditure plans. Debt and equity capital had a combined limitation prescribed by the Public Sector Borrowing Requirement. Within this latter government budgetary control, BA had its own external financing limit. This particular system began in 1977. In the first place a limit was set on the total capital expenditure. In the second place a limit was set upon the total of new capital, whether in the form of public dividend capital or loans from the government or other sources. This, of course, directly constrained company expansion because BA had to stand in line with other recipients of government funds.

Public dividend capital (equity) was originally granted to BOAC as part of a capital restructuring in 1965. The principle was continued on a temporary basis for the new British Airways Board by the Civil Aviation Act of 1971 and made a permanent feature of BA funding by the British Airways Board Act of 1977.

Throughout the history of the airline company(s), all loans were underwritten by the government, which also offered until April 1, 1981 a foreign exchange hedging facility called the "treasury exchange cover scheme."

The long-term capital structure was relatively simple, containing straight loans and public dividend capital. There seemed less room for innovative financial instruments since the government, in its attention to the debt/equity proportion, also monitored the nature of debt and equity financing.

In November 1979 the Thatcher government introduced legislation to "privatize" some nationalized industries. BA began planning for its own public share offering at some future date and paying off its debt, notably the National Loan Fund. The practical effect of the formation of British Airways Plc on April 1, 1984 was to prepare accounts for privatization by reclassifying public dividend capital as 180 million shares at £1 each. The privatization exercise was completed successfully in February 1987, with the government divesting its total shareholding.

**Group Investments**

BA has very large investments in computer and airport facilities. BA's operations are centered at Heathrow, which is one of the world's busiest airports with the most international passengers and destinations on offer.

---

[1] See Exhibits 8 and 9.

One of BA's largest investments was in the Concorde, an aircraft developed by British and European interests. The original idea to buy a Concorde had been an ambitious one, fraught with risks. On May 25, 1972, the Minister for Aerospace announced the government's approval for the company's decision to buy a Concorde and, referring to the risks involved, gave the assurance that the government would do all it could at the appropriate time to ensure the successful operation of the Concorde. On the same day, the Minister for Aerospace announced an increase in public dividend capital of £200 million. The succeeding government also committed itself to the same undertaking.

As a result of early losses, in February 1979 the government canceled £160 million of public dividend capital to allow Concorde assets to be fully written-off. (The Concorde, however, was eventually very successful.)

### Labor Relations

The general climate of labor relations in the United Kingdom (UK) had an impact on BA operations which was sometimes indirect, but nevertheless severe. For example, operating losses resulted from the steel strike of 1979–1980, a strike by air traffic control staff during the summer of 1981, a strike of ramp staff in early 1982, and the coal strike of 1984–1985.

BA considered labor relations management a matter of utmost importance throughout the company's history, maintaining that its labor relations performance was superior to British industry in general. In 1972 the new board of directors took advantage of the creation of British Airways to propose a new initiative to the trade unions, which it called an "Industrial Relations Charter". This led to the setting up of a Joint Manpower Advisory Council to examine manpower needs and policies.

However, annual reports registered complaints regularly about difficulties in labor relations. Attempts to improve operations often encountered resistance to change. For instance, the 1976–1977 Annual Report revealed one aspect of the problem between the company and its unions: "The urgent need is to move towards a higher productivity/higher wage organization. Given the complicated union structure of British Airways, the large number of agreements and the multiplicity of pay grades, the problems will require time and considerable goodwill to resolve." The complexity of the task of rationalizing pay structures was due to the proliferation of interested pressure groups over the years. For example, in 1978–1979 BA had to negotiate with eleven national selection panels on which seventeen trade unions were represented.

In 1978–1979 BA tried unsuccessfully to grow out of an overmanned position by increasing traffic volumes based on existing personnel. Redundancies were seen as politically unacceptable. From 1974 to 1980, labor disputes cost BA an average of 25,000 man-days per year.

### Regulatory Environment

The company's relationship with its governmental overseers was perhaps best expressed in the 1980–1981 chairman's statement, which declared that "when we find ourselves at issue with them we shall argue our case."

This ongoing adversarial approach was evident in the annual reports, which were replete with examples of open debate with national government, governmental bodies, and local interest groups.

### Outlook

Even before the privatization of BA in early 1987 there was an evident change in mood on the part of the government overseers as to the nature of the relationship that should be fostered with BA and the other nationalized industries. Nevertheless, statutory requirements dictated certain procedures and responsibilities in the relationship between the government and the nationalized industries that ruled out a *laissez faire* policy.

Indeed, it was still entirely possible that BA could revert back to nationalized industry status. As late as the October 1994 Labor Party conference, that party was steadfast in its long-standing determination to extend "social ownership" to key industries.

## Epilogue: The Post-Privatization Experience

Now in 1995 it is possible to look back and assess the post-privatization performance and behavior of BA and SIA.

### Singapore Airlines (SIA)

For SIA, privatization still did not remove the government's controlling interest, which stood at 54 percent. In fact, the only apparent change was the availability of equity, which was publicly tradable. SIA was able to utilize this new financial instrument to very good advantage in exchanging shares to cement cooperative relationships with other enterprises. For example, in 1991 SIA and Swissair exchanged shares in order to strengthen each party's commitment to an agreement on joint cooperation activities. In October 1989 SIA had announced a similar agreement with Delta Air Lines. SIA followed the industry trend by going on the acquisition trail, although Chairman Pillay repeatedly stressed that the company had no interest in going on a "diversification spree" or trying to become a "global mega-carrier" and would maintain a "disciplined approach to expansion." The 1992 annual report expressed SIA's interest in investing in Qantas Airlines, but that bid lost out to a bigger bid by British Airways.

Another advantage of marketable equity was increased financial strength. Because SIA shares were so attractive, the company was able to substitute debt with equity. The chairman's statement in the 1987–1988 annual report said, "For the first time in our history, we are free of debt."

The long-standing policy of fielding a young, modern fleet was still in place. In June 1994, SIA announced an order for 52 new aircraft (including options) worth US$10.3 billion, its largest order ever.

SIA continued to excel in its performance, despite the recessionary conditions of the early 1990s. In 1990 SIA was one of the top ten airlines in the world in terms of scheduled passengers carried (ranking tenth) and passenger-kilometers flown (ranking sixth); and among these ten industry leaders SIA ranked first in operating profits (Vandermere and Lovelock, 1991). In that year *Air Transport World* magazine named SIA "airline of the year" and *Business Traveler International* called SIA the "best international airline." By fiscal year-end March 31, 1994, SIA had moved up to rank 5 in passengers carried (from 10 in 1990) and was still number 1 in operating profits despite profitability consistently shrinking since 1990. The airline made a clean sweep at that year's Pacific Asia Travel Association award ceremony. Among other figures at an all-time high were capacity (ton-kilometers), revenues, staff strength, shareholder funds, and total assets. Unit costs were at an all-time low.

Finally, SIA's relationship with the government was essentially the same. The chairman was still J Y Pillay, who was still permanent secretary in the Ministry of Finance. An example to illustrate the ongoing intra-government cooperation was the Service Quality Centre, officially opened in July 1991. This training enterprise was a joint venture between SIA and the National Productivity Board dedicated to improving service quality in all areas of commercial life in Singapore.

### British Airways (BA)

Like SIA, BA was one of the world's few profitable airlines during the recessionary years of the early 1990s. Among the key performance measures for 1990 cited above concerning SIA, BA ranked first in scheduled passengers carried, first in scheduled passenger-kilometers performed, and fourth in operating profits.

BA's exploits since privatization, driven by a new mission statement "to be the best and most successful company in the airline industry," manifested an evident intent to become the top global "mega-carrier." Any role of government was now subdued as BA pursued an aggressive acquisition policy. In 1993 it beat out SIA in a bid for a 25-percent stake in Qantas for A$665 million, and finally obtained U.S. government approval to buy 24.6 percent of USAir for $300 million. In December 1992 BA purchased 49.9 percent of a French regional carrier. BA also set up fledgling airlines in Germany and Russia.

Also in 1993 a rather demoralizing row with a tiny British rival, Virgin Atlantic, was winding down. BA had been successfully sued by Virgin Atlantic's chairman for a "dirty tricks" campaign which, among other things, used illegal access to Virgin Atlantic's computers to steal customers. Although no BA directors were held responsible (there were only a small number of employees), this raised a discomforting question: Would BA have behaved so shamefully as a state-owned enterprise?

## Comparative Analysis of National Airlines

The focus of the following analysis is on the evaluation of the Singapore and British governments' role in their respective enterprises. The government role evolves essentially from the requirements of the "public enterprise" system such as the provision of public finance, and consequently the influence of politics and the bureaucracy, including the prevalence of noneconomic corporate goals.

### Origins

The original objectives of public enterprises (PEs) have been suggested in the literature (Millward and Parker, 1983; Aharoni, 1986) to have important explanatory power for behavior and performance. SIA's predecessor started out as a colonial venture, and the governments of Singapore and Malaysia stepped in to establish local ownership and control. When SIA became a Singapore firm it was an instrument in the national strategy to develop export markets. The Reconstruction Agreement of 1972 awarded SIA most of the international routes. Malaysia at that time was interested in regional routes, adhering more to an "import substitution" policy for development. In contrast, Singapore's economic policy, since separation from Malaysia in 1967, had evolved to an export-oriented strategy. This suggests an essential difference in the origins and initial corporate goals of SIA compared to BA.

BA had evolved from statutory corporations which were created partially for military-strategic purposes and partially with public service priorities. Specifically, in BEA's case, the task was to develop regional, economical air services, and BOAC's initial mission was to support the war effort. The development of both BEA and BOAC went hand-in-hand with the development of the British aircraft manufacturing industry, which gave rise to cross-subsidization. BEA's market was confined to Europe, while BOAC was assigned foreign policy objectives in the Commonwealth. BEA was charged with the social mission of developing cheap mass transportation for Britain. Here is ample evidence of a political, social orientation, whereas the Singapore government's long-standing purpose was more oriented on competitive strategy. Of course, international competitiveness must naturally be considered the underlying concern of BA's predecessor companies, and the normal business objectives of profitability, increased market share, and the like would be pursued. We see, however, some evidence of the "multiple objectives" problem of PEs described so frequently in the literature (see also later section on Objectives). Multiple objectives derive from social missions and the malleability of such priorities in a politically contentious society. Certainly, the "flurry of white papers" which set up BOAC and BEA after the war suggests competing forces at work. Nevertheless, wider objectives were more affordable in those early days, and the British airlines prospered.

Later evolution of the air transport industry in the U.K. developed around a policy to "divide the world" between BOAC and BEA, where the overall boundaries and rules of competition were decided by government edict. This policy was reinforced during the 1970s and 1980s because operating areas were repeatedly shuffled between BA and British Caledonian for the purpose of structural balance. The results were seldom happily accepted as indicated by frequent complaints in annual reports. And the government overseers were not always in agreement on airline and airport policy, such as in 1984 when the central government countermanded a Civil Aviation Authority idea to reduce the size of BA. It will be a central thesis, as this discussion progresses, that U.K. governmental interference was ongoing, inconsistent, and disruptive. The Singapore government's role, in contrast, was more proactive, unequivocal, and consistent toward long-term goal development.

### Management and Control

The organizational context that promoted such outstanding management teams as both companies manifested seemed to have several important aspects. One factor that may have contributed is public expectations. Both companies were national leaders in corporate performance and accepted that role confidently, rising to the occasion. This was made possible by good leadership, clearly a strength at SIA, and generally a healthy "organizational culture" in both companies. Another factor that may have contributed is high pay. As Millward and Parker (1983) have suggested, if management positions are well-paid, then the employment market will provide the best performers. The SIA chairman described his company's pay as being quite high, and it did not seem necessary to prove that fact for either company, as it was generally known to be the case in both countries. Indeed, "generous treatment of staff" was stated as an SIA corporate objective, and BA had a goal to be a "good employer." Anyway, top management was recruited on the open market at competitive remuneration.

The technological aspect also contributed to the favorable organizational culture in both enterprises. However, the case information indicates one distinction between the companies' performance, that BA was a world-pioneering company in air transport, while SIA was a follower company, albeit a close follower. SIA depended on BA specifically for some technology transfer, from inception throughout its corporate development. It has been suggested in the literature that follower countries have an advantage, as long as their costs are lower, in simply imitating successful leaders (Gerchenkron, 1962). As Singapore proceeded to catch up with the U.K. stage of development, this advantage evidently might subside, as indicated by worries expressed by Lee Kuan Yew.

In his Prime Minister's National Day Rally speech of August 1986, Lee reminisced about a conversation he had with Joe Pillay. Pillay had said, half in jest, that the government should divest its ownership in SIA because it was no longer a sunrise industry. Prime Minister Lee rephrased his old friend: "Our wages are going up so high we're already going up to high noon. We may go into sunset." Lee observed that neighboring airlines were emulating SIA's experience. "You ask SIA to compete with them . . . what will happen? It worries SIA's management and it worries me."

The primary means of government control in SIA was through the civil service members of the Board of Directors, although other means were apparent in the case. These included market control and *ad hoc* interventions (though interventions in support of, rather than to interfere with, company operations). The control mechanisms at BA were much more bureaucratic, as approval by the Minister of State is required for specific company actions. The Survey on Centralisation of Decision-Making (see Exhibit 11) also indicated that SIA had much more operational autonomy from the government. On the other hand, only BA had the nerve to openly question national policy matters which affected the company.

The fact that SIA was led by civil servants while BA directors were from the private sector would imply that SIA might be more encumbered by government bureaucracy. However, this interface with the government seems to be to SIA's advantage because the Singapore civil service is an elite corps of professionals and is more in tune with the national leadership than private directors would be. While British civil servants were certainly an excellent corps, the role of the British government in its enterprises is distinctly less productive than was the case in Singapore, as we will stress in the continuing analysis here. Indeed, the proximity to political and bureaucratic concerns was precisely the reason the U.K. did not often appoint civil servants as PE directors.

In Singapore that proximity is actually an advantage in that civil servants are important members of a cooperative national team. For example, Pillay was Managing Director of the government investment company that invested Singapore's foreign reserves and of the Monetary Authority of Singapore, Singapore's quasi-central bank, as well as Chairman of DBS and Temasek Holdings, among other positions. In the U.K., there is little evidence of intra-government cooperation; in fact the opposite circumstance was cited in Abromeit (1986): "The relationship [in the U.K.] between the various nationalized industries is by no means harmonious . . ." Therefore, the integration advantages that would result from putting civil servants on the board would be more than offset by the disadvantages ensuing from joining the company to the national bureaucracy.

Training is considered important by both companies. Training costs for SIA in the early 1980s averaged 2 percent of operating expenses, over 10 percent of total staff costs, and amounted to an average of nearly S$3,000 per employee annually. SIA's training priorities are also in line with national manpower development concepts, such as adopting the government's human relations and courtesy campaign ideas.

A courtesy drive program initiated at SIA in 1982 illustrates the well-known paternal character of manpower development in Singapore. A government-wide courtesy campaign had been well-publicized, commencing several years earlier. Many societies would consider such elaborate cajoling and coaching of a population to instill proper manners, work ethics, and the like to be an imposition, but social engineering is commonplace in Singapore (see, for example, Sikorski,1991). It may also seem surprising that both state-owned and private businesses would take up the government's slogans and appeals. For example, some of the country's leading private banks mimicked the courtesy campaign. A private company, Fraser & Neave Limited (whose chairman Michael Fam was also a SIA director), paid half a million dollars to sponsor a song, "Count on Me, Singapore," for the August 1986 National Day celebrations. This is one instance of behavior suggesting a significant sociocultural difference which, it may be argued, was itself a competitive advantage for Singapore. BA's annual reports did sometimes voice nationalistic sentiments, but SIA was more clearly "at one" with its government.

**Performance**

At the outset of this analysis of comparative performance of the two PEs, it must be noted that BA was operating out of an often struggling U.K. and European economy, while the Singapore and ASEAN economies outperformed most of the world. However, since the majority of ticket sales for both companies were overseas, and the overseas markets were not much confined to the airlines' respective regions, it did not seem necessary to account for different environmental economic conditions.

In terms of assets and net worth, both airlines have grown rapidly throughout their history, with brief hiccups in the 1980s. SIA grew faster, but from a much smaller base. SIA's profit margin was more consistent than BA's and frequently even higher, though not in the mid-1980s when BA was advertising itself, with some vindication, as "the most profitable airline in the world." In 1988, it was SIA that was ranked as the world's most profitable airline by *International Business Week*.

SIA's modern fleet was sustained by profits. The fact that the higher investment in aircraft was condoned by Temasek in the first place reveals an interesting characteristic of the Singapore government, that it was wealthy enough and aggressive enough in its desire to market national commercial services and upgrade its technology. The "high technology" aspect of SIA also contributed favorably to organizational culture.

It is clear that for SIA maximum financial viability was important while social obligation was not. Although it does not follow that for BA the opposite was true, there was a difference in "public purpose" between the two countries and hence their PEs. While SIA could concentrate exclusively on business efficiency, customer service, and other such "enterprise" concerns, BA had to address social issues and contend with political forces. Certainly both companies were ultimately most concerned with competing in the international marketplace, but BA operated in an environment where the "public purpose" was of a different character; at worst, the British and even their political parties were somewhat hostile to capitalism and business enterprise. This may have detracted from financial viability, as certainly was true in the instance of overmanning.

There is also a need to analyze non-financial factors in public enterprises. Menon and Jha (1980) suggested product quality, marketing effort, and human resource development. The quality of services at SIA and BA may be measured indirectly by their high ratings in market surveys. Marketing efforts bore clear results, that is, revenue increases and overall success.

Human resource management is reflected in training efforts. Although training was emphasized in both companies, Singapore PEs emphasized national training priorities, contributing to overall Singapore manpower development. This would seem to be an important advantage in less-developed countries using PEs as a development strategy.

Most productivity indicators were better for SIA than BA, at least up until BA's privatization. SIA's record in cost containment was especially good, with unit costs falling by 32 percent from 1981 to 1994. BA stated justifiable concern in the 1976–1977 Annual Report that it suffered from "the low productivity which is a feature of so much of the British economy."

### Objectives

If politics and social priorities are added to the enterprise's business objectives, surely some confusion must result. At BA this problem of "multiple objectives" was manifest. There were relatively frequent changes in the U.K. political leadership and an ongoing rotation of BA's directors. Throughout SIA's history the political scene in Singapore remained unchanged, and the only change in stated goals of the company represented a gradual, subtle shift in emphasis from national to commercial priorities. Even this change was of no real consequence because national priorities in Singapore were oriented anyway on national commerce.

An SIA objective which was not duplicated by BA concerned the airline's role in the national tourism effort. This provides an example of the national network of cooperative relationships that existed in Singapore among the key institutions. There could be no doubt about the synergistic relationship between SIA and the Singapore Tourist Promotion Board (STPB). In 1984 SIA's deputy chairman was appointed deputy chairman of the STPB, where he moved up to chairman in 1986.

BA's financial objectives entailed compliance with government-specified criteria, which may be seen as a constraint on the company's flexibility to decide its own operational priorities. Since governments would tend to use an overall cost/benefit analytical approach, profitability may have been a secondary criterion in deciding on required return on investment. Even financial viability may have been sacrificed for political considerations in the process of the formulation of financial targets by the minister of state and their approval by Parliament.

### Growth and Investment

Prior to privatization by both companies there seemed to be the same limited degree of restraint in diversification strategies, which may be characteristic of government ownership. In BA, the government might have been expected to object to an acquisition that may be perceived as predatory or anti-competitive. The perception may be political, or a particular competitor may object and bring unwanted attention to the government. BA's postprivatization behavior was much more free-wheeling (see epilogue). SIA's history does not provide much evidence of the government's response to group expansion, except that the company's strategy was to diversify only into activities which seem generally related to the airline business. That policy continued into the 1990s.

SIA's airport facilities and computer center illustrate the national scale of the company's investments and the pioneering position of the company in the country's development. The same was characteristic of BA also. Both companies could be presumed to operate generally at arms-length with the aviation/airport authorities, but both companies were the dominant concern of their respective authorities. In Singapore, there were "interlocking directorates" uniting SIA and the Civil Aviation Authority of Singapore (CAAS), another example of the network of cooperative relationships in the PE system.

Temasek Holdings provided a buffer for SIA whereby the airline was more free to formulate strategies and conduct its operations without direct interference by government. This represents one step towards decentralization, but where goals and constraints can still be established at a political level. In a democratic society, goals and constraints are implicitly reviewed by citizens. There was thus no sacrifice of "public purpose" at SIA, even after (partial) privatization.

### Privatization

The "privatization" concept was not mooted in Singapore until it was clearly known to be official policy, half a decade after the Thatcher Government's 1979 legislation was introduced, but SIA still preceded BA's public flotation of shares. The Singapore policy was deliberate and cautious, yet executed with a precision and decisiveness unimaginable at BA. While in Britain privatization meant a major ideological and practical change, in Singapore it was more a means of raising capital and strengthening the local equity market in addition to reinforcing market discipline over government enterprises.

Without a doubt, in Singapore both the government, through Temasek, and the company had benefited from the privatization exercise. One news caption a year after the flotation read, "SIA share sale pays off for government: Temasek stands to make $4 billion" (**The Straits Times**, October 31, 1986). This "paper" profit represented roughly the excess of share market value over Temasek's net cash cost since the inception of SIA. There was no devolution of government control at SIA — the Board of Directors was still 100-percent government-appointed. A further reduction in the Singapore government's ownership below 50 percent would reduce its formal hold on the company, but neither party seemed inclined to change a company-government relationship that had always been beneficial for all concerned.

**Financing**

Compared to the labor relations circumstance (analyzed later), the situation evident in financing was quite the obverse. In labor relations, the government of Singapore was intimately involved, while the U.K. government could seldom grapple successfully with their labor movement. In finance, the opposite situation prevailed as the U.K. government controlled BA's purse strings in minute detail, while the Singapore government was relatively detached from the everyday financial decision-making. (However, little is known about what went on behind the scenes in Singapore).

Debt/equity ratios at BA were dictated by the government. This important indicator is the classic measure of financial risk, that is, the risk of long-term viability. The British government, as guarantor of all long-term debt in addition to being the sole owner, would understandably want to dictate the level of risk. On the other hand, such business management procedures are hardly a usual tool of fiscal policy. The Singapore government did not make it a practice to guarantee debt, but certainly there was still a very real concern with SIA's level of risk. We may wonder what intervention would have occurred if SIA had ever come upon really hard times. Nevertheless, the fact remains that in BA's case the government prescribed the debt/equity ratio, while in SIA's case the government let Temasek and SIA do the worrying. A comparison of the debt/equity ratios between the two companies indicates that BA, where management control of the ratio was by the Minister of State, was far more conservative. A common prediction in the literature is that government managers may be more risk-averse.

Since both the absolute amount and the proportion of all financing at BA was controlled by the government, there was less room for financial maneuvering. The variety of financial instruments employed by SIA was impressive when compared to the larger and more sophisticated company, BA (until after its privatization). At BA, even foreign exchange losses were initially covered by a government plan, whereas SIA had to develop its own expertise in foreign exchange hedging. SIA's self-reliance in financial management enhanced its position of national leadership in management.

Temasek was not noted for generosity in the provision of capital. There were periods, such as prior to the 1981–1982 flotation, when equity capital was required but not readily provided. When finally the funding was provided it was at a price that was less generous, compared to the amount of asset backing per share, than the price of the public issue of 1985. The issue price paid was less than this very conservative measure of book value per share. Thus, contrary to SIA's critics, government provision of capital was not a subsidy, indeed quite the opposite as the government itself, through Temasek, benefited handsomely from its investment in SIA.

BA, like SIA, also seemed to find the government reluctant to provide equity. Both companies had been without all the tools available to publicly listed companies, such as rights issues, and raising new equity was difficult.

Debt financing in PEs seemed a more flexible process in SIA than in BA. SIA had more variety in its debt instruments, and particular borrowings did not seem to involve approval at political policy-making level. Bonds were not an available financing option at BA. Initial lease financing required explicit ministry approval in the U.K., while in Singapore Temasek alone provided approval. Temasek was interested as an investor rather than as a policy-maker.

Although Singapore has a well-developed financial center with an ample selection of foreign and local banks, the government-formed Development Bank of Singapore (DBS) seemed to occupy the pivot position in much of SIA's financing. An earlier study in Singapore also discovered that most of the public enterprises obtained credit from DBS (Lee,1978). Casual evidence suggests DBS itself was at the forefront of financial innovation in Singapore, making that bank a likely choice for new financing experiences by companies. DBS was SIA's bank for such first-time flotations as lease financing and the privatization share issue.

Both SIA and BA had some access to national loan funds. The purpose behind the government funding was different, for in Singapore money was provided for specific approved investments where the criteria for approval was the contribution toward national development. For BA, provision of funds was based on social needs. Budgeting processes in such countries as the U.K. were widely understood by political scientists to be an outcome of political competition between pressure groups representing the various interested potential recipients. In Singapore, such decision-making was more centralized, and interest group pressures are not welcomed by the government.

**Labor Relations**

In Singapore capital holds sway over labor. This was a major advantage for Singapore companies in general, the difference that is crucial in comparing SIA and BA.

At SIA, the balance of power clearly rested with the company, as illustrated by the pay negotiations. There were several notable differences between BA and SIA in the climate for negotiations. First, Singapore unions saw themselves in partnership with the company through the government, rather than in an adversarial relationship. The confrontational approach of "collective bargaining" was institutionalized, but union leaders had a milder approach, and there was not the obstructionist, resistance to change so evident in BA negotiations. Any strident disagreeableness would have been out of place in Singapore, even foolhardy, in the face of a government which does not tolerate the union's only real weapon, work stoppage. Second, wage policy is still largely dictated by government guidelines emanating from the National Wages Council (NWC). Although there was an announced intention to wean companies away from dependence on the NWC and toward independent company negotiations, neither management nor unions had developed a track record, and both were cautious to stand on their own. Third, the much less complex pay structure (and the smaller political sensitivity to unemployment) made the negotiation task considerably simpler at SIA. Undoubtedly SIA had an easier time than BA, resulting in considerable savings in several ways. Work stoppages were avoided, there was less need for elaborate negotiation machinery, and pay agreement packages, such as severance allowances, were probably less costly.

Both companies were in a position of national leadership in labor relations. In the general case it seems reasonable to suppose that any advantage or disadvantage for PE depended on the power and popular support of the government. BA purported to do better than the national record, and there was indirect support in the literature that this contention has historical validity. Pryke (1971) examined BA's predecessor companies, BOAC and BEA, and other nationalized industries, concluding that such enterprises might have an advantage in labor relations due to superior negotiating machinery.

In Singapore, it is doubtful the government would have been inclined to attempt such a direct role in a private company as they did in the SIAPA incident at SIA. Singapore's tough stand against pilot pay which preceded by several years similar cost-cutting measures by airlines in the advanced Western countries, illustrated how effectively change can be initiated from the top. This event was a convincing demonstration of government power and willingness to act decisively on behalf of national enterprises. Both BA and SIA may have had a collective bargaining advantage in their respective nations, but the overall advantage in labor relations was definitely Singapore's.

**Overt Government Participation**

The case studies and the survey response indicated a much greater (formal) government role in decision-making at BA than at SIA. However, the Singapore government did indeed participate, more often on an *ad hoc* basis, often to provide strategic or operational assistance.

In contrast to the numerous government-coordinated deals for Singapore PEs, there were evidently no early instances in the U.K. of the government playing such a direct or personalized role in the securing of new markets, or any "business agent" type of activity. The Thatcher government was known to engage in business negotiations abroad, for example, in a 1985 trip to Saudi Arabia which resulted in some help for the British aerospace industry. However, there was no record of any deals for BA secured by bureaucrats or politicians.

The U.K. government's major business venture in partnership with its airline (and its aerospace industry) was the investment in Concorde. By first putting up the required equity and then later allowing a write-off closely equivalent to the initial investment, the government was indeed indulgent. In contrast, Temasek provided partial funding, but no direct subsidy, for SIA's major fleet modernisation. The British government's rationale was partly to cross-subsidize its nationalized aerospace industry.

In labor relations, the British government found the labor movement to be a powerful adversary whenever it attempted to intervene. There did seem to be a difference between the two governments's ability and willingness to act on behalf of its business interests. Prime Minister Lee Kuan Yew, in his missions abroad for "Singapore Inc", resembled the venerable Armand Hammer, longtime (now deceased) Chairman of Occidental Petroleum in the U.S., combining statesmanship with business opportunism. An advantage that Lee had over Hammer was that he had an entire nation's resources in support and he was a government leader dealing with foreign government leaders who could match his proposals with requisite resources. This seemed an important competitive advantage favoring PE, especially when dealing with nations like China whose government, more so than Lee's, was at the helm of the nation's enterprises. An advantage Lee had over Thatcher was a smaller and less complex country to represent, which had a more tightly knit PE system, and a less political nation where the primary political concern was "business as usual."

There is some support here for the notion that PEs may have an advantage in securing business with socialist countries. In Lee Kuan Yew's 1985 trip to China we have an illustration of the very important role of civil service board members in Singapore's PEs. Ngiam Tong Dow, who was an SIA board member, coordinated the opportunities set up by the Prime

Minister. Indeed, through Ngiam it is likely that SIA played a proactive role in creating the proposals in the first place. Ngiam formerly chaired the Economic Development Board, which is Singapore's central development strategy coordinator, so a neat web of mutual support is easily perceived.

However, this advantage may be counterbalanced with a disadvantage in securing business with certain capitalist countries which have a bias against state ownership of enterprises. This possibility was underscored by Lee Kuan Yew in the 1986 Prime Minister's National Day Rally speech when he observed that Neptune Orient Lines, the national shipping company, should be divested of government ownership to avoid discrimination in America. U.S. laws originally aimed at communist countries affected all shippers with government ownership.

In contrast, BA manifests no similar intra-government or intra-national network of cooperative relationships: "The relationship, at least in Britain, between the various nationalized industries is by no means harmonious — a fact which, considering the lack of coordination between their 'sponsors', is hardly surprising . . ." (Abromeit, 1986:98)

**Business Environment**

There was an interesting contrast in the competition policies of Singapore vis-à-vis the U.K. with respect to their national airlines. The example of the creation of another government company, Changi International Airport Services (CIAS), illustrates the Singapore government's early use of competition as a means of control, contrary to a hypothesis of Cassesse (1981) that governments might preach but seldom actually utilize this means. CIAS was incorporated in December 1977, a joint venture between the Port of Singapore Authority (PSA) and seven private carriers which were not clients of SIA's own subsidiary Singapore Airport Terminal Services (SATS). The Prime Minister said in his August 1981 National Day speech, "We insisted against SIA's wishes that there shall be competition and PSA will move in." Once the competitive arrangement was in place, there did not appear to be any regulatory role for the government. In the small city-state of Singapore there is little room for the use of this formula on a much grander scale. Singapore is primarily concerned with national competition against the outside world, and internal competition is a means to that end. There is a strong respect in Singapore for market discipline, where it was in vogue long before Reagan and Thatcher made it part of their election platforms.

In the U.K., government went a step further than the creation of internal competitive arrangements; it attempted to prescribe what markets could be exploited, even how big the companies should be. Singapore's governmental role may be seen as pro-business, development-oriented, and pragmatic, while the U.K. government's role was ideological, erratic, and more concerned with regulatory control and "fair" distribution rather than development of enterprise. In Singapore, the competitive environment seemed more supportive than that in the U.K. where the Civil Aviation Authority, British Airports Authority, national and local governments, and special interests frequently were pulling in different directions, and not necessarily for the good of the company. In Singapore, there is more evidence of teamwork, and the only difficult encounters are with overseas authorities and international competitors.

BA's government overseers were not always in agreement on airline and airport policy, such as when the central government countermanded the Civil Aviation Authority's idea to reduce the size of BA. BA appealed to the government on other matters less successfully, such as an appeal for approval for financial reconstruction made publicly in successive annual reports. BA repeatedly objected about airport policy and allocation of markets, and some of these issues are still unresolved. There was even a major political controversy as to the future of nationalized industries as a whole. Thus, government interference was ongoing and inconsistent.

The most significant impact of the adversarial, checks-and-balances relationship among BA and its overseers was instability in the planning environment. The company complained plaintively and often about "uncertainty." Debates were open, arms-length attempts at resolution among all parties concerned, and the company never seemed to know its future until the government, sometimes amidst considerable acrimony, deliberated on the arguments and passed judgement. Even this decision could be reversed by a new government or even the existing one if there was a change in political opinion in the Parliament. The Concorde decision required endorsement by successive governments, despite financial commitments having already been made. Even privatization could be reversed, as had happened to some of the firms which had been denationalized by Winston Churchill's postwar government. The Singapore approach seemed to allow a less contentious, less political, and more business-like deliberation of practical business matters.

### Recapitulation and Outlook

The two case studies provide insight into the nature of centralization and autonomy of decision-making in state enterprise systems. Although both SIA and BA were excellent companies, the impact of government ownership was decidedly different in each case. The Singapore PE had much less political and social orientation except that the government was ready to act to protect the organization's financial viability or other interests. In contrast, BA was seriously inhibited by government and pressure groups. At privatization in 1987 BA's chairman observed, "Our newly won independence gives us the opportunity to exploit for the first time the full potential of the company."

Throughout its history SIA had been one of the few consistently profitable airlines in an industry that had been through extremely turbulent conditions. The mid-1970s and early 1980s had been disastrous times for world airlines, but the early 1990s were nearly as bad. Members of the International Air Transport Association (IATA) lost $1.7 billion in 1981 and $500 million in 1992. Although the 1993 loss was projected as only half that, profit margins everywhere were squeezed. With the vicissitudes of the international economy since the 1970s, the sensitivity of international competitors to any perceived advantage held by particular participants was especially marked in the airlines industry. Charges abounded of governments providing "structural and other market support to [their] own airlines" (Tillinghast, 1979:4). Amid a clamour of allegations that competing with state-owned airlines was "like getting in a bleeding contest with a blood bank" (Meyer, 1982), SIA steadfastly denied any unfair practices and countered with a staunch advocacy of "open skies" policies. SIA still was controlled by government owners and thereby had the competitive advantage of its position in a cooperative network of people and institutions.

EXHIBIT 1

**PERFORMANCE OF SINGAPORE AND BRITISH AIRLINES**

SINGAPORE AIRLINES LIMITED: Performance
(million S$)

| | *Group: Total Revenue* | *Net Profit* | *Net Worth* | *Company: Operating Revenue* | *Operating Profit* | *Fixed Assets* | *Capacity (million ton-km)* |
|---|---|---|---|---|---|---|---|
| 1973–74 | — | 23.3 | 95.6 | 404.4 | 57.3 | 326.4 | 649.6 |
| 1974–75 | 589.4 | 38.5 | 170.5 | 543.3 | 44.3 | 480.9 | 853.8 |
| 1975–76 | 751.8 | 37.8 | 198.2 | 695.5 | 44.7 | 434.8 | 1,064.4 |
| 1976–77 | 962.4 | 42.3 | 231.2 | 867.8 | 74.6 | 335.3 | 1,267.2 |
| 1977–78 | 1,250.2 | 42.6 | 269.1 | 1,132.0 | 93.1 | 488.3 | 1,567.1 |
| 1978–79 | 1,605.3 | 60.8 | 310.3 | 1,472.7 | 119.1 | 765.6 | 2,050.0 |
| 1979–80 | 2,034.3 | 88.7 | 394.4 | 1,861.3 | 25.7 | 1,591.3 | 2,537.8 |
| 1980–81 | 2,458.4 | 116.5 | 503.4 | 2,262.9 | 70.7 | 2,132.8 | 2,923.3 |
| 1981–82 | 2,707.1 | 120.6 | 1,026.4 | 2,497.2 | 78.0 | 1,800.4 | 3,338.2 |
| 1982–83 | 2,813.7 | 100.7 | 1,126.9 | 2,596.3 | 38.6 | 1,640.3 | 3,614.5 |
| 1983–84 | 2,947.4 | 136.9 | 1,255.2 | 2,683.7 | 57.5 | 2,336.3 | 3,778.8 |
| 1984–85 | 3,161.5 | 176.0 | 1,625.6 | 2,831.3 | 25.6 | 3,137.0 | 4,172.0 |
| 1985–86 | 3,174.6 | 285.0 | 2,267.6 | 3,006.0 | 121.7 | 3,608.2 | 4,393.1 |
| 1986–87 | 3,483.0 | 451.2 | 2,666.9 | 3,274.1 | 385.8 | 3,554.4 | 4,702.7 |
| 1987–88 | 4,010.9 | 602.6 | 3,207.7 | 3,778.2 | 476.6 | 3,617.8 | 5,136.5 |
| 1988–89 | 4,566.1 | 985.3 | 4,097.8 | 4,271.8 | 865.1 | 3,925.8 | 5,682.7 |
| 1989–90 | 5,093.1 | 1,200.6 | 5,499.4 | 4,730.7 | 1,128.9 | 4,515.2 | 6,280.3 |
| 1990–91 | 4,948.1 | 912.8 | 6,233.4 | 4,601.7 | 841.5 | 4,959.8 | 6,644.3 |
| 1991–92 | 5,421.0 | 928.4 | 7,045.9 | 5,012.7 | 863.7 | 5,875.7 | 7,624.4 |
| 1992–93 | 5,648.2 | 850.6 | 7,688.8 | 5,134.6 | 655.0 | 6,728.6 | 8,982.3 |
| 1993–94 | 6,236.4 | 801.0 | 8,279.2 | 5,560.5 | 534.1 | 7,641.6 | 10,156.0 |

EXHIBIT 1 (cont'd)

## PERFORMANCE OF SINGAPORE AND BRITISH AIRLINES

BRITISH AIRWAYS: Performance
(million £)

| | *Group: Total Revenue* | *Net Profit* | *Net Worth* | *Company: Operating Revenue* | *Operating Profit* | *Fixed Assets* | *Capacity (million ton-km)* |
|---|---|---|---|---|---|---|---|
| 1973–74 | 646.9 | 16.6 | 236.1 | — | — | 468.1 | 6,077 |
| 1974–75 | 748.1 | –9.4 | 305.9 | 671.0 | 1.3 | 511.2 | 5,832 |
| 1975–76 | 916.1 | –16.3 | 343.0 | 813.5 | 2.3 | 566.1 | 6,247 |
| 1976–77 | 1,247.9 | 35.1 | 377.9 | 1,125.8 | 88.3 | 620.0 | 6,555 |
| 1977–78 | 1,355.3 | 36.9 | 528.6 | 1,206.4 | 56.5 | 767.6 | 6,793 |
| 1978–79 | 1,640.3 | 77.3 | 455.6 | 1,454.5 | 76.2 | 766.6 | 7,557 |
| 1979–80 | 1,919.6 | 10.5 | 473.5 | 1,688.9 | 12.6 | 951.7 | 8,153 |
| 1980–81 | 2,060.6 | –145.1 | 349.7 | 1,806.2 | 108.7 | 1,058.8 | 8,243 |
| 1981–82 | 2,241.3 | –544.2 | –192.1 | 1,924.7 | 0.9 | 882.4 | 7,522 |
| 1982–83 | 2,496.5 | 88.6 | –117.4 | 2,080.9 | 163.1 | 1,005.5 | 7,208 |
| 1983–84 | 2,513.7 | 214.5 | 126.5 | 2,267.9 | 271.4 | 1,186.6 | 7,194 |
| 1984–85 | 2,942.5 | 176.1 | 286.9 | (no longer reported) | | 1,171.3 | 7,837 |
| 1985–86 | 3,149.0 | 181 | 482.0 | | | 1,239.0 | 8,601 |
| 1986–87 | 3,263.0 | 152 | 606.0 | | | 1,263.0 | 8,751 |
| 1987–88 | 3,756.0 | 151 | 634.0 | | | 1,773.0 | 10,083 |
| 1988–89 | 4,257.0 | 175 | 750.0 | | | 2,396.0 | 11,868 |
| 1989–90 | 4,838.0 | 246 | 1,232.0 | | | 2,357.0 | 12,445 |
| 1990–91 | 4,937.0 | 95 | 1,278.0 | | | 2,990.0 | 13,351 |
| 1991–92 | 5,224.0 | 395 | 1,604.0 | | | 3,425.0 | 13,818 |
| 1992–93 | 5,566.0 | 178 | 1,534.0 | | | 3,472.0 | 15,424 |
| 1993–94 | 6,303.0 | 286 | | | | | 16,913 |

Source: Annual reports.

## EXHIBIT 2

## PRODUCTIVITY OF SINGAPOREAN AND BRITISH AIRLINES

| | Singapore Airlines | | | | | British Airways | | | |
|---|---|---|---|---|---|---|---|---|---|
| | (1) | (2) | (3) | (5) | (6) | (1) | (2) | (4) | (7) |
| 1974 | 63.0 | 54.0 | 53.0 | 99.2 | 81.1 | 55.4 | 49.9 | 8.4 | — |
| 1975 | 60.0 | 55.0 | 58.0 | 106.4 | 99.0 | 55.6 | 55.8 | 11.4 | — |
| 1976 | 64.0 | 60.2 | 61.0 | 101.5 | 109.8 | 55.5 | 55.3 | 12.8 | — |
| 1977 | 66.2 | 59.4 | 61.1 | 102.9 | 127.1 | 57.9 | 52.5 | 14.9 | — |
| 1978 | 68.1 | 59.2 | 62.2 | 105.1 | 153.1 | 57.9 | 55.0 | 16.2 | 72 |
| 1979 | 70.0 | 60.4 | 61.6 | 102.0 | 168.3 | 61.6 | 58.2 | 17.6 | 84 |
| 1980 | 70.6 | 67.9 | 70.2 | 103.4 | 187.7 | 64.6 | 64.0 | 20.1 | 96 |
| 1981 | 68.8 | 65.8 | 73.7 | 112.0 | 223.7 | 60.7 | 64.5 | 22.6 | 94 |
| 1982 | 71.5 | 68.3 | 71.2 | 104.3 | 241.6 | 63.0 | 62.7 | 24.8 | 100 |
| 1983 | 68.6 | 67.3 | 70.3 | 104.5 | 246.0 | 63.4 | 58.0 | 26.1 | 117 |
| 1984 | 70.6 | 66.1 | 66.3 | 100.3 | 278.8 | 63.4 | 55.2 | 27.1 | 129 |
| 1985 | 71.5 | 68.7 | 65.1 | 94.7 | 293.3 | 66.1 | 58.2 | 29.8 | 143 |
| 1986 | 71.1 | 69.4 | 64.3 | 92.7 | 294.2 | 64.8 | 59.8 | 30.4 | 146 |
| 1987 | 72.4 | 64.3 | 59.2 | 92.0 | 314.2 | 64.7 | 60.4 | 30.9 | 146 |
| 1988 | 73.4 | 63.3 | 61.8 | 97.6 | 350.2 | 67.3 | 62.2 | 30.5 | 161 |
| 1989 | 74.3 | 58.8 | 58.3 | 99.2 | 371.9 | 67.0 | 61.1 | 30.0 | 164 |
| 1990 | 73.9 | 58.3 | 57.8 | 99.2 | 381.3 | 68.9 | 62.8 | 32.5 | 171 |
| 1991 | 71.0 | 61.3 | 58.4 | 95.2 | 344.6 | 66.8 | 64.3 | 32.7 | 165 |
| 1992 | 69.9 | 60.5 | 54.9 | 90.8 | 355.2 | 65.6 | na | 32.2 | 181 |
| 1993 | 67.8 | 62.2 | 50.6 | 81.3 | 428.2 | 66.2 | na | 30.1 | 211 |
| 1994 | 69.5 | | 49.8 | | | 66.5 | | | 228 |

Notation of productivity measures:
(1) = capacity utilization (%)
(2) = capacity breakeven (%)
(3) = unit costs (cents/ton-km)
(4) = unit costs (pence/ton-km)
(5) = unit yield (cents/ton-km)
(6) = revenue per employee (S$ '000)
(7) = revenue ton-km per employee (£ '000)

Source: Annual reports.

## EXHIBIT 3

## SINGAPORE AIRLINES' EQUITY FINANCING UP TO PRIVATIZATION

| *Date* | *Instrument* | *NBVPS** | *Shares (mil)* | *Price* | *Amount (mil S$)* |
|---|---|---|---|---|---|
| 1972 | capitalization of net worth | S$1.00 | 61.0 | S$1.00 | 61.0 |
| 1974–1975 | share issue | S$1.35 | 30.0 | S$1.00 | 30.0 |
| | share dividend | | 24.4 | S$1.00 | |
| 1981–1982 | rights issue | S$4.12 | 103.86 | S$3.89 | 400.0 |
| Dec 1985 | share dividend | | 284.8 | S$1.00 | |
| | non-rights public offering | S$3.66 | 50.0 | S$5.00 | 250.0 |

*NBVPS stands for "Net Book Value Per Share" based on year-end figures. SIA announced "net tangible assets per share" for the privatization issue of S$3.27, based on internal calculations.

Source: Annual reports.

EXHIBIT 4

## SINGAPORE AIRLINES' DEVELOPMENT FUND LOANS

| *Disbursed* | *Paid off* | *Amount (mil S$)* | *Interest* |
|---|---|---|---|
| 1972–1973 | 4/1/79 | 5.0 | 6.5% |
| 1973–1974 | 4/1/79 | 0.35 | 6.5% |
| 1974–1975 | 4/1/78 | 30.0 | 9.0% |
| 1976–1977 | 4/1/89 | 24.6 | 5.5% |
| 1977–1978 | 4/1/87 | 146.4 | 6.95% |

Note: Foreign exchange was borrowed on the international market by the government and passed on to SIA in terms of local currency. Interest was determined from the original instrument. As of March 31, 1986, S$128,456,448.13 was outstanding.

Source: Singapore Accountant-General Financial Statements.

EXHIBIT 5

## SINGAPORE AIRLINES DEBT/EQUITY RATIOS BEFORE PRIVATIZATION

| | |
|---|---|
| 1973 | 3.59 |
| 1974 | 3.57 |
| 1975 | 2.29 |
| 1976 | 1.92 |
| 1977 | 1.59 |
| 1978 | 1.91 |
| 1979 | 2.82 |
| 1980 | 4.35 |
| 1981 | 4.64 |
| 1982 | 2.94 |
| 1983 | 2.46 |
| 1984 | 1.94 |
| 1985 | 1.62 |
| 1986 | 0.90 |
| 1987 | 0.52 |

Source: Calculated from financial statements (loans/net worth).

EXHIBIT 6

## BRITISH AIRWAYS PLC
## BOARD OF DIRECTORS AS OF APRIL 1, 1994

| *Name* | *Position* |
|---|---|
| Lord King of Wartnaby | President |
| Sir Colin Marshall | Chairman |
| Sir Michael Angus | Deputy Chairman |
| Robert Ayling | Managing Director |
| Derek Stevens | Finance Director |
| Captain Colin Barnes | |
| Michael Davies | |
| Sir Francis Kennedy | |
| Charles Mackay | |
| Baroness O'Cathlan | |
| The Hon CH Price II | |

| *Members Who Have Departed from the Board Since Privatization* | |
|---|---|
| Lord King of Wartnaby, President (formerly Chairman) | Resigned 1993 |
| Robert Henderson | Resigned July 1989 |
| Basil Collins | Resigned 1988–1989 |
| Gordon Dunlop | Resigned 1988–1989 |
| Jack Jessup | Resigned March 1991 |
| Henry Lambert | Resigned December 1989 |
| Lord White of Hull | Resigned 1992–1993 |

EXHIBIT 7

## SINGAPORE AIRLINES LTD
## BOARD OF DIRECTORS AS OF APRIL 1, 1994

| *Name* | *Position* |
|---|---|
| J Y Pillay | Chairman |
| Lim Chin Beng | Deputy Chairman |
| Cheong Choong Kong | Managing Director |
| Michael Yo Fam | |
| Ngiam Tong Dow | |
| Wan Soon Bee | |

There have been no departing board members or new members since privatization.

EXHIBIT 8

## BRITISH AIRWAYS: EQUITY FINANCING BEFORE PRIVATIZATION

(in million £)

| *Instrument* | *1974* | *1975* | *1976* | *1977* | *1978* | *1979* | *1980* | *1981* | *1982* | *1983* | *1984* | *1985* |
|---|---|---|---|---|---|---|---|---|---|---|---|---|
| Public Dividend Capital | | | | | | | | | | | | |
| Net annual amount | 11 | 80 | 64 | 10 | 10 | –150 | 10 | 10 | 10 | | | –180 |
| Balance | 136 | 216 | 280 | 290 | 300 | 150 | 160 | 170 | 180 | 180 | 180 | 0 |
| Called Up Share Capital | | | | | | | | | | | | 180 |

EXHIBIT 9

## BRITISH AIRWAYS: DEBT FINANCING BEFORE PRIVATIZATION

(in million £)

| *Instrument* | *1974* | *1975* | *1976* | *1977* | *1978* | *1979* | *1980* | *1981* | *1982* | *1983* | *1984* | *1985* |
|---|---|---|---|---|---|---|---|---|---|---|---|---|
| National Loan Fund | | | | | | | | | | | | |
| Net annual loan | –36 | –36 | 28 | –24 | –23 | –15 | –6 | –6 | 7 | 1 | –42 | |
| Balance | 116 | 80 | 108 | 84 | 61 | 46 | 40 | 34 | 41 | 42 | 0 | |
| Capital borrowings (commercial banks) | | | | | | | | | | | | |
| Net annual loan | 7 | –4 | 4 | 28 | 99 | 54 | 162 | 295 | 231 | 32 | –110 | –252 |
| Balance | 110 | 106 | 110 | 138 | 237 | 291 | 453 | 748 | 979 | 1011 | 901 | 649 |

## EXHIBIT 10
## BRITISH AIRWAYS PLC: DEBT/EQUITY RATIOS BEFORE PRIVATIZATION

| | |
|---|---|
| 1974 | 0.96 |
| 1975 | 0.61 |
| 1976 | 0.64 |
| 1977 | 0.59 |
| 1978 | 0.56 |
| 1979 | 0.74 |
| 1980 | 1.04 |
| 1981 | 2.24 |
| 1982 | undefined |
| 1983 | undefined |
| 1984 | 7.12 |
| 1985 | 2.25 |
| 1986 | 0.79 |
| 1987 | 0.49 |
| 1988 | 1.34 |

Source: Calculated from financial statements (loans/net worth).

EXHIBIT 11

## A MARKET SURVEY

To obtain an assessment of the nature of centralization or autonomy in Singapore, a questionnaire was distributed. It was administered by interview to Singapore Airlines and British Airways, before privatization in each case. Results are shown in the table below.

TABLE: SURVEY ON CENTRALIZATION OF DECISION-MAKING

| | Response to Questionnaire | |
|---|---|---|
| *List of Decisions* | *Singapore Airlines* | *British Airways* |
| Corporate plan | F1 | A3 |
| Operational budgets | E1 | E1 |
| Corporate objectives | F1 | E1 |
| Pricing strategy | F1 | F1 |
| Pay structure: labor | F1 | F1 |
| Pay structure: management | F1 | F1 |
| Pay change: company | F1 | E1 |
| Pay change: executive | F1 | E1 |
| Union agreement | F1 | F1 |
| New company union | F1 | F1 |
| Retrenchment | F1 | E2 |
| Hiring/firing management | F1 | F1 |
| Hiring/firing CEO | E1 | E4 |
| Expand existing operations | E1 | E2 |
| Diversification | C2 | E2 |
| Rationalization | E1 | E2 |
| R&D | F1 | E/F1 |
| Commercialize R&D | F1 | E/F1 |
| Overseas investment | E1 | E2 |
| Joint venture: local | E1 | E/F1 |
| Joint venture: foreign | E1 | E2 |
| Vendor: local | F1 | E/F1 |
| Vendor: foreign | F1 | E/F1 |
| New customer | — | F1 |
| New bank: ST credit | E1 | A4 |
| New bank: LT credit | E1 | A4 |
| Flotation | C1 | A3 |
| Dividend | C1 | A3 |

The table summarizes the letter-number responses to a questionnaire which asked, "Who was the last person whose assent must be obtained before legitimate action is taken even if others have subsequently confirmed the decision?" Choices were listed as follows:

*Last person*: (A) Ministry, (B) Other government, (C) Holding company, (D) Company Board of Directors, (E) Company executive management, (F) Other company management.

*The decision is*: (1) Made by enterprise, (2) Made by enterprise in consultation with government, (3) Made jointly be enterprise and government, (4) Made by government in consultation with enterprise, (5) Made by government.

At each company a meeting was held with an executive, who suggested a particular letter-number combination to describe the nature of the decision-making process for each policy issue listed.

The obvious conclusion of the survey exercise: In the United Kingdom the government was clearly much more involved in operational decision-making, while the Singapore state-owned enterprise seemed relatively autonomous. A review of the table reveals that in the U.K., the government had to approve more decisions and at higher levels (as indicated by more frequency of the letter A): and the government participated more in the formulation of decisions (as indicated by higher numerical responses).

Inaccurate answers were certainly possible in these interviews. An obvious instance was the SIA answer concerning the hire/fire decision for the Chief Executive. SIA's Chairman Pillay was a close associate of Lee Kuan Yew even before the latter became Prime Minister. Pillay's appointment likely was a very personal choice of the Prime Minister, yet the data indicates a decision by the Board of Directors without government influence.

In an attempt to alleviate the bias of only one response, the same questionnaire was modified for mailing to a sample of 32 Singapore PEs, which was accomplished during 1987–1988. This resulted in only 11 usable responses. Most companies did not answer at all, two responded that the questionnaire was not applicable to them, and one (the national shipping line) declined response "due to the sensitivity of the issue." Such sensitivity was a real obstacle to researching government activities in Singapore and probably explains the fact that few questionnaires were returned at all.

All PEs surveyed were commercial firms. There was no control for deviations in responses resulting from different percentages of government ownership, which ranged from 12 to 100 percent.

In terms of the letter response ("Last person"), over 90 percent of all decisions did not require government approval. A government role was reported at Ministry level by one company for the corporate plan, hiring/firing the Chief Executive Officer (CEO), as well as "Other government" approval for domestic joint ventures. That particular company was one of the largest manufacturing firms in Singapore, and evidently there was a perceived scrutiny from top government officials. One other firm required Ministry approval for new share and bond issues and dividends. The need for approval by the government's holding company was a more commonly cited centralizing factor, which was generally confined to financial decisions including new share and bond issues, dividends, joint ventures, foreign investment, and acquisitions.

In terms of the numerical response (Who makes the decision?), only numbers 1 and 2 were reported, except for one 5 by the abovementioned large firm which had indicated that its CEO was selected by the Ministry. Still, less than 7 percent of the decisions had any government input (number 2, 3, 4 and 5 responses). Three of the 11 firms responding reported government involvement in hiring/firing the CEO.

The mailed survey was not statistically useful but did serve to confirm the general, if not the specific results, of the interview at SIA. The overall exercise leads to a conclusion that the Singapore public enterprise system is quite autonomous in its everyday operations, though the government exerts an extremely strong influence indirectly, as in selecting key personnel.

Though not explicitly tested, the question of power is crucial. Of course, it is the power of the central government that explains how very effective control could be maintained over the public enterprise system, often on an *ad hoc* basis without requiring explicitly legislated supervisory systems to cover all contingencies as in the U.K. Indeed, the underlying implication is that the power of the executive branch of the Singapore government is the basis for competitive advantage — for PEs, and for the country as a whole.

# Malaysia Airlines and Its Media Image in the "Visit Malaysia Year"* 7

When the government declared 1990 as the "Visit Malaysia Year" (VMY), it was an effort to boost tourism in the country. As the national flag carrier, Malaysia Airlines had a significant role to play in ensuring the success of Visit Malaysia Year. By all indications, it had the capacity to do so. By then MAS had spread its wings to over 70 destinations around the world; it had acquired the most modern aircraft; its cabin crew were widely acclaimed for their charm and courtesy; and its participation in international activities organized locally and abroad have placed Malaysia on the tourism map. These achievements were in line with the airline's corporate objectives (see Exhibit 1).

Malaysia Airlines, or the Malaysian Airline System (MAS) as it was then known, took to the skies on October 1, 1972. Its history began in 1937 when Malaysia Airways Ltd was incorporated but it was 10 years later that the airline began operations. The early routes covered domestic and regional destinations (see Appendix A in this case for background information on MAS).

Up until October 1, 1972, the airline was run jointly with Singapore. But on that date, the partnership was dissolved and the Malaysian Airline System (MAS) spread its wings to fly on its own. Saw Huat Lye from the Ministry of Transport was appointed General

---

* This case was written by Sharifah Mariam bte Syed Mansor to serve as a basis for class discussion rather than to illustrate either effective or ineffective handling of an administrative situation. 

Manager and was given the task of ironing out the legalities involved in the splitting of the Malaysia-Singapore Airlines (MSA). Encik Abdul Aziz bin Abdul Rahman, then 39, from the Malaysian Judicial and Legal Service was appointed Secretary and Legal Affairs Manager. About that time too, a 29-year-old graduate with a Bachelor of Commerce degree from the University of Melbourne resigned from Shell to join the infant airline. That young man was Jaafar Abdul Manaf.

In March 1982, Tan Sri Abdul Aziz was appointed Managing Director (MD) of the airline. From the outset, he was aware that MAS was a high-profile company and that its public image should always be protected and promoted. In March 1984, Jaafar Abdul Manaf was appointed Public Affairs Manager. Prior to the appointment, he was Human Resources and Development Manager in the Personnel Division (see Appendix B in this case for information on Tan Sri Abdul Aziz and Encik Jaafar and Appendix C in this case for information on the Public Affairs Department).

Recalling his appointment, Jaafar, or Jeff, as he was more popularly known, said:

> I had been in the personnel division for almost 10 years and felt that I had gained enough experience as airport manager (Kuala Lumpur) and manager of the MAS London Office. In December 1983, I informed the managing director concerning my desire to move to another department, and 3 months later I was appointed public affairs manager (PAM). The managing director told me that he expected change. I promised him delivery within 3 months. And this I did.

One of the main areas that Jeff addressed his energies to was that of the image of the airline — MAS had to be seen as being at par with or better than the other airlines in the region. The MAS image suffered much in the 1970s. In 1977, an MAS plane was hijacked and bombed, killing all on board. Two years later, MAS experienced the worst ever strike which crippled all operations.

His experience as airport manager taught Jeff about the importance of customers while his experience in personnel helped him to develop good rapport with staff of all levels. He is the listening ear, the counselor, and the confidante. He recognizes that people are a company's strongest asset and that they have the capacity to grow with the company. Thus, the importance of training and human resource development.

Jeff knows that for the airline to succeed, all divisions, departments, and sections have to cooperate and play their part. To that end, he obtained the managing director's approval to set up a corporate image committee which comprised division, department, and section heads.

Together with the public relations manager, Siew Yong Gnanalingam, Jeff built up a strong relationship with the press and the broadcast media, which generated extensive publicity for the airline.

**Smooth Sailing**

By 1990, MAS had demonstrated tremendous growth. Its 10-year statistical review showed the airline expanding in all areas. Financially, it had generated a total revenue of \$2.4 billion by 1990 compared to \$825.7 million in 1980–1981. In 1981, the company made a loss of \$35.2 million, but in 1983, a year after Tan Sri Abdul Aziz was made Managing Director, it recovered to gain a profit of \$95.19 million. From then on it has been smooth sailing for MAS. By the first quarter of 1990, profit after tax was \$221.9 million.

In terms of network size (total distance of routes covered), MAS expanded from 87,467 km to 191,243 km. As of December 1989, the route network of MAS was 71 destinations

(38 international and 33 domestic, including 16 rural destinations). This was a far cry from the 33 domestic destinations at the time of the split of the Malaysia-Singapore Airlines in 1972.

In terms of passengers carried, 1980 charted a total number of 4,151,000 but by 1989–1990, the number almost doubled to 7,873,000. Significant increases were also seen in the amount of cargo and mail carried. In terms of employment, MAS had a total of 14,013 employees by March 31, 1990, as compared to 9,327 in 1980–1981 (see Exhibit 2).

In 1987 the MAS logo of a solid red "Wau Bulan"[1] was changed to a more aerodynamic shape of red, blue and white, the colors of the Malaysian flag. The name of the airline was also changed from Malaysian Airline System to Malaysia Airlines.

Up to 1989, the image of the airline had been strong. During that year, MAS won the Pride of Excellence Award by Boeing; Managing Director Tan Sri Abdul Aziz was accorded recognitions and honors locally and abroad among management, academic, and aviation circles. The airline's successful negotiations for new landing rights and increases in landing frequencies were widely acclaimed by the media.

The staff was always reminded to strive for excellence. As early as 1982, the Esprit de MAS committee, which was represented by all unions, staff associations, and management launched a campaign on the theme "Better Always." The campaign sought to inculcate in the staff a sense of commitment and loyalty based on mutual respect for one another regardless of rank and department, to strive for greater efficiency and productivity, to encourage a positive attitude and to preserve the good name of the company.

In October 1988, a "Towards Service Excellence" campaign was launched, also by the Esprit de MAS Committee. A three-pronged corporate philosophy was incorporated during the campaign covering service, staff, company, and corporate aspects. The aim was to imbue in the staff the need for excellence in customer service, to be service-conscious, and to project an orientation toward customers (see Exhibit 3).

Tan Sri Abdul Aziz in one of his speeches said,

> The purpose of a business is to get and keep customers. Without customers in sufficient and steady numbers, there is no business and profit. No business can function effectively without a clear view of how to get customers, what its prospective customers want and need, and what options its competitors give them.

Up until late 1989, media coverage accorded to MAS had been extensive in terms of frequency, amount of space given, and the use of photographs. In 1989 alone the media highlighted MAS' generous donations in support of various activities such as tourism, sports, culture, and the arts.

The airline's efforts to promote tourism included the MAS Celebrity Tennis, the Malaysia Kite Festival, and the International Kite Festival. It also contributed toward sporting activities such as the Mount Kinabalu Climbathon, the Trans-Borneo Rally, the MAS Penang Bridge International Marathon, the Terengganu Marathon, the TDC-MAS Tour of Malaysia Golf Series, the World Sepak Takraw Championship and the MAS Tourism Cup Soccer Tournament. In the arts arena, MAS played a significant role in the Golden Voices of Kuala Lumpur, World Golden Kite Song Festival, the Asian Folk Festival,

---

[1]An impressive and beautiful kite originally from the state of Kelantan.

Titian MAS, the Malaysia Fest activities, and the promotion of Malaysian food and culture in Vienna, Taipei, Fukuoka, Perth, Mauritius, Dubai, and Bandar Seri Begawan. All these were given wide media coverage. The media also highlighted a special performance by the MAS Orchestra, the MAS Gamelan Troupe, and the MAS Cultural Group at the historic Commonwealth Heads of Government Meeting (CHOGM).

National radio and television stations also provided extensive coverage of MAS in the news and documentary programs. The popular Radio Malaysia Ibu Kota gave MAS an exclusive one hour (9:00–10:00 am) musical program slot for publicity purposes.

**Storm Clouds**

Around December 1989, storm clouds of trouble began brewing. The MAS Employees Union (MASEU) met with Tan Sri Abdul Aziz to air their grievances regarding staff welfare, remuneration, service policies, and other matters.

The media began publishing more letters of complaints. These were mainly directed at the ground and traffic services. The customer relations section, which monitored letters of complaints and compliments found that while the cabin crew had been complimented for good courteous service, ground crew like the traffic, passenger, baggage, telephone sales and ticketing counter staff "could do with a lot of improvement."

However, by December 1989, even the cabin crew drew more letters of complaints than compliments. In April 1989, in-flight compliments numbered 66 compared to 37 complaints. In December of the same year, compliments had dropped to 19 while complaints had risen to 30. There were only 2 letters complimenting the ground/traffic services while letters of complaint increased to 21 (see Exhibit 4).

Management's recruitment of foreign pilots came under heavy fire from the MASEU. Among the issues raised by the union was why local engineers and pilots were paid much less than the expatriates. It was reported in a local newspaper that of MAS' 600 pilots, 100 were foreigners and out of this number, 72 were Australians. Three weeks later the same paper reported that 12 engineers had resigned for better pay abroad. The Malaysian Cabinet demanded an explanation.

On January 2, just two days into Visit Malaysia Year, a major local newspaper published an extensive editorial feature on MAS's deteriorating service. The article said that about a year ago MAS was well-known for its "charming cabin crew, good food and a fine wine and beer list. It was punctual too." "But today," the article continued, "MAS is characterized by flight delays, overbookings, mechanical problems and inferior aircraft." The article claimed that these facts "were freely admitted by senior managers in the face of a barrage of questions from media editors in a recent dialogue at the MAS headquarters." The following day, several other newspapers highlighted on their front page the frustration of Minister of Transport Dato' Ling Liong Sik, on the frequent flight delays, overbookings, cancellations of confirmed seats, and the deterioration in the standards of service on board and on the ground.

The next day, a Malay daily in its editorial reiterated that this was no longer an internal problem but had become public knowledge. It applauded the MAS management for admitting its weaknesses. Although the solution would not be easy, it said that every effort should be made to improve the quality of service so that MAS could live up to the "Golden Service Image," which was its slogan. The editorial maintained that the airline's failings also affected the national image, especially in relation to the public's perception of its privatization policy (MAS was the first government department in Malaysia to be privatized). The editorial warned that once the public questions the credibility of the airline, it would be difficult for MAS to restore its image.

The editorial of another newspaper was written in a similar vein. It said that the restoration of the airline's image was not only to ensure better service for passengers but also to guarantee the future of the airline, in view of the upturn in the global economy which had sparked the interest to travel. During the Visit Malaysia Year, the airline should capitalize on this trend, the editorial said.

Henceforth, MAS experienced a vigorous onslaught from the press. Negative reports on MAS were featured in the front pages, editorials, and letters to the editor. The quality of service had deteriorated; expansion had been too fast and incommensurate with the airline's capacity; flight delays and arrivals were too frequent and there were too many cases of overbooking, which resulted in the cancellation of confirmed seats.

The minister of transport made no bones about the government's dissatisfaction with the state of affairs and announced that he would investigate the matter. Weekly meetings were to be held with MAS management to iron out problems that the company faces.

Jeff felt that the problems MAS faced could have been anticipated:

> There were undercurrents. I knew that one day the bubble would burst. Feedback through letters of complaints to MAS pointed clearly to apathy and blind indifference by staff, principally at the airport. But as a result of this apathy, this lack of sensitivity and understanding of customer and media needs, there has been a serious communication fallout.

**More Turbulence**

But more was to come. On January 8, 1990, MASEU sought a meeting with the minister of transport. The union maintained that the shortage of cabin crew, baggage handlers, and security staff was the cause of delay and inefficiency. It claimed that the airline had expanded operations without a proportionate increase in staff recruitment.

But this was refuted by an MAS technician who wrote in an open letter to a major newspaper that there was no shortage of staff. The problem, he alleged, was under-utilization of staff, lack of proper control, no manpower planning, unnecessary wastage of expensive items, indifferent attitude of workers, and pay not being commensurate with training.

A newspaper report on the meeting of the union and the minister of transport said that the issues raised by the union revolved around problems of "mismanagement," "excessive spending," and "improper planning." The union also expressed no confidence in some of the company directors.

Letters to the editor (from locals as well as foreigners) were published in the newspapers. One letter complained of transit passengers not being provided free transportation to Terminal 2. Passengers have to shuttle by taxi instead.

A West German in a letter headlined "Where Is The Golden Service?" complained bitterly of the delays on all flights he had taken from Germany to Kuala Lumpur and on all internal flights; of the attitude of the ground staff who gave either poor or wrong information, their unwillingness to help, their lack of interest and knowledge; and of the garbled information and announcements of pilots and staff through the PA system.

"Throughout the confusion, no one seemed to know anything or was interested," he lamented.

**Damage Control**

Even before the January 2 article, Tan Sri Abdul Aziz had already moved "to check the rot." Following a meeting with the union in late December, he sent a telex to all his top management teams at the head office and all MAS stations to quickly identify and rectify problems relating to flight delays and overbooking of seats. He urged them to "bypass bureaucratic procedures to hire more staff and buy new equipment to improve its service and image." He added:

> As a result of the frequent delays and unsatisfactory services, both on the ground and air during the last few months, MAS's image has been severely affected, both at home and abroad.

He said that the press was more or less determined "to portray a negative image of MAS and would continue to hound us until we improve."

Tan Sri Abdul Aziz had an open door policy with the press. He explained to the press and on television the problems besetting MAS. These included the late delivery of the B747-400 Combis, which would have increased seating capacity in accordance with the projected demand; as well as defects in the "wet-leased" aircraft, which MAS was not in a position to remedy.[2]

At this time too, the government directed the airline to move its domestic departures and arrivals from Terminal 1 to Terminal 2.

> We were given only a month to move. Naturally, there were problems in getting Terminal 2 ready to handle all domestic arrivals, training some 200 staff recruited for the purpose and providing the necessary facilities like buses and canopied steps for passengers.

December also coincided with the school holidays and it was an unusually busy time such that "a few hundred extra flights" had to be mounted to cater to this demand.

"It was a strain on the airline and all the staff involved," explained Gnanalingam, the public relations manager.

In line with his open policy, Tan Sri Abdul Aziz together with the public affairs manager met with members of the press several times to explain the airline's predicament.

He granted an exclusive interview to the *Utusan Malaysia* which appeared as a question-and-answer feature on January 11, 1990, headlined "MAS at Par With the Biggest Airlines in the World" (translated to the English language). The article gave him an opportunity to explain MAS's side of the story.

"Our stance was to be open and candid with the media. We even showed the media statistics of aircraft delay. Most airlines face the problem of flight delays due to weather conditions, technical faults, and sometimes waiting for VIPs who don't show up. SIA and the other airlines have this problem too. The only difference is that it is not blown out of proportion by the media," Tan Sri Abdul Aziz said.

---

[2]Wet-leased aircraft means that the lease includes the engineers and technical crew.

Meanwhile, Tan Sri Abdul Aziz moved fast to correct some of the internal problems. Spot checks were often carried out. In one of the spot checks, he discovered that a RM2.5 million computer which had been purchased to tabulate and record in-flight sales had been left idle for 7 months. The cabin crew claimed that they were not trained to use the equipment. On further investigation, he discovered that the software was not suitable. He directed that new software be developed to solve the problem.

On the engineering side, the engineering crew was instructed to carry out extra checks on the aircraft at the end of each day to minimize delays in early morning flights.

Jeff agreed with the swift action by management to correct the problems and its complete openness with the press. He said, "The press will be a part of any cover-up."

Besides arranging for meetings between newspaper editors and the MD, Jeff also organized a forum to enable direct interface among press editors and MAS managers and section heads. "This achieved its purpose and they became less critical. Goodwill was restored because we showed that we wanted to improve," Jeff said. For the time being, the press was appeased.

**The Bubble Bursts Again**

Just when all seemed well, the *New Straits Times* of January 29, 1990, carried a 5-column article headlined "MAS Passengers to Australia Stranded." Two photographs accompanied the story. One of the photographs showed a group of stranded passengers crowding around the ticketing counter and another had 2 dejected-looking passengers sitting on the floor. The article claimed that 73 Australia-bound passengers on MAS, including "many who had their flights confirmed," were stranded at the Subang (Kuala Lumpur) Airport. The article reported that they had been stranded for a week. During that time some had been sleeping at the balcony. Others became guests of local families who offered them the hospitality of their homes. One of the passengers alleged that passengers with confirmed seats were put on stand-by because there were no seats available. He also claimed that some were given new departure dates. They also had to check at the counter daily if they wanted a flight out. The last paragraph of the report said that "MAS officials could not be reached for comment."

The following day, Gnanalingam explained that only seven of the 73 passengers actually had the OK status stamped on their tickets (i.e., they had confirmed seats). This statement was supported by Tan Sri Abdul Aziz.

Meanwhile, Jeff called an urgent meeting of the corporate image committee to decide what to do with the passengers.

> I suggested that for the sake of our image, a special chartered flight should be arranged for those involved. The damage has already been done. This at least would have a good PR rub-off.
>
> The decision was agreed upon and endorsed by the MD. A press conference was called and the next day (January 31, 1990), the *New Straits Times* reported that a special B747-200 KL-Melbourne-Sydney flight would be mounted for all the stranded passengers. It was also explained that 19 had confirmed seats but did not reconfirm within the stipulated 72 hours. Of these, 11 had been put on the next flight.

To ensure that the press would not be given the runaround, four public relations officers were stationed at the airport, two at each terminal for 11 weeks.

**An Uneasy Calm**

The highly critical treatment of MAS by the press was a blow to the public relations department. The PR department staff felt that they had put a lot of effort in cooperating and building a good relationship with the press; then this happened.

In addition to the normal press releases and press conferences, MAS also began conducting a series of courses for the press in 1984. These courses were intended to familiarize the press with the organization and with aviation jargon, and to give them the opportunity to ask questions regarding various issues. The courses also included visits to the hangar complex, the training complex, the flight simulator areas, and so on.

This program was not able to solve the problems completely. The main reason was that unlike big newspapers in the west, the local newspapers did not have a special desk for the reporting of aviation matters.

> "We were training various levels of press people, from rookies to senior reporters and there was no incentive from the press to develop expertise in aviation matters and to know our executives personally. We held the courses to help them to be more knowledgeable about relevant issues so that their reporting would be more accurate, balanced, and fair. But under the circumstances, it was impossible," said Gnanalingam.

There were also goodwill activities like the Annual Press Night in which senior editors from all over the country were invited for a dinner hosted by the chairman of the board. For the younger reporters, fun parties were organized. In 1990 for example, a party based on the theme "Back To Nature" was held to reflect the company' s concern for the protection and preservation of the environment.

While these activities helped generate goodwill, they did not always guarantee positive reportage when a reporter filed in his story.

Jeff recalled a conversation he had with a senior editor of a major newspaper:

Editor: It is quite rare for the mainstream media to openly criticize against a large corporation, particularly one that is linked with the government. But there were several reasons why we decided to go ahead. We received over 100 letters in a period of two months complaining about those problems that we had highlighted, mainly frequent flight delays, cancellations of reservations and poor cabin service. Only a small number of these letters were published.

Jeff: You know, we do have a customer relations section which handles customer complaints. Each time we receive a complaint, we acknowledge it, investigate with the department concerned, get feedback, and dispatch the final replies. For standard cases, we take only about a week to respond. Of course, for more complicated cases we take a little longer, but no longer than 20 days (see Exhibit 5 for Customer Relations Investigation Standards).

Editor: Jeff, some of the letters that we received were carbon copies of letters that had been sent to the management of MAS and even senior ministers, including the prime minister and the minister of transport. This seems to indicate that they are not confident that MAS would act on theft complaints unless a third party, i.e., the press, was involved. Some of the letters complained about the nonresponse to their earlier complaints, others about the condescending way that the complaints were answered, for instance by ridiculing the passengers and throwing the conditions of ticket purchase to the customers.

Jeff: That is unfair. We have always cooperated fully with the press. Why do you keep hounding us this way without any letup?

Editor: Jeff, I am a reporter. My responsibility is to my readers. When it comes to a question of public interest, I know which way I have to choose. Besides, I am personally convinced that there is indeed a deterioration in MAS service, especially in sticking to schedules and in the poor cabin service. Further, the complaints I received from MAS staff, mainly the union, were quite true. Their allegations are not unfounded.

Jeff: Look, why don't I arrange for you to meet with our managing director so that you can explain all this to him? I'll be there too.

Editor: No problem, Jeff, anytime at all. I'm prepared to spend whatever time it takes to meet the management so that there is no misunderstanding. After all, MAS is as much my airline as it is yours. But big corporations must realize that the way the press responds to issues is governed largely by the significance of the issue to the public. Relations with the press must be built on mutual respect, honesty, and forthright exchange. Just as MAS has a responsibility to the public, so does the press to its readers and to its profession.

Thus following this conversation, Tan Sri Abdul Aziz had a three-hour session with the editor to help clarify matters.

## Heading Back on Course

When the dust had settled, Jeff sent a letter to the press to assure the public that the problems faced by MAS in late 1989 and early 1990 would soon be solved through a program of fleet modernization, recruitment, and training of pilots, flight engineers, cabin crew and ground staff, automation and computerization, and continued improvements in Terminal 2 facilities. The letter highlighted the fact that MAS was doing well financially and that despite problems, the airline had also received many letters of compliment. This letter was published in the *New Straits Times* under the headline "MAS Plan For Smooth Flying" (February 24, 1990).

MAS continued to improve the airline but the tone of media coverage remained uncertain. While the press continued to highlight the recurring flight delays, disagreements between management and the union, and the vacillating management position on whether there would be a major revamp, the press also provided strong support to MAS' corporate sponsorship programs, recruitment drives, and route expansion structure.

By the end of March 1990, the operational problems had not been completely solved as evidenced by a March 27, 1990, *New Straits Times* report which highlighted that there were 2,424 flight delays from January 1 to February 25 due to technical faults, breakdowns, weather conditions, and operating problems.

On April 4, 1990, the minister of transport announced that the weekly meetings with MAS management had been scrapped, a move which many interpreted to mean that all was well with MAS. Ten days later the government announced that Tan Sri Abdul Aziz had been reappointed managing director for one more year.

Jeff still wonders how to ensure that the MAS image will no longer be tarnished by bad press coverage. How could he make management realize that the root of the PR problem lies with every staff member — from the top managers to the blue collar workers in the company — and how they handle their responsibilities. He identified 10 conditions which, if implemented, would considerably smoothen the kinks in the MAS image and restore the luster to its name.

As public affairs manager, it was Jeff's duty to ensure that MAS did not receive bad press again the coming year.

EXHIBIT 1

## MALAYSIA AIRLINES
## Corporate Objectives

The corporate objectives of MAS as laid down by the Government are:

1. To provide the people of Malaysia with an efficient and profitable air transport system which enhances the standing of the nation and the policies of its government.

2. To develop an efficient service within Malaysia which also directly links Sabah and Sarawak with Peninsular Malaysia and contributes to the economic and social integration of the country as a whole.

3. To select, train, and develop personnel using the most up-to-date and appropriate managerial techniques.

4. To provide simultaneously competitive and profitable international services which support Malaysia's trade, tourism, and other activities.

5. To contribute meaningfully to national aspirations and foster an organization which is in harmony with the multiracial objectives of Malaysia.

EXHIBIT 2

**MALAYSIA AIRLINES**
**Ten-Year Statistical Review of the Company**

| | | *1989–1990* | *1988–1989* | *1987–1988* | *1986–1987* | *1985–1986* | *1984–1985* | *1983–1984* | *1982–1983* | *1981–1982* | *1980–1981* |
|---|---|---|---|---|---|---|---|---|---|---|---|
| **Financial** | | | | | | | | | | | |
| Total Revenue | ($000) | 2,402,890 | 1,939,196 | 1,613,913 | 1,432,770 | 1,326,003 | 1,314,437 | 1,237,302 | 1,183,514 | 995,345 | 825,734 |
| Total Expenditure | ($000) | 2,255,340 | 1,738,957 | 1,458,495 | 1,316,937 | 1,218,849 | 1,179,685 | 1,140,141 | 1,170,791 | 1,028,979 | 817,053 |
| Taxation | ($000) | 2,806 | 45,857 | 3,962 | 3,622 | 2,250 | 3,168 | 1,971 | 2,682 | 1,534 | 1,704 |
| Profit/(Loss) tax and Extraordinary Item | ($000) | 221,939 | 154,382 | 151,456 | 112,211 | 104,904 | 131,584 | 95,190 | 10,041 | (35,16) | 6,977 |
| Shareholders' Funds | ($000) | 1,147,939 | 954,438 | 828,494 | 720,788 | 643,402 | 371,494 | 239,910 | 144,713 | 134,678 | 169,846 |
| Profit/(Loss) as a % of Revenue | (%) | 8.01 | 7.96 | 9.38 | 7.83 | 7.91 | 10.01 | 7.69 | 0.85 | (3.53) | 0.84 |
| Return on Shareholders' Funds | (%) | 16.8 | 16.2 | 18.3 | 15.6 | 20.1 | 35.42 | 39.68 | 6.94 | (26.11) | 4.11 |
| Earnings/(Loss) Per Share | (Sen) | 55 | 44 | 43 | 32 | 51 | 188 | 136 | 14 | (50) | 10 |
| **Production** | | | | | | | | | | | |
| Network Size | (km) | 191,243 | 128,258 | 115,889 | 101,763 | 91,776 | 91,288 | 88,512 | 87,653 | 87,467 | 87,467 |
| Time Flown | (hours) | 137,585 | 118,055 | 108,589 | 99,824 | 94,886 | 95,025 | 94,692 | 95,570 | 98,547 | 93,761 |
| Distance Flown | (000 km) | 71,279 | 57,855 | 53,467 | 48,637 | 45,048 | 44,429 | 43,722 | 44,143 | 44,685 | 42,829 |
| Available Capacity | (000 tkm) | 1,994,493 | 1,579,122 | 1,430,429 | 1,257,844 | 1,085,170 | 1,056,419 | 1,022,806 | 1,030,229 | 828,372 | 763,329 |
| Available Passenger Capacity | (000 seat km) | 14,189,005 | 11,495,805 | 10,319,998 | 9,313,545 | 8,494,894 | 8,221,762 | 7,935,831 | 7,958,333 | 6,844,460 | 6,170,601 |

EXHIBIT 2 (cont'd)

**MALAYSIA AIRLINES**
**Ten-Year Statistical Review of the Company**

| | | *1989–1990* | *1988–1989* | *1987–1988* | *1986–1987* | *1985–1986* | *1984–1985* | *1983–1984* | *1982–1983* | *1981–1982* | *1980–1981* |
|---|---|---|---|---|---|---|---|---|---|---|---|
| **Traffic** | | | | | | | | | | | |
| Passengers Carried | (000) | 7,873 | 6,811 | 6,138 | 5,597 | 5,520 | 5,625 | 5,232 | 5,018 | 4,838 | 4,151 |
| Passengers Carried | (000 pax km) | 10,514,260 | 8,931,629 | 7,828,266 | 6,589,990 | 6,195,474 | 6,134,053 | 5,624,476 | 5,588,615 | 4,810,862 | 4,206,004 |
| Passenger Load Factor | (%) | 74.1 | 77.7 | 75.9 | 70.8 | 72.9 | 74.6 | 70.9 | 70.2 | 70.3 | 68.2 |
| Cargo Carried | (000 tkm) | 439,763 | 376,316 | 352,080 | 288,283 | 212,216 | 196,076 | 178,519 | 143,979 | 132,925 | 112,693 |
| Mail Carried | (000 tkm) | 14,617 | 13,022 | 11,886 | 10,549 | 8,300 | 7,361 | 7,730 | 7,299 | 7,403 | 7,108 |
| Overall Load Carried | (000 tkm) | 1,390,270 | 1,213,756 | 1,101,276 | 916,734 | 803,513 | 779,648 | 713,785 | 670,603 | 587,579 | 513,456 |
| Overall Load Factor | (%) | 69.7 | 76.9 | 77.0 | 72.9 | 74.0 | 73.8 | 69.8 | 65.1 | 70.9 | 67.3 |
| **Staff** | | | | | | | | | | | |
| Employee Strength | (as of March 31) | 14,013 | 11,928 | 11,249 | 11,136 | 10,798 | 10,632 | 10,055 | 10,124 | 10,248 | 9,327 |
| Revenue per Employee | ($000) | 171 | 163 | 144 | 129 | 123 | 124 | 123 | 117 | 97 | 89 |
| Available Capacity per Employee | (tkm) | 142,332 | 132,388 | 127,160 | 112,953 | 100,497 | 99,362 | 101,721 | 101,761 | 80,833 | 81,841 |
| Load Carried per Employee | (tkm) | 99,213 | 101,757 | 97,900 | 82,322 | 74,413 | 73,330 | 70,988 | 66,239 | 57,336 | 55,050 |

EXHIBIT 2 (cont'd)

**MALAYSIAN AIRLINES**
**Graphical Presentation**

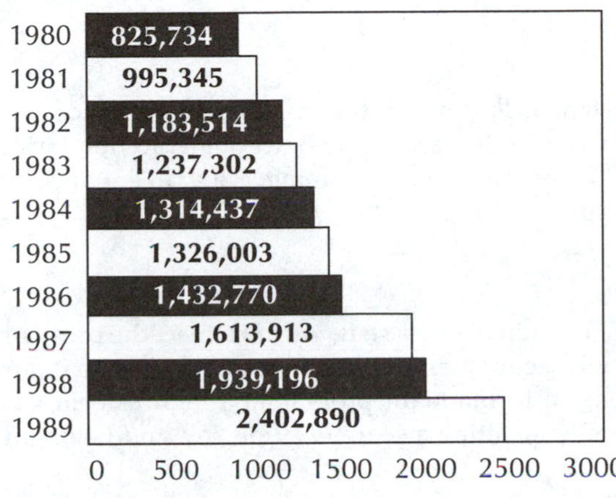


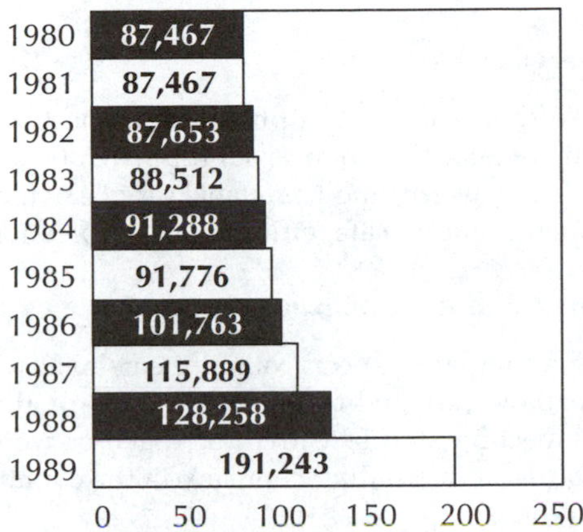


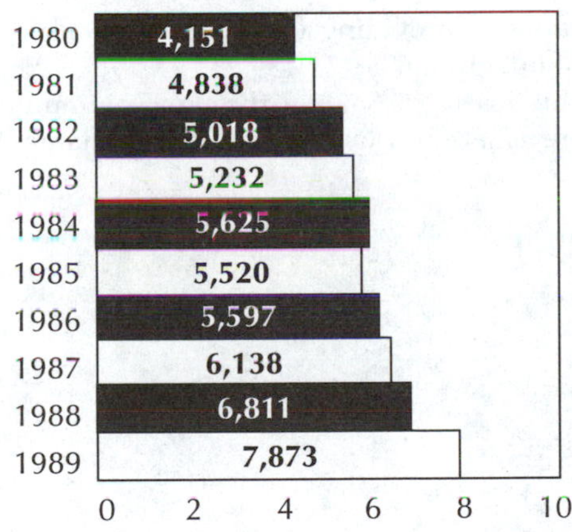


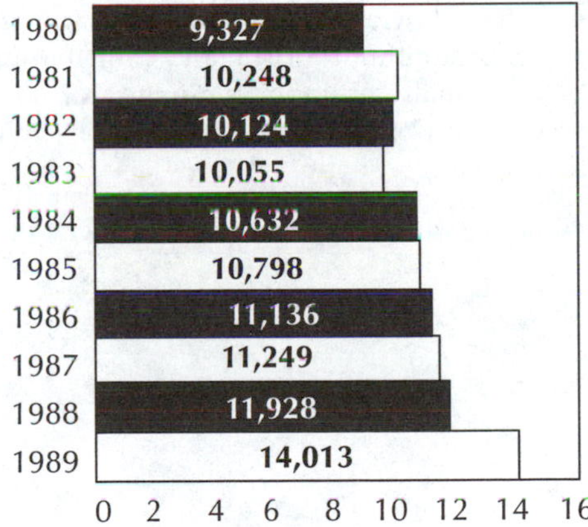

EXHIBIT 3

## MALAYSIA AIRLINES
## Corporate Philosophy

Befitting our status as a national airline, we hereby adopt a Malaysian philosophy in achieving standards of excellence in everything we do.

**Service**

We shall constantly uphold the highest service standards through the pursuit of excellence with customer satisfaction as our ultimate purpose of existence. Toward this end, we shall provide caring, sincere, warm, and hospitable service in the true Malaysian style. In so doing, we shall enhance our operation of a safe, efficient, and professional airline.

**Staff and the Company**

The company expects commitment, loyalty, and dedication from its staff. We too expect the company to show care and responsibility by providing us job security, ensuring personal development, and respecting staff sensitivities. Together we shall strive to maintain profitability, high esteem, and status as the leading company in the country, thereby instilling a sense of pride, joy, and belonging to the Company.

**Corporate Responsibility**

We shall lead by example in fulfilling our national aspirations by providing an efficient air transport service, promoting tourism, and contributing to national integration.

We shall continue to pursue our social responsibilities to the nation through community projects, sponsorships, and patronage of activities which are in harmony with the multiracial character of Malaysia.

EXHIBIT 4

**MALAYSIA AIRLINES**
**Complaints and Compliments (April–December 1989)**

| | *Apr* | *May* | *Jun* | *Jul* | *Aug* | *Sept* | *Oct* | *Nov* | *Dec* |
|---|---|---|---|---|---|---|---|---|---|
| Complaints | | | | | | | | | |
| In-flight services | 37 | 08 | 12 | 26 | 19 | 12 | 24 | 12 | 30 |
| Ground/traffic services | 27 | 18 | 11 | 29 | 26 | 13 | 17 | 12 | 21 |
| Total | **64** | **26** | **23** | **55** | **45** | **25** | **41** | **24** | **51** |
| Compliments | | | | | | | | | |
| In-flight services | 66 | 44 | 41 | 24 | 41 | 45 | 49 | 39 | 19 |
| Ground/traffic services | 04 | 04 | 03 | 03 | 02 | — | 01 | 01 | 02 |
| Total | **70** | **48** | **44** | **27** | **43** | **45** | **50** | **40** | **21** |

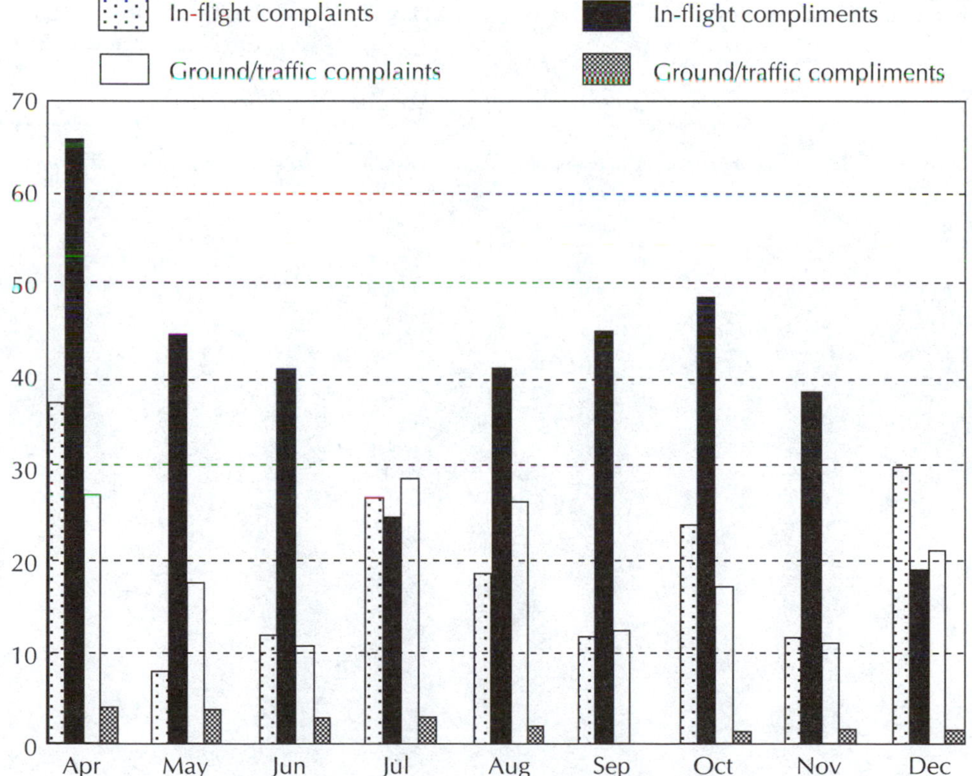


Source: Customer Relations, Malaysia Airlines.

EXHIBIT 5

**MALAYSIA AIRLINES**
**Customer Relations Investigation Standards**

| | *Date* | | |
|---|---|---|---|
| *Action* | *Commencing* | *Target* | *Remarks* |
| 1. Receipt and Acknowledgment of Complaint | | Day 1 | Letters from MD/divisional directors/urgent cases |
| 2. Investigation with other departments/stations (via CRAR/Telex/OUS or phones) | | Day 2 | Others |
| 3. Receipt of feedback from departments/stations | | Day 6 | For letters from MD/ directors/urgent cases (via Telex/OUS/phones) |
| 4. Dispatch of final replies | | Day 7 | For letters from MD/ directors/urgent cases |
| | | Day 10–15 | Standard cases* |

*For more complicated cases needing thorough investigation, this target shall not exceed Day 20.

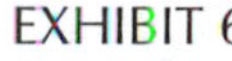

EXHIBIT 6

**MALAYSIA AIRLINES**
**Organizational Chart**
**As of April 1988**

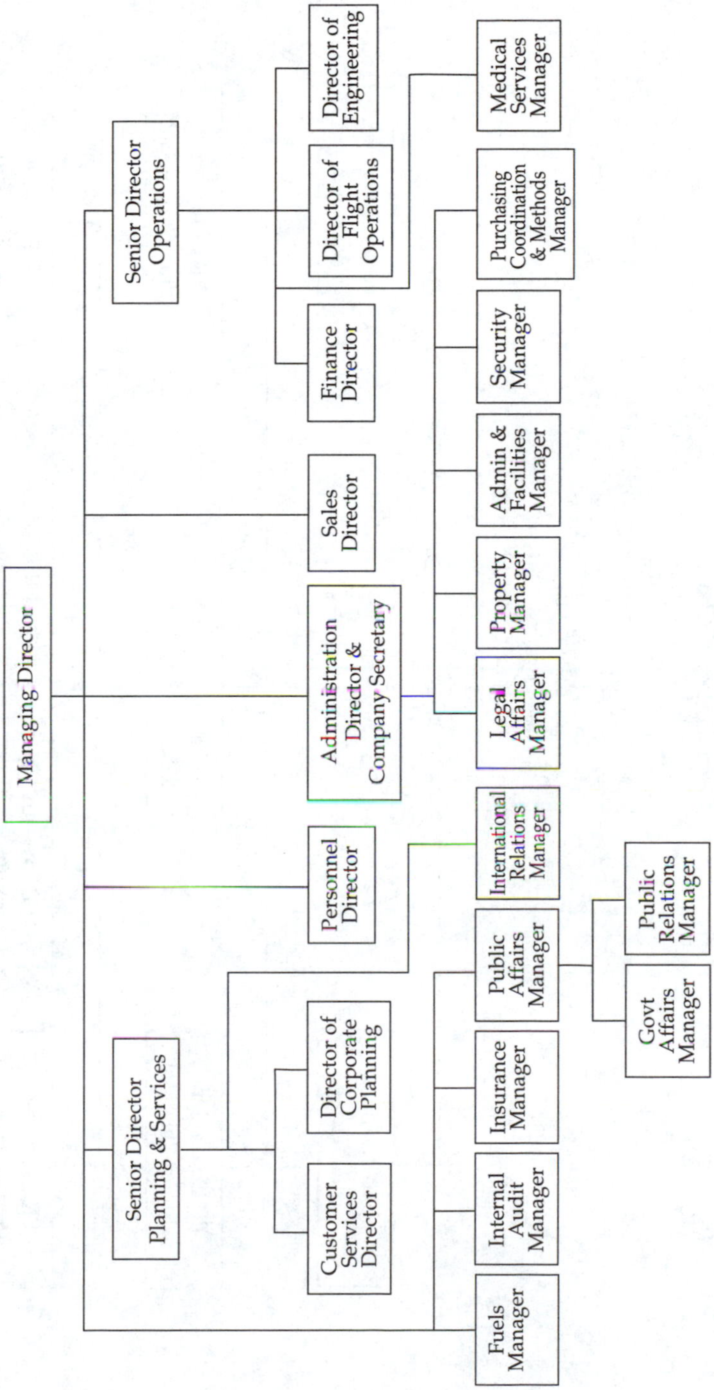

- Managing Director
  - Senior Director Planning & Services
    - Customer Services Director
    - Director of Corporate Planning
    - International Relations Manager
  - Personnel Director
  - Administration Director & Company Secretary
    - Legal Affairs Manager
    - Property Manager
    - Admin & Facilities Manager
    - Security Manager
    - Purchasing Coordination & Methods Manager
  - Sales Director
  - Senior Director Operations
    - Finance Director
    - Director of Flight Operations
    - Director of Engineering
    - Medical Services Manager
  - Fuels Manager
  - Internal Audit Manager
  - Insurance Manager
  - Public Affairs Manager
    - Govt Affairs Manager
    - Public Relations Manager

EXHIBIT 7

**MALAYSIA AIRLINES**
**Public Affairs Department**
**Organizational Chart**

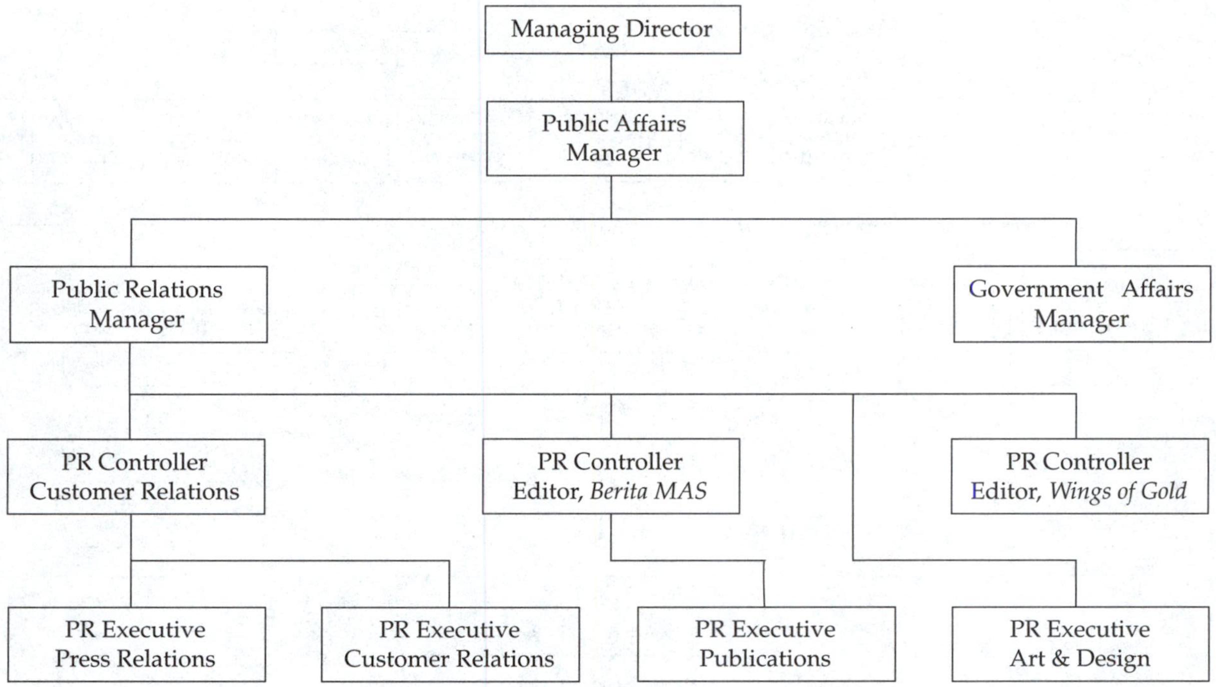

- Managing Director
  - Public Affairs Manager
    - Public Relations Manager
      - PR Controller Customer Relations
        - PR Executive Press Relations
        - PR Executive Customer Relations
      - PR Controller Editor, *Berita MAS*
        - PR Executive Publications
      - PR Executive Art & Design
      - PR Controller Editor, *Wings of Gold*
    - Government Affairs Manager

## APPENDIX A

## INDUSTRY NOTES: BACKGROUND ON MALAYSIA AIRLINES

Malaysia Airlines (MAS) is a public-listed company. A Board of Directors comprising a Chairman, Deputy Chairman, and 10 members with four alternate members is responsible for policy formulation and the corporate development of the company. The management of the company is headed by a managing director.

As a corporation, MAS had a total of 9 subsidiary and associate companies whose primary activities ranged from helicopter, trucking, and coach transportation to software management. MAS' equity in these companies ranged from 11 percent to 100 percent.

The history of MAS dates back to 1937 when the Malayan Airways Ltd was formed. It began operations only in 1947, flying mainly along the Singapore–Kuala Lumpur and Penang sectors. By 1958, the first long-haul flight to Hong Kong was made, marking its entry into international aviation. Five years later, when Malaysia was formed, the airline was renamed Malaysian Airways. Following Singapore's separation from Malaysia, the airline was renamed Malaysia-Singapore Airlines (MSA). By 1972, MSA was flying to Taipei, Sydney, Phnom Penh, Tokyo, Colombo, Madras, Melbourne, London, Osaka, Athens, Zurich and Frankfurt, in addition to the regional capitals of ASEAN.

MSA was dissolved on October 1, 1972 and in its place grew two separate airlines, Singapore International Airlines (SIA) and Malaysian Airline System (MAS). While SIA took over all the international routes, MAS operated services to 38 destinations (5 regional and 33 domestic) with a fleet of 19 aircraft.

By 1975, MAS had built up its international network to Hong Kong, Tokyo, London and Melbourne. By 1980, it had spread its wings to Taipei, Perth, Frankfurt, and Amsterdam.

In 1982, Tan Sri Abdul Aziz bin Abdul Rahman was appointed the first Managing Director (formerly, General Manager). In November 1985, MAS became the first government agency to be privatized and its shares were listed on the Kuala Lumpur Stock Exchange. The year 1986 saw the completion of its new 34-story corporate headquarters in Kuala Lumpur's Golden Triangle on Jalan Sultan Ismail. In the same year the new Hangar Complex at Subang Airport was opened.

In 1988, MAS added a sixth frequency to the Frankfurt andAmsterdam services through Dubai, to Madras and Taipei. New flights to Phuket and Mauritius were inaugurated jointly with Thai Airways and Air Mauritius, respectively.

Two B747-400s which came into service in late 1989 helped increase seat kilometers capacity by 23.4 percent. There were also increases in flight frequencies to existing destinations such as Tokyo (9 times a week), London (7 times a week), Seoul (3 times a week), and Bangkok (additional 2 times a week). New destinations, namely, Fukuoka, Guangzhou, Ho Chi Minh City, Pontianak, Brussels, Istanbul, Auckland, and Kuwait came on line in December 1989.

When Honolulu was added to the MAS destination, flights to Los Angeles increased to 5 times a week with the inauguration of twice weekly flights to Honolulu in January 1990 on the B747-400. MAS began joint services to Teheran and Yangon with Iran Air and Myanmar Airways respectively in March and January 1990.

Forecasts for 1990–1991 appear bright with stronger demand in international and domestic travel which have been spurred by the strength of the economy worldwide. The acquisition of more sophisticated aircraft would help to increase seat and cargo capacity consistent with this demand.

# APPENDIX B

## MAIN PERSONALITIES IN THE CASE

### Tan Sri Abdul Aziz bin Abdul Rahman, Managing Director

Hailed as the "corporate pilot" who brought MAS out of debt, Tan Sri Abdul Aziz bin Abdul Rahman has been recognized and honored by local and foreign professional bodies, the government, and the King.

Tan Sri Abdul Aziz joined MAS in 1971 as its Legal Affairs Officer and Secretary. In 1982, after he took over as managing director, Tan Sri Abdul Aziz turned the fortunes of the airlines from a loss of $35 million in the financial year of 1981 to chart a record earning of $95.2 million in 1983. By 1984, the airline was able to offer its staff an annual bonus. In June 1990, MAS gave its staff a 3-month bonus.

The corporate publication "The Sky is the Limit" said of his management style:

> Dato' Aziz' forte is his way with people: staff, customers, the press, and the public. He practices an open door policy in which the staff can come to him directly with their problems."

On public relations, he had this to say:

> Every individual in the company should consider himself a PR person and should always strive to uphold the company's good reputation both during and after office hours. PR is something very comprehensive . . . one's behavior must be right; one must be efficient and helpful; and one must have a positive attitude. Above all, one has to be courteous and helpful at all times, no matter what his position in the company is.

### Jaafar Abdul Manaf (Jeff), Public Affairs Manager

Jeff completed his Bachelor of Commerce degree at the University of Melbourne in 1969 under a Shell scholarship. After serving at Shell for 3 years, he resigned in 1972 to join the newly formed Malaysian Airline System.

His experience in MAS includes being airport manager (Kuala Lumpur) up to 1974; manager (London) until 1975; then back to Kuala Lumpur to take charge of purchasing aircraft and ground fuel. Jeff was later posted to the personnel division as its Training and Development manager. He became the personnel services manager and then human resources and development manager. In March 1984, Jeff was appointed public affairs manager.

Outside of MAS, Jeff has been president of the Institute of Public Relations Malaysia (IPRM) since 1988.

He says of the public relations function:

> "Having a PR department is not good enough. It must be given the authority to act, even encroach on other departments. For if the PR role is merely advisory, then it will not be able to live up to its responsibility as the corporate conscience which demands from management the highest standards of ethical responsibility to the public."

APPENDIX C

## PUBLIC AFFAIRS IN MALAYSIA AIRLINES

The Public Affairs Department is grouped under general management. Together with four other departments (i.e. Insurance, Internal Audit, Fuels, and Cargo Sales Projects), the Public Affairs Department comes directly under the supervision of the managing director.

Within the total management setup, the Department has more staff than a line function, coordinating freely with other divisions and departments, namely, Planning and Services, Operations, Customer Services, Corporate Planning, Personnel, Administration, Sales, Finance, Flight Operations and Engineering (see Exhibits 6 and 7).

The public affairs manager reports directly to the managing director and is responsible for the overall supervision of the PAD, the orchestra, and the *Mega Hiburan 9-10*, a daily radio entertainment program aired over the popular city network of Radio-Television Malaysia (RTM).

Under him are the public relations manager and the government affairs manager. Together, they supervise almost 50 staff and handle a budget of almost $10 million. The Department is responsible for counseling management and giving ideas and creative recommendations on public relations implications of management decisions and activities as well as dealing with the media, general public, stockholders, customers, government agencies, staff, and so on, to maintain a positive image.

The public affairs manager chairs the corporate image committee comprising heads of divisions, departments, and sections. The committee meets about once a month to identify and plan activities that would enhance the image of the airline, evaluate public relations problems, and make decisions so that speedy action could be taken on matters affecting corporate relations.

### Public Relations

The Public Relations Manager, Siew Yong Gnanalingam, is responsible for conducting activities that would project the right corporate image of the company. She is the company spokesperson and is responsible for five major subsections. These are:

#### 1. Corporate Activities/Projects

This subsection identifies community projects worthy of MAS support, which would enhance the airline's image. For instance, it collaborates with the Tourist Development Corporation (TDC) for the Visit Malaysia Year programs and donates generously to activities which promote tourism, sports, arts, and culture.

#### 2. Publications

Three major publications are produced by the Department. These are *Berita MAS*, a newsletter for employees; *Esteem*, a corporate magazine distributed internally as well as externally, and *Wings of Gold*, the airline's in-flight magazine.

#### 3. Customer Relations

This subsection monitors feedback relating to customer complaints and compliments, in particular from corporate clients and esteemed passengers of whom profiles and records are kept. In addition, customer relations staff visit various business chambers and send out questionnaires on a quarterly basis regarding various aspects of customer services. The staff also seek ideas for improvement, assist in press projects, and plan and initiate activities to enhance customer support. With the assistance of the publications subsection, the customer relations subsection produces information brochures and leaflets on company procedures, products, and services. It evaluates appeals for MAS contributions and assistance. Three officers are especially assigned to look into enhancing relations with the Bumiputera, Chinese, and Indian communities.

The subsection recommends the appropriate reimbursement of claims where claims are due. It conducts briefings and schedules talks for other staff (e.g., traffic liaison officers, supervisory cabin crew) on aspects of customer services relevant to them. This is done through case studies in which the cost implications of poor customer relations (not merely in financial terms, but more in terms of the detrimental effects to the airline's image) are stresed.

#### 4. Press Relations

The main function of this subsection is to establish and maintain positive relations with the mass media to ensure a fair and balanced coverage that would enhance the image of the airline.

According to Gnanalingam, in addition to the regular press releases sent and the press conferences organized from time to time, a number of familiarization courses are organized and designed to "make them understand us better." These 3-day courses in which some journalists from the local papers are briefed by MAS top personnel on the operations of the company also offer journalists the opportunity to ask questions on various issues and to visit various parts of the complex.

Similar courses are also conducted for groups such as consumer groups, tourist industry personnel, chambers of commerce, and other special interest groups. The public relations officers often meet with press editors to clarify issues and provide background information to assist in the writing of news in mass media.

Press nights are organized annually, one for senior editors of newspapers in Peninsular and East Malaysia; and the other, fun parties for the general reporters.

#### 5. Art and Design

This subsection, which is handled by a Public Relations controller, is responsible for providing the graphic and creative support for all MAS publications, including *Berita MAS*, *Esteem*, and *Wings of Gold*, as well as other materials such as leaflets, souvenir programs, invitation cards, posters, and photographs. This subsection also works together with the Advertising and Promotions Department, especially in the area of design.

### Employee Relations Program

It should be noted that the Public Affairs Department does not have an employee relations arm. This is handled by the personnel division as part of its industrial relations function.

However, in view of the many associations in MAS (some of them with union status, namely the MAS Management Association [MASMA], MAS Pilots Association [MAPA], MAS Flight Engineers Association [MAFEA], Association of MAS Aircraft Licensed Engineers [AMALE], MAS Executive Staff Association [MESA], and MAS Employee Union [MASEU]), the Esprit de MAS Committee was set up to provide a sense of belonging and to foster goodwill. Among the work of the Esprit de MAS were the launching of campaigns (e.g., the "Better Always" and the "Towards Service Excellence" campaigns), selection of the winner of the Employee of the Month Award, formation of the cultural dance troup, and involvement in various community projects.

### Government Affairs

A second major section is the Government Affairs section, which is responsible for all interactions with government departments and agencies. This section mainly channels appropriate reports and information on the airline to the government. In matters relating to negotiations, technical cooperation, trade and consular matters, the Government Matters Subsection is to advise management on the implications of such matters with regard to the government. The government affairs manager also supervises the archives.

## References

1. "The Sky is the Limit." A Profile of Dato' Abdul Aziz bin Abdul Rahman, Managing Director of Malaysia Airlines, October 1988.

2. MAS Annual Reports, 1988/89 and 1989/90.
3. Hawa D Abg Hj Abdul Rahim. "Towards Service Excellence." Unpublished project paper for the Malaysian Institute of Management, May 31, 1989.
4. Ho Shuh Mool, "The Role of MAS in Promoting Tourism in Malaysia." Unpublished paper for the Malaysian Institute of Management, June 22, 1989.
5. Interview with Tan Sri Abdul Aziz bin Abdul Rahman, Managing Director, Malaysia Airlines.
6. Interviews with Jaafar Abdul Manaf, Public Affairs Manager, Malaysia Airlines.
7. Interview with Mrs Siew Yong Gnanalingam, Public Relations Manager, Malaysia Airlines.
8. Interview with Puan Zawiah Aruf, Customer Relations Controller, Malaysia Airlines.
9. Interview with Hj Jumaat Yusoff, President, Malaysia Airlines Employees Union.
10. Geoff Easton, *Learning From Case Studies*. London: University of Lancaster and Prentice-Hall International, 1982.

# The Deluxe Hotel Industry in the Philippines in 1989* 8

The hotel industry in the Philippines was a vital factor in the government's push for tourism and foreign investments. In 1989, the industry accounted for a total of 90 percent of tourist establishments. Consequently, it was a principal dollar earner for the Philippine economy. Tourists and foreign businessmen will not come to a country which does not have the facilities to accommodate them. Thus, the hotel industry was part of a system geared to draw in tourists and foreign investments.

After several years of lackluster performance, the industry achieved a turnaround in 1988. Hotel occupancy rates reached record highs, and the industry was transformed from a buyers' market into a sellers' market (see Exhibit 1). With the tourism boom, the problem became the shortage of hotel rooms to accommodate the large influx of tourists. With promising prospects in the years to come, plans were drawn up for the construction of several new hotels, the expansion of existing hotels, and the revitalization of moth-balled hotels.

* This case was written by Maria Virginia Cruz, Margaret Sanchez, Wilfred Son Keng Po, and Simeon Yap, (MBA, University of the Philippines, 1989), under the supervision of Visiting Professor Luis Ma. R. Calingo. This case was prepared to serve as a basis for class discussion rather than to illustrate either effective or ineffective handling of an administrative situation.

## Background on the Philippine Hotel Industry

### Definition of a Hotel

A "hotel" can be defined as any building, edifice or premises, or a completely independent part thereof, used for the regular reception, accommodation, or lodging of travelers and tourists and the provision of incidental services.

### Classification of Hotels

For purposes of registration and licensing, the Philippine Department of Tourism (DOT) classified hotels into four categories, namely: deluxe class (5-star), first class (4-star), standard class (3-star), and economy class (1- and 2-star). The standards for a five-star hotel are set out in Exhibit 2.

### History

Prior to 1976, there were only four five-star hotels in Metro Manila. The turning point came in October 1976 when Manila hosted the joint conference of the International Monetary Fund (IMF) and the International Bank for Reconstruction and Development (IBRD/World Bank). As a result, new hotel projects were started in 1975 with encouragement coming from the Philippine government and the Central Bank of the Philippines. Most of these hotel projects availed themselves of long-term loans from the Development Bank of the Philippines (DBP) at the then prevailing concessional rate of 12 to 14 percent. These five-star hotels were funded by peso loans mostly through Central Bank flotations.

By 1976, 10 new five-star hotels were built. Most of these hotels started their operations late into 1976. However, by 1977, the market dwindled and the deluxe hotels were suddenly faced with undercapacity. Even when the hotel occupancy rate increased to 62 percent in 1978 and 71 percent in 1979, most of the hotels incurred substantial financial losses. To survive, hotels undercut standard minimum rates imposed by the Philippine Tourism Authority (PTA), thus directly competing with lower-class hotels. Realizing that they could no longer rely on tourists, the five-star hotels shifted their emphasis to local customers. Thus, food and beverage sales became the bread and butter of hotel operations.

By this time, DBP controlled 90 percent of the five-star hotels. In 1982, it started divesting its investments in hotels, among them the Manila Peninsula, the Manila Mandarin, the Manila Garden, Holiday Inn, Silahis (Filipino for "jewel") International, and Century Park Sheraton.

From 1980 to 1986, the country's tourism industry experienced its ups and downs in arrivals, mostly downs. This was mainly due to a continuing barrage of negative publicity abroad, which reached its peak after the assassination of Senator Benigno Aquino Jr in August 1983.

When the Aquino government took over in February 1986 following the ouster of the Marcos regime, industry leaders were ecstatic that this would signal the start of a revival in Philippine tourism. The February 1986 Revolution spawned a new "age" for the hotel industry, with the increase in tourist arrivals. The industry could not completely take off, however, because the political and economic situation continued to be unstable. Gains were set back by the negative publicity generated by the spate of coups d'état, urban terrorism, labor unrest, bombing incidents, and kidnappings.

Toward the end of September 1988, however, it appeared that the hotel industry was really on its way to the much anticipated "boom." From January to September 1988, the number of tourist arrivals was at 733,357, compared to 1987's 599,488 covering the same period. By the end of 1988, tourist arrivals exceeded one million, the first time in eight years. Five-star hotels, in particular, experienced a rosy year in 1988 with an overall average occupancy of 77.09 percent, reflecting an increase of 9.21 percent over the level of the same period in 1987 (see Exhibit 3).

**Tourist Arrivals**

Tourist arrivals in the Philippines have always been considered low by Asian standards, averaging just about 150,000 prior to the 1970s. All this changed after the imposition of martial law by former President Ferdinand Marcos in September 1972, which saw tourist arrivals reaching over half a million by 1975 and over a million by 1980.

A declining trend in tourist arrivals then followed with average percentage drops of about five percent per year. The situation reversed, though, in 1986 following the establishment of a new government in the Philippines (see Exhibit 4).

The number of tourist arrivals in the country also followed a seasonal pattern. The number of visitors reached its highest levels during the latter months of the year (October to December), as well as in January (see Exhibit 5). This was followed by the lean months of February to May. It must be noted that during the rainy season (i.e., the months of June to August), the number of tourist arrivals increased significantly. Thus, two peak seasons could be considered, namely, the rainy season and the holiday season.

**Customers**

The hotels' customers consisted of both foreigners and locals (including "balikbayans," or returning overseas Filipinos). Foreigners were the primary target market. Based on the statistical figures provided by the DOT (see Exhibits 6 to 9), the typical foreign visitor to the country had the following characteristics:

1. Businessperson (i.e., professional, administrative, or managerial)
2. Japanese, Hong Kong Chinese, American, or European in origin
3. Typically a male, independent traveler
4. Primary purpose of stay was either leisure or business

However, locals could sometimes be equally important as they provided the revenues during periods of downturn in the tourism industry. Other local customers consisted largely of corporate and government accounts. In terms of the hotels' food and beverage outlets, local residents were their biggest clients, especially in terms of wedding receptions and local conventions or professional meetings.

Most of the hotels' customers were Foreign Individual Travelers (FITs) from Asia, North America, and Europe (see Exhibits 10 to 12 for a profile of major travel markets by country of origin per hotel).

A substantial portion of the foreign business was also accounted for by tour groups. These provided lower margins for the hotels, because of the discounted rates given to this type of customers. It should be noted here that, with the current tourism boom, most of the five-star hotels were gearing away from tour groups. The trend shifted to FITs, which provide higher margins for the hotels.

**Suppliers**

The hotels' suppliers consisted mostly of food and beverage wholesalers. Since food and beverage costs comprised a substantial portion of total costs, most hotels normally monitored various supplier prices through the regular canvassing procedures of their purchasing departments as a control procedure. The hotels, of course, were also very particular about the quality of their purchased items because quality must be consistent with the standards of a deluxe hotel.

The hotels also had various suppliers for amenities, furniture, appliances, and operating equipment (chinaware, silverware, glassware, linen, and uniforms). A substantial portion of purchased items, such as special wines and liquors, special food items, silverware, and glassware were imported from abroad. There were a large number of local suppliers and distributors who tried to maintain or get hold of the hotel business. Consequently, prices of goods in general were competitive.

**Channels of Distribution and Sources of Business**

The most important sources of the hotels' foreign business were the wholesalers such as travel agents and tour companies. Although each person or group booked through these wholesalers cost the hotel a 10-percent commission, they handle a large volume of travelers. As a result, most hotels found it good business to work closely with them. A hotel might often arrange a package plan with the travel agent in which the latter sells the customer a package that includes: transportation, lodging, and often, visits to tourist attractions within the country. It should be noted, though, that travel agents normally did not deal exclusively with any single hotel.

The airlines were another important source of business. Because airline agents were also sources of information about hotels, the sales department worked closely through these representatives in order to generate business.

Each of the hotels maintained a local sales force which made regular sales calls to these traditional contacts. Field sales personnel conducted a sales "blitz," or traveled to foreign countries specifically to promote the hotel.

Aside from these field personnel, the hotels also had a sales force that conducted business from their office using the telephone or received visits from prospective customers. These included sales personnel for banquets and catering services.

**Substitutes**

The hotels' major services were in the form of lodging and food and beverage. In the area of lodging, five-star hotels indirectly competed with four-star hotels and remotely with lower-category hotels (see Exhibit 13 for the list of hotels under each classification; Exhibit 14 for the percentage occupancy of each category of hotels).

A significant percentage of the travel market did not stay in hotels or other similar establishments (see Exhibit 15 for a breakdown of the accommodation alternatives taken by travelers).

In the area of food and beverage, including entertainment services, the years 1987 to 1988 gave the market a host of new, first-class places — various gourmet and specialty restaurants, bars, discos, and music lounges. These new and exciting places, which proliferated in the Makati and Manila areas, gave the local and foreign market more alternatives for their dining, entertainment, and relaxation needs.

**Hotel Services**

All twelve five-star hotels in Metro Manila offered the standard sources/facilities required of a deluxe hotel. These included the following:

Room Features

- Direct-dial telephone with a bathroom extension
- Radio/television
- Refrigerator/mini-bar
- Individually controlled central air-conditioning system
- Tub/shower bath combination with 24-hour service

Guest Facilities

- Laundry and valet services
- Medical and dental services
- 24-hour room service
- Swimming pool
- Health club with sauna and gymnasium facilities
- Communication facilities
- Business center
- Barber shop and/or beauty parlor
- Newsstand
- Shopping facilities
- Baby sitting service
- Limousine/car rental services

It was also standard practice among hotels to undertake major renovations every five years in order to upgrade their facilities. Aside from bedroom facilities and guest services mentioned above, hotels had a variety of food and beverage outlets which served as dining and entertainment facilities. There were also convention and banquet facilities, which included a ballroom and a number of function rooms.

The trend among hotels was the computerization of their operations to enable them to provide quicker service to their customers. All the five-star hotels were planning to eventually link up all their outlets to the front office so as to come up with up-to-date guest ledgers and facilitate information requirements from the different departments.

Room rentals accounted for 45 to 48 percent of the hotel revenues and the remaining 38 to 42 percent was generated from the sale of food and beverages. The balance of the revenue came from telephone, laundry services, foreign exchange transactions, and concessionaires (operators of shops who rent hotel space). The house guests contributed to some 25 percent of the hotels' food and beverage sales, with the rest being accounted for by the local residents.

### Pricing

Room rates varied among the five-star hotels (see Exhibit 16 for hotel rates for September 1988). The Manila Mandarin currently had the highest rate, charging US$130 for a single room and US$150 for a double room, while the Manila Garden had the lowest rate, charging US$52 for a single room and US$60 for a double room.

Food and beverage prices were comparable among the five-star hotels, although prices were generally higher compared to other first class restaurants in Metro Manila. The relatively higher price charged by hotels for food enabled them to cover their enormously high overhead.

### Promotions

Promotions among the five-star hotels were quite standard. Advertising was usually done in print, specifically through local newspapers, and to a limited extent, foreign business and travel magazines. In addition, brochures and leaflets were used to inform the market of the complete array of services and facilities, available rates, and other pertinent information.

Local advertising on print encouraged local patronage of a hotel's food and beverage outlet. Advertisements were usually about ongoing special promotions such as discounts on room rates or food fairs, the opening of a new restaurant or a newly renovated disco, wedding packages, and the like.

Publicity was also a common tool among five-star hotels. All these hotels had their own public relations department tasked with creating favorable publicity for their respective hotels. One could frequently find periodic press releases pertaining to the inauguration of a new restaurant, the promotion or an appointment of a general manager or director of sales, or the hotel's public relations officer welcoming newly arrived well-known celebrities or public figures.

### Employment

The hotel industry accounted for 42.8 percent of total employment in all tourist establishments. A deluxe hotel employed 1.6 employees per room.

While these establishments got most of their employees locally, the top managerial positions of most hotels were mostly occupied by expatriates. Among the positions commonly occupied by the expatriates were the following: General Manager, Executive Assistant Manager, Executive Chef, Executive Sous Chef, Specialty Sous Chef, and Food and Beverage Manager. This could be explained by the fact that most of these five-star hotels were managed by foreign hotel chains, and food and beverage operations require highly trained and experienced chefs of international calibre.

### Ownership, Management and Franchising Arrangement

The standard practice in the industry is to have franchising arrangements with transnational hotel chains. Under the franchising arrangement, there is a management contract whereby the owner employs the operator (the international chain) to assume full operational responsibility for the property. As an agent, the operator pays all property and operating expenses from the cash flow generated from operation, retained its management fees, and remits the remaining flow. The owner, on the other hand, provides the hotel property, including the land, building, furniture, fixtures, and equipment and assumes legal and financial responsibility for the project. This type of arrangement enabled the local hotel to use the name of the international chain, as well as to take advantage of the international chain's worldwide reservation network, professional and experienced management in hotel operations, and technical assistance.

In return for these services, the management company is paid a certain fee. In general, there were three types of fee structure:

1. A basic fee structure ranging up to five percent of gross revenue is paid to the managing company.
2. A basic fee plus incentive, in which the management company is paid a basic fee as above but also gets an additional incentive of up to 10 percent of income before fixed charges. These fixed charges include rent, interest, depreciation, property, and income taxes.
3. A basic fee or incentive, whichever is greater.

Aside from this, the hotel is also charged with certain expenses incurred by the management company on a regional, centralized, or chain-wide basis. For example, the local hotel is commonly charged with its "share" of corporate marketing and promotion expenses.

### Government Regulation

As tourism establishments, hotels are under the jurisdiction of the DOT. The department is vested with the authority to promulgate rules and regulations governing the operation and activities of all persons, firms, entities, and establishments that cater to tourists.

Aside from providing standards for accreditation and for classification of hotels, the DOT has prescribed rules regarding registration of hotel guests, provisions for ensuring the safety of tourists, building sanitation, discipline and training of hotel staff, and immoral and illegal acts such as prostitution.

The DOT conducts periodic inspections of the hotels and their immediate premises. The purpose of these inspections is to find out whether hotels are being kept and/or managed in a manner that conforms with the licensing and registration standards set by the DOT for a given hotel accreditation or classification. A hotel might be promoted or demoted from one class to another as the facts may warrant. As a tourist-registered enterprise, hotels are also granted certain tax incentives.

Since the hotel regularly deals with foreign exchange in the conduct of its business, it is also subject to certain rules and regulations of the Central Bank of the Philippines. For example, as an authorized foreign exchange agent, the hotels are required to sell all foreign exchange to the local banking system for Philippine pesos. Hotels are also not allowed to purchase foreign exchange.

## Competition

### Rivalry Among Existing Firms

There are currently twelve five-star hotels in Metro Manila. Four of these hotels are located in Makati, which is the heart of Manila's commercial and business district. The rest are located at or near the Manila Bay Area, within easy reach of the Philippine International Convention Center (PICC), Manila's central business district, and entertainment districts, commonly referred to as the "Tourist Belt" (see Exhibit 17 for the percentage share of total guests of five-star hotel establishments, and Exhibits 18 to 19 for the monthly occupancy rates per deluxe hotel).

Competition among five-star hotels can be characterized as "friendly" since they normally exchange information and statistics regarding hotel operations. All the deluxe hotels are members of the Hotel & Restaurant Association of the Philippines, a forum where industry practices and problems are discussed.

This friendly relationship can best be illustrated when a hotel is victimized by a "skipper" (i.e., a hotel guest who runs away without paying his bills). The hotel normally furnishes the other hotels with information on the identity of the skipper and a description of the skipper.

While competition can be characterized as friendly, there is nevertheless intense competition during slack periods. During these lean times, hotels attempt to fill up vacancies through heavy promotions, special discounts, and advertising.

In general, the financial performance of the five-star hotels within Metro Manila provide some insights into the current conditions of the hotels in the area. Almost all hotels were hit hard by the downtrend in tourist arrivals during the late 1970s and early 1980s, resulting in net losses for most hotels. However, by 1986, the booming tourist industry enabled most hotels to generate positive net incomes.

## Profile of Leading Deluxe Hotels

**Manila Hotel.** The Manila Hotel, apart from being the most established five-star hotel in the Philippines, is also the most recognized and most rewarded for its outstanding facilities and services.

It is the only hotel to have been ranked consistently among the 50 best hotels of the world and the top 10 hotels in Asia in recent years by the *Institutional Investor*, a prestigious international business publication which conducts annual surveys of hotels. Manila Hotel's "historical" reputation has made it more appealing to the U.S. market (General Douglas MacArthur stayed in one of its rooms, later renamed the MacArthur Suite).

In October 1988, the Manila Hotel had an average occupancy rate of 60.11 percent with gains of more than 5 percent over the same period in 1987. Actual gross revenues obtained amounted to a hefty PHP50 million increase over the past year.[1] The year 1988 was a very good year for the hotel as it saw its room revenues go up by PHP20 million and its food and beverage revenues by PHP20 million. These figures may be the real indicators of the hotel's profitability and not room occupancy.

The Manila Hotel adhered to a philosophy stressing a commitment to excellence. As such, the hotel's respected status in the international hotel industry did not leave any room for compromising its excellent standards and quality.

**Century Park Sheraton.** The Century Park Sheraton is one of the most sought-after hotels in the country, with an average occupancy rate of 76.2 percent in October 1988. It

[1]In 1989, the exchange rate between the Philippine Peso (PHP) and the U.S. Dollar was US$1 = PHP20.

is associated with the Sheraton group of hotels, which has been voted as the world's number one hotel chain in 1987 based on a survey of 30,000 airline passengers conducted by the International Federation of Airline Passengers Association. Its high rating was attributed primarily to its hotels' good location, quality rooms and service, "value for money", and fast check-in and check-out services.

The Century Park Sheraton is situated in the heart of Manila's business, cultural, shopping, and entertainment districts. It is located across from the Central Bank and the Ninoy Aquino Stadium, beside Harrison Plaza (a very busy shopping center complex in Manila) and within walking distance of the PICC.

The Century Park Sheraton had been on a renovation program which started late in 1987. The first phase of its plan, which includes the upper lobby and adjacent public areas, reception facilities, and function rooms has already been completed. In addition, new guest facilities have been incorporated, such as the separate tour group lounge and a bar-equipped VIP lounge to allow for a smooth check-in. Also, the cashier's counter was expanded to expedite check-out procedures, and the Business Center in its new location is also now equipped with a computer to complement its existing facilities, which include a facsimile, and cable and telex facilities.

The second phase of the renovation involved the refurbishing of 500 rooms. This phase extended up to the hotel's restaurants and bars, as well as its dining and entertainment plaza.

In 1989, the hotel also established financial linkages with a leading Japanese airline, which owned some amount of stocks. Further, the superb guest services and excellent facilities made Sheraton one of the top four hotels in the Philippines.

**Manila Garden Hotel.** The Manila Garden Hotel came into being during 1976 as a joint venture among the Fernandez and Ayala groups of companies, the Japan Airlines Development Company, the Mitsui group of Japan, and the Bank of Japan with a paid-up capital of PHP60 million. A long-term loan of PHP172.9 million was borrowed from the DBP and the 16-story, 525-room hotel was constructed in the Makati Commercial Center. The Manila Garden Hotel was part of the Japan Air Lines chain of hotels linking some 65 hotels all over the world. It also has a computerized reservation system (JALCOM #3), which is one of the most advanced in the world and can confirm reservations from any part of the globe.

The Manila Garden Hotel's unique tri-winged superstructure sets it apart from the standard hotel structure. Further, it enjoys the highest occupancy rate among all hotels at 93.38 percent (October 1988) due to its contacts with tour groups. Moreover, it has less expensive room rates vis-à-vis the competition.

**Manila Midtown.** The Manila Midtown stands amidst a giant seven-hectare complex that includes a department store, specialty shops, a fast-food center, travel agencies, an airline office, and moviehouses right in the heart of Manila's tourist and entertainment district.

The Manila Midtown has the largest ballroom among the five-star hotels in Manila, with a capacity of 2,200 people for a sit-down dinner and 3,300 for cocktails. It also boasts of 600 newly renovated guest rooms and suites, many of which have extra-large beds. In addition, Manila Midtown has the latest in key systems. Its computerized key system, the

VING card, was the first and only one of its kind in the Philippines. VING Card takes away the use of the lock key and provides the utmost security and convenience for the user. The VING card has holes in it which are programmed to fit into the door's opening. The holder does not need to return it after his or her stay (thus possibly serving as a souvenir item) since the next occupant of the room would have a different key card, programmed for his or her own personal use.

A close look at its financial statements would show that Manila Midtown has a relatively low overhead. Unlike the majority of hotels, it does not pay management fees because it is locally managed.

**Manila Pavilion Hotel.** This hotel, formerly known as the Manila Hilton, was recently bought by the Acesite group of Hong Kong. It is managed by the CIM Hotel Management Company Limited of Hong Kong (a sister firm), following the expiration of a management contract between Hilton International and the Delgado group on December 31, 1988.

The 406-room Manila Pavilion Hotel was completed in 1968 and, with 22 stories, was one of Manila's tallest buildings at that time. It is located along United Nations Avenue, which is in the heart of Manila's tourist district. It is also one of only two deluxe hotels in Metro Manila authorized by the government to operate a casino.

In January 1989, the Manila Pavilion Hotel embarked on an expansion plan on an adjacent lot along United Nations Avenue. This would cost about PHP200 million and would involve the addition of 120 rooms to the existing 406 rooms of the hotel. The planned building would also be as tall as the old one and there could be provisions to connect the two.

**Mandarin Oriental.** Formerly called the Manila Mandarin, the Mandarin Oriental was associated with the world famous Oriental Bangkok, recently voted as the second best hotel in the world. The hotel's character and style echoes an image which management has successfully developed — that of a businessperson's hotel. It is then reputed to be the best hotel in terms of service.

Offering all the amenities of a five-star businessperson's hotel, the Mandarin caters mostly to foreign businessmen from Asia and the Pacific (60 percent of total occupants), the U.S. (17 percent) and Europe (9 percent). In 1988, the Mandarin Oriental began undergoing a three-year renovation program to upgrade the hotel's public areas, restaurants, and existing rooms. It had also begun to computerize operations, with a total cost of US$11.5 million.

With the continued upswing in visitor arrivals expected to occur in 1989, the hotel posted an unprecedented 69.23 percent average occupancy rate for the first quarter of 1988. However, in May 1988, the Mandarin Oriental had the lowest occupancy rate at 60 percent. This might be attributed to its then ongoing renovation and expansion program, which prompted guests to change hotels due to the inconvenience caused by the renovation.

Room rates offered by the Mandarin Oriental are competitive with those offered by other hotels catering to the business crowd, namely the Manila Hotel, the Manila Peninsula, and Hotel Intercontinental.

**Westin Philippine Plaza.** The Westin Philippine Plaza is the country's largest hotel, featuring 675 exotically furnished rooms offering world-class amenities. It is part of the Cultural Center Complex and is right next to the US$100 million PICC. The Cultural Center Complex comprises the Folk Arts Theater, the Convention Center, the Cultural Center, and the International Trade & Exhibit Center, structures built under the patronage of the former First Lady, Imelda Marcos.

The hotel is also known as Manila's only seaside resort and has a pillarless banquet ballroom, which has the second largest capacity in the country. Also, the Philippine Plaza is managed by Westin Hotels and Resorts, America's oldest operating hospitality firm. Westin owns or manages 61 hotels worldwide, including the Plaza in New York, the Westin St Francis in San Francisco, the Westin Stamford in Singapore, and Kowloon Shangri-La in Hong Kong.

The Government Service Insurance System (GSIS), which owns the Philippine Plaza, plans to privatize it by 1989 and gain some PHP1.3 billion in the process.

**Manila Peninsula.** The Manila Peninsula Hotel is one of the classiest hotels in the country and is a member of the worldwide association of independently operated luxury hotels, that is, the Preferred Hotels. It is managed by the Hong Kong and Shanghai Hotels Limited, which manages the Peninsula group of hotels. It is located right across from the Makati Commercial Center and the country's financial district.

Within the international market, the Manila Peninsula is primarily known as a businessperson's hotel. It caters to business travelers coming from the United States, Australia, and Europe since, relative to other nationalities, these people were potentially bigger revenue sources for the company. Consequently, it also has one of the highest room rates in the country.

The Manila Peninsula is also well-known for its huge lobby, which projects a classy ambiance and for its restaurants, which provide superlative cuisine. Thus, guests usually refer to the Manila Peninsula as the "place to see and be seen."

**Silahis International Hotel.** The Silahis International Hotel is one of the few five-star hotels without any management contract from any transnational firm. It is managed by the Sulu group of hotels, which also manages the Puerto Azul Beach Club and other resorts in the country. It acquired a franchise with Playboy Products and Services International, which granted it the privilege to operate a Playboy Club. It is also one of only two hotels in Metro Manila with a casino. Another unique feature is its space-capsule elevator leading to the Stargazer, the longest-running disco in Manila.

The Silahis International Hotel, however, has been beset with problems after the February 1986 Revolution. In May 1986, the Presidential Committee on Good Government (PCGG) issued a sequestration order based on the owners' connection with the wealth, shares, and interest allegedly acquired illegally by certain stockholders of the company. As of January 1989, there was still no decision as to the fate of this sequestration.

**Hotel Inter-Continental Manila.** The Hotel Inter-Continental is the oldest hotel in the Makati area. It is backed by a strong stockholder group that maintains a policy of plowing back its earnings to continually upgrade the hotel. It is known as a businessperson's hotel and definitely does not entertain tour group accounts.

The hotel is located within the Makati commercial complex and has links with the Punta Baluarte Inter-Continental resort in Batangas and the Davao Insular Inter-Continental Inn in Mindanao.

**Hyatt Regency.** Hyatt Regency was acquired in 1988 by the Chan group of companies from GSIS in line with the privatization thrust of the Philippine Government. It is a member of the Hyatt chain of hotels and has links with Hyatt Terraces in Baguio and Hyatt Rafols in Palawan. It is the smallest five-star hotel in terms of area and accommodation, having only 265 rooms. Its biggest clients come from diversified areas such as Europe (15.75 percent), Japan (14.17 percent), and the Middle East (14.27 percent).

Hyatt's exclusive accommodations at the Regency Club are known the world over as a "hotel within a hotel" (one floor was devoted to this club).

**Holiday Inn Manila.** The hotel has strong links with the United States' Holiday Inn chain, which boasts of over 200 hotels worldwide and is one of the most respected names in the hotel business.

Holiday Inn Manila is located along the Manila Bay Area and has 570 rooms. It caters mostly to Japanese clients, which account for 25 percent of its total guests.

As with the Silahis International Hotel, Holiday Inn is also under sequestration from PCGG for shares of stock that were allegedly acquired illegally.

**Potential Entrants**

The Hong Kong–based Kuok Group, whose Shangri-La hotel chain was rated as among the best in the world, plans to build two deluxe hotels in Metro Manila. One of these would be built in Makati and the other in Mandaluyong at a combined cost of US$158 million.

The Shangri-La Manila, to be built at the intersection of Ayala and Makati Avenues, would be a 27-storey structure with 667 rooms modules and suites, and parking facilities for more than 350 vehicles. The Shangri-La Manila would become the 17th member of the Shangri-La chain of hotels throughout Asia and the Pacific.

The Shangri-La EDSA (Epifanio de los Santos Avenue) Plaza, on the other hand, will be constructed at the corner of EDSA and Shaw Boulevard in Mandaluyong. It would be a joint undertaking with the Ramos group, which owns the two-hectare hotel site and the country's largest bookstore chain, the National Book Store. The first phase would house 440 rooms and would cost about US$50 million to complete, while the second one would cost US$30 million. The construction of the Shangri-La EDSA Plaza is expected to start during the first half of 1989. It plans to open in 1991 and would be part of a complex of shopping areas, two office towers, and two apartment towers. Its vicinity is believed to be the next business center of Metro Manila, particularly with the transfer of major business institutions such as the Asian Development Bank (ADB).

Another hotel whose construction is in full swing is the PHP2 billion Robinson's Galleria hotel shopping complex. This hotel is to be located at the corner of Ortigas Avenue and EDSA in Pasig. The hotel is expected to be completed by December 1989. It was designed by Hellmuth, Obata, and Kassebaum of San Francisco and would be a 30-storey deluxe hotel. It would be unique from the other hotels in the sense that the gross floor area would cover about 26 hectares and would house mini-anchor shops, a dry goods shop, a supermarket, a department store, six cinemas, and an amusement center.

### Rejuvenation of Mothballed Hotels

Aside from these plans of building new hotels, there are talks of revitalizing the Philippine Village Hotel (PVH) and the Regent of Manila, two "mothballed" hotels. PVH is situated near the Manila International Airport and thus has the advantage of capturing check-in traffic provided by stranded or delayed flight passengers. It was closed in 1986 due to financial difficulties.

The Regent of Manila, on the other hand, is situated in the bay area and was partially gutted down by fire in early 1985. It is owned by the Philippine National Bank, which foreclosed it from the previous owners. With the government's thrust toward privatization, there are ongoing negotiations for the sale of the building and property. It is being eyed by a Taiwanese group, which plans to restore it to meet expected demand for more hotel rooms in Manila.

## Prospects for the Future

### Department of Tourism

The year 1988 marked the most successful year for the tourism industry since 1980 as it saw its tourist arrivals hit one million for the first time in eight years. The primary factors that led to this overwhelming success have much to do with improving the Philippines' image problem and concentrating tourism marketing efforts on Japan and Hong Kong.

The long-term goal of the DOT was to establish the Philippines as a national and international convention country. It therefore declared 1989 as "Fiesta Islands Year" to launch its new five-year program. Some of the plans lined up for this program included intensifying the role played by the Philippine Tourism Authority as the developing arm of the Department of Tourism, as well as lining up international conferences for the Philippines.

The fiesta theme is intended to capture the epitome of Filipino culture. It is supposed to encapsulate everything that is positive about the Philippines: the music, the hospitality, the cuisine, and the religious aspects of the country. These factors or characteristics are seen as giving the Philippines a distinctive edge over its Asian neighbors.

The Philippines still has some catching up to do if it expects to match the tourism receipts of its Asian neighbors. Improvements needed to boost tourism prospects are expected to be achieved through such campaigns as the "Barangay Bidahan sa Kalinisan" (Neighborhood Competition for Cleanliness) program, a road improvement campaign which would facilitate more passable roads and well-lit highways, a beautification program that hopes to transform Metro Manila into a fiesta city, an information and education campaign on Philippine tradition and heritage, and an airport campaign which would seek to ease the flow of visitors through customs, quarantine, and immigration at the Ninoy Aquino International Airport, including crowd and vehicular traffic control outside the terminal area.

Another area that also needs much improvement concerns some of the practices and attitudes Filipinos hold toward tourists. Some practices which need to be changed include taxi drivers ripping off tourists through tampered meters and vendors overcharging for their goods when tourists are the buyers.

The ultimate goal of the project is to bring in a total of two million visitors to the Philippines by 1991, as well as to increase tourism receipts to about PHP2 billion by the same year. DOT predicted that an additional 700 deluxe rooms alone may be needed by 1991 in order to service the lodging needs of the potential inflow of tourists. The campaign also hopes to develop higher awareness and a deeper appreciation of local traditions among Filipinos and foreigners.

Most tourism industry experts, including Eugene Sullivan (Executive Director of the Hong Kong Tourist Association) and the president of a U.S. travel agency, agree that there had been an increasing trend of North American and Western Europeans visits to the Far East in the late 1980s. The visits usually involved more than one stopover.

Thailand was the first to take advantage of this trend by launching its "Visit Thailand Year" in 1986. In 1988, Thailand boasted arrivals of over four million tourists, a figure four times larger than the figure for the Philippines that same year. Following Thailand's success, Malaysia designated the year 1990 as "Visit Malaysia Year." In fact, the Philippines started feeling the positive effects of this shift of tourists to the Asian market only in 1988 because the country was previously beset by image problems.

**The Philippine Economy**

The Philippine economy is expected to slow down in 1989 after recording its strongest GNP growth rate performance for the decade. The reasons for the lower growth hinges on the fact that there will be a recession that might hit the United States, which is one of the country's biggest trading partners. Also, the consumer-led economic recovery might be over, and now the nasty effects of higher inflation, higher interest rates, and likely depreciation of the peso vis-à-vis the U.S. dollar are likely to take place in 1989.

Despite the projected slowdown, the growth momentum is expected to be sustained in 1989 as businesses in the Philippines remain motivated and bullish. This is a good sign because a good economy would attract the needed revenues generated by the tourism industry which, in turn, would ultimately have a positive effect on the five-star hotel industry.

EXHIBIT 1

**THE DELUXE HOTEL INDUSTRY IN THE PHILIPPINES IN 1989**
**Average Level of Occupancy of Hotels, 1979–1988**

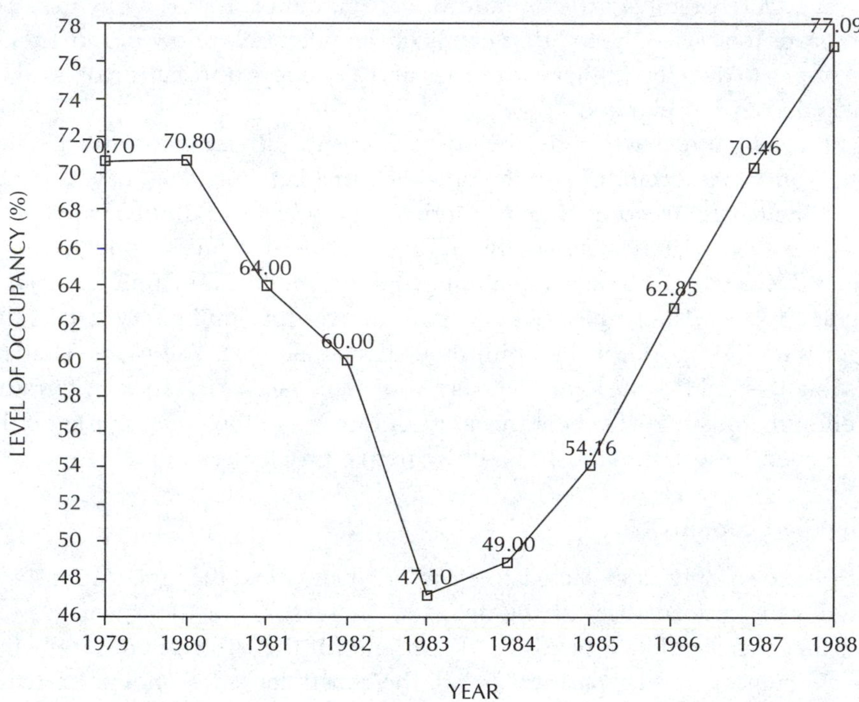


Note: The survey was carried out from 1979 to October 1988.

Source: Philippine Department of Tourism.

EXHIBIT 2

## THE DELUXE HOTEL INDUSTRY IN THE PHILIPPINES IN 1989
## Requirements for a Deluxe Class Hotel

The Philippines' Hotel Code of 1987 (Chapter II, Section 4) prescribes the following minimum requirements for the establishment, operation, and maintenance of a deluxe class hotel:

1. Location
   a. The locality and environs, including approaches, should be suitable for a luxury hotel of international standard.
   b. The facade, architectural features, and general construction of the building should have the distinctive qualities of a luxury hotel.

2. Bedroom Facilities and Furnishings
   a. Size
      All single and double rooms should have a floor area of not less than 25 square meters, inclusive of bathrooms.
   b. Suites
      There should be one suite per 30 guest rooms.
   c. Bathrooms
      (1) All rooms must have bathrooms which should be equipped with fittings of the highest quality befitting a luxury hotel with 24-hour service of hot and cold running water.
      (2) Bathrooms must be provided with bathtubs, showers, and telephones.
      (3) Floors and walls should be covered with impervious material of elegant design and high-quality workmanship.
   d. Telephones
      There should be a telephone in each guest room.
   e. Radio/Television
      There should be a radio, a television, and relayed or piped-in music in each guest room.
   f. Vacuum Jugs or Flasks
      There should be vacuum jugs or thermos flasks with ice-cold drinking water and glasses in each bedroom.
   g. Refrigerator/Mini-Bar
      There should be a small refrigerator and a well-stocked bar in each guest room.
   h. Room Service
      There should be a 24-hour room service (including provisions for snacks and light refreshments).
   i. Furnishings and Lighting
      (1) All guest rooms should have adequate furniture of the highest standard and elegant design; floors should have superior quality wall-to-wall carpeting; walls should be well-furnished with well-tailored draperies of rich materials.
      (2) Lighting arrangements and fixtures in the rooms and bathrooms should be so designed as to ensure esthetic as well as functional excellence.
   j. Information Materials
      Room tariffs shall be prominently displayed in each bedroom plus prominent notices for services offered by the hotel, fire exit guidelines, and house rules for guests, including meal hours and charges.

3. Front Office/Reception
   There should be a reception, information counter, and guest relations office providing 24-hour service and attended by highly qualified, trained, and experienced staff.
   a. Lounge
      There should be a lobby and a well-appointed lounge with seating, reading, and writing facilities, the size of which is commensurate with the size of the hotel.

b. Porter Service
There should be a 24-hour porter service.

c. Foreign Exchange Counter
There should be a duly licensed and authorized foreign exchange counter.

d. Mailing Facilities
Mailing facilities, including sale of stamps and envelopes, should be available in the premises.

e. Long Distance/Overseas Calls
Long-distance and overseas telephone services should be available in the establishment.

f. Reception Amenities
There should be a left-luggage room and safe deposit boxes in the establishment.

g. Telex Facilities
There should be telex-transceiver facilities in the establishment.

4. Housekeeping
Housekeeping should be of the highest possible standard.

a. Linen
There should be a plentiful supply of all linen, blanket, towels, and the like, which should be of the highest quality available and be spotlessly clean. Linen and towels should be changed everyday.

b. Laundry/Dry Cleaning Service
Laundry and dry cleaning services should be available in the establishment.

c. Carpeting
All public and private rooms should have superior quality carpeting, which should be well-kept at all times.

5. Food and Beverage

a. Dining Room
There should be a coffee shop and at least one specialty dining room which are well-equipped, well-furnished, and well-maintained, serving high-quality cuisine and providing entertainment.

b. Bar
Wherever permissible by law, there should be an elegant and well-stocked bar with an atmosphere of comfort and luxury.

c. Kitchen
(1) The kitchen, pantry, and cold storage should be professionally designed to ensure efficiency of operation and should be well-equipped, well-maintained, clean, and hygienic.
(2) The kitchen should have an adequate floor area with nonslip flooring, tiled walls, and adequate light and ventilation.

d. Crockery
(1) The crockery should be of elegant design and superior quality.
(2) There should be an ample supply of crockery.
(3) No piece of crockery should be chipped, cracked, or grazed. The silverware should be kept well-plated and polished at all times.

6. Recreational Facilities

a. Swimming Pool
There must be a well-designed and properly equipped swimming pool.

b. Tennis, Golf, Squash, and Gym Facilities
There should be at least one recreational facility or tie-up with one within the vicinity of the hotel.

7. Entertainment
Live entertainment should be provided.

8. Engineering and Maintenance
   a. Maintenance of all sections of the hotel (e.g., building, furniture, fixtures) should be of superior standard.
   b. Air-Conditioning
      There should be centralized air-conditioning for the entire building (except in areas which are at a minimum of 3,000 feet above sea level).
   c. Ventilation
      There should be technologically advanced, efficient, and adequate ventilation in all areas of the hotel.
   d. Lighting
      There should be adequate lighting in all public and private rooms.
   e. Emergency Power
      There should be a high-powered generator capable of providing sufficient lighting for all guest rooms, hallways, public areas/rooms, operating elevators, food refrigeration, and water services.
   f. Fire Prevention Facilities
      The fire prevention facilities must conform with the requirements of the Fire Code of the Philippines.

9. General Facilities
   a. Outdoor Area
      The hotel premises must have a common outdoor area for guests. Examples are a garden, a roof garden, or a spacious common terrace.
   b. Parking/Valet
      There should be adequate parking space and valet service.
   c. Function/Conference Facilities
      There should be one or more of the following: conference rooms, banquet halls (with a capacity of not less than 200 people, seated), and private dining rooms.
   d. Shops
      There should be a barber shop, recognized travel agency and tour counter, beauty parlor, and sundries shop.
   e. Security
      Adequate security on a 24-hour basis must be provided at all entrances and exits of the hotel premises.
   f. Medical Services
      A medical clinic to service guests and employees should have a registered nurse on a 24-hour basis and a doctor on call.

10. Service and Staff
    a. Professionally qualified, highly trained, experienced, efficient, and courteous staff should be employed.
    b. Staff should be in smart and clean uniforms.

11. Special Facilities
    A business center, gym facilities, limousine service, and airport transfers should be provided.

12. Insurance Coverage
    There should be adequate insurance against accidents for all guests.

EXHIBIT 3

## THE DELUXE HOTEL INDUSTRY IN THE PHILIPPINES IN 1989
### Average Hotel Occupancy Rates, 1986–1988

| | *1986* | *1987* | *1988** |
|---|---|---|---|
| Sheraton | 75.63% | 77.60% | 76.18% |
| Holiday Inn | 72.48% | 81.35% | 88.90% |
| Hotel Inter-Continental | 60.31% | 66.78% | 79.89% |
| Hyatt | 52.50% | 70.91% | 69.68% |
| Manila Garden | 74.63% | 85.99% | 93.38% |
| Manila Pavilion | 56.49% | 54.29% | 65.76% |
| Manila Hotel | 48.01% | 55.97% | 60.11% |
| Mandarin Oriental | 63.92% | 68.53% | 66.40% |
| Manila Midtown | 67.58% | 76.33% | 86.58% |
| Manila Peninsula | 52.64% | 63.39% | 72.53% |
| Silahis International | 57.47% | 75.13% | 81.40% |
| Philippine Plaza | 68.26% | 69.80% | 80.64% |
| Overall average | 62.85% | 70.46% | 77.09% |

*Up to October 1988 only.

Source: Philippine Department of Tourism.

EXHIBIT 4

**THE DELUXE HOTEL INDUSTRY IN THE PHILIPPINES IN 1989**
**Tourist Arrivals, 1970–1987**

| *Year* | *Arrivals* | *% Change* |
|---|---|---|
| 1970 | 144,071 | — |
| 1971 | 144,321 | 0.17% |
| 1972 | 166,431 | 15.32% |
| 1973 | 242,811 | 45.89% |
| 1974 | 411,138 | 69.32% |
| 1975 | 502,211 | 22.15% |
| 1976 | 615,159 | 22.49% |
| 1977 | 730,123 | 18.69% |
| 1978 | 859,396 | 17.71% |
| 1979 | 966,893 | 12.51% |
| 1980 | 1,008,159 | 4.27% |
| 1981 | 938,953 | −6.86% |
| 1982 | 890,807 | −5.13% |
| 1983 | 860,550 | −3.40% |
| 1984 | 816,712 | −5.09% |
| 1985 | 773,074 | −5.34% |
| 1986 | 781,517 | 1.09% |
| 1987 | 794,700 | 1.69% |

Source: Philippine Department of Tourism.

EXHIBIT 5

## THE DELUXE HOTEL INDUSTRY IN THE PHILIPPINES IN 1989
## Monthly Distribution of Visitor Arrivals, 1986–1987

| | *1986* | *% Change* | *1987* | *% Change* |
|---|---|---|---|---|
| January | 63,981 | — | 72,038 | — |
| February | 46,330 | –27.59% | 62,867 | –12.73% |
| March | 54,393 | 17.40% | 65,643 | 4.42% |
| April | 58,410 | 7.39% | 73,002 | 11.21% |
| May | 59,946 | 2.63% | 59,551 | –18.43% |
| June | 62,989 | 5.08% | 63,356 | 6.39% |
| August | 78,729 | 10.27% | 77,474 | 6.10% |
| September | 58,258 | –26.00% | 52,540 | –32.18% |
| October | 65,445 | 12.34% | 58,744 | 11.81% |
| November | 72,601 | 10.93% | 56,558 | –3.72% |
| December | 89,140 | 22.78% | 79,910 | 41.29% |

Source: Philippine Department of Tourism.

EXHIBIT 6

## THE DELUXE HOTEL INDUSTRY IN THE PHILIPPINES IN 1989
## Percentage Distribution of Visitor Arrivals in the Philippines, 1983–1988

| *Travel Market* | *1983* | *1984* | *1985* | *1986* | *1987* | *1987* | *1988* |
|---|---|---|---|---|---|---|---|
| Asean | | | | | | | |
| Brunei | 0.00% | 0.25% | 0.28% | 0.26% | 0.24% | 0.29% | 0.29% |
| Indonesia | 0.90% | 0.76% | 0.78% | 0.81% | 0.72% | 0.83% | 0.84% |
| Malaysia | 2.11% | 1.78% | 1.89% | 1.64% | 1.51% | 1.82% | 1.89% |
| Singapore | 3.19% | 2.74% | 2.26% | 2.27% | 2.26% | 2.66% | 2.67% |
| Thailand | 1.36% | 1.53% | 1.26% | 1.07% | 1.17% | 1.41% | 1.19% |
| Subtotal | 7.57% | 7.06% | 6.46% | 6.05% | 5.90% | 7.02% | 6.88% |
| Australia | 6.26% | 6.16% | 6.33% | 5.83% | 5.56% | 6.05% | 5.52% |
| Hong Kong | 8.18% | 7.75% | 6.83% | 9.69% | 10.22% | 12.62% | 15.92% |
| Japan | 20.78% | 19.72% | 19.86% | 17.18% | 15.96% | 18.65% | 22.41% |
| North America | | | | | | | |
| Canada | 1.85% | 2.11% | 2.25% | 2.38% | 2.49% | 2.45% | 2.24% |
| United States | 21.48% | 24.16% | 25.72% | 25.92% | 26.52% | 26.18% | 25.56% |
| Subtotal | 23.33% | 26.27% | 27.96% | 28.30% | 29.02% | 28.63% | 27.80% |
| Taiwan | 4.99% | 4.95% | 4.64% | 4.42% | 4.52% | 5.46% | 6.67% |
| Western Europe | | | | | | | |
| France | 0.98% | 0.96% | 1.01% | 1.03% | 0.87% | 0.98% | 0.91% |
| West Germany | 3.36% | 3.03% | 3.01% | 3.14% | 3.01% | 3.04% | 3.08% |
| Italy | 0.97% | 0.86% | 0.71% | 0.70% | 0.76% | 0.81% | 0.81% |
| Spain | 0.46% | 0.27% | 0.25% | 0.19% | 0.23% | 0.25% | 0.27% |
| Switzerland | 1.30% | 1.25% | 1.24% | 1.14% | 1.05% | 1.05% | 1.02% |
| United Kingdom | 2.81% | 2.72% | 2.66% | 2.62% | 2.62% | 2.75% | 2.90% |
| Other W. Europe | 2.80% | 2.73% | 2.57% | 2.77% | 2.89% | 2.07% | 2.24% |
| Subtotal | 12.67% | 11.83% | 11.46% | 11.60% | 11.43% | 10.96% | 11.25% |
| Other Unspecified Residences | 16.22% | 16.25% | 16.45% | 16.92% | 17.39% | 9.82% | 10.43% |
| Grand Total | 100.00% | 100.00% | 100.00% | 100.00% | 100.00% | 100.00% | 100.00% |

Source: Philippine Department of Tourism.

EXHIBIT 7

## THE DELUXE HOTEL INDUSTRY IN THE PHILIPPINES IN 1989
## Percentage Distribution of Air Visitor Arrivals
## By Major Travel Market, 1986–1987

| | *By Sex* | | | | | | *By Travel Arrangement* | | | | | |
|---|---|---|---|---|---|---|---|---|---|---|---|---|
| | *1986* | | | *1987* | | | *1986* | | | *1987* | | |
| *Travel Market* | *Male* | *Female* | *Not Stated* | *Male* | *Female* | *Not Stated* | *Package* | *Indep* | *Not Stated* | *Package* | *Indep* | *Not Stated* |
| Asean | | | | | | | | | | | | |
| Brunei | 78.50% | 19.74% | 1.76% | 76.98% | 20.71% | 2.31% | 9.99% | 83.99% | 6.02% | 9.44% | 81.75% | 8.31% |
| Indonesia | 71.58% | 26.57% | 1.85% | 73.85% | 24.10% | 2.05% | 8.58% | 82.78% | 8.64% | 8.08% | 79.86% | 12.46% |
| Malaysia | 75.87% | 22.79% | 1.34% | 76.80% | 22.25% | 0.95% | 20.47% | 73.58% | 5.95% | 22.90% | 70.19% | 6.51% |
| Singapore | 77.23% | 21.98% | 0.79% | 77.97% | 21.37% | 0.66% | 17.64% | 78.63% | 3.73% | 15.93% | 79.51% | 4.56% |
| Thailand | 68.07% | 30.59% | 1.34% | 69.18% | 29.42% | 1.40% | 6.98% | 81.28% | 11.74% | 10.68% | 73.02% | 16.30% |
| Subtotal | 74.58% | 24.21% | 1.21% | 75.55% | 23.35% | 1.10% | 15.05% | 78.48% | 6.47% | 15.63% | 76.01% | 8.36% |
| Australia | 71.67% | 28.03% | 3.00% | 72.13% | 27.48% | 0.39% | 18.60% | 77.60% | 3.80% | 15.59% | 79.18% | 5.23% |
| Hong Kong | 62.04% | 36.45% | 1.51% | 62.57% | 35.97% | 1.46% | 51.65% | 40.87% | 7.48% | 46.35% | 44.37% | 9.23% |
| Japan | 81.31% | 17.02% | 1.67% | 85.17% | 13.26% | 1.57% | 50.48% | 45.51% | 4.01% | 42.50% | 51.58% | 5.52% |
| North America | | | | | | | | | | | | |
| Canada | 53.78% | 45.95% | 0.27% | 54.47% | 45.09% | 0.44% | 11.08% | 81.12% | 7.80% | 9.80% | 80.55% | 9.45% |
| United States | 56.62% | 43.13% | 0.25% | 57.10% | 42.55% | 0.35% | 10.89% | 83.48% | 5.63% | 11.46% | 81.10% | 7.14% |
| Subtotal | 56.37% | 43.37% | 0.26% | 56.87% | 42.77% | 0.36% | 10.91% | 83.27% | 5.82% | 11.31% | 81.06% | 7.43% |
| Taiwan | 54.67% | 42.74% | 2.59% | 61.19% | 36.31% | 2.50% | 61.88% | 27.67% | 10.45% | 52.70% | 33.08% | 14.32% |

EXHIBIT 7 (cont'd)

**THE DELUXE HOTEL INDUSTRY IN THE PHILIPPINES IN 1989**
**Percentage Distribution of Air Visitor Arrivals**
**By Major Travel Market, 1986–1987**

| | *By Sex* | | | | | | *By Travel Arrangement* | | | | | |
|---|---|---|---|---|---|---|---|---|---|---|---|---|
| | *1986* | | | *1987* | | | *1986* | | | *1987* | | |
| *Travel Market* | *Male* | *Female* | *Not Stated* | *Male* | *Female* | *Not Stated* | *Package* | *Indep* | *Not Stated* | *Package* | *Indep* | *Not Stated* |
| Western Europe | | | | | | | | | | | | |
| France | 67.55% | 31.86% | 0.59% | 71.97% | 27.42% | 0.61% | 14.17% | 73.02% | 12.81% | 13.72% | 73.12% | 13.36% |
| West Germany | 71.04% | 27.30% | 1.66% | 72.36% | 26.21% | 1.43% | 13.37% | 74.13% | 12.50% | 13.51% | 70.67% | 15.92% |
| Italy | 69.91% | 28.81% | 1.28% | 70.79% | 28.04% | 1.17% | 20.06% | 64.75% | 15.19% | 22.18% | 59.27% | 18.35% |
| Spain | 60.52% | 38.11% | 1.37% | 64.48% | 34.15% | 1.37% | 16.19% | 70.08% | 13.73% | 17.38% | 65.08% | 17.54% |
| Switzerland | 71.73% | 26.96% | 1.26% | 71.95% | 26.87% | 0.18% | 13.51% | 76.41% | 10.08% | 14.97% | 72.01% | 13.02% |
| United Kingdom | 69.95% | 29.32% | 0.73% | 72.26% | 27.14% | 0.60% | 10.87% | 84.03% | 5.10% | 11.14% | 82.77% | 6.09% |
| Other W. Europe | 72.20% | 27.61% | 0.19% | 72.67% | 26.25% | 1.08% | 11.67% | 78.47% | 9.86% | 11.04% | 75.69% | 13.27% |
| Subtotal | 70.58% | 28.25% | 1.17% | 72.08% | 26.88% | 1.05% | 12.96% | 76.88% | 10.16% | 13.16% | 74.13% | 12.71% |
| Other Unspecified Residences | 67.50% | 29.73% | 2.77% | 67.19% | 30.42% | 2.39% | 13.82% | 69.02% | 17.16% | 14.74% | 64.50% | 21.76% |
| Grand Total | 66.69% | 31.09% | 1.32% | 67.70% | 31.06% | 1.24% | 25.64% | 66.17% | 8.19% | 23.31% | 66.14% | 11.53% |

Source: Philippine Department of Tourism.

EXHIBIT 8

**THE DELUXE HOTEL INDUSTRY IN THE PHILIPPINES IN 1989**
**Percentage Distribution of Air Visitor Arrivals**
**By Major Travel Market and Occupational Group**
**1986–1987**

| *Travel Market* | *Professional, Managerial, Administrative* | | *Clerical Sales Services* | | *Fishery, Husbandry, Agriculture* | | *Industrial Workers/ Laborers* | | *Civilian/ Military/Gov't Personnel* | |
|---|---|---|---|---|---|---|---|---|---|---|
| | *1986* | *1987* | *1986* | *1987* | *1986* | *1987* | *1986* | *1987* | *1986* | *1987* |
| Asean | | | | | | | | | | |
| Brunei | 54.06% | 50.86% | 8.08% | 8.97% | 0.29% | 0.42% | 5.53% | 2.99% | 8.57% | 11.33% |
| Indonesia | 37.86% | 39.43% | 9.43% | 10.61% | 0.37% | 0.55% | 1.17% | 1.02% | 11.04% | 11.96% |
| Malaysia | 57.90% | 60.69% | 9.56% | 10.59% | 0.63% | 0.67% | 4.16% | 4.20% | 2.82% | 2.75% |
| Singapore | 63.67% | 64.67% | 8.65% | 8.84% | 0.12% | 0.10% | 3.85% | 3.37% | 1.68% | 1.52% |
| Thailand | 33.63% | 34.52% | 21.01% | 23.93% | 0.20% | 0.26% | 1.02% | 1.11% | 16.10% | 14.70% |
| Subtotal | 53.11% | 54.63% | 11.18% | 12.23% | 0.34% | 0.34% | 3.17% | 2.89% | 6.03% | 5.86% |
| Australia | 40.00% | 42.74% | 10.71% | 10.23% | 0.92% | 0.75% | 14.71% | 11.25% | 1.64% | 1.33% |
| Hong Kong | 35.73% | 37.79% | 16.15% | 16.38% | 0.11% | 0.17% | 6.94% | 5.71% | 1.87% | 1.29% |
| Japan | 45.45% | 43.47% | 27.02% | 28.16% | 0.73% | 0.53% | 1.76% | 1.72% | 1.01% | 0.83% |
| North America | | | | | | | | | | |
| Canada | 37.34% | 36.76% | 10.41% | 11.46% | 0.58% | 0.51% | 9.32% | 8.71% | 0.78% | 0.66% |
| United States | 34.50% | 33.00% | 10.58% | 13.09% | 0.40% | 0.35% | 6.52% | 6.09% | 3.70% | 2.98% |
| Subtotal | 34.74% | 33.33% | 10.57% | 12.95% | 0.41% | 0.37% | 6.77% | 6.32% | 3.45% | 0.28% |

EXHIBIT 8 (cont'd)

**THE DELUXE HOTEL INDUSTRY IN THE PHILIPPINES IN 1989**
**Percentage Distribution of Air Visitor Arrivals**
**By Major Travel Market and Occupational Group**
**1986–1987**

| *Travel Market* | *Professional Managerial, Administrative* | | *Clerical Sales Services* | | *Fishery, Husbandry, Agriculture* | | *Industrial Workers/ Laborers* | | *Civilian/ Military/Gov't Personnel* | |
|---|---|---|---|---|---|---|---|---|---|---|
| | *1986* | *1987* | *1986* | *1987* | *1986* | *1987* | *1986* | *1987* | *1986* | *1987* |
| Taiwan | 48.11% | 51.82% | 2.80% | 3.12% | 1.69% | 1.12% | 1.71% | 1.50% | 3.40% | 0.22% |
| Western Europe | | | | | | | | | | |
| France | 48.42% | 50.37% | 8.14% | 7.56% | 0.57% | 0.66% | 3.57% | 4.50% | 1.16% | 0.81% |
| West Germany | 41.65% | 42.50% | 8.25% | 8.03% | 0.21% | 0.30% | 5.76% | 5.57% | 1.35% | 1.19% |
| Italy | 44.39% | 45.54% | 10.00% | 9.13% | 0.51% | 0.26% | 5.72% | 4.52% | 1.21% | 0.74% |
| Spain | 46.38% | 43.39% | 6.70% | 8.58% | 0.27% | 0.38% | 5.87% | 4.70% | 1.50% | 1.15% |
| Switzerland | 37.86% | 38.06% | 10.65% | 10.61% | 0.54% | 0.41% | 8.50% | 7.08% | 0.78% | 0.74% |
| United Kingdom | 51.32% | 53.16% | 9.11% | 8.68% | 0.20% | 0.57% | 7.20% | 6.03% | 1.66% | 1.56% |
| Other W. Europe | 45.80% | 46.11% | 8.02% | 7.33% | 0.38% | 0.47% | 6.14% | 5.71% | 1.31% | 1.16% |
| Subtotal | 45.32% | 46.24% | 8.71% | 8.29% | 0.36% | 0.44% | 6.25% | 5.68% | 1.33% | 1.16% |
| Other Unspecified Residences | 36.54% | 35.04% | 10.28% | 11.27% | 0.67% | 0.62% | 5.98% | 5.80% | 2.88% | 2.43% |
| Grand Total | 40.27% | 40.02% | 13.42% | 14.32% | 0.54% | 0.49% | 5.72% | 5.19% | 2.44% | 2.04% |

EXHIBIT 8 (cont'd)

**THE DELUXE HOTEL INDUSTRY IN THE PHILIPPINES IN 1989**
**Percentage Distribution of Air Visitor Arrivals**
**By Major Travel Market and Occupational Group**
**1986–1987**

| | *Housewife* | | *Student* | | *Retirees/ Pensioners* | | *Others* | | *Not Stated* | |
|---|---|---|---|---|---|---|---|---|---|---|
| *Travel Market* | *1986* | *1987* | *1986* | *1987* | *1986* | *1987* | *1986* | *1987* | *1986* | *1987* |
| Asean | | | | | | | | | | |
| Brunei | 5.00% | 4.93% | 8.23% | 6.97% | 0.39% | 0.58% | 5.44% | 5.61% | 4.51% | 7.34% |
| Indonesia | 8.37% | 7.83% | 12.59% | 10.09% | 0.29% | 0.26% | 8.31% | 7.79% | 10.50% | 10.46% |
| Malaysia | 6.13% | 5.48% | 9.42% | 6.29% | 0.49% | 0.43% | 4.48% | 4.84% | 4.40% | 4.06% |
| Singapore | 5.96% | 5.02% | 4.95% | 4.81% | 0.66% | 0.64% | 6.12% | 5.93% | 4.30% | 5.10% |
| Thailand | 6.39% | 5.25% | 10.20% | 8.85% | 0.42% | 0.27% | 4.73% | 4.66% | 6.60% | 6.45% |
| Subtotal | 6.28% | 5.51% | 8.21% | 6.65% | 0.51% | 0.47% | 5.67% | 5.62% | 0.55% | 5.80% |
| Australia | 6.94% | 6.77% | 8.52% | 8.17% | 4.23% | 4.14% | 8.40% | 9.83% | 3.93% | 4.79% |
| Hong Kong | 6.72% | 7.09% | 7.05% | 6.76% | 0.28% | 0.36% | 4.92% | 5.27% | 20.20% | 19.18% |
| Japan | 2.89% | 2.34% | 4.62% | 4.99% | 0.11% | 0.09% | 4.39% | 5.14% | 11.90% | 12.73% |
| North America | | | | | | | | | | |
| Canada | 7.58% | 6.98% | 14.04% | 13.85% | 4.00% | 3.96% | 5.99% | 6.74% | 9.90% | 10.37% |
| United States | 9.21% | 8.60% | 14.27% | 14.18% | 4.82% | 4.77% | 6.14% | 6.91% | 9.70% | 10.03% |
| Subtotal | 9.14% | 8.45% | 14.26% | 14.16% | 4.75% | 4.69% | 5.12% | 6.89% | 9.80% | 10.06% |

EXHIBIT 8 (cont'd)

**THE DELUXE HOTEL INDUSTRY IN THE PHILIPPINES IN 1989**
**Percentage Distribution of Air Visitor Arrivals**
**By Major Travel Market and Occupational Group**
**1986–1987**

| *Travel Market* | *Housewife* | | *Student* | | *Retirees/ Pensioners* | | *Others* | | *Not Stated* | |
|---|---|---|---|---|---|---|---|---|---|---|
| | *1986* | *1987* | *1986* | *1987* | *1986* | *1987* | *1986* | *1987* | *1986* | *1987* |
| Taiwan | 16.31% | 12.43% | 3.19% | 2.66% | 0.27% | 0.38% | 4.17% | 4.79% | 22.00% | 21.96% |
| Western Europe | | | | | | | | | | |
| France | 0.94% | 1.21% | 7.38% | 5.64% | 2.03% | 2.13% | 15.05% | 14.52% | 13.00% | 12.60% |
| West Germany | 4.67% | 4.22% | 7.91% | 8.78% | 1.03% | 0.97% | 14.44% | 13.91% | 14.70% | 14.53% |
| Italy | 3.49% | 3.41% | 6.48% | 6.76% | 1.96% | 1.74% | 17.98% | 19.30% | 8.20% | 8.60% |
| Spain | 7.38% | 6.98% | 8.33% | 9.95% | 1.16% | 1.26% | 14.28% | 14.43% | 8.10% | 9.18% |
| Switzerland | 5.15% | 5.32% | 5.06% | 4.94% | 0.64% | 0.78% | 19.06% | 18.94% | 11.70% | 13.12% |
| United Kingdom | 5.87% | 5.46% | 8.52% | 8.40% | 1.76% | 1.61% | 6.76% | 7.60% | 7.40% | 6.93% |
| Other W. Europe | 3.02% | 2.82% | 10.52% | 10.00% | 0.80% | 1.01% | 11.16% | 11.87% | 1.29% | 13.52% |
| Subtotal | 4.22% | 4.02% | 8.25% | 8.28% | 1.25% | 1.26% | 12.67% | 12,87% | 11.64% | 11.76% |
| Other Unspecified Residences | 9.25% | 8.87% | 12.32% | 12.08% | 1.82% | 1.84% | 6.59% | 7.19% | 13.67% | 13.86% |
| Grand Total | 7.29% | 6.80% | 9.63% | 9.55% | 2.11% | 2.13% | 6.54% | 7.15% | 12.04% | 12.31% |

Source: Philippine Department of Tourism.

EXHIBIT 9

## THE DELUXE HOTEL INDUSTRY IN THE PHILIPPINES IN 1989
## Percentage Distribution of Air Visitor Arrivals
## By Major Travel Market and Purpose of Visit
## 1986–1987

| | *Holiday* | | *Business* | | *Official Mission* | | *Convention* | |
|---|---|---|---|---|---|---|---|---|
| *Travel Market* | *1986* | *1987* | *1986* | *1987* | *1986* | *1987* | *1986* | *1987* |
| Asean | | | | | | | | |
| Brunei | 70.32% | 69.86% | 18.92% | 10.96% | 8.47% | 8.86% | 32.30% | 4.46% |
| Indonesia | 42.17% | 39.97% | 13.06% | 13.83% | 15.36% | 17.82% | 5.31% | 7.02% |
| Malaysia | 67.78% | 64.52% | 12.54% | 15.38% | 4.18% | 5.45% | 4.31% | 5.72% |
| Singapore | 60.35% | 56.91% | 28.57% | 32.09% | 2.44% | 2.77% | 2.48% | 2.73% |
| Thailand | 40.98% | 38.44% | 14.49% | 15.86% | 17.72% | 20.59% | 38.00% | 6.55% |
| Subtotal | 57.10% | 54.11% | 19.00% | 21.70% | 7.51% | 8.72% | 3.95% | 4.79% |
| Australia | 70.90% | 76.18% | 12.81% | 15.27% | 3.94% | 1.36% | 1.42% | 0.94% |
| Hong Kong | 77.95% | 77.05% | 13.87% | 15.00% | 0.28% | 0.55% | 0.54% | 0.49% |
| Japan | 77.95% | 79.80% | 10.93% | 11.75% | 1.54% | 2.00% | 0.50% | 0.42% |
| North America | | | | | | | | |
| Canada | 75.21% | 76.58% | 7.54% | 0.82% | 1.37% | 1.38% | 1.11% | 0.66% |
| United States | 81.72% | 57.12% | 11.07% | 10.89% | 3.21% | 3.12% | 1.26% | 0.90% |
| Subtotal | 56.16% | 58.82% | 10.77% | 10.66% | 3.05% | 2.97% | 1.25% | 0.88% |
| Taiwan | 80.37% | 77.01% | 10.19% | 12.34% | 0.76% | 0.90% | 0.43% | 0.61% |
| Western Europe | | | | | | | | |
| France | 71.97% | 68.13% | 15.95% | 22.15% | 2.10% | 2.19% | 1.31% | 0.83% |
| West Germany | 77.42% | 76.69% | 14.00% | 14.67% | 1.54% | 1.83% | 0.75% | 0.43% |
| Italy | 69.06% | 69.63% | 16.17% | 16.29% | 2.38% | 2.76% | 1.27% | 1.34% |
| Spain | 66.73% | 64.73% | 15.03% | 16.67% | 4.10% | 3.22% | 2.19% | 3.28% |
| Switzerland | 84.01% | 82.78% | 6.59% | 9.44% | 2.11% | 2.54% | 0.74% | 0.58% |
| United Kingdom | 66.22% | 66.70% | 22.12% | 23.26% | 1.14% | 1.54% | 1.12% | 0.83% |
| Other W. Europe | 69.16% | 69.73% | 18.74% | 19.77% | 1.93% | 2.33% | 2.13% | 0.99% |
| Subtotal | 72.38% | 71.83% | 16.74% | 18.15% | 1.75% | 2.08% | 127.00% | 0.83% |
| Other Unspecified Residences | 55.73% | 56.19% | 9.47% | 9.99% | 3.87% | 3.72% | 131.00% | 1.53% |
| Total | 67.51% | 66.72% | 12.18% | 13.02% | 2.55% | 2.74% | 1.20% | 1.09% |

EXHIBIT 9 (cont'd)

**THE DELUXE HOTEL INDUSTRY IN THE PHILIPPINES IN 1989**
**Percentage Distribution of Air Visitor Arrivals**
**By Major Travel Market and Purpose of Visit**
**1986–1987**

| | *Health* | | *Others* | | *Not Stated* | |
|---|---|---|---|---|---|---|
| *Travel Market* | *1986* | *1987* | *1986* | *1987* | *1986* | *1987* |
| Asean | | | | | | |
| Brunei | 0.05% | 0.11% | 3.92% | 3.30% | 3.00% | 3.25% |
| Indonesia | 0.42% | 0.17% | 15.98% | 13.43% | 7.70% | 7.76% |
| Malaysia | 0.21% | 0.29% | 67.30% | 5.42% | 4.25% | 3.22% |
| Singapore | 1.00% | 0.06% | 3.10% | 2.98% | 2.96% | 2.46% |
| Thailand | 1.40% | 0.09% | 12.52% | 10.99% | 8.53% | 7.48% |
| Subtotal | 1.70% | 0.14% | 7.40% | 6.31% | 4.87% | 4.23% |
| Australia | 16.00% | 0.20% | 340.00% | 3.94% | 2.37% | 2.11% |
| Hong Kong | 11.00% | 0.07% | 110.00% | 1.28% | 6.15% | 5.56% |
| Japan | 0.70% | 0.08% | 161.00% | 2.18% | 3.58% | 3.77% |
| North America | | | | | | |
| Canada | 1.11% | 0.70% | 9.06% | 8.31% | 4.65% | 4.12% |
| United States | 1.30% | 1.22% | 18.59% | 19.03% | 8.41% | 7.72% |
| Subtotal | 1.28% | 1.17% | 17.77% | 18.09% | 80.80% | 7.41% |
| Taiwan | 0.20% | 0.05% | 1.98% | 2.65% | 6.25% | 6.44% |
| Western Europe | | | | | | |
| France | 0.15% | 0.09% | 3.58% | 2.33% | 4.94% | 4.28% |
| West Germany | 0.24% | 0.25% | 2.24% | 2.63% | 3.81% | 3.50% |
| Italy | 0.55% | 0.33% | 4.75% | 4.55% | 5.82% | 5.10% |
| Spain | 0.41% | 0.60% | 3.89% | 5.46% | 7.65% | 6.39% |
| Switzerland | 0.48% | 0.56% | 1.43% | 1.70% | 2.64% | 2.40% |
| United Kingdom | 0.10% | 0.13% | 3.71% | 3.34% | 5.59% | 4.20% |
| Other W. Europe | 0.20% | 0.16% | 2.87% | 2.91% | 4.97% | 4.11% |
| Subtotal | 0.24% | 0.23% | 2.95% | 2.94% | 4.67% | 3.94% |
| Other Unspecified Residences | 1.21% | 1.23% | 9.67% | 10.80% | 18.74% | 16.54% |
| Total | 0.63% | 0.61% | 8.05% | 8.57% | 7.88% | 7.25% |

Source: Philippine Department of Tourism.

EXHIBIT 10

**THE DELUXE HOTEL INDUSTRY IN THE PHILIPPINES IN 1989**
**Percentage Share of Occupants' Countries of Origin, 1987**

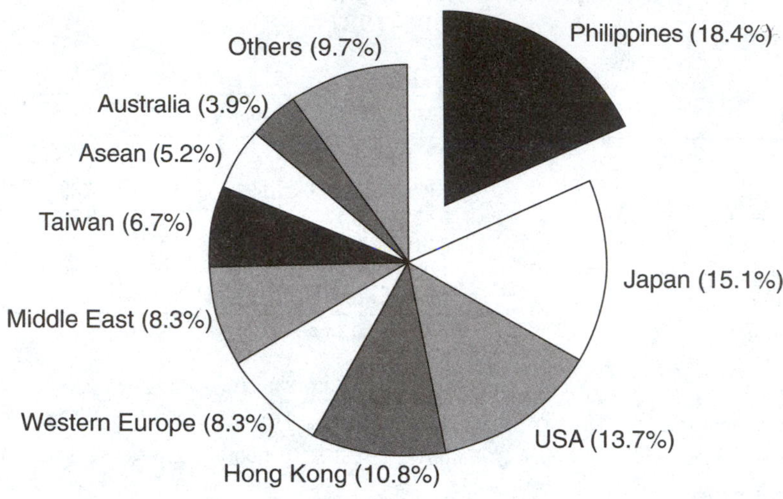


Source: Philippine Department of Tourism.

EXHIBIT 11

**THE DELUXE HOTEL INDUSTRY IN THE PHILIPPINES IN 1989**
**Top Five Countries/Regions of Origin**
**By Deluxe Hotel, 1987**

| *Hotel* | *Country of Origin* |
|---|---|
| Manila Hotel | U.S., Philippines, Western Europe, Hong Kong, Japan |
| Century Park Sheraton | Japan, Hong Kong, Philippines, Taiwan, Middle East |
| Manila Garden | Hong Kong, Philippines, Taiwan, Japan, Asean |
| Manila Midtown | Philippines, Japan, Middle East, U.S., Western Europe |
| Manila Pavilion | Philippines, Japan, Hong Kong, U.S., Taiwan |
| Mandarin Oriental | U.S., Japan, Hong Kong, Taiwan, Philippines |
| Westin Philippine Plaza | U.S., Japan, Philippines, Middle East, Hong Kong |
| Manila Peninsula | Hong Kong, U.S., Philippines, Western Europe, Japan |
| Silahis International | Hong Kong, Philippines, Japan, U.S., Middle East |
| Hotel Inter-Continental | Western Europe, U.S., Philippines, Taiwan, Asean |
| Hyatt Regency | Philippines, Western Europe, Middle East, Japan, U.S. |
| Holiday Inn | Japan, U.S., Middle East, Philippines, Hong Kong |

Source: Philippine Department of Tourism.

EXHIBIT 12

## THE DELUXE HOTEL INDUSTRY IN THE PHILIPPINES IN 1989
**Percentage Share of Each Country/Region of Origin**
**By Deluxe Hotel, 1987**

| | *Century* | *Inter* | *Hyatt* | *Mla Pav* | *Mla Ori* | *Mla Pen* | *Silahis* | *Hol Inn* | *Garden* | *Manila* | *Midtown* | *Plaza* | *Total* |
|---|---|---|---|---|---|---|---|---|---|---|---|---|---|
| Asean | 6.88% | 5.67% | 3.57% | 7.05% | 6.61% | 7.75% | 2.79% | 6.64% | 6.27% | 4.82% | 3.69% | 4.81% | 5.18% |
| Australia | 6.19% | 5.56% | 4.49% | 3.15% | 3.49% | 2.80% | 2.82% | 6.66% | 0.87% | 5.29% | 2.82% | 3.31% | 3.86% |
| Hong Kong | 17.69% | 1.17% | 6.85% | 13.51% | 14.58% | 21.91% | 22.93% | 8.22% | 20.22% | 8.00% | 0.01% | 10.77% | 10.75% |
| Japan | 18.98% | 3.43% | 14.17% | 13.92% | 15.82% | 9.34% | 12.41% | 24.17% | 13.60% | 7.34% | 24.82% | 16.64% | 15.08% |
| Canada | 0.41% | 2.15% | 1.11% | 0.54% | 0.73% | 1.91% | 0.25% | 0.89% | 0.89% | 1.24% | 0.72% | 0.78% | 0.95% |
| United States | 4.64% | 17.72% | 10.71% | 9.70% | 16.49% | 19.65% | 7.12% | 12.13% | 4.90% | 24.07% | 5.11% | 24.81% | 13.72% |
| Taiwan | 12.65% | 15.32% | 0.71% | 9.68% | 13.42% | 1.82% | 0.52% | 1.10% | 19.64% | 4.01% | 3.32% | 1.25% | 6.74% |
| Western Europe | 3.78% | 21.48% | 15.75% | 7.57% | 8.65% | 9.43% | 3.34% | 5.28% | 3.55% | 11.79% | 5.14% | 6.31% | 8.27% |
| Middle East | 11.18% | 3.24% | 14.27% | 4.62% | 3.25% | 2.41% | 4.37% | 11.37% | 0.17% | 2.27% | 18.06% | 12.02% | 8.27% |
| Philippines | 12.82% | 17.11% | 18.60% | 25.46% | 11.87% | 18.39% | 13.14% | 11.09% | 19.98% | 17.70% | 33.82% | 14.72% | 18.44% |
| Others | 4.78% | 7.15% | 9.77% | 4.80% | 5.09% | 4.59% | 30.31% | 12.45% | 9.91% | 13.47% | 2.49% | 4.58% | 8.74% |
| | 100.00% | 100.00% | 100.00% | 100.00% | 100.00% | 100.00% | 100.00% | 100.00% | 100.00% | 100.00% | 100.00% | 100.00% | 100.00% |

Source: Philippine Department of Tourism.

EXHIBIT 13

## THE DELUXE HOTEL INDUSTRY IN THE PHILIPPINES IN 1989
## List of Hotels by Classification

| *Hotels* | *Number of Rooms* | *% of Total Rooms* |
|---|---|---|
| Five-Star Hotels | | |
| Century Park Sheraton | 500 | |
| Holiday Inn | 308 | |
| Hotel Inter-Continental | 384 | |
| Hyatt Regency | 265 | |
| Manila Mandarin | 470 | |
| Manila Garden | 523 | |
| Manila Hilton | 400 | |
| Manila Hotel | 532 | |
| Manila Midtown | 600 | |
| Manila Peninsula | 494 | |
| Silahis International | 452 | |
| Philippine Plaza | 673 | |
| Subtotal | 5,601 | 65.24% |
| Four-Star Hotels | | |
| Admiral | 110 | |
| Ambassador | 225 | |
| Bayview Prince | 258 | |
| Hotel Mirador | 264 | |
| Subtotal | 857 | 9.98% |
| Three-Star Hotels | | |
| Aloha | 94 | |
| Boulevard Mansion | 184 | |
| Camelot | 114 | |
| Hotel Aurelio | 102 | |
| Hotel Las Palmas | 100 | |
| Sundowner Hotel | 104 | |
| Hotel MacArthur | 48 | |
| Manila Manor | 67 | |
| Midland Plaza | 226 | |
| Midland Plaza | 126 | |
| Rothman Inn | 56 | |
| Solanie | 38 | |
| Sulo | 49 | |
| Town & Country | 33 | |
| Subtotal | 1,341 | 15.62% |

EXHIBIT 13 (cont'd)

## THE DELUXE HOTEL INDUSTRY IN THE PHILIPPINES IN 1989
### List of Hotels by Classification

| *Hotels* | *Number of Rooms* | *% of Total Rooms* |
|---|---|---|
| Two-Star Hotels | | |
| Danarra | 27 | |
| Hotel Carston | 111 | |
| Kamalig Inn | 16 | |
| Keyser Hotel | 34 | |
| Merchants Hotel | 72 | |
| Swagman Hotel Manila | 46 | |
| Tower Hotel | 45 | |
| Uptown Hotel | 38 | |
| Subtotal | 389 | 4.53% |
| One-Star Hotel | | |
| Hotel Soriente | 49 | |
| Iseya Hotel | 26 | |
| Manila Tourist Inn | 14 | |
| New Fortune | 90 | |
| Philippine First | 90 | |
| Premiere | 83 | |
| Tayabas | 45 | |
| Subtotal | 397 | 4.62% |
| Grand Total | 8,585 | |

Source: Philippine Department of Tourism.

EXHIBIT 14

## THE DELUXE HOTEL INDUSTRY IN THE PHILIPPINES IN 1989
## Percentage Occupancy of Each Class of Hotels
## 1985–1988

| | *Five-Star* | *Four-Star* | *Three-Star* | *Two-Star* | *One-Star* | *Overall* |
|---|---|---|---|---|---|---|
| 1985 | 54.16% | 43.91% | 51.82% | 41.61% | 49.81% | 51.91% |
| 1986 | 62.85% | 50.25% | 58.62% | 44.31% | 55.62% | 59.96% |
| 1987 | 70.46% | 58.03% | 58.55% | 56.36% | 53.00% | 65.99% |
| 1988* | 77.09% | 65.06% | 67.64% | 56.94% | 52.66% | 66.05% |

Source: Philippine Department of Tourism.

EXHIBIT 15

## THE DELUXE HOTEL INDUSTRY IN THE PHILIPPINES IN 1989
## Percentage Distribution of Air Visitor Arrivals
## By Major Travel Market and Intended Place of Stay
## 1986

| *Travel Market* | *Hotels* | *Rented Homes/ Apartments* | *With Relatives/ Friends* | *Military Camps* | *Religious Educ Inst* | *Others* | *Not Stated* |
|---|---|---|---|---|---|---|---|
| Asean | 65.47 | 2.90 | 12.32 | 0.70 | 1.39 | 9.24 | 7.98 |
| Australia | 53.03 | 4.25 | 25.65 | 0.11 | 0.31 | 9.51 | 7.14 |
| Hong Kong | 84.78 | 1.05 | 5.35 | 0.05 | 0.08 | 3.47 | 5.22 |
| Japan | 76.52 | 2.70 | 8.85 | 0.13 | 0.25 | 6.77 | 4.78 |
| North America | 24.49 | 4.00 | 49.59 | 3.79 | 0.37 | 10.15 | 7.61 |
| Taiwan | 86.60 | 0.95 | 5.50 | 0.03 | 0.14 | 2.37 | 4.41 |
| Western Europe | 50.54 | 5.02 | 22.06 | 0.13 | 0.53 | 11.35 | 10.37 |
| Others | 46.55 | 5.20 | 26.71 | 0.96 | 0.63 | 11.20 | 8.75 |
| Total | 53.27 | 3.60 | 25.40 | 1.31 | 0.43 | 8.75 | 7.24 |

Source: Philippine Department of Tourism.

EXHIBIT 16

**THE DELUXE HOTEL INDUSTRY IN THE PHILIPPINES IN 1989**
**Hotel Rates of Five-Star Hotels, September 1988**
(in U.S. Dollars)

| *Hotel* | *Single* | *Double* |
|---|---|---|
| Manila Garden* | 52 | 60 |
| Holiday Inn | 100 | 110 |
| Manila Midtown | 60 | 68 |
| Century Park Sheraton | 105 | 110 |
| Hotel Inter-Continental | 96 | 106 |
| Westin Philippine Plaza | 75 | 87 |
| Silahis International Hotel | 75 | 75 |
| Hyatt Regency | 84 | 84 |
| Mandarin Oriental | 130 | 150 |
| Manila Peninsula | 125 | 140 |
| Manila Pavilion | 72 | 82 |
| Manila Hotel | 95 | 105 |

* 11th Anniversary Special Rate effective until March 1989.

Notes: 1. These rates are subject to change based on promotional activities of the hotels.
2. Peso equivalents are based on existing foreign exchange rates (US$1 = PHP21.09).

Source: Philippine Department of Tourism.

EXHIBIT 17

**THE DELUXE HOTEL INDUSTRY IN THE PHILIPPINES IN 1989**
**Percentage Share of Total Guests**
**by Deluxe Hotel, 1987**

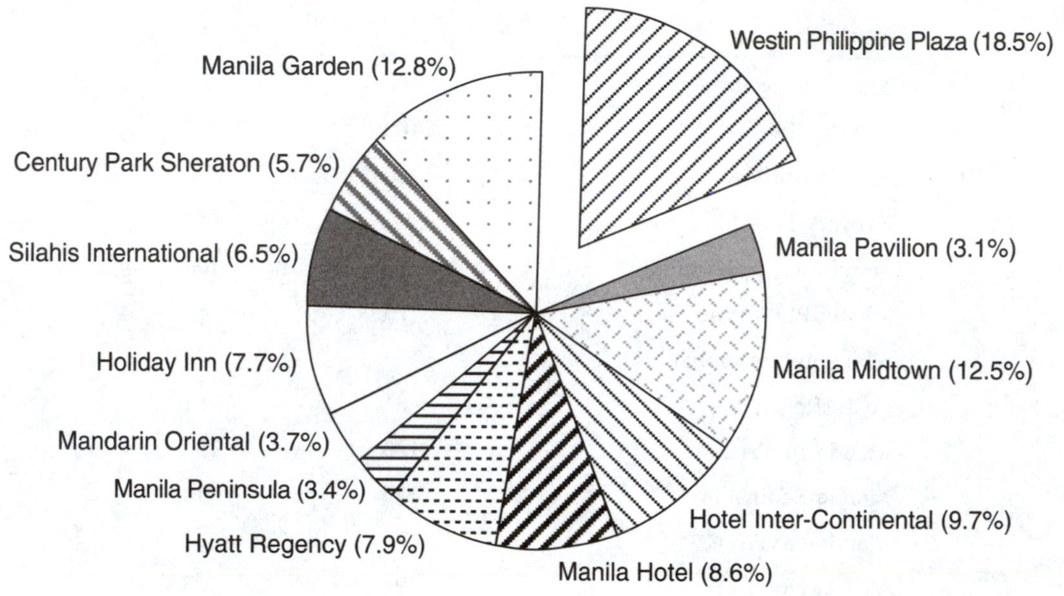


Source: Philippine Department of Tourism.

EXHIBIT 18

## THE DELUXE HOTEL INDUSTRY IN THE PHILIPPINES IN 1989
## Monthly Occupancy Rates and Average Length of Stay (Nights) of Five-Star Hotels in Metro Manila
## January–December 1987

| *Category* | *Jan* | *Feb* | *Mar* | *Apr* | *May* | *Jun* | *Jul* | *Aug* | *Sept* | *Oct* | *Nov* | *Dec* | *Average Occupancy* 1987 | 1986 | 1985 |
|---|---|---|---|---|---|---|---|---|---|---|---|---|---|---|---|
| Sheraton | | | | | | | | | | | | | | | |
| Occupancy Rate | 85.7 | 78.9 | 79.3 | 77.6 | 67.9 | 75 | 75.8 | 84 | 74 | 76 | 77 | 80 | 77.6 | 75.63 | 68.63 |
| Length of Stay | 3.5 | 2.98 | 3.46 | 3.21 | 3.19 | 3.16 | 2.89 | 3.07 | 3.21 | 3.42 | 3.25 | 3.6 | 3.25 | | |
| Holiday Inn | | | | | | | | | | | | | | | |
| Occupancy Rate | 86.04 | 77.02 | 71.96 | 80.37 | 79.54 | 78.55 | 87.14 | 94.25 | 83.31 | 77.1 | 80.26 | 80.65 | 81.35 | 72.48 | 64.76 |
| Length of Stay | 2.81 | 2.41 | 2.73 | 2.63 | 2.81 | 2.45 | 2.64 | 2.62 | 2.94 | 2.67 | 3.23 | 3.11 | 2.75 | | |
| Inter-Continental | | | | | | | | | | | | | | | |
| Occupancy Rate | 60.04 | 78 | 77.2 | 72.6 | 60 | 61.1 | 64.6 | 67.4 | 59.2 | 65.9 | 70.3 | 65.05 | 66.78 | 60.31 | 57.25 |
| Length of Stay | 2.08 | 2 | 2.8 | 2 | 2.3 | 2.4 | 1.8 | 1.5 | 2.4 | 3 | 3.4 | 2.9 | 2.38 | | |
| Hyatt Regency | | | | | | | | | | | | | | | |
| Occupancy Rate | 74.80 | 69.3 | 60.4 | 70.6 | 71.9 | 70.13 | 74.1 | 82.8 | 62.14 | 68.63 | 72.83 | 73.24 | 70.91 | 52.54 | 37.15 |
| Length of Stay | 2.50 | 2.2 | 2.4 | 2.5 | 2.9 | 2.7 | 3.2 | 2.71 | 2.8 | 2.7 | 2.3 | 2.34 | 2.6 | | |
| Manila Garden | | | | | | | | | | | | | | | |
| Occupancy Rate | 87.65 | 92.35 | 86.89 | 89.42 | 88.35 | 90.22 | 88.2 | 89.98 | 76.54 | 75 | 79.3 | 88 | 85.99 | 74.63 | 59.97 |
| Length of Stay | 2.56 | 2.49 | 2.97 | 2.41 | 2.73 | 2.55 | 2.71 | 2.55 | 3.43 | 3.7 | 3 | 2.8 | 2.83 | | |
| Manila Pavilion | | | | | | | | | | | | | | | |
| Occupancy Rate | 68.03 | 73.51 | 50.87 | 56.64 | 50.94 | 49.02 | 46.67 | 65.91 | 42.08 | 41.84 | 48.37 | 57.6 | 54.29 | 56.49 | 49.49 |
| Length of Stay | 2.76 | 2.81 | 3.2 | 2.31 | 3.07 | 2.73 | 2.44 | 2.11 | 2.84 | 2.64 | 2.7 | 2.65 | 2.69 | | |

EXHIBIT 18 (cont'd)

## THE DELUXE HOTEL INDUSTRY IN THE PHILIPPINES IN 1989
## Monthly Occupancy Rates and Average Length of Stay (Nights) of Five-Star Hotels in Metro Manila
## January–December 1987

| | | | | | | | | | | | | | Average Occupancy | | |
|---|---|---|---|---|---|---|---|---|---|---|---|---|---|---|---|
| *Category* | *Jan* | *Feb* | *Mar* | *Apr* | *May* | *Jun* | *Jul* | *Aug* | *Sept* | *Oct* | *Nov* | *Dec* | *1987* | *1986* | *1985* |
| Manila Hotel | | | | | | | | | | | | | | | |
| Occupancy Rate | 55.08 | 64.15 | 52.04 | 59.49 | 57.58 | 45.88 | 51.35 | 62.44 | 46.43 | 54.44 | 56.65 | 65.32 | 55.97 | 48.01 | 39.39 |
| Length of Stay | 2.8 | 4.33 | 3.09 | 2.63 | 3.26 | 2.47 | 2.55 | 2.38 | 2.64 | 2.98 | 2.68 | 2.59 | 2.85 | | |
| Mandarin Oriental | | | | | | | | | | | | | | | |
| Occupancy Rate | 67.7 | 78.9 | 80.4 | 74.3 | 62.5 | 66.9 | 70.5 | 76 | 60.1 | 57.2 | 66.7 | 61.1 | 68.53 | 63.92 | 55.37 |
| Length of Stay | 2.4 | 2.5 | 2.8 | 2.2 | 2.64 | 2.5 | 1.9 | 2 | 2.8 | 2.2 | 2.7 | 2.4 | 2.42 | | |
| Manila Midtown | | | | | | | | | | | | | | | |
| Occupancy Rate | 85 | 79 | 73 | 74 | 76 | 74 | 78 | 83 | 70 | 68 | 75 | 81 | 76.33 | 67.58 | 65.33 |
| Length of Stay | 3.29 | 2.95 | 3.23 | 3.21 | 2.97 | 3.07 | 3 | 3.28 | 2.99 | 2.83 | 2.95 | 2.74 | 3.04 | | |
| Manila Peninsula | | | | | | | | | | | | | | | |
| Occupancy Rate | 47.35 | 59.68 | 73.13 | 58 | 63.5 | 65.56 | 62.28 | 68.24 | 63.5 | 63.82 | 73.25 | 62.28 | 63.39 | 52.64 | 43.99 |
| Length of Stay | 2.84 | 3.05 | 3.82 | 3.67 | 3.58 | 3.7 | 3.28 | 2.97 | 3.91 | 3.66 | 3.78 | 3.73 | 3.5 | | |
| Silahis International | | | | | | | | | | | | | | | |
| Occupancy Rate | 90 | 74 | 69 | 83.51 | 70 | 49 | 80 | 91 | 73 | 75 | 70 | 77 | 75.13 | 57.47 | 45.86 |
| Length of Stay | 1.5 | 1.4 | 1.7 | 1.3 | 1.7 | 1.3 | 1.4 | 1.2 | 1.7 | 1.5 | 1.5 | 1.37 | 1.46 | | |
| Philippine Plaza | | | | | | | | | | | | | | | |
| Occupancy Rate | 75.2 | 71.2 | 64 | 71.5 | 64.4 | 72.3 | 74.5 | 90 | 62 | 70.6 | 63.4 | 58.5 | 69.8 | 68.26 | 61.48 |
| Length of Stay | 2.6 | 2.2 | 2.4 | 2.2 | 2.1 | 2.3 | 2.4 | 2.8 | 2.1 | 2.5 | 2.4 | 2.5 | 2.38 | | |
| Overall | | | | | | | | | | | | | | | |
| Occupancy Rate | 73.61 | 74.74 | 70.13 | 72.23 | 67.62 | 66.91 | 71 | 79.62 | 64.08 | 66.02 | 69.12 | 70.52 | 70.46 | 62.85 | 54.16 |
| Length of Stay | 2.62 | 2.61 | 2.88 | 2.52 | 2.77 | 2.61 | 2.52 | 2.43 | 2.81 | 2.82 | 2.82 | 2.73 | 2.68 | | |

Source: Philippine Department of Tourism.

EXHIBIT 19

**THE DELUXE HOTEL INDUSTRY IN THE PHILIPPINES IN 1989**
**Monthly Occupancy Rates and Average Length of Stay (Nights)**
**of Five-Star Hotels in Metro Manila**
**January–October 1988**

| | | | | | | | | | | | *January–October* | | |
|---|---|---|---|---|---|---|---|---|---|---|---|---|---|
| *Category* | *Jan* | *Feb* | *Mar* | *Apr* | *May* | *Jun* | *Jul* | *Aug* | *Sept* | *Oct* | *1988* | *1987* | *1986* |
| Sheraton | | | | | | | | | | | | | |
| Occupancy Rate | 86.90 | 84.90 | 78.00 | 74.00 | 71.80 | 72.70 | 72.70 | 76.60 | 73.50 | 70.70 | 76.18 | 77.42 | 74.23 |
| Length of Stay | 3.63 | 2.81 | 3.19 | 2.97 | 3.05 | 2.88 | 3.53 | 3.05 | 3.08 | 2.87 | 3.21 | 3.21 | |
| Holiday Inn | | | | | | | | | | | | | |
| Occupancy Rate | 88.17 | 86.00 | 90.39 | 88.70 | 84.52 | 90.84 | 89.90 | 94.25 | 87.28 | 88.96 | 88.90 | 81.53 | 71.31 |
| Length of Stay | 3.53 | 2.51 | 2.85 | 2.86 | 2.72 | 2.63 | 2.60 | 2.27 | 2.37 | 2.33 | 2.67 | 2.67 | |
| Inter-Continental | | | | | | | | | | | | | |
| Occupancy Rate | 64.00 | 87.10 | 84.00 | 86.40 | 78.30 | 70.80 | 80.00 | 76.50 | 79.60 | 81.30 | 79.89 | 66.60 | 56.92 |
| Length of Stay | 3.40 | 3.10 | 3.30 | 3.30 | 3.10 | 3.00 | 3.30 | 3.30 | 2.90 | 3.40 | 3.21 | 2.23 | |
| Hyatt Regency | | | | | | | | | | | | | |
| Occupancy Rate | 70.97 | 71.20 | 73.57 | 73.89 | 72.77 | 67.69 | 55.69 | 73.85 | 67.27 | 72.90 | 69.68 | 70.48 | 49.74 |
| Length of Stay | 2.40 | 2.30 | 2.37 | 2.53 | 2.66 | 2.66 | 3.46 | 2.03 | 2.06 | 1.34 | 2.38 | 2.66 | |
| Manila Garden | | | | | | | | | | | | | |
| Occupancy Rate | 85.00 | 96.08 | 96.19 | 96.14 | 90.59 | 92.18 | 93.31 | 95.79 | 94.13 | 94.34 | 93.38 | 86.46 | 71.56 |
| Length of Stay | 2.50 | 2.30 | 2.40 | 2.30 | 2.50 | 2.20 | 2.20 | 2.30 | 2.40 | 2.70 | 2.38 | 2.81 | |
| Manila Pavilion | | | | | | | | | | | | | |
| Occupancy Rate | 51.57 | 70.09 | 53.29 | 66.70 | 61.48 | 57.51 | 69.87 | 79.96 | 73.73 | 73.37 | 65.76 | 54.55 | 53.86 |
| Length of Stay | 2.56 | 2.19 | 2.51 | 3.14 | 2.39 | 3.40 | 2.60 | 2.70 | 3.50 | 2.40 | 2.74 | 2.69 | |

EXHIBIT 19 (cont'd)

**THE DELUXE HOTEL INDUSTRY IN THE PHILIPPINES IN 1989**
**Monthly Occupancy Rates and Average Length of Stay (Nights) of Five-Star Hotels in Metro Manila**
**January–October 1988**

| | | | | | | | | | | | *January–October* | | |
|---|---|---|---|---|---|---|---|---|---|---|---|---|---|
| *Category* | *Jan* | *Feb* | *Mar* | *Apr* | *May* | *Jun* | *Jul* | *Aug* | *Sept* | *Oct* | *1988* | *1987* | *1986* |
| Manila Hotel | | | | | | | | | | | | | |
| Occupancy Rate | 47.43 | 64.86 | 54.88 | 70.17 | 64.69 | 53.20 | 57.11 | 70.00 | 60.01 | 58.79 | 60.11 | 54.97 | 45.12 |
| Length of Stay | 2.47 | 2.37 | 2.37 | 3.02 | 2.82 | 2.55 | 2.67 | 2.35 | 2.71 | 2.47 | 2.58 | 2.89 | |
| Mandarin Oriental | | | | | | | | | | | | | |
| Occupancy Rate | 59.99 | 86.60 | 67.10 | 71.20 | 60.00 | 61.00 | 60.70 | 70.40 | 58.30 | 68.70 | 66.40 | 69.45 | 61.53 |
| Length of Stay | 2.87 | 2.20 | 2.30 | 2.20 | 2.10 | 2.10 | 2.00 | 1.90 | 2.40 | 2.60 | 2.27 | 2.39 | |
| Manila Midtown | | | | | | | | | | | | | |
| Occupancy Rate | 88.00 | 86.00 | 89.00 | 91.00 | 89.00 | 86.00 | 88.78 | 89.00 | 78.00 | 81.00 | 86.58 | 76.00 | 65.60 |
| Length of Stay | 3.29 | 2.46 | 3.12 | 3.05 | 2.96 | 2.97 | 2.91 | 2.73 | 3.12 | 2.84 | 2.95 | 3.08 | |
| Manila Peninsula | | | | | | | | | | | | | |
| Occupancy Rate | 50.91 | 70.25 | 69.32 | 72.63 | 70.32 | 73.50 | 76.06 | 79.91 | 77.61 | 84.82 | 72.53 | 62.51 | 52.13 |
| Length of Stay | 3.34 | 3.11 | 3.26 | 3.22 | 3.27 | 3.55 | 3.75 | 3.61 | 3.77 | 4.03 | 3.49 | 3.45 | |
| Silahis International | | | | | | | | | | | | | |
| Occupancy Rate | 67.00 | 85.00 | 77.00 | 83.00 | 86.00 | 84.00 | 68.00 | 93.00 | 81.00 | 90.00 | 81.40 | 75.45 | 53.96 |
| Length of Stay | 1.90 | 1.60 | 1.70 | 1.50 | 1.50 | 1.50 | 1.20 | 1.30 | 1.30 | 1.40 | 1.62 | 1.47 | |
| Philippine Plaza | | | | | | | | | | | | | |
| Occupancy Rate | 78.10 | 84.00 | 69.20 | 82.80 | 75.70 | 80.10 | 82.60 | 89.10 | 80.00 | 84.80 | 80.64 | 71.57 | 66.96 |
| Length of Stay | 2.50 | 2.40 | 2.10 | 2.40 | 2.10 | 2.40 | 2.40 | 2.30 | 2.30 | 2.30 | 2.19 | 2.36 | |
| Overall | | | | | | | | | | | | | |
| Occupancy Rate | 70.22 | 81.43 | 75.00 | 80.22 | 75.67 | 75.03 | 75.46 | 82.81 | 75.99 | 79.21 | 77.09 | 70.59 | 60.64 |
| Length of Stay | 2.87 | 2.45 | 2.62 | 2.71 | 2.60 | 2.65 | 2.72 | 2.49 | 2.66 | 2.56 | 2.63 | 2.66 | |

Source: Philippine Department of Tourism.

# Shangri-La Hotel Ltd* 9

If attainment of industry awards was any indicator of a company's strength and leadership position, then the Shangri-La Hotel had once again confirmed its role as a leading hotel in the Asia-Pacific lodging industry. Throughout 1993, the five-star hotel was the recipient of a collection of travel industry awards, including Best Hotel in Singapore and Best Hotel in the World (*Euromoney*), Hotel of the Year, Best Hotel in the Asia-Pacific, and Best Conference Hotel In the World (*Executive Travelers Magazine*). The Shangri-La Hotel's success continued into 1994, with the hotel's chefs winning the coveted "Best Hotel Team" award at the prestigious Salon Culinaire 1994 competition.

## Historical Background

Shangri-La Hotel Ltd is owned by the Kuok Brothers, operating under Leo Properties, and is part of the diversified group of companies collectively known as the Kuok Group. It had been jointly owned by two brothers, Robert and David Kuok, Malaysians of Chinese descent.

---

*This case was prepared by Professor Luis Ma. R. Calingo on the basis of student reports submitted by Chan Seet Meng, Albert Ee Oon Sun, Lee Wai Fai, Jeffrey Ong Yeng Keng, Phan Thanh Truc, Shen Shu Qiao, Stephen Sum Ngai, and Tay Lip Guan (MBA, Nanyang Technological University). This case was developed wholly from published materials. It is designed to serve as a basis for class discussion rather than to illustrate either effective or ineffective handling of an administrative situation.

The beginnings of the Kuok empire started with the father, who owned a commodities trading firm. But it was Robert Kuok who started the expansion and the diversification from its humble beginnings. After taking over from his father, Robert Kuok succeeded in achieving control of 30 percent of the world's sugar supply, thereby earning him the nickname "Sugar King." As an entrepreneur, Robert Kuok was not content with these achievements. He started diversifying into such industries as manufacturing, timber, flour mills, shipping, insurance, construction, and real estate.

An avid student of the theories of modern business, Robert Kuok applied the concepts of vertical integration and the value chain as he added one business to another. Through a series of vertical integration moves, Kuok was able to enhance the profitability of his business holdings.

Shangri-La Hotel Ltd was incorporated in 1962 under the name "Guan Thong Ltd". It went public in 1968 and changed its name to Orange Grove Hotel and took the name Shangri-La Hotel in 1969. The hotel was initially managed by Westin Hotels and Resorts under an assistance plan arrangement (with Leo Properties) until the early 1980s, when both parties mutually ended the collaboration. The philosophy of Westin — "People Make a Difference" — was regarded as having influenced the shaping of the Shangri-La Hotel's "people-oriented" vision: its preoccupation in striving to be a hotel "where guests and staff enjoy a genuine sense of belonging" had become almost like its trademark, and was certainly one of the most important success factors of the company.

The background of the Kuok brothers was a major factor in the success of their hotel ventures. David Kuok served as an ambassador for Malaysia for many years and has extensive political connections. Robert Kuok was the chairman of MSA (Malaysian Singapore Airlines) before the two airlines went their separate ways in 1972 to form the Malaysian Airlines System and Singapore Airlines. As he was already well-versed in the travel industry, Robert Kuok naturally went into the hotel business.

Because the Westin Group was managing the hotels, Robert Kuok quickly learned the tricks of the trade. He formed the management company, Shangri-La International and took over the management of the hotel in the early 1980s. With the exception of Shangri-La Kowloon, which was still on existing contract with Westin, all the rest of the Shangri-La Hotel properties were managed by the management company in 1993. This meant that more profits stayed within the Kuok Group.

Having the reputation of being a shrewd visionary, Robert Kuok saw beyond the hotel industry as a stand-alone business. What he really wanted was to control a land bank. Observers had credited him with the foresight to predict that land prices in the fast-growing Asian countries would soar and that he would be richly rewarded for his pioneering investments. The operations of the hotel business contributed to the cash flow of the company. The first two hotels that he started were the Rasa Sayang in Penang, Malaysia and the Shangri-La in Singapore, which opened its doors on April 23, 1971.

The common business concept of the Shangri-La Hotels was that of an image of resplendence, charm, and tranquility. Most of the Kuok's hotels are located very near the city center and yet they always have sprawling, well-landscaped gardens that give the guests the feeling that they are living in a tropical paradise. In fact, David Bellemy, a world-renowned botanist, described the Shangri-La Hotel as "Singapore's Other Botanic Gardens" in a 1993 hotel advertisement.

In 1995, the company was listed in the main board of the Stock Exchange of Singapore. About a quarter (22 percent) of its shareholdings is owned by Kuok (S) Ltd, with members of the Kuok family also sitting in the board of directors. Almost all (96 percent) of the company's business is in hotel activities. The company also has stakes in numerous hotels and resorts around the world (mostly in the Asia-Pacific region).

## The Hotel Industry in Singapore

In 1994, the Singapore Hotel Association (SHA) reported a total of 78 hotels with a total of 24,573 rooms in Singapore. Singapore is strategically located in a booming ASEAN region, which has a strong potential for the tourism and travel industry. Singapore was expected to continue to attract its fair share of tourists. The Singapore Hotel Association (SHA) estimated in 1987 that the multiplier of the tourism dollar was as high as 3.2.[1] Given that the tourism industry was the third largest foreign exchange earner for Singapore, the Singapore government has been supporting the industry primarily through the Singapore Tourist Promotion Board (STPB).

**Performance.** During the first quarter of 1995, visitor arrivals to Singapore rose by 2.9 percent to 1.75 million. The average occupancy rate dropped to 84.3 percent, and the average room rates increased by 3 percent. The revenues generated from room rentals, food, and beverages sales dropped by 2.2 percent to S$454.7 million (see Exhibit 1).

**Supply.** The Singapore Urban Redevelopment Authority forecasted that there would be an increase of 2,163 and 5,019 rooms in 1995 and 1996, respectively, representing about a 15-percent increase in 5-star hotel rooms over 2 years (see Exhibit 2).

**Demand.** Singapore's influx of Asian tourists has been on the rise, relative to Western travelers. The January 1995 figures posted an increase in visitor arrivals from Asia by 10.6 percent, while its share of total arrivals grew by 3.7 percent to 71 percent (see Exhibit 3). Interestingly, Asian travelers tended to stay more to a room, and had second homes or relatives to provide for their accommodation in Singapore. The bottom line was that with increasing arrivals, the occupancy rate need not increase correspondingly. Generally, tourists stayed an average of three days a year in 1994, as compared to 3.9 days in the 1990. With the opening in 1995 of the Singapore International Convention Center (Suntec City), Singapore has positioned itself as a premier business center in the region. This was expected to bring in higher-spending business and convention tourists.

**Tourism Unlimited.** The STPB made the concept of "Tourism Unlimited" the cornerstone of its strategies for the 21st century and with it the idea of "Bringing the World to Singapore, Bringing Singapore to the World." The challenge for the hotel industry is to take advantage of the government initiatives and exploit mutually beneficial strategies.

---

[1] *The Straits Times*, November 26, 1987.

**Slowdown in earnings.** Rising rentals, high labor costs, and a strong Singapore dollar had somewhat exerted a strain on revenues and earnings in the hotel industry. Coupled with a huge potential increase in the supply of hotel rooms during the 1996–2000 period, room rates and occupancy rates for the hotels were expected to be under pressure. The expected growth in visitors' arrival into Singapore would not be sufficient to absorb the excess supply in 1996, if all new hotels come onstream as planned.

**Competition.** Singapore's stronger currency had increased the attractiveness of less expensive destinations such as Malaysia, Indonesia, the Philippines, and Thailand. These neighboring countries have embarked, on their own, aggressive tourism drives, improved on their shopping facilities, and offered more natural attractions as compared to Singapore. Because they are bigger countries growing from a smaller tourism base, they are more likely to see a higher growth in visitor arrivals and a higher rate of repeat visitors compared to Singapore. In short, Singapore hotels, while competing against one another, were also competing on a regional level.

**Expensive tourist destination image.** A related development is that Singapore is increasingly no longer perceived as "an inexpensive tourist destination," based on comments from many an overseas tour operator. The importance of this image becomes more apparent after considering that new markets from within Asia, such as China, ASEAN, Hong Kong and Taiwan, were growing rapidly. In comparison to the traditional high-yield markets such as the United States, Japan, and Europe, the new travelers tended to seek less frills and more "value for money," rather than deluxe accommodations.

**ISO 9000 in the hotel industry.** The SHA, STPB, and Singapore Institute of Standards and the Industrial Research (SISIR) had been advocating that hotels implement quality management systems that meet the ISO 9000 series standards. By June 1995, five hotels in Singapore had received ISO 9000 certification: Mandarin Orchard, Marina Mandarin, Le Meridien, Phoenix, and Westin Stamford. Although ISO 9000 registration was no guarantee of a high quality service offering, hoteliers have expected ISO 9000 certification as a *de facto* requirement for doing business in Singapore's hotel industry.

## Industry Success Factors

Although several factors influenced a hotel's operation, six factors have been considered as the key ingredients for success in the hotel industry: an effective reservation system, the actual choice of locations, the facilities and amenities offered at each hotel location, the friendliness and efficiency of hotel staff, pricing policies, and aggressive marketing practices.

While it might seem unnecessary to emphasize the importance of an effective reservation system, no single factor could cause the equivalent loss of goodwill in potential guests than lost hotel reservations, incorrect dates, and errors in requested room types. Even if the hotel can accommodate the guest by effecting adjustments at the check-in registration, the negative start to the guest's stay at that location might never be overcome.

Similarly, intuition would suggest that the actual physical location chosen for a hotel would be extremely important to the success of its operations. For example, a resort hotel in Bali, Boracay, or Pattaya located on the beach would be expected to have a more advantageous location than one situated several blocks further inland. Other locational factors relevant are the proximity of the hotel location to other desirable amenities (e.g., golf courses and after-hour social activities) and the types of customer segments expected to be chosen as the dominant segments targeted for marketing efforts, among others.

A third critical success factor included the actual facilities available at each location, both in-room facilities such as bed sizes, bath and dressing room configurations, and cable television, as well as overall facilities such as swimming pools, tennis courts, exercise rooms, restaurants, meeting rooms, business center services, computer and fax hookups, and so on. This list continued to expand in length with changing lifestyles and technology.

The friendliness and efficiency of the hotel staff were also extremely important success factors. The friendliness and efficiency must be a pervasive staff attitude. It must begin at the initial guest/staff contact point, be it the doorman or reception desk clerk, and continue through all other guest/staff contact situations for the entire duration of the guest's stay.

The final few success factors of pricing policies, advertising, and special promotional activities are all related to an aggressive marketing program as important keys to success. With the advent of convention, business and other group pricing plans, pricing has recently become far more segmented and competitive than in the past. In addition, these pricing strategies must be coordinated with other marketing activities such as advertising themes and special promotion programs and activities. To summarize, what appeared to be necessary for success in today's highly competitive hotel industry is a well-crafted and coordinated aggressive marketing program which stresses media advertising coupled with a relatively sophisticated approach to multiple pricing schemes.

## Hotel Features

The Shangri-La Hotel is well-known for the lush tropical greenery and is sometimes referred to as "Singapore's Other Botanical Garden." To highlight the beauty of the tropical gardens at twilight, Mr John Watson, a world-recognized landscape illumination expert, created a new lighting system. The Tower Wing is 24-stories high and has 500 tastefully decorated rooms and 21 suites. Located in this wing are the food and beverage outlets, a 24-hour business center, a flower shop, an impressive pillarless Island Ballroom, and eight smaller function rooms. The 837-square-meter tower wing lobby has a 10-meter-high white marble (from Italy) ceiling with green marble flooring from China. Four 8-meter-long Austrian chandeliers, from world-famous company E Bakalowits Sohn, flank the lobby and the lobby court. Costing S$850,000, these chandeliers descend impressively from a ceiling of timber cornices and marble columns to complete the luxurious furnishing and fine Oriental adornments.

The 9-story garden wing, built in 1978, added 151 guest rooms and 10 suites to the hotel. The building was designed around a spectacular open-atrium garden where over 100 varieties of palms, trees, and vines are planted. The cool rhythmic sound of water tripping over rocks and falls was welcome music to those seeking natural tranquility. The Valley Wing, opened in 1985, has 112 deluxe guest rooms and 24 suites. Spanning the east side of the Shangri-La and facing Cuscaden Road, a lightly traveled street in downtown Singapore, this S$78 million luxurious wing ensures total exclusivity. With a land area of 2,368 square meters, the Valley Wing has its own entrance and driveway, separate lobby on the third level and an exclusive function room called the "Summit Room" on the lobby level.

The hotel also boasts some of the finest restaurants in town, offering a wide range of food selections. Nadaman Japanese Restaurant brought to Singapore a 150-year tradition of fine cuisine dating back to 1830 in the Edo of Japan. Nadaman specializes in traditional Japanese cuisine like Kaiseiki, which has been described as "the art of transforming blessings of nature into food." Built at a cost of S$4.5 million by Japanese craftsmen with tool-crafted material from Japan, Nadaman sits on the 24th floor and commands a spectacular view of the city. For French food lovers, the Shangri-La boasts the top french restaurant with the best wine selection. Restaurant Latour was designed by famous international interior decorator Don Ashtun. Its very special elegant interiors form an impressive setting for an exquisite meal for fine continental dining. The restaurant was awarded the Excellence in Service Award by STPB in 1993.

One of the most popular Chinese restaurants in Singapore, the Shang Palace was designed as a replica of a Shang Emperor's palace courtyard, with most of the material imported from mainland China. Here, one can dine on Cantonese delicacies in the privacy of cozy pavilions and feast in the resplendence of a traditional Chinese courtyard.

Set amidst the lush tropical greenery, the Waterfall Cave with its cheerfully clad staff is a tropical haven overlooking the pool. Located by the cascading waterfall and rockpool, the Coffee Garden has a refreshing look after a S$1.6 million construction cost. Fashioned in the style of an English conservatory, the 24-hour restaurant allows abundant sunlight to stream through its glass-roofed alcoves, overlooking the hotel's swimming pool and garden.

To cater to the night owls, the Shangri-La has different entertainment spots to meet the demands of the discerning guests. It created a new spectrum of entertainment and fun in the Singapore nightlife scene.

The Rose Veranda Lounge is an elegant room for the idyllic enjoyment of tea and pastries. The Rose Veranda serves the widest range of tea from around the world, including Chinese, Japanese, and the traditional English tea which are exclusively supplied by Fortnum and Mason of London.

Voted "Bar of the Year" by *Newsweek* magazine in the early 1980s, the Lobby Court is an elegant cocktail lounge, providing live entertainment. Finally, the famous Xanadu is an entertainment center which has a fascinating jukebox, snazzy electric guitars, antique Coke machine, and original gold and platinum records adorning the walls.

Recreational facilities at the Shangri-La are simply unsurpassed in variety. In the midst of 6.1 hectares of lush greenery and beautifully landscaped ground are tennis and squash courts, a swimming pool, an outdoor Jacuzzi, and a 3-hole pitch and putt green. A health club is located in the lower lobby of the Valley Wing.

The Shangri-La offers superior facilities for meeting and party planners. Conventions, meetings, reception, banquets, and exhibitions are handled professionally by a team of expert banquet, convention, and incentive service staff. The Island Ballroom is one of the biggest functions rooms in Singapore, hosting a large majority of annual corporate functions.

**Shangri-La Hotel's Operations**

> The difference between a good hotel and an outstanding one lies in the attention to detail and the level of service offered. For us, it is the collective difference made by all the little things done by the many people who work behind the scenes to ensure that every guest has a memorable stay. These are the people that make the hidden difference that distinguishes us from the rest.
>
> — Shangri-La Hotel Ltd Annual Report, 1992

## Principal Activities

The principal activities of Shangri-La Hotel Ltd consisted of carrying on the business of a hotelier and investment holding. The principal activities of its subsidiaries are investment holding and retail of general merchandise. Exhibit 4 lists hotels in the region in which the Shangri-La has a stake as of 1995.

In the local scene, the Shangri-La Hotel has majority stakes in two other hotels: Traders Hotel and Rasa Sentosa. Other than lodging, the Shangri-La has also invested in property via its subsidiaries: Midpoint Properties and Cuscaden Properties. The Shangri-La also plans to diversify into resort developments and service apartments as well.

From its early beginnings in 1962, the Shangri-La has come a long way in its steady progression and expansion to reach its present-day position. The result of continuing its tradition of service and attention to detail in all aspects of the hotel operation, the Shangri-La has enjoyed many successful years, with special guests such as Mr George Bush, then President of the United States, and Mr F W De Klerk, then President of South Africa, choosing to stay in Shangri-La Hotel during their visits to Singapore.

It was not uncommon to see foreign heads of state staying at the Shangri-La during their visits to Singapore. President Bush had this to say during his stay in February 1992:

> I am sure that you worked overtime to prepare for my stay at the Shangri-La Hotel, and it was thanks to your efforts that my time at the hotel was so pleasant and memorable.

Other unsolicited comments like the following from Emma Francis in February 1993 are not uncommon:

> Your hotel had something special. Letting location, most of all, superb staff. If ever someone needs an opinion on your property . . . I would be happy to give a glowing report.

Accordingly, the Shangri-La received several international awards in 1992 for its unique blend of outstanding service and beautiful surroundings. The Shangri-La hotel was ranked second in a survey conducted by *Business Traveller* magazine for "Most Favorite Hotel in the Asia-Pacific Region" and third place on the "Best Hotel in the World" in the *Institutional Investor*'s 12th annual hotel survey. The *Nikkei Trends* (Japan) rated their Valley Wing the "Best Hotel in the World." Similarly, it was ranked "Best Business Hotel" by *Asian Review* magazine.

## Staff

In an industry which has been suffering from high employee turnover, the Shangri-La has a staff strength of approximately 1,300, of whom more than 40 percent have been with the hotel for over ten years. The Shangri-La recognizes that having loyal and well-trained staff is the key to a healthy and successful organization. Thus, it is dedicated not only to creating an environment where its employees have an enthusiastic attitude toward serving customers, but also provides them with challenging and rewarding opportunities for advancement, personal growth, and fulfillment. To this end, staff training programs conducted by professional foreign and local management consultants are regularly organized.

Looking ahead to the future, Shangri-La managers developed a "total training plan" for each of their employees. The plan aims to update the professional skills of all employees through a wide range of courses which include guest satisfaction training, institutional training, management development, sales training, quality circle training, as well as language, safety, and computer training.

The Shangri-La also has a Hotel Scholarship Program through which outstanding employees are sent to leading management schools like Cornell University, Michigan State University, Washington State University, and the University of San Francisco.

As for employee relations, the hotel's Recreation Committee continues to implement programs and activities for the benefit of its employees and their families. At the same time, the Shangri-La stepped up employee communication to enable its staff to be constantly kept up-to-date in the latest developments in Shangri-La.

January 1994 heralded the launch of the Shangri-La's Vision of "Where Guests and Staff Enjoy A Genuine Scene of Belonging." This vision aimed to introduce and establish a new working culture in which the Shangri-La delivers an unparalleled level of service and product quality which not only meet guests' expectations but actually exceeds them. The implementation and realization of the vision was driven by small task forces comprising members of staff from both senior and middle managerial levels with the objective of simplifying and improving every aspect of the hotel's operations.

## Renovation and Expansion

In its continuing efforts to provide a higher quality of service to the guests and to enhance the hotel's performance, several renovations and expansions have been done. In 1988 and 1989, an extensive refurbishment program occurred in the Tower Block guest rooms, the Main Lobby, the Coffee Garden, and the outdoor Waterfall Cafe. The hotel also added a new reception for the main lobby and an attractive shopping arcade in the lower lobby. In 1991, the hotel opened a new tea lounge called "The Rose Veranda," which had the distinction of offering the widest range of fine teas in Singapore, and a new flower shop which served both guests and members of the public. The hotel also undertook a complete refurbishment of the Xanadu discotheque, one of the top night spots in Singapore, believed to be the first of its kind in Asia. Others due for renovation shortly were the Garden Wing guest rooms, Nadaman Japanese Restaurant, and the Business Center.

In 1992, guest lifts in the Tower Wing and the hotel's escalators were replaced. The hotel's Health Center which offered a wide range of sophisticated recreational and health facilities was refurbished and provided Cable News Network (CNN) news broadcasts as well. In working toward greater efficiency, the hotel implemented a new microcomputer system during the year. This system interfaced all point of sales directly to guests' accounts, making these transactions more convenient and faster.

In 1993, in line with its policy of offering the best in service and facilities, the Shangri-La embarked on a S$90 million full-scale renovation program which covered most of its accommodation and entertainment outlets.

In 1994, all the 136 rooms in the Valley Wing and function rooms were refurbished, as was the Valley Wing lobby. The Shangri-La was determined to position its product offering as Singapore's most luxurious room accommodation. Shang Place Restaurant was extensively renovated (both the restaurant and supporting kitchens) in the same year.

Projects in 1995 included the renovation of Nadaman Restaurant and the recreation of a Horizon Club in the Tower Wing. The Horizon Club was built around key operation concepts such as luxury, privacy, excellent service, and "value for money," and offered the discerning business traveler an attractive recluse from urban living. The hotel's entertainment outlet, Xanadu, was to be renovated as part of its upgraded image to the selective local customer base and relaunched in mid-1995.

## Market Segmentation

The Shangri-La Hotel occupies five hectares of prime Orchard Road district of Singapore. Strategically located, it is well-positioned to increase its market share. The Shangri-La is the hotel for the "well-heeled traveler," especially the corporate and business traveler. The new 543-room, 4-star Traders Hotel offers "no-frills" accommodation for the budget business traveler. Rasa Sentosa is positioned to cater to resort-goers, including Singaporeans who want a short break. Effectively, the Shangri-La's offerings are targeted to meet the needs of various types of hotel guests.

With its proven track record as an industry leader, the Shangri-La had carved for itself a niche among high-worth travelers. In addition, there is an element of prestige associated with the hotel, which made it a much favored venue for high-profile company and social events.

Main patronage is hence derived from business travelers and convention guests. The hotel is also highly favored among Japanese tour groups. The Shangri-La's clientele pool is generally not price-sensitive because most of their arrivals are dictated by business opportunities in the region rather than leisure factors (except the Japanese tour groups). With the booming Asian economies a current phenomenon, this niche apparently would work well for the hotel.

The Shangri-La's strength is its ability to attract the high-paying corporate clients. This segment formed about 65 percent of the clientele, as opposed to 34.2 percent for the general industry. High-paying corporate clients are the most lucrative market segment for the hotel. The room tariffs for corporate accounts were normally about 50 percent more than those offered to tour operators. As corporations bear the cost, hotel guests are less likely to be careful with their spending. Tourists form the other 35 percent of the clientele mix. Most of these are from Japan and Europe and it is this segment that was of growing importance to the Shangri-La as competition for the corporate clients intensified.

Corporate clients' needs typically included the basic hotel room plus meal services and basic communication facilities. Additional needs related to meeting rooms, special clerical, reproduction, special communications, recreation, and entertainment, are also frequently desired. Tourist travelers' needs are often more basic and mostly related to hotel rooms and meal services. Tourist travel is generally viewed as being quickly affected by changes in the economy, whereas corporate travel more typically followed the turns in the economy by 3 to 6 months.

## Performance

The hotel's strong performance could be attributed to the following factors: an increase in revenue due to high occupancy, improved room rates, and increased food and beverage sales.

**Rooms.** Currently, the Shangri-La has three wings: the Tower Building, the Garden Wing, and the Valley Wing, with a total of 821 rooms complete with 5-star facilities. It had, in 1993, just undergone a S$90 million renovation and was still on the track for further refurbishment and renovations. Hotel occupancy was 77 percent on average for the past 5 years. The average occupancy for the year 1994 finished at 82.2 percent — an increase of 6.8 percentage points over the previous year with gross room revenues totaling S$76 million, which represented an improvement of S$9.6 million over 1993.

**SHANGRI-LA HOTEL LTD**
**Occupancy Rate and Room Rate**

| *Year* | *1990* | *1991* | *1992* | *1993* | *1994* |
|---|---|---|---|---|---|
| Occupancy rate (%) | 84.3 | 68.9 | 75.2 | 75.4 | 82.2 |
| Room rates (S$) | 262.4 | 287.8 | 250.4 | 234.5 | 251.2 |

**Food and beverage outlets.** The Shangri-La has seven food and beverage (F&B) outlets: Shang Place, Latour, the Rose Veranda, the Waterfall Cafe, the Coffee Garden, the Lobby Court, and Nadaman. The Pool Bar was a new outlet in 1995, positioned to complement the operation of the Waterfall Cafe and providing snacks and beverages through the day. The hotel recorded a constant average growth of 28.1 percent of revenue for the past three years ending in 1995. This segment of the operation was less sensitive to tourist arrivals because it does not rely on hotel guests alone.[2] F&B revenues had grown steadily from 1992 to 1994: S$31.6 million in 1992, S$34.7 million in 1993, and S$36.4 million in 1994.

**Conventions and conferences.** The year 1994 saw a series of high-profile events being hosted at the Shangri-La. These high-profile gatherings and many others contributed to convention revenues increasing from S$2.4 million in 1993 to S$4.1 million in 1994, an impressive achievement of an additional S$1.7 million or 71 percent over the previous year. In 1994, the Tower Ballroom (the second largest in Singapore, with a 1,600-seating capacity), the Tower Foyer, and the approaching corridor were refurbished, resulting in a brighter and fresher look to the Tower Ballroom facilities. There are plans of converting the outside banqueting venue of the Pavilion into a fully operational seminar venue, complete with soundproofing, audio and visual services, and conference facilities.

[2] From 1992 to 1993, when tourism was hard hit, the Shangri-La's F&B outlet still managed to show steady growth.

**Banqueting.** The Shangri-La offers organizers a choice of two ballrooms and 11 function rooms. Its banqueting revenues for 1994 posted a healthy increase of S$6.8 million, or 44 percent, from S$13.1 million in 1993 to S$18.9 million in 1994. The opening of the new Island Ballroom in September 1993 greatly increased the hotel's banqueting facilities and was the main reason for the dramatic increase in banqueting sales. The Island and Tower ballrooms continue to be Singapore's most popular venue for society events, private weddings, corporate banqueting functions, and international gala dinners. Annual growth has averaged 27.3 percent since 1991, when banquet revenues amounted to S$11.2 million.

## Awards

Individually and collectively, the Shangri-La's awards provide an additional enforcement to its market positioning as Singapore's premier hotel within the political, industrial, and social sectors.

In 1989, as a testimony to its constant effort to provide the highest quality in both accommodation and service, the hotel was honored to receive the 1989 National Productivity Board Award for its outstanding performance and achievements.

In 1991, the *Institutional Investor*'s 11th annual hotel survey revealed the Shangri-La to be the fourth best hotel in the World, while readers of the *Business Traveler* magazine had put it at second place.

In 1992, the Shangri-La Hotel was ranked second in a survey conducted by *Business Traveler* magazine for the "Most Favorite Hotel in the Asia-Pacific Region", and secured third place as the "Best Hotel in the World" in the *Institutional Investor*'s 12th annual hotel survey. The *Nikkei Trendy* (Japan) rated the Shangri-La's Valley Wing the "Best Hotel in the World." The hotel was also ranked "The Best Business Hotel" by *Asian Review* magazine and received the "Successful Meetings Pinnacle Award" from *Successful Meetings* magazine.

In 1993, the Shangri-La received the following additional awards: *Euromoney*'s "Best Hotel In The World" and "Best Hotel in Singapore," and *Executive Traveler Magazine*'s "Hotel of the Year," "Best Hotel in Asia-Pacific," and "Best Conference Hotel in the World."

In 1994, the Shangri-La improved its position within various internationally recognized rankings. The Shangri-La was rated the number one hotel in either the world or the Asia-Pacific by a number of magazines, including *Executive Traveler* in Europe, *Successful Meetings* in the United States, and *Business Traveler* in New Zealand. It also received the American Express Service Excellence Award in the food and beverage category. Within the hotel industry in Singapore, the Shangri-La performed well, achieving the "best hotel" position in the rankings by *Euromoney* (Europe), *Business Traveler* (Asia-Pacific), and *Institutional Investor* (U.S.).

## Material Contracts with Company

The Singapore hotel had a Management Service Agreement with Shangri-La International Hotel Management Private Limited to manage the hotel for a period of ten years starting 1984 with an option on the part of the company to renew the contract for an additional term of ten years.

The company had also made out a Project Management Service Agreement with Leo Property Management Pte Ltd to undertake hotel renovation projects.

## Community Contributions

The Shangri-La continues to be a strong community contributor through its numerous sponsorships and other contributions to education, cultural, and artistic activities in Singapore. The Universities Endowment Fund, which support the National University of Singapore and the Nanyang Technological University in their programs to stimulate research and scholarship, is a beneficiary of its community sponsor program.

In support of cultural and artistic activities, the Shangri-La also made financial contributions to the Singapore Labour Foundation, Singapore Festival of Arts, and the Directory of Singapore Artists.

## Company Properties

### Residential and Commercial Properties

In 1995, the company undertook a condominium development project on its properties just across the hotel. The 10-storey, 127-unit luxury serviced apartment project will be completed in mid-1997. The Shangri-La expected to generate an annual rental income of about S$4.9 million from this investment. The Shangri-La also participated in the Great-World project, off River Valley Road in downtown Singapore, with its Tiara Condominium — the only investment that was contributing to profits as of 1995. One of its retail outlets, Tanglin Place, had to close down shortly after it was opened. Tanglin Mall, Tanglin Place, and Traders Hotel are all owned by Cuscaden Properties, a subsidiary of the Shangri-La. The Shangri-La had a strong asset base with 7,785 square meters of freehold land at Orange Grove Road and Anderson Road, just outside Singapore's central business district. This prime site appreciated in value to an estimated S$42 million as of 1995.

### Hotel Properties

Losses incurred by the Shangri-La Rasa Sentosa Resort in 1994 did not prevent Shangri-La Hotel Pte Ltd from opening another hotel targeted at the budget business traveler, the Traders Hotel. As the forecast of tourists and business travelers from the Asia-Pacific region increases, budget hotels will gain a fair share of the market. Rasa Sentosa was targeted at the leisure travelers and Singaporeans who wanted an easily accessible getaway. The three hotels under the wing of the Shangri-La underscored its resolve to cover the entire spectrum of travel accommodation business.

### International Investments

The Shangri-La had recognized the importance of expanding beyond the one-hotel operation and tapping into the growing business opportunities in the region. By the end of 1994, it had a very diversified portfolio of investments, ranging from property development to resort development. Being associated with the Kuok group, an East Asia conglomerate, the Shangri-La had many opportunities to participate in property and hotel development projects. Shangri-La Hotel Pte Ltd's shareholdings in two of its major subsidiaries netted about S$13.5 million in dividends.

Hong Kong/China Shangri-La Hotel Pte Ltd has major interests in the Asean region, China, Hong Kong, and Canada. Its presence in the Hong Kong and China market was represented by Shangri-La Asia Pte Ltd, incorporated in Bermuda, and listed in the Hong Kong Stock Exchange in June 1993. In January 28, 1995, Shangri-La Hotel Pte Ltd increased its shareholdings in Shangri-La Asia by transferring all its interests in other subsidiaries to Shangri-La Asia. Shang Holdings Ltd, which has a group of subsidiaries spread over the whole of China then comes under Shangri-La Asia. Shangri-La Asia is poised to take on a greater presence in China.

In addition to its already prominent presence in the hotel business sector in Hong Kong, Shanghai and Beijing, there are projects in new hotel and property development in China, the ASEAN countries, and Myanmar (Burma). The Shangri-La also ran a 389-room Shangri-La Hotel in Surabaya, Indonesia. In Malaysia, the company focused on a new beach resort and golf club development to be opened by mid-1996. A new Shangri-La Hotel is to be opened in the city center of Johor Bahru, Malaysia. A 470-room Traders Hotel will also be opened in Yangon (Rangoon) in late 1996. The company hotels in Manila and Cebu, Philippines have shown encouraging results. It even has equity interest in the Pacific Palisades Hotel in Vancouver, Canada.

**Strategic Outlook for the Shangri-La**

In January 1995, visitor arrivals increased by five percent. There has been an increasing number of tourists from the Asian countries, while the visitors from traditional high-yield sources such as America and Europe has dropped (see Exhibit 5). The Shangri-La had been perceived as a luxury hotel which catered to American and European travelers. Hence, the Shangri-La had to rethink its strategies and attract the high-spenders from Asia amidst stiff competitions from other luxury hotels. As the convention business grows in Singapore, the Shangri-La intends to get a fair share of the pie by joining forces with Traders Hotel and Regent Hotel to boost its convention hosting capabilities.

Industry analysts have noted that as early as 1988 Singapore's hotel industry was already in the maturity phase of its product life cycle.[3] However, the annual Singapore Food Festival and the Great Singapore Sale, both launched by the Singapore Tourist Promotion Board, have been successful in drawing more tourists to Singapore. Closer cooperation between STPB and the hotels would increase the occupancy rate of the hotels in Singapore in general. The Shangri-La plans to be an active sponsor of these activities.

The Singapore government is actively engaging in formalizing tourism agreements with India, Vietnam, and Indonesia. The physical amenities are no longer sufficient to pull in crowds. Governments of these countries are exploring the possibility of expanding "tourism space" and taking advantage of the collective attractiveness of the region by offering a diverse range of tourist attractions. Opportunities are open for the Shangri-La to leverage its international network of hotels and leverage off governmental agreements in order to offer a total tourist package.

---

[3] Lee Weng Kee, B C Ghosh, and J Oliga, *Strategies for Hotels in Singapore*, ENDEC Practice Monograph No 2 (Singapore: NTI-Peat Marwick Entrepreneurship Development Center, 1988): 26–27.

### Financial Performance

The financial highlights of Shangri-La Hotel Ltd from 1983 to 1992 are presented in Exhibit 6. While the general trend indicated by these figures are by no means phenomenal (e.g., sales turnover increased by about 38 percent over the 10-year period), they reflected instead the steady growth of the company, and somewhat consistent health in areas of profitability, leverage, and asset management. The financial summary of the company for financial years 1993–1994 is presented in Exhibit 7.

### Competitive Pressures

The new 612-room super de luxe Ritz-Carlton Millennium Singapore is due to open in 1996; it will target high-end travelers. A 1992 winner of the U.S. Malcolm Baldrige National Quality Award, the Ritz-Carlton promises to be a formidable competitor in the area of service quality. In addition, the upcoming Ritz-Carlton Millennia will open with a huge 1,555-square-meter ballroom.

Other mid-range hotels like Negara Hotel, Grand Central, and Pontiac Marina will compete very closely with Traders Hotel. Nevertheless, the Shangri-La is losing out in the tussle for conference visitors to the newly launched Suntec City. Suntec City has signed an agreement with the Pacific-Asia Travel Association to host the annual travel mart for the next ten years. Singapore's first six-star hotel, Four Seasons Hotel, opened in 1994. All of these have been threatening the Shangri-La's position as Singapore's luxurious hotel accommodation provider.

The company is also facing the problem of a glut of retail space in Singapore. The continuing drop in domestic residential property prices has not been encouraging to its property development businesses. While facing some problems in the domestic market, the international investment of the Shangri-La is going to rise with the emerging economies in the region.

### Market Segmentation

As the Singapore hotel industry enters the maturity phase of its product life cycle, several industry analysts believe that the international hotel chains will be utilizing market segmentation strategies. These segmentation strategies, which had been identified as budget-priced operations, all-suite operations, premium full-service operations, and the like are necessary if the chains are to retain their market shares and ensure future profits. Meanwhile, the smaller players are intent on creating a market niche for themselves — a niche that separates their operations from the major chains. In fact, the all-suite hotel (such as Singapore's Raffles Hotel) and the budget-priced operations were started by small players searching for a market niche to give themselves a competitive advantage.

Clearly, market segregation was of prime importance to the Shangri-La. With the three different wings, the Main Tower, the Garden Wing, and the Valley Wing, it could capitalize on its unique product differentiation. The million-dollar question that all hoteliers have been facing is, how do you strike a balance between average room rate and occupancy? Since the 1980s, the Shangri-La has been enjoying an average occupancy of 70 percent; this is slightly below Singapore's average of 75 percent for big deluxe hotels. However, they are leaders in terms of average room rate of $300 and above for the three different wings combined. With travelers more discerning in terms of budget, the Shangri-La might have to lower its hold in terms of average room rate so that occupancy could be on par with the national average.

**Future Challenges**

The opening of Traders Hotel marked the move by the company from serving exclusively the high-end market segment to entry into the lower-end segment since Traders Hotel is specifically targeted at budget travelers. Business conventions in Suntec City will draw travelers which, in turn, would benefit the Shangri-La and Traders Hotels. The stronger Japanese yen would benefit the tourism industry, especially the Shangri-La, which has a big Japanese following.

Initially, STPB had forecasted a 6 to 7 percent increase in the number of ASEAN tourists to Singapore in January 1995. However, in the second half of 1995, STPB posted a downward revision of its forecast of visitor arrival. Much of the public hype about a boom of tourism industry in the first half of the year had been drained.

Figures from STPB have always shown positive growth in tourism. However, how much of this percentage growth is relevant to the Shangri-La's unique market representation? Would the 20-percent increase in the China market have any relevance for the Shangri-La? In order to maintain its stature, should Shangri-La Hotel hold on only to the limited and shrinking high-yield market?

EXHIBIT 1

## SHANGRI-LA HOTEL LTD
## Singapore Hotels' Average Occupancy and Room Rate, 1981–1996

| *Year* | *Average Occupancy Rate (%)* | *Average Room Rate (%)* |
|---|---|---|
| 1981 | 85.5% | 100 |
| 1982 | 81.0% | 112 |
| 1983 | 75.5% | 116 |
| 1984 | 75.5% | 112 |
| 1985 | 66.0% | 96 |
| 1986 | 65.0% | 76 |
| 1987 | 69.0% | 70 |
| 1988 | 79.0% | 72 |
| 1989 | 86.0% | 82 |
| 1990 | 84.0% | 138 |
| 1991 | 76.5% | 148 |
| 1992 | 80.0% | 144 |
| 1993 | 84.0% | 138 |
| 1994 | 86.0% | 142 |
| 1995 | 85.5% | 156 |
| 1996 | 82.0% | 160 |

Source: Estimates from Singapore Hotel Association data.

EXHIBIT 2

## SHANGRI-LA HOTEL LTD
## Supply of Hotel Rooms, 1988–1996

| *Year* | *Gazetted Hotels* | *Average Rooms* | *Additional Rooms* | *Change in Supply (%)* |
|---|---|---|---|---|
| 1988 | 68 | 24,669 | 1,238 | 5.3% |
| 1989 | 64 | 22,457 | 2,212 | 9.0% |
| 1990 | 66 | 23,453 | 996 | 4.4% |
| 1991 | 68 | 24,102 | 649 | 2.8% |
| 1992 | 69 | 24,573 | 471 | 2.0% |
| 1993 | 71 | 25,489 | 916 | 3.7% |
| 1994 | 78 | 25,440 | 49 | 0.2% |
| 1995 | 88 | 28,422 | 2,982 | 11.7% |
| 1996 | 97 | 31,561 | 3,139 | 11.0% |

Source: Singapore Hotel Association.

EXHIBIT 3

## SHANGRI-LA HOTEL LTD
## Profile of Visitors, 1989 and 1994

| *Country of Origin* | *1989* | *1994* |
|---|---|---|
| Asia | 44% | 56% |
| Europe | 19% | 16% |
| Japan | 17% | 16% |
| US | 5% | 5% |
| Others | 15% | 7% |

Source: Singapore Hotel Association.

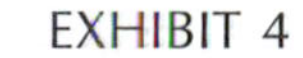

EXHIBIT 4

## SHANGRI-LA HOTEL LTD
## Corporate Investments as of April 22, 1994

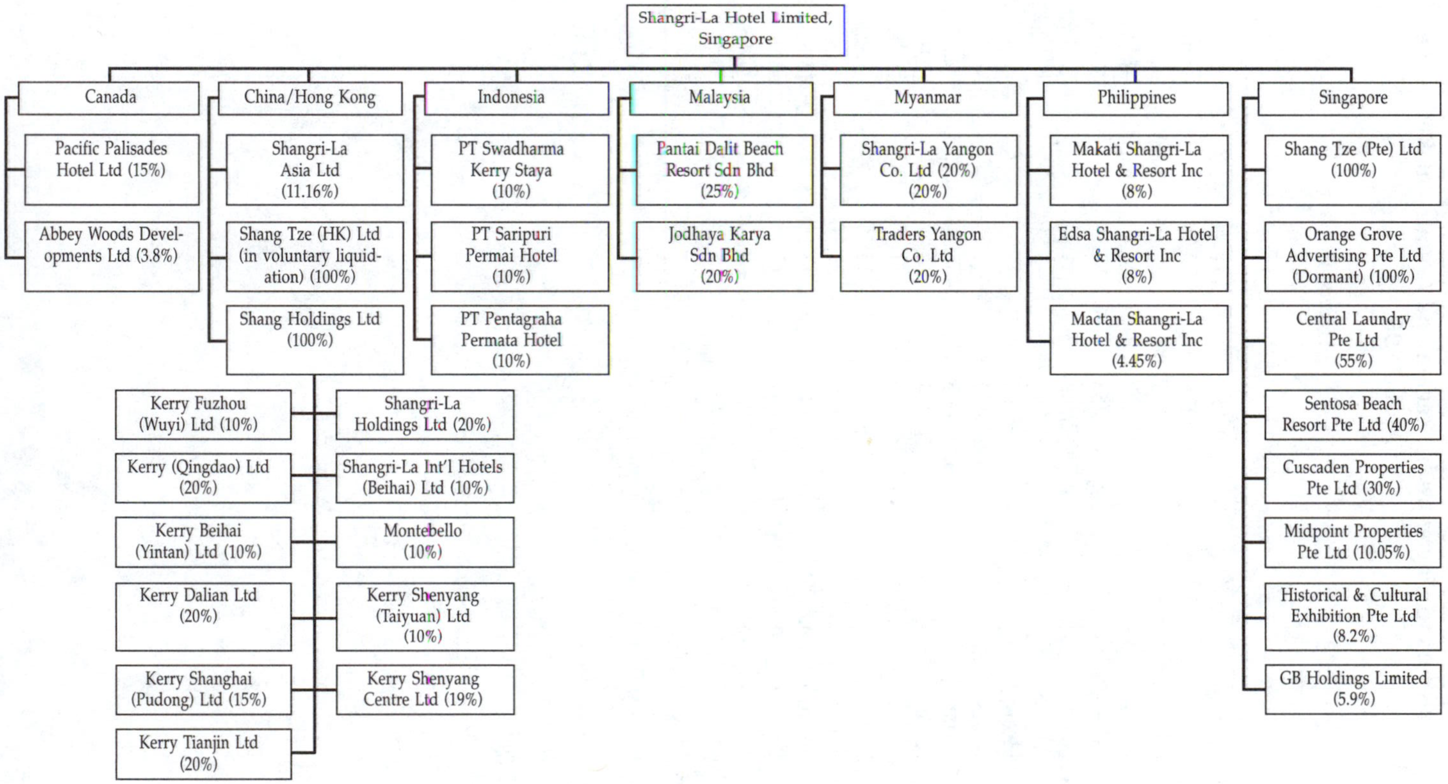

- Shangri-La Hotel Limited, Singapore
  - Canada
    - Pacific Palisades Hotel Ltd (15%)
    - Abbey Woods Developments Ltd (3.8%)
  - China/Hong Kong
    - Shangri-La Asia Ltd (11.16%)
    - Shang Tze (HK) Ltd (in voluntary liquidation) (100%)
    - Shang Holdings Ltd (100%)
      - Kerry Fuzhou (Wuyi) Ltd (10%)
      - Shangri-La Holdings Ltd (20%)
      - Kerry (Qingdao) Ltd (20%)
      - Shangri-La Int'l Hotels (Beihai) Ltd (10%)
      - Kerry Beihai (Yintan) Ltd (10%)
      - Montebello (10%)
      - Kerry Dalian Ltd (20%)
      - Kerry Shenyang (Taiyuan) Ltd (10%)
      - Kerry Shanghai (Pudong) Ltd (15%)
      - Kerry Shenyang Centre Ltd (19%)
      - Kerry Tianjin Ltd (20%)
  - Indonesia
    - PT Swadharma Kerry Staya (10%)
    - PT Saripuri Permai Hotel (10%)
    - PT Pentagraha Permata Hotel (10%)
  - Malaysia
    - Pantai Dalit Beach Resort Sdn Bhd (25%)
    - Jodhaya Karya Sdn Bhd (20%)
  - Myanmar
    - Shangri-La Yangon Co. Ltd (20%) (20%)
    - Traders Yangon Co. Ltd (20%)
  - Philippines
    - Makati Shangri-La Hotel & Resort Inc (8%)
    - Edsa Shangri-La Hotel & Resort Inc (8%)
    - Mactan Shangri-La Hotel & Resort Inc (4.45%)
  - Singapore
    - Shang Tze (Pte) Ltd (100%)
    - Orange Grove Advertising Pte Ltd (Dormant) (100%)
    - Central Laundry Pte Ltd (55%)
    - Sentosa Beach Resort Pte Ltd (40%)
    - Cuscaden Properties Pte Ltd (30%)
    - Midpoint Properties Pte Ltd (10.05%)
    - Historical & Cultural Exhibition Pte Ltd (8.2%)
    - GB Holdings Limited (5.9%)

EXHIBIT 5

**SHANGRI-LA HOTEL LTD**
**Visitors to Singapore by Region and Country of Residence**
**April 1995**

| *Country of Origin* | *Number* | *Change Over Month (%)* | *Change Over Year (%)* |
|---|---|---|---|
| Grand Total | 548,967 | –11.4% | 1.5% |
| Total — Americas | 31,138 | –20.5% | –5.8% |
| Canada | 4,607 | –25.8% | –10.4% |
| US | 25,337 | –20.3% | –4.7% |
| Total — Asia | 395,263 | –13.3% | 4.9% |
| Asean | 172,924 | –14.5% | 2.3% |
| China | 16,344 | –6.2% | 40.2% |
| Hong Kong | 26,798 | 45.9% | 19.0% |
| India | 15,415 | 14.7% | 1.6% |
| Japan | 71,615 | –35.5% | –2.2% |
| Korea | 20,974 | –36.3% | 2.9% |
| Pakistan | 3,760 | 4.2% | 31.1% |
| Sri Lanka | 5,106 | 35.5% | 8.2% |
| Taiwan | 48,130 | 28.3% | 6.3% |
| Saudi Arabia | 940 | –24.1% | –15.8% |
| United Arab Emirates | 1,061 | –25.1% | –5.0% |
| Total — Europe | 82,050 | –5.5% | –5.4% |
| Total — Oceania | 32,262 | 3.7% | –6.8% |
| Total — Others | 8,254 | 17.3% | 55.3% |

Note: By air, sea and land (excludes arrivals of Malaysians by land).

Source: Singapore Hotel Association.

EXHIBIT 6

**SHANGRI-LA HOTEL LTD**
**Income Statements**
**For the Years Ended December 31, 1993, and 1994**
(in S$ thousands, except per-share data)

| | *The Group* | | *The Company* | |
|---|---|---|---|---|
| | *1994* | *1993* | *1994* | *1993* |
| Revenues | 150,885 | 119,306 | 139,407 | 115,487 |
| Operating profit | 35,360 | 20,098 | 29,448 | 20,334 |
| Share of losses of associated companies | (2,395) | (2,983) | — | — |
| Profit before taxation | 32,965 | 17,115 | 29,448 | 20,334 |
| Taxation | (8,667) | (6,240) | (8,670) | (6,255) |
| Profit after taxation | 24,298 | 10,875 | 20,778 | 14,079 |
| Minority interests | 242 | 460 | — | — |
| Profit after tax & minority interests but before extraordinary items | 24,540 | 11,335 | 20,778 | 14,079 |
| Extraordinary items | 17,888 | 75,560 | 2,197 | 97,675 |
| Profit attributable to the shareholders | 42,428 | 86,895 | 22,975 | 111,754 |
| Retained profits at beginning of year | 215,764 | 139,819 | 215,589 | 114,785 |
| Profits available for appropriation | 258,192 | 226,714 | 238,564 | 226,539 |
| Dividends | (13,140) | (10,950) | (13,140) | (10,950) |
| Retained profits at end of year | 245,052 | 215,764 | 225,424 | 215,589 |
| Earnings per ordinary share of $1 each (cents) | 16.36 | 7.56 | | |

Source: Company records.

EXHIBIT 7

## SHANGRI-LA HOTEL LTD
## Balance Sheets
## As of December 31, 1993, and 1994

(in S$ thousands)

| | *The Group* | | *The Company* | |
|---|---|---|---|---|
| | *1994* | *1993* | *1994* | *1993* |
| Share capital | 150,002 | 150,002 | 150,002 | 150,002 |
| Capital reserves | 209,756 | 209,755 | 199,461 | 199,460 |
| Revenue reserve | | | | |
| Retained profits | 245,052 | 215,764 | 225,424 | 215,589 |
| Interest of the shareholders of the company | 604,810 | 575,521 | 574,887 | 565,051 |
| Minority interests | 1,098 | 1,340 | — | — |
| Noncurrent liabilties | | | | |
| 5% unsecured bonds due 1997 | 100,000 | 100,000 | 100,000 | 100,000 |
| Loans from minority shareholders | 900 | 900 | — | — |
| Deferred taxation | 14,643 | 13,433 | 14,643 | 13,433 |
| | 115,543 | 114,333 | 114,643 | 113,433 |
| Current liabilities | | | | |
| Trade creditors | 23,833 | 20,896 | 22,651 | 19,121 |
| Provision for repairs, renewals & maintenance | 379 | — | 379 | — |
| Due to subsidiares — trade | — | — | 168 | 234 |
| Provision for taxation | 6,208 | 1,797 | 6,101 | 1,705 |
| Bank overdrafts | 1,588 | 6 | 1,501 | — |
| Bank loans | 10,748 | 17,587 | — | — |
| Proposed dividend | 7,665 | 5,475 | 7,665 | 5,475 |
| | 50,421 | 45,761 | 38,465 | 26,535 |
| Total Share Capital, Reserves, Minority Interests, & Liabilities | 771,872 | 736,955 | 727,995 | 705,019 |
| Noncurrent assets | | | | |
| Fixed assets | 418,417 | 417,812 | 407,871 | 407,292 |
| Subsidiaries | — | 4,808 | 39,724 | 32,093 |
| Associated companies | 74,038 | 60,833 | 79,510 | 63,910 |
| Long-term investments | 267,204 | 234,925 | 189,914 | 184,359 |
| Preliminary & preoperating expenses | 162 | 213 | — | — |

EXHIBIT 7 (cont'd)

**SHANGRI-LA HOTEL LTD**
**Balance Sheets**
**As of December 31, 1993, and 1994**
(in S$ thousands)

| | *The Group* | | *The Company* | |
|---|---|---|---|---|
| | *1994* | *1993* | *1994* | *1993* |
| Current assets | | | | |
| Inventories | 1,418 | 1,305 | 1,066 | 987 |
| Trade debtors | 6,379 | 6,117 | 5,907 | 5,765 |
| Advances to associated companies | — | 5,591 | — | 5,591 |
| Short-term investments | 3,521 | 3,811 | 3,521 | 3,811 |
| Bank & cash balances | 733 | 1,540 | 482 | 1,211 |
| | 12,051 | 18,364 | 10,976 | 17,365 |
| Total Assets | 771,872 | 736,955 | 727,995 | 705,019 |

Source: Company records.

# Johan Cement Bhd and Utara Cement Sdn Bhd* 10

## Introduction

"Cement is a heavy product, therefore incurring high transportation costs. It is also a government-controlled item. Fortunately, we have distributed the cost of transportation to our distributors. Competition is tight and competitors are so numerous. The cement industry competition in Malaysia can be grouped into several regions. In the north (or *utara*) of Malaysia, our competitors are Utara Cement Bhd and Kemuncak Cement (KC); in the midwestern region, P Hanjoong (PH); while in the east coast, Cement Industries (CI). The 1990 decade definitely necessitates a thorough and refined planning," lamented the general manager of Johan Cement (the largest cement manufacturer in Malaysia) to his newly recruited deputy marketing manager.

## Cement Industry and the Economy

In 1988 and 1989, the Malaysian economy grew at 8.79 percent and 8.5 percent, respectively. Bank Negara Malaysia, the central bank of Malaysia, predicted that the economy would grow at 8.3 percent in 1990. Public investment in road infrastructure projects is

---

*This case was prepared by Professor Siti Maimon Kamso Wan Rafaei, Dean of the School of Business and Economics, Universiti Malaysia Sabah. At the request of the companies, financial data and the names of organizations, people, and some places have been disguised but essential relationships have been preserved. The case was designed to serve as a basis for class discussion rather than to illustrate either effective or ineffective handling of an administrative situation. 

estimated to amount to RM2 billion for 1989–1990.[1] The economic recession of 1984 to 1987 had severely affected the cement industry at the time that the cement manufacturers operated only at 40 percent capacity. However, since the end of 1988, the cement industry has slowly improved and most cement manufacturers have been operating at full capacity.

### Raw Materials

The local raw materials used to produce cement are available within Malaysia (i.e., lime and sand clay) except for gypsum, which has to be imported from Thailand. Malaysia imported RM198,000 worth of gypsum in 1989 and RM340,000 in 1990. These raw materials, however, constituted only seven percent of the total cost of production. The remainder of the cost consisted of energy (from coal) and maintenance charges. Coal is imported from Indonesia, China, and Australia. There is a need to obtain new sources of energy (besides petroleum) among cement manufacturers given that energy costs comprise the single largest cost item in total production costs.

### Competition

There are eight cement producers in Malaysia, six in West Malaysia, and one each in Sabah and Sarawak (see Table 1). The total capacity of all these plants is 7.7 million tons. Among the plants, there are six with integrated plants which produce *clinker*.[2] Clinker needs to be purchased for cement production. The remaining two plants are grinding plants.

TABLE 1

**Cement Producers and Their Capacities**

| *Company* | *Capacities (000 tons)* |
|---|---|
| Integrated Plants | |
| Johan Cement (JC) | 2,100 |
| Utara Cement (UC) | 1,200 |
| Kemuncak Cement (KC) | 1,200 |
| P Hanjoong (PH) | 1,200 |
| Cement Industries (CI) | 1,000 |
| Mayang Cement (MC) | 60 |
| Total | 6,760 |
| Nonintegrated Plants | |
| Malaysia Cement Corporation (MCC) | 450 |
| Ilham Cement Corporation (ICC) | 500 |
| Total | 7,710 |

[1]In 1989, the exchange rate between the Malaysian Ringgit (RM) and the US Dollar was US$1.00 = RM2.7088.
[2]Clinker is the hard mass of fused stony matter which is later ground to produce cement.

## Industrial Structure

The state governments own two of the eight cement producers in Malaysia, KC, and PH. A northern state government owns 25 percent of KC and the Perak state government (mid-west region) owns 60 percent of PH. The others are either under the ownership of some cement holding companies or listed under the Kuala Lumpur Stock Exchange.

The Malaysian government closely controls cement production through the Ministry of Domestic Affairs. A 50 percent import tax (or RM80 per ton) is levied on cement imports. The price of cement has been fixed much higher than the production cost in order to protect producers from the threat of a fall in demand. Following the recovery in the construction industry, producers were able to recoup a high profit level which they reaped before the economic recession of 1985 to 1989. Table 2 shows the profits of some publicly listed cement companies.

Although the total number of cement producers is small, the total combined capacity or production is sufficient to meet Malaysia's needs. A potential producer who wishes to apply for a manufacturing licence or incentive may not be given it in view of the excess capacity that has not been fully utilized.

TABLE 2

**Profits Before Tax for Publicly Listed Comnpanies**
(million RM)

| *Company* | *1986* | *1987* | *1988* | *1989* |
|---|---|---|---|---|
| MC | 23.2 | 18.1 | 19.3 | 39.6 |
| PMCW | 16.8 | 9.3 | 7.4 | 19.1 |
| Tasek | 31.6 | 14.2 | 11.6 | 23.1 |
| CIMA | 7.3 | 0.5 | (0.4) | 5.7 |
| CMS | — | 5.6 | 7.6 | 9.1 |

### Supply and Demand

During the period 1980 to 1985, there was a shortage of cement supply in Malaysia. Since then, imported cement has met excess demand. From 1986 onward, supply exceeded demand (see Table 3).

Cement needs for 1990 were estimated to reach 5.0 million tons whereas supply amounted to 7.6 million tons. Amounts exceeding domestic needs (surplus supply) would be exported mainly to Thailand and Singapore.

### Local Market

The cement industry produces enough to meet local requirements, as well as to export some surplus. Most of the local demand is concentrated in the central region of West Malaysia. The Klang Valley, where Kuala Lumpur is located, alone represents 50 percent of the total demand. This is followed by the northern region (Penang) with 20 percent, the southern region (Johor) with 20 percent, and the eastern region with 10 percent. A strategic geographical location is an important factor in determining a cement supplier's ability to secure a good market share.

TABLE 3

**Supply and Demand of Cement**
**1986–1995**
(000 tons)

| *Year* | *Supply* | *Demand* | *Surplus/Export* |
|---|---|---|---|
| 1986 | 3,569 | 2,985 | 584 |
| 1987 | 3,204 | 3,061 | 143 |
| 1988 | 3,828 | 3,362 | 466 |
| 1989 | 4,774 | 4,344 | 430 |
| 1990* | 7,600 | 5,000 | 2,600 |
| 1991* | 7,900 | 5,750 | 2,150 |
| 1992* | 7,900 | 6,612 | 1,288 |
| 1993* | 8,000 | 7,273 | 727 |
| 1994* | 8,000 | 7,927 | 72 |
| 1995* | 8,000 | 8,640 | (640) |

*Estimates.

Source: Cement and Concrete Association of Malaysia.

In order to achieve an equitable distribution of cement supplies, the government devised a region-based price scheme for cement. The farther away from the central region, the higher the price. In order to avoid influence on their positions, CI, KC, and PH set up a marketing joint venture known as the National Cement Marketing (NCM). This marketing joint venture has three depots in the central region and one each in Kota Bahru and Penang.

## Supply

At this stage the cement producers are experiencing problems in supplying cement for local needs due to inadequacies in the transportation system. The rail and truck transportation systems represent the main means used to transport final products, whereas barges are used to transport clinker. It was reported that Keretapi Tanah Melayu (KTM), the Malaysian railway company, was not able to meet the transportation needs due to a limited number of locomotives and carriages. In addition, KTM was estimated to have raised the transportation charges in August that year based on the final review made in the month of July 1989. This transportation problem resulted in some regions in Malaysia experiencing a shortage in cement supply. The double railway track from Kuala Lumpur to Port Klang and Rawang to Seremban was estimated to help reduce transportation problems.

The official government price for local cement (for a 50-kg bag) ranges from RM8.80 to RM9.60, depending on the region. The lowest priced (RM8.80) cement is to be found in Perak and the Eastern Region. Kelantan and Terengganu have the highest priced (RM9.60) cement. The actual local cement price ranges from RM186 to RM217 per ton.

## Export Market

With the surplus supply in 1986, Malaysia started to export cement. The export destinations were Singapore, Bangladesh, Vietnam, Thailand, Sri Lanka, and Tahiti. The total amount exported depended on local needs; only surplus supplies were exported. Hence, if the Malaysian construction industry grew, less cement would be exported (balancing it with the capacity utilization rate). This determined the total amount that would be available for the international market.

It was evident that a majority of the Asian nations that were planning or implementing large construction projects experienced a shortage of cement supply. The usual cement exporters to Malaysia (i.e., South Korea, Taiwan, and Japan) were tied up with their own local demands. In addition, environmental regulations limited the cement output of these countries (see Exhibit 1 for cement demand in selected Asian countries).

In the Southeast Asia region, the Philippines sells the lowest-priced cement at RM133 per ton, followed by Thailand at RM125 to RM150 per ton. It was reported that the market price for cement would increase by 10 to 20 percent. However, all producers located in the interior rural areas except for KC (in Langkawi Island) attempted to operate as economically as possible by setting up depots in every port. The marketing joint venture PSN had depots in Port Klang and Johor Bahru (southern region), while KC attempted to export through the Langkawi Port.

## Future Demands

### Development Expenditure

Growth figures for the cement industry increased in line with overall national economic growth figures. The construction industry showed impressive growth in the late 1980s — the growth rate rebounded from a decline of 11.8 percent in 1987 to a positive growth rate of 2.7 percent in 1988. The growth rate accelerated to 9 percent in 1989 and an estimated 14.5 percent in 1990.

Under the Fifth Malaysia Plan (1985–1990), the government allocated RM74 billion for development expenditure; however, this sum was reduced to RM57.5 billion due to the economic recession. In June 1989, only 49.2 percent of the allocated expenditure was utilized, leaving a remainder of RM28 billion. Net expenditure was actually much reduced, thereby leaving about RM15 billion brought forward into the Sixth Malaysia Plan (1991–1996).

Based on past experience, usually about 42 percent of development expenditure was allocated for transportation, communication, energy, and public utilities (construction). Hence, every year, there would be RM76 billion to be spent on construction for the forthcoming five years, compared with only RM3 billion a year during 1985 to 1988.

### Population Policy

The government's policy of encouraging population growth and achieving a large population base by the 21st century is expected to increase the demand for housing. One of the factors currently favoring accelerated growth rates for the housing construction industry is generational: 53 percent of the population lies in the 20- to 49- year age group category. Under the Special Low-Cost Housing Scheme of the government, 340,000 housing units would be constructed every year. Buying facilities and attractive loan rates by financial institutions would further increase demand for housing.

### Construction by Large Private Corporations

High demand by the private sector in the commercial and industrial sectors resulted in an increased demand for office space and factories. Large private corporations have planned and implemented large development projects such as Hotel Istana by Pernas, Bangsar Shopping Complex by Bandaraya and Cold Storage, and the Bazaar of Bandar Mid-Valley by IGB. It is estimated that more than a billion ringgit (Malaysian dollars) would have been spent on the development of new industrial areas which form about 130,000 to 140,000 square meters of built-up space every year.

The construction industry is projected to play an important role in the economy in the 1990–2000 decade. Indirectly, the cement industry would continue to obtain the development benefits. Cement producers of Malaysia realized the potential opportunities ahead. Some four of the eight producers (i.e., UC, JC, CI, and KC) are looking for new approaches to increase output whether by replacing old plants or through modernisation. Activities are focused on meeting local demands and also supplying export markets.

### Government Protection

The Malaysian government has protected the cement industry for the past 30 years through controlled pricing and by levying import duties. If the government withdraws the above protection, cement producers would have to face the challenges of having to compete in the open market with foreign competitors. However, large producers (e.g., Japan, Taiwan, and South Korea) which export to Asean countries are believed not to pose such a challenge since they have to cater to their own respective large local demands. In fact, Korea and Thailand were predicted to increase their capacities of production by 60 percent and 100 percent, respectively in 1993.

The cement industry also faces difficulties in transportation, especially in rail transportation. Not only are the number of carriages and locomotives limited, but the transportation charge will be revised upward — with a 50 percent charge hike. Before privatization, the transportation charge was controlled by the government. The Malayan railway company, KTM, might bring in a new era in terms of cement transportation charges.

## Johan Cement Bhd

### Background

Johan Cement (JC) was established in 1970. It produced and distributed cement as its main activity. JC is not allowed to diversify into other industrial activities because it is a subsidiary company especially set up for the production of cement. Johan Cement has an authorized capital of RM500 million and paid-up capital of RM230 million. With total assets of RM400 million, it is the largest cement company in Malaysia. JC has two factories, one in Seremban (central region) and another in Tampin, Malacca (southern region). JC has a production capacity of 1.5 million tons per year.

JC's technology represents one of the most modern in terms of the clinker drying process, thereby achieving the most economical energy consumption. JC is also in the process of changing to burning charcoal as a source of energy in an effort to save energy from consuming petroleum. Its dust control system was sophisticated and has exceeded the minimum environmental standards stipulated by the authorities.

"We will continue to finance technological improvements and research on the final output. This has been allocated for in the budget and also in our long-term plan," said the JC General Manager to the Ministry of Energy officials.

**Production and Distribution**

The cement quality of JC could be said to have more than met the standard requirements set by the Standards and Industrial Research Institute of Malaysia (SIRIM). A computer system was introduced for quality control so as to determine the exact rate of utilization of raw materials at each processing level.

JC has appointed an associated company as one of its agents for its cement distribution, thereby enabling it to concentrate fully on its production process. JC owns the largest network in Malaysia with four depots for packaging in several strategic locations: Alor Star, Kedah; Taman Maluri, Kuala Lumpur; Lukut, Negri Sembilan; and Kluang, Johor. The physical distribution of cement is partly conducted by its commercial transportation group, and partly by various transportation contractors and the Malaysian Railways.

**Mission and Objectives**

The JC mission is to continue overall growth in accordance with the nation's economic growth. With the foresight, vision, and full vigor of its management team, JC hopes to continue to commit itself to the economic and social development of the nation.

**Main Objectives**

JC has the following five main objectives:

1. To produce maximum clinker tonnage and cement at optimum efficiency.
2. To ensure consistent clinker and cement quality at all times.
3. To control cost for all divisions through productivity and efficiency improvements.
4. To continue with the development and motivation of human resources to bring about corporate superiority.
5. To contribute effectively to national economic development and maintain a responsible image.

**Corporate Strategy**

The main strategies adopted by the company include the following:

1. To build more plants in the factories using additional assets to increase production capacity and efficiency so as to gain a share of the rising demand in the local market.
2. To improve a planned maintenance system so as to reduce unscheduled machinery and equipment breakdowns.
3. To increase productivity levels and operational efficiency through automation and machinery.
4. To ensure the availability of the required raw material sources in the long run.
5. To increase efforts in encouraging and motivating every worker to participate

actively in Productivity Improvement Programs (PIPs) so as to improve the quality of human resources and productivity at the company.

6. To increase efforts in training and developing qualified workers IN ORDER to prepare them for heavier responsibilities and management in the future.

### Image

JC has a very well-known brand for its cement — *Sutera* (silk), which symbolizes very fine cement. For over two decades, the Sutera brand has enjoyed widespread acceptance among developers. Its competitors regarded JC as having a well-founded philosophy on quality and accuracy which cannot be emulated. Malaysians view its headquarters in Jalan Kilang, Seremban as a national landmark. The external architectural configuration of the building is unique and can be viewed as signifying a concrete and cohesive corporate culture.

The chief executive of one of Malaysia's housing developers, JC's major consumers, stated that: "We are happy with Sutera brand cement as it has been shown to be suitable for heavy-duty uses. Our projects have never failed as that brand is a quality product. In addition, it is available everywhere as JC's cement distribution network is the largest in Malaysia."

### Operating Systems

The marketing manager complained to JC's general manager: "Although we use various systems of transportation, purchasing, and stocking, our scheduling for distribution is done manually. This is ineffective for a full transportation haulage that is very complex. We need to computerize our system." Further, the marketing manager said, "We could do with more distributors to strengthen our company because we depend a great deal on them. For our purchasing system, we have decided to install the Just-In-Time (JIT) system. This system would also help our stocking system which, at the moment, is not carried out by trained technicians."

## Utara Cement Sdn Bhd

### Background

Utara Cement (UC) is a government-owned company under the economic development corporation of one of Malaysia's northern states. It was established in the 1970s to produce and distribute ordinary cement or "Ordinary Portland Cement" (OPC) and "Masonary Cement" (Walcrete). OPC is made of calcerous materials such as lime, shale, and clay. The mixture of the above materials is baked at a very high heat of about 1,400°C in a tile kiln to turn it into clinker. This clinker is then cooled and ground with a sufficient amount of gypsum so that it could be transformed into fine cement termed as "portland" cement. Portland cement is gray in color and can be used to stick small chips to a compact mass when the cement is mixed with water. "Masonary" cement, on the other hand, is a mixture containing more sand (see Exhibit 2).

UC was established for the purpose of supplying cement to developers of industrial estates in the northern states of Malaysia. It also sought to supply hotel and tourism development projects.

### Production

The production capacity of UC is 1,200 million tons per year. It represents the second largest economic-size factory in Malaysia. Three other cement companies have this capacity size. The largest capacity factory produces 2,400 million tons a year, and is owned by Johan Cement. UC can obtain its cement materials from Kedah, Langkawi, and Pernas due to its location in one of the northern states.

Cement production at UC uses the wet technology process. It is a traditional process which is partially dry, a technology adopted since the late 1970s. This technology incurs high energy costs. About 40 percent of UC's production capacity has not been utilized and the company has not achieved the level at which economies of scale can be realized. The factory often experiences production disruptions despite its long experience in cement production.

The market share of UC is only 20 percent compared to JC's 33 percent. The total market share of UC can be broken down into: 8.5 percent for the northern region, 8.5 percent for the central region, 2.0 percent for the southern region, and 1.0 percent for the eastern region of Malaysia. Since the price of cement is controlled by the government, UC makes only small promotional efforts through government agencies and chambers of commerce.

### Distribution

UC not only produces cement but also distributes its products, especially in the northern region of Malaysia. Due to the high transportation costs of cement, UC appointed numerous distribution agents to cover the Penang region, Kedah, Perlis, Langkawi, Perak, Selangor, Negri Sembilan, Malacca, Johor, and some parts of the east coast. Agents for this region have their own distribution groups, which mostly use trucks and the railway system. Cement and packaging depots would be insufficient if UC goes into full production capacity. Transportation costs to the central, southern, and eastern regions of Malaysia are high and competition is stiff. Competition comes not only from KC; JC, PH, and Tasek Cement compete with UC as well since they are located right in the central region of Malaysia.

### Management and Innovation

Human Resource Development is very important for UC, but a majority of its workers are very senior. "We are seldom given a chance to attend short courses or given exposure to interact with the Kuala Lumpur community," said a middle-aged manager who has served for more than 10 years. Research facilities are not available and the development of new products is never financed.

### Finance

Cement manufacturing is expensive to set up. It cost UC more than RM100 million in terms of equity and loan. The government sources financed 60 percent and the private sources, 40 percent of the total sum.

The finance manager of UC observed, "Escalation of costs on energy will require UC to use other energy sources in the future." On other costs he stated, "Labor costs could be inexpensive, including that of distributors provided we can limit ourselves to the northern region of Malaysia. This will help achieve a better rate of return as has been achieved in the past. We used to be the envy of our competitors, including JC, in terms of profitability. Selling cement to Thailand would be cheaper than to the southern region or the east coast of Malaysia. There is a difference of 50 percent in terms of cost between the two above-mentioned regions."

UC made history in terms of sales in 1985 when it yielded RM50 million worth of profits. Its scale of operation was optimal and its long-term experience paid off. UC still aimed to achieve a high level of profits as in the past. Profits actually fell since 1988. In 1989, profits rose as a result of efforts to increase productivity (see Exhibits 3 and 4 for the Five-Yearly Financial Summaries of JC and of UC; and Exhibit 5 for a brief comparison of sales and profits of JC and UC). The past data from 1980 to 1985 indicated very good levels of profitability for UC, something which even JC, the largest cement company, could not achieve at that time.

**Future Perspectives**

UC conducts a long-term planning process every five years. The last long-term plan was for the 1986–1990 period. At the time this case was written, UC was embarking on a new long-term plan in approaching the 21st century. UC had received a government directive that all plans were to be in line with the corporation's other subsidiaries. The corporation has 12 other subsidiaries, including two in housing construction, one in the manufacture of bricks, and another in transportation (which helps to transport UC cement to packaging depots).

EXHIBIT 1

**JOHAN CEMENT BHD AND UTARA CEMENT SDN BHD**
**Consumption of Cement in Some Asian Countries**
**For the Period 1986–1990**
(in million tons)

| *Country* | *1986* | *1987* | *1988* | *1989* | *1990* |
|---|---|---|---|---|---|
| Japan | 68.9 | 71.2 | 77.5 | 78.7 | 79.0 |
| Korea | 20.4 | 22.8 | 26.2 | 28.2 | 33.1 |
| Taiwan | 11.3 | 12.7 | 14.2 | 16.3 | 17.9 |
| Philippines | 3.1 | 4.4 | 5.6 | 6.1 | 7.7 |
| Thailand | 7.9 | 9.7 | 11.6 | 15.2 | 18.3 |
| Indonesia | 9.5 | 9.9 | 10.1 | 11.4 | 13.1 |
| Malaysia | 3.1 | 3.0 | 3.4 | 4.4 | 5.0 |

Source: ACPAC Data, Cement Consumption.

EXHIBIT 2

**JOHAN CEMENT BHD AND UTARA CEMENT SDN BHD**
**Walcrete Mix Known to Yield Best Results**

| *Applications* | *Walcrete Proportions by Volume* | *Sand Proportion by Volume* |
|---|---|---|
| Plastering | 1 | 5 or 6 |
| Arranging bricks and concrete blocks | 1 | 5 or 6 |
| Layering and cementing tiles | 1 | 3 |
| Layering of floor and ceiling | 1 | 3 |

EXHIBIT 3

## JOHAN CEMENT BHD AND UTARA CEMENT SDN BHD
### Johan Cement Bhd
### Five-Year Financial Summary
(in million RM)

| *Item* | *1990* | *1989* | *1988* | *1987* | *1986* |
|---|---|---|---|---|---|
| Reserves | 230 | 153 | 153 | 153 | 153 |
| Share capital | 104 | 113 | 103 | 94 | 98 |
| Shareholders' fund | 334 | 266 | 256 | 247 | 251 |
| Deferred tax | 67 | 75 | 94 | 95 | 73 |
| Term loans | 57 | 78 | 112 | 160 | 208 |
| Pension benefits | 5 | 4 | 4 | 3 | 3 |
| Long-term debt | 129 | 157 | 210 | 258 | 284 |
| Fixed assets | 462 | 389 | 412 | 436 | 458 |
| Current assets | 162 | 140 | 128 | 151 | 154 |
| Current liabilities | 123 | 110 | 83 | 93 | 90 |
| Net current assets | 39 | 30 | 45 | 58 | 64 |
| Sales | 315 | 248 | 211 | 249 | 285 |
| Profit before tax | 75 | 37 | 26 | 27 | 30 |
| Income taxes | 25 | (2) | 4 | 11 | 14 |
| Extraordinary items | (10) | 0 | 0 | 0 | 0 |
| Profit after tax and extraordinary items | 90 | 35 | 30 | 38 | 44 |
| Dividend rate | 16.1% | 19.6% | 7.2% | 7.2% | 9.8% |
| Total dividends | 37 | 30 | 11 | 11 | 15 |
| Asset backing per share | 2.18 | 2.74 | 2.99 | 3.23 | 3.41 |

EXHIBIT 4

## JOHAN CEMENT BHD AND UTARA CEMENT SDN BHD
### Utara Cement Sdn Bhd
### Five-Year Financial Summary

(in million RM)

| *Item* | *1990* | *1989* | *1988* | *1987* | *1986* |
|---|---|---|---|---|---|
| Share capital | 150 | 150 | 150 | 150 | 112 |
| Reserves | 31 | 26 | 25 | 25 | 45 |
| Shareholders' fund | 181 | 176 | 175 | 175 | 157 |
| Deferred tax | 8 | 12 | 11 | 14 | 17 |
| Term loans | 0 | 0 | 0 | 0 | 0 |
| Pension benefits | 7 | 7 | 6 | 6 | 6 |
| Long-term debt | 196 | 195 | 194 | 200 | 189 |
| Fixed assets | 111 | 119 | 127 | 135 | 121 |
| Subsidiary companies | 0 | 0 | 0 | 0 | 0 |
| Associated companies | 13 | 13 | 12 | 11 | 8 |
| Investments | 10 | 12 | 9 | 9 | 4 |
| Noncurrent assets | 134 | 144 | 148 | 155 | 133 |
| Current assets | 103 | 90 | 105 | 127 | 125 |
| Current liabilities | (41) | (41) | (61) | (83) | (70) |
| Net current assets | 62 | 49 | 44 | 200 | 55 |
| Sales | 130 | 101 | 127 | 158 | 189 |
| Profit before tax | 23 | 12 | 14 | 31 | 50 |
| Income taxes | (7) | 5 | 8 | (14) | (25) |
| Extraordinary items | (4) | (1) | 0 | 0 | 1 |
| Profit after tax and extraordinary items | 12 | 16 | 6 | 17 | 26 |
| Dividend rate | 8.0% | 5.0% | 7.5% | 15.0% | 20.0% |
| Total dividends | 8 | 5 | 7 | 13 | 13 |
| Acquisition per share | | | | | |
| Shares (cents) | 10.8 | 4.6 | 4.6 | 11.5 | 17.0 |
| Asset backing per share | 1.21 | 1.18 | 1.17 | 1.17 | 1.05 |

EXHIBIT 5

## JOHAN CEMENT BHD AND UTARA CEMENT SDN BHD
### Sales and Profits of Johan Cement and Utara Cement For the Period 1980–1985

(in million RM)

| *Company* | *1980* | *1981* | *1982* | *1983* | *1984* | *1985* |
|---|---|---|---|---|---|---|
| Johan Cement | | | | | | |
| Sales | 131 | 151 | 248 | 316 | 318 | 327 |
| Profit before tax | 12.8 | 6.8 | 11.2 | 49.6 | 56.4 | |
| Utara Cement | | | | | | |
| Sales | 158 | 195 | 196 | 201 | 194 | 189 |
| Profit before tax | 31.8 | 30.2 | 32.8 | 35.2 | 37.4 | 50.3 |

# Uraco Holdings Limited* 11

"Being able to build our own machines has given us an edge over our competitors because they have to rely on others," said a satisfied Mr Lim Ee Ann, Managing Director and Cofounder of Uraco. But this competitive advantage had its price because it drove the company to run at full capacity. Based on a survey of the disk drive industry (see Exhibit 1), demand for disk drives is expected to increase by as much as 20 percent. So how can Uraco capitalize on this growing demand when it is already operating at full capacity?

Ng Kok Heng, Chairman and the other Cofounder of Uraco Holdings Limited pondered over this issue. Uraco's high dependence on the disk drive industry, which makes up 90 percent of Uraco's business is a constraint for any major immediate diversification. Uraco must come up with something fast, otherwise competitors would use this opportunity to capture more market share and eat into Uraco's share. What strategy should Uraco then follow? What costs must Uraco be prepared to pay? These are tough questions which the two founders have to address, and their decisions would eventually determine the fate of Uraco.

---

*This case was prepared by Lee Teck Meng, Lin Ling, Mario Alain Gonzalez Hernandez, Seah Yen Goon, and Tan Ai Tong (MBA, Nanyang Technological University, Singapore, 1995–1996) under the supervision of Professor Luis Ma. R. Calingo to serve as a basis for class discussion rather than to illustrate either effective or ineffective handling of a managerial situation. This case was developed wholly from published materials. Most quotations are paraphrased creations of the case authors for educational purposes and cannot be considered actual statements by Uraco's management and employees.

## Background of Uraco

### The Early Years

In November 1981, two entrepreneurs, Ng Kok Heng and Lim Ee Ann, jointly started Uraco Precision Engineering (UPE) as a tool-and-die workshop using secondhand toolroom machines. Toward the end of 1982, the two founders saw potential in the market for precision-machined metal parts in Singapore. Disk drive multinational companies (MNCs) which had established their manufacturing base in Singapore were unable to obtain precision parts of acceptable quality from within Singapore. Recognizing this niche potential, UPE diversified into the precision-machining business, targeting the floppy and hard disk drive industry as its main customers. UPE's first few years were very trying and the partnership, started with S$200,000 scraped together from friends and relatives of the two partners, almost did not succeed during the first couple of years.[1]

The first break for UPE came when they secured their first contract with Tandon, a floppy disk drive manufacturer. UPE became one of the first local companies to achieve the quality standards required to supply directly to the floppy and hard disk drive industry. UPE was then incorporated as a private company in 1983 with precision-engineering services as its main focus.

### Expansion of Uraco's Business

In late 1984, UPE acquired a 20-percent strategic stake in Aluputer, a company providing metal plating services. With this acquisition, UPE was able to exercise greater control over the quality of the final product because a large portion of UPE's products require this service.

As UPE grew, it invested in more factory space and equipment in order to satisfy increasing demand for its services. In 1987, UPE expanded into the die-casting business. Uraco Die Casting Pte Ltd (UDC) was incorporated to handle the die-casting operations. This vertical integration gave UPC more control over the supply and quality of die cast because UPE's business involved the machining of raw castings.

In 1990, in response to customer requests, UPE started to do some subassembly work. Acura Manufacturing Pte Ltd (AM) was then incorporated to provide clean room and mechanical subassembly services. The range of services that AM provided gradually increased since its inception and by 1994 AM had its principal businesses in the mechanical and clean room subassembly of disk drive and computer tape components, as well as die-cutting services such as the die-cutting of Kapton, aluminium foil, copper foil, and polyester materials.

In 1991, both partners decided to capitalize on the lower production costs available in Malaysia by shifting some of the production to this country. Uraco Manufacturing Sdn Bhd (UM) was incorporated and started production in July 1991, serving as a second production base for Uraco. This move also brought Uraco closer to some of its customers in Malaysia and allowed Uraco to benefit from Malaysia's status within the United States' Generalized System of Preferences (GSP). UM was awarded pioneer status in Malaysia for five years commencing July 1991.

[1]In 1994, the exchange rate between the Singapore Dollar and the US Dollar was US$1.00 = S$1.47.

In 1993, Kapitas (Malaysia) Sdn Bhd (KM) was established in the state of Johor, Malaysia, to specialize in die-casting activities and to serve as a key supplier to UM. KM's role paralleled that of UDC in Singapore: supplying die castings to UM.

The founders saw potential in the precision metal-stamping business in Singapore; Singapore Precision Stampings Pte Ltd (SPS) was set up to specialize in precision metal-stamping to cater for this service. With the establishment of SPS, Uraco's range of products was further expanded to include connector pins, leadframes, terminals, and motor stators (laminates).

### Joint Ventures and Strategic Alliances

Besides investing in vertical integration, Uraco also went into strategic alliances with counterparts around the globe. Uraco intends to diversify its business in other related and unrelated areas through joint ventures with other parties.

On May 6, 1994, SPS entered into an agreement with Katoh, a Japanese firm specializing in die-making and metal-stamping in which Katoh would acquire a 30-percent stake in SPS by the end of August 1995. This agreement would allow SPS access to Katoh's transfer press technology. This transfer of technology to SPS significantly increased its capabilities.

In May 1994, Uraco started Vision Venture Pte Ltd (VV) to explore investment opportunities in China and other parts of Asia. VV's efforts bore fruit in September 1994, when Uraco embarked on a joint venture with a Chinese motor manufacturer, the Changzhou Group of Best Models ("Best Models") to produce micro stepper and DC motors. Best Models has been manufacturing AC, DC, servo, and stepping motors since 1959.

In November 1994, Uraco ventured into a new unrelated business through another joint venture with a China firm. This alliance was with Chongqing Sida Experiment Instrument Factory ("Sida"), under which VV would set up a subsidiary company in China to be called Chongqing Yuanda Appliance Co Ltd (CYA). This subsidiary would manufacture clothes dryers for the local market and low-temperature testing equipment for the domestic and export markets.

Later that same year, Uraco acquired a 25-percent stake in Maxplas Singapore Pte Ltd, a plastic injection molding company. This acquisition served to further enhance Uraco's range of services and was another step toward Uraco's objective of offering a comprehensive suite of services to its customers. Uraco then established other subsidiaries in Malaysia, seeking to parallel the functionality of SPS and AM in Singapore to serve UM.

## Principal Business Activities

Through its subsidiaries, Uraco is engaged in the following principal activities: aluminum die-casting, precision-machining, clean room and mechanical subassembly, and precision metal-stamping. Through its associated companies, Uraco is also involved in stepper and DC-motor manufacturing, plastic-injection molding, and metal plating (see Exhibit 2 for Uraco's organizational chart).

UPE's major products are disk drive components, especially disk drive plates and covers, which account for about 90 percent of the turnover (see Exhibit 3 for an illustration of UPE's production process). The first stage of the process starts with castings made by

UDC and KM from aluminum ingots; the second stage is the precision-machining process done by UPE and UM, which process these castings according to their customers' requirements.

In some cases, subassembly of mechanical parts, manufactured by SPS, onto the machined castings forms the third stage in Uraco's production chain. Uraco has over 215 CNC machines in operation and believes in continued investment in modern equipment. Uraco saw more future involvement in the contract manufacturing projects. SPS would be involved in the stamping of components for these projects.

Hence, Uraco could offer its customers a complete service, with its full range of die-casting, machining, stamping, and subassembly skills augmented by its associated companies' skills in plating and plastic injection moulding. The founders believed that this vertical integration of all the associated businesses of Uraco to provide total services is one of the key differential advantages they have over their competitors.

## Production Facilities

Uraco's production facilities are mainly based in Malaysia and Singapore. The group has invested heavily in modifying its old machines, buying new machinery, hiring skilled workers to operate them, and expanding its production capacity. This practice has allowed Uraco to increase its productivity with high-quality standards.

To perform its precision-engineering operations, Uraco owns two manufacturing buildings in Johore Bahru, Malaysia. The company plans a further increase in its production capacity by building a third site in the same city on a freehold property. This new building would have an area of approximately one-and-a-half times the floor space of the two current buildings. When this facility is finished, Uraco's plans are to move all its machining operations into it. Later, the company would move its entire Malaysian die-casting operations into the two existing buildings. The objective of grouping the die-casting and precision-machining operations is to increase the efficiency through the reduction of material handling. Further plans include investment in automated die-casting technology to provide the projected die-casting plant with automatic molten aluminum delivery systems.

Uraco's subassembly operations are performed by Acura Manufacturing, a wholly owned subsidiary that operates both in Singapore and Malaysia. In order to accomplish the company's strategies of offering a full range of services and embarking on more contract manufacturing projects, Acura Manufacturing applied for new factory space in Singapore.

Singapore Precision Stampings was incorporated in 1993 to perform stamping operations — to increase the range of services that the group offers. At the time when this case was written, the company had twelve stamping machines and expected to purchase two more. The customer base served by Uraco's stamping facility included multinational corporations like Texas Instruments, AMP, JTS, and Sony.

## Staff Training

Uraco places strong emphasis on training its workers toward quality assurance. Machine operators undertake a training program where they are taught not only how to operate the machines but also the safety measures to take and how to check the output from the machines. After this training, the operators are able to check basic quality assurance measures. Uraco also sponsors its workers for National Trade Certificate Courses and its experienced engineering assistants for external courses such as the Diploma in Production Engineering.

## Quality Assurance

Uraco's founders believe that quality is the responsibility of every member in the group and they stress quality assurance throughout the entire manufacturing process. Before production starts, Uraco's engineers spend a large amount of effort in the design of the production process and in the preproduction tests to ensure that the process meets the required quality. Once the production has started, quality is checked during the production process itself instead of simply inspecting the products at the end of the production line. Furthermore, Uraco uses a statistical monitoring process to detect and rectify any deviation from the specifications. Finally, the quality assurance department ensures that all the tests required by the customers are applied.

Uraco continuously improves its quality standards. This fact attracted Uraco's main customers like Seagate Technology, Western Digital, Micropolis, and Hewlett Packard to admit the company into their just-in-time (JIT) inventory control system, which requires high quality and on-time delivery. Another evidence of Uraco's devotion to quality is the customer acceptance of its products without performing the standard incoming inspection procedures. Uraco's subsidiaries performing manufacturing operations either have been or are expected to be awarded the ISO 9002 certification for their quality management systems.

## Tax Concessions

In Singapore and Malaysia, companies that invested heavily in capital goods are normally awarded with government incentives to continue their expansion activities. This is the case of Uraco which, owing to its investments in new plant and equipment, enjoys tax rates below the corporate levels. Since the future plans of the group include further capital investments, it is expected to continue enjoying these lower tax rates. Further, Uraco was awarded Pioneer status for five years for its Uraco Manufacturing and Kapitas companies in Malaysia.

## Marketing

The market base of Uraco comprises multinational corporations operating in Singapore and Malaysia. The company's strategy in this field is to build long-term relationships with its customers by offering them quality products and on-time delivery. The top managers are personally involved in the marketing activities, including regular consultations with its main customers. Uraco had gotten companies based in the United States, Switzerland, and Germany as customers through their procurement offices in Singapore. The reputation built by Uraco has led some of its customers to approach the company directly to contract its services.

Many of Uraco's customers have been doing business with Uraco for over five years. The percentage of Uraco's turnover derived from repeat customers has been consistently above 70 percent for the past three years. Uraco has also been bestowed with many awards (listed in Table 1) from its customers for quality products and delivery.

TABLE 1

**Quality and Customer Satisfaction Awards Received by Uraco Holdings Ltd**

| *Customer* | *Award* |
|---|---|
| Micropolis | Excellent Support and Quality Performance Award |
| Hewlett Packard | Appreciation for Outstanding Support |
| Seagate Technology | Quality Excellence and Certified Supplier Achievement Award |
| Western Digital | Strategic Partner in Western Digital's Success |
| Texas Instruments | Responsiveness and Excellent Support |

## Performance of Uraco's Core Businesses

Based on a 1994 Dataquest survey of worldwide disk drive market, Uraco's market share of base plates sold to the total number of disk drives is as follows:

| *Hard Disk Drive Format* | *Percentage* |
|---|---|
| 2.5 inches or less | 19.4 |
| 3.5 inches | 11.6 |
| 5.25 inches or larger | 72.0 |

### Turnover and Profits of Different Business Activities

The different companies that form Uraco's Group are engaged in three main activities. First, Uraco Die Casting (Singapore) and Kapitas (Malaysia) are involved in the die-casting business. Uraco Precision Engineering (Singapore) and Uraco Manufacturing (Malaysia) competed in the precision-machining business. Due to the degree of vertical integration attained by Uraco and its experience in these two activities, the management has combined them as one business. Second, Acura Manufacturing (Singapore and Malaysia) participates in the electronic and mechanical subassembly business. Third, Singapore Precision Stampings (Singapore and Malaysia) performs the precision-stamping activities. Tables 2 and 3 provide Uraco's turnover and profit before tax by activity for five years.

The die-casting and precision-machining business is the original and most profitable activity of Uraco. Table 2 presents a stable growth in the business turnover from 1992 to 1994, after a decrease from 1990 to 1991. This decrease was due to a slowdown in the disk drive industry in 1990–1991, when Uraco's customers lowered their selling price, thus affecting the company's margins. The decrease in turnover is also due to heavy investments made by the company on new machinery and equipment. After 1991, the disk drive industry recovered, and in 1994 it experienced a boom. Uraco's expansion in Malaysia in

TABLE 2

**Turnover by Activity, 1990–1994**

(in thousand dollars)

| Segment | 1990 $ | 1990 % | 1991 $ | 1991 % | 1992 $ | 1992 % | 1993 $ | 1993 % | 1994 $ | 1994 % |
|---|---|---|---|---|---|---|---|---|---|---|
| Die-casting & precision-machining | 42,644 | 100.0 | 42,136 | 99.6 | 45,997 | 97.9 | 58,028 | 97.7 | 79,718 | 95.1 |
| Mechanical subassembly | | | 160 | 0.4 | 1,000 | 2.1 | 1,339 | 2.3 | 2,830 | 3.4 |
| Precision stamping | | | | | | | 22 | 0.0 | 1,283 | 1.5 |
| Total | 42,644 | 100.0 | 42,296 | 100.0 | 46,997 | 100.0 | 59,389 | 100.0 | 83,831 | 100.0 |

TABLE 3

**Profit Before Tax by Activity, 1990–1994**

(in thousand dollars)

| Segment | 1990 $ | 1990 % | 1991 $ | 1991 % | 1992 $ | 1992 % | 1993 $ | 1993 % | 1994 $ | 1994 % |
|---|---|---|---|---|---|---|---|---|---|---|
| Die-casting & precision-machining | 5,333 | 100.0 | 1,352 | 114.4 | 4,297 | 99.2 | 11,627 | 99.5 | 13,034 | 98.4 |
| Mechanical subassembly | | | (170) | (14.4) | 36 | 0.8 | 174 | 1.5 | 45 | 0.3 |
| Precision stamping | | | | | | | (119) | (1.0) | 164 | 1.2 |
| Total | 5,333 | 100.0 | 1,182 | 100.0 | 4,333 | 100.0 | 11,682 | 100.0 | 13,243 | 100.0 |

1993 allowed its profits before tax to increase in that year since production costs were lowered significantly.

The mechanical subassembly activity was started in 1991 by AM. The year 1992 was the first full year of operations for AM, attaining the S$1 million sales mark. After this year, the sales activity of this business increased since AM had established a good reputation in the industry. In 1994, however, profits declined. This was due mainly to the decision of a customer to stop consigning materials for one of its products. AM started sourcing these materials itself, and these expenses now had to be included in the cost of goods sold.

Uraco entered the precision-metal stamping business at the end of 1993. By 1994 the business reached S$1.3 million in sales. The profit before tax in this activity was S$164,000.

### Turnover by Customer

Seagate Technology International's sales was forecasted to reach US$4.4 billion sales during the fiscal year ending June 30, 1995. Seagate also invested another S$200 million to increase its Singapore plant capacity, which accounted for 70 to 75 percent of Seagate's total disk drive production. With an expected increase in production and a good customer relationship with Seagate, Uraco would continue to supply to Seagate the required products and services. Table 4 summarizes Uraco's turnover by customer.

TABLE 4

**Customer Purchases as a Percentage of Total Sales Fiscal Years 1992–1994**

| *Customer* | *1992* | *1993* | *1994* |
|---|---|---|---|
| Seagate Technology International | 34.2% | 36.8% | 39.4% |
| Maxtor Peripherals (S) Pte Ltd | 23.5% | 19.2% | 11.3% |
| Western Digital (S) Pte Ltd | 5.5% | 11.1% | 9.3% |
| Micropolis Ltd | 11.6% | 10.5% | 4.7% |
| Archive Singapore Pte Ltd | 11.8% | 9.2% | 3.8% |
| Hewlett Packard S'pore (Pte) Ltd | 6.3% | 7.1% | 1.7% |

## Group Profitability

The year 1991 was characterized by a slowdown in the disk drive industry (see Exhibit 4 for financial statements). The Group's customers were forced to reduce their selling price in order to boost demand. In consideration of their long-term relationships, Uraco had to cooperate with its customers by lowering its price so as to ease the burden on its customers' margins. Thus, both the Group's turnover and profit margin declined in 1991.

The disk drive industry recovered in 1992. Uraco's turnover increased at an annual compounded rate of 26 percent from 1992 to 1994. The growth in turnover was attributable to the following reasons:

1. The robust demand in the disk drive and computer industries after 1991.
2. The Group's progressive expansion of its matching capacity with the expansion of the Group's machining operations into Johor Bahru (Malaysia's southernmost city).
3. The Group's expansion into its new businesses of subassembly and metal stamping.

In 1993, the Group began to expand rapidly. The Group's machining facilities in Johor and its subassembly operations both came fully on line. The relocation of part of the Group's manufacturing operations to Johor reduced the operating costs significantly. At the same time, the Group was trying to phase out the lower margin products and phase in the higher margin products progressively. This move increased the profit margins.

Profit before tax increased over 150 percent in 1994 compared to 1990 due to the strong growth in turnover combined with increases in profit margins as well as general improvements in operating efficiency. The Group had kept on investing in new machinery and developing and modifying the existing ones, which resulted in increased efficiency and productivity.

Ninety-five percent of Uraco's revenue was denominated in US dollars and the remainder in Singapore dollars. But 60 percent of its purchases and operating expenses were denominated in Singapore dollars, 33 percent in US dollars and the remaining 7 percent in Malaysian Ringgit. The U.S. exchange rate was negotiated with the customers based on the exchange rate forecasted during the contract period with clauses for renegotiation should the exchange rate materially deviate from the original forecast. Table 5 presents the foreign exchange gains/losses for the past three years.

TABLE 5

**Foreign Exchange Gains and Losses**
**Fiscal Years 1992–1994**
(in thousand Singapore dollars)

| | *FY 1992* | *FY 1993* | *FY 1994* |
|---|---|---|---|
| Exchange Gain/(Loss) | (471) | 234 | (465) |
| Percentage of Sales | 1.0% | 0.4% | 0.5% |
| Percentage of Profit Before Tax | 10.8% | 2.0% | 3.5% |

To minimize the foreign exchange rate fluctuations, Uraco hedged the US dollars with forward contracts. It had been monitoring its exposure to Malaysian Ringgit and would hedge with appropriate forward contracts if required.

## Looking into the Future

A 1994 report of the Singapore Economic Development Board (EDB) indicated that there were 960 companies in the precision-engineering industry. However, only TPW of Thailand, Kenseisha of Japan, and Cam Mechatronic Ltd of Singapore were regarded as main competitors to Uraco's business. This industry requires high capital investment to produce a significant capacity and a long lead time for establishing good customer relationships; both posed barriers to new entry.

Ninety percent of Uraco's turnover was accounted for by the disk drive industry. The growth prospects of this industry remained favorable. The International Data Corporation (IDC) expected demand for disk drives to grow by almost 30 percent in 1995. Thus, the Group has no plans to shift its focus away from this industry. However, Uraco will continue to improve in the disk drive's performance/price ratio, which is the key competitive advantage of disk drives over other forms of data storage. According to Ng, innovative uses of disk drives and personal computers like video servers and multiple disk drive storage systems are not a threat to Uraco's business because they do not require significant changes to the disk drives themselves. Ng also considered that there are few new storage media or products that have the potential to replace the current disk drives technology. However, marketing for other business to broaden its spread and further increase its customer base would be continued.

Uraco currently offers its products and services to a customer base of 19 customers in the electronics industry. Out of the six top disk drive manufacturers, which shipped more than two million hard disk drives in 1994, Uraco serves five of them. Uraco also constantly invests in new equipment and upgrades its staff so as to minimize the risk of technological obsolescence and improve its quality service to the customers.

Demand for the Group's precision-machined products is derived from the demand for computers in general and disk drives in particular. On the other hand, demand for the Group's stamped and assembled parts is derived from the demand for the electronic products that they eventually become part of.

Considering the following perspectives, Ng is quite optimistic about the prospects for the Uraco Group:

1. **Global economic recovery.** The global economy continues to recover. The economies of the Asia-Pacific region are expected to show a higher growth rate in 1995. The global economic recovery would contribute to stronger demand for the electronic products that are manufactured by the Group's customers, which should in turn benefit the Group.
2. **Good prospects for precision engineering industry.** The strong demand from Asia-Pacific emerging markets has contributed significantly to the 12-percent growth in 1994 in the precision- engineering industry. The outlook for the industry in 1995 is bright, with output growth expected to again reach 12 percent.
3. **Good prospects for disk drive and computer industries.** With a predicted growth rate of 30 percent in 1995, 29 percent in 1996, and a compounded annual rate of 18.5 percent from 1997 to 1999, the disk drive industry continues to show good growth potential. The demand is fueled by increases in the price and/or performance of disk drives and the boom in the demand for personal computers. In addition to the recent increases in investment by many disk drive manufacturers in Singapore, up to ten more foreign disk drive media companies are expected to announce investment plans here over the next two years, according to the EDB. The Group is well-positioned to benefit from this.
4. **Good prospects for electronics industry.** It is predicted that the electronics industry would enjoy an average annual growth rate of 14.5 percent during the period 1996–2000. The contract manufacturing operations in countries such as Malaysia, Indonesia, Thailand, and China would benefit most because they serve the local markets and provide lower cost manufacturing for export markets. The Group is going to further widen its range of services in order to take advantage the opportunities. Its new subsidiaries, SPS and AM (Malaysia), are geared towards this industry.

EXHIBIT 1

## URACO HOLDINGS LTD
## A Survey of the Disk Drive Industry

### Manufacturing Sector's Performance and Outlook

The disk drive industry is optimistic about its performance for 1995. The disk drive makers, in particular, are confident that the introduction of new products would boost their output. Reflecting on this optimism is the plan to increase investments in Singapore by Seagate (S$200 million) and by IBM (S$150 million).

However, there are other factors to be considered, such as the weak US dollar, the strong Singapore dollar, and the strong Japanese yen. These would affect not only the terms of trade for Singapore (which in turn affect export) but also the profitability of the industry. In fact a recent study conducted by Kay Hian James Capel found that 38.67 percent of the 75 companies surveyed would be "poorly to terribly affected" by the recent currency turmoil. This is of particular concern to the disk drive industry, which sells mainly in US dollars and buys in a stronger currency such as the Singapore dollar or the yen.

Therefore for the next two quarters or so, the manufacturing sector is expected to continue to grow. However its growth rate would depend on, besides the fundamentals of the sector, the relative strength of the US dollar, Singapore dollar, and Japanese Yen.

### Industry's Performance/Development and Outlook

In 1994, Singapore's disk drive industry grew by 44 percent to 29.6 million rigid disk drives, and the worldwide disk drive market was worth some US$17 billion and growing at a rate of 20 percent a year. Besides, there is great potential for the PC market in the Asia-Pacific region given the low penetration rate for Indonesia, Philippines, Thailand, and Malaysia.

Despite the positive outlook for the industry, there are still several major players who were not able to reap the benefits of this growth. Maxtor Peripherals had its eighth quarter of successive losses totaling US$360 million, and Micropolis suffered losses for two years in a row totaling US$51 million. However, Seagate, Conner, and Western Digital enjoyed a profit in all of the four quarters during 1994. The net worth of Conner increased by 21.70 percent over the last six months to $592 million. Maxtor, on the other hand, lost some 25.25 percent of its net worth in the last three months. This vast difference in performance goes to show the intensity of the competition within the industry.

Competition from the Japanese is expected to increase because Toshiba Corporation announced in 1995 its intention to market two types of new 2.5-inch hard disk drive, which it claims has the world's largest storage capacity. Therefore, players in this industry have to cope not only with the rapid changes in technology; they also have to deal with decreasing margin, brought about by major OEMs producing their own disk drives and shortages in key components.

The success of a company also depends on its ability to compete on the following: price, early new product availability, product performance, product quality, storage capacity, and responsiveness to customer demands, which increasingly include schedule predictability.

Some of the major players in the disk drive industry are beginning to change their business strategy. They had focused not solely on disk drives but toward providing a "total storage solution." It is expected that, with this new strategy, volatility in the company's business would be reduced. This is because the demand for other products such as supporting software is less volatile. This strategy would thus inject more stability in their profit and stock prices.

The new strategy would also allow companies to diversify into other areas which have great potential (e.g., software development). Among those who are actively pursuing this strategy are Seagate and Conner. Both have acquired businesses engaged in software development.

## Recent Trends in Disk Drive Requirements

1. The shift from centralized computing based on mainframes and minicomputers to networks and client-server architectures has resulted in an increased demand for compact, high-capacity, high-performance storage devices and systems for use in networks of personal computers and workstations.
2. Increasing complexity of personal computers, application software operating systems (e.g., Windows, OS/2), and the software applications designed to support them have resulted in the demand for greater storage capacity in individual computers.
3. The substantial storage requirements necessary to store high-resolution images, and sound and video data applications are adding significantly to the amount of storage required on personal computer systems.

In short, the demand would be for compact, higher capacity and higher performance storage devices. Therefore, the demand for 1.8-inch and 2.5-inch disk drives looks optimistic if their storage capacity and performance improve.

## Other Developments

Although the low demand for 1.8-inch disk drives does not justify new investments for many major disk drive manufacturers, demand for 1.8-inch disk drives in 1995 is expected to increase by 30 percent this year because of the great demand for portable computers. Therefore, competition in the manufacturing of 1.8-inch disk drives is expected to heat up as more current major disk drive manufacturers are expected to go into its production. Among those who are either researching or already producing the 1.8-inch drives are Maxtor and Seagate. This would mean that Integral Peripherals, the main supplier of 1.8-inch disk drives in 1995, is likely to face fierce competition from the "bigger players."

Conner Peripherals and Human Interface Engineering signed a memorandum of understanding to carry out R&D projects with the Gintic Institute of Manufacturing Technology at Nanyang Technological University. The project will develop technical knowledge on overcoming production bottlenecks and modular stations along the production line, thereby allowing it to make a variety of products without scrapping the whole line. Cost savings, if the project were successful, is estimated to be S$1 million every six months. Although the resulting technology would not belong to Conner exclusively, the company is expected to reap the first fruits from the project.

EXHIBIT 2

## URACO HOLDINGS LTD
## Organizational Chart

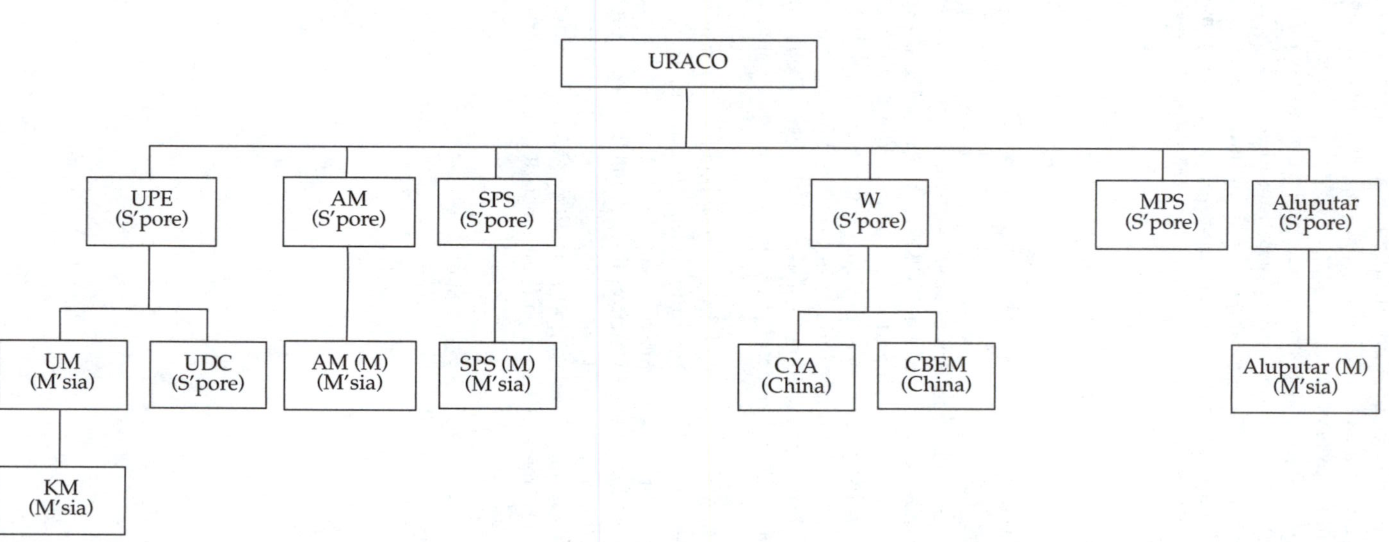

EXHIBIT 3

**URACO HOLDINGS LTD**
**Flow Chart of Production Process**

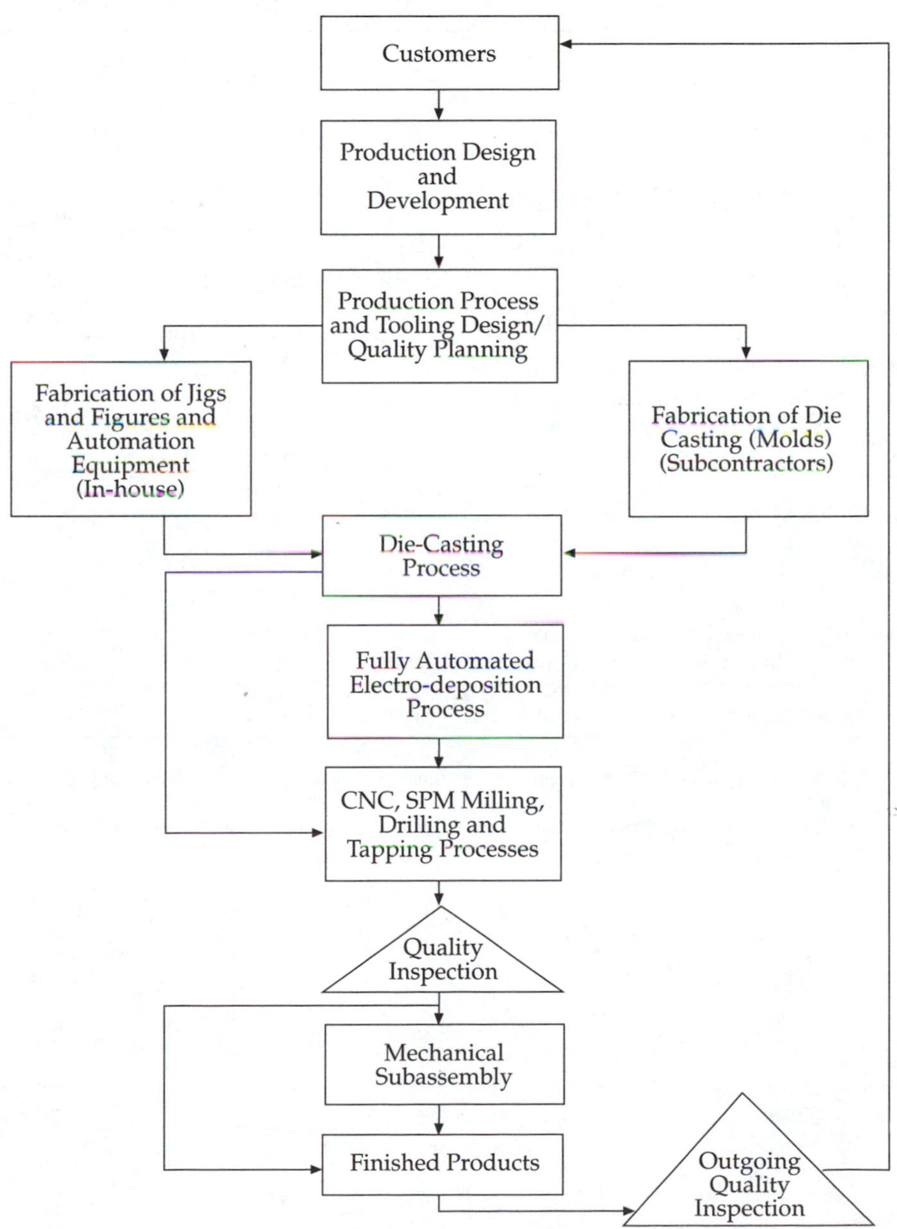

EXHIBIT 4

**URACO HOLDINGS LTD**
**Financial Statements, 1990–1994**
(in thousand dollars, except EPS)
**Income Statement**
**For the Period 1990–1994**

| | *1990* | *1991* | *1992* | *1993* | *1994* |
|---|---|---|---|---|---|
| Sales | 42,644 | 42,296 | 46,997 | 59,389 | 83,831 |
| Operating profit | 5,333 | 1,182 | 4,333 | 11,682 | 13,243 |
| Share of profit (loss) of associated companies | 9 | 0 | 12 | (29) | 168 |
| Profit before tax | 5,342 | 1,182 | 4,345 | 11,653 | 13,411 |
| Taxes | (1,267) | (228) | (628) | (1,952) | (1,842) |
| Profit before tax, minority interests, and extraordinary items* | 4,075 | 954 | 3,717 | 9,701 | 11,569 |
| Minority interests | (346) | (96) | (246) | (329) | (523) |
| Extraordinary items | 0 | 0 | 0 | 0 | (4,400) |
| Profit attributable to the shareholders of the company | 3,729 | 858 | 3,471 | 9,372 | 6,646 |
| Earnings per Share (cents)** | 1.66 | 0.38 | 1.54 | 4.17 | 4.91 |

*The extraordinary items in FY 1994 represent provision for diminution in value and a write-off of long-term unquoted equity investments.

**For comparative purposes, the net earnings per share was based on profit after minority interest and the pre-flotation share capital of 225,000,000 shares.

EXHIBIT 4 (cont'd)

## Balance Sheet
## As of July 31, 1990–1994

(in thousand dollars, except per-share data)

| | *1990* | *1991* | *1992* | *1993* | *1994* |
|---|---|---|---|---|---|
| Fixed assets | 10,787 | 14,153 | 15,265 | 17,465 | 23,427 |
| Interests in associated companies | 143 | 135 | 132 | 93 | 206 |
| Long-term investments | 748 | 1,225 | 1,463 | 4,462 | 2,301 |
| Investment Properties | 0 | 0 | 0 | 0 | 9,064 |
| Expenditure carried forward | 6 | 6 | 0 | 3 | 237 |
| Current assets | 13,764 | 8,924 | 14,932 | 21,140 | 33,663 |
| Current liabilities | 13,102 | 11,946 | 15,729 | 15,918 | 28,581 |
| Net current assets/(liabilities) | 662 | –3,022 | –797 | 5,222 | 5,082 |
| Noncurrent liabilities | –2,415 | –1,772 | –1,621 | –3,104 | –4,613 |
| | 9,931 | 10,725 | 14,442 | 24,141 | 35,704 |
| Represented by: | | | | | |
| Shareholders' equity | 9,008 | 9,706 | 13,177 | 22,547 | 33,314 |
| Minority interests | 923 | 1,019 | 1,265 | 1,594 | 2,390 |
| | 9,931 | 10,725 | 14,442 | 24,141 | 35,704 |
| NTA per Share (cents) * | 4 | 4.31 | 5.86 | 10.02 | 14.7 |

*For comparative purposes, the net tangible assets per share is based on the pre-flotation share capital of 225,000,000 shares.

# Cycle & Carriage Limited* 12

Boon Yoon Chiang, group managing director of Cycle & Carriage Ltd, was sitting at his desk one late Friday evening in January 1995 reflecting on the past phenomenal success of Cycle & Carriage Ltd and the recent wide-scale expansion of the group into the Asia-Pacific region. He wondered if the group had not spread itself too thin by its diversification into unrelated businesses and markets.

## Company Background

The Cycle & Carriage Group dates back to 1899. It had its beginnings in a small store in Kuala Lumpur repairing bicycles and selling diverse products. The store was formed by two brothers, Chua Cheng Tuan and Chua Cheng Bok.

At the turn of the century, motorized cars rapidly gained popularity in Singapore and Malaysia. The Chua brothers, realizing the enormous potential of motorized vehicles, acquired sole distributorship for several European and American cars and trucks. They opened their first Singapore branch in 1916. So successful was the company that it became public in 1926 under the name Cycle & Carriage (1926) Limited.

---

*This case was prepared by Alicia Cheung Wai Lai, Sarah Chng, Sujata Ramakrishna, and Tan Geok Cheng (MBA, Nanyang Technological University, Singapore, 1995–1996) under the supervision of Professor Luis Ma. R. Calingo to serve as a basis for class discussion rather than to illustrate either effective or ineffective handling of an administrative situation. This case was developed wholly from published materials. Most quotations are paraphrased creations of the case authors for educational purposes and cannot be considered actual statements.

In the 1930s, Cycle & Carriage was badly hit by the depression. The company closed their Malaysian businesses, reducing operations to Singapore alone. It ceased business during World War II. After the war, the company resumed business and acquired the Mercedes-Benz franchise in 1951. In 1969, Cycle & Carriage Limited was incorporated and listed on the stock exchanges of Singapore and Malaysia. Its major shareholders were Jardine Strategic Holdings Limited (23.6 percent), Employees Provident Fund Board (11.5 percent), and Edaran Otomobil Nasional Bhd (20.0 percent).

In 1995, the Cycle & Carriage Group was involved principally in three core fields: motor vehicles, properties, and food and retail businesses. The Group's operations spanned Singapore, Malaysia, Australia, New Zealand, Thailand and Vietnam (see Exhibit 1).

**Management**

The Cycle & Carriage Group was led by an impressive board of directors from a diverse range of backgrounds. In April 1993, Tan Sri Dato' Paduka Sallehuddin was appointed Chairman of the Board. He was previously Chief Secretary to the Government of Malaysia, Secretary to the Cabinet, Head of Civil Service, Director General of the Economic Planning Unit for the Malaysia Prime Minister's Department, and, in 1995, the Executive Chairman of the Employees' Provident Fund, Malaysia (see Exhibit 2).

The outstanding management of Cycle & Carriage Limited and the quality of its products and services were evident by the company's high rankings in various comparative analysis reports. It received the Financial Management Award for the second year running in the 1993 Asian Management Awards organized by the Asian Institute of Management. It was also rated the 10th most admired company in Singapore in the article "Asia's Most Admired Companies" published by *Asian Business* magazine. In a survey conducted by the magazine in nine Asian countries, it was ranked 137th among 250 companies for the quality of its products and services, management, contribution to the local economy, record as enlightened employers, potential for growth, ethics, and honesty.

**Regional Venture**

To broaden its earnings base, the Group ventured beyond its traditional boundaries of Singapore and Malaysia. In Australia, the Group had a joint venture company for the distribution of Hyundai and Chrysler vehicles. In New Zealand, the Group's 70-percent-owned Sri Temasek improved its market share and was now represented in all major cities. Results from this subsidiary was expected to improve in line with the improvement of the economy.

In October 1993 the Group commenced the distribution and retailing of Ford vehicles in Thailand, a country which held great promise with its buoyant economy and rising affluence. In joint venture with the Saigon Tourist Company, the Group started car rental operations in Vietnam.

**Financial Performance**

Over a five-year period from 1990 to 1994, the Group's turnover and profit before taxation grew by 204 percent and 141 percent, respectively. Net operating assets of the Group increased by 215 percent over the same period (see Exhibit 3).

The relative financial performance of the various business operations in terms of turnover, profit before taxation, and net operating assets employed by industry and by geographical location for the last three financial periods are indicated in Exhibit 4. Vehicle operations continued to be the dominant contributor to Group profits with increasing contribution seen from the property operations.

## Motor Division

### Singapore

Cycle & Carriage Ltd's main motor vehicle operation was in Singapore, where it distributed the Mercedes-Benz, Proton Saga (Malaysia's national car), and Mitsubishi lines. The Singapore vehicle operation remained the dominant contributor to Group profits in 1994 although actual earnings is slightly down on an annualized basis. This was due to the exceptionally strong results in 1993, when the government implemented a one-off increase in the number of Certificates of Entitlement (COEs).[1]

Total passenger car registrations in 1994 were 31,200, a 14-percent drop from the 1993 figure. Although operating in a highly competitive market, the Mercedes-Benz performed exceptionally well in 1994, whereas the Proton line and especially the Mitsubishi line found difficulty in matching Mercedes-Benz's performance in 1993. Nonetheless, Cycle & Carriage maintained its 26-percent market share of the passenger car market. In 1994, for the fifth consecutive year, Cycle & Carriage had the highest market share of any distributor in Singapore.

In an evening in November 1993, traffic almost came to a virtual halt along Orange Grove Road when more than 1,000 people (many chauffeured) made their way to Shangri-La Hotel — not for a prestigious high-class dinner — but for the launch of the Mercedes-Benz C-class. And that was not all. Cycle & Carriage, the Mercedes distributor, received 1,300 prelaunch bookings for its C-cars and needed 12 months to fulfill its orders. But this did not deter buyers, who had each to part with S$10,000 in deposit and would have to bear most, if not all, COE costs.[2] As Philip Eng, General Manager of Cycle & Carriage's motor division said, "The company was unwilling to take positions on COEs because of current unpredictable conditions." Cycle & Carriage has long been associated with the Mercedes-Benz franchise. Through its aggressive marketing efforts and its tradition of providing quality after-sales service, the Group had established Mercedes-Benz as the undisputed leader in the luxury car market.

### Changing Customer Profile

Cycle & Carriage was not scared off by tough car markets. Its home base was Singapore, where car prices are among the highest in the world. This, however, has not dampened the

[1]On May 1, 1990, the Singapore Government introduced a Vehicle Quota System to regulate the vehicle population in Singapore. Under this system, purchasers of new cars must first obtain a Certificate of Entitlement (COE), via a process of monthly tenders, for the category of vehicle they wish to purchase. Successful bidders only have to pay the lowest successful bid. A vehicle can then be registered with a COE, which is valid for 10 years from the date of registration.

[2]The exchange rate between the Singapore Dollar and the US Dollar was US$1.00 = S$1.59 in 1993 and S$1.43 in 1995. In November 1995, the price of the lowest successful COE bid ranged from S$4,006 for motorcycles to S$60,002 for automobiles in the above-2,000cc category.

desire of most Singaporeans to own a Mercedes as could be seen by the big Mercedes sedans that have started to pack the roads in Singapore.

Mercedes-Benz was the second highest selling automobile in Singapore with a market share of 13 percent. Singaporeans were becoming more and more affluent, and this can be seen by the number of well-heeled Singaporeans who are snapping up Mercedeses at a record rate. Its sales of 3,425 units (each costing more than S$200,000) in 1993 and over 4,000 units in 1994 was a remarkable level for a luxury automobile achieved by a car distributor in the Singapore market, prompting *Drive* magazine to say: "We know there were many rich Singaporeans around but we didn't know there were that many."

In 1994, the luxury European car outsold Nissan, Mitsubishi, Suzuki, and Mazda in Singapore by almost two to one, even though its cheapest vehicle costs two to three times as much as a Japanese car. Cycle & Carriage's assistant general manager for marketing, S K Ho, said in an interview in mid-1994 that a good portion of 1994's sales would simply be the delivery of cars already booked. Demand is so strong that it took Cycle & Carriage an average of 14 months to deliver a Mercedes-Benz from the time a sale was made. The Mercedes was seen as a symbol of success in Singapore, a tangible way for people to show others they have "arrived". Unsurprisingly, most local Mercedes buyers were mature businessmen and executives. But professionals — and more women — were fast becoming a new breed of Mercedes owners as the car introduced new, more racy designs. Women now make up about 15 percent of new Mercedes owners, up from less than 5 percent eight years ago. Ho said that this reflected local women's growing economic success.

### Trends in Demand

Sustainable strong economic growth and increasing affluence increased the demand for luxury cars. Mercedes sales in 1993 were fueled by demand for E-class sedans. The waiting list on these had been more than a year — and there were so many around in 1995 that owners had to book a service up to one month ahead, compared with two weeks in 1994. According to carmaker Daimler-Benz, in 1994, the brand had a 9.6 percent share of Singapore's passenger car market, the highest share in any country outside Germany. In 1993, it had 26 per cent of the Singapore market. Singapore was often said to have more Mercedes-Benzes per kilometer of road than any other country in the world, including Germany where the car was made.

Cycle & Carriage's earnings, which came mostly from its motor division, saw phenomenal growth in car sales from January to March of 1993 from buyers trying to beat the 3 percent Goods and Services Tax (GST), which the government instituted in April 1994. But this performance is unlikely to be repeated for several reasons. One is the decline in the number of COEs released this year. Also, Mitsubishi and Proton lines did not launch any new models so the growth in the number of cars sold in 1994 would be relatively low. The longer-term picture is more worrying because the number of COEs appears to be decreasing.

Like most competitors within the Japanese and economy passenger car segments, Mitsubishi and Proton suffered the brunt of high COE prices and the reduction in available vehicle quotas. Both Mitsubishi and Proton experienced falls in unit sales in 1994 and a tightening of margins. The strength of the yen and strong competition from the European models also impacted the results for Mitsubishi, even though the 2.0-liter Space Wagon and

Libero were both well-received. As for the Proton, the launch of the Wira in 1993 was highly successful, with sales amounting to almost 2,000 units and accounting for a 6.3 percent share of the Singapore passenger car market.

### Growth in Other Sectors

In the commercial sector, Mercedes-Benz vehicles are also extensively used by the Singapore Bus Service (1978) Ltd, the major transport service company in Singapore. The Group continued to win major fleet contracts including customers like the Ministry of Defence, Trans-Island Bus Services, the Singapore Police Force, Singapore Bus Service, Singapore Airlines, and Singapore Telecom.

### Car Population and Government Controls

In December 1993, Singapore had a total of 584,322 registered vehicles (of which 306,216 are cars) sharing 2,989 kilometers of road space. Within the last 10 years, Singapore's motor vehicle population grew at a compounded rate of 2.7 percent. Though the growth was mainly controlled by the government, it was also dependent on the economic climate in the country at that time. For example, the motor vehicle population declined in the recession years of 1985–1987 and during the 1991 Gulf War. Local market sentiment and demand for vehicles, particularly passenger cars, were influenced by the Vehicle Quota System (VQS) and government measures on car ownership. The Singapore Government's controls on cars included the Additional Registration Fee (ARF) and import duty, the VQS, and the 10-year life span policy for private cars.

The government imposed an ARF and import duty of 150 percent and 45 percent of a vehicle's open market value (OMV), respectively. This increased the landed cost of the car by 195 percent. Induced by strong monetary incentives, the government also imposed a 10-year life span policy for private cars; that is, a car loses its scrap value after the tenth year. Scrap value is the rebate given by the government upon deregistration of a vehicle before or in its tenth year; a Prevailing Quota Premium (PQP, or the 12-month moving average of COE prices) has to be paid in order to keep the car on the road past its tenth year.

The government also regulated the number of cars on the roads through the Vehicle Quota System. Begun in May 1990, the number of COEs available for bidding each month was dependent on the number of cars deregistered (scrapped) and the allowable vehicle population growth rate. The 10-year age policy on cars results in a fairly distinct 10-year replacement cycle. Since the number of COEs allocated in each year is based on the deregistrations of the previous year, this one-year lag led to a shortage of COEs in 1992 (a year of higher replacement demand due to strong sales in 1982) and would result in a generous supply in 1993 when replacement demand started to taper off. In addition to this related deregistration, there was a surge in scrapping in April 1992 just prior to the end of the two-year grace period allowed to pay the PQP for existing cars older than ten years. This resulted in 10,400 more COEs available for the 12 months starting December 1992, which translated into a 30-percent increase in COEs in 1993.

The strong demand for COEs in 1992 pushed premiums up substantially. The big increases in COE premiums squeezed profit margins for most car distributors. Average profits per car for Cycle & Carriage declined 6.1 percent to S$10,283. Volatility in COE prices resulted in fluctuations in vehicle pricing.[3] However, the increase in selling prices seldom fully offsets increases in COE premiums. Unpredictability was further raised since there was a one-month lag between the imposition of a new price and the results of the COE bids. At the same time, the government's announcement that it was considering regulating the COE bidding system through a "pay-as-you-bid" system and the curbing of double transfers of COEs, created much uncertainty among both distributors and buyers. These adverse factors, together with the poor performance of regional stock markets, culminated in a very keen competition across all car categories.

In his 1992 National Day speech, Prime Minister Goh Chok Tong said that the government intended to increase the penetration of car ownership from one car for every ten persons currently to one car for every seven persons by the year 2000. If the population grew by 1.5 percent annually, Singapore would have about 3.2 million people and 456,900 cars by the year 2000. This worked out to an average compounded car growth rate of 6.1 percent per annum, which contrasts sharply with the previously stated policy of restricting growth to 3 percent a year. To accommodate the growth, the government has plans to improve the road and tunnel network. An underground ring-road is on the way and the introduction of the Electronic Road Pricing (ERP) system, targeted for 1996, aims to regulate road usage instead of car ownership.

Despite the government's plans, a sharp fall in the number of COEs available is expected during the period 1996–2000, and this forecast clouded the longer-term view for most car distributors. While new COEs were capped at 3 percent of the total car population each year, the replacement COEs depended on the number of old cars scrapped. Since fewer cars were bought during the mid-1980 recession, replacement COEs during the late 1990s were expected to drop sharply. It was estimated that the number of COEs would fall from 36,872 in 1995 to 22,087 in 1997. However, it hardly seemed possible that the COE squeeze would affect Cycle & Carriage, largely because of the strong performance of Mercedes, which had overtaken Honda as the second top-selling car in Singapore. The success of Mercedes sales can be attributed to two effects: the wealth effect from the bull-run and the surge in property prices, as well as its timely launch of new models. Although the upmarket Mercedes should be relatively immune to higher COE prices, the mid-priced Mitsubishi and Proton are likely to suffer a drop in sales. With one offsetting the other, industry observers expected the overall impact to be neutral for Cycle & Carriage's motor division.

**Malaysia**

Cycle & Carriage Bintang, the franchise holder for Mercedes-Benz and Mazda motor vehicles in Malaysia, was 49-percent owned by Cycle & Carriage Ltd. For two years, Cycle & Carriage Bintang suffered depressed profitability. This was due in part to the ongoing problem of rampant parallel importing of reconditioned Mercedes-Benz cars at a big discount compared to the new cars. This forced Cycle & Carriage Bintang to maintain prices despite the strong deutschemark, thus reducing profit margins.

[3]For instance, COE prices for automobiles in the 1,601cc–2,000cc range dropped from S$54,080 in October 1995 to S$45,200 in November 1995, while COE prices in the "open" category (in terms of ability to purchase any car, regardless of size) increased from S$60,200 to S$65,098 during the same one-month period.

Due to Malaysia's strong economic growth and improved road infrastructure, the total passenger car market grew by over 20 percent and Cycle & Carriage Bintang achieved substantial profit growth in 1994. The national car and luxury car segments were the principal beneficiaries. Discounting of older Mercedes models and Proton's dominance in Malaysia hurt profits from the company's Malaysian car operations. But Malaysia, where the car market grew about 10 per cent in 1993, was still the company's most promising market, according to Boon. The long-term growth prospects were encouraged by: the rise in disposable incomes, or the country's rapid economic growth; the car to population ratio of 1:8, which was still well below the 1:2 ratio in the U.S. and 1:4 in Japan; the improvement in road infrastructure such as through the February 1994 completion of the North-South Expressway; and the expectation of strong replacement demand in 1995.

In 1994, Cycle & Carriage Bintan started assembly of the Mercedes-Benz C-Class and S-Class models at the company's own plant at Petaling Jaya, the satellite district of Kuala Lumpur. Together with the merging of the vehicle operations of the Mercedes-Benz and Mazda franchises, greater operational efficiency and reduced costs were achieved. To reduce waiting lists, the company also had plans to continue increasing production. This improved level of production directly led to increased sales, with Mercedes-Benz passenger car sales rising 59 percent in 1993. Several new Mercedes-Benz models were introduced in 1994; the C-Class in Kuala Lumpur, as well as the multi-valved E-Class and the new 1827S/32 heavy truck which reached the Malaysian market for the first time. Mercedes-Benz commercial vehicles experienced sales growth of 11 percent in 1994, mainly in the truck sector. The demand for Mercedes bigger bus models was expected to remain favorable especially with the emphasis on a cleaner environment and better commuter services, which would indirectly call for the replacement of the present old buses.

The Mazda passenger car franchise had a difficult 1994 due to the continued strength of the Japanese yen and increased competition. Cycle & Carriage Bintan indicated that it would concentrate on developing niche markets where Mazda could compete more effectively. Cycle & Carriage Ltd also owned 70 percent of Cycle & Carriage (Malaysia), the remaining 30 percent being held by Cycle & Carriage Bintan. Cycle & Carriage (Malaysia) is an authorized dealer for Proton and Mazda passenger cars and Mitsubishi, Mazda, and Isuzu commercial vehicles. It was also the Malaysian distributor for Mitsubishi passenger cars. Cycle & Carriage Bintan had also developed a nationwide network comprising six branches offering sales, after-sales service, and parts. Like Singapore, the vehicle repair and maintenance business in Malaysia had good growth potential. Cycle & Carriage Bintan would benefit from the newly opened RM13 million, 2.1-hectare workshop-cum-showroom complex in Johor Bahru; a new RM10 million, 161,600-square-meter, 3-storey workshop consisting of 92 work bays in Petaling Jaya; and another new RM12 million, 5,376-square meter, 2-storey workshop.[4]

**Australia**

The Group had a 49-percent interest in Astre Investments, which held the Hyundai and Chrysler distributorships in Australia. Aided by economic recovery and resultant improvement in consumer confidence and buyer sentiment, Cycle & Carriage Ltd's Australian associate company, Hyundai Automotive Distributors Pte Ltd (Hada), became

[4]In 1995, the exchange rate between the Malaysian Ringgit (RM) and the US Dollar was US$1.00 = RM2.46.

the world's top Hyundai distributor with the fastest growing sales in the first half of 1994, grabbing 5.2 percent of the Australian passenger car market. It was on track to sell a record 25,000 cars by the end of 1994, commented Cycle & Carriage's Philip Eng. The company beat 140 distributors around the world for the title, awarded by Hyundai Motor Corporation of Korea. With a network of 136 authorized dealers, the Group was putting extensive efforts into its marketing and promotional activities, staff training, and customer service improvements.

Hada, a joint venture among Cycle & Carriage Ltd, Singaporean entrepreneur Ong Beng Seng via Rizona (Hongkong) Ltd, and Komoco Auto Pte Ltd, Hyundai's Singapore distributor, entered the Australian market in 1990. Since then it has enjoyed significant sales increases every year. Hada boasted one of the best distribution networks in Australia in terms of quality. A recent independent survey which covered dealers of all makes voted Hyundai as one of the three most desirable franchises for the next five years. Hada's Hyundai Elantra also won the New South Wales NRMA Small/Medium Car of the Year Award for the second straight year.

The distribution of Chrysler Jeep, even though it had just begun in April 1994, met with immediate success with 49 dealers appointed and almost 1,600 units being sold by the end of 1994. To improve sales further, a wider product range was planned, including the Grand Cherokee, which should broaden the appeal for the Chrysler Jeep.

### New Zealand

Sri Temasek, a 70-percent-owned subsidiary, retailed Mazda motor vehicles through five dealerships, three in Auckland and one each in Wellington and Christchurch. It accounted for over half of Mazda's sales in New Zealand, an automobile which held over 4.8 percent of the market. Sri Temasek's sales grew by almost 37 percent in 1994, doubling the national rate and leading the company to make a profit for the first time.

### Thailand

Cycle & Carriage had a 52-percent interest in New Era Cycle & Carriage, one of two Ford distributorships in Thailand. The company now has a network of 61 dealers, the majority of which were concentrated in and around Bangkok. The year 1994 was not a particularly good year because of the inconsistent supply of Aspire from the factory in Korea. This has resulted in low actual deliveries while considerable efforts were made to sustain interest in the product. The company had invested in building up showroom and after-sales service capacity.

Thailand was seen as one of the most important markets in Southeast Asia, growing by over six percent in 1994, with vehicle sales of almost half a million. Traditionally dominated by Japanese cars, Ford was committed to expansion, initially with its European and Asian-made models, but ultimately through local assembly and manufacture of both passenger cars and light commercial vehicles. New Era Cycle & Carriage was committed to supporting Ford in these expansion plans.

### Vietnam

Cycle & Carriage Ltd was granted an investment license by Vietnam's State Committee for Cooperation and Investment in March 1993. In July of the same year, Cycle & Carriage Ltd formed a 50-50 partnership with state-owned hotel operator Saigontourist. The Singapore firm's eventual investment in a vehicle workshop and car rental joint venture was expected to total US$600,000 (S$948,000). Cycle & Carriage Ltd set up CCL Indo-China (a wholly owned subsidiary of issued and paid-up capital of $3.1 million) to hold its investment in the joint venture called CCL Saigon Joint Venture Company. CCL Saigon would operate a fleet of 20 new cars for rental and a vehicle workshop with 11 bays and a paint booth. CCL Saigon was looking to expand this fleet. The workshop, which was under construction, is expected to begin operations in May 1995 and would service all types of vehicles.

Shares in Singapore's Cycle & Carriage Ltd rose after the company said it would have the exclusive right to distribute cars and commercial vehicles from Ford Motor Co in Vietnam. Cycle & Carriage was awarded the Ford franchise for Vietnam in 1994 and had formed another joint venture with Saigontourist for the distribution of Ford vehicles throughout the country. Plans were under way for the first showroom for Ford sales to be opened in Ho Chi Minh City in the first half of 1995 and a sales operation for Hanoi was planned for later in the same year. Analysts said the joint venture demonstrated Cycle & Carriage Ltd's commitment to expansion outside its home base. The company received about 90 percent of its S$112 million in 1993 profits from Singapore, while its ventures in Australia, New Zealand, and Malaysia brought in most of the rest. "Myanmar would be its next target," according to Managing Director Boon Yoon Chiang.

Analysts believed that the Vietnam venture might not contribute to earnings until at least the end of the 1990s. This was largely because most Vietnamese did not have the money to purchase a new car. The country's yearly gross domestic product was just US$200 per person. Vietnam is "not really a developed market," said Soon Teck Onn, an analyst at Baring Securities. Major car dealers and distributors are "looking at Vietnam as a long-term prospect," he continued.

In December 1994, Cycle & Carriage also entered into an agreement to acquire a 35-percent stake in Autostar, the Mercedes-Benz passenger car distributor for southern Vietnam (Ho Chi Minh City). British Virgin Islands-registered Autostar is owned by Peregrine Capital and another Vietnamese firm, Dainam. Cycle & Carriage would provide Autostar with parts, servicing, and staff training support.

## Toward a One-Stop Shop

Cycle & Carriage believed that its quality of service was what had and would set it apart from its competitors, and the Group was continuing to seek excellence in this field. A new Customer Service Audit initiative was launched, which would assess the performance of sales representatives, after-sales service staff and all administrative support personnel. This means that Cycle & Carriage would continually monitor the level of service satisfaction provided to customers both during and after a sale.

Cycle & Carriage's new S$19.5 million showroom and service center at Eunos Link (located in the eastern part of Singapore) became operational in January 1995. Group Managing Director Boon Yoon Chiang said that the center would allow the company to "penetrate into the fast-expanding residential and commercial market in the eastern region of Singapore." The center occupies 6,800 square meters of land and house offices, a showroom, and a workshop with 56 work bays and 89 holding bays. Built-up area totaled about 8,800 square meters spread over three levels. "All three brands we handle —

Mercedes-Benz, Mitsubishi, and Proton — will be displayed together for the first time at the showroom on the first level," Mr Boon said.

Construction was also completed at Cycle & Carriage's Alexandra Road headquarters, which became operational in June 1995. The spacious showrooms and a modern parts and service center improved Cycle & Carriage's accessibility for vehicle sales and after-sales service for both Mercedes-Benz and Mitsubishi. Cycle & Carriage expected growing contribution from its workshop services.

Cycle & Carriage sold its car-financing subsidiary to an associated company, Associated Merchant Bank (AMB), as part of a plan to convert the latter from a merchant bank to a credit company. The plan was to expand AMB's business to include consumer financing. AMB now provides commercial equipment and car finance. Cycle & Carriage would then refer half of its car financing needs to AMB, a 36-percent associate with a small operation in Singapore, on a best-efforts basis.

## Competitors

### In Singapore

In Singapore, the main source of competition comes from the following distributors and their respective automobiles:

| *Company* | *Make* |
|---|---|
| Borneo Motors (S) Pte Ltd, an Inchcape Company | Toyota, Suzuki |
| Sime Singapore Group | BMW, Ford |
| Intraco Ltd | Rover |
| SAE Autocentre, a division of Singapore Automotive Engineering Ltd | Opel |
| Kah Motor Co Sdn Bhd, a wholly owned subsidiary of Oriental Holdings Berhad | Honda |
| Tan Chong & Sons Motor Co (S) Pte Ltd | Nissan |

In Singapore's luxury car segment, Toyota is Mercedes' main competitor and its sales in 1995 are expected to improve when its new Corolla range is delivered. Rover and BMW sales were also healthy; increased sales for both brands are predicted with the release of their new 416 model and 316 compact model, respectively. However, the market for Mercedes-Benz is pretty much loyal and distinct. For the lower-end brands of Cycle & Carriage (Mitsubishi and Proton), the demand is relatively elastic and there is no firm following.

Apart from the above, parallel importers are threatening to become a formidable force. In Singapore, there is no law in force that restricts parallel imports. Cycle & Carriage faced a potential dip in sales due to the proliferation of such importers. Quick delivery is the main reason why car buyers go to parallel importers. With the short waiting period, an average of two weeks, the uncertainty of COE prices was reduced. Some customers are also wooed by the additional features that parallel-import Mercedes-Benzes are typically fitted with. Hence, they deem it worthwhile to pay 2 to 5 percent more for these cars.

There were different opinions in the market regarding these parallel importers. They were seen as opportunists with no long-term interest in the business and not as a professional organization with comparable expertise and well-trained personnel to provide the service, maintenance, and repairs required.

Veteran motoring writer Winston Lee said there is "always a risk" in buying parallel-import cars. Although all Mercedes-Benzes come with a worldwide warranty and Cycle & Carriage also services cars not sold by it, Lee sees "no reason why the company should give priority to such a car." Members of the Motor Trade Association of Singapore have strong feelings against parallel importers. "They plow nothing back into the industry for the end user," said Association President Michael Wong, citing the huge sums authorized dealers invested in spare parts, workshops, and training. On the other hand, the Automobile Association of Singapore's Vice President Gerard Ee, commenting on the reported risk of buying a parallel-import Mercedes, says that the Association has not come across any such complaint. He says that the make is relatively trouble-free and simple to service and, "At the end of the day, a Merc is a Merc, no matter who it comes from!"

### In the Region

Cycle & Carriage Ltd is not without its competitors in Vietnam since the United States lifted its 19-year-old trade embargo on the country in February 1994. In fact, Vietnam's car industry is starting to get crowded and new entrants face the heat of competition. Other major automobile companies have moved into the heretofore untapped market. Chrysler Corporation was looking to establish a service center in Vietnam before it started importing and was eventually planning to set up an in-country assembly line. General Motors was also looking into the market but has not made any specific announcements. "It's pretty much an open field," said James Rockwell, Managing Director of U.S. investment consultancy Vatico, which advises Chrysler in Vietnam. The country already had one active car maker, Mekong Motors. This was a joint venture among South Korea's Tongil, Japan's Sailo Machinery, and a Vietnamese firm. Mekong is licensed to produce 10,000 cars a year. Another firm, state-run Vietnam Motor Corporation, has yet to start production but has also been licensed to produce 10,000 cars a year. Both these firms could tie up with American carmakers.

Competition in regional markets also comes from local manufacturing joint venture companies. To protect their interests and to ensure that the national car manufacturer was not put out of the business by these new entrants, they could lobby the government to increase import duties to help boost sales. Vietnamese authorities, for instance, are not keen on allowing too many carmakers into the country because the market is far too small. A Mitsubishi-funded survey showed that the market would be able to absorb only 60,000 cars annually by the year 2000.

## External Factors

External factors as much as local ones are to blame for what appeared to be the start of a price war in the Singapore car market. These factors range from macro developments like recent shifts in world trends to micro events like the restructuring of the parent company of an automobile manufacturer. The bottom line is that car distributors all over the world are under great pressure to meet ever-rising targets. One effect of the U.S.-Japan friction over car imports was "preemptive moves" by Japan carmakers to secure a bigger market share in Asia — in case the U.S. decides to restrict foreign cars further.

The looming threat of recession in Singapore has also caused prices to spiral downwards. Industry observers expected the non-premium brands to go down the tube faster. Toyota and Mercedes-Benz are also expected to hold their own in this trying period. As in all markets, sentiment also played a part. Buyers tended to stay on the sidelines in the hope that COE prices would fall. The plunge in premiums in 1994 threw the used-car market into disarray. The dealers, many of whom were individual operators, took big bank overdrafts to buy stock. They were now afraid to take in cars. Hence, those who wanted to change their cars could not find ready buyers with realistic offers for their old vehicles.

COEs are now a major factor in the profitability of listed motor dealerships. This is only to be expected with the keen competition in Singapore. The best edge a motor distributor has is to read COE prices correctly and package its car prices accordingly. Those forecasting the performance of a motor vehicle distributor now cannot avoid factoring in whether the company is able to do well on its COEs. Motor stocks are fast becoming a speculative pursuit, with prices moving according to fast-changing COE prices. This is definitely not a game for the fainthearted.

## Property Division

The Group's second core business is property development and investment. Cycle & Carriage's long-term goal is to create a balanced commercial and residential portfolio of investment and development properties. Opportunities abroad, particularly in China, are being explored.

### Organizational Structure

Cycle & Carriage's involvement in properties started only in 1985, a relative latecomer. Its property activities stem from its holdings in two subsidiaries: Cycle & Carriage Ltd Group Properties Holdings (CCLPH, 60-percent direct interest) and Malayan Credit Ltd (MCL, 57-percent owned and publicly listed). In total, Cycle & Carriage holds a property portfolio valued at over S$1 billion comprising investment and development properties and a massive 64.1-hectare land bank, nearly 90 percent of which is located in Malaysia.

CCLPH is the result of a restructuring exercise where all property interests owned by Cycle & Carriage, Cycle & Carriage Bintang (CCB), and Cold Storage Malaysia (CSM) are grouped under one company. The objectives of the restructuring are:

1. Property development and investment activities have been identified as a core business of the Group. The restructuring exercise has formed a distinct property division with a separate management team to supervise and manage the Group's property interests that have been identified for development in Malaysia and Singapore.
2. Property development and investment activities have management, operating, and financial requirements which differed from the Group's motor vehicle business and food and retail business. In addition, the development of properties require considerable financial resources. Separation of property activities from the Group's other businesses has enabled its property personnel to achieve a better focus of the property development and investment activities.

3. A separate property division would enhance the public image of the Group's property development and investment activities.
4. The restructuring enabled CCB and CSM to concentrate their resources in their core business.

Under the new structure, the property division of the Group consisted of:

1. A property investment holding company established in Malaysia, CCLPH(M), in which Cycle & Carriage, CCB, and CSM hold 60 percent, 20 percent, and 20 percent, respectively of the issued capital.
2. A property investment holding company incorporated in Singapore, CCP P/L, has become a wholly owned subsidiary of CCLPH(M) to hold Singapore property interests.
3. A property investment holding company established in Malaysia, CCLP S/B, has become a wholly owned subsidiary of CCLPH(M) to hold the Malaysian properties interests.

## Malayan Credit Ltd

Malayan Credit Ltd (MCL) is responsible for the management and development of CCLPH's properties as well as its own. MCL was acquired by Cycle & Carriage in a hostile takeover launched in April 1992, together with Hotel Properties Ltd, as part of its move to strengthen its presence in the property sector with immediate effect. By 1995, Cycle & Carriage already controlled MCL's land bank of approximately 483,080 square meters (48.3 hectares) in Malaysia and 34,953 square meters in Singapore, as well as a large portfolio of investment and development properties.

Since its acquisition, MCL has shifted its focus from receiving rental income from investment properties to being active in the local residential market. It has actively begun realizing the potential of the land bank with condominium development as well as five landed property projects in the pipeline. In 1995, nearly all the group's property portfolio was concentrated in Singapore. However, the vast land bank in Malaysia, which stretched from Johor Bahru (south) and Port Dickson (west) to Penang (north) was yet to be unlocked. Should development proceed on these sites, they are likely to be a mix of residential, commercial, and hotel developments.

The cost of the Malaysian land bank is very minimal, purchased for about RM3 million in the 1970s. Therefore the risk of developing the land bank is low and earnings potential is expected to be significant. Together with an estimated rental income of RM40 million a year from investment properties, MCL would contribute significantly to Cycle & Carriage's profitability in the long run and help achieve a 50-50 ratio between the car and non-car sectors targeted by the end of the decade.

## Food and Retail Division

Cycle & Carriage's food manufacturing and retailing business is concentrated in Malaysia through 42-percent-owned Cold Storage Berhad (CSM), the only publicly listed food retailing and manufacturing operation in Malaysia. Profit contribution from this segment has been insignificant but strategic plans are underway to expand its operations through alliances with global industry leaders to ensure long-term growth.

### Manufacturing

Activities include a dairy and beverage factory producing consumer products such as ice cream and butter, a separate meat-processing plant manufacturing "halal"[5] and non-halal meat products under the Angus and Gourmet brands; and ice factories to meet the needs of the Malaysian fishing and food industries.

CSM recently tied up with Nestle SA to manufacture and distribute a new range of ice cream and dairy products in Malaysia and Singapore. Production would initially be based in CSM's existing Petaling Jaya Plant, with plans to build a new plant in the future. The tie-up would replace CSM's ice cream manufacturing arrangement with Magnolia, which expired in October 1994. Through Nestle, one of the two biggest players in the global ice cream industry, CSM sought to make Nestle ice cream the market leader in Malaysia's RM120 million ice cream industry by the year 2000. The combination of Nestle's technological know-how and CSM's marketing network and expertise was expected to enhance Cycle & Carriage's role as a major player in the regional marketplace.

### Retailing

With rising affluence and increasing per capita income in Malaysia, shopping habits are already changing in favor of supermarket shopping. CSM owns only four Jaya supermarkets in Malaysia, and there is a sense of urgency for Cycle & Carriage to capture this growing market and to improve its market share. Cycle & Carriage plans to expand its Jaya outlets by more than tenfold, to 30–40 during the period 1996–2000 aided by its recent 50-50 tie up with Jardine's 46-percent-owned Dairy Farm, Asia's largest food retailer outside of Japan. Dairy Farm also owns Cold Storage Singapore (1983) Pte Ltd (Singapore's largest supermarket chain), Guardian Pharmacies (Singapore's largest drug store chain), and 7-Eleven convenience stores in Singapore. Both parties would inject an initial S$11 million each into the expansion program, with Dairy Farm providing the technical expertise and marketing skills.

### Pharmacy

In 1995, Guardian Pharmacy retailed a comprehensive range of pharmaceutical, cosmetic, and other personal care products through its 28 outlets in Malaysia. Cycle & Carriage plans to add ten outlets every year from 1996 to 2000. It also hopes to enhance future earnings by aggressively looking for new agency lines for its distribution operations and new pharmacy outlets.

### Other Activities

CSM also manages shopping centers in and around Kuala Lumpur:

1. The newly upgraded Jaya Shopping Complex, a 4-storey retail podium block (total retail floor area of 12,077 square meters) with a 10-storey office tower (with a total leasable office area of 6,040 square meters).
2. Bangsar Shopping Center (total retail floor area of 7,432 square meters), which is situated in a prime residential area, hence enjoying good customer traffic.

[5]"Halal" food is food prepared according to the traditions of Islam, the state religion of Malaysia.

## Future Plans

Managing Director Boon Yoon Chiang is well aware of the effects of external factors and the rising competition in Singapore's automobile market. He has began seriously considering moving quickly into unexplored regions like Myanmar and China to preempt the company's competitors and reap any first-mover advantages.

On the other hand, Cycle & Carriage is concentrating its effort in its food operations by teaming up with Nestle and Dairy Farm to aggressively establish itself as a serious player and market leader in this fast growing sector. Boon started wondering what contingency plans the company should prepare if the joint venture does not work out.

# EXHIBIT 1

## CYCLE & CARRIAGE LIMITED*
## Group Structure

**Vehicles**
*Singapore*
- Cycle & Carriage Industries
- Cycle & Carriage Automotive
- Cycle & Carriage Proton

*Malaysia*
- Cycle & Carriage Bintang**
- Cycle & Carriage (Malaysia) (Subsidiary)

*Australia*
- Astre Investments+

*New Zealand*
- Sri Temasek (Subsidiary)

*Thailand*
- New Era Cycle & Carriage (Subsidiary)

*Vietnam*
- CCL Saigon
- C&C Saigon Tourist Automotive (Subsidiary)
- Autostar

**Property**
*Singapore & Malaysia*
- Malayan Credit**
- CCL Group Properties

**Food & Retail**
*Malaysia*
- Cold Storage (Malaysia)**

**Others**
*Singapore*
- UMF Private
- MTU Asia
- Robert Bosch (SE)
- Maritime Holdings

*Malaysia*
- Ampang Investments

Subsidiaries (shaded)
Associates (unshaded)

*Listed on the Stock Exchange of Singapore.
**Listed on the Kuala Lumpur Stock Exchange.
+Holding company for Hyundai & Chrysler distributor.

Source: Company Records.

EXHIBIT 2

## CYCLE & CARRIAGE LIMITED
## Board of Directors

**Tan Sri Dato' Paduka Sallehuddin bin Mohamed**, *Chairman*

Tan Sri Dato' Paduka Sallehuddin became the Chairman of the Board in April 1993. He was the Executive Chairman of the Employees' Provident Fund, Malaysia and was concurrently Chairman of the Council for the University of Technology, Malaysia. Previously he was Chief Secretary to the Government of Malaysia, Secretary to the Cabinet, Head of Civil Service, Director General of the Economic Planning Unit for the Malaysian Prime Minister's Department and had held several senior posts in the Ministry of Finance, Malaysia.

**Boon Yoon Chiang**, *Group Managing Director*

Boon assumed responsibility as the Group Managing Director of the Cycle & Carriage Group in July 1993. He was the Chairman of Jardine Matheson (S) Limited and sits on the boards of several companies in the Jardine Group. Active in the Singapore business scene, he served on the Council of the Singapore Federation of Chambers of Commerce & Industry and the Board of the Singapore International Chamber of Commerce and was Honorary Secretary of the Singapore National Employers' Federation. He was also a member of the Executive Board of the Paris-based International Chamber of Commerce.

**Rin Kei Mei**

Rin joined the Board in July 1993 and was the Chairman of Malayan Credit Limited. He was the Chairman of EON Berhad and EON Bank Berhad and Deputy Chairman of EON Finance Berhad.

**Anthony J L Nightingale**

Nightingale joined the Board in February 1993. He was a Director of Jardine Matheson Holdings Limited, Chairman of Jardine Pacific Limited, and Joint Managing Director of Jardine International Motor Holdings Limited. He also sat on the board of several other companies in the Jardine Group.

**Hassan Abas**

Hassan was appointed to the Board in December 1993. He trained as a chartered accountant and was director of several other public companies in Malaysia and Singapore.

**Alan Yeo Chee Yeow**

Yeo has been a Board member since 1977. He was Chairman of Rothmans Industries Limited; he was also a director of Inchcape Berhad, Neptune Orient Lines Limited, and Keppel Bank of Singapore Limited. Awarded the Public Services Star by the Government of Singapore in 1969, Yeo was named Businessman of the Year in 1987.

**Philip Eng Heng Nee**

A certified accountant by training, Eng joined the Group in 1982 and was appointed to the Board in May 1993. At the time of the writing of the case, he was the Executive Director responsible for the motor vehicle operations of the Cycle & Carriage Group.

**Vimala a/p V R Menon**

Menon was appointed to the Board in August 1994. She was the Executive Director, Finance & Corporate Services, EON Berhad, and also sat on the board of most companies in the EON Group.

**Hasni bin Harun**

Hasni was appointed as the alternate director to Dato' Paduka Sallehuddin bin Mohamed in June 1994. An accountant by profession, Hasni also holds a Master in Business Administration degree. He was senior manager in the Employees' Provident Fund, Malaysia, and previously was the Senior Treasury Accountant in the Accountant General's Office, Ministry of Finance.

**Owen P Howell-Price**

Howell-Price was appointed as the alternate director to Nightingale in July 1993. He was formerly Chief Executive of Dairy Farm International Holdings Limited, a large international retail group, and, at the time of the writing of the case, was a director of Dairy Farm and Cold Storage (Malaysia) Berhad.

Source: Company Records.

EXHIBIT 3

## CYCLE & CARRIAGE LIMITED
## Five-Year Financial Profile

| | 1990 S$m | 1991 S$m | 1992 S$m | 1993* S$m | 1994 S$m |
|---|---|---|---|---|---|
| Group Profit & Loss | | | | | |
| Turnover | 813.4 | 1,149.3 | 1,544.7 | 2,298.3 | 2,477.0 |
| Profit before taxation | 83.2 | 105.6 | 95.2 | 171.9 | 200.8 |
| Taxation | (29.3) | (33.6) | (30.2) | (52.4) | (64.2) |
| Profit after taxation | 53.9 | 72.0 | 65.0 | 119.5 | 136.6 |
| Minority interest | 0.0 | 0.0 | 0.9 | (7.5) | (12.9) |
| Profit after taxation & minority interests | 53.9 | 72.0 | 65.9 | 112.0 | 123.7 |
| Extraordinary items | 17.0 | (1.5) | (6.7) | 0.0 | 0.0 |
| Profit attributable to shareholders | 70.9 | 70.5 | 59.2 | 112.0 | 123.7 |
| Dividends | (17.8) | (20.6) | (25.0) | (39.4) | (39.2) |
| Retained profits | 53.1 | 49.9 | 34.2 | 72.6 | 84.5 |
| Earnings per share (cents) | 33.0 | 41.1 | 34.1 | 49.8 | 53.1 |
| Gross dividend per share (cents) | 16.1 | 17.0 | 17.0 | 23.0 | 23.0 |
| Group Balance Sheet | | | | | |
| Fixed assets | 40.9 | 46.6 | 55.2 | 87.4 | 113.5 |
| Investments properties | 23.2 | 22.8 | 769.4 | 951.7 | 713.3 |
| Development properties | 78.8 | 66.6 | 246.2 | 127.4 | 243.3 |
| Interests in associates | 151.0 | 169.5 | 163.1 | 177.0 | 187.7 |
| Other noncurrent assets | 53.4 | 37.3 | 30.4 | 21.6 | 10.6 |
| Net current assets (liabilities) | 164.8 | 207.0 | (49.9) | 83.8 | 280.2 |
| Borrowings due after one year | (50.0) | (52.8) | (91.4) | (158.0) | (122.4) |
| Other noncurrent liabilities | (10.3) | (9.5) | (10.0) | (7.7) | (3.5) |
| Net operating assets | 451.8 | 487.5 | 1,114.0 | 1,283.2 | 1,422.7 |
| Share capital | 175.0 | 175.2 | 211.4 | 232.3 | 233.1 |
| Share premium | 104.3 | 54.9 | 186.4 | 231.2 | 235.1 |
| Revenue and other reserves | 171.4 | 255.9 | 342.8 | 417.5 | 569.3 |
| Shareholders' funds | 450.7 | 486.0 | 740.6 | 881.0 | 1,037.5 |
| Minority interest | 1.1 | 1.5 | 373.4 | 402.2 | 385.2 |
| Capital employed | 451.8 | 487.5 | 1,114.0 | 1,283.2 | 1,422.7 |
| Net tangible assets per share (S$) | 2.58 | 2.77 | 3.49 | 3.79 | 4.45 |
| Key Ratios | | | | | |
| Gearing | — | — | 25.00% | 12.00% | — |
| Interest cover | 20.8 | 28.1 | 12.8 | 11.1 | 15.4 |
| Return on shareholders' funds | 14.20% | 15.40% | 10.70% | 11.00% | 12.90% |
| Number of employees | 649 | 829 | 1,089 | 1,314 | 1,460 |

*1993 figures were for a 15-month period.

Source: Company records.

EXHIBIT 4

## CYCLE & CARRIAGE LIMITED
## Segment Performance

| | *31.09.92 S$m* | *31.12.93* S$m* | *31.12.94 S$m* |
|---|---|---|---|
| *By Activity* | | | |
| Turnover | **1,564.4** | **2,298.3** | **2,477.0** |
| Vehicles | 1,243.5 | 1,909.6 | 2,081.7 |
| Property | 66.0 | 144.6 | 159.0 |
| Food & Retail | 58.6 | 73.6 | 52.7 |
| Others | 196.3 | 170.5 | 183.6 |
| Profit before Tax | **95.2** | **171.9** | **200.8** |
| Vehicles | 80.3 | 143.5 | 133.1 |
| Property | 12.7 | 24.6 | 58.1 |
| Food & Retail | 1.1 | 4.5 | 3.0 |
| Others | 1.1 | (0.7) | 6.6 |
| Net Operating Assets | **1,113.9** | **1,283.2** | **1,422.7** |
| Vehicles | 194.0 | 281.0 | 299.9 |
| Property | 940.9 | 953.7 | 1,162.1 |
| Food & Retail | 45.7 | 51.2 | 36.8 |
| Others | (88.7) | (2.7) | (76.1) |

| | *31.09.92 S$m* | *31.12.93* S$m* | *31.12.94 S$m* |
|---|---|---|---|
| *By Geographical Locations* | | | |
| Turnover | **1,564.4** | **2,298.3** | **2,477.0** |
| Singapore | 1,093.0 | 1,663.3 | 1,701.6 |
| Malaysia | 280.8 | 371.1 | 366.5 |
| Australasia | 182.4 | 238.1 | 346.3 |
| Others | 8.2 | 25.8 | 62.6 |
| Profit before Tax | **95.2** | **171.9** | **200.8** |
| Singapore | 92.5 | 167.2 | 168.1 |
| Malaysia | 4.1 | (0.4) | 23.7 |
| Australasia | (1.8) | 2.2 | 14.2 |
| Others | 0.4 | 2.9 | (5.2) |
| Net Operating Assets | **1,113.9** | **1,283.2** | **1,422.7** |
| Singapore | 885.6 | 1,011.2 | 1,126.9 |
| Malaysia | 192.2 | 240.7 | 254.9 |
| Australasia | 16.2 | 19.1 | 29.6 |
| Others | 19.9 | 12.2 | 11.3 |

Source: Company records.

## SECTION THREE

# Strategy Implementation

| *Case Number* | *Case (Country)* | *Nature of Situation* | *Complexity* |
|---|---|---|---|
| 13 | Sahaviriya OA Group of Companies (Thailand) | SBU integration | High |
| 14 | Gateway Technology Singapore (Singapore) | Headquarters-subsidiary relationships | Low |
| 15 | Panyu Security Gate Company Guangdong (Guangdong, China) | Socialist market economy | Medium |
| 16 | Nan Feng Household Appliance Co (China) | Socialist market economy | Medium |
| 17 | Rayalaseema Biscuits Company, Kurnool (India) | Turnaround | Low |
| 18 | Kum Fook Press (Hong Kong) | Leadership in transition phase | Medium |

| Products/ Services | Sector | Financial Data | US$ Sales (000) | Industry Conditions |
|---|---|---|---|---|
| ormation technology | Manufacturing | Yes | 260 | Growth |
| k drives | Manufacturing | Yes | 2,700,000 | Growth |
| ricated structured tal products usegates) | Manufacturing | No | 1,111 | Growth |
| ctric housewares l fans | Manufacturing | Yes | 17,118 | Growth |
| kery products | Manufacturing | Yes | 223 | Mature |
| nting and publishing | Manufacturing | No | 10,400 | Mature |

# Sahaviriya OA Group of Companies* 13

Being with the Sahaviriya OA Group of Companies (SVOA) since the beginning Mr Jack Min Chun Hu, the President and Corporate Executive Director, had enjoyed the success of SVOA in the past decade. The big show was at the "Management 2000" conference that honored SVOA as one of the ten most outstanding companies in Thailand. SVOA was ranked number 10 and was one of the only two firms in the technology industry in the conference.

SVOA's strategy of "Win! Win! Win!" had paid off handsomely. Helping customers to win and winning the loyalty and steady business from the customers has made SVOA a real winner so far. Yet, with new developments in the world market, Mr Min wondered what impacts agreements such as the General Agreement in Tariffs and Trades (GATT) and the Asia-Pacific Economic Cooperation (APEC) would have on the computer-related technology in Thailand and on SVOA. He pondered how to maneuver SVOA into the next century with a better record of success. Mr Min also contemplated the extent of opportunities a new high-tech building, the "Intelligent Building", would create after an

---

*This case was prepared by Dr Uthai Tanlamai, the Chair Professor of the Lumsum Foundation and Dr Achara Chandrachai, Associate Professor and Head of the Department of Management. The case writers are from the Faculty of Commerce and Accountancy, Chulalongkorn University, Thailand. The case was designed to serve as a basis for classroom discussion rather than to illustrate either effective or ineffective handling of an administrative situation. The case write-up was initiated and supported by Sasin Graduate Institute of Business Administration of Chulalongkorn University and Sahaviriya OA Group of Companies. 

unfortunate fire to the corporate headquarters (rented) on February 10, 1993 caused a loss of 86 million baht. Another one of the firm's success stories was getting listed in the Stock Exchange of Thailand (SET). Joining SET in July 1993 was an important strategic move that had yet to be capitalized on a full scale. After December 1993, about 5 months after its initial public offering, not all stocks issued by SVOA had been fully subscribed.

Mr Min used to talk to everybody in the course of a day, but now the firm had grown over tenfold. He felt that SVOA's people knew him, but he wished to know and talk to them like in the good old days. Mr Min believed in communications and he had made that the number one priority throughout his management career. He had put time and energy into the development of communication systems within the organization and with the others outside. He had published down-to-earth management and philosophy books with some even taking the form of cartoons, in an effort he thought would help communicate with SVOA's constituencies (i.e., employees, customers, suppliers). Mr Min wanted SVOA's personnel to get to know him personally and the people outside the company to know SVOA as more than just a corporate name. With stacks and stacks of "must-do" things, Mr Min missed the good-old-days when he knew everyone in the organization on a more personal basis.

The business opportunities waiting to be tapped in this industry were tremendous, especially with the end of political unrest in the Indochina region; Vietnam, China, Myanmar, Laos, and other countries were opening up their doors to everything, including computer- and telecommunications-related technology. Mr Min felt that the time had come to get SVOA's executives to step back and assess the overall situation faced by the group and to identify a new corporate vision and strategies that would lead SVOA to be within the circle of winners in the next decades.

## The Company

Sahaviriya OA Group of Companies (SVOA) was founded in 1982 as a company in the Sahaviriya Group of Companies, a diverse conglomerate involved in various industries. SVOA was formed to serve the emerging computer and office automation markets in Thailand. SVOA's initial foray into the market was as the sole Thai distributor of OKI microcomputers. This venture was extremely successful and the company soon expanded into all areas of office automation and telecommunication.

SVOA, encompassing 13 subsidiary companies, was Thailand's leading office-automation supplier with the largest distribution network in the country. Computers and peripherals accounted for 74 percent of sales, while telecommunications equipment (mostly Oki mobile phone handsets) accounted for another 15 percent. The group was the sole distributor of ACER, EPSON, OKI, ROLAND, Hitachi Data System (HDS), Tandem, Lotus, and Apple brands and was an authorized distributor for Hewlett-Packard, Autocad, Novell, Borland, Creative Technology, and others (see Figure 1). The corporations strategy of targeting every segment of the market and concentrating on the world's most popular brands was highly successful. Nationwide distribution was conducted through 55 Sahaviriya OA Center showrooms, 300 dealers, 8 value-added resellers (such as the Shinawatra Group), 14 Mini OA showrooms, and direct sales.

SVOA was listed in the Stock Exchange of Thailand (SET) in 1993. Mr Min Chun Hu, SVOA's President and Corporate Executive Director, stated that the money derived from the registered capital increase would be used to keep its office automation business

FIGURE 1

**SVOA's Leading Products**

growing. The capital raised would make it possible for the company to build their new corporate headquarters, the "Intelligent Building," and to invest in subsidiary companies as well as working capital. SVOA offered five million shares to the public and a further six hundred thousand shares to staff members. The stock's offering price was set at 85 baht.

To become a very successful company, SVOA invested in its people. The company had a policy of non-stop human resource development that involved all manner of staff training and education. SVOA had a fully integrated teamwork style of management. From teamwork that encouraged each individual to reach his or her full personal potential, SVOA was able to build the solid infrastructure of its human resource systems.

The dynamic environment that SVOA was operating in had provided SVOA with ample opportunities to grow. One example was the Copyright Bill awaiting the Thai Parliament's approval; its imminent passage would change the fate of "legitimate 333 software" sales. This situation was particularly promising for SVOA, which already had contracts with popular software producers such as Lotus, Novell (which produced the industry- benchmark Local Area Network software), and Borland. Major institutions such as Bank of Ayudhya, Krung Thai Bank, and Siam Cement recently upgraded their software by purchasing over 1,000 copies of these legitimated software packages.

The competitor environment was also changing such that rivals might become friends. Shinawatra Corp, one of SVOA's fierce competitors, recently launched Thailand's first satellite. SVOA was exploring the possibility of taking part in the telecommunication projects to be initiated by Telecom Asia, TAC, and Advanced Info Services, Shinawatra's subsidiaries and many other companies. SVOA has formed strategic alliances with these organizations.

## Economy and Related Industry

The prospect of computer-technology-related business is bright, especially for software-related business. The software market was projected to be worth more than 5 million baht in the second half of 1994 when enactment of a copyright law was closer to becoming a reality. The important technology in 1994 and beyond as perceived by IBM's customers, surveyed in 1993 during IBM's reengineering process, was Networking, Electronic Data Interchange, Expert Systems, Graphics, and Portable technology respectively. The highest growth in hardware was in personal computers and workstations. Yet the most immediate need in the technology market is for technological know-how personnel.[1]

SVOA operated in two major industries, computer equipment and telecommunications-related equipment. The two industries are closely related and both appear to have had an increasing influence on Thailand's economic development.

### Computer Equipment Market[2]

The majority of the computer-related industry in Thailand dealt with importing from and supplying products to foreign countries, such as the U.S., Japan, Taiwan, Singapore, and so on. However, one segment of the computer-related industry was involved in the assembly of computer equipment within the country. Yet, parts needed for the assembly of computer equipment were not only sourced domestically but also imported from foreign countries.

The total import value of computer equipment was increasing from 240 million baht in 1982 to 9,530 million in 1991, about 50 percent per year. The trend of using computers in business was definitely increasing. As a whole the economy in this part of the world has been expanding in the past decade, and there was an intense competition that put a demand on businesses to use computer equipment in order to increase their efficiency. The computer technology was also improving a great deal in terms of the wide variety of applications and the decrease in price.

Two segments of computer markets were the microcomputer (PC), and mini and mainframe. In 1990 the total number of microcomputers sold was 63,820 units, amounting to 3,190 million baht and a 30-percent increase from the prior year. In 1991 the total sales volume was 93,956 units, amounting to 4,632 million baht, a 47-percent increase from 1990. The growth in the mini/mainframe market was from 538 units (3,573 million baht in 1990) to 558 units (4,900 million baht in 1991). The growth rate was only 4 percent in unit sales, but it was a 37-percent increase in total sales value.

Many factors recently boosted the computer industry in Thailand, including the strong economic expansion of the region and the decrease in import taxes for computer-related products. Although the number of new entries in this industry is increasing swiftly, the impact of an increasing pool of competitors has been mitigated by the fact that many business institutions now recognize the need to use computers in order to increase their efficiency. Taking into consideration the foregoing factors, the International Data Corporation found that the microcomputer market in Thailand grew 40 percent annually until 1996 and the mini/mainframe market would grow 12 to 15 percent a year.

### Telecommunications Equipment Market[3]

All telecommunications equipment was imported into Thailand. Japan, Taiwan, the United States, South Korea, and Europe were the major sources of equipment. The telecommunications market grew as various governmental agencies worked to build an infrastructure of communication networks for the country.

---

[1] "Thailand's Software Market: A Waiting for the Copyright Law." *Bangkok Business IT*, July 28, 1994.
[2] *Thailand Equity Review*, November 16, 1993.
[3] *Thailand Equity Review*, November 16, 1993.

Two major telecommunications equipment product categories in major demand were terminal equipment and networking equipment. The terminal equipment category included products such as small office telephone systems (key telephone) and large office telephone systems (EPABX), facsimile, cellular telephone, MODEM, and other transformation equipment. Thailand's Seventh Economic Development Plan has projected an upward trend in the import values for all of these products. The networking equipment was mainly used by governmental agencies such as the Telephone Authority of Thailand, the Police Department, the Electricity General Authority of Thailand, large banks, and various businesses in the telecommunications industry that provide communication and networking services to the public. These telecommunication businesses included Public Switching, International Switching, Satellite, Optical Fiber, and Mobile Telephone Network businesses.

Telecommunications equipment had been an important component of the infrastructural foundation needed to develop the country. As seen from substantial investment from the government and from joint ventures between government and private industries, there would be more and more developments in this market and its rapid growth was inevitable.

### SVOA's Place in the Industry[4]

In 1989, IBM was the leader in the PC computer equipment market with a market share of 18.6 percent. Following closely were ACER, the PC product from SVOA; and NEC, the PC from Datamat Ltd, with an 11.4 percent and 6.5 percent share of the market respectively. In 1990, SVOA was able to maintain its number 2 position for ACER and moved its APPLE sales to number 3, with 10.9 percent and 5.0 percent market shares respectively. The competition got more acute in 1991. Although SVOA's ACER still maintained its number 2 position (7.7 percent), the APPLE position (4.9 percent) was slightly eroded by a Taiwanese brand, TWINHEAD (5.0 percent).

On a lighter note, SVOA was able to compete in the mini/mainframe market more vigorously. It was successful in luring TANDEM, the number 3 seller in this market; the group became TANDEM's sole distributor in Thailand with a market share of 6.2 percent. SVOA was also able to move its long-standing product, HITACHI, to entertain number 5 in the share of the mini/mainframe market with 3.2 percent.

Although the competition in the telecommunications equipment market was more keen, SVOA has a 6.7 percent (number 4) market share of the Key Telephone and EPABX products market, a 13.1 percent (number 2) share of the Mobile telephone product market, and a 14.2 percent (number 3) share of the Facsimile products market.

## The Parent — Sahaviriya Group[5]

Originally established in the early 1950s as a small iron workshop, the Sahaviriya Group of Companies (the Group) diversified into a broad range of key areas, including steel, finance, real estate, technology, and international business. Today, the Group comprises 43 affiliate companies (see Exhibit 1), employing approximately 5,000 staff and billing around 40 billion baht annually.

[4] *SVOA's Initial Public Offering Prospectus*, June 30, 1993.
[5] Sahaviriya Group's 1993 Annual Report.

**Steel** is the oldest business in which the Group has expertise and sophisticated facilities. Offering optimum flexibility in both input and output were three separate steel complexes, at Bangsaphan, Bangpakong and Prapradaeng. Each comprises several distinct subsidiary companies and each of these employs different raw materials and processes to produce different steel products designed to meet an optimum range of end uses, one of the biggest being the automobile industry.

Equipped with a private deep-sea port operated by Prachuap Port Corporation, the Bangsaphan Complex is one of the most modern sites employing advanced technology from Italy and Japan. With a total combined investment of around 30 billion baht, the Group's Bangsaphan Steel Complex produces hot rolled coils, high-quality finished steel rolls and electrogalvanized coils. The total annual combined capacity is 3.5 billion tons. The Complex is equipped with efficient environmental protection systems.

The Group's two other steel complexes at Bangpakong and Prapradaeng mainly produces Plate Mill with annual capacity of 360,000 tons, and some shape steel, and wire rods and bars. Although the Prapradaeng Complex is the oldest facility, it was equipped with up-to-date technological developments.

In order to deal with imported steel which could not be produced locally, the Group had its own trading and logistic companies including the Sahaviriya Panich Co Ltd, Sahaviriya Transportation Co Ltd, Siam Nana Transportation Co Ltd, Sahaviriya Nittan Co Ltd, and Tec-Sahaviriya Co Ltd. These vertically integrated operations allowed the Group to be self-sufficient in the entire process, from production to trading, through an extensive network of channel distribution in local markets.

**Finance** has always been important to the Group. The Group founded the Sahaviriya Trust in 1964, subsequently, the Sahaviriya Credit Foncier in 1976, and the latest, CL Sahaviriya Finance and Securities Co, Ltd (CLSV), a joint venture with French banking giant Credit Lyonnais. The Group's financial assets had risen steadily to a current total of 5 billion baht.

CLSV provided a variety of finance and security services including business loans, consumer and housing loans, financial advice on loan structuring and foreign exchange services, brokerage service and security trading services. One major conviction of CLSV was an ongoing effort to promote the Thai Government's policy to encourage investment funds so as to better local living standards and to achieve a healthy economy for Thailand.

**Real Estate** is another business of the Group that is viewed as being important to the Thai economy. The Group's property portfolio is impressive. SV City was conceptualized as a city within a city. This riverside development included eight residential towers, three office buildings, and a range of shopping, recreational, and service amenities. SV Garden, another riverside development which had the feel of a resort, sought to meet the strong need for a residential area within the city. Wellgrow Industrial Estate was a different type of success. Located in Bangna-Trad Highway, Wellgrow served the large market of people who worked in the many industrial parks along the highway. Further diversification was witnessed in the redevelopment of the Hang Zhou Eastern Dragon Hotel. Conducted as a joint venture with the Tourism Bureau of Zhejiang in southern China, the project involved transforming an existing hotel property into a top country resort.

**Technology** has enabled Sahaviriya OA (SVOA) to forge stronger links with leading international partners around the world. Being a major distributor of top-brand microcomputers and office automation such as EPSON, ACER, APPLE, and OKI, the Group also had a competitive edge in serving a growing number of high-end customers as a professional systems integration and mainframe consultant. Primarily focused in the banking, telecommunications, industrial, and government sectors, SVOA concentrated on Tandem, Hitachi, and other mainframe connectors in the development of integrated "turn-key" systems.

OA Centers, a revolutionary concept in the marketing of high-tech products, work as a large franchise network to promote the benefits of computers and office automation. Mini OA Centers, a concept ahead of its time, were also established to provide convenient sales and service facilities for the customer in key retail locations. The commitment to satisfy the customer's needs is the key to the Group's continuing growth and success.

Only ten years after its conception, SVOA was listed in the Stock Exchange of Thailand in 1993 offering 5,000,000 plus shares at 85 baht per share. SVOA, under the leadership of Mr Min Chun Hu, the President and Corporate Executive Director, had planned an unprecedented local venture and a massive diversification into international and regional markets.

One of the corporation's greatest strengths lies in its ability to assemble tightly knit and efficient teams to operate according to the company policy, "There is always a way to make it better!" This visionary management network allowed SVOA to offer the most comprehensive set of computer-related product lines in Thailand.

**International trading and globalization** are vital to sustaining the growth of the Group. Listed in the Stock Exchange of Hong Kong, Linkful International Holdings Ltd (founded in 1990) is the Group's strategic unit to link suppliers in steel-rich countries such as the Commonwealth of Independent States, Brazil, Venezuela, Mexico, South Africa, and Eastern European nations with the booming markets of the Far East. Matalsrussia Corp was also established to deal with the import and export of steel worldwide.

The Group was committed to its steel trading core business and strategically planned to integrate vertically. The group set up a joint-venture operation to secure priority access to the strategic North Asia seaport of Nakhodka; acquired their own vessel; co-invested in the Odessa Seaport, Ukraine; built a steel plant in Zhejiang, China; and set up a joint-venture operation to send engineers to advise on the building of a steel furnace in Pakistan.

Systematic and continuous growth is the key strategy used by the top management, shepherded by Dr Prapa Viriyaprapaikit, the Honorary Chairman of the Group; Mr Wit Viriyaprapaikit, the Chief Executive Officer; and more than fifteen other executive officers and directors. According to Dr Prapa, the Group sought to enhance the quality of life of the Thai people, to conduct business responsibly with an eye to fostering the development of Thai society, and to contribute to the development of essential infrastructure in the country.

## The Success

SVOA's success could be attributed to its confidence in its business directions. According to Mr Min, SVOA had not just painted and followed "dreams," but had actively worked to realize its "hopes and prospects."[6] The business directions that SVOA had taken did not always just follow the flow, or current, of business; the firm had many times reversed the business current successfully. Against all the beliefs of many industrial players, SVOA developed an auspicious franchise system for its office automation business. This was a great example of reversing the current.

In the special supplement jointly published by *Money & Banking* and the *Far Eastern Economic Review*, the Sahaviriya Group of Companies was ranked number 10 among Thailand's most outstanding companies. SVOA was one of the only two firms that were included in the technology segment. Unlike SVOA, which was more diversified, the other firm, the Shinawatra Group, focused its business only in telecommunications-related markets.[7]

The Sahaviriya Group of Companies was ranked number 5 for its Marketing-driven feature, number 9 for being Visionary, number 12 both for Quality of Products and Services and for Being Good Examples to Other Companies, and number 21 for its Financial Stability attributes. The technology division, SVOA, was one of the Sahaviriya Group's best-known areas. These rankings appeared to concur with the way the organization had prioritized its efforts. In his book, *Toward the Year 2000*, Mr Min discussed the four factors that have made SVOA the leader in its industry: dedicated teamwork, satisfied customers, visionary investors, and confident suppliers. SVOA was not proud of itself as a sole producer of a specific technology, product, or brand. Its greatest pride was its ability to provide "customer satisfaction." To do so, its most important asset was people. SVOA valued its people, its unique corporate culture, and its spirit. Mr Min believed that SVOA's employees should feel that working for SVOA is not just a job but a way of living and achieving a fulfilling career.

## The Beginnings

The Office Automation (OA) business was one of the first successful areas taken up by the Sahaviriya OA Group. Under Mr Min's directorship as the OA Group's President, the area expanded rapidly. In the mid-1980s, OA became one of the most important symbols of modernity. Companies in every industry had found that office automation could open the door to a world of new opportunities. SVOA seriously took on the role of helping Thai companies open this door through the establishment of Sahaviriya Infortech Computer Co, Ltd in 1982. This company serves as the import agent and distributor/service provider for OKI computers in Thailand.

Sahaviriya Infortech Computer Co Ltd began as a single computer importer with a staff of seven. It had total sales of 1.6 million baht in its first year. The company's total sales increased over 2,000 percent the next year. Since then the SVOA Group has evolved into Thailand's largest diversified OA Group, comprising over ten companies. The OA Group's

---

[6] Jack Min Chu Hu, *Toward the Year 2000*, SVOA Publication, March 1994.

[7] "Review 200 Asia's Leading Companies and 30 Leading Thai Companies." *Money & Banking* in association with the *Far Eastern Economic Review*, January 1994. The data was collected from interviewing 25 top administrators from 11 countries in Asia, including Singapore, Malaysia, Thailand, Indonesia, Taiwan, Philippines, Australia, Japan, India, Hong Kong, and Korea. Also 4,042 survey questionnaires were received from businessmen and women who subscribe to the leading journals in their respective countries. From 140 questions asked, the questions were filtered into 5 main areas that characterize successful companies. The five areas are 1) Having Quality Products and Services, 2) Being Visionary, 3) Being Marketing-driven, 4) Having Financial Stability, and 5) Being a Good Example to the Others.

revenues grew at a rate of more than 30 to 50 percent per annum. Exhibit 2 shows the chronological order of the individual companies' establishment, their capitalization as of March 31, 1993, and a brief description of the individual businesses.

## Growing Up

As shown in Exhibit 3, SVOA had expanded rapidly to cover 7 groups of products and services. The largest number of employees was in the Software & Service Business Group (SSBG) — 205 people, about 20 percent of SVOA's personnel. From merely seven employees at the beginning of operation in 1982, SVOA's staff grew into almost a thousand people, including more than a dozen expatriates.

SVOA also evolved to have one of the most diversified shareholder structures within its industry (Exhibit 4). The structure had evolved constantly to reflect the strategic growth of the group. Joint ventures with other companies allowed the SVOA group to offer a variety of products and services to its customers. Joint ventures with companies in the SVOA group enabled the group to strengthen their pooled resources in areas such as personnel and distribution systems.

According to Mr Min, one of the reasons why SVOA had been so successful was that the firm constantly, briskly analyzed the life cycle of its products as well as monitored its environment. One of SVOA's successful product strategies was to make sure that its products can provide a maximum life span. Figure 2 shows how SVOA managed the life cycles of their products in terms of the relationship between the contribution margin of an individual product and its associated size of the market. Early in its life cycle, a product might make a 20 to 30 percent margin; the margin got smaller when the size of the market became larger. SVOA had a product-mix that covered different stages of the life cycle. SVOA continually monitored the product life cycle of individual product lines and added value features to the line so that it would be able to maximize its life. With this management, the company would always have some products with at least an 18 percent contribution margin.

FIGURE 2
**Product Life Cycle Management**

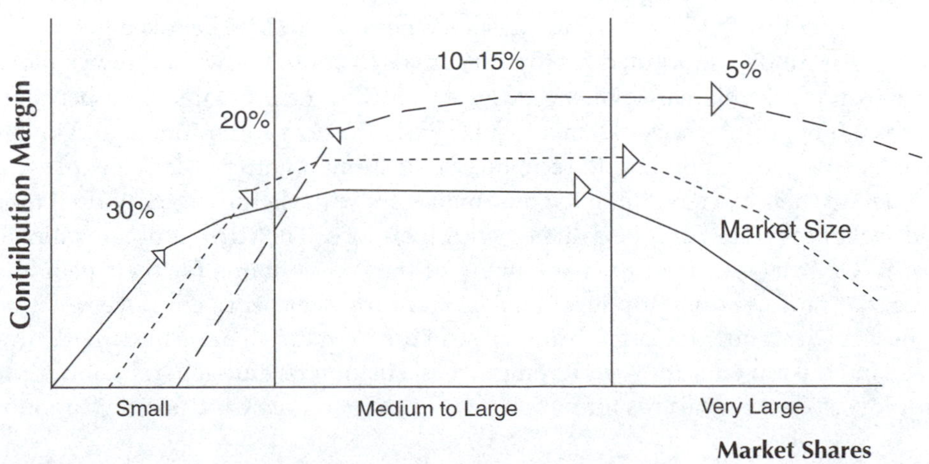

To monitor its environment, the Marketing Research & Information Department published and circulated a bimonthly clipping of articles from newspapers and magazines. This collection of bimonthly clippings was called *Opponent* and was neatly organized into sections such as Sahaviriya's News, Competitor Movement, New Products, Telecommunications & Transportation, Foreign News, and so on. SVOA's personnel also had access to this information on a daily basis via its internal communication mode, a video media system located next to elevators that provided the Opponent news continuously. Other similar electronic media used for organizational communications have been used since 1991.

In the past decade SVOA had diversified to add many new products and services to the corporation. Although it had been the first to offer the newest technology and enjoyed high contribution margins from an early stage in its life cycle, the group's strength also lies in the fact that they were able to capture a good portion of the market through their innovative distribution channels. According to Mr Min, SVOA viewed suppliers worldwide as SVOA's suppliers; thus the Group had no immediate need to invest in the manufacture of its own products. By being very careful in choosing top-of-the-line world products, SVOA established its reputation of carrying only quality products. By being very keen on the needs of customers, SVOA established its reputation of providing quality services.

"Being There First" was how SVOA planned to position itself in the Indochina, North Asia, and East Asia markets. SVOA strategically invested in Malaysia to position itself in a gateway to India, and in Kunmin (close to the northern part of Thailand) to gain a foothold in a gateway to mainland China and Indochina. SVOA hoped to aggressively expand its regional business by becoming an opinion leader through a strategy of positioning itself as the pioneer supplier of hi-tech products and services.

## Doing Things Right

The Group's organizational structure (Exhibit 5) captured the essence of both its product lines and its functional specialty. This short pyramid structure facilitated maximum communication and linkages across subunits' boundaries. Like a butterfly, each subunit would be very flexible in maneuvering through a rapidly changing technological environment. Yet these small butterflies, or subunits, could metamorphose into a giant which could take control of any situation effectively.

The structure of SVOA was flatly designed because Mr Min believed in "management by walking around." He wanted his top executives to get to know their own subordinates. In terms of top-level management positions, SVOA had a large number because it believed in rewarding its people on a regular basis. To earn commitment and loyalty from its people, an organization had to recognize basic human nature. Many people wanted to be "tigers" in their own mountains. Thus, managers with their own individual mountains should feel empowered and be satisfied with their jobs. The current organizational structure of SVOA was designed to create many of these mountains for their people. On the average, the ratio was one top-level management for every fifty employees.

Besides designing the organizational structure to nourish basic human nature, SVOA believed in nonstop education for its employees, customers, and general public. Education for employees came in various forms: job rotation, Marco Polo Club (similar to a mini-MBA program), study abroad, and internal communication systems (providing total economic environment, industry movement, and competitor analysis on a weekly and as-needed basis). Customers and public education took the form of newsletters that contained technical knowledge researched by the Marketing Research and Information Department.

The financial position of SVOA as shown in the consolidated financial statements of the SVOA for the past two years (Exhibits 6 and 7) was very strong. SVOA managed to be in the right place at the right time. Part of its success lay in the innovative channel development strategy, Sahaviriya OA Center, the heart of the Systems Network, which was established in 1989. This revolutionary concept in the marketing of high-tech products has been vital to SVOA's continuing success. The centers were one of Southeast Asia's largest franchise networks instituted to promote the benefits of computers and office automation by providing a place where managers could explore technology that would enhance their companies' performance. The OA center concept was "low-key" rather than "hard-sell", with specialists providing answers and advice to customers.

Another step closer to their customers were Mini OAs established in retail outlets, department stores, and shopping malls around Thailand. These centers sold and serviced office automation and computer equipment in a way that matched the changing lifestyles of consumers.

## In Control

Many of SVOA's operational and information systems had evolved to ensure the effectiveness of the group's management control mechanism. The group devised its control processes by using self-control principles. Each subunit would set its own targets or performance criteria. These targets or criteria would then be used as benchmarks of the subunit's achievement. Although the targets or criteria were set using a bottom-up approach, they also conformed with industrial norms embodied in the group's top-down business plans.

**Marketing and Distribution Systems.** SVOA had the following marketing policies:

1. Use the "One-Stop Shopping" concept. Give customers the convenience they need by providing them with a full cycle of quality and fair price products and services. Also provide before and after sales service to customers.
2. Develop "Value Added" products and services. Find quality products and services and develop them into commercialized software packages or specialized software packages.
3. Focus on providing "Solutions" to customers, more than merely selling products and services.
4. Build the most comprehensive distributing channel to cover every part of the country.

These policies led SVOA to develop an extremely effective marketing operation and control system, its distribution channels. Five channels were used including Dealer, Direct Sales, Sahaviriya OA Centers, Value Added Resellers, and Mini OAs. Usage figures for these channels varied: from 34 percent for Dealer Channel to 32 percent for Direct Sales, 18 percent for Sahaviriya OA Centers, 14 percent for Value Added Resellers and 2 percent for Mini OAs.

1. Dealers. A total of about 300 dealers of which 34 were large ones, 31 were in Bangkok, and 3 were up-country.
2. Direct Sales. SVOA had about 80 sales staff members servicing large customers such as banks, governmental agencies, and petrochemical companies.
3. Sahaviriya OA Centers. These centers were operated as a franchise system. With a total of 40 centers as of March 31, 1993, there were 11 in Bangkok and 29 up-country. SVOA received 4 to 5 million baht per year on franchise fees. Using the same standard, OA centers were designed to be the "Best Buy OA Shop" with "One Price Policy." Before and after sales service were important attributes of the OA centers. SVOA monitored the quality of service of their centers by sending direct mail to customers soliciting their opinion.
4. Value Added Resellers (VARs). This setup allowed these retail stores to add Sahaviriya's authorized products to their own products. In 1994, there were 8 VARs, mostly in Bangkok, such as Shinawatra Computer Co, and Control Data Co Ltd.
5. Mini OAs. These centers were designed to provide services to home and personal users. The four centers are located in department stores and shopping centers.

To promote these centers, SVOA set up trade shows, field trips, and regional centers. These regional centers assisted SVOA's dealers and the OA centers in all aspects of sales and services, including the provision of education programs for all personnel.

SVOA has a very comprehensive customer database. It keeps performance information as well as detailed personal data on each individual customer. The ten largest SVOA's customers are shown in Exhibit 8. The group's major customers are in the finance/banking and dealer businesses. Their combined sales contributed 19 percent and 22 percent of SVOA's total sales in 1991 and 1992, respectively.

## The Scarecrow Leader

Theorizing the scarecrow as a metaphor for management, Mr Min wrote a philosophical book delineating his cumulative managerial experience.[8] He compared scarecrows with business administrators, whose duty was to safeguard the well-being of their organizations (Figure 3). Administrators should not boast about their vital role in the organization but should simply carry their work and work as hard as they could, just like the scarecrows. To be effective, these administrators have to be able to do their best in their different roles. These roles included being a teacher, a fortune-teller, an artist, a family person, an equalizer, a professional, a militant, and a sportsman. Blending these roles into one grand marshal required a flexible outlook on everything surrounding an administrator's domain.

A good manager had to be a "great" teacher, one who was able to inspire, encourage, follow up, and evaluate his or her subordinates fairly. According to Mr Min, a charismatic leader should be able to forgive and forget the mistakes made by his subordinates. Empathy would transform mistakes into valuable experience. Also, management should be able to bring about professionalism and create an arena for its people to achieve their potential to the fullest.

---

[8] *Scarecrow* is a book by Jack Min Chun Hu.

FIGURE 3

**Jack Min Chun Hu, SVOA's Scarecrow Leader**

Although the art of administration depended on the artistic talent of a particular individual, it is a "must do" in the scarecrow management philosophy. One of the major challenges facing administrators was to teach their subordinates the skills of recognizing, absorbing, and withholding details. To understand and reveal to others the true nature of work activities is also an art that helps to bridge the gap between leaders and their people.

In his book, Mr Min viewed the business organization as a large family, one that succinctly designated roles and duties to its subunits and members. With loosely defined roles and duties, the subunits would be flexible in dealing with a changing environment. Being part of the same happy family, the subunits would be able to unite into a strong clan. In order to create SVOA's family culture, one very challenging role of management was to maintain the balance between the happiness of its people and the demand for exemplary contributions from its people.

SVOA's employees viewed Mr Min as being a very effective leader. He was very demanding of his people and of himself. As one ex-employee said, "He was a true leader, especially in a time of crisis." She recalled the day she went to work at the old corporate headquarters. When she got there at 7:00 am, smoke from the fire at the old corporate headquarters still permeated the air. People began piling up at the site wondering what they should do. By 8:00 am, Mr Min distributed a flier telling his employees to keep their hopes up. By 10:00 am, he issued another flier telling them to meet at the new temporary headquarters (Chaopraya Tower) the next day. She later found out that Mr Min was in an emergency executive meeting and was working through the night when he was advised about news about the fire. He was working with his executive teams while the fire was burning away at the old headquarter building. His major concern at the time was his people and how to make sure that they would not feel lost in a time of crisis.

Aside from the motto — "there is always a way to make it better" — Mr Min stressed the importance of professional ethics and integrity. He communicated these views in various publications: from a philosophical book like the *Scarecrow* to a cartoon book like the *Rainbow*,[9] from corporate vision statements to employee newsletters, from annual reports to technology newsletters. SVOA prospered in the last decade under the guidance of Mr Min's leadership.

## Killing Instinct: The Best People

Since people who were committed to excellence constituted the core of SVOA's success, the group spent a great deal of effort in staffing and skill development. Each employee attended a variety of education programs, with all managers undertaking extensively technical and service-oriented training both in Thailand and abroad. The single theme running through the heart of all human resource training was "How to Best Serve SVOA's Customers."

Realizing the rapid growth in the number of SVOA's employees, Mr Min was instrumental in developing an employee handbook. Pictures and schematic diagrams were used to portray everything an employee needed to know as an SVOA employee and more. The employees handbook provided detailed information on processes such as applying for insurance benefits, requesting maternity leave, making a reservation for the firm's vacation houses, borrowing equipment, qualifying for educational funds, and so on. Exhibit 9 illustrates a few pages from the employee's handbook. Each employee would receive one of these copyrighted handbooks when he or she joined the Group. An employee was required to return the handbook when he or she left the organization. The handbook also outlines the rights and duties of employees, and the authority and responsibilities inhering in each management position.

A typical employee's handbook is usually written in formal language and is somewhat difficult to comprehend; SVOA's handbook was easy to understand. According to Mr Min, the book has served its purpose thus far. He also plans to apply this novel idea to other aspects of organizational procedures.

## All for One and One for All

"There is always a way to make it better." This was Mr Min's philosophy, which appeared to be shared by everyone in the corporation and it became SVOA's way of life. SVOA's success was not built upon a single individual or a small group of talented executives, but on teamwork. "How to best serve our customers" is also the motto hummed by every individual in the firm.

One shared commitment of SVOA under the guidance of the Sahaviriya Group was its dedication to bettering Thailand's social and economic welfare. SVOA participated in many social service projects such as a youth education project and an environmental preservation project entailing the application of hi-tech hardware and software. SVOA also

---

[9] *Rainbow* is a cartoon book that Jack Min Chun Hu wrote in order to communicate his managerial ideas to his people.

believed that technology belonged to everyone and not just the elite; thus, all company activities, such as exhibitions and seminars, have always been open to the public. Equipment and software packages are donated on a regular basis to public and private schools and universities.

## The Bright Future

Recognizing Thailand's continuing economic expansion, SVOA has already taken advantage of numerous opportunities for technology-oriented companies. It has sought to expand sales and manufacturing through internal expansion, joint international partnerships, and acquisitions of other companies. One major international joint venture is Sahaviriya AOKI (Thailand) Co Ltd, a factory investment between Thailand and Japan. The company manufactures rubber items (black rubber parts, silicone rubber). SVOA intends to expand this manufacturing facility into the manufacturing of computers, facsimile machines, and other office automation equipment.

The increasing number of competitors entering the market will increase the importance of customer services multifold for SVOA. Sahaviriya Centers will be established to take care of the after-sales service, installation, repair, and maintenance of the equipment. These centers will maintain spare parts and product information that will be distributed to the customers. The centers will provide services in all regions of Thailand.

"Win! Win! Win!" was the strategy Mr Min visualized for SVOA. As Mr Min put it, one of SVOA's major goals was to first "win" over its customers. Thus, SVOA would do whatever it could to help its customers to "win". SVOA wanted its customers to be the "first winners". SVOA would be the "second winner" and Thailand's economy as a whole would be the "third winner".[10]

Besides his vision of total customer satisfaction and success, Mr Min saw the rapid, continuing development of information technology as the greatest opportunity for SVOA. Educament, a combination of education and entertainment, would also provide abundant opportunities for SVOA to gain a big piece of public and personal home markets.[11] Systems Integrator and its value-added services would become important to SVOA's Number 2 winning streak. By being ready to customize these services to its customers, SVOA would also be ready to capitalize on the increasingly popular activity of outsourcing the information technology of business organizations.

SVOA plans to turn misfortune into new opportunities. Costing 1,066 million baht, the new 34-storey Intelligent Building (see Figure 4) will house the Group's new corporate headquarters. The new building was designed to have all the latest technology in office management, providing network connections between offices within and outside the country. It will use the integration of three major technologies: Building Automation, Office Automation, and Telecommunication. Building automation and management comprises the Centralized Fireguard System which interlocks with the Other System, Emergency Information/Refuge Guidance System; Building Entry/Exit Control System which interlocks with the Centralized Security System; and the Energy Saving System. Office automation will consist of the Voice Mail System, Electronic Mail System, Videotex System, Shared

[10]Excerpt from Jack Min Chun Hu's presentation at the Management 2000 Conference on July 28, 1993.
[11]Excerpt from Jack Min Chun Hu's presentation at the Management 2000 Conference on July 28, 1993.

Database, and Data Processing Facilities. Advanced communication features include Digital EPABX with ISDN Interface, Teleconference and Video Conference System, TV Phone, Wireless Telephone System, and Gateway to Outside-Building and Worldwide Telecommunications. The building will be ready for operation in August 1995. When completed, office space in the new building could be sold for about 40,000 to 45,000 baht per square meter or rented for about 450 baht per square meter. SVOA has estimated the net return on the building investment to be 33 million baht in 1996, 33 million in 1997, 45 million in 1998, and a 10-percent increase per year thereafter.[12]

Mr Min's down to earth philosophy has guided his plans to make SVOA a "global" company with a "local" touch. He believes in using local people to do the work, whether it be an expansion of operations to different parts of the up-country of Thailand or to Indochina and other regions of the world (Exhibit 10 shows the planned network of business operations). He estimated 100 percent plus growth in terminal products such as calculators, mobile phones, and notebook computers for the northern and northeastern regions of Thailand. Mr Min foresees all possible forms of business integration and joint ventures to be established with SVOA in the next decade.

Since Thailand is the ideal gateway to the economic opportunities of Indochina, Sahaviriya is ready to provide its technological expertise and full range of products to this region. With Seiko Epson Corporation of Japan, Epson Electronics (Thailand) Co was established to develop information technology specifically for business and governments

FIGURE 4

**The Artist's Concept of the New Intelligent Building**

[12]SVOA Prospectus on June 30, 1993

in Indochina. In Vietnam, this partnership led to the formation of Viettronimex Company, which distributed Epson products in Indochina. SV Acer, a joint venture with Acer of Taiwan, was formed in July 1993 specifically to handle the distribution of products in Indochina. SVOA holds a 51-percent stake in this joint venture, its fourteenth subsidiary.

Besides using joint ventures as a means for SVOA to expand internationally, SVOA plans to establish its own successful network of distribution channels on a regional and global basis. Sites in Singapore, Malaysia, and Indonesia are currently being studied as SVOA looks to the future.

EXHIBIT 1

**List of Companies**

## Steel Business

**Bangsaphan Steel Complex**

1. Sahaviriya Steel Industries Co, Ltd
2. Thai Cold Rolled Steel Sheets Co, Ltd
3. Thai Coated Steel Sheets Co, Ltd
4. Prachuap Port Corp, Ltd

**Bangpakong Steel Complex**

1. Sahaviriya Plate Mill Co, Ltd
2. Sahaviriya Wire Rod Co, Ltd
3. Sahaviriya Shape Steel Co, Ltd
4. Sahaviriya Bright Bar Co, Ltd
5. Sahaviriya Steel Service Co, Ltd

**Prapradaeng Steel Complex**

1. Sahaviriya Metal Industries Co, Ltd
2. Sahaviriya Steel Works Co, Ltd
3. Sahaviriya Steel Bar Co, Ltd
4. Sahaviriya Light Gauge Steel Co, Ltd
5. Sahaviriya Steel Products Co, Ltd
6. Sahaviriya Steel Center Co, Ltd

**Steel Trading**

1. Sahaviriya Panich Co, Ltd
2. Sahaviriya Transportation Co, Ltd
3. Siam Nana Transportation Co, Ltd
4. Sahaviriya Nittan Co, Ltd
5. Tec-Sahaviriya Co, Ltd

## Finance

1. CL Sahaviriya Finance and Securities Co, Ltd
2. Sahaviriya Credit Foncier Co, Ltd

## Real Estate

1. Sahaviriya City Co, Ltd
2. Prapawit Co, Ltd
3. Western Housing Co, Ltd

## Technology Business

1. Sahaviriya OA Co, Ltd
2. Sahaviriya Infortech Computer Co, Ltd
3. Sahaviriya Systems Co, Ltd
4. Sahaviriya Data Systems Co, Ltd
5. Sahaviriya Advance Products Co, Ltd
6. Sahaviriya Telecom Co, Ltd
7. Sahaviriya Communications Co, Ltd
8. Sahaviriya Comservice Co, Ltd
9. Sahaviriya Aoki (Thailand) Co, Ltd
10. SV Acer Co, Ltd
11. Epson Electronics Co, Ltd
12. Spectrum House Co, Ltd
13. Thai Soft Co, Ltd
14. Automatic Networks Service Co, Ltd
15. Thanawat Information Systems Co, Ltd
16. Institute of Thai Information Technology

## International Business

1. Linkful International Holdings Limited
2. Metalsrussia Corp, Ltd

EXHIBIT 2

## Sahaviriya OA Group of Companies

| | *Year Estab-lished* | *Capital as of 3/31/93 (million baht)* | *Type of Business* |
|---|---|---|---|
| 1. Sahaviriya OA Co, Ltd | 1982 | 184.0 | Distributor of microcomputers and equipment, EPSON and ACER. |
| 2. Sahaviriya Infortech Computer Co, Ltd | 1982 | 20.0 | Joint venture with Infortech (Japan) Inc. (93:7). Distributor and dealer of minicomputers, TANDEM and DEC, workstation and associated software. |
| 3. Sahaviriya Telecom Co, Ltd | 1985 | 20.0 | Distributor and dealer of telecommunication equipment, mobile phone, FAX, switching boxes: OKI and SAHAVIRIYA. |
| 4. Sahaviriya Systems Co, Ltd | 1986 | 20.0 | Distributor of microcomputer and equipment: APPLE. |
| 5. Sahaviriya Advance Products Co, Ltd | 1987 | 2.5 | Distributor and dealer of cash registers, CASIO; hand-held computers, IBS, and MSI. |
| 6. Tanawat Information Systems Co, Ltd | 1988 | 5.0 | Distributor of microcomputers and equipment: HEWLETT PACKARD. |
| 7. SV Comservice Co, Ltd | 1988 | 2.0 | Document processing services: Microfiche. |
| 8. Spectrum House Co, Ltd | 1989 | 1.0 | Sahaviriya OA Center, model store. Dealer and distributor of SVOA's products. |
| 9. SV Data Systems Co, Ltd | 1990 | 10.0 | Distributor of mainframe computer and equipment: HITACHI DATA SYSTEM. |
| 10. Epson Electronics (Thailand) Co, Ltd | 1990 | 10.0 | Joint venture with SEIKO EPSON (Japan) Co Ltd (51:49) Distributor and dealers of microcomputer equipment, EPSON, to Indochina market. |
| 11. Thaisoft Co, Ltd | 1990 | 5.0 | Developer of Thai language software and distributor of well known software packages: GENEUS, LOTUS, DBASE, and Novell's NETWARE |
| 12. Institute of Thai | 1990 | 5.0 | Joint venture with Advance Research (60:40). Provides training to customers and public. |
| 13. SV Communication Co, Ltd | 1991 | 12.5 | Distributor and System Integrator of Intelligent Building Products: TC-Technology, AMP. |
| 14. SV AOKI (Thailand) Co, Ltd | 1992 | 41.0 | Joint venture with Saviriya Telecom and C.ITOH and AOKI RUBBER (Japan) (55:45), equipment manufacture using rubber for interior of cars and for electronics. |
| 15. SV-ACER Co, Ltd | 1993 | 20.0 | Joint venture between Sahaviriya OA and Acer Computer International. Distributor of Acex products in Indochina market. |
| 16. SV-EDS Technology Services Ltd | 1994 | 50.0 | Information technology services: consulting, systems development, systems integration, systems management and process management. |

## EXHIBIT 3

### Group's Products and Services

| *Group* | *Number of Employees* | *Products and Services, or Activities* |
|---|---|---|
| The SSCB Group | 152 | ACER computers<br>EPSON computers and printers<br>Roland Plotters<br>Quantum Hard Disk<br>Summagraphic Digitizers<br>Verbatim Diskette<br>American Power Conversion (UPS)<br>Sahaviriya OA Center Channel |
| The SSVB Group | 95 | Desktop Publishing<br>Desktop Presentation<br>design, pagination and printing services to leading newspapers and magazines<br>POS management<br>Management of financial systems for chain retailers and department stores |
| The SSB Group | 205 | Find effective solutions through a computer managed filing/ retrieval system.<br>Perform systems analysis, design and implementation services.<br>Specialized training. |
| The SIB Group | 83 | Mini-mainframe computers<br>Hitachi Data Systems Mainframe Computers<br>Tandem OLTP Computers<br>UNIX Systems and Workstations<br>Develop "turn-key" systems for use in banking and financial sectors, manufacturing and energy sectors and telecommunications and government Sectors. |
| The TB Group | 108 | Provide telecommunication terminal equipment such as facsimile, mobile telephone, key telephone and microwave telecommunication equipment.<br>OEM<br>Voice/Data Private Communication Network through dealers<br>Mini OA Channel |
| Office of Executive Group | 86 | Coordinate all groups. Consists of 7 departments including personnel, advertising & public relations, new business, marketing research & information, customer relations, local purchasing, and legal & internal audit. |
| Financial and Administration Group | 157 | Control and support functions in areas of OEM (Original Equipment Manufacturing). Consists of four subunits consisting of logistics, finance, accounting, and MIS. |

EXHIBIT 4

**SVOA's Shareholders' Structure**

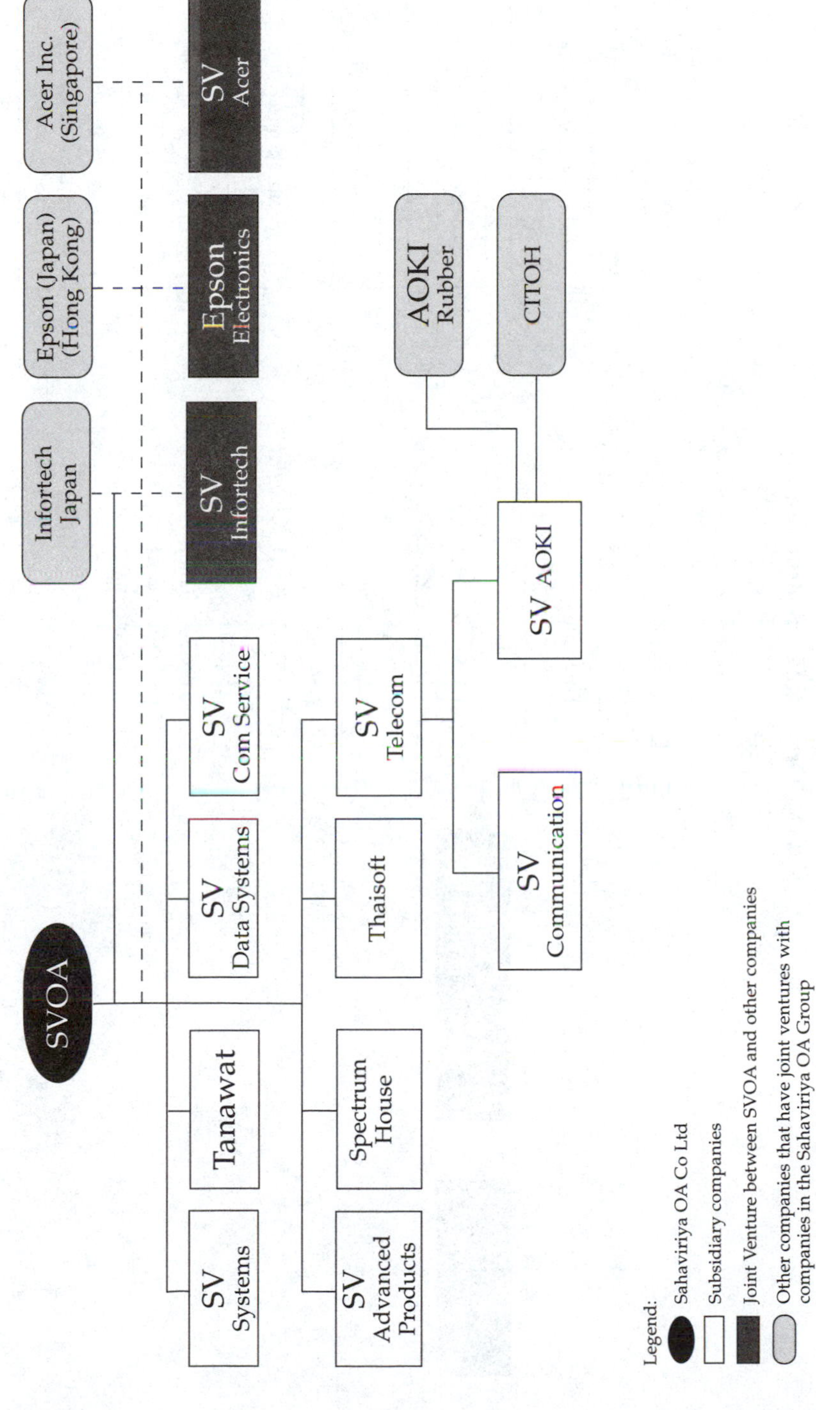

EXHIBIT 5

**SVOA's Organizational Structure**

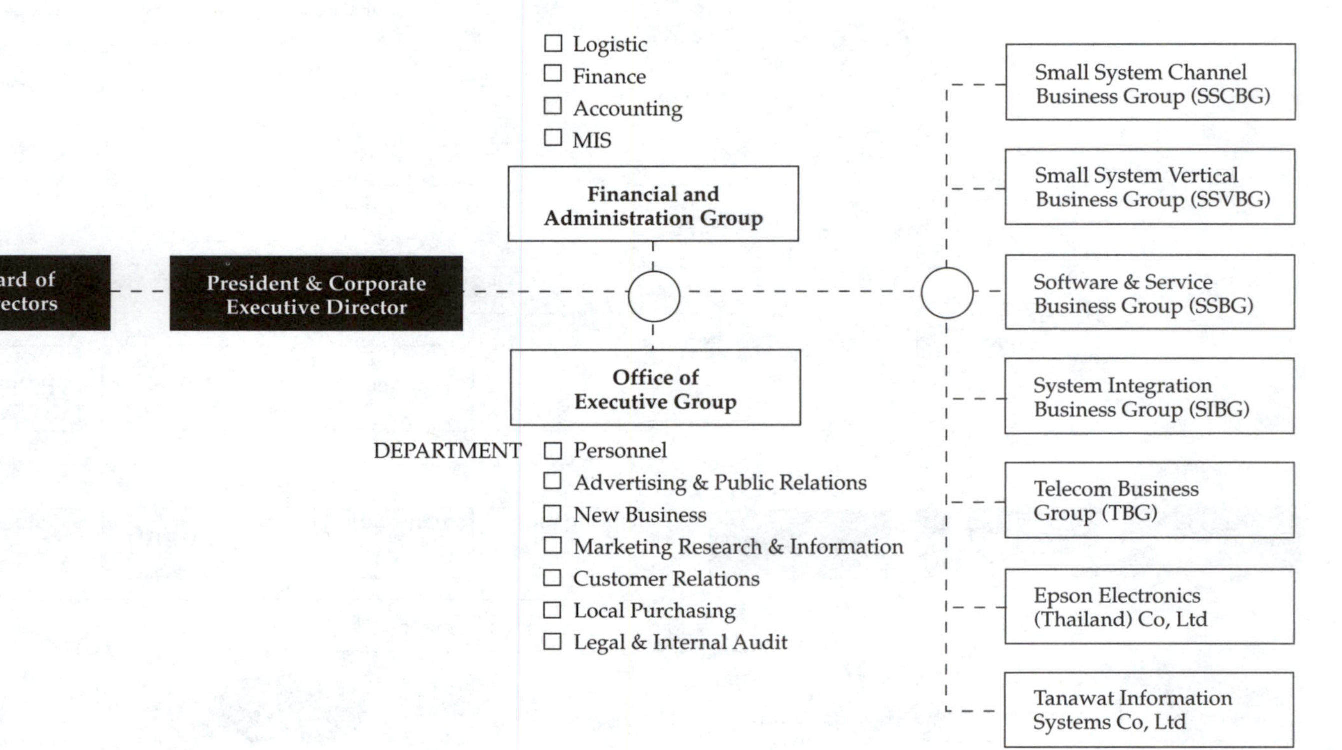

EXHIBIT 6

## Condensed Income Statements
## Years Ended December 31, 1989–1993

(Thai Baht in thousands, except per share)

| *Item* | *1989* | *1990* | *1991* | *1992* | *1992 Consolidated* | *1993 Consolidated* |
|---|---|---|---|---|---|---|
| Net sales | 339,835 | 438,270 | 490,417 | 1,139,848 | 2,336,586 | 3,094,526 |
| Cost of goods and service selling | 279,016 | 336,607 | 379,022 | 855,795 | 1,667,756 | 2,292,243 |
| Administrative and general expenses; interest and other expenses | 63,372 | 87,626 | 107,448 | 214,318 | 567,666 | 689,465 |
| Operating profit | (2,553) | 14,037 | 3,947 | 69,735 | 101,164 | 112,818 |
| Other income | 2,910 | 4,518 | 9,411 | 14,596 | 35,385 | 74,013 |
| Earnings before taxes | 357 | 18,555 | 13,358 | 84,331 | 136,549 | 186,831 |
| Income tax | 156 | 6,533 | 4,770 | 26,506 | 51,638 | 63,270 |
| Net income after tax and before extraordinary items | 201 | 12,022 | 8,588 | 57,825 | 84,911 | 123,561 |
| Extraordinary item | – | – | – | – | – | (19,618) |
| Net income after extraordinary items but before minority interest | 201 | 12,022 | 8,588 | 57,825 | 84,911 | 103,943 |
| Minority interest | – | – | – | – | 3,566 | (3,734) |
| **Net Income** | **201** | **12,022** | **8,588** | **57,825** | **88,477** | **100,209** |
| Net earnings per share | 0.18 | 6.01 | 4.29 | 4.63 | 7.09 | 4.83 |

EXHIBIT 7

## Condensed Balance Sheets
## Years Ended December 31, 1989–1993

(Thai Baht in thousands, except per share)

| *Assets* | *1989* | *1990* | *1991* | *1992* | *1992 Consolidated* | *1993 Consolidated* |
|---|---|---|---|---|---|---|
| Current assets | 252,076 | 318,182 | 269,233 | 675,573 | 1,449,747 | 1,987,115 |
| Fixed assets | 7,889 | 8,187 | 30,226 | 65,901 | 202,650 | 220,300 |
| Investments | – | – | – | 87,646 | 1,100 | 2,100 |
| Other assets | 1,347 | 5,044 | 3,463 | 47,824 | 84,185 | 382,333 |
| Total assets | **261,312** | **331,413** | **302,922** | **876,944** | **1,737,682** | **2,591,848** |
| Liabilities and equity | | | | | | |
| Current liabilities | 217,599 | 263,210 | 226,136 | 632,997 | 1,430,977 | 1,752,209 |
| Loan from Director | – | 12,670 | 12,665 | – | 8,245 | 7,157 |
| Other liabilities | – | – | – | – | 4,386 | 2,240 |
| Total liabilities | 217,599 | 275,880 | 238,801 | 632,997 | 1,443,608 | 1,761,607 |
| Minority interest | – | – | – | – | 19,476 | 25,660 |
| Issued share capital | 20,000 | 20,000 | 20,000 | 184,000 | 184,000 | 240,000 |
| Premium on share | – | – | – | – | – | 412,200 |
| Retained earnings | 23,213 | 35,033 | 43,621 | – | – | – |
| Legal reserve | 500 | 500 | 500 | 2,000 | 2,000 | 5,826 |
| Unappropriated retained earnings | – | – | – | 57,947 | 88,598 | 146,555 |
| Total shareholders' equity | 43,713 | 55,533 | 64,121 | 243,947 | 294,074 | 804,581 |
| Total Liabilities and shareholders' equity | **261,312** | **331,413** | **302,922** | **876,944** | **1,737,682** | **2,591,848** |

EXHIBIT 8

**SVOA's Largest Customers**

| | *Customer* | *Type of Business* | *Sales in 1991 (million baht)* | % | *Sales in 1992 (million baht)* | % |
|---|---|---|---|---|---|---|
| 1. | Bangkok Bank | Finance/Bank | 92 | 5 | 86 | 4 |
| 2. | Microhouse Co, Ltd | Dealer | 80 | 4 | 120 | 5 |
| 3. | SPV Co, Ltd | Dealer | 51 | 3 | 61 | 3 |
| 4. | Krungthai Hitech Co, Ltd | Dealer | 46 | 2 | 33 | 1 |
| 5. | Thai Farmer Bank | Finance/Bank | 42 | 2 | 21 | 1 |
| 6. | Thai Military Bank | Finance/Bank | 35 | 2 | 11 | – |
| 7. | Phonex Co, Ltd | Dealer | 34 | 2 | 67 | 3 |
| 8. | STS Supercom Co, Ltd | Sahaviriya OA | 30 | 2 | 38 | 2 |
| 9. | SVP Import & Export Co, Ltd | Dealer | 29 | 1 | 65 | 3 |
| 10. | GF Fuinance & Security Co, Ltd | Finance/Bank | 29 | 1 | 8 | – |
| | Total | | 468 | 24 | 510 | 22 |

## EXHIBIT 9

## Sample Pages from SVOA's Employee Handbook

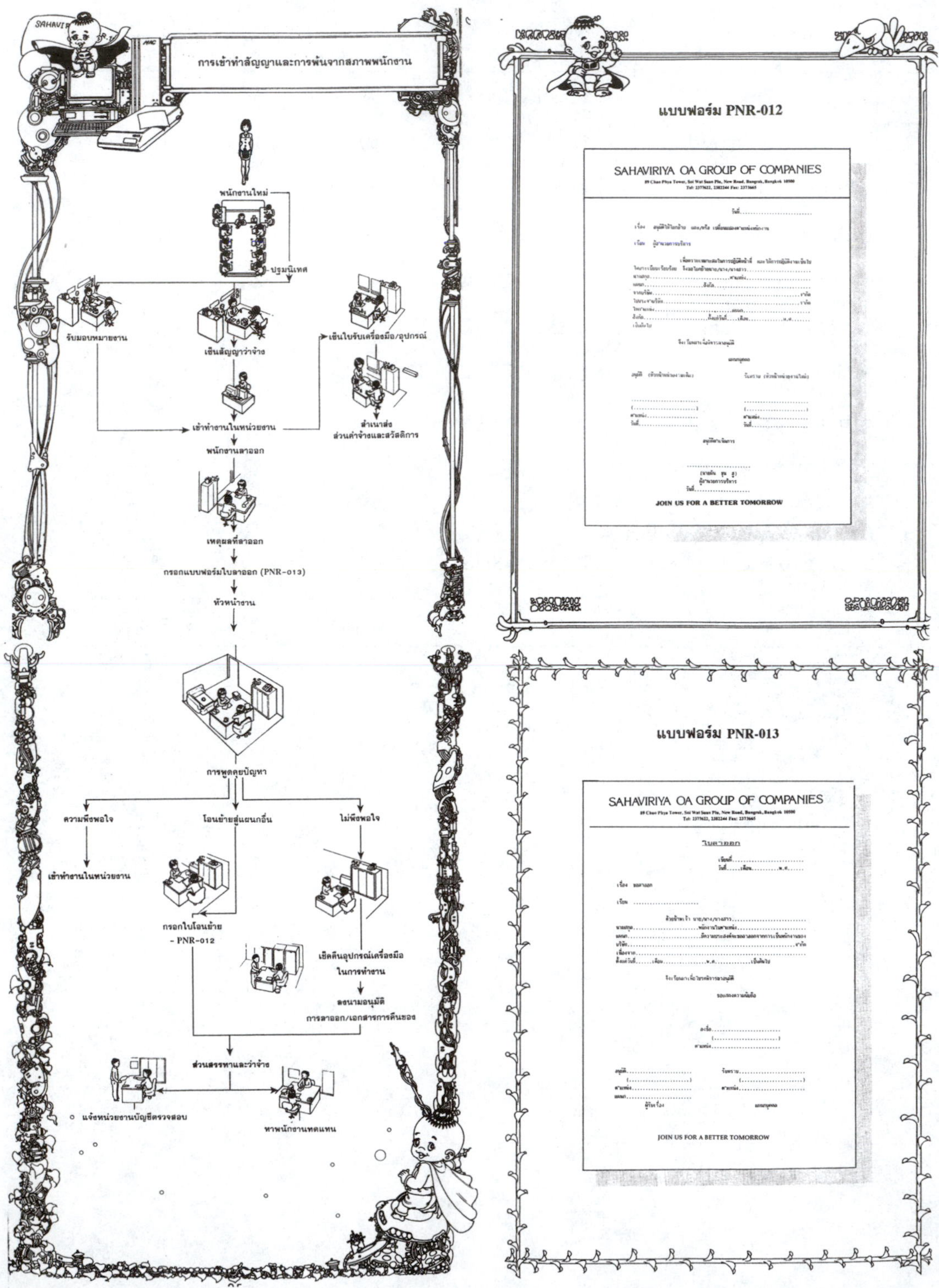

EXHIBIT 10

**Planned Networks of Business Expansion**

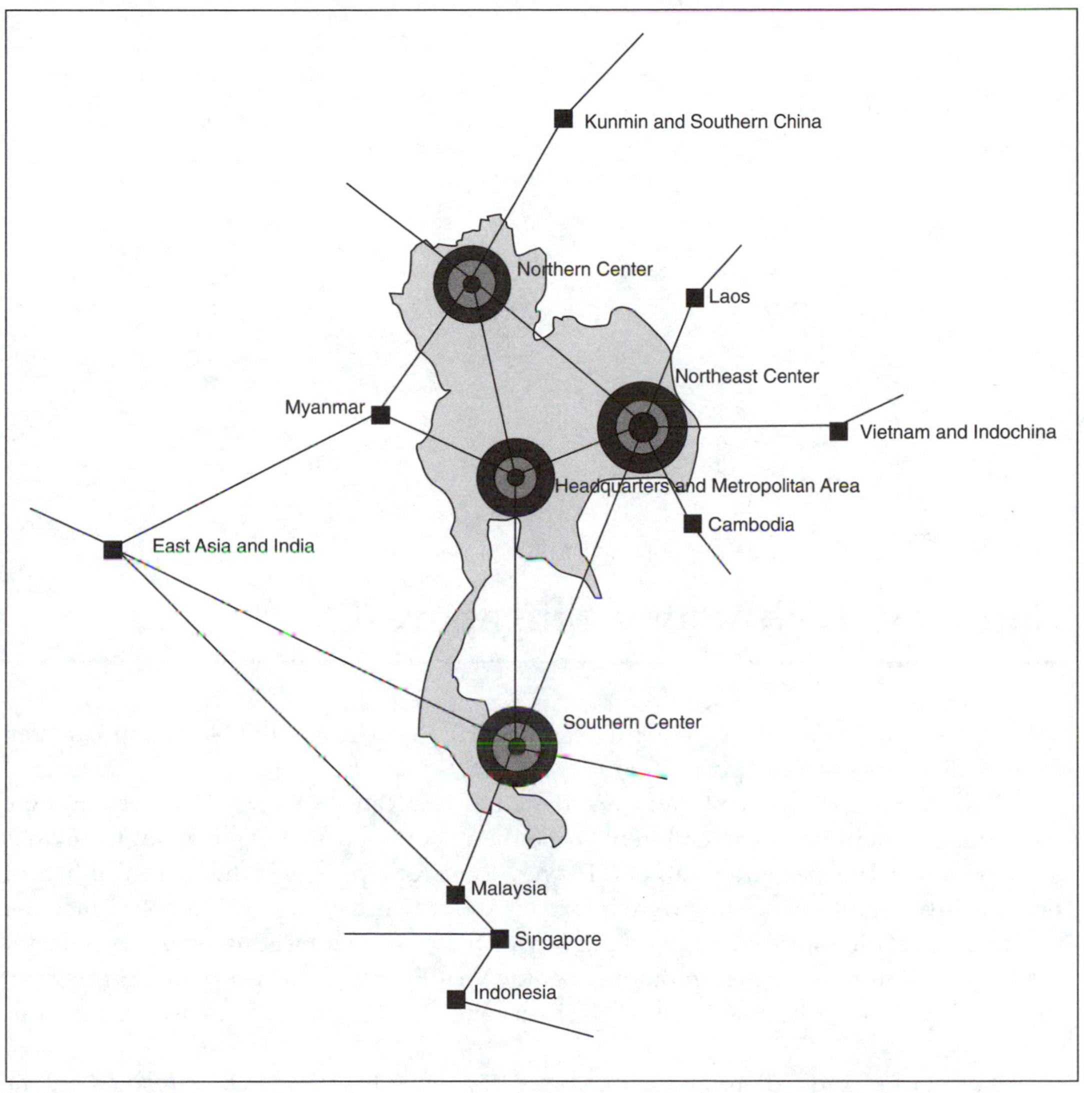

# Gateway Technology Singapore* 14

Setting: 9:00 pm; December 31, 1993; 10 Nassim Hill; Residence of the Managing Director, Gateway Technology Singapore (GTS).

Many of the management staff were invited to Don Tan's New Year's Eve celebration. They brought their wives and children. While their spouses were talking about the events of the past year, the managing staff of GTS were there for a purpose other than waiting for the New Year countdown. They were informed about two days ago that a board meeting had been scheduled for the first working day of the year. The meeting would be chaired by George Clinton, the newly promoted Senior Vice President for Corporate Strategy of Gateway Technology International (GTI). Everyone was feeling apprehensive about this board meeting.

Tan started the ball rolling by commenting on why they were informed of the meeting only two days ago. He said: "This is typical of headquarters's behavior — never letting us know until the last minute and never giving us a choice. Heck, a board meeting on the first day of the year? And what for?"

Don Tan has been the Managing Director (MD) of GTI's operations in Singapore for the last six months. He started with GTI as the Vice President for Sales and Marketing.

---

*This case was prepared by Chiam Fong Sin, Loh Yuh Por, Wendy Loo Siu Ho, Law Lay Geok, and Wong Wee Kim (MBA, Nanyang Technological University, Singapore) under the supervision of Professor Luis Ma. R. Calingo. At the request of the company, financial data and the names of organizations, people and some places have been disguised, but essential relationships have been preserved. The case is designed to serve as a basis for class discussion rather than to illustrate either effective or ineffective handling of an administrative situation.

Among his accomplishments were a 45-percent increase in sales volume for the 3.5-inch RDD (rigid disk drive) disk. His sales record made him rise up GTS' corporate ladder very fast. His previous experience in production operations had made him both technically and personally competent as MD. He was well-liked and respected.

Mary Steiner surprisingly vented her frustration by saying, "Hey, I am supposed to be on vacation because it is my son's first day at school. Where does that leave me?" Mary has been with GTS for the last 7 years. As one of the pioneers of GTS, she even knew GTI's Chief Executive Officer personally.

Messrs Heng Poh San (VP, Sales and Marketing), Chow Seng Mong (VP, Operations) and Alan de la Cruz (VP, Personnel) all nodded in agreement. Of key concern in everyone's mind was the purpose of the board meeting and its implications in terms of new work activities.

Heng went on to say: "Hey, Don, is something going to happen? I heard from the KL (Kuala Lumpur, Malaysia) guys that some restructuring is occurring on the U.S. side. Will we see another 1987 when GTI retrenches some workers? The experience was a painful one as it cut across levels and divisions. I was lucky the first time, but do I have to go through that again?"

Chow totally agreed with Heng and remembered the sleepless nights he had in 1987. He silently regretted his decision and wondered if he should have taken up that headhunter's offer two months ago.

De la Cruz was quietly telling himself that he would have to be personally and deeply involved if indeed there would be a reorganization.

As the others continued to complain, Steiner, the oldest serving employee, sat at a corner and began to reflect on GTS' history.

## Gateway Technology International

### Historical Background

Managing the boom-to-bust business of making personal computers (PCs) was hard enough. But it was a cinch compared with trying to earn a living from supplying hard-bargaining computer manufacturers with components — especially such tricky devices as hard disk drives, the spinning magnetic disks that store megabytes of data inside computers.

With PC prices down by almost half from 1991 to 1993, profit margins of hard disk drive manufacturers have also been squeezed. Of the 100 or more firms that were in the business over the last decade, fewer than a dozen remained. Fewer still were profitable.

One of them was Gateway Technology International (GTI), founded in 1979 and based in San Joaquin Valley, California. From July to September 1993, GTI reported a net profit of US$48 million on sales of US$1.04 billion in an environment of intense competition and pricing pressure (see Exhibits 1 and 2 for GTI's financial performance from 1991 to 1993). Its main competitors, Conner, Micropolis, Maxtor, Quantum, and Western Digital all reported losses during the same period. Conner, once the high flyer of the hard disk flock, plunged to a loss of US$372 million. GTI's top management believed that, clearly, GTI had been doing something better than its competitors.

Making hard drives is one of the most exacting jobs in the computer industry. The magnetic disks inside a drive would spin at 5,000 revolutions per minute and have surfaces machined to a tolerance of 0.001 millimeter. The slightest irregularity would cause the head to crash into the disk, splattering data everywhere.

In the rigid disk drive (RDD) industry, GTI had been ranked second after IBM Corporation in technological advancement. Only IBM could offer comparable products; however, being a large PC manufacturer itself, it had trouble persuading rival computer companies to buy its wares. IBM's recent decision of not spinning off its RDD business was indeed a piece of good news for GTI. In recent months, GTI introduced a new range of hard drives that had left its rivals scrambling to catch up. Micropolis, Hewlett Packard, and Fujitsu had a chance of coming close, although not for some time.

GTI was founded in 1979 by Bob Smith. Like many in the industry, Smith cut his technological teeth on hard drives during the early days of their development at IBM. Notwithstanding this background, it was not technology that allowed GTI to become one of the 200 largest industrial companies in the United States. Indeed, in the 1980s, the company was better known for hard selling than for innovative products.

This image started to change in 1989 when GTI bought Prism Technology, a maker of high-performance hard drives. GTI had bought companies for their know-how before. But Prism, with its high-quality manufacturing methods and skill at making the thin film heads that read and write data on the disk, brought a new level of engineering to the mass marketer. This led GTI to rethink its whole way of doing business.

Two trends could have spelled disaster for GTI had it not been for its new corporate way of thinking. The plunging prices of PCs was turning GTI's leading customers into ruthless cost-cutters; suppliers like GTI were the first to suffer.

The other trend was fast growth in the storage capacity of hard drives. In just slightly over a decade, the average drive's size had shrunk by two-thirds, while the amount of data it could store had grown a thousandfold. This annual doubling of capacity was punishing even for the giants like IBM, Fujitsu, and Hitachi. For small hard drive manufacturers without their own technology base, it was often fatal. Faced with dwindling margins, American companies at the time were being advised by management gurus to cut costs by "outsourcing" their manufacturing to subcontractors in Southeast Asia. However, as Quantum (which started manufacturing all its drives in Japan) had learned, outsourcing cuts costs by three percent at best.

The real answer, GTI concluded, was to own an expanding body of know-how and then raise the technological stakes. In so doing, it could set the standards for performance, reliability, and price. This meant deciding what the company should be doing in a decade's time and working out how to get there.

GTI realized that, although it must remain the master of a core set of skills, it would also have to learn how to apply them to more products. As the challenges of a changing global economy and constantly evolving industry continue, GTI positioned itself to engage the new opportunities presented by these challenges through a broadened corporate vision as a "data technology company." GTI aimed to meet the growing needs of not only the data storage markets, but also the increasing demands for the components, software, and technology related to the communication and management of data. As modernization continued to broaden the forms of data, GTI had to cease being simply a manufacturer of hard drives and had to learn to become a supplier of products for handling text, graphics, audio, and video. GTI planned to offer everything from mass storage devices to the software for managing databases and networks. The target was to double sales from US$4 billion in 1993 to US$8 billion by 2000.

GTI attributed much of its success under the current market adversities to the soundness of its business strategy and exceptional strength in numerous core technical competencies. GTI spent two years remaking itself in its new mold, explaining its mission in staff meetings around the world.

### Corporate Mission and Business Philosophy

Gateway Technology International is a leading independent designer, manufacturer, and marketer of data storage products for the computer systems industry. GTI offered the broadest spectrum of innovative data storage products in the industry, and its main line of products was the rigid magnetic disk drive. The company pursued data storage opportunities in virtually all market segments, including pen-based systems, notebooks, laptop, and portable computers; personal computers and technical workstations; mainframes and supercomputers. The company sold its products to original equipment manufacturers (OEMs) for inclusion in their computer systems or subsystems; to systems integrators; and to distributors, including industrial distributors, resellers, and dealers. GTI also pursued a strategy of vertical integration and manufactures disk drive components such as heads, disk, substrates, printed circuit boards, motors, and custom semiconductors.

Since 1979, GTI had shipped more than 44 million disk drives. With total revenue of US$4.08 billion in 1993, GTI was ranked among America's 200 largest industrial corporations. In 1993, GTI employed more than 40,000 professional, technical, administrative, and manufacturing personnel in 17 countries.

GTI had always believed in viewing itself as a "portfolio of core technologies and capabilities," rather than simply a portfolio of products. GTI's vision as a data technology company involved harnessing the company's core technologies to create innovative products that could inspire evolutionary change in the industry.

In a recent speech, CEO Bob Smith affirmed GTI management's strong commitment to providing opportunities for employees to develop their creative and entrepreneurial drive. Its employees' commitment to innovate had placed GTI in a position of strength to develop many new products. He also said, "GTI believes in working together, managing today's business and planning for tomorrow's opportunities."

Smith had been known to be a good manager in terms of people management and getting the best out of a person's potential. But he had been known to only hang on to the best and to "put to cold storage" some of the less productive employees. On the other hand, he rewarded good performance handsomely.

## GTI's Strategies

### Marketing Strategy

GTI believed that economic results were accomplished through long-term relationships between sellers and buyers; doing business was no longer a matter of simply getting and then holding on to customers. It was a matter of giving the customers what they want, when they want it. GTI practiced this belief by providing its customers with maximum after-sales satisfaction through toll-free telephone support, electronic bulletin boards, fax services, warranty programs, and rapid service and distribution operations conveniently located around the world. It also actively participated in customer-design-cycles in order to know customers' needs in advance so as to design and manufacture products to exact specifications.

### Research and Development Strategy

Through cooperative research programs like Stanford University's Integrated Manufacturing Association, GTI collaborated with educational institutions to discover, develop, and put to practice its capabilities in order to achieve excellence in science, technology, and manufacturing.

**Actuators.** Early GTI products used only stepping motors for head positioning. These motors supported track densities of up to 255 tracks per inch and were relatively slow. These stepping motors had since been replaced with motors that were not only significantly faster but also supported track densities over 1,000 tracks per inch and were much less costly. Voice coil positioning was being used in many GTI products in both linear and rotary forms to obtain higher track densities and faster access times.

**Electronics.** The desire to cope with smaller drive sizes and to include more functions in the drive has led GTI to design custom integrated circuits.

**Heads.** From 1979 to 1989, the recording densities of GTI products rose from 3 million bits per square inch to nearly 30 million. This was made possible when GTI learned to construct magnetic heads with different materials, smaller dimensions, and better process control. Improvement in the mechanical characteristics of both the recording head and the suspension system permitted heads to fly closer to the surface of equally improved disks.

**Disks.** When small hard disk drives were first shipped by GTI in the 1980s, the magnetic layer on the disks was obtained by spraying an emulsion of gamma ferric oxide onto the aluminum substrate. Since then, thin film disk technology has enabled GTI's drives to support significantly higher recording densities than the earlier oxide-coated disks.

**Spindle motors.** GTI recognized that improving the accuracy of spindle motors was fundamental to increasing track densities in new product designs. Accordingly, GTI maintained a substantial motor research, development, and pilot production effort in Watsonville, California.

GTI's product cycle from concept, research phase, design, testing, and into manufacturing have been the foundation of the company's success. GTI attributed that success to a process that did not rely on the vision of just one or two people. The company's design team leveraged knowledge and technologies from the company's four disk drive development centers in the U.S., namely Fresno (Calif), St Paul (Minn), Oklahoma City (Okla), and Santa Monica (Calif); magnetic recording head and media operations; and semiconductors and motors development operations. Product development expenditures in 1993 increased by US$28 million a 16 percent rise over 1992's expenditures.

### Restructuring Operations

To enhance its competitive position, GTI continued to introduce changes into its operations. The recent consolidation of its high-volume, low-capacity drive repair in the Far East had resulted in reducing its workforce in both Scotland and Del Rey Beach, Florida. GTI continued to look for cost reduction opportunities as a response to the ongoing price erosion.

In Thailand, GTI's plant was involved in the manufacture of subassemblies such as spindle motors, in-head stack and head gimbal. It began operations in 1987 and by 1993, was also producing very mature and high-yield 5.25-inch and 3.5-inch RDDs. GTI found the Thailand plant to be very attractive for its inexpensive and abundant labor.

## Key Success Factors

### Quality

Speaking of product quality, Smith emphasized:

> There is one area where there is no compromise, calling for not only extra effort, but for continuous improvement; and that area is *quality*. Everyone has a role to play in customer satisfaction. Quality, continuous improvement, and total customer satisfaction require all of us to have a passion to be the best and feel that being second is not good enough.

Doing business in the disk drive industry had changed over a span of only two years — the approach used in 1993 was different from that used in 1991. GTI recognized the evolutionary changes necessary to survive in this competitive industry. The shift in philosophy, particularly in the areas of quality and customer service at GTI went beyond what the employees had seen internally. The shift had also been observed by many of GTI's customers. GTI was no longer regarded as the high-volume, low-end, low-price manufacturer. It was a company on the cutting edge of technology, offering a wide variety of quality products for virtually every computing environment. Many of GTI's strategic customers began referring to GTI as the "new GTI."

FNC Corporation, one of GTI's customers, was dedicated to quality, and GTI's management teams assured the company of exactly that. Carl Thomsen, the Group Manager of Supplier Engineering for FNC, recalled:

> Two years ago, GTI could not compete in FNC's market because of quality and response issues. Looking at GTI's improvements in those areas, it's almost unbelievable. GTI has taken large steps in its ability to provide high quality products, support our needs, and meet our time-to-market window.

Higher quality was not the only positive modification Thomsen has experienced from GTI. Feedback from his customers also indicated an improvement in GTI's customer service and engineering as well. Joe Johnson from Advanced Microsystems had this to say:

> By fully understanding customers' requirements, I believe GTI has successfully identified what is necessary to become a world class supplier. At Advanced Microsystems, we are always exploring new ways to improve our products and business strategies. GTI's dedicated team has given us that opportunity by adapting to our needs and focusing on our long-term goals. In terms of its commitment to helping Advanced Microsystems meet market demands, GTI is leading our supplier base.

Johnson had witnessed the restructuring of GTI's upper management in 1991 and observed a transformation in the way GTI approached its customers and delivered quality products. With time-to-market windows shrinking and qualification processes drawing from valuable resources, Sun looked to suppliers who could provide time-to-volume, quality products. Johnson believes this to be one of GTI's strengths.

GTI's proficiency in "reinventing the relationship" seems to be reaping success. It stems from GTI's capacity to draw on the depth of its resources to successfully leverage product platforms, and to open communication to adapt to changing requirements. With this new long-term strategic relationship, GTI and its customers are prepared for any new challenges, focusing on making the right things happen at the right time.

Monica Richmond, GTI's Vice President for Strategic Accounts, who was responsible for developing and maintaining the crucial relationships between GTI and its strategic OEM customers, had this to add:

> Doing business with OEMs is much different today. The product is ultimately what causes the OEM to make the phone call to GTI. The single most compelling factor that really got us into some key OEM accounts was quality and the design of the products has kept us there. Determining the optimum product solution for our customers is truly a process, rather than just an event. We get into finding the solution, and this is where the real selling takes place. The customer is mainly concerned with tradeoffs, whether it be performance, cost, or schedule timing. It's a matter of determining what is truly important to the customer. Our methodology is to spend a great deal of time analyzing and identifying a customer's need. We then jointly determine solutions. That's primarily how we sell into an account. We approach this type of methodology knowing that we're establishing a long-term relationship. I believe we must always continue to get closer to our customers. The creative synergy of jointly developing GTI's products alongside our OEMs would truly be a large step.

GTI has a tremendous advantage in that it offers a balanced product line comprising reliable entry-level and high-end products. OEMs recognized this ability and sought to capitalize on GTI's depth and product migration capability.

GTI was increasingly being recognized for world-class product performance, quality, and service. All this was made possible because every GTI employee played a role in Total Customer Satisfaction for GTI's customers.

**Worldwide Customer Support**

In the fast and furious world of disk drives, differentiators among products are dwindling, but at the same time becoming more important. A manufacturer's product could be the fastest, cheapest or smallest, but one factor would separate it from the rest — customer support. Customers range from OEMs to distributors to dealers to end users. GTI had realized this shift toward customer support and, since 1991, has answered the call of its customers by improving its customer support organization, worldwide.

Daniel Buckley, GTI's Vice President for Field Engineering, asserted:

> I believe that customer support and quality are the two biggest differentiators today. Yes, in the long run the customer makes a decision based on the product, but if they don't have the support, then it is all for naught. We're aiming to make customer service to end users more automated. If a customer in a most remote town has an issue, we will have the representative for that region on the next plane to address the issue. In that respect, I think we have a better organization than our competition. Even countries that are behind in technology are buying disk drives and need support like everyone else, so we installed telexes for these customers.

There is little leeway for error in the world of customer support. It is one of the key differentiators in the disk drives and cannot be stressed enough. GTI sought to make its customer support organization the best in the industry and in the world, and early results showed that they are going in the right direction. GTI has a worldwide network of customer support organizations which covers virtually every region of the world (see Exhibit 3).

## Gateway Technology Singapore

In December 31, 1993, GT Singapore operations employed a workforce of approximately 14,000, making GTS the largest private-sector employer in Singapore. GTS had three plants in Singapore, located in Jurong, Woodlands, and Toa Payoh. Jurong and Toa Payoh were drive assembly plants and GTS Woodlands was a printed circuit board (PCB) plant.

### Human Resources

GTS policy on salary was to remain competitive and provide benefits to maintain a spirited workforce. Singapore was known for high turnover rates in the manufacturing sector, but GTS was not experiencing the high turnover rate other industry participants were facing. GTS' success in Singapore has been attributed to the Singapore management team's wanting to make and support the changes toward a new GTS. In 1990, GTS began an employee retention training function for front-line supervisors. One of the most important lessons was simply to "listen." Employees were free to talk to their supervisors. Among the programs introduced to meet the needs of GTS employees were child care assistance and educational benefits, including financial assistance for school fees and book expenses.

The Human Resources Department was trying to create an environment where working for GTS was not just a job, but a contribution to the current success of GTS. In turn, the Human Resources Department hoped that the employees' experience and responsibilities contributed to their personal career growth and future opportunities. Training was the key. GTS provided not only the work experience necessary for employee growth, but specific training in the areas of manufacturing process and technology that helped them achieve the goals they had set for themselves. Training was provided to employees at all levels, from operators to top managers.

GTS' most significant changes have been in the level and extent of communication. In the past, top management handed down decisions without communicating organizational goals and how those decisions contributed to the overall objective of the company. By 1993, communication at all levels of management had drastically improved. In addition to quarterly visits by Smith, GTI Far East management held general business communication sessions every two months with all exempt staff members. Through broad communication of the company's objectives and its organizational goals, employees were able to feel a stronger sense of ownership and commitment in knowing how their work contributes to the success of the company. Management obtained feedback through sessions with the director of Human Resources.

A few years ago, when Human Resources interviewed a potential employee, the perception was that GTS was a "pressure cooker" and job security was poor. In 1987, because of a sharp fall in demand for RDD, GTI turned in huge losses. The following year,

GTI implemented a major restructuring program, which was primarily a cost-reduction program. In that program, plants where optimum economic efficiencies no longer existed were closed, and there was a significant reduction in workforce in all set-ups and across all levels. At the time this case was written, the perception had changed and potential job candidates made very positive comments about the company, particularly in relation to the high quality of GTS drives. Herman Tan, GTS' Executive Director of Human Resources, said in an in-house newsletter that GTS had made a transition to a more communicative, open environment.

### Quality

GTS' management placed a strong emphasis on quality in every aspect of doing business. In 1991, GTS launched a Singapore-wide quality program for all levels of employees and across all departments. Starting from the very top, all directors, managers, supervisors, and operators were trained in Statistical Process Control (SPC). By 1993, GTS had very active Continuous Process Improvement (CPI) teams at all sites, working on various projects to improve quality. SPC/CPI training programs had been instituted for GTS employees, and GTS was looking into "Service Quality" training starting with Human Resources staff.

### Automation

With the trend toward decreasing form factors and increasing customer demand, automating the disk drive production helped the company maintain its competitive edge as a world-class manufacturer of disk drives. Automating the production process had given the company the flexibility to compete in the industry. An automated line could be reprogrammed to produce other products of the same form factor. The line was also not restricted by the life span of the drive it was first designed for. Another advantage was that technicians and operators working on the line need not be retrained for each new drive to be assembled on the line.

GTS began updating much of its equipment, making it more automated. The smaller drives coming into volume production could not be effectively assembled with human hands. Engineers sent to learn the operation of the automated systems were required to pass training onto the line workers through in-house training.

### Materials Management

The Material Management Department plays an important role because about 70 percent of the cost of the disk drive is made up of materials. Singapore Materials Management was involved in purchasing, planning, storing, and distributing production materials from the raw material state to the finished product state. This intricate operation comprised various functions such as materials planning, production, scheduling, shipping, purchasing, inventory control, stores, and in-plant materials movements. GTS' procurement policy was to locate the best buys with a view to ensuring availability, quality, reliability, and competitive pricing. This policy did not restrict procurement of parts to GTI components plants if good sources could be located elsewhere. This created tremendous pressure on GTS' components manufacturing plants.

Good relationships between GTS and its suppliers, especially its local subcontractors, have been important factors which helped GTS bring its products to the market in a very short time frame.

#### Manufacturing

With four design centers, GTS had to standardize raw card specification to the general design of the PCB. The presence of multiple designs originating from four different design centers had limited GTS Woodlands' efficiency in PCB manufacturing. With the approval of GTI, GTS Woodlands established the Advanced Technology Department, the first of its kind in Singapore. This new department consisted of Product Management, Document Control, and Advanced Engineering, and focused on key issues of standardization and low-cost manufacturing. It worked closely with GTI's design centers in the U.S. to identify, study, and offer new technology and techniques that would ensure that leverage, technology, and no duplication of resources took place.

#### Product Transfer

Because GTI anticipated that the competitive pressures would continue to be severe, the company took additional steps toward improving efficiency, managing its expenses, and reducing costs. As a major part of these efforts, there were plans to move some additional production and repair activities to Singapore. Engineers sent overseas to be trained on previous product transfer programs had commented that they faced much resistance, thus learning was not in-depth.

#### GTS' Short-Term and Long-Term Challenges

Trends indicate that the disk drive industry is headed toward reducing form factors and increasing areal density while at the same time reducing cost of ownership to customers. Before the year 2000, the industry would be likely to witness more than one gigabyte on a single 3.5-inch disk and in excess of 500 megabytes on a single 2.5-inch disk. Smaller form factors would also benefit from this increase in areal density. Improvements in Mean Time Before Failures of over one million hours combined with power reduction to subwatt and ruggedness to over 300 G's would be possible.

The short-term challenge for GTS is to complete its current product developments on schedule and cost targets. This will ensure GT's profitability while it transitions its products to the new technologies such as the MR head.

In the longer term, GTS sees the need to implement a series of new enabling technologies and lead the areal density growth curve. At the same time, GTS needs to expand the data storage horizon into new products and services, as well as new markets in order to increase the revenue base. From 1994 to 1999, GTS would concentrate on expanding the data storage part of the company by approximately 30 percent in order to achieve GTS's strategic objectives.

### Staff Meeting at GTS

Setting: 9:30 am; January 3, 1994; First working day of the year; GTS Board Room; Board Meeting with George Clinton.

All the executive managers were gathered in the board room to meet George Clinton, the new Senior Vice President (SVP) for GTI's Corporate Strategy Division. This division was set up in 1990 following the successful acquisition of Prism Technology. Clinton was instrumental in structuring this acquisition.

Clinton was scheduled to meet these managers as part of his global tour of all the offices outside the U.S. and to explain GTI's new mission and corporate objectives. As part of this meeting, Clinton had prepared, with the help of William Lee, one of the deputies and a Taiwanese immigrant working in the U.S., a quick description of current industry specifics in a folder (see Exhibit 4). Lee, in his years working in Asia before immigrating to the U.S. in 1991, had advised Clinton on his perceptions of the RDD market in Asia.

Clinton had never worked in Asia, except on a few business trips over the last two years. He graduated with an MBA degree from Harvard Business School where he was one of the top of his class. He was even called a "financial whiz" by people who have worked with him. At 38 years of age, Clinton is the youngest of the senior management of GT International. Some have even dubbed him the heir apparent.

GTS managers were given a copy of the briefing document only when they met half an hour ago. They were told by Lee to review this information before the meeting started. They were also told that they were expected to give feedback to Clinton after he had finished addressing the various issues on his agenda.

At 10:45 am Chow, the Operations Manager who was educated in Chinese schools, was still halfway through the briefing document. Although he had exactly the same folder, he could not read as fast as Heng did. He started to panic and again regretted not leaving GTS. He looked at Managing Director Don Tan, and saw Tan shaking his head away and frowning. He guessed that everybody was having the same apprenhensions about the short time given to review the material.

At 11:00 am sharp, Clinton arrived at the boardroom and was introduced to everyone. He started the meeting by presenting his agenda as follows:

1. Long-range Strategic Business Plan of GTI
2. Business Objectives
3. Feedback

Before he went on, Clinton commented that this meeting would be an informal one. Although an agenda was prepared, he felt that open interaction was a better way of getting feedback from the local operations.

Clinton summarized GTI's long-range business strategy and growth objectives as follows:

**GTI's Long-Range Strategic Business Plan**

By the year 2000, targeted sales growth from US$4 billion to US$8 billion.

Redefining GTI business from being merely a hard disk manufacturer to a company which now deals in data management, including its repertoire products for handling text, graphics, audio and video. To do this, GTI would have to offer everything from mass storage devices to software for managing databases and networks.

Clinton cited as an example GTI's entry into new markets such as the software market through its recent acquisition of Datatex, a small Texan database firm whose main product (known as D, "The Data Language") is 10 times faster than any comparable software on the market. This business is expected to generate a revenue of close to US$1.5 billion by the end of this decade.

**Growth Rate Objectives**

Corporate: To double sales from US$4 billion to US$8 billion by the year 2000. The US$8 billion sales will be achieved as follows: disk drive business to grow to US$5 billion, software business by US$1.5 billion, and components to US$1.5 billion.

GTS: By 1995, US$2.7 billion; by 2000, US$4 billion.

Corporate: Through acquisition, GTI hopes to expand its current body of technical know-how and thus maintain its stronghold by introducing new applications as well as new products.

Clinton commented further, "Various acquisitions such as Prism and the latest, Silicon Storage (SS), have helped to further put GTI ahead of its competitors in its technology standing." With SS, GTI now entered the flash memory products market by marketing and distributing SS products. More interestingly, GTI and SS had longer-term plans to jointly develop data storage products. The plan included exploring the two different technologies, rotating and solid state memory, to create new products.

Being financially strong, or cash-rich, was the key to supporting acquisitions of related companies so that GTI could begin a new chapter in its corporate history of being a data management company.

At this juncture, Tan commented to Heng, who was sitting beside him that, actually, no one in the U.S. ever thought about acquisitions in this part of the world, especially Singapore.

Clinton flipped to his next transparency and went on to talk about market orientation objectives:

**Market Orientation Objectives**

To achieve Total Customer Satisfaction by focusing on meeting the needs of the customers and getting their feedback, especially with OEM. Every GTI employee is expected to have a role to play in giving our valued customer Total Satisfaction.

Concentrate on building the leadership position of being the strategic storage supplier of choice for a large number of leading OEMs.

Clinton quoted Valerie Harper, SVP for Global Sales when asked what spurred GTI's recent growth in OEM business: "Quality." She continued to promote GTI's ability to provide a balanced product line of reliable entry level and high-end products, that is, to capitalize on GTI's depth and product migration capability.

Clinton believed that customer support and quality were the two biggest and most important differentiators which, he felt, most of the GTI geographic divisions other than the U.S. had not been emphasizing enough.

At 11:30 am Heng wrote in his note pad: "That's what he thinks. How did we come up with 45 percent of GTI's international sales if we didn't understand the importance of these two differentiators?" He was frustrated and needed to vent out his grouses right there and then quietly in his note pad.

In the meeting, Clinton also presented the following profit improvement objectives:

**Profit Improvement Objectives**

Develop a more effective cost-accounting program. Work for a more effective cost-reduction program, especially in the areas of material expenses, as well as non-recurring expenses such as product returns, which had significantly offset almost US$7 million of last year's profits.

Through various restructuring of overseas operations, a reduction of almost 1,000 jobs in both temporary and independent contractor sectors will help to reduce staff costs. Cost efficiency through consolidating certain operations is a key objective.

Setting up an International Treasury Division to better control the flow of funds among all the overseas operations. Advice from overseas operations will help GTI to make acquisitions as some overseas companies are under consideration. Thus, translation risk may be a factor for future consideration. Also, there is a need to better control the exchange risk as Net Foreign Currency transaction losses amounted to as much as US$1.8 million for the last fiscal year.

Clinton ended his agenda by listing the following critical variables affecting GTI's future:

**Critical Variables**

Dealing with price erosion. Price erosion will significantly affect revenues and profit margins.

Main variables are very important for GTI to remain competitive and profitable. They are continued efficiency improvement, expense management, and cost reduction.

Differentiated products are getting fewer but at the same time more important. The only factor that will separate GTI from the rest is customer support.

The need to maintain a long-term positive relationship with your buyers is of paramount importance in the disk drive industry.

How to stay ahead of competitors in pricing without losing quality.

The need to be technologically ahead of competitors.

At 12:05 pm Clinton smiled at everyone and said that he was still suffering from jet lag and wanted to go back to the hotel to take a nap during lunch time. Everyone laughed, thinking it was a joke. They arrived at the restaurant and learned from Tan that Clinton and Lee had gone back to the hotel to rest as both of them had arrived at 3.00 that morning. They would join them back at GTS after lunch.

At 12:30 pm the staff were all seated at one table. At lunch, the local management team started to exchange their thoughts about the morning presentation when the two HQ corporate SVPs were not around. Tan was trying to figure out how GT Singapore was going to fit into the entire corporate objective of GTI. He started to identify the strengths of GTS and began to question the feasibility and reality of meeting the corporate objectives laid by Clinton.

Heng started the ball rolling: "See, I told you guys two days ago. I knew they were talking about restructuring again. Wasn't Clinton hinting that GTS will be affected?"

Chow recalled a workforce that had felt threatened after the retrenchments in 1988. In one of his latest addresses, the CEO had mentioned that one key variable for GTI worldwide to diligently look out for was cost reduction. He was also quoted as saying, "There are no guarantees, but I am working diligently, along with the rest of GTI's executive management, to keep the impact on people's personal lives as minimal as we can." Some of the lower-ranking employees felt some unease because of a possible hint of retrenchments once GTI hits the red again.

Chow surprisingly commented that, in a way, it would actually make sense for GTI to want to consolidate the two plants in Singapore if that was what they intended to do. Shifting some of the operations to Thailand would benefit GTI because of the relatively lower labor costs. De la Cruz agreed because he knew that the Singapore Government would be announcing higher wage and salary scale recommendations and the cost structure of the labor market would be affected. Also, if they intended to relocate the Woodlands plant to Toa Payoh, most of their staff who were Malaysians and lived in Johor Bahru (the first Malaysian city across the border) might not continue with GTS as they would have to travel farther.[1]

Tan said: "Singapore has been making excellent profits and has shown higher growth and productivity due to an efficient workforce. Government policies have also helped, especially its tax incentives for high-value products. "Heng, don't get excited because you were around at the last retrenchment. Corporate headquarters has learned a lot from the last retrenchment and will not necessarily do this without considering the long-term impact."

Tan emphasized that their GTS product was reputable in terms of quality and time delivery. Heng interrupted: "Hey, Clinton seemed to say that only the U.S. operations concentrate on these two differentiators. What does he think we have been doing over in this part of the world?"

De la Cruz pointed out: "As usual, these American guys think that things can get done only in the U.S. Like acquisitions of technical knowledge, I guess they never thought about Singapore or regional opportunities. For a start, I am sure it would be cheaper to buy these over here. The expertise of some local software houses is comparable to that held by software houses in the U.S. Look at Creative Technology; they made a name for themselves globally and their design was done in Singapore."

Tan mentioned that from the customer orientation point of view, it might be good to relocate the design centers to the Asia-Pacific region. Meeting the customer's need in terms of design and delivery time was crucial.

---

[1]Being the northernmost district in the city-state of Singapore, Woodlands is the location closest to the Malaysian border.

Chow commented that most of the industry's design awards were awarded to GTI's inventors and this had helped to give GTI some patents in the U.S. Inventors who applied for a patent would receive a plaque and a check. After ten contributions, an inventor's name would be entered into the Hall of Fame. So far, Singapore had not contributed any names. Perhaps this state of affairs was due to the emphasis placed on the U.S. centers as key design centers and the lack of emphasis placed on centers in the rest of the world.

Tan reminded them that the afternoon would be spent obtaining input from local management regarding the future of GTS. Heng suggested that they give personnel headquarters their frank opinions. It was obvious that GTI had decided what they wanted to do. But in dishing out some of these objectives and long-term goals, did GTI look at its operations in the Asia-Pacific before deciding on the path they would take?

Setting: 2:30 pm, Board Conference Room. Clinton was already seated in the room and looked more refreshed than this morning. He stood up as the local management staff walked in.

Don proposed that the local management team could start off the afternoon discussion by giving Clinton feedback based on the local perspective. From there, he hoped that GTI's corporate objectives could factor in the local conditions when setting up the strategies for various overseas operations.

EXHIBIT 1

**GATEWAY TECHNOLOGY INTERNATIONAL**
**Condensed Operating Statements**
**Years Ending June 30, 1991–1993**
($ millions)

| | *1993* | *1992* | *1991* |
|---|---|---|---|
| Net sales | $4,078.4 | $3,852.9 | $3,587.2 |
| Cost of goods sold | 3,176.7 | 3,199.4 | 2,937.9 |
| Gross margin | 901.7 | 653.5 | 649.3 |
| Product development | 206.4 | 178.1 | 184.2 |
| Selling & administrative | 297.6 | 270.5 | 290.5 |
| Amortization of intangibles | 17.2 | 17.3 | 17.3 |
| Restructuring costs | 20.1 | 45.4 | 8.1 |
| Operating income | 360.4 | 142.2 | 149.2 |
| Other operating income | 34.7 | 17.7 | 25.4 |
| Earnings before interest & taxes | 395.1 | 159.9 | 174.6 |
| Interest on debt | 31.5 | 45.4 | 65.2 |
| Earnings before taxes & extraordinary gain | 363.6 | 114.5 | 109.4 |
| Income taxes | 101.8 | 29.7 | 25.1 |
| Income before extraordinary gain | 261.8 | 84.8 | 84.3 |
| Extraordinary gain on repurchase of debt | | | 6.2 |
| Net income | $ 261.8 | $ 84.8 | $ 90.5 |
| Primary net income per share | $ 3.12 | $ 1.03 | $ 1.14 |
| Fully diluted net income per share | $ 2.86 | $ 1.01 | $ 1.13 |
| Number of shares used in per share computations (in thousands) | | | |
| Primary | 83,785 | 82,632 | 79,368 |
| Fully diluted | 91,518 | 83,766 | 79,901 |

EXHIBIT 2

## GATEWAY TECHNOLOGY INTERNATIONAL
## Condensed Balance Sheets
## June 30, 1992, and 1993

($ millions)

| | *1993* | *1992* |
|---|---|---|
| Assets | | |
| Current assets | | |
| Cash | $ 571.0 | $ 579.3 |
| Short-term investments | 272.2 | 95.8 |
| Accounts receivable (net) | 479.3 | 537.9 |
| Inventories | 534.3 | 406.8 |
| Other current assets | 114.8 | 67.2 |
| Total current assets | 1,971.5 | 1,687.0 |
| Plant, property, and equipment (net) | 469.1 | 489.1 |
| Goodwill and other intangibles (net) | 186.6 | 204.1 |
| Other assets | 94.6 | 54.1 |
| Total assets | $2,721.8 | $2,434.2 |
| Liabilities and Net Worth | | |
| Current liabilities | | |
| Accounts payable | $ 335.4 | $ 310.2 |
| Long-term debt due in one year | 2.0 | 3.3 |
| Accrued income taxes | 46.6 | 23.7 |
| Other accrued liabilities | 344.9 | 334.8 |
| Total current liabilities | 729.0 | 672.1 |
| Long-term debt | 376.9 | 429.5 |
| Deferred income taxes | 165.6 | 130.2 |
| Other liabilities | 49.7 | 47.3 |
| Total liabilities | 1,321.2 | 1,279.1 |
| Common stock | 0.9 | 0.9 |
| Additional paid-in capital | 422.9 | 404.5 |
| Foreign currency translation adjustment | (0.6) | 1.8 |
| Income retained in business | 978.1 | 752.1 |
| Less Treasury common stock at cost, 60,000 shares in 1992 | | (1.1) |
| Deferred compensation | (0.6) | (3.1) |
| Total net worth | 1,400.6 | 1,155.2 |
| Total liabilities and net worth | $2,721.8 | $2,434.2 |

EXHIBIT 3

**GATEWAY TECHNOLOGY INTERNATIONAL**
**Worldwide Customer Support Organization**
**As of September 1993**

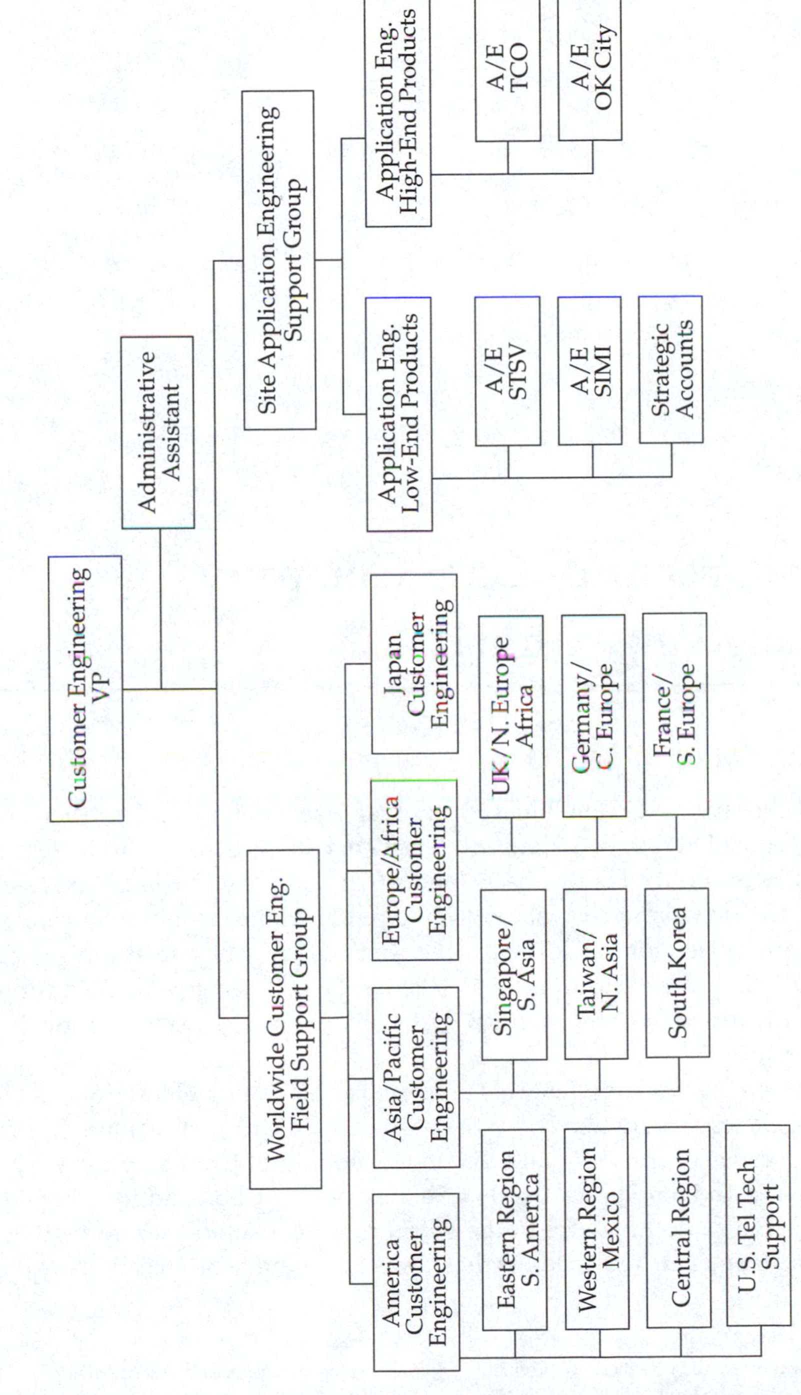

# Panyu Security Gate Company (Guangdong, China)* 15

## Introduction

It was February 1991 and Chinese New Year was barely over. Mr Chen was mulling over what he considered to be a significant challenge in his career — to increase the sales of the product he introduced to the market more than four years earlier. While sitting in his office sipping tea, he wondered what he would tell his three deputy managers whom he called to a planning session on Monday, the first working day in the New Year. Among the thoughts that crossed his mind was whether he still had the enthusiasm he had when he became the top man of his company. At 42, he thought he still had much to contribute to his company.

In 1984, Xin Zheng Chen was promoted as Manager of Panyu Second Metal Company (PSMC). He was recommended to the position by the former manager, who thought highly of him because of his vigor and his understanding of technology.

Young and ambitious, the then 36-year-old Mr Chen had long hoped for the promotion: There was nothing else in the world that he wanted than to be the manager of the company. However, he also knew that it was not going to be an easy job, given the problems

*This case was prepared by Reuben Mondejar and Chen Zhen Xiong with research assistance provided by Cai Wei Quan. Reuben Mondejar is Senior Lecturer at the Department of Business and Management of the City Polytechnic of HongKong. Chen Zhen Xiong is Lecturer at the School of Management of Zhongshan (Sun Yat Sen) University in Guangzhou, Guangdong, China. Cai Wei Quan is a Research Assistant at Zhongshan University. The case was prepared to serve as a basis for class discussion rather than to illustrate either effective or ineffective handling of an administrative situation.

faced by the company. Sales were declining, competition was getting stiffer, and the company's financial resources were becoming depleted. The company's top level management, unsure of Mr Chen's ability to save the company from the crisis, did not give him a free hand. Mr Chen therefore expected many restrictions and pressures that would make it impossible for him to carry out reforms smoothly.

Mr Chen, however, took on the challenge. Determined to perform well, he intended to bring his intelligence and capability into play to pull the company through.

## Company Background

The 30-year-old PSMC is a small-sized collective enterprise under the administration of the Second Light Industrial Bureau (SLIB). Located in the capital of Panyu county in the province of Guangdong, PSMC is within the Pearl River Delta Economic Open Zone. Panyu is a bustling county with a population of some 800,000 and is considered one of the so-called "Little Tigers" of the Pearl River Delta Region.

PSMC started by making articles from bamboo. Later, it produced louver windows, iron beds, and other metal appliances. When it began operations, PSMC was run using funds provided by the SLIB as well as those generated from the workers' capital and loans. By 1979, it had fixed assets valued at 3 million yuan (equivalent to US$2 million). The company tried to expand its production by using funds obtained from internal sources such as staff individual stock, the enterprise replacement and transforming fund, and the production development fund.

Although the government provided an incentive for output expansion (i.e., if the company succeeded in developing new products that met set standards, it could apply for tax reduction and use the savings to expand its output), PSMC could not avail itself of this plan then because of the company's backward technology and inefficient operation. Moreover, the size of its manpower proved to be a heavy burden on the company's finances. In 1984, it had a total of 338 staff and workers, more than 170 of whom were retired. In fact, at the time of Mr Chen's promotion, the company had not paid its workers for more than a year.

When Mr Chen assumed the manager position, he was aware of the company's problems. However, he also knew that as a collective enterprise under the growing market economy in China, PSMC could operate according to market demand without intervention from the state. It could also exercise more decision-making power, and had more leeway in its financial operations, that is, the manager could utilize part of the company's profits as he saw fit. Mr Chen knew that he must take full advantage of the greater flexibility of collective enterprises to bring back life to the company.

## A New Development Strategy

When he took office, Mr Chen was convinced that developing new products was the only workable way of saving PSMC. Thus with some knowledge of modern management and his practical experience, he set out to carry a series of big reforms in his company.

**Developing a new product.** The first step he took was to conduct market research. He found out that as economic reforms progressed in China, the people's living standards rose correspondingly. More and more people owned durable consumer goods such as refrigerators, color television sets, video tape recorders, and washing machines. With their acquisition of these luxury items, people became more concerned about their security at home and in the office. Mr Chen also paid particular attention to the observations made by the local security department in its annual report. According to the report, "Of the total number of theft cases, 60 percent involved burglary. Moreover, 65 percent of burglary cases involved the breaking down of doors. This situation illustrates that the door is the most vulnerable part of the house."

Thus, a new product came to Mr Chen's mind — a different type of security gate, one that would provide extra protection to homeowners. Security gates were usually installed right before the main door of the house for additional security. At that time, there was only one kind of security gate in the home market — the rolling type, which was not very effective in preventing thefts. What Mr Chen had in mind was a security gate similar to that commonly used in Hong Kong. This type gave more solid security since it was usually made of a strong combination of iron and copper grills and plates. Mr Chen was confident that this type of security gate had good prospects in China not only because of its greater effectiveness but also because of the big potential market, considering that the construction of residential buildings was flourishing due to the growth of the Chinese economy.

With the technology and type of equipment available in the company, the production of the security gate did not require a big investment. Thus at the end of 1985, after he and his colleagues studied the process of manufacturing the security gates used in Hong Kong, Mr Chen decided to introduce the product in China.

In June 1986, the first generation of PSMC's security gates was produced on trial and placed in the market. Mr Chen gave the new product its brand name "Lucky Star," designed a logo for it, and changed the name of the company to Panyu Security Gate Company (PSGC).

**Reorganizing the company.** The successful development of the new product was a great encouragement to all the staff and workers of the company. All hoped to see their company become prosperous under the leadership of the new manager.

For his part, Mr Chen knew that for an enterprise to develop and thrive, it must have the right organizational structure. Only then can it develop new products, enter the market, and compete effectively.

The old organizational structure was relatively simple and loose (see Exhibit 1). While it worked under the previous production-oriented set-up, it was not effective under the market-oriented environment that the company had now moved into. After careful consideration, Mr Chen made the following changes in the company's organizational structure (see Exhibit 2):

1. The sales section was separated from the purchase section and placed directly under a deputy manager. The separation of the two sections was aimed at reinforcing the company's selling and marketing operations.
2. A public relations (PR) section under the direct supervision of the manager was set up to increase external relationships and improve the company's image.
3. A total quality control (TQC) section was established to ensure a continuously high level of product quality.

Mr Chen carried out the company's reorganization by dismissing incompetent managers and promoting the vigorous and competent ones. He also stipulated the company's administrative regulations, defined the responsibilities of each section manager, and carried out a management-by-objective system in the company. As a result of these moves, the company took on a completely new look. Everyone knew his responsibilities and the company's goals, and worked hard to accomplish them.

**Modifying the wage structure.** Under the traditional wage system, the basis for computing wages varied according to a three tier worker's categorization scheme. In general, the staff members and workers of a collective enterprise fell into three categories. The formal workers were those registered with the authorities. Called the "iron bowls," these workers enjoyed several benefits and could not be dismissed. The contractual workers were those employed by the enterprise through contracts and were dismissed when their contracts expired. The temporary workers had no security of tenure since the company could dismiss them anytime.

Of the total income received by formal workers, only about 30 percent represented the basic wage; the balance consisted of bonuses. The basic wage was set by the SLIB, while the amount of the bonus was decided by the enterprise, depending on the profit made as well as on the worker's workload, position, and responsibilities. On the other hand, the bonus for the contractual and temporary workers was paid according to the number of pieces they were able to produce.

Mr Chen rejected the traditional system of paying wages. He thought that since all workers performed the same type of work, it was unfair not to pay them uniformly. To get the best out of every worker in the company, Mr Chen decided to apply the piecework system for everybody so as to give each one the opportunity to earn income under equal terms. Those who worked more could get more money, and those who worked less would have to settle for less income. As a result of this change, workers became much more interested in improving their productivity.

**Developing the market.** Mr Chen often said that the survival and development of an enterprise depended on how strong it linked up with the market. The company must be able to sell the goods that it produced. To develop the market, Mr Chen changed his marketing strategy from one that was passive to one that was more aggressive. He thus carried out reforms in the following areas:

1. **Market segmentation.** Mr Chen segmented the market by consumer group, namely: urban construction development system, security and fire control systems, government office buildings, city commercial buildings, and individual customers. The security gate could be made according to the requirements of these different groups.

   Mr Chen also targeted the cities and counties in Guangdong Province and the other relatively rich provinces around it (e.g., Fujian) where the consumption levels were high. The proximity of these areas also lowered the transportation cost.

In July 1986, the first batch of security gates was placed in the market. Initial sales were small. Low sales figures were expected given that the product was still in its introductory marketing stage, which was generally the most difficult period for marketing. Mr Chen, however, realized that he must not lose time in tapping the potential of the product and formulating a strategy that would maximize sales.

2. **Pricing.** Pricing was a major concern. After collecting and assessing a lot of information about the market, Mr Chen decided to give up the usual pricing policy and adopted a high-price, high-promotion strategy. He cited several reasons for using this strategy:

   a. He was certain that the product would become popular in the market and, hence, must be priced high in order to enable the company to earn big profits from it.
   b. The company's production capacity was not enough to attain economies of scale. But increasing the capacity would require additional financing, which could be sourced only from the company's profits. A break-even analysis conducted by the company's finance department indicated a break-even volume of 30,000 square meters of security gates a year, as shown below:

| *Item* | *Amount (in yuan)* |
|---|---|
| Total fixed cost (per year) | 2,180,000 |
| Unit variable cost (per square meter) | 98 |
| Price (per square meter) | 172 |
| Breakeven volume = 2,180,000/(172–98) = 30,000 square meters | |

Even if this sales level was achieved, the company would still be losing money because it had to pay its 200 retired workers some 500,000 yuan for their retirement fund and health welfare.

Thus Mr Chen thought that he was left with no choice but to price the product high. He hoped for an immediate acceptance of the product but unfortunately, the initial market reaction was not that good, as evidenced by the low sales volume.

3. **Distribution.** Mr Chen believed that good products still needed a good distribution network. He asked the PR section to develop informational pamphlets introducing the company and its products. These pamphlets were then distributed to every city in Guangdong Province. He also went personally or sent salesmen to different places to look for qualified sales agents. The selected agents were usually given preferential prices, extended credit (but only until the delivery of the next order), and provided transportation facilities.

The security gates were sold to the agents at prices ranging from 134 yuan to 172 yuan per square meter. After some time, however, this flexible pricing policy led to some problems, particularly with regard to price control. Some agents would price the products very high in order to earn more. The policy also led to regional differences in the wholesale and retail prices. On the whole, the policy tended to damage the company's reputation.

4. **Advertising and promotion.** Under the old socialist economic system, market competition was hardly emphasized and advertising and promotion were regarded as unnecessary. Some people thought it was not worth investing money to advertise their products. They believed people would buy their products as long as these were of good quality.

   However, with economic reform and market opening, major attitudinal changes had taken place. People were now willing to take a certain degree of risk to achieve the desired results.

   Mr Chen realized that it was impossible for his product to become popular in the market without some kind of promotion. He knew that the right advertising could not only influence consumption but also make the company well-known. Mr Chen decided to conduct a series of promotional activities:

   a. In 1986, the company held a conference in Guangzhou where representatives of construction companies and fire control and public security departments were invited to a launching of the company's new product. As an offshoot of the conference, PSGC was invited to Beijing to take part in a national exhibition of home interior decor and furnishing products and an exhibition on construction and fire control products.
   b. The company also took part in the Guangdong province exhibition of products produced by companies with foreign investments. Here the "Lucky Star" security gate received a high product rating.
   c. In November 1986, the company took part in a high-quality product appraisal meeting held by the Guangzhou Economic Committee. In this meeting, the "Lucky Star" security gate was given the "Guangzhou 1986 Novel Product" award.
   d. The company also became a member of the Guangzhou Urban Construction Development Group, Ltd, which subsequently required all its members to use the "Lucky Star" security gate.
   e. To promote sales, the company sent its salesmen to every big city of the country to find big customers and sign sales contracts. The company also held various product display exhibits and sales conferences in Beijing, Guangzhou, Shenzhen, Zhuhai, and in other big cities.
   f. Because the cost of television advertising was very high in China, the company promoted its product mainly through newspapers such as the *Yangchen Evenings* and *Southern Daily.*
   g. It carried out other promotional programs such as slogan contests; kept long-term relationships with the local news media and advertising departments; and sent product materials to governmental departments, construction and architecture colleges, construction material agencies, and real estate development companies around the country.

   The company's advertising and promotion programs proved to be very effective. More and more customers came to know about the new product from the radio, television, and direct mailings from the company. As a result, sales increased from 3.49 million yuan in 1986 to 19.45 million yuan in 1989, as shown below:[1]

| *Year* | *Sales (in million yuan)* |
|---|---|
| 1986 | 3.49 |
| 1987 | 3.26 |
| 1988 | 18.40 |
| 1989 | 19.45 |
| 1990 | 13.13 |

5. **After-sales service.** To strengthen the company's image, Mr Chen and his colleagues placed great importance on after-sales service and customer feedback. Complaints regarding quality, delivery, or installation were received by the Public Relations Section and passed on to the concerned department for appropriate action. The company would then send service men to repair or replace the security gates in question.

## Coping with the Changes

As the company's sales grew, so did its problems. For instance, despite an increase in the product's price per square meter from 130 yuan to 170 yuan, supply still fell short of demand. Subsequently, some firms began to manufacture and sell the same type of security gate. Since the company had not applied for a patent on "Lucky Star," it could not stop other manufacturers from counterfeiting the product. With more than ten factories producing and selling security gates at lower prices in the market, the demand for "Lucky Star" began to drop. People bought other brands. Some sales agents of the company even began to sell the products of its competitors.

The situation turned from bad to worse when the Chinese government, in a move aimed at slowing down the overheating economy, controlled investments, scaled down infrastructure projects, and restricted group purchases. As the market demand for security gates declined further, inventories piled up, prompting the company to convert its workshops into storehouses.

The company inevitably encountered cash flow problems. Bank credits were hard to come by. The company's financial position became very tight due to the following reasons:

1. Some of the company's salesmen failed to remit their collections on time.
2. The company had to extend credit to some customers, particularly after 1990, when it became more and more difficult to sell the product.
3. Some customers paid their accounts only after delivery or installation of the product.
4. Customers who complained about the product's quality would ask for a refund even after their complaints had been attended to.

[1]At the beginning of 1991, the exchange rate was 0.66 yuan to one HongKong dollar, while the HongKong dollar was traded at US$1.00 = HK$7.80.

5. Samples sent to customers remained unpaid.
6. Some salesmen ran off with their sales collections.

Each salesman was put in charge of a certain area. Sales varied from one area to another. In areas where consumption was high, supply sometimes fell short of demand; in areas where demand was still weak, particularly those where the market was still being developed, business was slow. The disparity in sales among the various areas led to disputes and competition among the company's salesmen. Some salesmen, in their desire to earn higher income, tried to find customers outside their assigned areas, thereby encroaching on the areas of other salesmen.

Mr Chen attributed the trend toward declining sales which started in 1990 to several factors. First, since its introduction in 1986, the company's product had not undergone any modifications in either style or design. Consumption subsequently leveled off as customers began looking for product variety. Second, the emergence of competitor firms dented the company's market share.

Mr Chen, however, was unfazed by the declining sales. He remained optimistic about the market, seeing instead the potential of other untapped areas in the country such as Shanghai and Henan Province. He, therefore, pursued new strategies to develop these new markets and boost sales to record levels.

The company began to produce new varieties of security gates to meet the changing requirements of customers. The prices per square meter of the new varieties ranged from 153 yuan to 183 yuan, depending on their features. The company also organized a technical force that developed a new type of electronically controlled security gate. Although these newly developed security gates were already being produced in batches, they had not gained wide market acceptance due to some technical problems.

Despite the more intensified marketing efforts of Mr Chen and his colleagues, the sales of PSDC continued to decline. Mr Chen was thus faced with the formidable problem of formulating new strategies that would revive the company's sagging sales.

EXHIBIT 1

**PANYU SECURITY GATE COMPANY OF GUANGDONG**
**Original Organizational Structure**

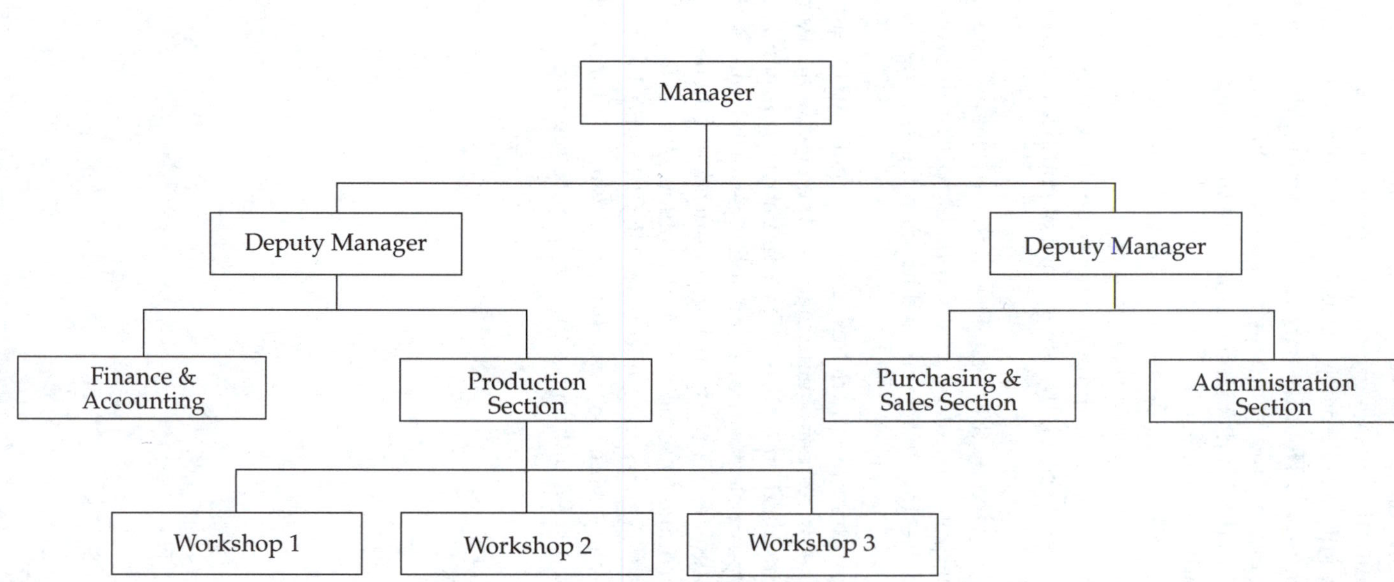

EXHIBIT 2

**PANYU SECURITY GATE COMPANY OF GUANGDONG**
**Revised Organizational Structure**

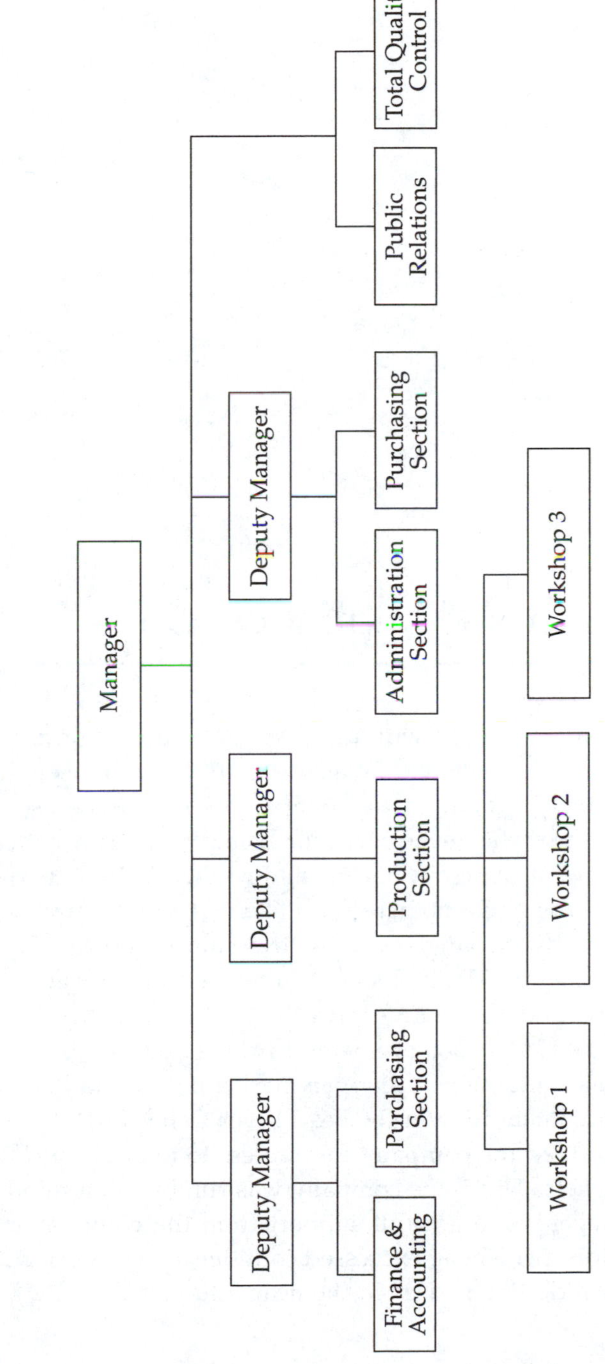

# Nan Feng Household Appliance Co* 16

As he prepared himself for an interview with a newspaper reporter on the morning of October 16, 1990, Jiang Zheng, the General Manager of Nan Feng Household Appliance Co (NFHAC), had reason to be proud of his company. For three consecutive years, NFHAC was consistently cited by the government for exemplary performance. In 1988, it won two awards: one for being "The Best Exporting and Foreign Exchange-Making Enterprise in Guangdong Province," and another (the "Flying Dragon Award") for being the "Best Exporting and Foreign Exchange-Making Township Enterprise in China." The following year, it was given the title "The Advanced Enterprise in Guangdong Province," and in 1990, the "National Second Grade Enterprise."

Mr Zheng attributed NFHAC's achievements to three factors. First, the business environment following China's adoption of an open market policy had been favorable to NFHAC's operations. Second, its location in the Pearl River Delta (PRD), which was near Hong Kong and Macao, provided the company easy access to international capital, technology, equipment, and markets. Third, the company was run by open-minded, pioneering, and hardworking managers who got full support from the company's cooperative employees. Given these factors, Mr Zheng expressed confidence that NFHAC would earn the title of "National First Grade Enterprise" in the near future.

---

*This case was prepared by Reuben T Mondejar, City University of Hong Kong and Chen Zhen Xiong, Zhongshan (Sun Yat Sen) University, Guangzhou, China. The case was prepared to serve as a basis for class discussion rather than to illustrate either effective or ineffective handling of an administrative situation.

## Company Background

The predecessor of the company was a small manual operation workshop set up by the town government in 1968 to produce plastic products and automobile parts. Because the development of township enterprises was restricted by the Government at that time (the time of the Cultural Revolution), the workshop failed to grow over the years. It operated with obsolete equipment and inadequate technicians, and as a result, cranked out low-quality products.

Starting in 1979, however, when China began to carry out its economic reforms, the Government encouraged the growth and development of all types of enterprises. The more open policy fired up the entrepreneurial spirit of many Chinese businessmen, including Mr Zheng's.

Mr Zheng saw opportunities for new business ventures under the more liberal environment created by the Government. He anticipated that with the economic reforms, the living standard of the Chinese people would rise continually, and so would the demand for household appliances, particularly electric fans. At that time, however, there were only a few factories producing electric fans in the whole of China. In fact, there was only one in Guangdong Province: the Yuangdong Fan Factory, which produced, in limited volume, electric fans under the brand name "Diamond." The dearth in manufacturers led to a shortage in domestic supply, forcing consumers to source their electric fans from "back door" suppliers.

Under these circumstances, Mr Zheng was convinced that it was the best time for the enterprise to move away from plastic products and automotive parts and into household appliances. Thus, in 1980, NFHAC was established, and began designing and assembling its first metal electric fans. Soon after that, the Company started production on a commercial scale. Ten years later, NFHAC had become one of the biggest electric fan manufacturers in China. Its annual output had grown from 16,116 units valued at 3.83 million yuan in 1980 to 1.95 million units valued at 202.3 million yuan in 1990.[1] Profits from sales of its products rose from 32,000 yuan to 6.03 million yuan during the same period. The number of employees had increased by more than ten times, from 168 to 1,787, with the 1990 manpower complement already consisting of 96 technicians and 121 administrative staff.

As of 1990, NFHAC's total assets stood at 66.5 million yuan. Its offices and factory occupied a land area of 40,000 square meters (sq m) and covered a total floor area of 47,800 sq m. It owned about 300 sets of advanced equipment, including four high-speed Japanese-made pushing machines, 10 electric fan production lines, and 6 electric fan checking lines.

Because of their good quality and novel designs, the company's electric fans had been favorably received not only in the home market but also abroad. NFHAC had been shipping to about 20 countries in North America, Europe, Southeast Asia, Hong Kong, and Macao. In 1990, the company's export shipments totaled 1.5 million units valued at US$15.86 million.

[1]At the beginning of 1991, the exchange rate was 0.66 yuan to one HongKong dollar, while the HongKong dollar was traded at US$1.00 = HK$7.80.

## Three Stages of Development

It was not an easy climb for the company, however. Success was achieved only after it overcame a series of obstacles and surmounted intense market competition. In fact, the company's development over the past ten years can be broken down into three stages.

**First Stage: 1980–1982.** The company began its business in 1980 by assembling metal electric fans with spare parts bought from the Guangzhou Yuangdong Fan Factory. It operated under this arrangement for the next two years, yielding a monthly output valued at only 3,000 yuan and making a very low profit. With the entry of more middle- and small-size manufacturers into the market, the situation turned from bad to worse. By 1982, a supply glut had developed, resulting in an intense price war among manufacturers. The increased competition led to the closure of about 70 percent of the electric fan factories. NFHAC survived, however, sustained by the better quality of its products.

**Second Stage: 1983–1985.** To improve competitiveness, Mr Zheng concluded that the company needed to develop new products using advanced technology and equipment. With this idea in mind, he visited Hong Kong in 1983 to gather market information on electric fans. When he returned to China, he brought with him a Japanese-made National 12-inch electric fan, which was made of plastic parts. At that time, plastic electric fans were not being manufactured in China. He asked his technician to disassemble the fan and study and compare its features with those of the metal fans. Shortly thereafter, his technician reported the following findings:

1. The technological process involved in producing plastic electric fans was simpler than that for the metal ones. While the key parts of plastic fans could be finished in one step by injection mould, those of metal fans involved 20 working procedures.
2. The cost of producing plastic fans was half that of metal fans.
3. The plastic fans were better-looking than the metal ones.

Metal fans, however, edged out the plastic ones on one count: durability. But Mr Zheng was aware that durability was not a key factor considered by consumers when buying electric fans. A functional life of more than two years, which was the average functional life of a plastic bus, was already acceptable to the buying public.

After weighing these factors, Mr Zheng made a critical decision: to start manufacturing plastic electric fans instead of metal fans. Thus, in early 1984, the company acquired advanced injection mold machines and plastic electric fan molds from abroad. It began to produce 12-inch plastic electric fans, which soon proved to be popular among the local consumers because of their new design, high quality, and low price. Encouraged by the high level of market acceptance of its new product, the company expanded production. Output as of the end of 1985 reached 210,000 units while sales totaled 36.65 million yuan. With these figures, Mr Zheng gave himself a pat on the back for his decision to switch into plastic fan production.

**Third Stage: 1986–1990.** The company's success proved to be short-lived, however. Sales of its new product leveled off in 1986 as competitors, riding on the popularity of plastic electric fans, flooded the market with their own version of the product. Consequently, NFHAC's sales declined to 120,000 units during the year, its inventory swelled to 230,000 units, and its annual profit dropped to 23,000 yuan.

As the situation became more critical, Mr Zheng saw the urgent need to review the company's strategy for future development. He called the deputy general managers and the managers of the different departments to a meeting to solicit their ideas and suggestions regarding the future direction of the company.

The first to speak was Mr Xian Lin, Deputy General Manager in charge of the company's production and technology management. He said: "Since there is an oversupply of electric fans in the market, we cannot continue manufacturing this product. If we do, that will be the end of our company. We should instead shift to other household appliances, such as washing machines. The demand for washing machines is growing in the home market, and there are only a few local manufacturers to meet the rising demand. The shift will not pose too much of a problem since the technology and equipment used in producing plastic electric fans can also be used in producing plastic washing machines."

Mr Shen Li, Deputy General Manager in charge of Sales and Finance, disagreed: "We cannot give up the business of plastic electric fans halfway since we have invested a large amount of capital on it. The key to surviving market competition lies in the quality and style of our product. As long as we exert more effort in developing high-quality and well-designed electric fans, I am sure we can pull through with the current crisis and achieve success in the future."

Mr Qi Zhang, Manager of the Sales Department, added: "Although the domestic market for electric fans is currently saturated, there is ample room in the international market, now that most of the advanced countries have given up their production of electric fans due to its labor-intensiveness. We should take advantage of this opportunity to export our plastic electric fans and penetrate the international market with every possible means."

Mr Jinmir Fang, Manager of the Finance Department, concurred with Li and Zhang: "We should maintain our production of plastic electric fans and strive to go into exports. But we can break into the world market only if our prices are competitive. Right now, our production cost is quite high. We must, therefore, think of a good way to reduce cost. Otherwise, entering the foreign market will be very difficult."

After listening to his managers, Mr Zheng decided on what he thought was the correct strategy to save the company from its present predicament. Speaking in a formal tone, he told his managers: "We will continue producing plastic electric fans and strive to gradually enter the overseas market. As an ancient Chinese saying goes: 'When the east is dark, the west will be bright.' I believe that as long as we try our best, we will have a bright future in the world market even as our prospects in the local market have dimmed."

After the meeting, the company came out with a new model for its plastic electric fan that more or less followed the design popular in the world market. Shortly thereafter, this new model was successfully exported through the Import and Export Company of Light Industrial Products of Guangdong Province, which shipped some 80,000 units in 1986.

The success of the new model in the export market inspired the company to adopt bold measures that would enhance its market position. These measures included the following:

1. **To continue developing new products.** The company set up a new product development section staffed with its best technicians to develop new models that meet the requirements of foreign buyers. The new section came out with three new models in 1987 and five more in 1988. By 1990, the company's product line already consisted of more than 30 items, all of which catered to the tastes and preferences of the foreign market in terms of design, quality, and price.

2. **To have the authority for direct exportation.** Under the government's past export policy, manufacturing enterprises were not allowed to export directly. Instead, they were required to sell their products to the state-owned export/import company, which, in turn, sold them to foreign buyers. NFHAC soon realized that such an arrangement was disadvantageous to the company for several reasons. First, the lack of direct contact with the overseas customer prevented the company from obtaining firsthand information on the different requirements of the market. Thus, it could not respond immediately to the needs of foreign customers. Second, NFHAC had no control over the export price, since it was the state-owned export/import company which negotiated with the buyers. Third, the inefficiency of the export/import company often led to extended periods of negotiations or delays in export shipments.

   Realizing the difficulties under such an arrangement, Mr Zheng, using good public relations, requested government authorization to export directly. The request was partially granted in 1987. The company was allowed to sell 50 percent of its exports directly to foreign buyers, with the remainder coursed through the state-owned import/export company. Over the next three years, the proportion allowed for direct exports was gradually raised to 80 percent in 1988, 90 percent in 1989, and finally, 100 percent in 1990.

3. **To increase production scale, reduce operation cost, and enhance the company's economic benefits.** Mr Zheng understood clearly that only with competitive prices could the company enter the overseas market, and that prices could be made competitive only by keeping operation costs low. He also realized that an effective way of lowering costs was to expand production to a level where economies of scale could be attained.

   Thus, starting 1986, NFHAC increased its investments using funds borrowed from local banks. It built more factory buildings and acquired more advanced equipment, including fan motor and fan net casing assembly lines, high-speed pushing machines, and injection mold equipment. It also employed additional young workers from the nearby countryside. As a result of the expansion, production continuously increased. By 1990, total output was already 5.5 times the 1986 level (see Exhibit 1). Consequently, the ratio of sales cost to sales income declined from 93 percent to 86 percent during the period.

4. **To recruit the right people.** NFHAC believed that coming out with export-quality products required highly capable people. Thus, to attract talented

technicians and administrators, the company offered high salaries and other incentives, such as free housing. This strategy enabled the company to recruit five top-rate engineers, who later became major contributors to the development of new products. The company also "bought" from Jinan University one of its MBA graduates, Mr Tao Lo, at a price equivalent to the cost of his university education.[2] Mr Lo was hired as Director of the company's Business Administration Section and later became Consultant to the General Manager.

5. **To promote the company's products.** NFHAC allocated 21 percent of its annual sales income for advertising and other promotional activities. It advertised in the *Guangdong and Hong Kong Information Post*, put up outdoor advertising boards in downtown Guangzhou, and exhibited its products in the Guangzhou Export Commodity Fair, which was held twice a year.

These policies led to a further increase in the company's exports. In 1990, NFHAC shipped some 1.5 million units of its electric fans abroad, compared with only 80,000 in 1986.

## The Management System

Mr Zheng believed that much of the company's strength could be attributed not only to its decision to penetrate the export market but also to its continuous efforts to improve the management system, particularly with respect to the organizational structure, income distribution, and staff welfare.

**Organizational Reforms.** When the company shifted its economic operations toward exports in 1986, it also made some gradual adjustments in its organizational structure to make it more responsive to the new set-up. By the end of 1990, the company had taken on a significantly different organizational structure from what it had in 1986 (see Exhibits 2 and 3). The following additional sections and departments were established:

1. An Import and Export Department to manage the company's export business.
2. A Total Quality Control (TQC) Office to ensure product quality.
3. A Product Development Section to develop new products that respond to the changing needs of customers.
4. A Personnel Department to reinforce the company's personnel management (and relieve the general manager of this function).
5. A Business Administration Section to implement modern business administration methods in the company.
6. Six independent factories to replace the former workshops. These factories were independent accounting units which were given more decision-making power in their production.
7. A Public Relations Department to promote the public image of the company.

[2]Under official regulations, all university graduates were required to work for any of the government agencies or state-owned enterprises in return for the government's sponsorship of their tuition.

**Income Distribution.** NFHAC distributed its income to two groups: the Industrial Administration Office of the town government, and its employees. The distribution scheme for the two groups were as follows:

1. **With the town government** – The distribution plan for the town government was based on a system commonly followed by township enterprises in PRD. According to the system, Mr Zheng as General Manager of the company has to sign a contract with the town government every three years. In this contract, Mr Zheng stated his annual operational targets (e.g., output value, sales income, profit, and depreciation) during his tenure of office. The company would pay the town government two sums of money annually: one would be equivalent to 3 percent of its annual sales income, and the other equivalent to 20 percent of its annual net profit (see Exhibit 4).
2. **With the company employees** – The company followed two income distribution schemes for its employees: one for workers and another for managers and administrative staff. Workers were paid based on a piece-rate wage system. A worker generally works eight hours a day, 25.5 days a month. Managers and administrative staff were paid using a mixed salary system. Under this system, their salaries were broken down into three components: basic, floating, and position. The basic salary was fixed and of the same amount as those in state enterprises. The floating salary was determined on the basis of the previous month's profits; hence, this component varied from month to month. The position salary was based on the employee's position. There were 15 levels in the company's position scheme. Each position was assigned a position salary coefficient (see Exhibit 5). The position salary was equal to the standard position salary multiplied by the position salary coefficient. The standard position salary was about two to three times the worker's average wage.

The payment plan of the company was accepted well by its staff and workers and in fact, enhanced their enthusiasm to work. During summer when production was at its peak, many workers rendered overtime services. On the other hand, many administrative staff volunteered to do overtime work even without pay, since they knew they would get higher floating salaries if they could contribute more to the company's profits.

**The Welfare System.** The company offered its employees a number of benefits, including:

1. **Medical allowance** – The staff and workers could reimburse their medical bills either in full or in part, depending on their length of service, as follows:

| *Number of Years in Service* | *Reimbursable Amount (in %)* |
|---|---|
| 15 | 100 |
| 10–14 | 80 |
| 5–9 | 50 |
| Below 5 | 20 at most |

In special cases, if an employee with more than two years of work experience with the company were hospitalized for serious illness, he would be able to get a reimbursement of all of his hospitalization expenditures.

2. **Educational subsidy** – Employees were given a 100-percent subsidy for the school tuition of their children in kindergarten.
3. **Meal subsidy** – The company subsidized 60 percent of the cost of employees' lunch in the company's canteen.
4. **Lodging** – The company provided low-rent apartments to the administrative staff or technicians recruited from faraway places, and low-rent dormitories to the workers.
5. **Retirement benefits** – After retirement, administrative staff and technicians will continue to receive 100 percent of their basic monthly salary, while workers will receive 70 percent of their basic monthly wage. All retirees could reimburse their medical expenditures in full.

**Economic Responsibility System.** When the company decided to enter the export market in 1986, it implemented its economic responsibility system, which defined the areas of responsibility for the different units, set targets for each unit, and established an incentive system to encourage units to work hard in order to achieve their targets (see Exhibits 6 and 7).

Under the system, the managers or directors of the company's different units (departments, factories, and workshops) were given authority over the following matters:

1. **Personnel management** – They are authorized to appoint or remove their subordinate administrators or supervisors, or employ and dismiss their workers, following, of course, the procedures of the company's personnel department.
2. **Finance management** – They are authorized to approve expenditures of their units according to the budget. They are also entitled to the "manager's fund," which they could use to entertain clients or for other purposes that would promote their employees' enthusiasm to work. Furthermore, they had the authority to distribute bonuses to their employees when they achieved or surpassed targets.
3. **Quality control** – They have the right to reject the nonstandard semi-manufactured products from other factories in the company.

The implementation of its economic benefits system led to positive results, including:

1. **Reduction in raw material and energy consumption** – A good example was the savings made in the fan net casing factory. By changing its shift schedule and adopting other measures, the factory reduced its electricity consumption by one-third (or 400,000 kwh) a year, giving the company an annual savings of 200,000 yuan. It was also able to save, by as much as 100,000 yuan a year, on the cost of repairing broken down equipment.
2. **Increased capacity utilization** – The case of the fan motor factory exemplified the benefits derived by the company from its economic responsibility system. Before the implementation of the system, the factory's monthly production of 70,000 fan

motors fell short of the company's demand of 150,000 units every month. Thus, to improve output, the director of the factory organized the technicians, streamlined production procedures, and hired more workers (many of whom worked overtime). These measures eventually resulted in higher production (150,000 fan motors a month), better product quality, lower costs, and higher wages for the workers.

## New Challenges Ahead

While he took pride in the past achievements of the company and in the good reputation it had built up over the years both at home and overseas, Mr Zheng also felt some apprehensions about the future. He realized that there would be new challenges ahead. The company's rapid growth had necessitated changes in its operations and structure, changes that spawned new problems and created fresh conflicts:

1. **Modern production versus backward management** – As the company's capacity expanded to meet a growing demand, production planning and control became more complex, resulting in occasional imbalances in the company's operations. At times, delivery schedules could not be met. With the increase in the volume of financial transactions, the use of calculators and abacus would no longer suffice. Thus, unless the company resorted to computerization, the Finance Department could not effectively carry out financial analysis and control.

   Although Mr Zheng realized the need to computerize and adopt modern management methods, he also recognized the limited capability of the company's current staff. NFHAC did not have enough qualified managers or administrative staff and competent computer personnel to handle the new job requirements.

2. **The old managers versus the young** – Most of the department managers were pioneers in the company and had contributed considerably to its growth and development. They were the right-hand men of the general manager. But as the company slowly adopted the modern methods of management, the department managers became worried that they would soon be replaced by the more educated, talented young men recruited by the company from outside town to be junior administrative officers in their departments. Threatened and feeling insecure, the old managers refused to place the young "outsiders" in important positions.

3. **Difficulties in exports** – The company encountered many problems in exporting its product.

   First, export prices were low. At US$10 a set, the FOB export price of its electric fans was 50 to 70 percent lower than the domestic market price. In fact, according to an international grading of electric fans in the world market, China-made fans were classified under grade five – the lowest.

   Second, it took a long time before the company could get its export drawbacks. According to government regulations, drawbacks (equivalent to 18 percent of the FOB value of the shipment) would be given to the company upon shipment of its product. In practice, however, it would sometimes take months before the company got paid.

Third, it was not easy to get passports and visas for anyone to go abroad to market the company's product. The procedure for the passport application was long, and so was the waiting time for the visa. As a result, the company could not do business with foreign traders on time or missed out on business opportunities.

Fourth, most of the staff of the Export and Import Department did not have a good command of the English language and were, therefore, ineffective in dealing with foreign buyers.

4. **A sunset industry** — Electric fan manufacturing was turning into a sunset industry. Being highly labor-intensive, the industry was greatly affected by the rapid increase in wages in PRD brought about by the high economic growth in the area.

Faced with the above problems that threatened the future growth of the company, Mr Zheng asked the Business Administration Section to come up with a proposal outlining development strategies for the company over the next three years.

## NFHAC's Development Plan for 1991–1993

After an enthusiastic discussion, Mr Zheng and his deputy and department managers came up with a draft plan that had the following major features:

**Development Strategy.** The company would continue to produce and export electric fans at the current volume. However, no further expansion in capacity nor additional investments in equipment and buildings would be made for the manufacture of the product.

In the meantime, NFHAC would go into the production and export of air conditioners. For this purpose, a factory with an annual output of 100,000 units would be built in cooperation with the Hong Kong W F Air Conditioner Co.

The Company would also develop some new types of simple household appliances for the home market, such as electric warmers, range hood fans, and electric frying fans.

**Targets.** The total output value for the period 1991–1993 was targeted to reach 1 billion yuan, of which 60 percent would be accounted for by electric fans; 35 percent by air conditioners; and 5 percent by other household appliances.

About 70 percent of the total output of electric fans and 50 percent of the production of air conditioners would be exported.

After defining the company's development strategy and setting production and export targets for the next three years, Mr Zheng and his staff are now ready to recommend specific measures to help the company achieve its objectives.

EXHIBIT 1

## NAN FENG HOUSEHOLD APPLIANCE CO
## Selected Indicators of NFHAC's Operations
## For the Period 1980–1990

| *Year* | *1980* | *1981* | *1982* | *1983* | *1984* | *1985* | *1986* | *1987* | *1988* | *1989* | *1990* |
|---|---|---|---|---|---|---|---|---|---|---|---|
| Value of output (thousand yuans) | 3,830 | 4,010 | 2,930 | 6,540 | 16,780 | 19,500 | 31,680 | 41,860 | 103,680 | 196,660 | 202,260 |
| Sales income (thousand yuans) | 4,020 | 4,200 | 1,250 | 5,640 | 11,350 | 36,650 | 15,860 | 43,570 | 104,330 | 187,560 | 213,200 |
| Sales cost (thousand yuans) | 3,788 | 3,400 | 1,260 | 4,782 | 8,690 | 28,760 | 14,727 | 40,435 | 95,797 | 166,070 | 192,246 |
| Sales tax (thousand yuans) | 200 | 220 | 210 | 846 | 1,703 | 5,497 | 1,110 | 3,050 | 7,303 | 13,129 | 14,924 |
| Profit (thousand yuans) | 32 | 580 | –220 | 12 | 957 | 2,393 | 23 | 85 | 2,230 | 8,363 | 6,036 |
| Output (thousand units) | 16 | 18 | 14 | 33 | 170 | 210 | 350 | 600 | 1,360 | 1,950 | 1,940 |
| Export volume (thousand units) | 0 | 0 | 0 | 0 | 0 | 0 | 80 | 240 | 960 | 1,480 | 1,500 |
| Number of staff | 168 | 206 | 256 | 289 | 369 | 650 | 853 | 1,002 | 1,236 | 1,583 | 1,787 |

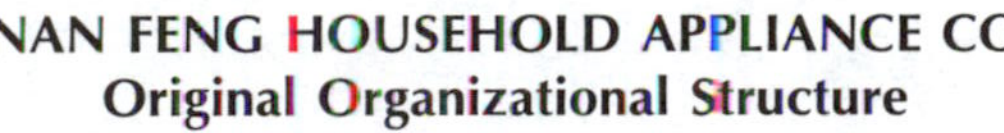

EXHIBIT 2

**NAN FENG HOUSEHOLD APPLIANCE CO**
**Original Organizational Structure**

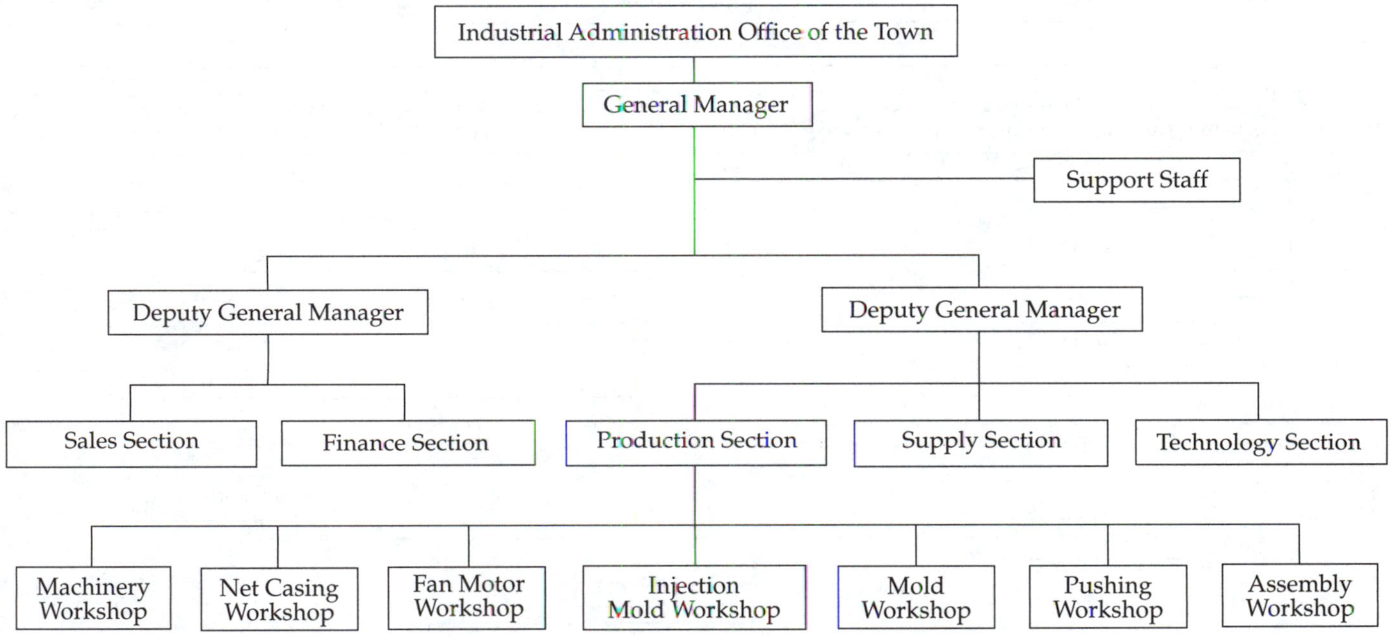

Industrial Administration Office of the Town
General Manager
Support Staff
Deputy General Manager
Deputy General Manager
Sales Section
Finance Section
Production Section
Supply Section
Technology Section
Machinery Workshop
Net Casing Workshop
Fan Motor Workshop
Injection Mold Workshop
Mold Workshop
Pushing Workshop
Assembly Workshop

EXHIBIT 3

**NAN FENG HOUSEHOLD APPLIANCE CO**
**Revised Organizational Structure**

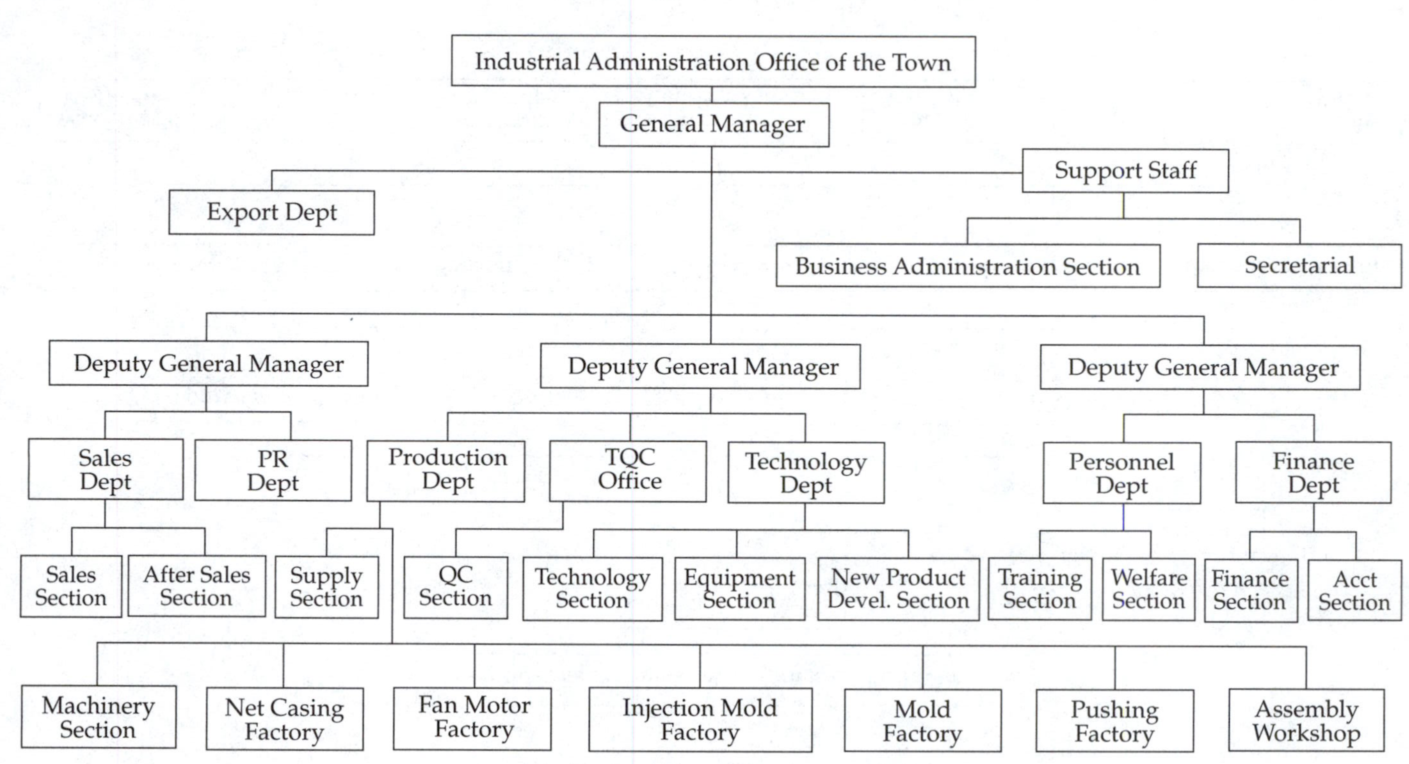

EXHIBIT 4

## NAN FENG HOUSEHOLD APPLIANCE CO
## Contract of Responsibility Between General Manager of NFHAC and Industrial Development Company (IDC), Town Government
## For the Period 1991–1993

1. The IDC appoints Mr Jiang Zheng as the General Manager of NFHAC for three years, from January 1, 1991 to December 31, 1993.

2. The General Manager will observe the following targets during his tenure of office:

| *Item* | *1991* | *1992* | *1993* |
|---|---|---|---|
| Total value of output (in thousand yuan) | 242,000 | 363,000 | 472,000 |
| % Growth | 20 | 50 | 30 |
| Total sales income (in thousand yuan) | 255,000 | 380,000 | 519,000 |
| % Growth | 20 | 49 | 36 |
| Total profit (in thousand yuan) | 9,680 | 16,150 | 23,600 |
| % Growth | 60 | 67 | 46 |
| Management fee to be turned over to the IDC | 3% of the annual sales income of the company. | | |
| Profit share to be handed over to the IDC | 20% of the annual net profit of the company. | | |
| Depreciation fund | To be drawn each year by the company at a rate of 10%. | | |
| Taxes | Company pays sales tax, income tax, and other taxes on time. | | |
| Safety | General Manager must ensure safety in the production area at all times. | | |

3. If the General Manager achieves or exceeds his targets, he will be rewarded with a bonus of 1,000–15,000 yuan by the IDC. If he falls short of his target in the first year, he loses 20 percent of his floating salary. If he still fails to reach his targets in the second year, he will be dismissed from his position. However, if failure to attain the targets is due to unforeseen reasons, the IDC will discuss and readjust the targets with the General Manager.

4. The General Manager will be given the authority to:
   a. employ and dismiss employees.
   b. determine the salary and wage structure for the company's employees, subject to the approval of the IDC.
   c. decide on the production and operation of the company, with the important decisions subject to the approval of the IDC.

Tom Huang
Director of the IDC of the
Town Government
December 10, 1990

Jiang Zheng
General Manager
of NFHAC
December 10, 1990

EXHIBIT 5

**NAN FENG HOUSEHOLD APPLIANCE CO**
**Salary Coefficients**

| *Position* | *Coefficient* |
|---|---|
| General Manager | 1.0 |
| Deputy General Manager or General Engineer | 0.9 |
| Manager of Department and Director of Factory | 0.8 |
| Deputy Department Manager | 0.7 |
| Director of Section or Engineer | 0.6 |
| Deputy Director of Section | 0.55 |
| Administrative Staff | 0.1–0.5 |

EXHIBIT 6

## NAN FENG HOUSEHOLD APPLIANCE CO
## Contract of Economic Responsibility Between Export Department and Management of NFHAC

To raise the work enthusiasm of the export staff, the Export Department and the Management of NFHAC agree on the following:

1. The Export Department must reach an annual export volume of 1.6 million electric fans and an annual export sales income of US$15.5 million.

2. The amount to be distributed as floating salary of the staff will be pegged at 0.1 percent of the total export sales income of the department. The Manager of the Export Department has the authority to distribute the amount to his staff according to their contribution, capacity, etc. He himself is entitled to 165 percent of the average amount received by the staff.

3. If the Department succeeds in exporting the electric fans at a price higher than the basic price set by the Management, then it gets as bonus 50 percent of the extra sales income derived from the price difference.

4. The total management expense of the Department is pegged at 0.2 percent of the total export sales income, and will be regulated as follows:

    a. The authorized expense items include: entertainment for clients, rice supplies, transportation cost, service charges of the customers, commodity inspection, advertising, and promotion.
    b. If the Department saves part of the amount allocated for management expense, it gets as bonus 20 percent of the amount saved. On the other hand, if the department spends in excess of the allocation, then the excess amount will be deducted from the Department's total floating salary.

This contract is valid from January 1991 to December 1991.

Jian Qiu
Manager
Export Department
December 10, 1990

Jian Zheng
General Manager
NFHAC
December 10, 1990

EXHIBIT 7

## NAN FENG HOUSEHOLD APPLIANCE CO
## Contract of Economic Responsibility Between the Fan Motor Factory and the Management of NFHAC

To encourage its workers and supervisors to reduce production costs, improve product quality, and increase economic benefits, the Fan Motor Factory enters into an agreement with the company management on the following:

1. The factory aims to reach the following annual production targets:
   a. 25–40cm motor ............... 2 million units
   b. 15–20cm motor ............... 500,000 units
2. The factory will function as an independent accounting unit, assuming sole responsibility for its profits or losses.
3. The Factory Director has the following authorities:
   a. to hire and dismiss his employees, except the accountant, who has to be appointed by the company's personnel department.
   b. to distribute the floating salaries of the administrative staff within the range set by the finance department.
4. The wage of the workers will take into account production cost. The standards for the piecework wage system should be set by the Finance Department.
5. The factory has to buy the main materials, supplementary materials, and spare parts from the company at transferred prices set by the latter. It can buy tools outside of the company at prices approved by the finance department.
6. The depreciation charges may take into account production cost, with the annual depreciation rate set at 12 percent.
7. The wastage rate for materials (enameled wires, wiring plates, etc) is set at 5.5 percent.
8. The factory is allocated a circulating fund of 600,000 yuan annually. If it exceeds its allocation, it will pay an interest to the company at the prevailing bank rate of 12 percent per annum. If it saves on the fund, the company pays the factory an interest at the same rate.
9. The factory will sell its products to the company at the transferred price set by the latter at the end of each month. The monthly profit of the factory will be equal to its monthly sales income minus its monthly production cost.
10. Half of the monthly profit will constitute the factory's floating salary, bonus, and director's fund. Of this amount, 6 percent will be allocated to the director's fund and 7 percent for the director's monthly floating salary. The deputy director will get a floating salary equivalent to 90 percent of the director's floating salary, and the other administrative staff, 40–60 percent. The remaining amount will be paid out at the end of the year as bonus for the administrative staff.

This contract is valid from January 1, 1991 to December 31, 1991.

Son Li
Director
Fan Motor Factory
December 10, 1990

Jiang Zheng
General Manager
NFHAC
December 10, 1990

# Rayalaseema Biscuits Company, Kurnool* 17

In mid-1988, Surya Narayan, who had recently assumed charge as the branch manager of Telugu Bank Ltd, Kurnool, was contemplating what legal action he should take against Rayalaseema Biscuits Company (RBC). As of June 30, 1988, RBC owed Rs 41.5 lakh to the bank, whereas its accumulated losses totaled around Rs 59 lakh against its share capital of Rs 11 lakh.[1] The chances of recovering the dues from the liquidation of stocks appeared bleak. Though the advances were partly secured by personal guarantees of the directors, the bank could hardly recover 70 to 80 percent of the dues. Surya Narayan was convinced that RBC could be turned around with a change in management. Nonetheless, he was contemplating enforcement of the personal guarantees given by the directors.

## The Company

RBC was established in 1980 as a private company to manufacture biscuits in the small-scale sector. It was promoted by two directors, Pratap Reddy and Kantha Rao. Pratap Reddy, a man of substantial means, was the correspondent of a college and a nonpracticing lawyer. Kantha Rao was an agriculturist turned successful civil contractor who had executed a number of projects for the Indian Railways, the Public Works Department, and

---

*This case was prepared by S Raghunath, Assistant Professor of Management, Lal Bahadur Shastri Academy of Administration, Mussoorie, India. Reproduced with permission from *Vikalpa: The Journal for Decision Makers*, 14:4 (October–December 1989), published by the Indian Institute of Management, Ahmedabad.

[1]In 1988, the exchange rate was US$1.00 = Rs 13.917. A "lakh" is a unit of 100,000; for example, Rs 1 lakh is equivalent to Rs 100,000.

other large companies. They entered into a technical and marketing tie-up with Benzer and Company Limited, Bangalore, which was to act as the clearing and forwarding agent for the biscuits manufactured by RBC. In addition, Benzer was to provide technical guidance for manufacturing quality biscuits and for training some of the employees.

## Finance

The total cost of the project was estimated at Rs 31 lakh. In September 1980, the promoters approached Telugu Bank for a term loan of Rs 19 lakh and a working capital finance of Rs 2.7 lakh. At that time, they did not submit a detailed project report to the bank but gave an outline of the project, details of machinery and equipment, and working capital requirements. On October 14, 1980, the branch manager recommended RBC's proposal to the regional manager. On October 30, 1980, the regional manager wrote to the head office that RBC's proposal could be accepted on the basis of the recommendation of the branch manager, subject to the condition that the promoters would bring in a capital of Rs 6 lakh and unsecured loans of Rs 2.2 lakh before the release of any bank loan. The regional manager highlighted in his letter "... the directors of the company are honest and creditworthy. They have been dealing with the bank for a long time in the past . . ." (see Exhibits 1 and 2 for the branch manager's and the regional manager's letters, respectively.)

In March 1981, the bank sanctioned a term loan of Rs 17.66 lakh, opened a cash credit limit of Rs 2.67 lakh and a key cash credit limit of Rs 3 lakh with the stipulation that promoters have to initially invest a capital of Rs 6 lakh before the release of any part of term loan.

The branch manager, however, did not insist on the stipulation mentioned by the regional manager and disbursed the amount sanctioned. Further, he made payments directly to the promoters when the sanction stipulated that payments were to be made to the suppliers of the machinery after collecting margins from the borrower. Most of the disbursements in the term loan were cash payments made to the promoters and the branch did not get copies of the invoices relating to the machinery purchased by the company. Further, the Bank did not create a charge on the assets of the company within 30 days of disbursing the loan as was statutorily required.

## Project Implementation

There was considerable delay in implementing the project because the State Electricity Board did not provide power connection to the unit. Moreover, the company did not send periodic progress reports to the Bank. However, bank officials occasionally visited the factory site to keep themselves abreast of the work-in-progress. The technical officer from the regional office inspected the unit during 1982 and reported as follows:

> The civil construction of the unit is complete and the machinery has been erected. The machinery has been verified as per the quotation of the suppliers and it is found that it has been properly installed.
>
> The company has applied to the Civil Supplies Department for supply of sugar and *maida*.[2] The branch manager has confirmed that the disbursement of loan amounts was made directly to the

[2]*Maida* is white flour.

suppliers and that the company paid an amount of Rs 1 lakh to the Civil Supplies Department for securing stocks of sugar and *maida*.

The unit is ready to commence production, but the main hurdle is the power connection, which has not yet been obtained. It was learnt from the applicants that power supply was delayed because neither the Rural Electrical Corporation nor the State Electricity Board could take any decision on whose jurisdiction this unit falls. After prolonged persuasion, the State Electricity Board has agreed to give power connection on August 20, 1982. The transformer for power connection has been erected.

The order for power connection was issued by the State Electricity Board on August 3, 1982 and was received by the company on August 30, 1982. The unit started production on December 22, 1982, well over two years behind schedule. The financial position of the company as of December 31, 1982 is shown in Exhibit 3.

## More Financial Assistance

Consequent to the delay in implementing the project, the company required more working capital. It also requested the Bank for a rescheduling of the term loan.

Agreeing favorably to the request, the Bank raised the open cash credit limit to Rs 10 lakh, provided a clean bills purchase limit of Rs 2 lakh, and canceled the key cash credit limit of Rs 3 lakh. During the year 1983, the company had a turnover of Rs 4.35 lakh and incurred a loss of Rs 5.46 lakh.

## Change in Marketing Arrangement

In November 1983, the company approached Benzer with a proposal that Benzer should purchase RBC's biscuits under the brand name of "Benzer." In the earlier arrangement, biscuits were dispatched to Benzer but the title of the stocks held by Benzer remained with RBC. Benzer distributed RBC's products to dealers/consumers, and collected and dispatched checks drawn in favor of the manufacturer. A late realization of these checks led to an increase in the working capital requirements of RBC. There was a substantial increase in the cost of materials and overheads too. Because the finished products were immediately dispatched to Benzer, RBC was unable to take advantage of the finance on finished goods stocked; the realization on receivables was also delayed. The bank would not consider any sort of demand bills purchase limit for the following reasons:

1. The goods delivered by the company to Benzer were distributed to dealers and/or consumers by the latter.
2. These parties were unknown to the company and the bank until the checks and/or bills were presented for realization.

In the revised marketing arrangement which came into effect starting November 5, 1983, Benzer agreed to purchase the biscuits under the brand name of Benzer, provided the quality control staff of Benzer had given its stamp of approval to the biscuits. RBC extended to Benzer a credit period of 60 days from the date of delivery. Benzer advised RBC to draw bills under the *hundi*[3] system for supplies made and such bills were to be accepted

[3]The *hundi* system refers to the interest-free credit facility extended by many merchants in India.

by Benzer for payment on the due dates. The supply price for each item and the commission payable to Benzer for its services were fixed through negotiations.

In 1984, RBC's turnover had increased to Rs 30.98 lakh but losses too had gone up to Rs 12.47 lakh (see Exhibit 4 for RBC's financial position for 1983 and 1984).

## Labor Unrest

The packaging department at RBC consisted of 30 workers, mostly female. In April 1984, the workers of RBC went on strike, demanding a wage increase of Rs 3 a day on the existing rate of Rs 12 a day for those workers who were categorized as unskilled labor. The union contested this categorization and argued that packing is a skilled job because it involved matching the packing speed with the speed of production. The union pointed out that it normally took 10 hours to pack 8 hours of production; if it were not a skilled job, any unskilled worker would have done the job in just 8 hours. After a month, the management revised the wage rate to Rs 15 per day and also offered an incentive of Rs 2 for extra work done every day. Thus, the labor problem was amicably settled.

## Financial Crisis

However, by June 14, 1984, the company closed down its operations on account of a cash crunch (see Exhibit 5 for the company's liability towards the bank).

There were overdues of Rs 7 lakh in the term loan account, Rs 8.87 lakh because of deficits in stock and Rs 0.72 lakh overdue bills, a total of Rs 16.78 lakh against the total liability of Rs 29.38 lakh. The directors tried to lease the unit to Leo Foods Limited, Hyderabad. But the terms of lease were not acceptable to the Company and the bank.

In September 1984, RBC approached the bank in an attempt to renew the open cash credit limit of Rs 10 lakh and to obtain a sanction of Rs 20 lakh against usance bills. Apart from an assurance to bring additional unsecured loans of Rs 10 lakh, the directors gave the following details to the bank:

1. RBC would like to start production in September.
2. The company proposes to appoint an experienced man as Executive director.
3. The company has recently secured an order for 83 tons of biscuits.
4. Benzer agrees to accept *hundies* and market at least 100 tons of biscuits every month.

Extracts from the technical officer's note to the regional manager regarding the above request are given below:

> . . . the liquidity of RBC is not satisfactory. There is a liquid deficit of Rs 8.38 lakh. There is a negative net worth of Rs 7.11 lakh and the total liability is Rs 38.21 lakh. Already, there is an amount of Rs 22.31 lakh under the long-term liability against fixed assets valued at Rs 23.58 lakh. The proposed bringing in of Rs 10 lakh as unsecured loans will be just sufficient to wipe off the liquid deficit and meet the margin for working capital. The company has realised that it lacks experience in the field and wishes to bring in an experienced man as executive director.
>
> The branch manager recommends the renewal of open cash credit of Rs 10 lakh and the sanctioning of additional documentary usance bills purchase limit of Rs 20 lakh. He is of the opinion that an early sanction of usance bills will avoid further loss. As the limits are interlinked with the financial

commitments of the unit and as it is also difficult for directors to invest fresh capital without assurance from our side, needless to say the unit will be in the doldrums once again if the necessary limits are not given. On September 11, 1984, the branch informed me over the phone that usance bills outstanding of Rs 72,000 had been realised and the company has also remitted a sum of Rs 70,000 toward open cash credit liability, which has come down to Rs 8.17 lakh.

However, the position of this unit is alarming and we may have to decide whether we have to recall the advance or to renew the limits and consider additional usance bills limit.

To renew the limits, we have to consider the following factors:

1. Whether the present management will be able to manage the unit properly.
2. The name of the new executive director and his experience in the line.
3. Unsecured loans of Rs 10 lakh.

As there is the time factor, we may recommend a renewal of limits and sanction Rs 20 lakh usance bills limit with the following conditions:

1. The company should wipe off the deficit in open cash credit immediately with unsecured loans.
2. The credentials and experience of the new executive director should be verified by the manager.
3. A special report should be submitted by the branch every fortnight covering the following information: stock on hand (copy of statement), liability, drawing power, production made, sales made, and bills position.

In response to this official note, the regional manager recommended a renewal of the open cash credit limit of Rs 10 lakh and usance bills limit of Rs 20 lakh with the three conditions as detailed above. But RBC failed in its attempts to bring in Rs 10 lakh as unsecured loans and the unit could not be revived. The directors pleaded for more time to revive the unit. Subsequently, the directors decided to split up and Kantha Rao opted to give full managerial control to Pratap Reddy. Meanwhile, the bank advertised for the disposal of the unit but met with poor response. Pratap Reddy was not in favor of selling the unit since he wanted to lease it to the Bangalore Biscuits Company (BBC).

## Leasing Arrangement

During November 1986, RBC got a sanction from the bank to lease the unit to BBC provided:

1. RBC paid at least Rs 3 lakh against its dues to the Bank before enforcement of the contract.
2. RBC agreed to pay Rs 50,000 a month to the Bank after the commencement of the job work.
3. The Bank reserved the right to increase the monthly payment. Though the monthly repayment of Rs 50,000 was meager, the Bank consented to this condition as there was a possibility of increasing it if RBC could lease out another two shifts.

The period of lease was two years. The raw materials and other input costs except power and labor were to be borne by BBC. RBC would receive Rs 1,600 a ton toward conversion charges and would undertake to manufacture 100 tons of biscuits a month on a single-shift basis. BBC agreed to provide a cash advance of Rs 4 lakh and post their supervisory staff for controlling the quality and movement of stocks; BBC would bear the salaries of their staff.

## Performance of the Contract

RBC paid Rs 3 lakh to the Bank and cleared its arrears with the State Electricity Board. The company made a trial run and informed BBC that it would take up the conversion job from February 15, 1987. However, production could not start owing to non-allotment of the ISI certificate. Ultimately, the certificate was obtained in June 1987 and production commenced in July. The Bank did not receive any payment until then.

Meanwhile, Kantha Rao requested the Bank to relieve him from the company's liability by taking the properties of Pratap Reddy. A meeting was held in the zonal office of the bank on May 20, 1987 and Pratap Reddy offered ancestral property worth Rs 10 lakh to the bank. The Kurnool branch of the Bank was advised to collect information relating to the property and to ask for legal opinion on it.

A charge on the company's assets was created and the charge registration certificates were obtained for a term loan of Rs 15.60 lakh and an open cash credit of Rs 10 lakh.

In October 1987, the new manager of the Kurnool branch along with the technical officer inspected the unit and obtained the following information on the performance of the company (see Exhibit 6).

RBC continued to be irregular in paying its monthly installments to the bank. In June 1988, its financial position worsened (see Exhibit 7). The branch manager reviewed the situation and concluded that the managing director was not showing interest in making good use of the lease arrangement with BBC. His conclusions were based on the following observations:

1. The managing director of the company had shifted his registered office outside the present location, leaving the affairs of the company to a manager who did not have any experience in the management and technical aspects of the unit.
2. When power cuts were imposed on all industrial units in the area by the State Electricity Board, the manager did not present his case before the Board for exemption as a sick unit under revival.
3. The manager had allowed the affairs of the company to drift. He did not accede to the request of BBC to increase the staff in the packing section to match the production rate of the finished products.
4. Instead of reducing the liability of the Bank and saving the interest burden on overdues, the manager had allowed the outstandings to pile up without making any arrangements for repaying.
5. The manager had defaulted on the installments to the Bank and had diverted part of the surplus amount to pay the electricity bills. Though he had shown interest in obtaining concessions which were available to sick units, he was not really keen on reviving the unit.

The biscuit industry was booming since 1986 and the company did not take advantage of this fact. The branch manager was, thus, of the opinion that unless there was a change in management, the unit could not become viable.

EXHIBIT 1

## RAYALASEEMA BISCUITS COMPANY, KURNOOL
## Letter from the Branch Manager to the Regional Manager of the Telugu Bank Ltd

October 14, 1980

The Regional Manager
Telugu Bank Ltd

Dear Sir:

Re: SSI—Term Loan and OCC Facility A/C
Rayalaseema Biscuits Company

Rayalaseema Biscuits Company, Kurnool, has approached us for credit facilities: a term loan of Rs 11,50,000 against machinery, a term loan of Rs 7,50,000 against land and building, and working capital facility of Rs 2,70,000. Earlier, we have issued a bank guarantee for Rs 1,10,000 favoring Benzer and Co Ltd, Bangalore. Sri Pratap Reddy, Managing Director of RBC, has entered into an agreement with Benzer to install this unit, with registered office at Kurnool and the factory at a small village in Kurnool district. Accordingly, the Company has acquired two acres of land in the village at a cost of Rs 48,000. Since this is a backward area, the Industries Department is giving a subsidy of 10 percent on the proposed plant, machinery, and other equipment. The total estimated cost of the project comes to Rs 31.09 lakh; the company requires financial assistance to the extent of Rs 21.70 lakh.

Rayalaseema Biscuits is venturing into establishing a biscuit manufacturing unit with the cooperation of Benzer, who will act as C & F agents and will market to the tune of 1,200 tons of biscuits a year. The capacity of the unit is more than 2,700 tons a year. The additional production of 1,500 tons could be supplied to Benzer or marketed by RBC itself through its distributing agencies. This unit is the first of its kind sponsored by Benzer in the backward districts and, from the economic point of view, it is feasible, viable, and profitable.

The Managing Director and the other Director, Mr Kantha Rao, have been known to our bank for a long time. The Directors propose to invest their own capital to the extent of Rs 5 lakh, collect Rs 3 lakh from subsidy sources, and the rest we have to consider by way of a term loan and OCC. The remaining amount of Rs 1.1 lakh toward technical know-how will be borne by the Directors of the Company or by Benzer. The proposed unit is capable of securing raw materials, power, and labor at reasonable rates. It has received approval from the Industries Department and a Provisional Registration Certificate has been granted on September 11, 1980. The area where the unit is located is eligible for incentives from the Industries Department. The state incentive of interest-free sales-tax loan will also be eligible on the fixed assets, land, building, and machinery worth Rs 20 lakh as per recent amendments.

For this proposed advance, the land, building, and machinery will be taken under equitable mortgage and stocks under hypothecation in addition to the personal guarantee of the directors. The loan is repayable within seven years from the commencement of the business with a grace period of one year. The borrowers have agreed to pay Rs 75,000 plus interest on a quarterly basis. They are agreeable to avail the open cash credit limits according to our normal rates.

The proposed unit will produce all varieties of biscuits. There is no problem in marketing as Benzer is undertaking the responsibility of purchasing the entire quantity of biscuits on the basis of the agreement entered into with the manufacturer. In turn, Benzer will effect payment directly to the bankers to the credit of Rayalaseema's account with us. Rayalaseema Biscuits is giving a letter of authorization to deduct the usual installments plus interest from the amounts so received. There will not be any problem in repayment of the loans since there is a good demand and marketability for the product.

If there is any deficiency in the total investment of the project, the Directors will meet it from their own resources. Kindly consider the application on our usual terms and conditions at an early date and communicate the limits to us at your earliest convenience.

Yours faithfully,

Manager
Kurnool Branch

EXHIBIT 2

## RAYALASEEMA BISCUITS COMPANY, KURNOOL
**Letter from the Regional Manager**
**Telugu Bank Ltd**

October 30, 1980

The General Manager
Central Office
Bangalore

Dear Sir:

Re: Kurnool Branch — SS1 New Proposal of
Rayalaseema Biscuits Company

We forward herewith a letter from the Kurnool branch dated October 14, 1980 along with the proposed project details. The Directors of the company are honest and creditworthy. They have been dealing with the branch for a long time. The project is economically viable and technically feasible. We recommend the following limits:

| *Nature of Facility* | *Limit (Rs Lakh)* | *Security* | *Margin* |
|---|---|---|---|
| Term Loan | 17.66 | Land measuring 2.21 acres situated near Kurnool valued at Rs 48,000 | 50% |
| | | Machinery valued at Rs 15.30 lakh | 25% |
| | | Building/property valued at Rs 8.77 lakh | 33½% |
| Open Cash Credit | 2.67 | Against stock in trade of biscuits, raw materials and other confectionery products | |

Repayment: The term loan is repayable in quarterly installments of Rs 75,000 in seven years, with an initial holiday of one year. Please communicate your sanction at an early date.

Yours faithfully,

Regional Manager

EXHIBIT 3

## RAYALASEEMA BISCUITS COMPANY, KURNOOL
## Balance Sheet
## As of December 31, 1982

(Rs in lakh)

| | | |
|---|---|---|
| Assets | | |
| Current Assets, Loans, and Advances | | 4.90 |
| Fixed Assets | | 22.20 |
| Preliminary and Pre-operating Expenses | | 4.80 |
| Total Assets | | 31.90 |
| Liabilities and Net Worth | | |
| Current Liabilities and Provisions | | |
| Outstanding liabilities | 0.03 | |
| Security deposit from employees | 0.13 | |
| Creditors for suppliers | 0.94 | 1.10 |
| Secured Loans | | |
| Term loan from Telugu Bank against hypothecation of fixed assets | 17.66 | |
| Open cash credit from Telugu Bank against hypothecation of stocks | 2.67 | 20.33 |
| Unsecured Loans from Directors and Their Relatives | | 0.18 |
| Total Liabilities | | 21.61 |
| Share Capital | | 10.29 |
| Total Liabilities and Net Worth | | 31.90 |

EXHIBIT 4

**RAYALASEEMA BISCUITS COMPANY, KURNOOL**
**Financial Position**
**For the Years Ending December 31, 1983, and 1984**
(Rs in lakh)

| *Item* | *1983* | *1984* |
|---|---|---|
| Assets | | |
| Current Assets | 11.51 | 7.33 |
| Investments | 0.45 | 0.07 |
| Suspense Account | 0.12 | 0.12 |
| Fixed Assets | 30.06 | 31.29 |
| Less Depreciation | (4.13) | (7.71) |
| Total Assets | 38.01 | 31.10 |
| Liabilities and Net Worth | | |
| Current Liabilities | | |
| From Bank | 8.35 | 12.96 |
| From Others | 3.73 | 2.94 |
| Term Loans | | |
| From Bank | 15.60 | 15.60 |
| From Others | 4.85 | 6.71 |
| Net Worth | | |
| Capital | 11.00 | 11.00 |
| Less Intangible Assets (e.g., preliminary expenditure) | (5.52) | (18.11) |
| Total Liabilities and Net Worth | 38.01 | 31.10 |
| Sales | 4.35 | 30.98 |
| Net Loss | 5.46 | 12.47 |
| Purchases | 9.24 | 19.51 |
| Stock | 6.00 | 2.50 |
| Current Ratio | 1:1 | 1:2 |
| Liquid Surplus | Nil | (8.38) |

EXHIBIT 5

**RAYALASEEMA BISCUITS COMPANY, KURNOOL**
**Details of Liabilities to Telugu Bank**
(Rs in lakh)

| *Facility* | *Limit* | *Liability* | *Demand Promissory Note* | *Deficit/Arrears of Installments* |
|---|---|---|---|---|
| Term loan | 15.60 | 19.79 | – | 7.19 |
| Open cash credit | 10.00 | 8.87 | 1.50 | 8.87 (as the stock was very old) |
| Clean bills purchase | 2.00 | – | – | – |
| Documentary usance bills purchase | – | 0.72 | – | 0.72 (overdue) |

EXHIBIT 6

**RAYALASEEMA BISCUITS COMPANY, KURNOOL**
**Financial Performance**
**For the Period July–September 1987**

| *Item* | *July 1987* | *Aug. 1987* | *Sept. 1987* |
|---|---|---|---|
| Production | | | |
| Sakti Cartons | 7,017.00 | 1,263.00 | 5,929.00 |
| Sakti Tins | 0 | 2,271.00 | 0 |
| Marie Cartons | 0 | 685.00 | 2,551.00 |
| Tonnage | 33.96 | 24.49 | 42.32 |
| Number of Working Days | 25 | 26 | 30 |
| Indent from M/S Bangalore Biscuits Company (Tons) | 30.00 | 30.00 | 40.00 |
| Expenditures | | | |
| Electricity Bill and Salaries | 48,910.75 | 72,251.80 | 76,486.10 |
| Wages | 12,574.00 | 11,872.00 | 18,800.00 |
| Other Expenses | 7,000.00 | 8,000.00 | 10,500.00 |
| Total Expenditure | 68,484.75 | 39,123.80 | 105,786.10 |
| Receipts | | | |
| Conversion Cost Recovered from Bangalore Biscuits Co. | 54,339.65 | 39,696.24 | 68,012.22 |

**RBC showed the following liabilities toward the bank**
**as of September 30, 1987**

| *Facility* | *Limit* | *Liability* |
|---|---|---|
| Open Cash Credit | 10.00 | 9.37 |
| Term Loan | 15.60 | 30.32 |
| Total Liabilities | | 39.60 |

EXHIBIT 7

## RAYALASEEMA BISCUITS COMPANY, KURNOOL
## Financial Position
## As of June 30, 1988

(Rs in lakh)

| *Assets* | | *Liabilities and Net Worth* | |
|---|---|---|---|
| Current assets, including sundry debtors outstanding for more than six months | 15.03 | Current liabilities provision, including trade creditors | 18.15 |
| | | Secured loans | 43.38 |
| Fixed assets | 15.95 | | |
| | | Unsecured loans | 17.79 |
| Loss | 59.34 | | |
| | | Share capital | 11.00 |
| Total Assets | 90.32 | Total Equities | 90.32 |

| | |
|---|---|
| Present value of securities, factory land, building, machinery: Market value as estimated in 1986 | 38.18 |
| Additional security of house site | 15.00 |
| Total | 53.18 |
| Bank liability as of December 31, 1988 | 41.50 |

# Kum Fook Press* 18

Lee Seng, the patriarch of the venerable Lee family whose Midas touch had launched a mega-print empire, sat dejectedly, gazing long and deep at the rosewood table. How could the family business break up so soon? Whatever had gone wrong with the family . . . they ate together, played together, and worked together these fifty odd years, and yet, he had never realized that the conflict between his son and his brothers had escalated to this state.

Was it really due to "that woman" whom his son had brought in to help turn around the company? Modern management was not new to Lee Seng. He had agreed with his son Frank that they should modernise and pave the way for eventual listing on the Hong Kong Stock Exchange. That way the family fortune would be preserved and the business could only get bigger.

Lee Seng in his wildest dreams had not envisioned the strong reactions of his brothers to his son's new management style. How could they split up the family business now that it was about to take off to greater heights? The old man sat thinking to himself.

---

*This case was prepared by Selene Lay Hoon Lim, Ng Lee Keng, Tony Chuen Teck Phua, and Anne Hon Mui Tan-Lee (MBA, Nanyang Technological University, Singapore) under the supervision of Professor Luis Ma. R. Calingo. At the request of the company, financial data and the names of organizations, people and some places have been disguised, but essential relationships have been preserved. The case is designed to serve as a basis for class discussion rather than to illustrate either effective or ineffective handling of an administrative situation.

# The Printing Industry in Hong Kong

## Introduction

The printing industry had been one of the oldest established industries in Hong Kong. It had grown progressively over the years as the economy expanded. In the 1970s and early 1980s, the industry was largely oriented to the domestic market with a large number of small firms surviving on a jobbing basis to serve many local customers and a few large modern firms which also catered to the export market.

As of the time of the case, Hong Kong had over 350 printers, ranging from small stationery print shops to large-scale commercial printers. Except for a few larger firms, many of the printing establishments were still being run as family concerns. Many of them were family businesses started decades ago. They normally began operations by catering to simple stationery requirements such as business cards. A firm would initially have one small machine and perhaps about three workers. As business improved and the owner(s) found it worthwhile to plow back profits, more investments were made in manpower and machines, thus extending the firm's capability. While such an arrangement might suffice for small-scale printing jobs, the introduction of modern management to the firm was necessary before there could be any significant expansion, especially for the purpose of penetrating export markets.

## Role of the Small Printer

Small companies were defined as those employing less than 100 workers and with less than $3 million paid-up capital assets.[1] Medium-size companies referred to those employing 100 to 200 workers and with paid-up capital assets of $3–$8 million.

Small printing companies had an acknowledged role to play in the Hong Kong economy and, indeed, they provided an important service to the community. Their role in the business community was to supply the local market with basic requirements for documentation in commerce and industry such as letterheads, envelopes, invoices, statements of accounts, delivery orders, and receipt books. They were quite provincial in nature as they catered to the needs of those carrying on business in their respective vicinities. Since small printers were provincial in outlook, they tended to adhere to their business approach of controlled service supply. Many such firms relied to a great extent on a consistent flow of orders from regular customers. They made a reasonable profit but practically did not make much attempt to stretch their market boundaries. Partly because many of them were family concerns, they did not employ many workers and, thus, were unable to allocate manpower for sales work. These printers depended on referrals from existing customers for additional business.

Some of these companies with limited production facilities were cautious enough not to take in too much orders lest they fail to meet delivery deadlines. In most instances, small printers found themselves inhibited in business development and subsequent business expansion. This did not mean that the small printers would have no opportunity to improve themselves. The answer lay in upgrading their technology to improve printing quality and in providing further training to their workers.

---

[1]All currency figures are in Hong Kong dollars. As of December 31, 1994, the currency exchange rate was US$1.00 = HK$7.7375.

**Allied Trades**

In every industry, the allied trades play an important role by supporting the manufacturers in achieving higher productivity with the maximum level of quality and service without incurring excessive capital investment. Without the allied trades, industries could not maximize their profitability to compete in the open market. In the printing industry, the trade houses played this supporting role. The firms performed all the peripheral functions that supported or complemented the printing industry. They specialized individually in block-making, die-cutting, book-binding, type composition, plastic lamination, color separation, and paper trading.

## Performance of the Industry

The printing industry had witnessed significant and important improvements over the years. It had maintained a steady growth since the early 1980s. The local printers were able to carve a niche for themselves with their reliable quality even though there was greater competition from low-cost regional printers.

Hong Kong's competitive advantage depends on whether its print products could match or better the quality of foreign publications and at a lower price. Improving the product, in turn, would hinge on whether the industry could attract and keep trained workers. Hong Kong printers were pushing to upgrade the technical competence of their staff to make them more productive. Printers were also investing heavily in new equipment. With new equipment, firms could increase capacity without adding manpower. However, printers had argued that better training and more technology were not boosting productivity enough to keep up with the demand for print products. A number of labor-starved printers had begun to move some of their more labor-intensive operations to other countries in the region.

The highly competitive domestic market was already saturated, thereby limiting opportunities for domestic expansion yet paving the way to regional and international markets. To survive in the international market, the printing companies must produce work which was of good quality and at competitive prices. The common experience of successful firms was that they must be equipped with the latest in printing technology and also be producing printing of high standard and quality. Most of these internationalization efforts were accomplished through joint ventures with foreign firms.

## Kum Fook Press Pte Ltd

Kum Fook (meaning "Golden Fortune") Press Pte Ltd was one of the many rags-to-riches corporate success stories in Hong Kong. With an annual turnover of $80 million, it was undisputedly the market leader in the colony's printing industry, holding its forte in print manufacturing and book binding (see Exhibit 1 for Kum Fook Press's organizational chart).

Founded in the late 1930s, it was no overstatement that Kum Fook was the crystallization of perennial, good old qualities of hard work, vision, and dogged entrepreneurial spirit. With multiple assets and property investments, no one knew for sure the exact magnitude of the company's wealth. The land where the factory was located was last estimated at a modest sum of HK$50 million.

Into its second generation of family business, Kum Fook had been managed along traditional Chinese values. Atmosphere at the work place was congenial and easy-going. Mirroring the family management team, the staff also functioned as a close-knit community. Older staff members, some of whom have been employed at Kum Fook for decades since the early days, were accorded respect by the younger members. Seniority was a valuable asset, especially when firing was never embraced as a personnel practice.

Though it might not make it to the list of Fortune 500, the mention of Kum Fook would conjure notions of a very well-to-do family business giant that offered security synonymous to that of lifetime employment. At the time of the case, the Lee family owned 90 percent of Kum Fook, with the remaining 10 percent of shareholdings owned by a joint-venture Japanese press.

## Founder Lee Seng

Patriarch Lee Seng, 78, is the Founder and retired Chairman of Kum Fook. His sons Frank and Harry worked in the company as Managing Director and Sales Manager, respectively.

Born in Guangzhou, China of a school teacher and a peasant's daughter, Lee Seng migrated to Hong Kong after completing a few years of education. Armed with some linguistic proficiency and a keenness of mind, Lee Seng obtained his first job as a printing apprentice.

Not satisfied with being an employee all his life, he struck it out on his own and set up a small printing company named Kum Fook with the savings that he and his wife had managed to amass. It was literally a one-man operation. Lee Seng was the owner, writer, typesetter, graphic designer, and salesman, all rolled into one. The going was tough and business was slow. All through those days, Lee Seng's wife had always been a great supporting figure behind him, taking care of the household budget and helping with the chores in the firm. Their perseverance paid off when after two years of working 14-hour days, Kum Fook began to gain recognition as a printing firm. Coupled with Lee Seng's willingness to experiment with new techniques and management skills, expansion was given a boost and staff strength grew from a paltry 10 to a whopping 1,000.

Over the years, Lee Seng planned for a smooth takeover of business by his sons. He had no intention of selling the business to outsiders, even though there had been some really attractive offers. To lay the path for succession, one of the things he did was to send his sons to top business schools in the United States.

After fifty years of leading at the helm, he decided to call it a day and stepped down a few years ago. By this time, Lee Seng and his two sons owned 45 percent of the shares of Kum Fook Holdings. Though not holding official position, it was common knowledge that Lee Seng still wielded considerable decision-making power from the sidelines.

## Brother Lee Ho

When Lee Seng retired, his brother Lee Ho, 70, assumed the position of Chairman. Of a benign nature, Lee Ho was easily a popular figure in the company. He was easy-going and was well-noted for his generosity toward long-serving staff. But there were times when he was viewed as having overextended his generosity. There had been more than one occasion when he lent money to staff on the company's account without documentation.

He also disregarded the established incentive plans and promised promotion and increment to staff based on his personal feelings, much to the chagrin of Frank and the human resource director.

The underlying philosophy for Lee Ho's kind acts was his belief that one had to care for one's employees as one would care for one's children. For him, this was the only way to garner life-long loyalty. And true to his conviction, he had a sizeable following of loyal staff who would "die" for him.

Although Lee Ho had three sons, much to his disappointment, they chose not to work in Kum Fook. He had secretly hoped that they would participate in the family business where he had invested much of his youth, energy, and efforts. Instead, they set up a paper trading firm and thrived on it. It was, however, obvious that the trading firm's good profits were in no small way attributed to the ties with Kum Fook. Lee Ho did not exactly like the working styles of his nephews, Frank and Harry. Much as he respected his brother Lee Seng, he always had the gnawing feeling that the youngsters did not consult him enough on company matters. Thus, despite his good nature, he would sometimes prove to be curt with his nephews.

Into his 70th year, Lee Ho was still a robust man with an alert mind. He breathed and lived the life of Kum Fook and had no plans to retire as yet. At the time of the case, Lee Ho owned 35 percent of the shares in Kum Fook Holdings.

## Brother Lee Kwong

Lee Seng's second brother, Lee Kwong, had been with the family business ever since he was old enough to help around the shop. Having only a few years of education, which was considered a lot in those early days of the company, Lee Kwong rose from the ranks. To reward him for the years of service in the company, Lee Seng appointed him Director of the Graphics Department ten years ago.

The promotion pleased Lee Ho as he was glad that Lee Kwong had at last received a measure of recognition in the company. As for Lee Seng, although he was aware of the shortcomings of Lee Kwong, he had to appear fair in his dealings with Lee Kwong because his brother had indeed given the better part of his life to the business. What would the relatives think of him if Lee Kwong was still a junior manager after all these years? Lee Seng thought Lee Kwong's assistants, Ah Guan and Lang Chai, would somehow prop up the Graphics Department should Lee Kwong run into difficulties.

An easy-going person by nature, Lee Kwong delegated almost all of his job responsibilities to Ah Guan and Lang Chai just as Lee Seng had thought would happen. Being a straightforward person, he never checked on the comings and goings of his staff. Ah Guan and Lang Chai worked hard almost every night long after most of the other staff in the department had gone home. They were always treated favorably by Lee Ho and Lee Kwong, who both held them high as exemplary model workers for the rest of the workers to follow.

Lee Kwong, unlike Lee Seng, enjoyed the simple pleasures of life — as long as his staff reported no problem to him, he was "happy as a clam." His staff, long accustomed to his effusive moods and affable character, had learned to keep matters, especially negative ones, from his knowledge. Over the years, he had come to rely more and more on his two deputies to run the Graphics Department. Almost all the rank-and-file staff regarded his deputies as the heads of the department ,whom all of them reported to, and looked upon Lee Kwong more as owner than as a supervisor. At the time of the case, Lee Kwong and other relatives owned 10 percent of Kum Fook Holdings.

## The Graphics Department

Ah Guan and Lang Chai, both armed with a tradesman's certificate, had no more than 8 to 10 years of formal schooling. Although they were skilled in the art of color separation and flatbed proofings, they managed the department on a day-to-day basis.

Firefighting was a daily affair. With increasing workload, the department neither kept records of jobs-in-progress nor recorded machine hours for each job done. The department functioned with the sales service people chasing outstanding jobs each day. The graphics staff claimed this was the best way to work for they did not have enough manpower to keep track of outstanding jobs.

It was market practice that a client could request proofings to be redone several times to his or her satisfaction. Hence, a specific job can flow through the Graphics Department several times in the space of a few weeks, or even months, before a color separation job could be considered closed. There was a perpetual feud between the graphics and the sales service staff; both parties felt that they were not solely responsible for tracking the jobs in hand.

Since records of incoming and outgoing jobs were not adequately kept, the Graphics Department did not know the actual work volume it performed throughout the year. The monetary value would appear in the financial year's accounts when items charged under graphics by the sales service personnel were invoiced to the clients for payments. Should the sales personnel overlook charging, there was no way of knowing a mistake had been done.

## Son Frank Lee

Lee Seng's eldest son, Frank Lee, was appointed Managing Director of Kum Fook Press when his father retired as Chairman and his uncle, Lee Ho, vacated the post to become the new Chairman.

On passing his 40th birthday, Frank had undergone a change from his flamboyant past to a more focused and mellowed personality. His colleagues were quite surprised by his apparent change; everyone who knew him agreed the change was for the better. This happened one year before he was made the Managing Director.

Frank married an American after his first marriage to a Chinese failed. His family had frowned upon the match, but Lee Seng later gave his blessings as he felt his strong-willed future daughter-in-law would provide him the stability to run the company without distraction. As time passed by, the family felt that the old man (Lee Seng), as in business, was proven right again even in matters of the heart! Frank was considered a "born again" entrepreneur after his marriage.

It was no surprise that he brought in a highly qualified Human Resource Director, Wen Si, to help him reorganize the company and to change its prevailing culture.

Frank used to tell his uncles that: "Running a company based on relationships and staff loyalty is not enough, Uncles. . . . We need to know profit centers and loss makers . . .

. . . We need to sell our vision of where the company is moving so that our staff would know what is expected of them if they want to keep up with us. Those who will not change can choose to leave. They can make room for new blood to join us, for those who can share in our vision, our corporate goals. We cannot protect the rice bowls for those who won't change."

## Retrenchment and Consolidation

An event which demoralized and shook up the old guards at Kum Fook Press was the selling out of the Color Separation Department, managed by Lee Seng's third brother, Lee Kwong, who was the Graphics Director. In the past, there was no accountability for profit and loss by departments. When recession hit in 1985, the new management bared the apparent shortcomings of the Graphics Department.

A quick diagnosis suggested that graphics was bleeding the company. An equally quick remedy was prescribed to close the section, retrench the 100-strong old staff and sell off the machines to Color Key, a "friendly" competitor in the color separation industry.

Lee Kwong and Lee Ho were against the idea from the start. A heated exchange over the matter took place in the Board Room:

*Lee Kwong:* "How could they say that Graphics is hemmorrhaging the company? The sales people never check the work they do for the customers, maybe never bill clients for work done by us. . . . Our department kept doing overtime; how come we're not making money? Perhaps, the Sales Department gives heavy discounts and makes us look bad."

*Frank:* "Lee Kwong, be reasonable! Your workers had to work overtime because they are not efficient. You and I know they simply took a longer time to complete the tasks because of overtime pay. We cannot afford to look after so many people just because they grew up with the company — they either shape up or ship out! We had all agreed to work by the principles of accountability and profitability; we have 5 years to show clear profit records before the listing and we cannot afford to be sentimental!"

Lee Kwong's arguments fell on deaf ears. Frank and Wen Si held little regard for Lee Kwong as they found him an unsuitable candidate for the running of such an outfit.

Frank was getting increasingly upset by his uncles' reactions to many of his ideas. Being Managing Director, he had to show results and capability in leading the company to a higher plane. His uncle was Chairman only in name after Lee Seng's retirement; the sole responsibility of running the business fell on his shoulders. Frank was getting the pressure of steering the "clumsy ship" (as he so often described Kum Fook in his private moments with his wife) and yet can he reach out for the star and get his firm listed as quickly as possible? He often wondered.

The debate over the fate of the Graphics Department went on intensely for a week longer before the decision was made to ax off the department. Frank and Wen Si were thoroughly convinced that they should divest the Graphics Department and concentrate on the printing and binding business instead. Even then, the heated arguments were emotional:

*Lee Ho:* "My nephew, you'll be sorry if it's the wrong decision. . . . Do you realize there are so many in there who will talk bad about us, curse us for retrenching them? They'll say we have no heart, how shall we put up our heads after this? Can we take a little more time to consider such a major decision? After all, we are not talking about five or ten workers, but a hundred of them!"

*Lee Kwong:* "Or worse, we could be wrong to say this department is unprofitable? Do you cut out your hand if it looks ugly and old? How are we going to explain this to the father and son who had worked here for the past 40 years?"

## Leung Wen Si, Human Resource Director

The entrance of Wen Si (meaning "refined silk") was often identified by the industry as the fatal jab to Kum Fook's harmony and prosperity. An intelligent and assertive lady, she was widely acknowledged to be one of the top professionals in Human Resource Management. Prior to being hired by Frank to help turn the company around, she was working as a Recruitment Consultant at a multinational corporation.

Armed with a degree and knowledge of modern management theories, she set to reform the company with an almost religious zeal. Her restructuring strategies for Kum Fook comprised a comprehensive program involving incentives, staffing, and training. For incentives, she implemented merit payment plans with productivity as the measuring variable. That implied that not every staff would be accorded the extra cash.

Her other more drastic strategy was to recruit an entire cohort of MBA degree-holders to take over practically all the functions, from production to planning, bindery, sales and accounting. The old managers, who had only elementary Chinese education, saw the threat very clearly. Unable to grapple with the new management theories and practices, they soon left one after another.

Wen Si valued the importance of training and invested efforts to arrange training sessions for the staff. The sessions included team-building games and outdoor seminars.

Wen Si's mode of management was alien to Lee Ho and angered him to no end. The old man felt he was losing power; he could not even act as a protective shield for his loyal followers. But Wen Si, strong-minded and determined by nature, brushed aside the negative remarks on her management tactics and pressed on with her reforms with Frank's support. She had only one goal and that was to establish her prowess as a Human Resource Specialist and to get Kum Fook Press listed. Ever so self-assured, she was confident that the company was being led onto the right tracks. Deep inside, she knew that one day, Kum Fook would have her to thank for all the incredible accomplishments that were to come.

## One Year After Consolidation

At the office of Lee Ho, the two Lee brothers discussed the company's state of affairs. As usual, they would complain about their nephew behind his back but would keep up a stoic front in front of him:

*Lee Kwong* (lamenting): "We were the stupid ones. Color Key is doing so well. . . . I told you it was our sales people who didn't charge for all the work the department had produced. Ah Guan and Lang Chai taunted us. . . ."

*Lee Ho* (rejoined in frustration): "We should have stood up to Frank and that woman.

What do they know that we do not equally know? Oh, and that British consultant who works with her all day long. . . . What does he know about us? Was he here when we built up the plant? Frank was in his diapers, and now he thinks he has eaten more salt and totally disregards our opinions. He doesn't come and see me even if they are planning to acquire new machines. . . . I won't sign the next proposal that comes in."

## The Great Showdown

At the next management meeting, Frank opened the meeting with the following revelations:

*Frank Lee*: "I'm afraid we axed the graphics department too hastily. Should have seen what the guys in sales were up to. . . . How could Alfred and Bernard not know what their sales staff were doing? The lax supervision in sales resulted in both the new and old staff not charging clients for graphics work done!"

Lee Ho merely smiled. He could no longer follow his nephew, who sounded more like a stranger. Such a revelation was hardly surprising as this was what they meant to tell him all along before the retrenchment. They had no records then in the graphics department to make their case.

The retrenchment day, a week before Christmas, was the most painful day of Lee Ho's life. For the first time, he felt powerless. He was no longer in a position to offer comfort to the long line of departing staff. "Why be Chairman and be cursed for a decision I didn't make?" he thought.

*Wen Si*: (glancing at Lee Kwong) "How could we be so blind as to allow those two — Lang Chai and Ah Guan — to work overtime all the time without checking whether they were working for their own pockets? I was told they made more than a million dollars working at night here for a publisher-friend . . . using our materials and machines. . . . Now that we have closed the department, we have no proof to enable us to press charges against them."

Lee Kwong exploded in anger at this time. Over the past year, he was made to feel that he was responsible for the debacle. How could he be held responsible for the two men who were bent on cheating the company? "Who could have foreseen that loyal employees would end up backstabbing them? It's all fated!" he thought.

*Lee Kwong*: *to Wen Si* "You better shut up and leave right now! Because of you, the family is bickering; the department closed down. Didn't we tell you about the sales people?"

*Wen Si*: "My going and staying is up to Frank."

*Frank Lee*: "Stay calm, Uncle. It's not Wen Si's fault."

Lee Ho, who had stood listening at the sidelines, could not take it anymore. He had meant to talk to his nephew and brother, Lee Seng, in private but felt that this was a good time to bring up the subject. Lee Ho had several discussions with other family members in the absence of Lee Seng on the conduct of his nephew. He knew this was the time to air their differences and to go their separate ways.

*Lee Ho*: "Frank, I don't need to sit here day in–day out listening to the shortcomings of my people. Yes, I did agree to spare no efforts in staff training in order that they be made more efficient in order for the company to get listed. But things are getting out of hand. . . . How many old staff have left us and set up equally successful ventures outside since we began our program? I want to put an end to this listing nonsense — I'll talk to Lee Seng tonight with the rest of the family."

Wen Si could hardly breathe. Lee Ho and Lee Kwong actually had the gall to blame her for the closing of the graphics department as well as for staff resignations that she felt were long overdue.

More than half the family did not share the vision of going public. Right now, there are two serious offers to buy over the company, which could turn most of the Lees into multimillionaires without the hassles of running a tight ship. What could she do now to help Frank hold on to the dream? How do you convince two uncles who are bent on frustrating the grand plan? How could she and Frank salvage the situation?

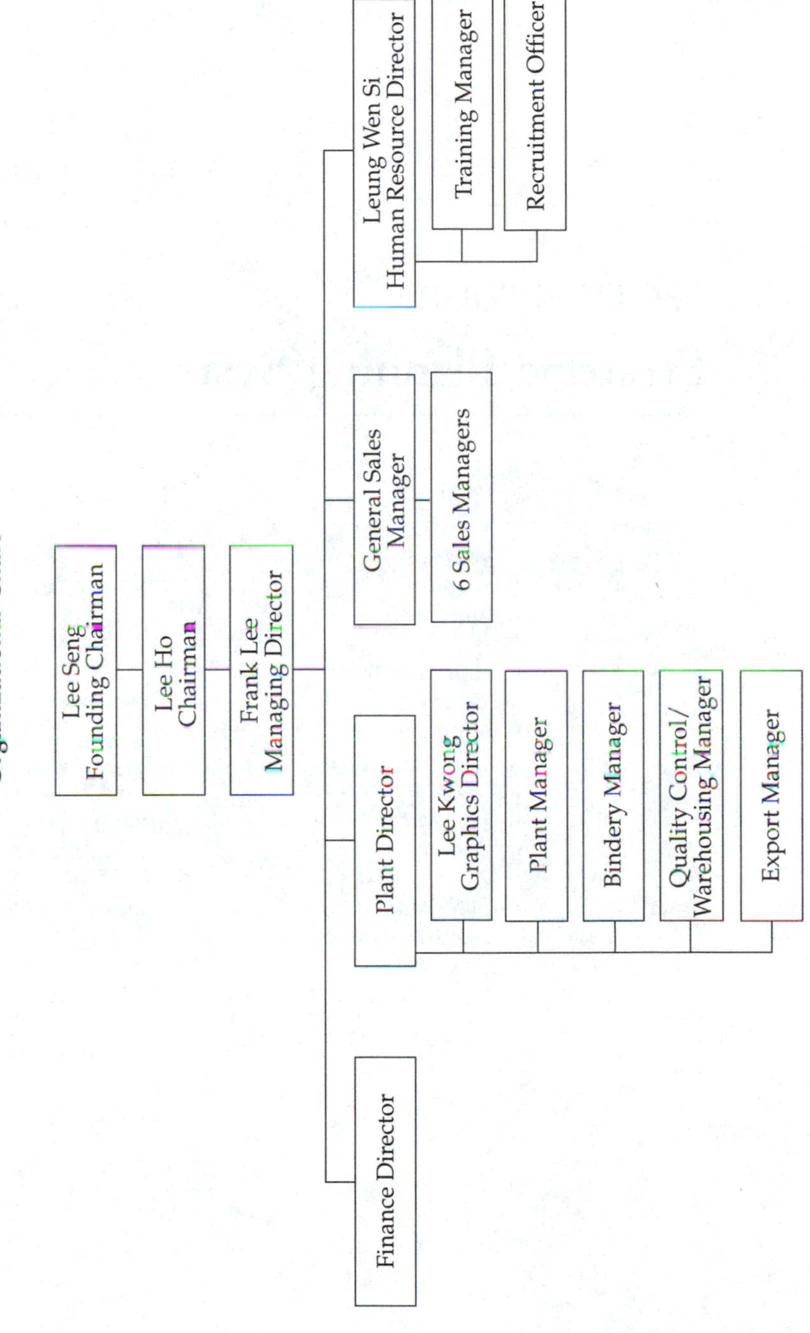
EXHIBIT 1
KUM FOOK PRESS
Organizational Chart
Lee Seng
Founding Chairman
Lee Ho
Chairman
Frank Lee
Managing Director
Finance Director
Plant Director
Lee Kwong
Graphics Director
Plant Manager
Bindery Manager
Quality Control/
Warehousing Manager
Export Manager
General Sales
Manager
6 Sales Managers
Leung Wen Si
Human Resource Director
Training Manager
Recruitment Officer

## SECTION FOUR

# Strategic Planning Systems

| *Case Number* | *Case (Country)* | *Nature of Situation* | *Complexity* |
|---|---|---|---|
| 19 | Ben Santos (Philippines) | Introducing strategic planning | Medium |
| 20 | Corporate Planning at Metro, Inc. (Philippines) | Implementing strategic planning | Low |
| 21 | La Tondeña Distillers, Incorporated (Philippines) | Introducing strategic planning | Low |
| 22 | British Banking Corporation (United Kingdom) | Business planning | Medium |

| *Products/ Services* | *Sector* | *Financial Data* | *US$ Sales (000)* | *Industry Conditions* |
|---|---|---|---|---|
| 'harmaceutical 'reparations | Manufacturing | Yes | 26,986 | Growth |
| .ight railroad ransportation | Transportation | Yes | | Growth |
| /ines and distilled iquor | Manufacturing | No | 106,399 | Mature |
| nvestment Banking | Finance, insurance, and real estate | Yes | 1,575,000 | Growth |

# Ben Santos* 19

In July 1986, 29-year-old Ben Santos was discussing with his former professor a set of materials he would present in a one-day planning workshop to be held by his company in Baguio City[1] the following week. The workshop was being held to discuss the institution of a corporate planning system designed by Santos. The system had already been endorsed by the company president and the division managers had been asked to comply with the new system. Mr Santos wanted to know how best to present and defend his proposed corporate planning system during the workshop.

## Company Background

H Braun, Philippines (HBP) was a wholly owned subsidiary of a West German multinational corporation which manufactured a line of medical and chemical products in Europe, Asia, and Latin America. The Philippine subsidiary was organized into five operating divisions, each distributing a selected line of products to institutional and retail outlets. The organizational chart of HBP is shown as Exhibit 1.

---

*This case was written by Professor Rafael A Rodriguez, College of Business Administration, University of the Philippines. At the request of the company, financial data and the names of organizations, people, and some places have been disguised but essential relationships have been preserved. The case was designed to serve as a basis for class discussion rather than to illustrate either effective or ineffective handling of an administrative situation. 

[1]Baguio City is a mountain resort city 300 kilometers north of Manila.

HBP had always been headed by a West German national. The current company president had no previous experience in the Philippines but was transferred from a Latin American assignment to assume the position in the Philippines in April 1986. Currently and historically, the five operating divisions of HBP were headed by West German nationals who reported to their counterpart product heads at company headquarters in West Germany, as well as to the president of the Philippine operation. Among the priority items in the announced agenda of the new head's presidency was the institution of a corporate planning system for H Braun, Philippines.

## Ben Santos

Ben Santos was an accountancy graduate from a leading university in Manila. After two years of work, he went back to school and obtained his MBA degree in 1982. Prior to joining HBP, Santos did financial analysis and staff planning work with three financial institutions in the Philippines.

In May 1986, Santos applied and was interviewed for the position of assistant to the president of HBP. During the interview, he learned that the president needed someone who would assist in the design and institution of a formal corporate planning system in HBP. Santos was hired shortly after these interviews.

Following his appointment, Santos had several discussions with the president concerning the need for a better planning system for the company. "How can we manage this company effectively if we do not have clearly stated strategies to guide us?" the president had asked Ben Santos in one of these meetings. Santos learned that there were preliminary discussions in HBP headquarters in Germany concerning the introduction of formal strategic planning for the whole company. Subsequently, the president formed a Strategic Planning Committee to coordinate the effort of designing a corporate planning system for HBP. The president was the Chairman of the committee. Santos as the Head of the Indent Division, as well as the Head of the Finance and Accounting departments also participated in the committee. The Head of the Indent Division was the most senior of the division heads in HBP. Santos was assigned the primary task of preparing the proposals for the corporate planning system for the company.

## The Planning System at HBP

As a first step in undertaking his assignment, Santos familiarized himself with the planning system currently in use at the company. Essentially, the current system consisted of the preparation of two-year revenue and cost budgets for each of the divisions based on planning guidelines coming from West Germany. These guidelines typically provided scant guidance and usually consisted of prescribed budget formats and a target return on "bound capital," which the Philippine subsidiary had to try to achieve. For the past few years up to 1986, Santos learned that the target had uniformly been set at 20 percent. Santos gathered that the target return represented headquarters's assessment of the "opportunity cost of capital." Occasionally, the planning guidelines included sales growth objectives for certain products, usually new products sold by specific divisions.

Divisional reports on actual performance are sent to the counterpart product divisions at the headquarters in West Germany every quarter. These reports served as the basis for updating the second year's budget forecast.

Bonuses for the managers and employees of HBP were paid when the Philippine subsidiary made profits. It was Mr Santos' impression, however, that although divisional profit targets were taken seriously by the division managers, they did not impose heavy sanctions if these targets were not met.

## Proposing a Corporate Planning System

Ben Santos went back to his personal files on the corporate planning systems of the companies where he had previously worked. He also read a number of the most recent American books on corporate planning. Finally, he compiled a set of macroeconomic indices and forecasts which he believed would be useful planning material for the company. Using the above, he prepared a proposal (see Exhibits 2 to 6) for the new planning system at HBP. When Santos presented these materials to the president for comment, the latter convened the Strategic Planning Committee, in which the proposal was discussed and approved with only minor modifications. Following this, the president issued a memorandum to the divisional managers (see Exhibit 2) announcing the adoption of the proposed system.

## Initial Reactions from the Division Managers

Santos spent the next few weeks interacting with the division managers concerning the proposed planning system. The reactions from the managers irritated him. "The division managers for Pharmaceuticals and Hospital Supplies gave childish reasons for criticizing my proposal. They implied that I copied the system straight out of a book, which of course is not true."

"The manager of Industrial Chemicals said he doesn't see the need for a new system. He explained that in his division, he uses estimated planned production of the textile mills, adds a factor for new mills and derives the bulk of his sales forecast in this manner. "I've been doing this for the last four years and so far, I've been able to hit the forecast, even allowing for the 10 percent growth rate targets for certain products coming from Germany. My method works. So what more do you want?" he told me."

When Santos reported these negative reactions to the president, the latter suggested that a one-day workshop to discuss the proposal be held. The president asked Santos to prepare well for the workshop and added that he was anxious to have a corporate planning system installed by the second half of 1986.

EXHIBIT 1

**BEN SANTOS**
**Partial Organizational Chart**
**H Braun, Philippines**

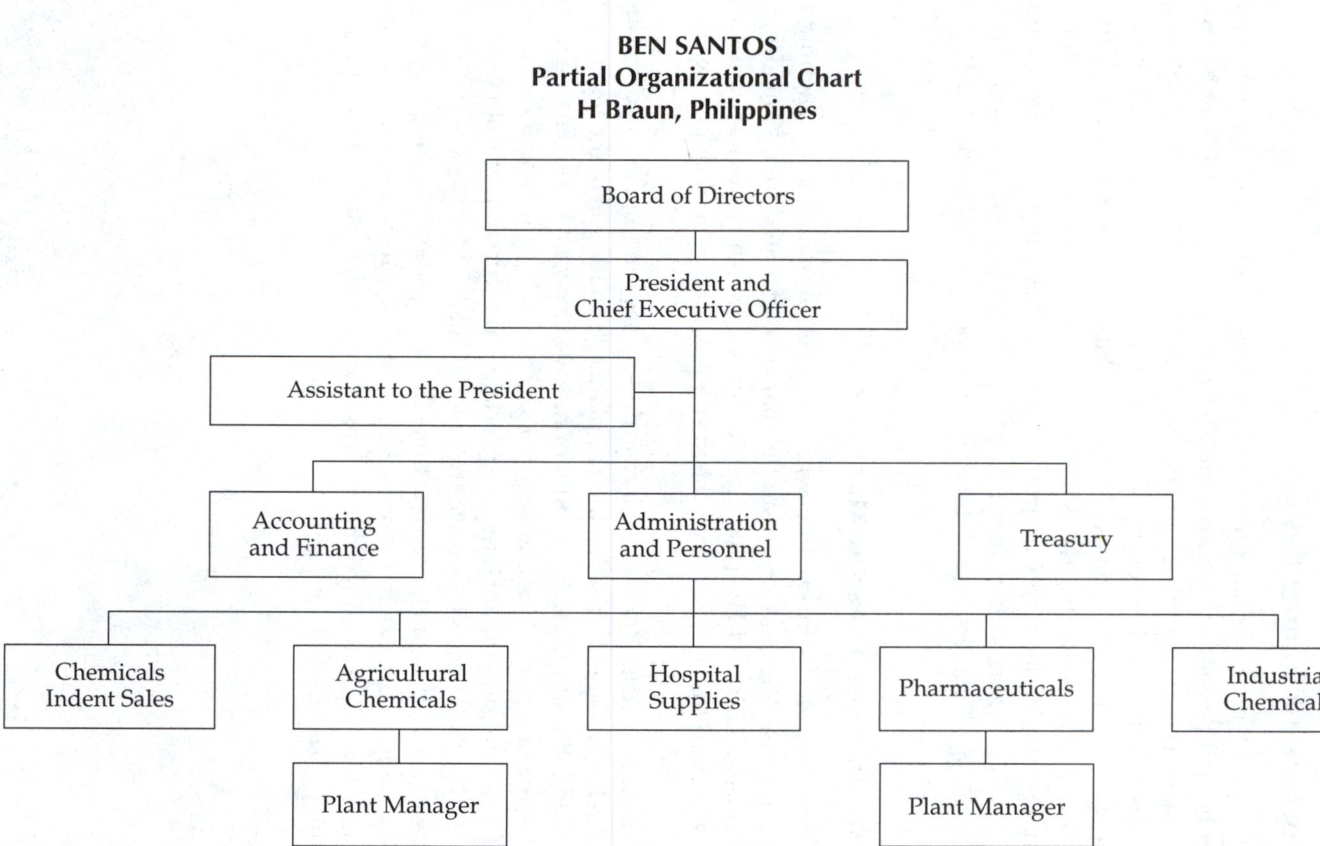

EXHIBIT 2

## BEN SANTOS
## President's Memorandum on Corporate Planning System

### MEMORANDUM

Date: June 29, 1986

To: ALL DIVISION MANAGERS

From: President

Subject: **Corporate Planning for H Braun, Philippines, 1987–1992**

Consonant with management's objective of defining appropriate strategies for HBP as discussed during the Division Managers' Meeting, I am pleased to inform you that the Strategic Planning Committee has already come up with general guidelines for the formulation of the respective divisional strategies for the next five years. They will serve as standard planning formats but are flexible, taking into consideration the nature of operations peculiar to your divisions.

Enclosed please find a summary of General Guidelines for Corporate Strategy Formulation for your ready reference.

As the preliminary step toward the implementation of an effective strategic planning system for HBP, the consensus arrived at by the committee members is that the strategy formulation process should start at the divisional level, and the consolidation thereof would represent HBP's overall corporate strategies.

Enclosed are the following standard planning formats and general assessment of the political and economic situation in the country for the period 1987–1990:

1. **General Economic Indicators for the Period 1983–1992.** Historical and projected figures were provided by the Economic Planning and Research Staff of the National Economic & Development Authority (NEDA).[1] Although still unofficial, the projected figures would, more or less, show the general growth pattern of the Philippine economy for the planning period.

2. **Overall Political Situational Analysis.** This will serve as the general background and would help explain future economic trends as set forth in the economic projections.

3. **Divisional Environmental Assessment.** This will cover the major parameters in the micro-environment of each division with the objective of identifying potential opportunities and/or threats in the external environment.

In view of the foregoing, we shall be able to come up with a critical analysis of our environment, which is the most important prerequisite to strategy formulation. I would appreciate it, therefore, if you could prepare and submit to the Strategic Planning Committee the following on or before July 30, 1986:

---

[1]NEDA is the national planning agency of the Philippine Government.

1. Definition of nature and scope of business pertaining to your respective divisions.

2. Indication of strengths and limitations of your respective divisions.

3. Divisional environmental assessment making use of the attached format allowing flexibility in terms of identification of other elements/parameters.

After submitting the above information, we will proceed to the second phase of the Strategic Planning Process as follows:

1. **Setting of Goals and Objectives.** This involves a definition of what is the company's desired future based on the company's present position, opportunities in the environment, the company's resources, and on the expectations of Central Headquarters in West Germany.

2. **Adoption of General Corporate Strategies.** This will be formulated at the divisional level, taking into consideration opportunities in the environment and at the same time, maximizing the company's utilization of resources to attain goals and objectives. The process of corporate strategy formulation involves the preparation of alternative approaches considering environmental opportunities/threats, strengths and limitations, and management values. (Attitudes toward risks, achievement, corporate climate, and social issues.)

3. **Financial Plan (Budget).** The financial plan is the translation of goals, objectives and strategies into quantifiable terms, or principally the profit and loss statement.

If you need additional information, please let us know.

Your full cooperation in this regard will be highly appreciated.

EXHIBIT 3

**BEN SANTOS**
**General Guidelines for Corporate Strategy Formulation**
**June 1986**

## I. OBJECTIVES OF STRATEGIC PLANNING

*Strategic Planning* is the design of a desired future for a business enterprise and the identification of effective ways to achieve it. It is called "strategic" because it gives major importance to the company's external environment as a major factor to consider in the process of corporate strategy formulation.

More specifically, the objectives of strategic planning are:

1. to allow constant awareness of both internal and external environmental developments and how they may affect the company's future growth;
2. to establish the company's overall direction and the specific targets that contribute to the achievement of the overall objectives;
3. to set priorities and maintain proper plan implementation; and
4. to monitor and control all activities to ensure the achievement of set targets and conformity with the planned direction of the enterprise.

## II. ELEMENTS OF STRATEGIC PLANNING

### A. Definition of the nature and scope of business

A definition of the business sets in broad terms the direction of the company. This involves answering the basic question, "What is our business?" This definition covers three aspects:

What has the business been?
What is unique about the business?
What should the business be?

The scope of business may be defined to include the product the company offers and intends to develop (this should be stated in terms of function instead of description), the market it serves or wishes to penetrate, and the technology it utilizes or desires to employ.

### B. Identification of corporate strengths and limitations

This involves a general review and evaluation of the entire company's strengths and limitations in terms of:

1. The company's present abilities relating to its business; and
2. the company's abilities in the future.

Evaluation should focus on such key areas as:

1. **Product** – what are the company's abilities to conceive, design, and modify the product.
2. **Production** – what are the company's plant and equipment capabilities; the technical processes and methods it employs; level of technology, etc.
3. **Market** – covers market share, distribution, sales force, and total marketing resource.
4. **Finance** – covers cash position, inventory levels, and financial stability.
5. **Human Resource** – includes personnel skills and abilities, organization, human relations, and turnovers.
6. **Management** – includes management style, values, and the organizational structure.

The objectives of such a review are to identify the company's resources needed to attain an expected future development and to compare resources with that of existing or future competitors.

## III. ENVIRONMENTAL ASSESSMENT

This involves an analysis of the external environment and the identification of different factors influencing the company's operation. Logically, the factors that should be considered as the main influence in the past operation should be identified. These areas should be monitored to see how they will affect the future. Other potential factors that could present opportunities or threats should also be monitored. A level of confidence for each envisioned factor should be determined — the probability that this will occur and the degree of its impact on operations.

Environmental assessment should include analyses of such areas as:

1. **Market** – present and envisioned markets.
2. **Competition**.
3. **Customer** – types, classification, needs and expectations.
4. **Technology** – developments in products, processes, machinery.
5. **Industry** – trends and prospects.
6. **Economic** trends and general business indicators.
7. **Monetary** and credit situation.
8. **Government** – Laws and restrictions.
9. **Social** Considerations.

## IV. BUSINESS SCREEN

The identification of corporate strengths and limitations and the assessment of the environment can be translated into a matrix called the "business screen." This matrix relates a business' or a product's industry attractiveness to the company's strengths. Its position in the matrix determines the relative expectation for such product or line of business, an important basis for strategy formulation. Each specific product or line of business should undergo this analysis so that its position in the business screen is established.

The business screen and its three categories are shown as follows:

INDUSTRY ATTRACTIVENESS

| STRENGTHS | HIGH | MEDIUM | LOW |
|---|---|---|---|
| HIGH | Invest/Grow | Invest/Grow | Selectivity/ Earnings |
| MEDIUM | Invest/Grow | Selectivity/ Earnings | Harvest/ Divest |
| LOW | Selectivity/ Earnings | Harvest/ Divest | Harvest/ Divest |

A. Portfolio Categories

The *invest/grow* category indicates products or lines of business with great potential and in which the firm is prepared to invest capital for long-term growth. The objective would be to achieve a strong market position for long-term profitability.

The *selectivity/earnings* category are products or lines listed for their short-term earnings. A product may remain in this category, move up, or decline.

In the *harvest/divest* category, the products are viewed as relatively weak and the industry only has a marginal interest in these products. The products are managed for immediate cash operations.

B. Evaluation Factors

The positioning of a portfolio should be based on the consensus of the company's executives. Product managers and top management may have varying perceptions of where a product is positioned. Once a product has been firmly established in the matrix, its treatment becomes almost automatic as dictated by its position. The significance of the categories in terms of strategies are discussed in Section VI.

As mentioned, the evaluation involves two sets of factors — the industry attractiveness (the external environment in which the product must compete) and business strength (the product by itself and the company's capability to handle the product).

Industry attractiveness is determined by the following factors:

1. **Industry size** – present and potential size to warrant the employment of management and other resources.
2. **Market growth** – indicates the stage of industry: mature or low growth, infant industry, or high-growth.
3. **Pricing** – competitiveness, control impositions.
4. **Market diversity** – number of segments, types of products, size per segment.
5. **Competitive structure** – relative strength of others in the same field.
6. **Industry profitability** – expected returns to be generated, considering size, competitiveness, etc.
7. **Technical role** – obsolescence of product, complexity of technical support required.
8. **Social, environmental, legal, and human aspects** – government legislations, environmental effect and moral expectations.

On the other hand, business strength is determined by:

1. **Size** – the volume the company can offer per segment.
2. **Growth** – volume and sales increases.
3. **Share** – market share per segment.
4. **Position/Image** – innovator, leader, etc.
5. **Profitability** – gross profit rate, fixed cost structure.
6. **Technology position** – innovator, R&D activities, competent back-up.
7. **Strengths/limitations** – strengths/limitations of the company in relation to the product.

In order to classify products into the high, medium and low categories, a scale can be drawn for each determinant factor in order to achieve an objective identification of product position. Prioritizing the factor will also determine the weight of each factor in the scale.

For example, the following weight may be assigned to determine product position in the industry attractiveness grid:

| *Industry Attractiveness Factor* | *Weight* |
|---|---|
| Industry size | 15 |
| Market growth | 15 |
| Pricing | 10 |
| Market diversity | 10 |
| Competitive structure | 13 |
| Industry profitability | 15 |
| Technical role | 8 |
| Social, environmental, and human | 7 |
| Legal aspects | 7 |
| Total | 100 |

Products/lines of business with scores of 85–100 are in the high industry attractiveness category; those with scores of 65–85 are in the medium industry attractiveness category; and those with scores below 65 are in the low industry attractiveness category.

A similar scale can be prepared for the business strength factor.

## V. SETTING OF GOALS AND OBJECTIVES

This involves a definition of what is the company's desired future based on the company's environment and the company's resources (business screen), and on the expectations of the various stakeholders. The goals and objectives will set the direction and pace of growth of the company.

Goals and objectives can be categorized as follows:

A. Long-term Objectives

Long-term objectives may be expressed in such terms as:

1. Attainment of certain industry status.
2. Continuing growth of sales.
3. Increase in market share.
4. Balanced satisfaction of the various "stakeholders" in the firm: managers, workers, stockholders, customers, suppliers and creditors.
5. Growth in earnings to provide resources for reinvestment.
6. Increase in the scope of market and service through new product lines and market penetration.
7. Contributions to social and economic development.

B. Short-term Goals

These may be expressed as specific percentages or values of the following:

1. Market share.
2. Plant capacity utilization.
3. Return on investment.
4. Return on stockholders' equity.

5. Growth in sales.
6. Growth in net income.
7. Earnings per share.

Short-term goals should be quantified.

## VI. ADOPTION OF GENERAL CORPORATE STRATEGY

General corporate strategies are formulated to take full advantage of opportunities in the environment and at the same time, maximize the company's utilization of resources in order to attain goals and objectives. The process of corporate strategy formulation involves the preparation of alternative approaches considering:

A. Environmental opportunities and threats.
B. The company's strengths and limitations.
C. Management values (attitudes toward risks, achievement, corporate climate, and social issues).

The first two factors, environment and corporate strengths and limitations, have been broadly considered in the business screen through the matching of industry (environment) and business strengths (corporate strengths and limitations). This determines the prospects for the product or line of business and hence the general expectations and course of action to be taken. On a broader level, this is called the *General Corporate Strategy*, as set forth below.

1. **Market Penetration** – offering the same products to the same markets.
2. **Market Development** – offering the same products to new markets.
3. **Product Development** – offering new products to the same markets.
4. **Diversification** – offering new products to new markets.

For products/lines of business within the selectivity/earnings category, a strategy of consolidation/rationalization of existing products and markets can be adopted. A divestment strategy can be adopted for the harvest/divest category.

The general strategies adopted for the three categories, broken down into the various strategy elements, are as follows:

| *Element of Strategy* | *Invest/Grow* | *Selectivity/Earnings* | *Harvest/Divest* |
|---|---|---|---|
| Capital Investment | Maximum feasible. | Selective/high yield segments. | Minimum. |
| Risk | Accept/contain. | Light. | Avoid. |
| Market Share | Build/diversify. | Target growth, protect position. | Forego share. |
| Pricing | Lead/determine price elasticity. | Stabilize for maximum contribution. | Maintain price even at the expense of volume. |
| Products | Lead/diversify. | Differentiate<br>• Specification<br>• Applications<br>• Performance | Preseve. |
| Costs | Determine reasonable level, not necessarily thrift. | Aggressive reduction of variable cost, economize on fixed costs. | Cut variable costs, consolidate. |
| Marketing | Build creativity/coverage. | Cut creativity/keepcoverage. | Reduce market activities. |

EXHIBIT 4

**BEN SANTOS**
**Philippine Economic Indicators**
**1983–1992**

| *General Economic Indicators* | *1983 Actual* | *1984 Actual* | *1985 Actual* | *1986* | *1987* | *1988* | *1989* | *1990* | *1991* | *1992* | *1987–1992* |
|---|---|---|---|---|---|---|---|---|---|---|---|
| Gross Domestic Product (Real Growth) | 0.9 | –5.7 | 4.0 | 1.0 | 5.3 | 5.3 | 5.4 | 6.0 | 6.3 | 7.0 | 5.9 |
| Gross National Product (Real Growth) | 1.1 | 6.8 | –3.8 | 1.5 | 5.0 | 5.5 | 5.5 | 6.0 | 6.0 | 6.5 | 5.8 |
| Investments (Real Growth) | –5.1 | –36.4 | –20.7 | –10.9 | 27.8 | 8.8 | 9.3 | 9.3 | 10.5 | 10.5 | 12.6 |
| Exports (Real Growth) | 10.2 | 8.2 | –7.2 | 0.6 | 3.5 | 5.3 | 6.5 | 7.6 | 8.0 | 9.0 | 6.7 |
| Imports (Real Growth) | 11.5 | –16.4 | –23.0 | 5.8 | 5.0 | 5.0 | 6.0 | 6.5 | 6.5 | 7.5 | 6.1 |
| Real Per Capita GNP (In Pesos) | 1,895.0 | 1,723.0 | 1,618.0 | 1,603.0 | 1,643.0 | 1,692.0 | 1,745.0 | 1,808.0 | 1,875.0 | 1,953.0 | 1,786.0 |
| Inflation Rate (%) | 10.0 | 50.0 | 23.1 | 6.0 | 8.0 | 8.0 | 8.5 | 8.5 | 8.5 | 8.5 | 8.3 |
| Exchange Rate (P/$) | 11.1 | 16.7 | 18.6 | 21.0 | 21.5 | 21.9 | 22.4 | 22.8 | 23.3 | 23.7 | 22.5 |
| Current Account Bal (Million US$) | –2,750.0 | –1,116.0 | 77.0 | 185.0 | –109.0 | –43.0 | –3.0 | 182.0 | 286.0 | 440.0 | 125.5 |
| BOP Deficit (Million US$) | –2,088.0 | 258.0 | –278.0 | –483.0 | –934.0 | –803.0 | –1,005.0 | –1,417.0 | –1,391.0 | –1,200.0 | –1,125.0 |
| Budget Deficit (Billion Pesos) | –7.4 | –9.8 | –11.2 | –27.0 | 11.6 | 12.4 | –13.3 | –14.2 | 15.0 | –14.5 | –13.5 |
| Interest Rates (%) | 19.2 | 26.7 | 28.2 | 16.5 | 16.5 | 16.5 | 17.3 | 17.3 | 17.3 | 17.3 | 17.0 |
| Unemployment Rate* (%) | 7.9 | 10.6 | 11.1 | | | | | | | | |
| International Reserves (Million US$) | 865.0 | 886.0 | 1,061.0 | 1,287.5 | 1,364.0 | 1,490.0 | 1,618.0 | 1,762.0 | 1,942.0 | 2,136.0 | 1,718.0 |

*Projections not yet available.
Data Source: Economic Planning & Research Staff, National Economic & Development Authority (Preliminary Projections only).

EXHIBIT 5

## BEN SANTOS
## Assumptions About the Political Situation in the Philippines and the Regulatory Environment

The economy is not expected to turn around by the end of 1986 as investors continue to take a wait-and-see attitude until after political stability has been achieved and after the government has come out with a coherent economic recovery program and the ratification of the Constitution.

As reflected in the economic projections prepared by the National Economic & Development Authority, the Philippines will start recovering in 1987. There will be political stability beyond 1986 for as long as Mrs Corazon Aquino remains President of the Republic. With the dismantling of crony capitalism, market monopolies, and excessive government regulation, all sectors in the economy are optimistic that recovery is sure to come.

The following are the major government policy reforms that will affect, directly and indirectly, the operations of business establishments in the future:

1. Removal of all export taxes except that on logging.
2. Increase in withholding tax on interest earnings from 17.5 percent to 20 percent.
3. Gradual phaseout of 15 percent tax on dividends with a 5 percent yearly reduction.
4. Elimination of 10 percent tax on intracorporate dividends.
5. Elimination of the 1.5 percent turnover sales tax and the lowering of the sales tax on non-essential articles from 50 percent to 30 percent.
6. Reduction of sales taxes on pesticides and fertilizers.
7. Central Bank plan to overhaul its rules on importation as part of the trade liberalization program of the government.
8. Elimination of marginal deposit requirements on import LCs.

EXHIBIT 6

## BEN SANTOS
## Planning Formats

Standard planning format to be accomplished by each division (may be flexible to suit divisional needs).

| *Element* | *Past (1981–1985)* | *Future (1986–1990)* | *Degree of Confidence** | *Political Opportunities/ Threats* |
|---|---|---|---|---|
| A. MARKET** | | | | |
| 1. Growth rate | | | | |
| 2. Segmentation (quality, price feature) | | | | |
| 3. Demand cycle | | | | |
| B. INDUSTRY*** | | | | |
| 1. Size | | | | |
| 2. Growth per year | | | | |
| 3. Industry cycle | | | | |
| 4. Entries and exits of companies | | | | |
| 5. Barriers to entry | | | | |
| 6. Major problems | | | | |
| C. COMPETITIVE ENVIRONMENT | | | | |
| 1. Number of competitors and market share | | | | |
| 2. HBP market share | | | | |
| 3. Major strategy adopted | | | | |
| 4. Indicated strengths/ limitations | | | | |
| D. CUSTOMERS | | | | |
| 1. Type — concentration | | | | |
| 2. Key customers | | | | |
| E. TECHNOLOGY | | | | |
| 1. Maturity —Life cycle | | | | |
| 2. Complexity | | | | |
| F. GOVERNMENT | | | | |
| 1. Restrictions | | | | |
| 2. Taxation | | | | |
| G. OTHER ELEMENTS RELEVANT TO DIVISION CONCERNED (Please Identify) | | | | |

*Medium, high or low level depending upon the overall assessment of the Division Manager concerned.

**Market refers to the target customers/buyers of H Braun's products. For example, the Pharmaceutical Division has, for its markets, drug stores, wholesalers, dispensing physicians, specialists, and government entities. Indirectly, however, the general market for H Braun's pharmaceutical products extend to the Philippine population.

***In contrast to Market, Industry is more specific, referring to Sales Performance of individual companies with the same target market.

EXHIBIT 7

**BEN SANTOS**
**H Braun, Philippines, Inc**
**Revenue and Employment Statistics**

| *Year* | *Gross Revenues (in thousand pesos)* | *Number of Company Employees* |
|---|---|---|
| 1985 | 441,768 | 406 |
| 1984 | 363,186 | 375 |
| 1983 | 214,505 | 380 |
| 1982 | 178,402 | 394 |

Note: In 1985, the official exchange rate was US$1 = PHP 17.

# Corporate Planning at Metro, Inc* 20

## Company Background

After years of studying mass transit options to alleviate the transportation problems in Metropolitan Manila, the Philippine Government decided during the late 1970s to establish a Light Rail Transit (LRT) System in Metro Manila. Shortly after the Philippine Government engaged the engineering and technical services of the Construction Development Corporation of the Philippines (now the Philippine National Construction Corporation) and a consortium of Belgian firms, the government designated the quasi-governmental Manila Electric Company (Meralco) to establish the first and only LRT System in the Philippines. Consequently, Meralco created a new subsidiary, the Meralco Transit Organization, Inc (Metro) on July 31, 1980.

Metro, Inc in the early stages of its existence focused mainly on the new and complex technology of the LRT. As the company grew, policies, systems, and procedures unique to the LRT were gradually prepared.

In January 1982, Metro and the Light Rail Transit Authority (LRTA), the legal owner of the railway system, signed the pre-operating agreement that set the guidelines on the

---

*This case was written by Teresita Espenilla, Noemi Gatmaitan, Cecilia Maldia, Romeo Orio, and Aurie Santiano (MBA, University of the Philippines, 1989) under the supervision of Visiting Professor Luis Ma. R. Calingo. This case was prepared to serve as a basis for class discussion and is not intended to illustrate either effective or ineffective handling of an administrative situation.

functions of both parties during project construction. As stipulated in the contract, some 36 key personnel of Metro were sent to Belgium for 3 to 6 months of technical training.

The "Metrorail," as the LRT was more popularly known, was inaugurated on September 12, 1984. Final tests of systems performance were conducted in November 1984. Commercial operations finally took off in December 1984. This occasion also marked the termination of the Pre-Operating Agreement, which put into effect the ten-year Operating Agreement.

By January 1989, Metro had been operating its single route, from Monumento in Caloocan City to Baclaran in Parañaque (both in Metro Manila), for four years. Plans were then drawn to augment Metro Manila's LRT System by increasing the number of coaches in this circumferential route and adding a radial route originating from Katipunan Road in Quezon City to Tutuban Station in Divisoria (Manila's old central business district). While new problems continued to surface, Metro was fast developing the expertise of running the system. With a workforce of less than 1,500, Metro took pride in its personnel who, in the words of a senior official, "always got their act together to provide the public a safe, fast, reliable, and comfortable mass transport service."

## Metro, Inc's Corporate Planning System

Established around September 1985, the corporate planning process of Metro, Inc consisted of two phases: Corporate Strategic Planning (Phase I) and Operational Planning (Phase II).

The Corporate Strategic Planning phase was the systematic process of formulating the overall strategies and thrusts of activities of the organization. It was the top-management level of planning where the president, the executive vice president and the heads of the different departments, all comprising Metro's Corporate Planning Committee, set the company's long- and medium-range objectives and formulated strategies and policies which served as guidelines and provided the structure for achieving corporate goals and objectives. These strategies and policies would then be further disseminated to the various operating units from which their operational plans and programs would be based.

The second phase, Operational Planning, started where strategic planning left off. Operational Planning was concerned with the detailed activities of each division. At this phase the division chief, guided by the plans and budget, sought to carry out the medium-range plans and programs. Exhibit 1 presents the organizational responsibilities for each phase of the corporate planning process.

In terms of analytical activities, Metro's corporate planning process started with an appraisal of the performance of organizational elements within the company and of relevant external developments outside the company. The results of the appraisal were summarized in two separate quarterly and annual reports, namely, the Corporate Performance Report and the Environmental Assessment Report.

These two reports served as the Corporate Planning Committee's main bases for the review of the corporate objectives and, subsequent formulation of the company's major strategies. The committee then disseminated these strategies and objectives by writing to each division chief who, in turn, translated them into more concrete and functional terms. Hence, every division chief developed the division's "Annual Goals and Plans," which was reviewed by his or her department manager. The Annual Goals and Plans served as the basis for the division's proposed budget. Exhibit 2 presents a flow chart of the corporate planning process at Metro, Inc.

## The Corporate Strategic Planning Process

Corporate Strategic Planning at Metro, Inc involved determining the company's future position with reference to a variety of factors. It included a close look at the corporate objectives and changes in Metro, Inc's external and internal structures which might warrant a modification of corporate objectives or the means to accomplish these objectives. Corporate strategic planning also included the formulation of major policies and strategies that would achieve the corporate mission.

Specifically, Corporate Strategic Planning at Metro, Inc involved the following analytical steps:

1. Environmental appraisal.
2. Corporate appraisal.
3. Formulation of objectives.
4. Strategy formulation.
5. Dissemination of corporate strategy.

## Environmental Appraisal

### General Description

Environmental appraisal involved identifying, analyzing, and reporting the external developments that had significant implications for Metro, Inc. operations. Environmental appraisal included some discussions on the Philippines' business environment, an evaluation of the past and forecasted performance of the various sectors of the economy, and an assessment of industry performance. This process ensured that the Corporate Planning Committee would be well-informed about relevant developments outside Metro, Inc.

### Responsibility Areas

The Corporate Staff Service Office, in coordination with other offices, was tasked with the preparation of the Quarterly and Annual Environmental Appraisal Reports of Metro, Inc and with the implementation of the accompanying activities necessary to produce these reports.

### Steps and Procedures

1. **Parameters for Environmental Appraisal**
   In appraising its environment, Metro investigated trends and developments during the year in the following areas: general economic conditions, foreign exchange rate, interest rate, inflation rate, wage orders, power rate, market profile, competition, technological environment, and other external factors. Exhibit 3 provides a brief discussion of each of these parameters.

2. **Data Gathering**
   Exhibit 4 summarizes the various offices and institutions utilized to provide the above input data.
3. **Data Analysis and Reporting**
   3.1. The data collected was organized and evaluated in light of the major goals or thrusts set for the same period.
   3.2. The results of the analysis were reported in the Quarterly Environmental Appraisal which, together with the Quarterly Performance Evaluation Report, served as the basis of the Corporate Planning Committee's overall corporate appraisal.
   3.3. The report contained not only an analysis of the previous data, but also of Metro, Inc's own projections on the rates of interest, inflation, foreign exchange, and LRT rates.
   3.4. For important external matters that had to be immediately reported, the Corporate Staff Services or any concerned office did not wait for the date of submission of the Quarterly Environmental Report and would instead immediately release this information. To illustrate, if the President of the Philippines decreed another general wage increase effective January, the predicted effects of this order might be immediately reported to top management. In addition, the information would be included in the first quarter report scheduled for submission at a much later date.

## Corporate Appraisal

### General Description

The aim of the internal appraisal was to frame the major parameters and to draw from them Metro, Inc's strengths and weaknesses, as well as to pinpoint the real resources the organization could deploy to exploit its strengths. Management would then know which areas needed to be improved and which could be exploited as opportunities for growth. The analysis emphasized what Metro, Inc had already done well in the past and what it could realistically do in the immediate future. Management measured how well it performed in meeting its objectives, especially in five key result areas: productivity, customer satisfaction, system reliability, financial position, and employee performance and welfare.

### Responsibility Areas

The Corporate Staff Services Office was responsible for consolidating the basic corporate performance information used for the Quarterly and Annual Corporate Performance Report. The Appendix discusses in detail the specific key result areas and also indicates the information gathered to monitor each key result area.

## Formulation of Objectives

### General Description

The third step in strategic planning involved the review of the corporate objectives and plan's assumptions to determine whether they were still relevant and realistic. The previous plan's assumptions and goals were compared with the actual results and were also tested for validity. Goals might have been set either too low or too high; this would warrant goal resetting or adjustment. The plan's assumptions and goals were also examined in light of the following:

1. Company mission.
2. Statement of major policies with regard to the different stakeholders, (e.g., the owners, the riding public, the employees, and the LRTA).
3. Specification of objectives with regard to the key results areas.
4. Present and anticipated business conditions affecting the company.

### Responsibility Area

The Corporate Planning Committee was responsible for the review of previously set corporate objectives and the formulation of new objectives that would become the overall targeted level of performance for the company during the planning period.

## Strategy Formulation

### General Description

Metro, Inc defined strategy as a major policy decision which embodies the general thrusts or program of activities for the company for a specified time frame. The objective of strategy formulation at Metro, Inc was to maintain a position of advantage by capitalizing on strengths and overcoming weaknesses. The strategy represented the course(s) of action selected by Metro, Inc from among alternatives as the optimal way to achieve the company objectives for the planning period.

### Responsibility Area

The Corporate Planning Committee was also responsible for the formulation of a corporate-wide strategy. All the activities of the organizational units would revolve around this strategy during the planning period. Normally, the planning period is the same as the period covered by the budget.

### Criteria for the Evaluation of Strategy

There are no infallible indicators that can be used to determine whether a proposed strategy is realistic and sound or otherwise. The Corporate Planning Committee is, however, provided with the following basic guidelines for evaluating a proposed strategy:

1. It must be explicitly stated and clearly defined.
2. It must be consistent with the established policies and goals and with the values and attitudes of Metro, Inc's management and employees.
3. It must be appropriate to the desired level of Metro, Inc's contribution to society and must fully exploit the market opportunities.
4. It must be consistent with corporate competence and resources.
5. Its risks must be feasible in economic and personal terms.
6. It must be applied at the proper time.
7. It must be workable.

### Steps in Strategy Formulation

1. **Comparison of Actual and Desired Performance**
   Metro, Inc's overall performance level was compared with the corporate objectives established. This enabled management to identify the gaps between the company's current position and, pursuant to corporate goals and objectives, where the company should be at the end of the planning period.
2. **Generation of Alternatives**
   Various ways could be generated to fill the gaps between the actual and desired performance. From among the alternatives identified, the Corporate Planning Committee chose the alternative which would best realize the company's goals and objectives. In evaluating and choosing the best alternative(s), the committee considered such factors as cost, economic feasibility, appropriateness in light of resources and capabilities, internal consistency, appropriateness of level of risk, and timing.
3. **Formulation of Major Policies and Guidelines**
   After choosing the best set of strategic alternatives, the formulation of major policies and guidelines was necessary for the effective execution of the plans and programs. In most cases, the policies and guidelines were reviewed to check for some possible conflicts.
4. **Setting of Priorities and Schedules**
   During this step, management sought to establish an order of accomplishment of goals, plans, and programs and developed the corresponding timetable. Metro, Inc found it helpful to classify the needs of the organization into "musts" and "wants." Normally, those classified under *musts* were areas where the performance level is way below standard. Those classified under *wants* were areas where the performance level was below standard but still within management's range of an acceptable standard.

### Dissemination of Corporate Strategy

The last step in Corporate Strategic Planning was the documentation and dissemination of the summary of the corporate strategy. This document, approximately 30 pages in length, serves as a guide to the various operating units in the development of their respective goals and plans. As communicated, the corporate strategy included the following information:

1. A summary of Metro, Inc's present position.
2. A statement of objectives to be reached at some point in the future (2 to 3 years).
3. A statement of corporate strategies, assumptions, and major policy guidelines.

## Operational Planning

### General Description

Operational Planning at Metro, Inc was the process wherein Metro's goals or strategies were translated into more concrete and functional terms. It encouraged the middle managers to:

1. Exercise their planning functions;
2. Assess their previous performance;
3. Identify all the factors or conditions affecting their respective activities;

4. Select and propose action plans for the future, and most important of all;
5. Draw their commitment to their set goals and plans.

**Responsibility Areas**

All division chiefs, assisted by their respective section chiefs, are responsible for preparing the Annual Goals and Plans of their respective offices prior to the preparation of their Budget for the same planning period. Exhibit 5 presents a sample format for these Annual Goals and Plans, each of which is about 5 to 10 pages in length. Each department manager evaluates his or her division chiefs' goals and plans to assess their consistency with corporate-wide strategies and objectives. The Corporate Planning and Budget Committees then review the Annual Goals and Plans and the proposed Corporate Budget of Metro, Inc, during the budget deliberation period. The Corporate Planning Committee would then approve the division's Annual Goals and Plans at the same time the corporate budget is approved.

**Steps and Procedures**

**Assessment by the Division**

The starting point of operational planning was the assessment of:

1. The plan's past performance vis-à-vis the set goals.
2. The problem areas that brought about the nonattainment of the goals.
3. The other attendant difficulties which might have hampered the division's operations.
4. The presently identified strengths and capabilities of the division.
5. The potentials and the capabilities that might be tapped for future needs.

For the division chief, the assessment process was an ongoing activity as he or she always monitored and reviewed the performance of his or her office's operations. The following questions guided the division chief in making this assessment:

1. How do you assess the general performance of your division as compared to the set goals and plans for the year?
2. How do you account for the discrepancy (if any) between the actual and the set goals?
3. Discuss your critical problem areas and the bottlenecks that need to be solved.
4. Discuss your division's presently identified capabilities, as well as the potentials that can considerably contribute to the company's efficiency.
5. Have there been any external developments or opportunities related to your division's operation that you must consider because they may somehow help Metro, Inc in the future?
6. What immediate or temporary remedies have been applied to the various problems that you encountered during the previous year?

**Goal Setting**

After the division chiefs have evaluated their respective offices' performance, problems, capabilities and potentials, they establish some targeted levels of performance that they wish their divisions to achieve in the future. These goals were reported in the "Annual Goals and Plans" which, if approved, would constitute the division's commitment during the planning period. The following guide questions were provided to the division chiefs to help them establish their respective division's goals:

1. In what areas of your operation have you set some goals?
2. Do these goals reflect the overall thrust of your division's performance?
3. Are these goals clearly stated, easily comprehended, and expressed in quantitative terms?
4. Are the targets consistent with Metro, Inc's strategies and objectives?
5. Are the targets realistically established such that they are neither too tight nor too loose from anyone's point of view?

### Action Plans

The Action Plans are the programs, projects, or set of future activities proposed by each division based on the corporate strategies and objectives set by the Corporate Planning Committee. The action plans were also included in the "Annual Goals and Plans", around which all the activities of the division in the immediate future would revolve. Just as in goal setting, the following guide questions assisted the division chiefs in the preparation of their action plans:

1. What specific course(s) of action, programs(s) and/or projects(s) do you plan to implement during the next period?
2. Will the implementation of these also mean the achievement of your set targets?
3. Are the plans consistent with Metro, Inc's strategies and objectives?
4. Are the plans also consistent with the division's competence and resources?
5. Are the plans feasible in economic and personal terms?
6. Are all the potentials and capabilities of the division considered?
7. Do the plans constitute a clear stimulus to the division's effort and commitment?
8. Will all the opportunities, both external and internal to the division, be exploited?
9. Will the plans resolve problems that hampered operations in the past?

### Budgeting

Although some of the action plans proposed by the divisions might not entail extraordinary expenditures (e.g., plans for tightening of supervision and shift rescheduling), many of them would require such expenditures. Thus, these plans were incorporated in the budget for the same period covered. These activities adhered to Metro, Inc's budgeting policies and procedures.

After the budget had been reviewed and certain plans had been scrapped or altered, the division chief concerned would prepare a revised Annual Goals and Plans that would suit the annual budget.

## Timetable of Corporate Planning Activities

Exhibit 6 illustrates the flow of Metro, Inc's corporate planning activities and their corresponding schedules. The objectives and strategies to be formulated would be implemented two years following plan adoption. Hence, at any year, the Corporate Planning Committee would base their assessment on the Environmental Appraisal and Corporate Performance Reports prepared during the first quarter of that year and all four quarters of the previous year.

Operational Planning commenced after corporate strategy and objectives had been disseminated to the individual division chiefs. Thus, the goals and plans set by each division during their own planning process would also govern the next two years of each division's operations.

APPENDIX I

## CORPORATE PLANNING AT METRO, INC
## Details of Metro's Key Result Areas

1. **Key Result Area: Productivity**

a. **General Description**

Productivity is the relationship between output and the input required to produce it. It is accomplishing more with the use of the same amount of resources. Productivity measures — or the measurable relationship between the input and the corresponding output of specific activities over a given period of time — are the indicators of the efficiency in the use of inputs in relation to actual outputs.

Productivity improvement measures are essential in aiding management establish productivity goals since these measures are supposed to indicate where productivity has been increasing or decreasing. Past operations were evaluated based on these measures, and subsequent goals and actions were identified. Aside from identifying the company's strong and weak points, productivity improvement measures are also essential in developing standards which will be used by management to monitor the performance of elements concerned.

b. **Indicators**

(1) Cost Efficiency Measures

| | |
|---|---|
| Source: | Monthly Reports |
| Units Responsible: | Financial Services, Depot, Materials Management |
| Frequency: | Monthly |
| Specific Objective: | To check if costs are kept at reasonable levels against different sets of output. |

These measures relate total cost and its components — operating, administrative, and maintenance costs — with total kilometers run and total passenger volume for a specific period (per month, usually). It is desired that costs be kept low, although, of course, a decrease (increase) in the values of these measures do not automatically imply that the company was more (less) cost-efficient.

(2) Labor Productivity

| | |
|---|---|
| Source: | Labor Utilization Summary: Monthly Report |
| Units Responsible: | Each department; Manpower Services |
| Frequency: | Monthly |
| Specific Objective: | To assess the effectiveness of human resource utilization. |

These measures were developed to facilitate further understanding of the factors which affect the productivity of the human resources.

(3) Income/Expense Forecasting Effectiveness

| | |
|---|---|
| Source: | Corporate Budget, Revenue and Expense Budget, Income Statement |
| Units Responsible: | Budget Section, Accounting Division |
| Frequency: | Monthly |
| Specific Objective: | To evaluate the effectiveness of concerned personnel in forecasting income and expenses. |

(4) Processing Time

| | |
|---|---|
| Source: | Monthly Reports |
| Units Responsible: | Engineering, Financial Services, Administrative Services |

Specific Objective: To measure and evaluate the degree variation of actual processing time from the set of standards.

For critical activities where standard processing times have been established, one way of assessing performance is by determining the variations of these standards. Standard times, set at reasonable levels, have to be met to ensure that the chain of work activities is followed through efficiently and promptly.

(5) Other Effectiveness Measures

Source: Monthly Reports
Units Responsible: All departments
Frequency: Monthly/Quarterly
Specific Objective: To evaluate the efficiency of concerned personnel in processing work requirements.

All other productivity measures not included in the above-mentioned classifications belong to this group. Examples of these indicators are Schedule Adherence, Inventory Level, Collection Efficiency, Cash Level Monitor, and Excess Funds Management.

2. **Key Result Area: Customer Satisfaction**

a. **General Description**

One way by which Metro, Inc could achieve its company mission of providing the best level of service to the riding public is through the monitoring and assessment of the responses of various sectors, specifically the riding public, to the level of service Metro could afford. Since much can be gained from customers' commendations, complaints and suggestions, this information has to be carefully gathered and objectively evaluated in order to come up with a necessary course of action.

b. **Indicators**

(1) Commendations and Complaints

Source: Log of Complaints, Suggestions, and Inquiries
Unit Responsible: Public Relations Office
Schedule: Daily/Monthly
Specific Objective: To assess the response of both media and the public to the company's performance vis-à-vis revenue operations.

(2) Service Level

Source: Daily Service Report
Schedule: Daily/Monthly
Specific Objective: To evaluate the level of service in areas where complaints would likely be directed.

The level of service considers all the abnormalities that may occur during revenue operations, which may or may not result in service interruptions. Defects on the LRT, tracks, substations, and signaling equipment have a different impact on the revenue service. Impact on passengers is evaluated and related to other factors such as duration of interruption and number of refund tickets issued.

3. **Key Result Area: System Reliability**

a. **General Description**

The overall objective of system reliability as a key result area is to evaluate the performance of the various physical and operational systems of the company with regard to train availability, breakdown/defects frequency and related factors. This area will provide management with a picture of how well the systems are working, to what extent these can be depended on, and at the same time alert management to alarms in the systems' performance which could affect, whether directly or indirectly, the transportation service for the public.

b. **Indicators**

(1) Light-Rail-Vehicle-Related Engineering Reliability Indicators

Source: Monthly Depot Report
Unit Responsible: Depot Division
Specific Objective: To determine the durability/reliability of the Light Rail Vehicles (LRVs) and to assess the effectiveness and adequacy of the maintenance and repair works and schedule for these.

These indicators will show how dependable the trains are and how efficient the maintenance work is. Train reliability is especially critical for train scheduling and revenue service. Examples of LRV reliability indicators are train availability data and kilometer-run per elections per day.

(2) Non-LRV-Related Engineering Reliability Indicators

Source: Reports of Divisions Concerned
Units Responsible: Workshop, Materials Management Division
Frequency: Monthly
Specific Objectives:
(a) To determine the durability of the company's physical resources and equipment.
(b) To monitor the amount of energy consumed by the trains and other systems.
(c) To assess the reliability of the materials consumption forecasts.

Some examples of non-LRV-related indicators are the frequency of defects in critical equipment such as tracks, catenary, substation, signaling, telecommunication equipment and facilities, AC and DC energy consumption per period, and the ratio of actual to forecasted materials consumption.

(3) Operating System Reliability Indicators

Source: Monthly Operations Summary Report
Unit Responsible: Operations Department
Frequency: Monthly
Specific Objectives:
(a) To determine the effectiveness of the train schedules and the reliability of the train system to meet these schedules.
(b) To determine the effectiveness and efficiency of concerned personnel in responding to breakdown incidents.
(c) To assess the reliability of the passenger demand forecasts.

Examples of Operation Systems Reliability Indicators are train scheduling indices, punctuality, coordination, normalization and disruption indices, and the ratio of actual to forecasted passenger volume.

(4) Safety System Reliability Indicators

Source: Accident/Incident Summary Reports
Unit Responsible: Safety and Security Office
Frequency: Monthly
Specific Objective: To evaluate the effectiveness of the safety rules and procedures.

Some safety indicators are the frequency of accidents per type of accident and the frequency of incidents per period. The indicators would show how adequate and good the existing safety rules and guidelines are, and how they are followed by Metro personnel.

4. **Key Result Area: Financial Position**
   a. **General Description**
   Analysis of the financial condition of the company is always among the top priorities for corporate appraisal. The financial statements and indicators reflect in monetary terms the performance and condition of the company in general and in specific areas of operation.
   b. **Indicators**
   (1) Liquidity Ratios

| | |
|---|---|
| Source: | Balance Sheet |
| Units Responsible: | Accounting Division; Financial Planning and Budget Control Division |
| Frequency: | Monthly, Yearly |
| Specific Objective: | To determine the capability of the company in paying maturing short-term obligations. |

The two most commonly used liquidity ratios are the current ratio and the acid-test ratio. For both ratios, the company has to establish a range of acceptable values. Too high a ratio means much excess or idle funds on hand, while too low a ratio implies the company's inability to meet short-term debts.

(2) Leverage Ratios

| | |
|---|---|
| Source: | Balance Sheet |
| Unit Responsible: | Accounting Division; Financial Planning and Budget Control Division |
| Frequency: | Monthly, Yearly |
| Specific Objective: | To measure the extent of debt financing by the company. |

The most commonly used ratios here are the total-debt-to-total-assets ratio and times-interest-earned ratio. High debt means that the company is heavily dependent on borrowings to operate. These reflect the owners' inability or hesitation to infuse more funds into the company, thereby resulting in a thin cushion for creditors in the event of insolvency. Too low debts reflect the inability or hesitation of the company to extensively use its borrowing power.

(3) Profitability Ratios

| | |
|---|---|
| Source: | Income Statement and Balance Sheet |
| Units Responsible: | Accounting Division, Financial Planning, and Budget Control Division |
| Frequency: | Monthly, Yearly |

The ratios used here are gross profit rate, return on total assets, net income rate, and return on equity. These ratios measure the level of income of the company as compared to various elements (e.g., assets, capital and expenses). Needless to say, any company desires high values in its profitability ratios.

5. **Key Result Area: Employee Performance and Welfare**
   a. **General Description**
   Employees are very important resources of Metro, Inc. As agents for implementation, they are geared toward the achievement of high levels of productivity, reliability, growth, and excellent financial position for the company. In this regard, management should not view the employee solely as an economic unit or factor for production, but more importantly as a human being with needs, wants, desires, attitudes, and feelings that will affect the company's performance. Employee performance and welfare assessment shall be oriented toward improving operational plans on how to develop employees to perform well.

b. **Indicators**

(1) Human Resource Utilization Reports

Source: Administrative Department's Monthly Report

Contents: Manpower status, attrition rate, seminars conducted, number of participating employees per seminar; turnover, absenteeism, tardiness, grievances, and infractions

Frequency: Monthly

Specific Objectives:
(a) To assess the performance of the employees and their development through the seminars given to them.
(b) To gauge employee satisfaction.

These indicators help management assess how Metro Inc's human resources have responded to the company's personnel development programs. They also enable management to gauge the general level of employee discontent with management policies and decisions so that proper future courses of action may be drawn.

6. **Key Result Area: Growth**

a. **General Description**

While all the other key result areas reflect the operational efficiency of the organizational elements, growth reflects the size and the extent and/or status of the financial, human, technical, and other resources and capabilities of the company. This does not mean, however, that growth is an entirely separate thing from operational efficiency. Growth is a necessary result of efficiency. Hence, an increase in the company's resources indicates a healthy position, unless, of course, the increase is brought about by capital infusion.

b. **Indicators**

(1) Growth of Assets

Source: Financial Statement; Reports of division concerned

Frequency: Monthly

Specific Objective: To inform the Corporate Planning Committee of the size of asset expansion or shrinkage both in qualitative and quantitative terms.

This indicator shall include the amount of assets, the type of assets, and a general discussion regarding the addition or reduction in assets, especially the technological assets, so that management may have a better grasp of the overall picture of Metro's resources.

(2) Growth of Capital

Source: Financial Statement

Unit Responsible: Accounting Division

Frequency: Quarterly, Yearly

Specific Objective: To appraise management of the volume and value of stocks invested in Metro, Inc so that management may be aware of the extent of exposure of capital investments that its owners have allowed and, in the process, estimate the desired level of returns.

As in asset growth, capital growth serves to simply inform management on the size of their primary resource — capital. Aside from the volume and value of stocks, this indicator also discusses where new capital investments have been used or are intended to be used.

(3) Manpower Growth

Source: Manpower Status Report

Unit Responsible: Manpower Service Division

Frequency: Quarterly, Yearly

Specific Objective: To gauge the level of manpower complement, their relative skills, and the approximate amount of wage and benefits per group so that excess human resources may be fully harnessed and their corresponding compensation may be assessed.

For reporting purposes, Metro, Inc's workforce is grouped according to skills (e.g., analysts, accountants, clerks) and according to other classifications (by sex, by division).

(4) Growth in Market Share

| | |
|---|---|
| Source: | Market Research Report |
| Frequency: | Quarterly, Yearly |
| Specific Objective: | To determine the extent of market penetration by Metrorail so that management may know where the company stands in the competitive transport business. |

This shall cover the market share (volume, percentages and growth rates) of Metrorail as compared with its competing transport modes. Shifts or major changes in the market share of each competitor are also explained here.

(5) Other Metro Ventures

| | |
|---|---|
| Source: | *Ad hoc* reports to management |
| Frequency: | As needed (usually quarterly and yearly) |
| Specific Objective: | To assess the operational efficiency and growth of the other ventures that Metro Inc has entered into so that management may decide whether they would further pursue or discontinue their operations. |

Each venture shall also have its own key result areas (e.g., productivity, system reliability) so that its performance may be properly evaluated.

Source: Company documents, 1989–1990.

EXHIBIT 1

**CORPORATE PLANNING AT METRO, INC**
**Organizational Responsibilities in the Planning Process**

PHASE I: CORPORATE STRATEGIC PLANNING
Positions in Corporate Planning Committee

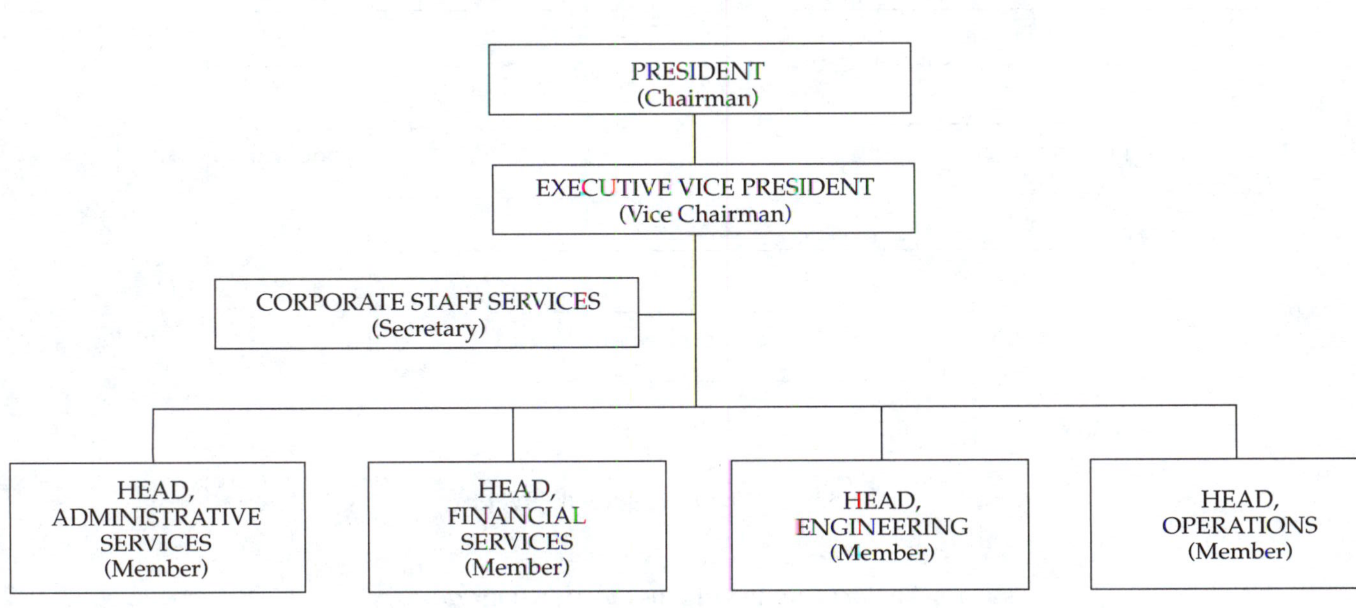

EXHIBIT 1 (cont'd)

**CORPORATE PLANNING AT METRO, INC**
**Organizational Responsibilities in the Planning Process**

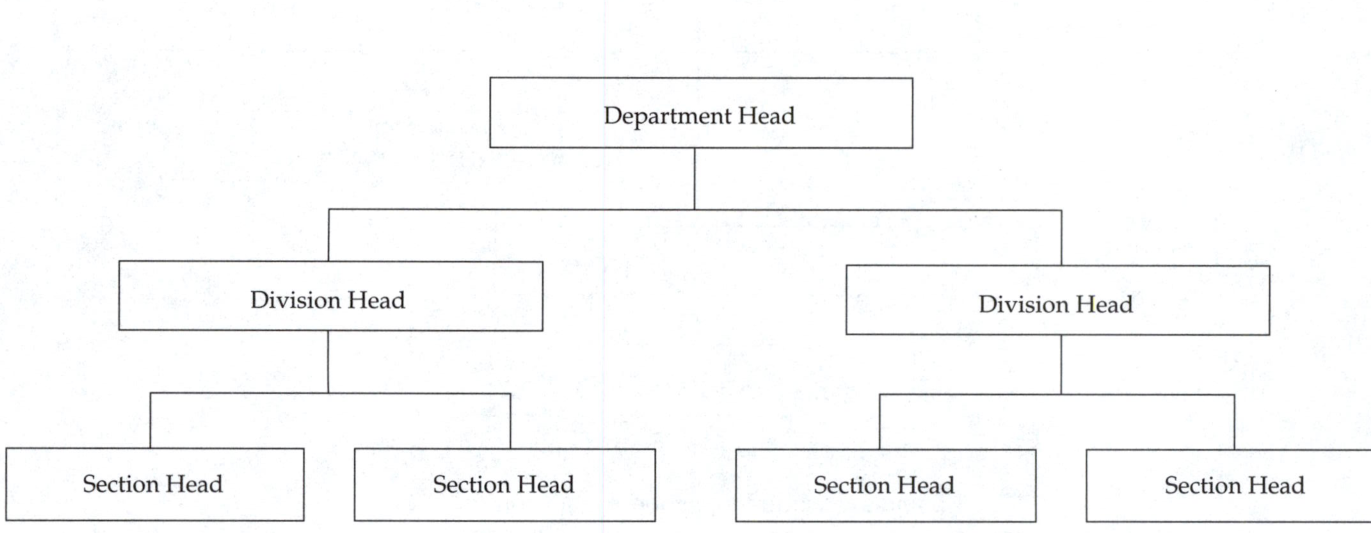

EXHIBIT 2

**CORPORATE PLANNING AT METRO, INC**
**Flow Chart of the Corporate Planning Process**

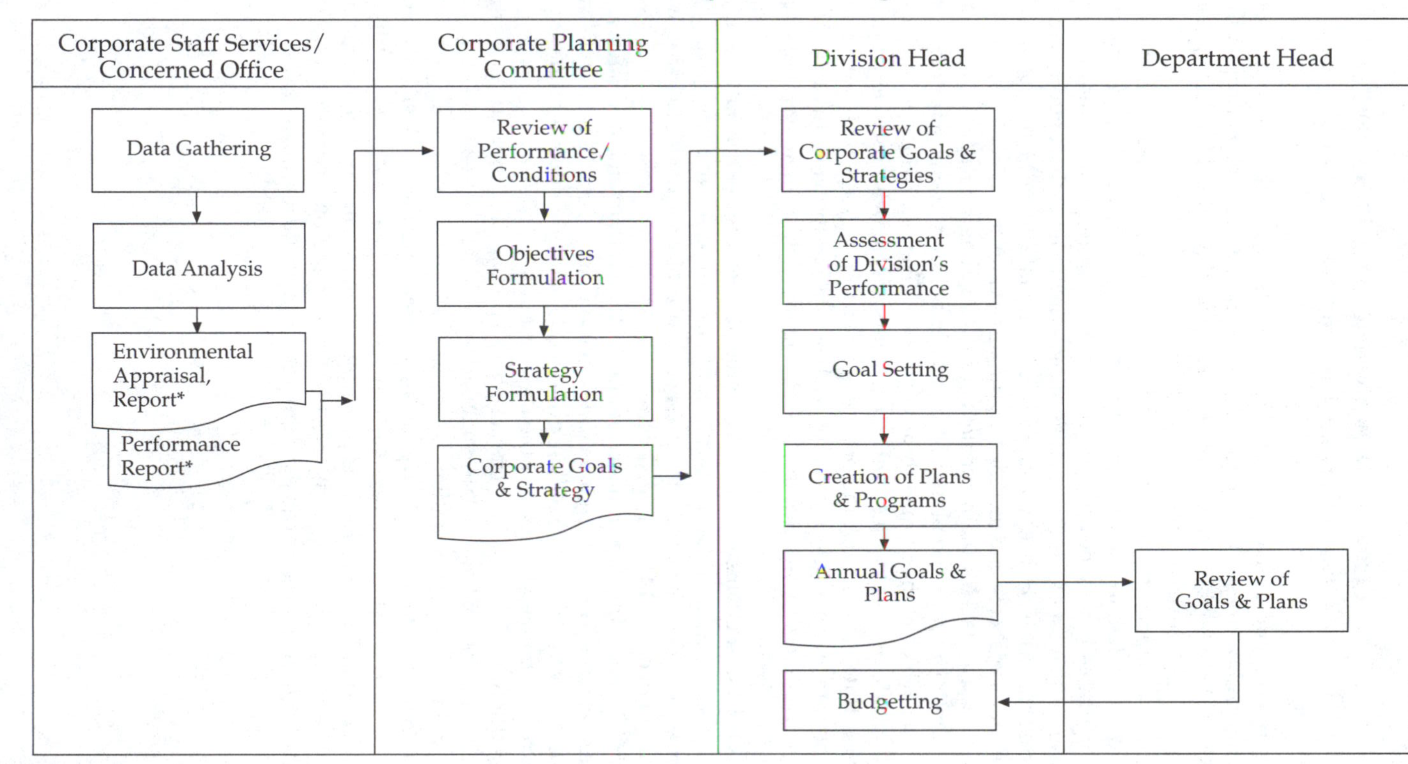


*Quarterly and yearly.

EXHIBIT 3

## CORPORATE PLANNING AT METRO, INC
### Parameters for Environmental Appraisal

1. **General Economic Condition.** Includes a discussion on the national, regional, and sectoral economic indicators such as gross national/domestic product, per capita income, population growth, international reserves money supply, domestic liquidity, personal expenditure patterns, and industrial growth.
2. **Foreign Exchange Rate.** Involves the analysis of the past, present, and forecasted Philippine peso to US dollar (or other currencies) exchange rates. Although any changes in foreign exchange rates have a bearing on Metro's expense items (i.e., peso depreciation meant an increase in the cost of gasoline and local materials), their direct effect is felt in the cost of the imported materials. Hence, the rate's fluctuation effects on Metro operations, with emphasis on the materials' cost, are included in the discussion here.
3. **Interest Rate.** Tackles the movements of the lending and borrowing rates of the financial institutions. The rates monitored here include not only the general prevailing rates but also those rates which Metro frequently avails itself of. The causes of their movements (if any), their effects on Metro's operations, and other points are likewise considered here.
4. **Inflation Rate.** Points out the pressures or factors that were identified to have caused the inflation rate levels of selected baskets (wholesale, consumer, industrial, etc) of goods. Also of particular interest to Metro is the basket of goods which really represents most of the items utilized by Metro.
5. **Wage Orders.** Pertains to the state-mandated salary, wage and/or benefit policies that have to be reckoned with in the computation of labor expense and labor overhead expenses.
6. **Power Rate.** Discusses the past, present, and projected power rates, as well as their corresponding effects on Metro's operations.
7. **Market Profile.** Includes an analysis of customer characteristics such as riding behavior, preferences and patterns, origin and destination, and age and gender distribution. This also includes a review of the population, growth rate, and other demographic indices related to the effective and potential market of the LRT System.
8. **Competition.** Highlights the market share comparison, capacity utilization analysis, and subjective assessment of the state competition of the LRT system and other modes of transportation in LRT's area of operation.
9. **Technological Environment.** Updates concerned parties, as well as management, on the various relevant technological and systems developments both in the Philippines and abroad.
10. **Other External Factors.** Reports pertinent developments that are not included in any of the above discussions but somehow affect Metro's operations. Examples of the subjects covered are tariff duties, new government regulations and policies, other taxes, licenses and fees.

EXHIBIT 4

**CORPORATE PLANNING AT METRO, INC**
**Sources of Input Data for Environmental Appraisal**

| | *Parameters* | *Sources of Data* |
|---|---|---|
| 1. | General Economic Condition | Center for Research and Communication, Philippine Chamber of Commerce and Industry, Bankers Association of the Philippines, Private Development Corporation of the Philippines. |
| 2. | Foreign Exchange Rates | Same as in No. 1. |
| 3. | Interest Rates | In addition to sources listed in No. 1, Financial Planning and Budget Control Division. |
| 4. | Inflation Rate | In addition to sources listed in No. 1, Purchasing Section of the Materials Management Division. |
| 5. | Wage Orders | Office of the President, Republic of the Philippines. |
| 6. | Power Rates | Meralco. |
| 7. | Market Profile | National Census and Statistics Office, Traffic Division, Public Relations Office, North/South Operations Division. |
| 8. | Competition | Department of Transportation and Communications and other operating divisions, Traffic Division. |
| 9. | Technological Environment | Research conducted by respective divisions. |
| 10. | Other External Factors | Concerned government offices or private institutions. |

EXHIBIT 5

## CORPORATE PLANNING AT METRO, INC
## Sample Format of Annual Goals and Plans

### ANNUAL GOALS AND PLANS: 1988–1989

**DIVISION:** General Services
**SECTION:** Purchasing
**DATE:** August 21, 1987

**A. Assessment: 1986 to 2nd quarter, 1987**

1. Comparison of Actual Performance and Goals
   a. Overtime Result: 20 percent average actual vs 15 percent set goal for the same period.
   b. Processing Time: One month processing for local purchases vs the goal of three weeks.
   c. Employee Welfare and Performance Results
2. Major Problems Encountered
3. Other Discussions: Strengths, weaknesses, opportunities, and threats.

**B. Goals for 1988–1989**

1. To set average overtime target at only 5 percent.
2. To cut local processing to two weeks.
3. To supervise well and motivate adequately the employees of the section.

**C. Action Plans/Programs**

1. To purchase additional facilities.
2. To increase manpower complement.
3. To conduct a study on internal operating procedures.
4. To enhance the monitoring system for individual performance.

EXHIBIT 6

**CORPORATE PLANNING AT METRO, INC**
**Time Table of Planning Activities**

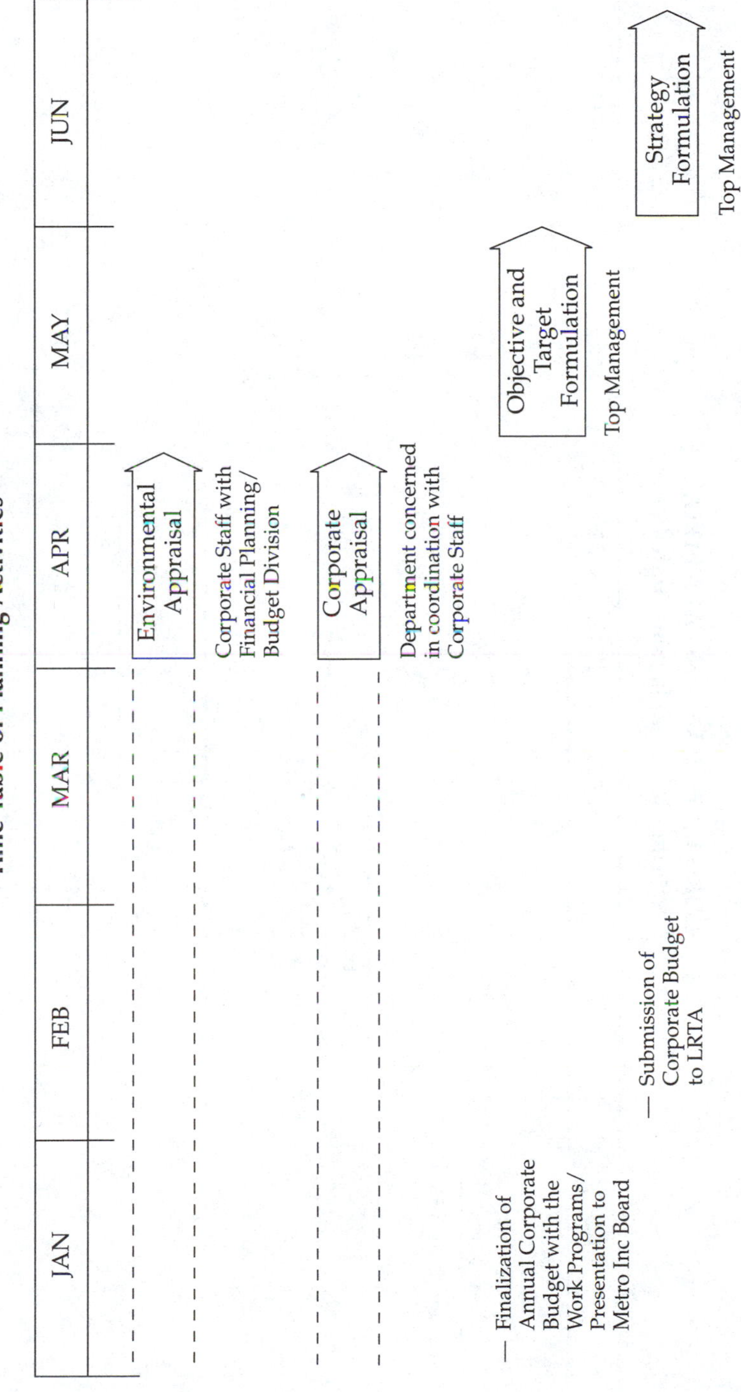

EXHIBIT 6 (cont'd)

**CORPORATE PLANNING AT METRO, INC**
**Time Table of Planning Activities**

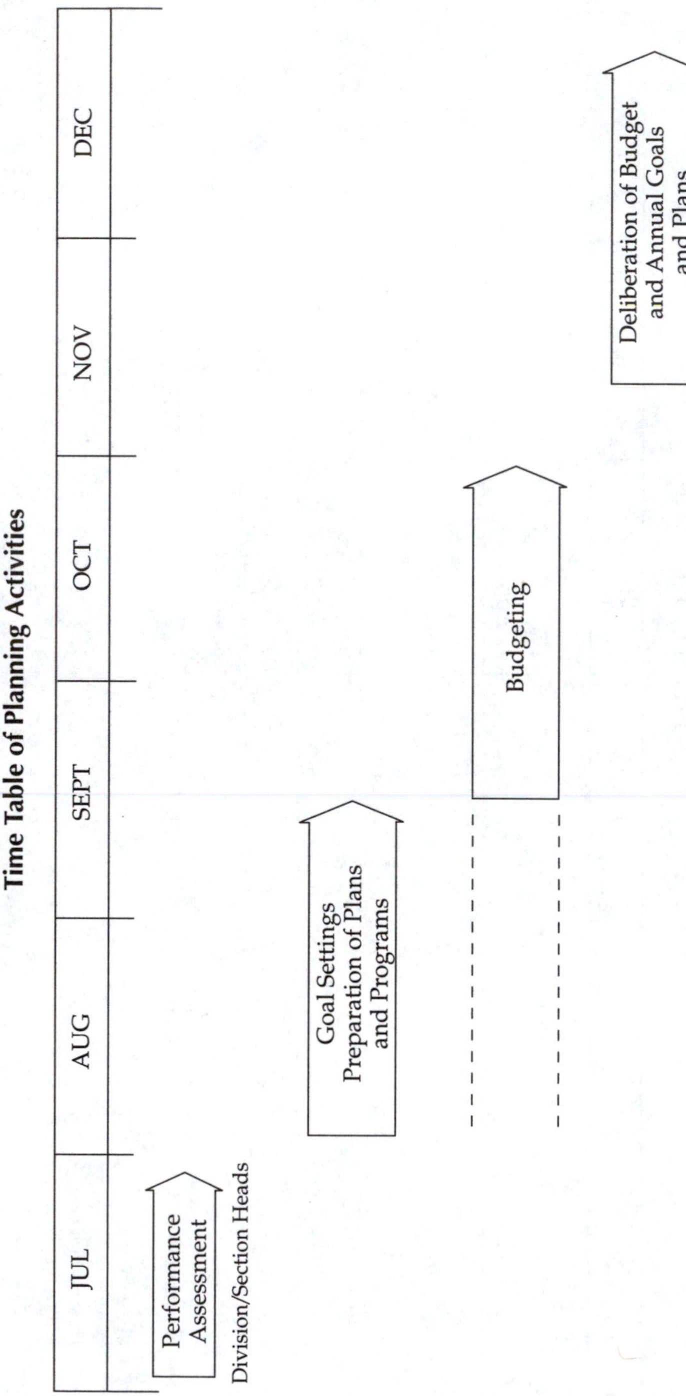

# La Tondeña Distillers, Incorporated* 21

In October 1987, Oscar Santos, a 33-year-old graduate from the University of the Philippines (UP), reported for his first day of work as Manager of the Corporate Planning Staff under the Senior Vice President (SVP) for Marketing Operations. Having five years of corporate planning experience with a consumer-products subsidiary of San Miguel Corporation (SMC), Santos was tapped by SMC management to assist in the institutionalization of a corporate planning system for La Tondeña Distillers, Incorporated (LTDI). He was deep in thought as he recalled the orientation meeting with his boss, the SVP for Marketing Operations.

> Welcome to LTDI, Oscar. I'm sure that with your experience you can do us a lot of good. However, let me warn you that you have to unlearn whatever you knew before — they just don't operate here the way you would expect people to. The systems you would generally expect to be basic are lacking and you just have to reinvent the wheel. On top of it all, the majority of the old managers will not know what you are talking about. The first thing you have to do is to reeducate them and be patient. I remember when we introduced Operation Radar (route-monitoring system) in Coke. It took us three years to be completely effective. I think we are in for tough times ahead.

---

*This case was prepared by Ruel Habaluyas and Marisol Ybañez (MBA, University of the Philippines, 1989) under the supervision of Visiting Professor Luis Ma. R. Calingo. Most quotations are paraphrased creations by the case authors for educational purposes and cannot be considered actual statements by officials and employees of La Tondeña Distillers, Incorporated. The case is designed to serve as a basis for class discussion rather than to illustrate either effective or ineffective handling of an administrative situation.

After a one-month orientation program involving a thorough visitation and briefing in all operational and support units of the company, Oscar Santos was preparing to meet with the President, Conrado Malixi, to present the LTDI corporate planning system that would serve as the guideline for the formulation of the 1988 Annual Plan and the 5-year Corporate Program.

The sentiments of the old LTDI managers with regard to the new corporate planning manager and the introduction of new systems were reflected in the reaction of Robert C So, the Vice President for Sales:

> Well, you are the new guy from SMC. What new systems will you introduce? A route monitoring system — is that necessary? Remember, we have a product different from beer. If people want to get drunk, then sales go up. That is all there is to it.

## Company History

La Tondeña Incorporada (LTI) was founded in 1902 by Tan Guin Lay, born on September 1, 1869, in Wily Village, Xiamen, Fujian Province, China. Forced by financial distress, Tan migrated to Manila in 1884 to seek his fortune. He worked as an apprentice in a textile store owned by a relative, opened his own dry goods store, learned Spanish and the local dialects, and acquired a thorough knowledge of local laws and legal procedures. Tan also acquired the name "Carlos Palanca" from the prominent governor who adopted him as his godson, as it was the custom at that time to be named after one's Christian godfather.

The small distillery, liquor, and spirits business on Juan Luna Street in Tondo, Manila was named LTI after its site, then a small suburban village of old Manila. By 1908, Carlos Palanca had acquired another distillery, the Destilerias La Locomotora, from Don Patricio Ubeda. In 1924, he acquired Destilerias Ayala, Inc, a company which had been manufacturing Ginebra San Miguel (the Philippines's most popular gin) since 1834.

Palanca ran LTI as a family corporation and his basic strategy was one of growth. Reflective of this, LTI was the only distiller which had two factories — one within Manila and the other based in Cebu to service the market needs of the Visayas region.

On September 2, 1950, Palanca Sr passed away and his son, Carlos Palanca Jr, took over management. The style of corporate management remained traditional and patriarchal in nature. For many years under Palanca Jr, LTI was the industry leader and consistent moneymaker until the start of the 1980s. The company placed a high priority on the quality of its products through the maintenance of good production and quality controls. Thus, high consumer acceptance for its products resulted. Moreover, constant and aggressive advertising and promotional efforts sustained customer loyalty for LTI's products.

In 1981, however, LTI started encountering difficulties in servicing its financial obligations with several banks due to the faulty implementation of one project — the multimillion distillery plant in Canlubang, Laguna (a province south of Manila). The plant was intended to supply the company's projected sales increase of 15 percent a year. At that time, LTI's existing facilities could supply 1.5 million cases of gin, which was enough to fill the annual market demand of 1.1 million cases. The anticipated projections and sales increase did not materialize and the original construction cost of PHP50 million[1] more than

[1]At the time of the case, the exchange rate between the US dollar and the Philippine peso was approximately US$1 = PHP10.

tripled, reaching PHP162 million. Completed in 1985, the plant was hardly used because of the decline in sales.

The Canlubang project thus became a "white elephant" project, causing a tremendous financial burden for LTI. LTI suffered losses as it had to shoulder interest payments of almost PHP500 million from 1983 to 1985. Sales remained strong, with a posting of PHP744 million in 1984. However this was negated by the huge interest payments resulting in a net loss of PHP17 million in 1984. In 1985 it made a PHP14 million profit from sales of PHP1.25 billion. In 1986 LTI made a profit of PHP114 million, from sales of PHP1.1 billion but its interest payments and other financial charges reached PHP133 million, mostly due to its PHP453 million worth of short-term liabilities. Shutdown expenses which arose from labor disputes in its manufacturing division also amounted to PHP16.4 million.

Aside from financial problems, LTI faced labor problems in the 1980s which affected largely its production capacity. The first two strikes in Tondo, Manila lasted for nine days and seven days, respectively. Workers went on strike from October 17, 1983 to January 30, 1984, and again from April 24 to June 7, 1986. The strike at the Canlubang plant started on March 17, 1986 and lasted up to April 30, 1986. The erratic production schedules in the plant failed to provide the necessary supply in the market. Consequently, LTI products disappeared from the retail outlets particularly in the Luzon area, which accounts for the greater proportion (70 percent) of the company's sales.

In February 1987 the company was plagued with financial problems and production setbacks and Palanca Jr, who was suffering from heart ailment, sought alternatives to ensure the continuous operation of LTI. After weighing the alternatives, he thought of selling the majority interest to SMC. Palanca Jr sought a private audience with Andres Soriano III, the Chairman of the Board of SMC, and told him of the problems he faced. Soriano asked him for time to study the matter. For two months, the Corporate Planning Staff of SMC gathered industry data on the hard liquor industry, analyzed the trends and forecasts, and examinedintensively the competition. Relating the acquisition to the present expansive thrusts of SMC, the Corporate Planning Staff recommended the acquisition of LTI as an SMC subsidiary through the infusion of additional working capital of PHP401 million in the form of long-term debt. On August 1, 1987, La Tondeña Incorporada was transformed into La Tondeña Distillers, Inc (LTDI), a joint venture company owned 70 percent by San Miguel Corporation (SMC) and 30 percent by LTI. Palanca Jr was named Chairman of the Board with Mr Soriano III as Vice Chairman, and Francisco Eizmendi Jr, Ramon del Rosario Jr, Conrado Malixi, Faustino Galang, Delfin Gonzales Jr, Carlos Palanca III, and Carlos Miguel Palanca as Board Members. SMC Beer Manufacturing Division Manager Malixi was appointed as LTDI President (see Exhibit 1 for a list of LTDI's principal officers).

The joint venture between the two corporate giants, SMC and LTI, was a distinct business partnership which brought together two companies whose products have become hallmarks of Filipino tradition and values. The new firm's business position was strengthened and fully reinforced by the manufacturing expertise, marketing and distribution network, and public goodwill of the owner companies. The joint venture ran in line with the strategic vision of Soriano III that SMC would "continue to expand its existing food, beverage and packaging business and build on its strengths, and explore new areas with attractive goals and earnings potential." Specifically, the acquisition of LTI assured SMC of a dominant position both in the beer market and in the hard liquor industry, which seemed to be complementary in terms of market demand. Beer sales are believed to be high during recovery and prosperity, while sales of hard liquor has been observed to be higher in times of depression or decline. Specifically, based on the econometric model for beer, beer sales was highly dependent on the farm gate price for copra (desiccated coconut). If the farm gate price exceeded PHP4 per kilogram, demand for beer increased until the price for copra would reach PHP8/kilo, at which level demand would flatten to give way to other demand for consumer goods. When the price of copra falls below the PHP4.00 mark, it is believed that the demand for hard liquor would increase. Thus, the acquisition of LTI provided SMC a greater leverage against the cyclical nature of the economy.

For his part, Palanca Jr said that the venture was "consistent with La Tondeña's new thrust of looking out for new investment opportunities in its efforts to diversify its investment portfolio." He added that the deal with SMC was tailor-fitted for LTDI's diversification move because of SMC's good track record in consumer marketing, "which blends with LTI's own expertise in the wines and spirits business."

## The San Miguel Corporation

The San Miguel Corporation is the Philippines' largest conglomerate in the food and beverage industry. Businesses include beer, packaging products, coconut oil milling and refining operations, agricultural operations, aquaculture operations, Magnolia dairy products, feeds and livestock, exports, and investments. In 1986, it had corporate resources of PHP12.9 billion and employed a total of 18,388 personnel, making it the country's largest private employer. With its subsidiaries, SMC generated about 4 percent of the country's gross national product. In terms of profits, it netted PHP 1.1 billion in 1986, with the flagship beer division contributing the biggest share.

SMC started in 1890 as the brewer of San Miguel Beer, Asia's oldest beer. It enjoyed a virtual monopoly of the beer market, thereby contributing largely to very profitable operations. In the 1970s, SMC embarked on a major diversification strategy which included Coca-Cola, Magnolia (dairy products), poultry, packaging, and agriculture, the perceived growth areas where the company could derive new businesses.

SMC had a divisionalized organizational structure in which each of the operating divisions was controlled as a profit center. There was autonomy in each of the divisions in terms of decision-making in the day-to-day operations. However, in terms of the corporate plans of the individual divisions, the corporate planning staff level monitored and synthesized these with those of the entire corporation.

## Industry Background

The hard liquor industry in the Philippines was made up of four major distillers — La Tondeña, Destileria Limtuaco, Tanduay, and Consolidated — which accounted for roughly 90 percent of the total sales in the industry. Nonetheless, there is a proliferation of backyard distillers and quite a few native wines which had been prevalent in the different barrios and towns of certain regions in the Philippines. As seen in Exhibit 2, La Tondeña accounted for the lion's share of the total volume of industry sales from 1979 to 1985. Due to the internal problems encountered, however, LTDI products disappeared from the marketplace in 1985 to 1986, leaving a vacuum. This opportunity was seized by Tanduay, LTDI's main competitor, which experienced a sudden rise in market share.

All of the four major distillers had plants in the Greater Manila Area. Only LTDI had production facilities outside of this area (i.e., Cebu, the country's second largest metropolis). In view of this factor, pricing in the different regions of the Philippines reflected greatly variations in transportation (shipping and trucking) and warehousing costs.

In terms of distribution, all four major distillers employed a booking method through major distributors and retailers. Orders were taken by salespersons from large-scale buyers and shipped to them. Chinese traders controlled the distribution network. Being of Chinese origin, Mr Palanca Sr had the advantage of access to the Chinese distributors.

Traditionally in the 1960s and 1970s, hard liquor products had a high alcohol content (normally 80 proof). This might have been due to the fact that native wines and spirits (e.g., *lambanog, basi, tuba*) were purely fermented from coconut, rice, or sugar. In the 1980s, however, probably due to the increasing health consciousness of the population, a trend had been identified toward lower alcohol content in hard liquor products. Tanduay launched in the mid-1980s a new 65-proof drink, Tanduay ESQ (Extra Smooth Quality). This new product easily caught on among the younger male population in the urban centers and threatened the supremacy of LTDI products.

## Organizational Structure

From 1902 to 1987, LTDI was operated as a family corporation. Although there was a formal organizational structure (see Exhibit 3), an informal structure based on personal relationships among the different officers prevailed. Although each vice president was responsible for a functional area, the Cebu operations functioned as an independent company from that of the central office. The company was highly patriarchal and decision-making was highly centralized in the president and general manager. There were no management systems in place, such as regular reports to monitor the performance of the various operating units. The following is a statement made by the EDP manager, which sheds some light on the control system in place at the time:

> I remember those times when the executive committee would pressure us to churn out volumes of reports that required long periods of overtime. After the reports were submitted, that was it. They never asked for it again until the time they might remember to have an update.

Financial controls were likewise very loose and there was no financial data base. Following traditional Chinese management style, the company's plans and programs were intrinsically based on the gut feeling and intuition of the Palanca family, in particular, Palanca Sr and later on Palanca Jr.

Upon the 1987 SMC takeover, a reorganization took place to pave the way for professional management. This functional set-up (see Exhibits 4 and 5) included three senior vice presidents who were responsible to the president and in charge of manufacturing, finance, and marketing. Manufacturing included supervision of the plant operations in Tondo and Cebu; marketing included monitoring of sales performance in Luzon, Visayas, and Mindanao. Also added under the new structure were the market research and information systems (MARIS), the public relations office, and the marketing logistics department (see Exhibit 5 for a detailed presentation of the Marketing organization). This new structure particularly revitalized the marketing function and was geared toward making LTDI more competitive against the other brands in the market.

Upon SMC's takeover in August 1987, the first move made to rehabilitate the company was to conduct an assessment of LTDI's manpower resources. A detailed evaluation of managers and the general labor force was undertaken to determine the proper match of personnel capability and their respective positions. Some managers, together with some militant workers, were terminated through an attractive compensation package. Those managers who remained had been assessed as trainable under the new systems patterned after SMC. Generally, they rose from the ranks; most of them did not have thorough professional management training, none possessed postgraduate degrees.

## Marketing Operations

**Products.** The major products of LTDI were hard liquor consisting of gin and rum (normally 80 proof). These products were dominated by Ginebra San Miguel (GSM), accounting for 70 percent of total sales, and Añejo Rum, which accounted for roughly 15 percent of total sales (see Exhibit 6). The other products are minor hard liquor products which found niches in certain regional and local municipalities. An example is Vino Kulafu, a Chinese herbal wine which is highly sellable in the Visayas region.

**Distribution.** Prior to SMC's takeover, LTDI's products, namely GSM and Añejo Rum, were distributed through major distributors and retailers throughout the Philippine archipelago. There were salespersons for each of the regions, but they booked orders only for the products. The company did not have any trucks for distribution nor did it have any logistics department to take care of shipping and warehousing the products. Generally, this system was true for the hard liquor industry; all the major distillers functioned through this distribution network wherein the major distributors and retailers were the Chinese businessmen.

Upon SMC's acquisition in August 1987, one of the major innovations introduced in marketing operations was the hiring of regional sales managers and district sales supervisors to strengthen the overall distribution network. A fleet of trucks was purchased and sent to major selling regions, and routing systems designed for each and every salesperson to follow religiously. Routing was never done on a systematic basis and the regular salespersons found it very difficult to adapt to the newer and more rigid distribution system.

**Price.** The prices of LTDI products were relatively competitive with the other major distillers. Since the target market for hard liquor was found to be the lower-income segments (referred to in the Philippines as the "C, D, and E" income classes), prices of hard liquor were kept within the reach of the market segment (see Exhibit 7 for a comparative pricing of hard liquor brands). The pricing practices, however, by the major distillers were a three-tiered pricing policy — one with the preferred discount policy for the major distributors, another set for wholesalers, and a third set for retailers. After the SMC takeover, LTDI management scrapped this set of prices and adopted only one set of prices with the variances among regions being accounted for only by differences in shipping and warehousing costs.

**Promotions and advertising.** In the 1970s, the main theme of promotional and advertising activities of the company was Ginebra San Miguel — "Ang Inumin ng Tunay na Lalaki" (literally "The Real Man's Drink" in Filipino). This was carried out in TV advertisements and radio commercials. This campaign, however, targeted the market segment in the far-flung barrios and towns. The impact on the consuming public was a general decreasing market share in the urban areas and a steady share in the provinces.

To signal the company's rebirth and to reintroduce it to the public with a new image, the company launched the "Magkasangga" (meaning "ally" in Filipino) television advertisement series. The first TV advertisement bannering the slogan "Ikaw at Ginebra, Magkasangga" ("You and Ginebra, allies") was aired in October 1987. The advertisements definitely had a profound impact on TV viewers since the slogan instantly gained popularity and acceptance all over the Philippines. It became a byword among Filipinos in their relationships with their family, relatives, and especially, friends.

## SMC Systems

San Miguel Corporation was the largest food and beverage conglomerate in the Philippines. It had the most extensive distribution network that spanned the entire 7,100 islands of the archipelago due to its basic consumer orientation. To SMC management, the company's slogan was "Availability is the mother of market share." Thus, in all the major operating divisions, sophisticated and well-planned systems were in place to design and effect the placement of products in all consumer-product outlets (*sari-sari* or neighborhood stores, *tiendas*, supermarkets, groceries, and restaurants).

The corporation followed the Louie Allen Corporate Planning Systems. Each division head was required to do an annual budget, a one-year plan and a five-year long-term plan for his or her respective divisions. This planning activity was normally done toward the end of the year, particularly the last quarter from October to December. All operating and staff managers were then called for an overall planning session which lasted 3 to 5 days in an out-of-town venue. After the divisional plans and forecasts were finalized by each division, they were then submitted to the SMC Executive Committee, composed of the president and three senior vice presidents (finance, corporate planning, and services), for approval. Normally, certain revisions on the submitted plans took place following meetings with the executive committee. These meetings were held on average 2 to 3 times before the plans were finalized and approved for implementation. Support systems for corporate planning included a good management and financial control system in the form of budgets and accurate financial accounting.

## LTI Culture

During the time of the Palancas, the company could be described, in the words of a manager, as "a nice place to work in." The working environment on the whole was a relaxed one, where one worked at his or her own pace. Executives came in generally by mid-morning and worked until after five. In terms of compensation, the salary scale of the company was below the industry. This was, however, compensated by other company benefits such as a very generous medical benefits program. For the LTDI employee, all expenses related to medical care were shouldered by the company. There was generally no policy for car loans or other benefits. Nonetheless, based on certain criteria such as loyalty and seniority, certain managers were given company cars that included gasoline and automotive repair allowances.

Channels of communication were open and managers were encouraged to exchange ideas and problems during lunch at the executive lounge. All meals taken within the normal office hours were shouldered by the company for all employees from managers to clerks. However, most decisions were centralized, emanating basically from the president and general manager. As a result, the managers were risk-averse, tending to concentrate on more short-term problems.

There was low turnover among the employees and the average length of service was about ten years. The average age of a manager was 45 years.

EXHIBIT 1

## LA TONDEÑA DISTILLERS, INCORPORATED
## Profile of LTDI Executive Officers

**President: Conrado R Malixi**

A graduate of Mapua Institute of Technology, Manila, Malixi served as Senior Vice President of SMC's Beer Division for eight years. Prior to that, he rose from the ranks as a production engineer and later on as a plant manager. Due to his fatherly concern for his employees, Malixi has been described as "wholesome and well-liked by subordinates." One manager has described his management style as "managing by walking around," in view of his personal visits to all operational units, whether they are located in the Manila area or in the far-flung barrios and towns.

**Senior Vice President (Finance): Bernabe L Navarro**

A BS Accounting graduate from the University of the East, Manila, Navarro served in the Controllers' Office of SMC for five years as Assistant Vice President. Prior to that, he was employed as a senior partner at Sycip Gorres Velayo & Co, the country's foremost public accounting firm. Navarro is a soft-spoken and mild-mannered person known for his penchant for details and accuracy.

**Senior Vice President (Marketing): Gregorio Ma. Villaseran III**

A graduate of Ateneo de Manila University in Management Engineering and BSc Economics (Honors), Villaseran came from the SMC Beer Division as Assistant Vice President. He was credited for competing in the Beer War with Asia Brewery Inc (ABI) and succeeded in reducing ABI's market share from 8 percent in 1983 to 3 percent in 1985. Prior to his SMC employment, Villaseran was Senior Advertising Eexecutive at McAnn Erickson, one of the most notable and aggressive advertising outfits servicing the top consumer manufacturing companies. Villaseran is seen as a highly dynamic individual. He is known to be a brilliant marketing man, although staff noticed his rather eccentric manner of approaching problematic situations. Villaseran is also known to be quicktempered and very direct in expressing his opinions.

EXHIBIT 2

**LA TONDEÑA DISTILLERS, INCORPORATED**
**Market Share, Historical to Current**
**From 1979 to March 1988**

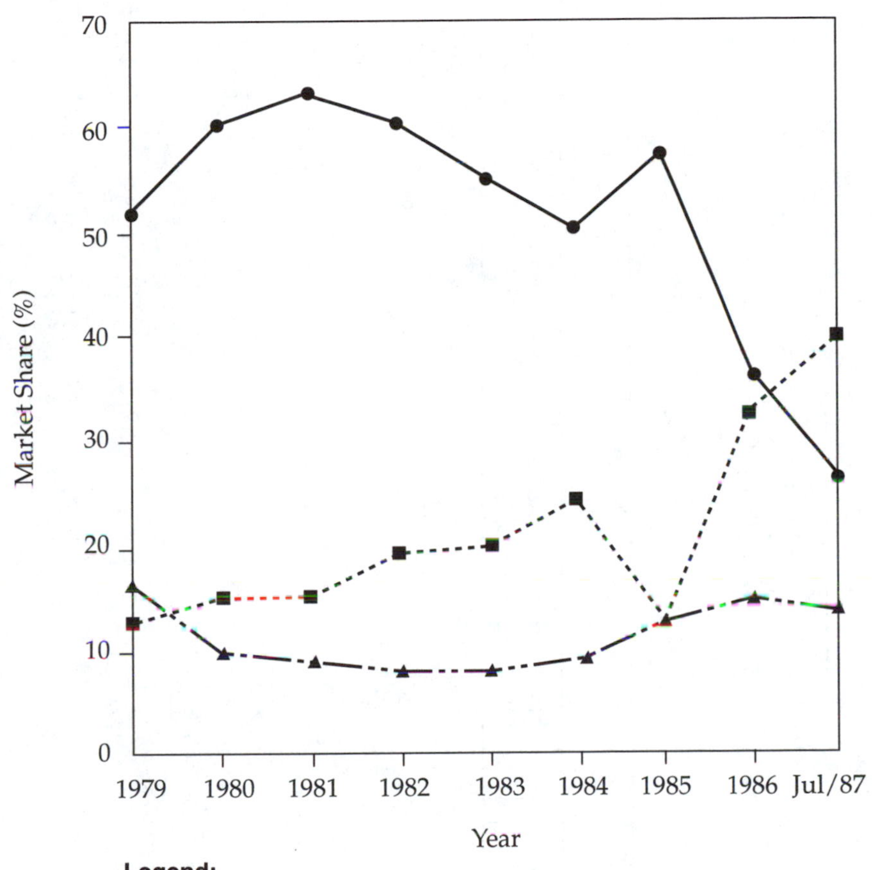


**Legend:**
- La Tondeña
- Tanduay
- Limtuaco

EXHIBIT 3

## LA TONDEÑA DISTILLERS, INCORPORATED
## Old LTDI Organizational Structure

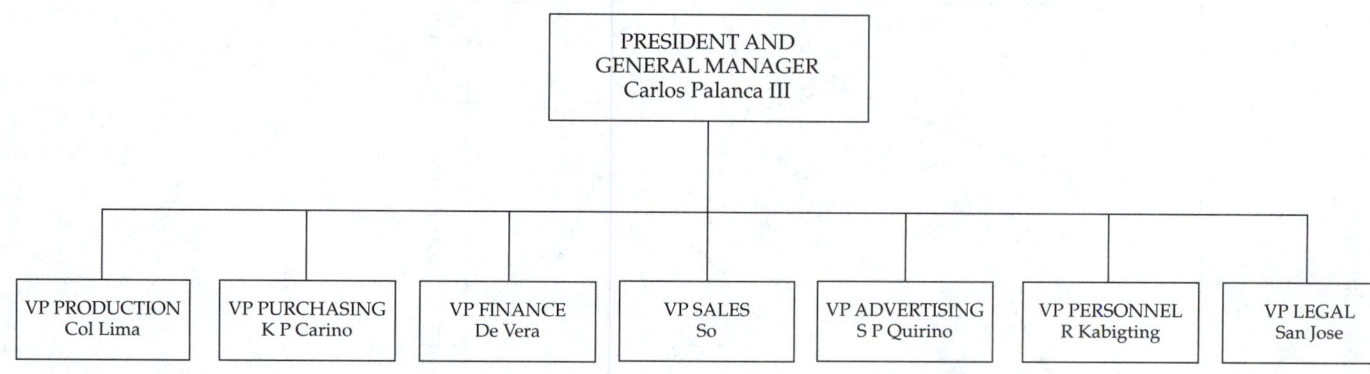


Note: Cariño and Quirino are sisters of Carlos Palanca III.

# EXHIBIT 4

## LA TONDEÑA DISTILLERS, INCORPORATED
## LTDI Organizational and Functional Chart
## As of April 6, 1988

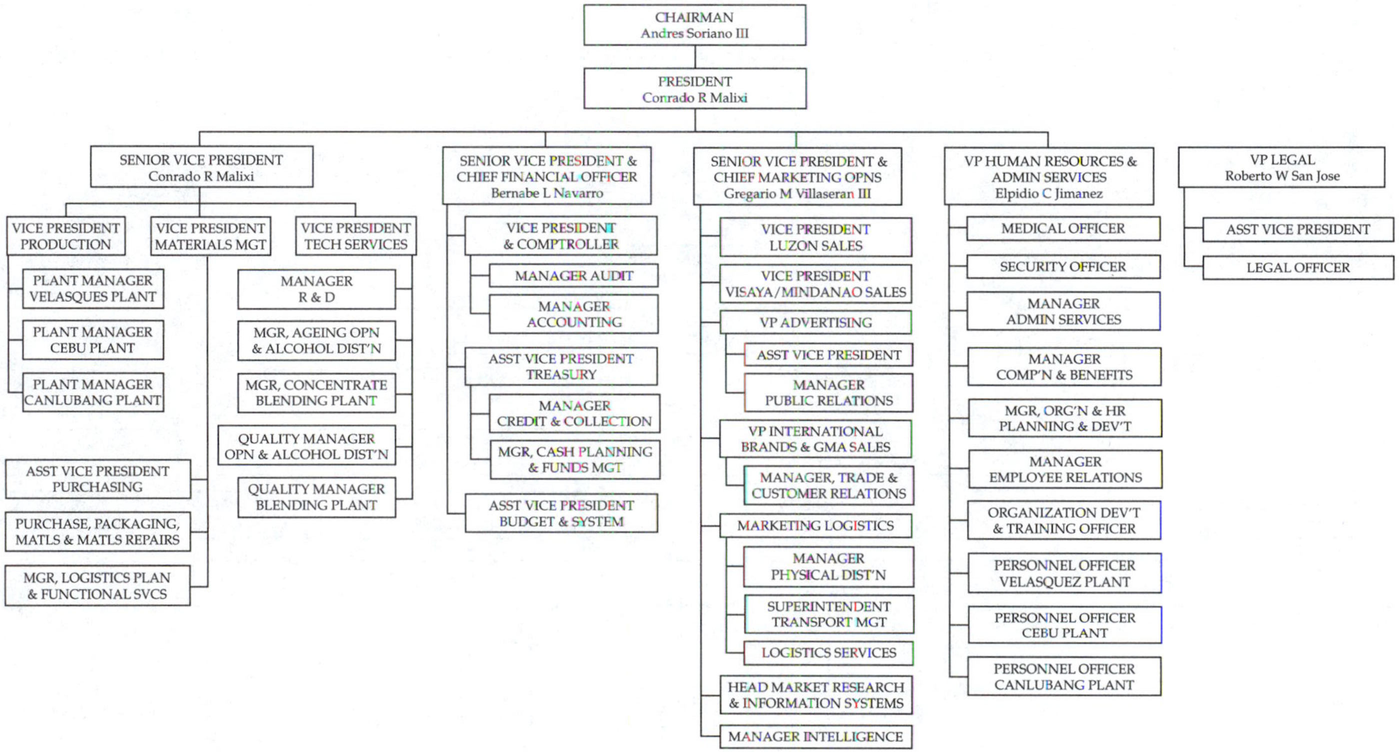

- CHAIRMAN — Andres Soriano III
  - PRESIDENT — Conrado R Malixi
    - SENIOR VICE PRESIDENT — Conrado R Malixi
      - VICE PRESIDENT PRODUCTION
        - PLANT MANAGER VELASQUES PLANT
        - PLANT MANAGER CEBU PLANT
        - PLANT MANAGER CANLUBANG PLANT
      - VICE PRESIDENT MATERIALS MGT
        - ASST VICE PRESIDENT PURCHASING
        - PURCHASE, PACKAGING, MATLS & MATLS REPAIRS
        - MGR, LOGISTICS PLAN & FUNCTIONAL SVCS
      - VICE PRESIDENT TECH SERVICES
        - MANAGER R & D
        - MGR, AGEING OPN & ALCOHOL DIST'N
        - MGR, CONCENTRATE BLENDING PLANT
        - QUALITY MANAGER OPN & ALCOHOL DIST'N
        - QUALITY MANAGER BLENDING PLANT
    - SENIOR VICE PRESIDENT & CHIEF FINANCIAL OFFICER — Bernabe L Navarro
      - VICE PRESIDENT & COMPTROLLER
        - MANAGER AUDIT
        - MANAGER ACCOUNTING
      - ASST VICE PRESIDENT TREASURY
        - MANAGER CREDIT & COLLECTION
        - MGR, CASH PLANNING & FUNDS MGT
      - ASST VICE PRESIDENT BUDGET & SYSTEM
    - SENIOR VICE PRESIDENT & CHIEF MARKETING OPNS — Gregario M Villaseran III
      - VICE PRESIDENT LUZON SALES
      - VICE PRESIDENT VISAYA/MINDANAO SALES
      - VP ADVERTISING
        - ASST VICE PRESIDENT
        - MANAGER PUBLIC RELATIONS
      - VP INTERNATIONAL BRANDS & GMA SALES
        - MANAGER, TRADE & CUSTOMER RELATIONS
      - MARKETING LOGISTICS
        - MANAGER PHYSICAL DIST'N
        - SUPERINTENDENT TRANSPORT MGT
        - LOGISTICS SERVICES
      - HEAD MARKET RESEARCH & INFORMATION SYSTEMS
      - MANAGER INTELLIGENCE
    - VP HUMAN RESOURCES & ADMIN SERVICES — Elpidio C Jimanez
      - MEDICAL OFFICER
      - SECURITY OFFICER
      - MANAGER ADMIN SERVICES
      - MANAGER COMP'N & BENEFITS
      - MGR, ORG'N & HR PLANNING & DEV'T
      - MANAGER EMPLOYEE RELATIONS
      - ORGANIZATION DEV'T & TRAINING OFFICER
      - PERSONNEL OFFICER VELASQUEZ PLANT
      - PERSONNEL OFFICER CEBU PLANT
      - PERSONNEL OFFICER CANLUBANG PLANT
    - VP LEGAL — Roberto W San Jose
      - ASST VICE PRESIDENT
      - LEGAL OFFICER

EXHIBIT 5

## LA TONDEÑA DISTILLERS, INCORPORATED
## Organizational Structure of Marketing Operations
## As of August 10, 1988

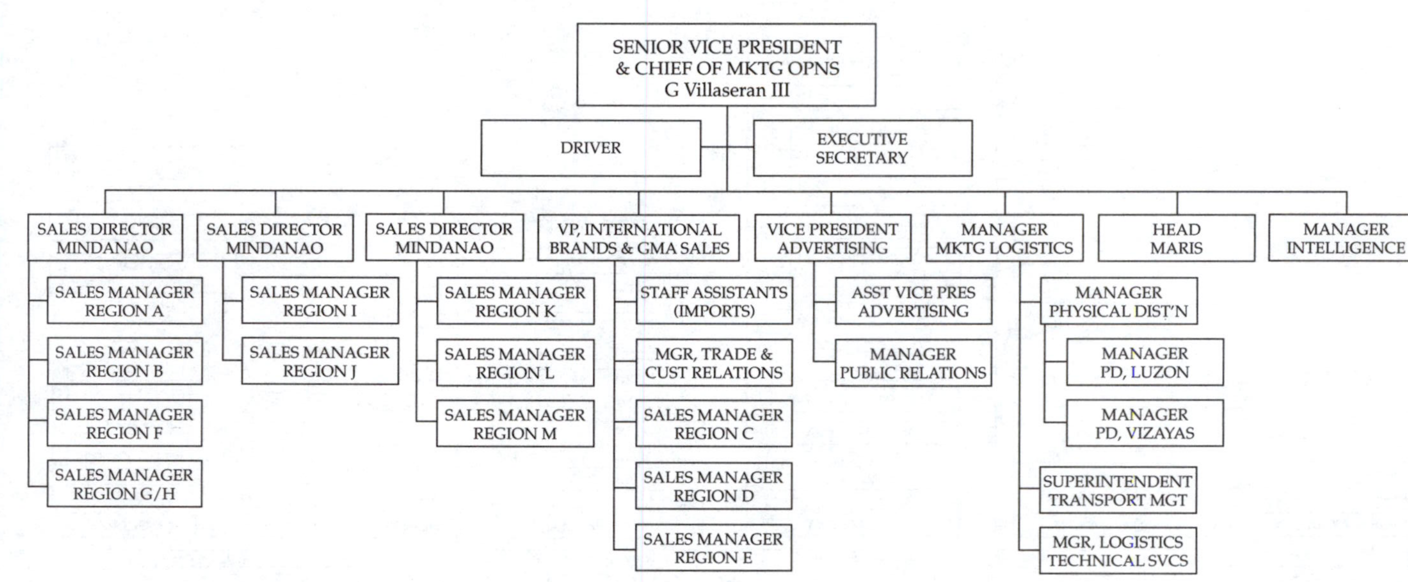


Note: This chart was designed to show reporting relationships and does not reflect seniority of positions.

EXHIBIT 6

**LA TONDEÑA DISTILLERS, INCORPORATED**
**LTDI Hard Liquor Sales**
**January–September 1987**

| *Product* | | *Size* | *Number of Cases Sold* |
|---|---|---|---|
| GSM | Frasco | 12' | 403,081 |
| | Frasquito | 24' | 184,378 |
| | Round | 24' | 3,442,684 |
| Añejo Rum 3 | | 12' | 56 |
| | | 24' | 1,793 |
| Anñejo Rum 5 | | 12' | 60,477 |
| | | 24' | 345,364 |
| Añejo Rum 65 | | 24' | 3,674 |
| Añejo Rum Oro | | 12' | 9,891 |
| | | 24' | 425,830 |
| Rum Cana 65 | | 12' | 68 |
| | | 24' | 43,086 |
| Vino Kulafu | | 24' | 485,931 |
| Vino Samson | | 24' | 1,087 |
| International Brands | | | 2,232 |
| Total | | | 5,409,632 |

EXHIBIT 7

**LA TONDEÑA DISTILLERS, INCORPORATED**
**Comparative Pricing of Hard Liquor Brands**
**As of September 30, 1987**
(in Philippine pesos)

| *Brand* | | *Size* | *Panel Per Case* | *Retail Per Bottle* |
|---|---|---|---|---|
| LA TONDEÑA | | | | |
| GSM | Frasco | 12' | 168.00 | 16.00 to 17.00 |
| | Frasquito | 24' | 176.00 | 8.00 |
| | Round | 24' | 168.00 | 8.00 to 8.50 |
| Añejo Rum 5 | | 12' | 266.00 | 24.00 to 25.00 |
| | | 24' | 266.00 | 12.00 to 12.50 |
| Añejo Rum 65 | | 12' | 152.00 | 15.00 to 16.00 |
| | | 24' | 164.00 | 7.50 to 8.00 |
| Vino Kulafu | | 24' | 136.00 | 6.00 to 7.00 |
| TANDUAY | | | | |
| ESQ | | 12' | 152.00 | 14.00 to 15.00 |
| | | 24' | 164.00 | 7.50 to 8.50 |
| LIMTUACO | | | | |
| White Castle | | 12' | 218.00 | 18.50 to 19.50 |
| | | 24' | 218.00 | 9.00 to 10.00 |
| CONSOLIDATED | | | | |
| Club Valentino | | 12' | 168.00 | 14.00 to 15.00 |
| | | 24' | 168.00 | 7.00 to 8.00 |
| Andy Player | | 12' | 224.00 | 19.00 to 20.00 |
| | | 24' | 224.00 | 10.00 to 10.50 |

# British Banking Corporation* 22

It was a misty morning as Cliff Forster walked into his office at the British Banking Corporation (BBC) in the heart of the city of London. Mr Forster was the Managing Director of BBC, a medium-size U.K. bank with an extensive high street retail banking network all over the country and wholly owned branches in New York and Hong Kong. The principal activities the BBC branches in New York and Hong Kong were treasury and stock trading.

Mr Forster had an important board meeting this morning. He was about to present his plan on the next strategic step for BBC.

Nine months ago, when he learned that BBC had shown a 10-percent improvement in its net profit after tax over the previous year, he was extremely pleased. However, his happiness proved to be short-lived as competitors subsequently announced better results. He then realized that BBC was out of line vis-à-vis its competitors. The financial press was not blind to this either and did not spare a moment to highlight the fact. The price of BBC shares fell. Mr Forster immediately initiated a review of BBC's operations with a view to correcting the situation.

Founded in 1930, BBC was a relatively young institution in the context of British banking. BBC was started by four industrialists and had grown from a modest retail bank

---

*This case was prepared by Chan Ying Lock, Chern Cher Hoon, Samuel Lim Siew Tee, Tsai Meow Ling, and Wong Meng Ling (MBA, Nanyang Technological University, Singapore) under the supervision of Professor Luis Ma. R. Calingo. At the request of the company, financial data and the names of organizations, people, and some places have been disguised but essential relationships have been preserved. The case is designed to serve as a basis for class discussion rather than to illustrate either effective or ineffective handling of an administrative situation.

to a nationwide retail bank in 1993. Its U.K. business also covered corporate banking, treasury business, trade financing, private and trust banking, and portfolio management.

While most other U.K. banks were struggling with ebbing capital adequacy ratios and a rising tide of bad loans, BBC had been expanding its retail banking aggressively. BBC had been able to pull this off, thanks to a cautious lending policy that had left it with below-average levels of bad loans and a low-cost approach to business expansion. "We decided that expanding the traditional U.K. customer base was more important than expanding the activities of our overseas offices activities," said Mr Forster recently.

To expand its retail business, the BBC had relied heavily on automated outlets instead of more expensive full-service branches and sited them in prime locations around the major cities' busy railway stations. Two-thirds of BBC's branches were unmanned, compared with an average of just one-third for the other big banks. Basically, BBC's cost controls were better than those of its competitors, and the retail business had helped contain overheads.

## Goal Formulation

The Board of Directors recently conducted an internal review of the BBC's group activities. The board had decided that its established U.K.-based retail banking activity should continue to be actively pushed because it was what the bank does best and was a profitable recurring business that required very little extra effort to keep it going. However, the review recommended that more attention be placed on wholesale banking business in all of its offices worldwide. The objective of this refocus was to diversify into corporate advisory banking, given that this was the profitable activity of the day and in the immediate future.

In addition, the review also recommended that BBC's overseas activities be expanded further. The problem for BBC was its limited resources. Given better prospects in Asia than in Europe and the U.S., BBC decided to concentrate its expansion efforts on Asia.

The new vision represented a significant new challenge for the bank. The bank's growth had been primarily on the back of its proactive retail banking business in the United Kingdom, with recent wholesale banking still a small and fledgling activity — an attempt to meet the needs of the bank's bigger corporate clients. The bank conducted a study of world economic trends and discussed with its bigger corporate clients their needs. As a result, the board was very convinced that future growth had to come from more corporate banking, not just traditional lending but corporate advisory services as well.

Such a proactive venture into mainstream corporate advisory banking would put the bank into direct competition with longer, established big names such as Baring Brothers, Hill Samuel, Morgan Grenfell, Goldman Sachs, Lehman Brothers, Salomon Brothers, and the like which had dominated the corporate advisory banking arena for a long time. The Board recognized that the task to join the game would not be an easy one.

## Environmental Analysis

### The U.K. Economy

The U.K. economy during the past five years was sluggish by all accounts. Unemployment still hovered above 10 percent, exports and industrial output were depressed, and these had put severe pressure on the earnings growth in the corporate sector of the country, which was reflected in poor corporate results from the domestic sector.

Demand for credit was weak as new investments into both the domestic and export sectors remained in the doldrums. In addition, a shrinking population and falling per capita disposable income had depressed consumer confidence and reduced purchases of durable goods. All of these factors had caused loan portfolios to shrink. To make matters worse, an increasing trend in domestic bankruptcies had forced banks to make higher write-off provisions for bad loans.

### Foreign Exchange Implications of a Pound Sterling Base

The weak U.K. economy was reflected in the weak exchange rate of the pound sterling, which was at its lowest level ever in its history. The most disastrous incident recently was the parity pressure on pound sterling which forced the Chancellor of the Exchequer (Great Britain's Minister of Finance/Treasury) to temporarily pull the pound sterling out of the European Monetary System (EMS), an action that further cast doubts on the pound sterling's underlying strength and value.

Ironically, the exceptional volatility of the pound sterling's exchange rate in the past year had brought in lots of business for the bank's Treasury department — volatility had resulted in an exceptionally high volume of foreign exchange transactions. The need of corporate clients to hedge against foreign exchange exposure risk arising from an unstable pound sterling had actually trebled the sales volume of treasury products this year compared to last year. This performance, however, was not expected to be repeated.

The strengthening of foreign currencies, particularly the U.S. dollar against the pound sterling, had enhanced the contributions of the bank's New York and Hong Kong branches' operations (the Hong Kong dollar being pegged to the U.S. dollar).

## Retail Banking Competition in the U.K.

The recent acquisition of Midland Bank by the HongKong and Shanghai Banking Corporation had given the latter, almost overnight, a significant presence in the U.K. Midland Bank had, in turn, been given a much-needed injection of capital to allow it to once again compete aggressively in the U.K. market.

Barclays Bank, the largest of the Big Four in the U.K., had been steadily holding on to its market share of the domestic market for both retail and wholesale banking businesses. The National Westminster Bank had similarly also held on to its market share of domestic banking business. Together they command over half the domestic banking business. Lloyds, the smallest of the Big Four, continued to trail behind.

The U.K. retail banking business could be considered to be in a mature stage with minimal growth potential. Hardly any major product had been introduced since the implementation of the electronic funds transfer system, BACS, back in the mid-1980s, the only other innovation being Standard Chartered Bank's sale and leaseback scheme for real estate which allows banks to reduce their fixed assets funding and the statutory capital ratio requirement significantly thus releasing funds to finance other operating needs.

Competition for traditional funds continued to be keen, but with little product differentiation.

### The Capital Market Worldwide

Years of poor U.K. corporate results and the prolonged recession in the West had taken its toll on the British securities market. The low returns on British company shares had caused investors to divert their funds into the higher-yield emerging markets, particularly of Asia. The recent strong contribution from the bank's Hong Kong branch's share trading activity substantiates this.

The Hong Kong stock market had been recently bullish in terms of both its breadth (volume) and its depth (variety of counters), due mainly to the robust business generated from trading in China stocks. This market performance pushed the growth rate of the bank's Hong Kong branch's contribution into double digits over the last three years. This was expected to continue into the immediate future.

The bank's New York securities trading activity continued to gain from the steady bull run on Wall Street. Basically, the integration of the major capital markets globally and the freeing of foreign exchange controls by the developing countries had allowed a more dynamic flow of capital funds internationally.

### Financial Products

The 1980s were known as the era of most innovative financial products in the history of banking to date. Starting in the United States, sophisticated financial engineering gave rise to a proliferation of new financial products, especially in the area of financial derivatives such as interest rate swaps and options.

The bank acquired an existing operation in the United States in 1973 when it decided to gain a foothold in the North American market. This proved to be a smart and timely move in the right direction, given the fact that financial products were spawned in the United States and had caught on all over the world. The expertise to master and market these products was, therefore, available within the Group.

### BBC's Strengths

In the U.K., BBC had a solid retail banking operation track record of profits. However, BBC was not yet a major player in the international banking circle. Nevertheless, its branch offices in New York and Hong Kong had made their presence felt in treasury activities and had participated in various loan syndications.

Having its head office in London, considered the most important financial center in the world, had given the bank considerable prestige. Being in the key international locations of London, New York and Hong Kong, BBC traded around the clock and had ready access to international funds. This further enhanced BBC's competitive advantage. With the world markets polarizing — in to the European Economic Community (EEC), North American Free Trade Area (NAFTA), and Asia-Pacific Economic Cooperation (APEC) group — BBC's three offices were ideally situated.

Another strength was its membership in the European banking fraternity. European banks had a long and rich experience in international banking due to their colonial histories. BBC as a European bank was well-positioned to take advantage of the connections and expertise of the more experienced European banks.

**Opportunities**

With the United States climbing steadily out of recession and Asia stepping into its second decade of dynamic growth, the opportunities for the Bank's New York and Hong Kong operations were plenty. It would take very little extra effort for BBC to step up a higher level of activities in its New York and Hong Kong offices.

BBC's main obstacle to exploiting these opportunities was financial resources. The recent response to rights issues in the London stock exchange had been short of pathetic, which meant that the bank was not able to raise additional equity funds for and would have to work within the limits of its current resources. This practically called for the board to decide between expanding either its North American or Asian operation. In short, BBC had to deploy its limited financial and managerial resources to areas of high demand, profit, and growth potential.

Being an EEC bank allowed BBC free entry into the EEC market, which the board had on its cards to enter at some later date, possibly when the EEC begins to climb out of its ongoing recession.

The volatile exchange rates and interest rates were not likely to subside in the foreseeable future. Such a scenario would require corporate clients to demand more treasury services. The treasury business was therefore expected to grow.

The volatile movements in interest rates would also affect fixed income instruments such as bonds and treasury bills. The ability to manage this portfolio was what private and corporate clients would also be seeking. Hence, professional portfolio management services were expected to be developed as a key component of the bank's new activities.

The dynamic rise of the ASEAN stock markets compared to the depressed Japan equity market was expected to cause massive flows of investment funds out of Japan, Europe, and North America into ASEAN. This augured well for all of BBC offices' securities trading activity.

The advent of new treasury products, especially in the area of derivatives, as a result of clever financial engineering offered yet another area of opportunity for the bank to move into and offer more services to its clients.

The developing countries of Asia had been relaxing their foreign ownership requirements in order to attract more investments from the more-developed countries. This had resulted in many British companies, including some of the bank's principal U.K. customers, investing in Asia. Here was another opportunity for the bank to service its customers at home as well as abroad.

## The Asian Opportunity

While London and New York had, for a long time, been the traditional key financial centers of the world, Tokyo had become the third giant financial center over the last 20 years. Lately, Hong Kong and Singapore have emerged as additional centres, a reflection of growth in Asia.

With the opening up of the China market since the early 1980s, business in Hong Kong had shot up in leaps and bounds. However, the handover talks between the British government and the Chinese authorities over Hong Kong's reversion to Chinese rule in 1997 was not proceeding smoothly and threatened the future of British businesses in Hong

Kong after 1997. Although the Chinese government had openly stated that it would continue to uphold Hong Kong's free market practices, such declarations offered little comfort to the board.

Aside from China, the more-developed economies of East Asia led by Japan showed promise of continued growth. However, it was the emerging economies of Southeast Asia led by Singapore which had been the hot favorites because of their very high growth rates. Not to be underestimated also were the newly emerging economies of South Asia led by India.

Western fund managers, hawkeyed for good "emerging market" prospects, had moved into Asia in a big way as populations of the West continue to gray and the private pensions business expanded by leaps and bounds so much so that no solid Asian company was short of funds. The capital was flowing predominantly toward middle-income emerging markets such as Taiwan, South Korea, Malaysia, and Thailand. This was only the beginning. The total market capitalization of the emerging Asian bourses was still small compared with their countries' share of world production, indicating the vast potential that had yet to be tapped.

**Strategy Formulation**

After considering the findings of the study, Mr Forster advised the board that: "The world is becoming one massive common market and the only way for any bank to survive into the future is to grow internationally. BBC must carve for itself a market niche where it had a competitive advantage and yet continues to maintain an above-average return on investment for its shareholders."

In the short term, the bank's strategy for its services business would have to be to compete against the established competitors on pricing for the same quality of service provided. The effect of such a strategy would be a low initial profit margin for services. It was important for this strategy to be explained to the shareholders.

The bank felt that it should first work on its existing client base, particularly its loan clients from all its three offices. Only after it had worked on its own client base would the bank be better positioned to become a challenger and grab market share from its competitors.

The market niche for both loans and services that Mr Forster believed the bank should carve was the up-and-coming new high growth businesses. Mr Forster suggested that the bank cultivate tie-in arrangements with various venture capitalists and their clients.

In the longer term, once the bank's reputation and its relationship with its clients were established, the bank should be able to charge higher service fees. The bank would also by then have a higher volume treasury business which would benefit it in terms of lower cost of funds. However, instead of passing all of this on to its clients, the bank could pass on part of it and retain part of it to post higher earnings for itself.

To date, the bank has been slow compared to its competitors in expanding its activities in the Asia region, thus suffering a competitive disadvantage in terms of time and client base. Mr Forster believed it was not too late to correct the situation. He thought that BBC merely had to act extra fast and innovatively in order to catch up with the established players in the market.

The board decided to be innovative by choosing to open up an office in Singapore in addition to expanding its Hong Kong branch activities. "We should have our cake and eat it too," said Mr Nick Allwyn, Chairman of BBC. Because of the uncertainty British banks in Hong Kong face after 1997, BBC decided to open a Singapore office as a safety measure just in case it had to wind down its operations in Hong Kong after 1997. In the meantime, Singapore itself was rapidly becoming an international financial center in its own right and had even been described by some analysts as the third leg in the Asian tripod link, together with Tokyo and Hong Kong. Besides, just as Tokyo had its Japanese hinterland and Hong Kong its China hinterland, Singapore regarded Southeast Asia as its hinterland.

The gearing-up period for new activities generally took 2 to 3 years. In order to shorten this in the case of setting up its office in Singapore, BBC decided to buy into an existing concern, similar to what it did in New York. Such a move would immediately give the bank a ready customer base in addition to cutting down the setup time.

Mr Forster was fully aware that such a route would require large acquisition monies and its success was highly dependent on the speed and ease with which both organizations were able to merge their corporate cultures.

A comprehensive search led to the identification of a Singapore-based stockbroking firm as the target for the bank to buy. For a start, the bank would purchase 49 percent of its equity with a put option for the balance in two years' time. The intention was to ultimately acquire full control; the bank obtained the necessary approval in principle from the Monetary Authority of Singapore to commence this planned acquisition.

### Implementation Strategy

BBC realized that a strong marketing staff was essential to the success of the business. The staff in the target stockbroking house had been assessed as having the right caliber to learn and cross-sell the new products that the bank intends to introduce. Selling new products to existing clients would be the Singapore branch's first thrust, simultaneously with the other offices.

## The Business Plan

Recognizing the need for strategic planning to survive and prosper in an increasingly competitive business environment, the board of directors voted in mid-1993 to direct Mr Forster to start formal strategic planning activities. The principal objective of BBC's business plan was to improve the competitive position of BBC vis-à-vis its competitors. Mr Forster worked with the bank's other senior executives throughout the balance of the year and, in January 1994, presented the following long-range business plan to members of the board of directors.

### Long-Range Strategic Business Plan

The Long-Range Strategic Business Plan for the British Banking Corporation covers the period 1994–1998, during which time the total billings of BBC worldwide are projected to increase from £1,575 million to £2,362 million. This rapid growth of 50 percent compares to 20 percent for the past three years from 1991 to 1993.

Most large banks and corporations had acknowledged the need for strategic planning in order to survive and prosper in an increasingly competitive business environment. Faced with the prospect of more intensive competition from all types of financial institutions, as well as the problem of accelerating operating costs, the officers of the British Banking Corporation have devoted considerable time and effort to preparing the Long-Range Strategic Business Plan. The following summarizes the major objectives and strategies of this plan.

Over the next five years, the major objectives and strategies of the British Banking Corporation will be to maximize the growth of income and assets by developing a full complement of commercial banking services and a stronger corporate bank image with the highest quality banking services for individuals as well as corporate customers. To minimize the need for alternative sources of funds to support portfolio growth, a major emphasis will be placed on developing and increasing demand and time deposits on the one hand, and on stepping up fee-related income on the other hand.

## Introduction

The management of the British Banking Corporation has committed itself to systematic planning for growth. This Long-Range Strategic Business Plan is the culmination of months of planning effort by Cliff Forster and his team of senior executives and their staff and has three main purposes:

1. To establish the long-range objectives of BBC.
2. Given those long-range business objectives, to define explicit courses of action.
3. Given those courses of action, to utilize the formal planning process within BBC for the modification and improvement of financial performance.

While the Long-Range Strategic Business Plan presents a framework of specific objectives and policies, it is also a "living" document which will evolve as the bank grows. The plan attempts to organize and coordinate the decision-making process to allow management to anticipate and plan for change, instead of merely reacting to it.

## Business Definition

Over the past 60 years, the British Banking Corporation has grown by adhering to the philosophy of sound, conservative banking principles and professional management responsibilities. The bank's primary concern is to fulfill its obligations to shareholders, customers, employees, and the public, and bases its business activities on a commitment to:

1. Safeguard the assets and deposits of the bank.
2. Provide quality services to customers while ensuring stable growth and a sufficient profit for the shareholders.
3. Create a meaningful work environment for the bank's employees.
4. Contribute to the welfare and prosperity of the communities served by the bank.

These same commitments have allowed the bank to grow in the past 60 years and will provide the foundation for growth in the next five years.

## Situational Analysis

Strategic planning begins with an assessment of current internal strengths and weaknesses, as well as environmental opportunities and threats. Before the planning objectives could be established, management needed to know what it had to work with, what problems needed to be resolved, and what alternative courses of action were available. In short, what was required was an assessment of BBC's current operating strengths and weaknesses, as well as the environmental opportunities and threats — a situational analysis.

The situational analysis recognizes the following competitive strengths of the British Banking Corporation:

1. An excellent reputation for high-quality consumer banking service.
2. A group of loyal core customers.
3. An excellent profit performance.
4. An extensive and well-coordinated national network.
5. An extensive data bank knowledge.

6. An experienced team of managers and executives.
7. A secure financial position with low leverage and high liquidity.

The situational analysis also recognizes the following competitive weaknesses or areas of improvement for the British Banking Corporation:

1. A low awareness of the bank's services potential.
2. A low awareness of the bank's overseas operations.
3. The lack of a cost accounting system to accurately price the services of the bank.
4. The lack of market research capabilities to introduce new products and services.
5. The low market value and minimal trading activity of the bank's stocks.
6. A high turnover of nonmanagerial personnel.

The situational analysis further recognizes two main strategic opportunities for growth and profit improvement:

1. Expand the "services" activity while maintaining the retail market share; that is, improve the profit margins by reducing the operating expenses and increasing fees and service charges.
2. Expand the geographic base by expanding each of the offices' activities.

Finally, the situational analysis recognizes the following concerns for the future:

1. Personnel costs worldwide are expected to increase, making it necessary to increase productivity, which is a difficult management task particularly in the service industry.
2. Inefficiencies are likely to arise from increased organizational and operational size requiring stringent cost control systems, which in turn are an added administrative expense.

To achieve the bank's objectives, management exercises control over a number of critical variables or factors that substantially affect the bank's performance. Six critical factors represent the focal points of the strategic plan:

1. Staffing levels
2. Budgetary allocations
3. Product/service decisions
4. Marketing policies
5. Expansion plans
6. Credit policies

The bank management recognizes that there are limits on the change in the critical variables without adversely affecting the Bank's stability or profit performance. These limits are the following:

1. Pre-set profit objectives
2. Banking regulations
3. Availability and cost of capital
4. Availability and cost of qualified employees

The use of critical variables under known constraints in strategic planning is dependent upon underlying assumptions about the future. Although it is impossible to predict events with certainty, bank management makes the following assumptions about the developed economies over the next five years:

1. Market interest rates will gradually rise, reaching an average of 7.5 percent in 1998.
2. Average annual inflation rate will be 3 percent.
3. Central banking authorities will ease monetary controls, although monetary policies will continue to be conservative.
4. Operating expenses, led by personnel costs, will continue to erode earnings.
5. New and innovative financial derivatives will be introduced into the market as competition gets keener among the numerous banks in the market.
6. Competition will become more keen as the banking industry becomes more deregulated with nonbank financial institutions such as brokerage firms and insurance companies being allowed to offer competing quasi-banking services.

## Long-Range Business Objectives

Overall corporate objectives for the British Banking Corporation may be classified into three groups: growth rate, market orientation, and profit improvement. Although these objectives overlap, each category represents a distinct area of emphasis, as described below:

**Growth rate objectives.** Through a controlled and well-planned program of growth, the British Banking Corporation seeks over the period 1994–1998 to:

1. Increase the total assets of the bank by 13 percent.
2. Establish four more retail outlets every year in the U.K. Increase the service income of New York and Hong Kong by 15 percent and 20 percent, respectively.
3. Increase the earnings per share by 30 percent.
4. Increase the equity of the bank by 13 percent.
5. Achieve a higher price-earnings ratio for its shares.

**Market orientation objectives.** The bank seeks to become a more market-conscious organization through:

1. Organizational restructuring to emphasize marketing and consumer service prior to 1998.
2. Increased market research prior to 1996.
3. Increased public relations program prior to 1996.
4. Introduction of investor relations program prior to 1996.

**Profit improvement objectives.** To improve BBC's profit performance, the bank shall:

1. Increase the deposits per £ of employee expense from the current £48,000 to £82,000 by 1998.
2. Reduce operating expense of the bank from the current 87 percent of operating income to 85 percent by 1998.
3. Increase the degree of computerization and automation of lending programs and accounting systems and reduce staff recruitment over the period 1994–1998.

## Summary of the Proposed Strategy

Management makes strategic decisions regarding critical variables subject to existing constraints in order to achieve the growth rate, market orientation, and profit improvement objectives given the assumptions on the bank's competitive strengths and weaknesses, and the environmental opportunities and threats. This section describes the decisions that have been made for accomplishing these objectives.

The British Banking Corporation shall grow primarily through international market development. The bank shall carve for itself a market niche where it has a competitive advantage and yet continue to maintain an above-average return on investment for its shareholders. The recommended market niche for both loans and services is the up-and-coming new high-growth businesses. The bank shall work out tie-in arrangements with various venture capitalists and their clients.

In the short term, the bank's strategy for its services business shall be to compete against the established competitors on pricing for the same quality of service provided. The bank's shareholders must understand that the effect of this short-term strategy will be a low initial profit margin for services. The bank shall first work on its existing base of clients, particularly its loan clients from all its three offices. Only after we have worked on our own client base will we position the Bank as a market challenger.

In the longer term, once the bank's reputation and its relationship with its clients are established, the bank shall charge higher service fees. By that time, the bank will have a higher volume treasury business, which should benefit the bank in terms of lower cost of funds. However, instead of passing all of this on to its clients, the bank shall retain part of it to post higher corporate earnings.

## Projected Results Over the Next Five Years

Proforma financial statements have been prepared for the five-year period 1994–1998, with actual results for 1991–1993 for comparison, to indicate the probable outcome of the improved long-term strategy of BBC (see Exhibits 1–4). These pro-forma statements are based upon the following assumptions and conventions:

1. Cash will be the "plug" figure in the balance sheet and will represent total assets minus securities (including U.K. Treasury), obligations of the Bank of England, net loans and leases, and miscellaneous assets.
2. Governmental securities will be 13 percent of total deposits.
3. Net loans (commercial, real estate, installment, direct lease, credit card and miscellaneous loans, less provision for loan losses) will be 68 percent of total deposits.
4. Total bank deposits are expected to grow at a minimum of 18 percent annually.
5. Shareholders' funds will increase 23 percent annually.
6. Income from fees will increase 7 percent annually, reflecting the bank's expanded service philosophy.
7. Loan-loss provision will be constant at 3 percent of net loans.
8. Miscellaneous expenses will be constant at 11 percent of revenues.
9. Income tax rates will be held constant at 33 percent of pretax profits in the U.K., 15 percent in New York, 15 percent in Hong Kong, and 27 percent in Singapore.

EXHIBIT 1

**British Banking Corporation (U.K.)**
**Consolidated Group Income Statement**
(In Thousand Pounds)

| | *Projected 1998* | *Projected 1997* | *Projected 1996* | *Projected 1995* | *Projected 1994* | *Actual 1993* | *Actual 1992* | *Actual 1991* |
|---|---|---|---|---|---|---|---|---|
| Interest on Loans | 1,519,834 | 1,347,843 | 1,201,542 | 1,115,570 | 994,065 | 983,308 | 943,453 | 821,367 |
| Income from Services | 842,322 | 753,910 | 684,044 | 634,279 | 580,599 | 518,484 | 495,769 | 430,144 |
| Total Income | 2,362,157 | 2,101,753 | 1,885,585 | 1,749,849 | 1,574,664 | 1,501,792 | 1,439,221 | 1,251,510 |
| Less Operation Expenses | 2,008,123 | 1,794,562 | 1,628,895 | 1,503,622 | 1,354,545 | 1,302,343 | 1,267,085 | 1,123,359 |
| Total Income Before Tax | 354,034 | 307,191 | 256,690 | 246,227 | 220,119 | 199,449 | 172,136 | 128,151 |
| Taxation | 84,904 | 75,145 | 64,124 | 61,194 | 56,262 | 51,988 | 45,212 | 34,558 |
| Net Income After Tax | 269,130 | 232,046 | 192,566 | 185,033 | 163,857 | 147,461 | 126,924 | 93,593 |

EXHIBIT 1 (cont'd)

**British Banking Corporation (U.K.)**
**Consolidated Group Balance Sheet**
(in Thousand Pounds)

| | *Projected* 1998 | *Projected* 1997 | *Projected* 1996 | *Projected* 1995 | *Projected* 1994 | *Actual* 1993 | *Actual* 1992 | *Actual* 1991 |
|---|---|---|---|---|---|---|---|---|
| Assets | 6,965,140 | 5,420,629 | 4,317,26 | 3,557,569 | 2,977,688 | 2,397,066 | 2,554,121 | 2,326,137 |
| Loans & Leases | 21,852,773 | 18,222,608 | 14,988,940 | 12,410,494 | 10,039,674 | 8,601,234 | 7,054,250 | 6,134,141 |
| Miscellaneous Assets | 5,908,109 | 5,465,715 | 5,039,493 | 4,634,929 | 4,292,421 | 3,102,088 | 2,554,129 | 2,115,222 |
| Total Assets | 34,726,021 | 29,108,952 | 24,345,700 | 20,602,992 | 17,309,783 | 14,100,388 | 12,162,500 | 10,576,100 |
| Represented by: | | | | | | | | |
| Total Liabilities | 32,379,729 | 27,031,790 | 22,500,584 | 18,950,442 | 15,842,266 | 12,847,868 | 11,057,468 | 9,598,129 |
| Shareholders' Fund | | | | | | | | |
| Share Capital | 900,000 | 900,000 | 900,000 | 900,000 | 900,000 | 850,000 | 850,000 | 850,000 |
| Capital Reserves | 20,000 | 20,000 | 20,000 | 20,000 | 20,000 | 20,000 | 20,000 | 20,000 |
| Retained Earning | 1,426,292 | 1,157,162 | 925,116 | 732,549 | 547,516 | 382,460 | 234,972 | 108,120 |
| | 2,346,292 | 2,077,162 | 1,845,116 | 1,652,549 | 1,467,516 | 1,252,460 | 1,104,972 | 878,120 |
| Total | 34,726,021 | 29,108,952 | 24,345,699 | 20,602,992 | 17,309,783 | 14,100,328 | 12,162,440 | 10,576,149 |

EXHIBIT 1 (cont'd)

**British Banking Corporation (U.K.)**
**Income Statement**
(In Thousand Pounds)

| | *Projected 1998* | *Projected 1997* | *Projected 1996* | *Projected 1995* | *Projected 1994* | *Actual 1993* | *Actual 1992* | *Actual 1991* |
|---|---|---|---|---|---|---|---|---|
| Interest on Loans | | | | | | | | |
| Consumer Loan Interest | 136,494 | 127,565 | 119,219 | 110,388 | 100,353 | 122,465 | 136,922 | 127,568 |
| Credit Card Loan Interest | 122,845 | 114,808 | 107,298 | 99,350 | 90,318 | 102,054 | 88,022 | 51,027 |
| Real Estate Loan Interest | 109,196 | 102,052 | 95,376 | 88,311 | 80,282 | 91,849 | 97,802 | 127,568 |
| Direct Lending Financing | 95,546 | 89,295 | 83,454 | 77,272 | 70,247 | 91,849 | 107,582 | 85,045 |
| Commercial Loan Interest | 81,897 | 76,539 | 71,532 | 66,233 | 60,212 | 91,849 | 127,142 | 127,568 |
| U.K. Treasury Securities | 122,845 | 114,808 | 107,298 | 99,350 | 90,318 | 61,232 | 58,681 | 42,523 |
| Municipal Securities | 109,196 | 102,052 | 95,376 | 88,311 | 80,282 | 81,643 | 39,121 | 17,009 |
| Obligations of Bank of England | 95,546 | 89,295 | 83,454 | 77,272 | 70,247 | 61,232 | 39,121 | 42,523 |
| | 873,564 | 816,415 | 763,005 | 706,486 | 642,260 | 704,173 | 694,392 | 620,829 |
| Income from Services | | | | | | | | |
| Treasury Income | 121,707 | 113,745 | 106,304 | 96,640 | 90,318 | 112,259 | 97,802 | 85,045 |
| Services Charges on Deposit | 108,184 | 101,107 | 94,492 | 85,902 | 80,282 | 51,027 | 48,901 | 42,523 |
| Funds Management Income | 67,615 | 63,192 | 59,058 | 53,689 | 50,177 | 40,822 | 29,341 | 25,514 |
| Loan Syndications | 94,661 | 88,469 | 82,681 | 75,164 | 70,247 | 61,232 | 58,681 | 42,523 |
| Project Financing | 54,092 | 50,553 | 47,246 | 42,951 | 40,141 | 30,616 | 29,341 | 17,009 |
| Corporate Advisory Services | 40,569 | 37,915 | 35,435 | 32,213 | 30,106 | 20,411 | 19,560 | 17,009 |
| | 486,830 | 454,981 | 425,216 | 386,560 | 361,271 | 316,367 | 283,625 | 229,622 |
| Total Income | 1,360,394 | 1,271,396 | 1,188,221 | 1,093,046 | 1,003,531 | 1,020,540 | 978,017 | 850,450 |

EXHIBIT 1 (cont'd)

**British Banking Corporation (U.K.)**
**Income Statement**
(In Thousand Pounds)

| | *Projected 1998* | *Projected 1997* | *Projected 1996* | *Projected 1995* | *Projected 1994* | *Actual 1993* | *Actual 1992* | *Actual 1991* |
|---|---|---|---|---|---|---|---|---|
| Less Operating Expenses | | | | | | | | |
| Interest on Time Deposit | 278,041 | 259,851 | 243,534 | 223,426 | 203,115 | 188,596 | 104,452 | 168,389 |
| Interest on Borrowing Funds | 193,420 | 180,766 | 169,415 | 155,427 | 141,297 | 116,750 | 121,861 | 183,697 |
| Provision for Bad Debts | 145,065 | 135,575 | 127,061 | 116,570 | 105,973 | 98,788 | 95,748 | 7,654 |
| Salaries & Benefits | 169,242 | 158,170 | 148,238 | 135,999 | 123,635 | 116,750 | 104,452 | 114,811 |
| Office-related Expenses | 108,799 | 101,681 | 95,296 | 87,428 | 79,480 | 98,788 | 104,452 | 68,886 |
| Equipment Related Expenses | 96,710 | 90,383 | 84,708 | 77,713 | 70,649 | 80,827 | 130,565 | 61,232 |
| Sales & Marketing Expenses | 72,532 | 67,787 | 63,531 | 58,285 | 52,986 | 62,865 | 87,044 | 76,541 |
| Miscellaneous Expenses | 145,065 | 135,575 | 127,061 | 116,570 | 105,973 | 134,711 | 121,861 | 84,195 |
| | 1,208,873 | 1,129,788 | 1,058,846 | 971,418 | 883,107 | 898,075 | 870,436 | 765,405 |
| Total Income Before Tax | 151,521 | 141,608 | 129,375 | 121,628 | 120,424 | 122,465 | 107,582 | 85,045 |
| Taxation | 50,002 | 46,731 | 42,694 | 40,137 | 39,740 | 40,413 | 35,502 | 28,065 |
| Net Income After Tax | 101,519 | 94,877 | 86,681 | 81,491 | 80,684 | 82,051 | 72,080 | 56,980 |

EXHIBIT 1 (cont'd)

**British Banking Corporation (U.K.)**
**Balance Sheet**
(in Thousand Pounds)

| | *Projected 1998* | *Projected 1997* | *Projected 1996* | *Projected 1995* | *Projected 1994* | *Actual 1993* | *Actual 1992* | *Actual 1991* |
|---|---|---|---|---|---|---|---|---|
| Assets | | | | | | | | |
| Securities | 566,089 | 435,453 | 340,198 | 274,353 | 228,627 | 290,628 | 331,200 | 216,000 |
| Cash & Due from Banks | 566,089 | 435,453 | 340,198 | 274,353 | 228,627 | 193,752 | 248,400 | 288,000 |
| U.K. Treasury Securities | 849,133 | 653,179 | 510,296 | 411,529 | 342,941 | 193,752 | 331,200 | 361,000 |
| Obligation of Bank of England | 2,830,443 | 2,177,264 | 1,700,988 | 1,371,764 | 1,143,137 | 968,760 | 828,000 | 721,000 |
| | 4,811,754 | 3,701,349 | 2,891,679 | 2,331,999 | 1,943,333 | 1,646,892 | 1,738,800 | 1,584,000 |
| Loans & Leases | | | | | | | | |
| Commercial Leases | 4,140,619 | 3,737,737 | 3,063,719 | 2,531,999 | 1,943,333 | 1,743,768 | 1,490,400 | 1,368,000 |
| Real Estate Loans | 4,242,285 | 3,535,237 | 2,897,735 | 2,394,823 | 1,829,019 | 1,453,140 | 1,407,600 | 1,296,000 |
| Installment Loans | 2,672,998 | 2,227,498 | 1,825,818 | 1,508,941 | 1,257,450 | 1,259,388 | 910,800 | 648,000 |
| Direct Lease Amount | 1,700,999 | 1,417,499 | 1,161,884 | 960,235 | 800,196 | 678,132 | 496,800 | 432,000 |
| Credit Card Amount | 1,943,998 | 1,619,999 | 1,327,868 | 1,097,411 | 914,509 | 678,132 | 496,800 | 361,000 |
| Miscellaneous Loans | 243,000 | 202,500 | 165,983 | 137,176 | 114,314 | 290,628 | 165,600 | 144,000 |
| | 14,943,898 | 12,740,470 | 10,443,008 | 8,630,585 | 6,858,821 | 6,103,188 | 4,968,000 | 4,241,000 |
| Less Provision for Bad Debts | (498,130) | (424,682) | (348,100) | (287,686) | (228,627) | (193,752) | (165,600) | (72,000) |
| Subtotal | 14,445,768 | 12,315,787 | 10,094,908 | 8,342,899 | 6,630,193 | 5,909,436 | 4,802,400 | 4,176,000 |
| Miscellaneous Assets | 3,093,420 | 3,032,765 | 2,973,299 | 2,914,999 | 2,857,842 | 2,131,272 | 1,738,800 | 1,441,000 |
| Total Assets | 22,350,942 | 19,049,901 | 15,959,885 | 13,589,897 | 11,431,368 | 9,687,600 | 8,280,000 | 7,200,000 |

EXHIBIT 1 (cont'd)

**British Banking Corporation (U.K.)**
**Balance Sheet**
(in Thousand Pounds)

| | *Projected 1998* | *Projected 1997* | *Projected 1996* | *Projected 1995* | *Projected 1994* | *Actual 1993* | *Actual 1992* | *Actual 1991* |
|---|---|---|---|---|---|---|---|---|
| Represented by: | | | | | | | | |
| Liabilities | | | | | | | | |
| Demand Deposits | 5,134,368 | 4,461,285 | 3,720,555 | 3,197,601 | 2,651,893 | 2,190,487 | 1,871,319 | 1,625,661 |
| Services Deposit | 4,296,026 | 3,724,950 | 3,233,575 | 2,864,045 | 2,386,704 | 1,825,406 | 1,202,991 | 651,264 |
| Other Time Deposits | 4,403,820 | 3,669,850 | 3,008,074 | 2,486,011 | 2,121,515 | 1,642,865 | 1,336,656 | 1,625,661 |
| Other Liabilities | 3,946,042 | 3,288,369 | 2,695,384 | 2,227,590 | 1,856,325 | 1,642,865 | 1,470,322 | 1,083,774 |
| Notes Payable | 3,382,322 | 2,818,602 | 2,310,329 | 1,909,363 | 1,591,136 | 1,642,865 | 1,737,653 | 1,625,661 |
| | 21,162,578 | 17,963,056 | 14,967,917 | 12,684,610 | 10,607,573 | 8,944,489 | 7,618,940 | 6,611,020 |
| Shareholders' Fund | | | | | | | | |
| Share Capital | 500,000 | 500,000 | 500,000 | 500,000 | 500,000 | 500,000 | 500,000 | 500,000 |
| Capital Reserves | 20,000 | 20,000 | 20,000 | 20,000 | 20,000 | 20,000 | 20,000 | 20,000 |
| Retained Earning | 668,364 | 566,845 | 471,967 | 385,286 | 303,795 | 223,111 | 141,060 | 68,980 |
| | 1,188,364 | 1,086,845 | 991,967 | 905,286 | 823,795 | 743,111 | 661,060 | 588,980 |
| Total | 22,350,942 | 19,049,901 | 15,959,885 | 13,589,896 | 11,431,368 | 9,687,600 | 8,280,000 | 7,200,000 |

EXHIBIT 2

**British Banking Corporation (NY)**
**Income Statement**
(In Thousand Pounds)

| | *Projected 1998* | *Projected 1997* | *Projected 1996* | *Projected 1995* | *Projected 1994* | *Actual 1993* | *Actual 1992* | *Actual 1991* |
|---|---|---|---|---|---|---|---|---|
| Interest on Loans | | | | | | | | |
| Corporation Loan Interest | 229,814 | 191,512 | 159,593 | 152,943 | 132,994 | 120,221 | 106,571 | 87,661 |
| Share Financing Loan Interest | 97,033 | 80,861 | 67,384 | 64,576 | 56,153 | 54,099 | 48,965 | 37,569 |
| | 326,847 | 272,372 | 226,977 | 217,520 | 189,147 | 174,320 | 155,536 | 125,230 |
| Income from Services | | | | | | | | |
| Treasury Income | 61,284 | 51,070 | 42,558 | 40,785 | 35,465 | 45,083 | 40,324 | 37,569 |
| Funds Management Income | 40,856 | 34,047 | 28,372 | 27,190 | 23,643 | 36,066 | 48,965 | 37,569 |
| Loan Syndications | 45,963 | 38,302 | 31,919 | 30,589 | 26,599 | 24,044 | 23,042 | 25,046 |
| Corporate Advisory Services | 35,749 | 29,791 | 24,826 | 23,791 | 20,688 | 21,039 | 20,162 | 25,046 |
| | 183,851 | 153,209 | 127,674 | 122,355 | 106,395 | 126,232 | 132,493 | 125,230 |
| Total Income | 510,698 | 425,582 | 354,651 | 339,874 | 295,543 | 300,552 | 288,029 | 250,460 |

EXHIBIT 2 (cont'd)

**British Banking Corporation (NY)**
**Income Statement**
(In Thousand Pounds)

| | *Projected* 1998 | *Projected* 1997 | *Projected* 1996 | *Projected* 1995 | *Projected* 1994 | *Actual* 1993 | *Actual* 1992 | *Actual* 1991 |
|---|---|---|---|---|---|---|---|---|
| Less Operating Expenses | | | | | | | | |
| Interest on Time Deposit | 95,923 | 78,625 | 66,072 | 62,537 | 55,060 | 53,017 | 29,725 | 49,591 |
| Interest on Borrowing Funds | 66,729 | 54,696 | 45,963 | 43,504 | 38,302 | 32,820 | 34,679 | 54,099 |
| Provision for Bad Debts | 50,047 | 41,022 | 34,472 | 32,628 | 28,727 | 27,771 | 27,248 | 2,254 |
| Salaries & Benefits | 58,388 | 47,859 | 40,217 | 38,066 | 33,515 | 32,820 | 29,725 | 33,812 |
| Office-related Expenses | 37,535 | 30,766 | 25,854 | 24,471 | 21,545 | 27,771 | 29,725 | 20,287 |
| Equipment-related Expenses | 33,364 | 27,348 | 22,981 | 21,752 | 19,151 | 22,722 | 37,156 | 18,033 |
| Sales & Marketing Expenses | 25,023 | 20,511 | 17,236 | 16,314 | 14,363 | 17,672 | 24,770 | 22,541 |
| Miscellaneous Expenses | 50,047 | 41,022 | 34,472 | 32,628 | 28,727 | 37,870 | 34,679 | 24,796 |
| | 417,055 | 341,848 | 287,268 | 271,899 | 239,390 | 252,464 | 247,705 | 225,414 |
| Total Income Before Tax | 93,643 | 83,733 | 67,384 | 67,975 | 56,153 | 48,088 | 40,324 | 25,048 |
| Taxation | 14,046 | 12,560 | 10,108 | 10,196 | 8,423 | 7,213 | 6,049 | 3,757 |
| Net Income After Tax | 79,596 | 71,173 | 57,276 | 57,779 | 47,730 | 40,875 | 34,275 | 21,289 |

EXHIBIT 2 (cont'd)

**British Banking Corporation (NY)**
**Balance Sheet**
(in Thousand Pounds)

| | *Projected 1998* | *Projected 1997* | *Projected 1996* | *Projected 1995* | *Projected 1994* | *Actual 1993* | *Actual 1992* | *Actual 1991* |
|---|---|---|---|---|---|---|---|---|
| Assets | | | | | | | | |
| Securities | 143,216 | 114,573 | 95,477 | 80,913 | 67,994 | 87,172 | 103,776 | 67,680 |
| Cash & Due from Banks | 143,216 | 114,573 | 95,477 | 80,913 | 67,994 | 58,115 | 77,832 | 90,240 |
| Treasury Securities | 214,824 | 171,859 | 143,216 | 121,369 | 101,991 | 58,115 | 103,776 | 112,800 |
| Obligation of Bank | 716,079 | 572,863 | 477,386 | 404,565 | 339,970 | 290,573 | 259,440 | 225,600 |
| | 1,217,335 | 973,868 | 811,556 | 687,760 | 577,949 | 493,974 | 544,824 | 496,320 |
| Loan & Leases | | | | | | | | |
| Commercial Leases | 1,646,982 | 1,317,586 | 1,097,988 | 890,042 | 747,934 | 668,317 | 570,768 | 473,760 |
| Real Estate Loans | 787,687 | 630,150 | 525,125 | 525,934 | 407,964 | 377,745 | 285,384 | 270,720 |
| Instalment Loans | 787,687 | 630,150 | 525,125 | 525,934 | 407,964 | 377,745 | 285,384 | 270,720 |
| Direct Lease Amount | 501,255 | 401,004 | 334,170 | 283,195 | 237,979 | 203,401 | 155,664 | 135,360 |
| Miscellaneous Loans | 71,608 | 57,286 | 47,739 | 40,456 | 33,997 | 87,172 | 51,888 | 45,120 |
| | 4,296,475 | 3,437,180 | 2,864,317 | 2,427,387 | 2,039,821 | 1,830,609 | 1,556,640 | 1,331,040 |
| Less Provision for Bad Debts | (137,487) | (114,573) | (95,477) | (80,913) | (67,994) | (58,115) | (51,888) | (22,560) |
| Subtotal | 4,158,988 | 3,322,607 | 2,768,840 | 2,346,474 | 1,971,827 | 1,772,494 | 1,504,752 | 1,308,480 |
| Miscellaneous Assets | 1,718,590 | 1,432,158 | 1,193,465 | 1,011,411 | 849,925 | 639,260 | 544,824 | 451,200 |
| Total Assets | 7,094,913 | 5,728,633 | 4,773,861 | 4,045,645 | 3,399,702 | 2,905,728 | 2,594,400 | 2,256,000 |

EXHIBIT 2 (cont'd)

**British Banking Corporation (NY)**
**Balance Sheet**
(in Thousand Pounds)

| | *Projected* 1998 | *Projected* 1997 | *Projected* 1996 | *Projected* 1995 | *Projected* 1994 | *Actual* 1993 | *Actual* 1992 | *Actual* 1991 |
|---|---|---|---|---|---|---|---|---|
| Represented by: | | | | | | | | |
| Liabilities | | | | | | | | |
| Demand Deposits | 1,631,102 | 1,314,943 | 1,078,359 | 910,624 | 763,583 | 638,716 | 574,156 | 500,044 |
| Services Deposit | 1,455,785 | 1,164,628 | 970,523 | 819,562 | 687,225 | 532,263 | 369,100 | 200,017 |
| Other Time Deposits | 1,294,031 | 1,035,225 | 862,687 | 728,499 | 610,866 | 479,037 | 410,111 | 500,044 |
| Other Liabilities | 1,132,277 | 905,822 | 754,851 | 637,437 | 534,508 | 479,037 | 451,123 | 333,362 |
| Notes Payable | 907,523 | 776,419 | 647,015 | 546,375 | 458,150 | 479,037 | 533,145 | 500,044 |
| | 6,483,718 | 5,197,036 | 4,313,437 | 3,642,497 | 3,054,332 | 2,608,088 | 2,337,635 | 2,033,511 |
| Shareholders' Fund | | | | | | | | |
| Share Capital | 200,000 | 200,000 | 200,000 | 200,000 | 200,000 | 200,000 | 200,000 | 200,000 |
| Retained Earning | 411,194 | 331,598 | 260,425 | 203,148 | 145,370 | 97,640 | 56,765 | 22,489 |
| | 611,194 | 531,598 | 460,425 | 403,148 | 345,370 | 297,640 | 256,765 | 222,489 |
| Total | 7,094,912 | 5,728,634 | 4,773,861 | 4,045,645 | 3,399,702 | 2,905,728 | 2,594,400 | 2,256,000 |

EXHIBIT 3

**British Banking Corporation (HK)**
**Income Statement**
(in Thousand Pounds)

| | *Projected 1998* | *Projected 1997* | *Projected 1996* | *Projected 1995* | *Projected 1994* | *Actual 1993* | *Actual 1992* | *Actual 1991* |
|---|---|---|---|---|---|---|---|---|
| Interest on Loans | | | | | | | | |
| Corporate Loan Interest | 143,848 | 115,078 | 95,899 | 91,903 | 79,915 | 72,240 | 64,038 | 52,675 |
| Share Financing Loan In | 60,736 | 48,589 | 40,491 | 38,803 | 33,742 | 32,508 | 29,423 | 22,575 |
| | 204,584 | 163,667 | 136,389 | 130,706 | 113,658 | 104,748 | 93,461 | 75,250 |
| Income from Services | | | | | | | | |
| Treasury Income | 38,359 | 30,688 | 25,573 | 24,507 | 21,311 | 27,090 | 24,231 | 22,575 |
| Funds Management Income | 25,573 | 20,458 | 17,049 | 16,338 | 14,207 | 21,672 | 29,423 | 22,575 |
| Loan Syndications | 28,770 | 23,016 | 19,180 | 18,381 | 15,983 | 14,448 | 13,846 | 15,050 |
| Corporate Advisory Services | 22,376 | 17,901 | 14,918 | 14,296 | 12,431 | 12,642 | 12,115 | 15,050 |
| | 115,078 | 92,063 | 76,719 | 73,522 | 63,932 | 75,852 | 79,615 | 75,250 |
| Total Income | 319,662 | 255,730 | 213,108 | 204,228 | 177,590 | 180,600 | 173,075 | 150,500 |

EXHIBIT 3 (cont'd)

**British Banking Corporation (HK)**
**Income Statement**
(in Thousand Pounds)

| | *Projected* 1998 | *Projected* 1997 | *Projected* 1996 | *Projected* 1995 | *Projected* 1994 | *Actual* 1993 | *Actual* 1992 | *Actual* 1991 |
|---|---|---|---|---|---|---|---|---|
| Less Operating Expenses | | | | | | | | |
| Interest on Time Deposit | 57,155 | 46,848 | 39,702 | 37,578 | 33,085 | 31,858 | 17,861 | 29,137 |
| Interest on Borrowing Funds | 39,760 | 32,590 | 27,619 | 26,141 | 23,016 | 19,722 | 20,838 | 31,786 |
| Provision for Bad Debts | 29,820 | 24,443 | 20,714 | 19,606 | 17,262 | 16,687 | 16,373 | 1,324 |
| Salaries & Benefits | 34,790 | 28,516 | 24,166 | 22,874 | 20,139 | 19,722 | 17,861 | 19,866 |
| Office related Expenses | 22,365 | 18,332 | 15,536 | 14,704 | 12,946 | 16,687 | 17,861 | 11,920 |
| Equipment related Expenses | 19,880 | 16,295 | 13,809 | 13,071 | 11,508 | 13,653 | 22,327 | 10,595 |
| Sales & Marketing Expenses | 14,910 | 12,221 | 10,357 | 9,803 | 8,631 | 10,619 | 14,884 | 13,244 |
| Miscellaneous Expenses | 29,820 | 24,443 | 20,714 | 19,606 | 17,262 | 22,756 | 20,838 | 14,568 |
| | 248,500 | 203,689 | 172,617 | 163,383 | 143,848 | 151,704 | 148,843 | 132,440 |
| Total Income Before Tax | 71,162 | 52,041 | 40,491 | 40,846 | 33,742 | 28,896 | 24,231 | 18,060 |
| Taxation | 10,674 | 7,806 | 6,074 | 6,127 | 5,061 | 4,334 | 3,635 | 2,709 |
| Net Income After Tax | 60,488 | 44,235 | 34,417 | 34,719 | 28,681 | 24,562 | 20,596 | 15,351 |

EXHIBIT 3 (cont'd)

**British Banking Corporation (HK)**
**Balance Sheet**
(in Thousand Pounds)

| | *Projected 1998* | *Projected 1997* | *Projected 1996* | *Projected 1995* | *Projected 1994* | *Actual 1993* | *Actual 1992* | *Actual 1991* |
|---|---|---|---|---|---|---|---|---|
| Assets | | | | | | | | |
| Securities | 78,099 | 62,479 | 52,066 | 42,677 | 35,564 | 45,209 | 51,520 | 33,600 |
| Cash & Due from Banks | 78,099 | 62,479 | 52,066 | 42,677 | 35,564 | 30,139 | 38,640 | 44,800 |
| Treasury Securities | 117,149 | 93,719 | 78,099 | 64,016 | 53,346 | 30,139 | 51,520 | 56,000 |
| Obligation of Bank | 390,496 | 312,396 | 260,330 | 213,386 | 177,821 | 150,696 | 128,800 | 112,000 |
| | 663,842 | 531,074 | 442,562 | 362,755 | 302,296 | 256,183 | 270,480 | 246,400 |
| Loans & Leases | | | | | | | | |
| Commercial Leases | 814,741 | 651,793 | 520,661 | 405,433 | 337,860 | 286,322 | 231,840 | 212,800 |
| Real Estate Loans | 759,495 | 607,596 | 494,628 | 384,094 | 320,078 | 256,183 | 231,840 | 201,600 |
| Instalment Loans | 507,644 | 406,115 | 338,429 | 320,078 | 266,732 | 241,114 | 193,200 | 156,800 |
| Direct Lease Amount | 273,347 | 218,677 | 182,231 | 149,370 | 124,475 | 120,557 | 90,160 | 67,200 |
| Miscellaneous Loans | 39,050 | 31,240 | 26,033 | 21,339 | 17,782 | 45,209 | 25,760 | 22,400 |
| | 2,394,277 | 1,915,422 | 1,561,982 | 1,280,313 | 1,066,928 | 949,385 | 772,800 | 660,800 |
| Less Provision for Bad Debts | (74,975) | (62,479) | (52,066) | (42,677) | (35,564) | (30,139) | (25,760) | (11,200) |
| Subtotal | 2,319,302 | 1,852,942 | 1,509,916 | 1,237,636 | 1,031,363 | 919,246 | 747,040 | 649,600 |
| Miscellaneous Assets | 695,791 | 685,589 | 650,826 | 533,464 | 444,553 | 331,531 | 270,480 | 224,000 |
| Total Assets | 3,678,935 | 3,069,605 | 2,603,304 | 2,133,855 | 1,778,213 | 1,506,960 | 1,288,000 | 1,120,000 |

EXHIBIT 3 (cont'd)

**British Banking Corporation (HK)**
**Balance Sheet**
(in Thousand Pounds)

| | *Projected 1998* | *Projected 1997* | *Projected 1996* | *Projected 1995* | *Projected 1994* | *Actual 1993* | *Actual 1992* | *Actual 1991* |
|---|---|---|---|---|---|---|---|---|
| Represented by: | | | | | | | | |
| Liabilities | | | | | | | | |
| Demand Deposits | 825,531 | 676,665 | 573,445 | 464,687 | 384,456 | 317,204 | 270,385 | 234,455 |
| Services Deposit | 755,242 | 619,051 | 516,100 | 418,218 | 346,010 | 264,337 | 173,819 | 93,7782 |
| Other Time Deposits | 610,724 | 540,465 | 458,756 | 371,749 | 307,565 | 237,903 | 193,132 | 234,455 |
| Other Liabilities | 577,872 | 473,665 | 401,411 | 325,281 | 269,119 | 237,903 | 212,445 | 156,303 |
| Notes Payable | 495,319 | 405,999 | 344,067 | 278,812 | 230,674 | 237,903 | 251,072 | 234,455 |
| | 3,264,687 | 2,715,845 | 2,293,778 | 1,858,747 | 1,537,823 | 1,295,251 | 1,100,853 | 953,449 |
| Shareholders' Fund | | | | | | | | |
| Share Capital | 150,000 | 150,000 | 150,000 | 150,000 | 150,000 | 150,000 | 150,000 | 150,000 |
| Retained Earning | 264,248 | 203,760 | 159,525 | 125,108 | 90,389 | 61,709 | 37,147 | 16,551 |
| | 414,428 | 353,760 | 309,525 | 275,108 | 240,389 | 211,709 | 187,147 | 166,551 |
| Total | 3,678,935 | 3,069,604 | 2,603,304 | 2,133,855 | 1,778,213 | 1,506,960 | 1,288,000 | 1,120,000 |

EXHIBIT 4

**British Banking Corporation (SIN)**
**Income Statement**
(In Thousand Pounds)

| | *Projected 1998* | *Projected 1997* | *Projected 1996* | *Projected 1995* | *Projected 1994* |
|---|---|---|---|---|---|
| Interest on Loans | | | | | |
| Corporate Loan Interest | 78,845 | 67,071 | 51,842 | 41,699 | 34,300 |
| Share Financing Loan Interest | 35,995 | 28,319 | 23,329 | 19,159 | 14,700 |
| | 114,840 | 95,389 | 75,171 | 60,858 | 49,000 |
| Income From Services | | | | | |
| Treasury Income | 18,854 | 17,885 | 19,441 | 15,778 | 14,700 |
| Funds Management Income | 11,998 | 11,924 | 15,553 | 19,159 | 14,700 |
| Loan Syndications | 13,712 | 13,414 | 10,368 | 9,016 | 9,800 |
| Corporate Advisory Services | 11,998 | 10,433 | 9,072 | 7,889 | 9,800 |
| | 56,563 | 53,656 | 54,434 | 51,842 | 49,000 |
| Total Income | 171,403 | 149,046 | 129,605 | 112,700 | 98,00 |
| Less Operating Expenses | | | | | |
| Interest on Time Deposit | 30,750 | 27,424 | 23,134 | 11,631 | 19,404 |
| Interest on Borrowing Funds | 21,391 | 19,078 | 14,321 | 13,569 | 21,168 |
| Provision for Bad Debts | 16,043 | 14,308 | 12,118 | 10,611 | 882 |
| Salaries & Benefits | 18,717 | 16,693 | 14,321 | 11,631 | 13,230 |
| Office-related Expenses | 12,032 | 10,731 | 12,118 | 11,631 | 7,938 |
| Equipment-related Expenses | 10,696 | 9,539 | 9,915 | 14,538 | 7,056 |
| Sales & Marketing Expenses | 8,022 | 7,154 | 7,711 | 9,692 | 8,820 |
| Miscellaneous Expenses | 16,043 | 14,308 | 16,525 | 13,569 | 9,702 |
| | 133,694 | 119,237 | 110,164 | 96,922 | 88,200 |
| Total Income Before Tax | 37,709 | 29,809 | 19,441 | 15,778 | 9,800 |
| Taxation | 10,181 | 8,048 | 5,249 | 4,733 | 3,038 |
| Net Income After Tax | 27,527 | 21,761 | 14,192 | 11,045 | 6,762 |

EXHIBIT 4 (cont'd)

**British Banking Corporation (SIN)**
**Balance Sheet**
(in Thousand Pounds)

| | *Projected 1998* | *Projected 1997* | *Projected 1996* | *Projected 1995* | *Projected 1994* |
|---|---|---|---|---|---|
| Assets | | | | | |
| Securities | 32,025 | 25,216 | 30,259 | 33,344 | 21,015 |
| Cash & Due from Banks | 32,025 | 25,216 | 20,173 | 25,008 | 28,020 |
| Treasury Securities | 48,037 | 37,824 | 20,173 | 33,344 | 35,025 |
| Obligation of Bank | 160,123 | 126,081 | 100,865 | 83,360 | 70,050 |
| | 272,209 | 214,338 | 171,470 | 175,055 | 154,110 |
| Loans & Leases | | | | | |
| Commercial Leases | 288,222 | 239,554 | 181,557 | 150,047 | 133,095 |
| Real Estate Loans | 288,222 | 239,554 | 181,557 | 158,383 | 126,090 |
| Instalment Loans | 208,160 | 151,297 | 161,384 | 108,367 | 84,060 |
| Direct Lease Amount | 160,123 | 113,473 | 80,692 | 66,688 | 56,040 |
| Miscellaneous Loans | 16,012 | 12,608 | 30,259 | 16,672 | 14,010 |
| | 960,739 | 756,487 | 635,449 | 500,157 | 413,295 |
| Less Provision for Bad Debts | (32,025) | (25,216) | (20,173) | (16,672) | (7,005) |
| Subtotal | 928,714 | 731,271 | 615,276 | 483,485 | 406,290 |
| Miscellaneous Assets | 400,308 | 315,203 | 221,903 | 175,055 | 140,100 |
| Total Assets | 1,601,232 | 1,260,812 | 1,008,650 | 833,595 | 700,500 |
| Represented by: | | | | | |
| Liabilities | | | | | |
| Demand Deposits | 367,186 | 288,963 | 226,641 | 187,794 | 158,001 |
| Services Deposit | 330,468 | 260,067 | 188,868 | 120,724 | 63,200 |
| Other Time Deposits | 293,749 | 231,171 | 169,981 | 134,138 | 158,001 |
| Other Liabilities | 257,030 | 202,274 | 169,981 | 147,552 | 105,334 |
| Notes Payable | 220,312 | 173,378 | 169,981 | 174,380 | 158,001 |
| | 1,468,746 | 1,155,853 | 925,452 | 764,588 | 642,538 |
| Shareholders' Fund | | | | | |
| Share Capital | 50,000 | 50,000 | 50,000 | 50,000 | 50,000 |
| Retained Earnings | 82,486 | 54,959 | 33,198 | 19,007 | 7,962 |
| | 132,486 | 104,959 | 83,198 | 69,007 | 57,962 |
| Total | 1,601,232 | 1,260,812 | 1,008,650 | 833,595 | 700,500 |

SECTION FIVE

# Strategic Management Across National Borders

| *Case Number* | *Case (Country)* | *Nature of Situation* | *Complexity* |
|---|---|---|---|
| 23 | P T Sepatu Bata (A) (Indonesia) | Turnaround | High |
| 24 | SIFCO Industries, Inc (China) (China) | Joint ventures | High |
| 25 | Purba-Paschim Trading Company: A Small Business Considers Expansion to Bangladesh (Bangladesh) | Market entry | Medium |
| 26 | DCM-Toyota Ltd (India) (India) | Joint ventures | High |
| 27 | Union Carbide Corporation: Industrial Plant Accident (Bhopal, India) | Corporate social responsibility | High |

| Products/ Services | Sector | Financial Data | US$ Sales (000) | Industry Conditions |
|---|---|---|---|---|
| bes | Manufacturing | Yes | 33,727 | Growth |
| el forgings | Manufacturing | Yes | 63,112 | Growth |
| parel and other tile products | Manufacturing | No | 13,000 | Growth |
| ht commercial nicles | Manufacturing | Yes | 60,327 | Growth |
| sticides | Manufacturing | Yes | 9,508 | Mature |

# P T Sepatu Bata (A)* 23

Giovanni Marchesi sat in his office in Jakarta one day in mid-1984 and shook his head. "Where should I start and what should I do with this company?" he wondered. Marchesi had recently moved from the head office in Canada of Bata Canada Limited (BCL), the largest shoe producer in the world, to become president-director of P T Sepatu Bata, BCL's 85-percent-owned subsidiary in Indonesia.

## BCL History and Operating Strategy

Based in Don Mills, Canada, Bata is the world's largest manufacturer and marketer of footwear. It has operations in more than 100 companies in 90 countries, 6,000 retail stores, 50,000 independent retailers, and employs more than 80,000 people worldwide to produce and sell more than 300 million pairs of shoes annually. The company started as a family business nine generations ago. In 1884, Thomas Bata laid the foundation for Bata as a multinational company in Zlin, Czechoslovakia. When he met his untimely demise in a plane crash in 1932, Thomas Bata had become one of his country's leading industrialists

---

* This case was prepared by Professor Donald J Lecraw, School of Business Administration, The University of Western Ontario and faculty members from the Institut Pengembangan Manajemen Indonesia (IPMI) with funding provided by USAID through DSPI under the supervision of a steering committee from Bappenas. The case is intended to serve as a basis for class discussion rather than to illustrate either effective or ineffective handling of an administrative situation. 

and Bata had spread its operations around the world. Thomas J Bata, the current chairman of the company, succeeded his father in 1932. During World War II, the original company in Zlin was lost and many of its factories and installations in Europe were destroyed. After World War II, the headquarters of the company was moved to Canada. Today, Thomas G Bata, the grandson of the founder, is the chief executive officer of Bata Canada Limited, the holding company for Bata.

One founding principle from which there is no deviation is that shoes, not politics, are Bata's business. Bata requires that its companies and managers participate fully in community affairs and development in the countries in which it operates. Bata's concern with contributing to the countries in which it operates has guided its fundamental operating strategy. Bata transfers product and process technology, and marketing and management skills throughout its units worldwide, but, to the extent possible, each unit in the country in which it operates is self-sufficient in production: each production unit supplies only the market in the country in which it is located and uses the maximum amount of domestically produced raw material inputs. In this way, Bata believes that it can make the maximum contribution to the economies of the countries in which it operates. Its key corporate strengths are impounded in its most important asset: Bata's internationally oriented managers and personnel. It is through them that Bata transfers its proprietary technology.

Bata's success depends on its managers worldwide. Headquarters staff in Toronto is comprised of less than 20 managers. Bata relies heavily on its managers, especially the general managers in individual country units, for its success. Through them it achieves the worldwide sharing, diffusion, and homogenization of product and process technology, management, and marketing skills while at the same time operating on a decentralized basis at the country level. Bata has created a corporate culture in which its employees are Bata people first and national citizens second. Bata's employees at all levels are proud of Bata and take pride in being a part of such an organization.

Every day each Bata country manager reports seven key operating results to five regional headquarters. These reports are then compiled and sent to headquarters in Canada on a weekly basis where they are reviewed every Friday. Country managers prepare six-month operating forecasts and budgets within the context of two- and five-year strategic plans. The accounting, production control, personnel, training, and purchasing systems of all Bata units have been standardized to allow the small head office staff to monitor, evaluate, and control performance of Bata's worldwide operations. By this means, Bata can achieve a system of decentralized decision-making at the country level which is not only responsive to individual country conditions, but which optimizes the performance of the company as a whole.

Bata has always been driven by marketing concerns. Bata's marketing strategy is to be quality-directed at all price points and at all levels. Its products are standardized around the world. Factories and stores are built and maintained to the same specifications wherever they are located. Employees throughout the world have access to the same management, technical, and sales training opportunities. Technology is maintained at competitive levels in all companies and information about new developments is constantly shared. Although factories are equipped with the most advanced machinery available, employment levels have remained relatively stable.

## P T Sepatu Bata — History

Bata first marketed imported shoes in Indonesia in 1931 and started production operations in Kalibata in 1939. Bata was nationalized in the early 1960s by the nationalist, socialist government of President Sukarno. After President Sukarno's fall from power in the mid-1960s, Bata was returned to its former owners by the government of President Suharto. In 1981, Bata was the second company in Indonesia to offer its stock to the public when it sold 15 percent of its shares. From 1981 to 1984, the returns to its original shareholders in stock appreciation and dividends averaged over 60 percent per year. By 1987, Bata had three plants in Indonesia (Jakarta, Medan, and Surabaya) and employed about 1,400 workers. P T Sepatu Bata believes its success rested on:

> Creating a healthy working environment where people can develop their full potential and being a company in which promotion depends only on the employee's achievement and performance. Achieving high productivity through well-prepared production and marketing plans with the best technology available.

In 1984, when Marchesi became President-Director of P T Sepatu Bata and in line with BCL's worldwide operating strategy, the company produced only for the domestic market, used 88 percent locally sou reed inputs, paid a 1.5 percent royalty on sales to BCL for technical services, and employed 13 expatriate managers.

### Marchesi's History

Giovani Marchesi was educated as a shoe designer in Italy. Upon graduation from design school in 1954, Marchesi worked in the design department of an Italian shoe company. In 1958, he joined Bata and worked in their design facilities in France. From 1959 to 1964, Marchesi worked in Bata's Middle East regional office in Beirut in product development. Following the expropriation of Bata operations in Egypt (1962) and Iraq (1964), the Middle East region was expanded to include West Africa. Marchesi was part of the management team responsible for product development that set up Bata's plant in Nigeria in 1964. This plant produced 75,000 pairs of shoes per day (compared to 45,000 in Bata's plant in Indonesia). In 1969, Marchesi moved back to Italy and started Bata's center for shoe design there. In 1975, Marchesi moved once again, this time to the head office in Canada where he had been in charge of product development for Bata. By 1984, when Marchesi became President-Director of P T Sepatu Bata in Jakarta, he had over 26 years of experience with BCL. Indonesia was his first general management position. Marchesi typified the manager on whose success Bata depended: his entire career has been with Bata; he had worked with Bata in Europe, the Middle East, Africa, and North America, and was now posted in Asia. Marchesi became a Canadian citizen while working for BCL in Toronto. Marchesi's goal over the five years of his prospective assignment in Indonesia was to make P T Sepatu Bata a "model example" for the Bata organization. As Marchesi remarked:

> When you're in a staff position in Toronto, you're like a priest: all you can do is preach and persuade. You can't make things happen directly. P T Sepatu Bata was my first chance to run my own show, to use my years of experience in the shoe industry to make this the best Bata unit in the world.

## Events in 1984

On his arrival at P T Sepatu Bata in June 1984, Marchesi did not like what he saw and liked what he heard even less. He recalled his first sight of Bata's plant in Jakarta:

> When I arrived at the factory for the first time as president director, the first thing that struck me as the driver pointed and said, "There it is," was that I couldn't see our plant at all. All I could see was an endless string of dirty, smelly food stalls jamming the fence from one end to the other. The factory buildings were nowhere to be seen! Across the street it was OK, even pretty, with many small nurseries selling all sorts of tropical garden plants. But on our side, it was a mess.
>
> Things improved somewhat when we managed to get past the food stalls and through the gates. But it still wasn't the Bata I'd known during my 25 years with Bata around the world. Things were dirty, cluttered, and run-down — from the shop floor, to the buildings, to the managers' desks. The production equipment was old, inefficient, highly labor-intensive, and poorly laid out. Finished goods and raw materials inventories were piled all over the place. I felt that something had to be done and that it was my job to do it.

## Finance

Marchesi's review of Bata's financial and profitability situation of the company yielded mixed results (see Exhibits 1 and 2). There he saw pluses and minuses. The results of this analysis were important to Marchesi since any actions he took to change the operations of P T Sepatu Bata would have to be undertaken within the financial boundaries of two constraints from the head office in Toronto. Marchesi remembered his last conversations with his superiors in Toronto before departing to Jakarta:

> Look, Giovanni, you've been working here at the head office for the past 10 years. Before that you were in Italy and reported directly to us. You know Bata, what Bata is, what Bata does, and what Bata wants to do. So in Indonesia, you'll run the show. We won't second-guess you. Of course we're here to help with any technical, marketing, or design assistance you need, but as far as day-to-day operations go, you're the boss. There are only two things we insist on.
>
> First, we won't provide any funds. If you want to do something out there, do it, just so long as you don't need money from us; if everything is OK then leave it as it is. Actually, we're quite satisfied with how things are going: profits and dividends have been satisfactory and they've been going up every year. Our Indonesian stockholders seem to be satisfied as well; the stock is listed on the stock market and we don't want to upset these people.
>
> Second, you'll have to meet the 1984 dividend target of Rp 2.1 billion and at least meet that level in Canadian dollars in subsequent years. We want this and the Indonesians want it too.

The devaluation of the Indonesian rupiah by 44 percent in 1983 meant that the rupiah dividend paid by P T Sepatu Bata would have to be increased by an equal percentage and any subsequent devaluations would have to be offset as well (see Exhibit 3). P T Sepatu Bata also had a general policy against long-term borrowing in the Indonesian market in accordance with Indonesian government policy in order to restrict access to Indonesian capital to Indonesian-owned firms.

## Marketing

On the marketing side, Marchesi's review of P T Sepatu Bata's operations identified several problem areas as well. Bata distributed its products through 150 independently owned retail stores bearing the Bata name. After an extensive tour of Bata Stores, Marchesi had concluded that, in general, they were not up to Bata's standards. But he wasn't sure what he should do. Indonesia was one of the lower-income countries in which Bata operated, so perhaps Bata's target customers were happy with its stores. In fact, if Bata modernized and upgraded its stores, its customers might be frightened away.

Marchesi had seen many new shopping centers in Jakarta and in the larger cities throughout Indonesia, but although they were crowded with shoppers, these customers seemed to be in a higher income bracket than the ones in Bata's stores. Bata's stores would need a major refurbishing if they were going to exhibit the bright, modern, clean, inviting image that was a Bata hallmark. Marchesi wanted each Bata store in Indonesia to look and feel the same so that Bata's long-time customers would feel comfortable and at home wherever they went. On the other hand, Marchesi believed that large, air-conditioned stores of the type Bata had in Canada and Europe were not appropriate for Indonesia since they would intimidate Bata's target customers. Marchesi estimated that he would have to invest about $6,000 per store in new signs, counters, shelves, and stock to bring them up to Bata standards. But was this action necessary or even a good idea?

## Distribution

Bata had followed a policy of widely separating the locations for its stores in order to allow each owner to enjoy a monopoly on Bata products over a large geographic area. This policy encouraged Indonesian entrepreneurs to invest their money in a Bata store; in fact, many of these independent owners were former Bata employees. Bata owned all the fixtures and merchandise in each store, with the store owner leasing or owning the store itself. In this way, if Bata were not satisfied with the store's operations, it could easily move out all its merchandise and displays, even the Bata sign in front.

Marchesi thought that Bata needed more market penetration in order to maintain or increase its sales. To reduce transportation costs, however, increasing the number of Bata stores would mean increasing the number of stores in one geographic area, rather than extending into previously untapped areas. If Marchesi decided to move Bata upmarket by improving its product quality, complexity, and design content, shoe prices would have to be raised as well. To do this, Bata would have to increase its market saturation by expanding the number of its stores substantially, perhaps even doubling their number, at a cost of $6,000 per store, about the cost of refurbishing an existing but run-down store. Marchesi wondered what to do about this situation.

## Product Quality and Design

In conversations with his managers and the owners of Bata stores, Marchesi was told that Bata's marketing problems might go beyond the quality of the stores, their merchandising methods, and their market coverage. Marchesi's review of Bata's product line gave some support to this view. Bata's product line was "old," at least by the standards that Marchesi had seen in Canada. The styles seemed to be several years behind what was being sold in Canada and elsewhere in the Bata organization. But this was not unusual for Bata or for other international marketers. It would introduce a shoe in Canada or Europe and see if it sold well there. Then, if it were successful, Bata would transfer the design to its subsidiaries in developing countries. After all, changes in style and types of shoes took time to spread and Marchesi knew that Bata did not want to get ahead of the market. Its target customers were often rather conservative and did not know or want the latest fads in shoes. Marchesi had noticed in his tours of shopping centers, however, that in many stores the latest worldwide fashions were available in shoes and other clothing.

Marchesi recalled a conversation with one of Bata's independent retailers:

> Some of our old customers aren't coming back to buy from us. Oh, yes, they'll come in with the whole family and look around. I've established a good relationship with them. But often one of the children will look disappointed and ask her mother if they can't try to look at another store in some shopping plaza to find some popular name-brand shoe.

Producing the latest fashions had its risks, however. At least at first, producing the "latest" fashion would mean producing a smaller number of shoes of many different types — and Bata would lose economies of scale and might not be competitive with smaller producers. There was also the risk that the market wouldn't accept the new styles and Bata would be left with unsold inventory. Also, higher fashion shoes produced in smaller batches meant more labor hours per shoe and more individual production steps for each shoe. This increased the labor content of such shoes and, hence, their cost of production. Higher fashion, more trendy shoes would also require more expensive materials. Bata would have to move out of plastics and synthetics into leather. Marchesi was worried about pricing Bata out of the market if Bata tried to follow this strategy.

Marchesi also noticed that Indonesians were very brand-name conscious, particularly when it came to clothing, but to a lesser extent for shoes. Imitations of brand-name products flooded the market with Pierre Cardin, Lacoste, and Polo shirts and Levi jeans in abundance. BCL produced three internationally known brand names: Power for athletic shoes, Northstar for leisure shoes, and Bubblegummers for children's shoes. Bata was also designated the official sponsor of the 1986 World Cup in Mexico and Power was the official sports shoes of the games.

Marchesi also saw that the quality of Bata shoes for sale, apart from their design, was below Bata standards even though the reject rate at the factory was also higher than standard. Yet if Bata moved upmarket into more stylish and complex shoes, the quality problem would be compounded.

## Production Technology

Beyond the generally run-down state of the factory and the equipment, Marchesi quickly saw that the equipment itself was old, inefficient, and labor-intensive. The ratio of new investment to sales had fallen from 0.06 in 1980 to 0.03 in 1983 (see Exhibit 2). If more efficient, more modern, and capital-intensive machinery were purchased, all else equal, workers would have to be laid off. Layoffs, combined with the current low morale of the workers, could very well lead to strikes and uncooperative workers. Yet if Bata was to improve its operations, it would need the full cooperation of all its workers.

In 1984, the average wage (including transportation, food, and rice allowance) of production workers was $1,085 (Rp1,242,319) per year while supervisors were paid $1,242 (Rp2,566,760). Because Bata owned the housing for its foreign managers, the total employment expense for each of its 13 expatriate managers was a relatively low $100,000 per year.

A full modernization of all Bata's factories and equipment would require an investment of $2.5 million, but since its three production units in its factory in Jakarta operated independently, everything did not need to be done at once. Perhaps the best way would be to first modernize one unit, then do the next one a year or so later. This would reduce investment needs and reduce labor displacement. Marchesi began to see the dilemma of the previous managing director.

## The External Environment

Two features of Bata's external environment were especially important to Marchesi, the overall economic performance of the Indonesian economy and the competitive environment. Through 1983, the Indonesian economy, buoyed by high oil prices, had performed well — real wages and real disposable income had risen. Since 1982, oil prices had fallen and the economy had begun to stagnate; lackluster economic growth began to affect Bata's sales adversely and more bad news was in sight — real wages were falling and unemployment was rising. The fall of Indonesia's oil prices during the 1982 to 1984 period was 20 percent and had brought about the 1983 devaluation of 44 percent. In 1983, oil and natural gas exports comprised about 75 percent of total exports. Through 1984, Indonesia was cushioned from part of the fall in oil prices on the spot market by the price schedules in its long-term supply contracts. If, as was widely predicted, oil prices continued to fall, Indonesia would experience a continued erosion in its terms of trade, increasing large deficits on its current account, and putting pressure on the government budget.

The strong economy through 1983 had helped Bata increase its sales revenue each year during the early 1980s (see Exhibit 4 for economic data). More money earned by more workers led to greater demand for shoes. As Marchesi had been told about Indonesian consumers: first comes food, shelter, and clothing, then comes shoes. Marchesi worried that, if the economy continued to stagnate, many of its customers would be thinking about food, not shoes (see Exhibit 5 for data on the price of Bata shoes in Indonesia).

For 1984, despite the downturn in the economy, it looked as if Bata would be able to maintain volume at 1983 levels while increasing revenues by about 16 percent (see Exhibit 6). The shortfall in oil revenues had had a dramatic effect on the government's budget and there was a widespread belief that the government would have to act in order to reduce its budget deficit by cutting spending and raising taxes. These actions, if they were taken, would further depress the economy and accelerate the recent trend toward falling real wages and rising unemployment.

In recent years domestically owned firms penetrated the lower end of the market, the market niche occupied by Bata. There was some entry of medium- and large-scale manufacturers (see Exhibit 7), but the bigger worry was the entry of small-scale manufacturers with less than 25 employees. Bata's store owners told Marchesi that they were not only losing customers to upscale stores but that these customers were not being replaced by new ones because working families realized that they could buy acceptable shoes at lower prices made by small Indonesian-owned companies. Several firms had been set up in Indonesia to produce solely for the export market. These firms, several of which were owned by firms based in Korea and Taiwan, produced low-quality shoes for the bottom end of the international market, using largely imported materials and combining them with low-cost Indonesian labor (and government export incentives) in order to be competitive in international markets.

These firms had been quite successful, and Bata's current product line was quite similar to the products produced by these export-oriented firms. On the other hand, Bata could try to produce and export for the medium-price, medium-quality segment of the market. But this would be very difficult for Bata, given its workers's current skills and capabilities and its current product and production technology. Moreover, Marchesi knew he could not rely on BCL's worldwide sales outlets as a ready-made, in-house distribution network, since BCL's overall corporate strategy did not encourage trade among its units in different countries. Whatever trade did occur was on an arm's-length basis and depended strictly on P T Sepatu Bata's ability to provide the right shoes at the right price for export. Nonetheless, this segment of the international market looked like it had potential since only Spain, Brazil, and Italy were major suppliers to this segment; Bata would have to upgrade its quality and design significantly if it were to compete in this segment.

With all these factors in mind, Mr Marchesi turned to the decision at hand: What should Bata's overall strategy be for the rest of the 1980s and what steps would Bata have to take in order to implement it? Should Bata remain on its present course? After all, the results over the past several years had been quite good and the head office was satisfied. In 1983, Bata earned 34.55 percent return on equity before tax. Average depreciation was 10 percent per year for plant, equipment, and store fixtures. If Bata were to upgrade its plant, equipment, and stores, this investment would have to be returned in increased profits. If Bata upgraded its line of shoes, the increased costs of production would have to be recovered in higher shoe prices. Taken together, Bata might have to increase the prices it charged for its shoes by 50 to 70 percent — quite apart from the effects of inflation on costs and prices. Two contradictory phrases ran through his head: "Time (and, he added, the competition and the market) waits for no man," and "Fools rush in where angels fear to tread."

Overall there seemed to be a sense of drift and decline in the company among the production workers, the office staff, and among the managers. There was less sense of pride in their work and in being a Bata employee than Marchesi had found in his career with Bata in other countries. Bata was having difficulties hiring managers. On the other hand, the head office of BCL seemed reasonably content with P T Sepatu Bata's performance. Marchesi remembered the famous phrase used so often in *Dear Abby*: "If ain't broke, don't fix it." After all, each country was different and to expect to operate in Indonesia the same way he had in Canada and Italy might not only be unrealistic, but counterproductive.

EXHIBIT 1

## P T SEPATU BATA (A)
## Balance Sheets, December 31, 1980–1983
(in million rupiah)

| | *1980* | *1981* | *1982* | *1983* |
|---|---|---|---|---|
| ASSETS | | | | |
| Current assets | | | | |
| Cash | 159 | 388 | 164 | 484 |
| Time deposits | 0 | 2,606 | 2,555 | 4,613 |
| Time deposits — other | 0 | 0 | 0 | 5,910 |
| Accounts receivable — trade | 706 | 961 | 1,018 | 1,550 |
| Due from affiliates | 5 | 2 | 3 | 19 |
| Current portion of notes receivable | 232 | 0 | 0 | 0 |
| Inventories | 3,208 | 3,486 | 3,640 | 4,753 |
| Advances for purchases | 251 | 60 | 62 | 167 |
| Deferred income tax — current | 183 | 79 | 107 | 12 |
| Total current assets | 4,744 | 7,582 | 7,548 | 17,508 |
| Time deposits, noncurrent | 0 | 3,816 | 4,071 | 0 |
| Notes receivable, noncurrent | 1,431 | 0 | 0 | 0 |
| Property, plant, and equipment | | | | |
| Buildings | 763 | 2,134 | 2,250 | 2,386 |
| Machinery and equipment | 2,431 | 5,510 | 5,453 | 6,278 |
| | 2,890 | 7,644 | 7,704 | 8,663 |
| Less: Accumulated depreciation | (299) | (1,837) | (2,112) | (2,871) |
| Net property, plant, and equipment | 2,591 | 5,807 | 5,592 | 5,792 |
| Intangible assets | | | | |
| Land rights | 27 | 5,635 | 5,635 | 5,635 |
| Other assets | | | | |
| Deferred charges | 535 | 711 | 824 | 1,109 |
| Deferred income taxes, non-current | 522 | 244 | 0 | 0 |
| Total assets | 9,849 | 23,795 | 23,670 | 30,043 |

The company was allowed by the Ministry of Finance to revalue its fixed assets on December 31, 1981 when it went public. Most of the increase in property, plant, and equipment does not represent any new investment.

EXHIBIT 1 (cont'd)

**P T SEPATU BATA (A)**
**Balance Sheets, December 31, 1980–1983**
(in million rupiah)

| | *1980* | *1981* | *1982* | *1983* |
|---|---|---|---|---|
| LIABILITIES AND SHAREHOLDERS' EQUITY | | | | |
| Current liabilities | | | | |
| Notes payable | 500 | 800 | 0 | 0 |
| Accounts payable | 444 | 412 | 428 | 1,611 |
| Accrued liabilities[a] | 585 | 556 | 568 | 0 |
| Short-term debt | 0 | 0 | 0 | 5,910 |
| Other taxes payable | 131 | 152 | 171 | 284 |
| Corporate income tax payable | 1,280 | 696 | 596 | 1,591 |
| Due to affiliates | 166 | 81 | 136 | 261 |
| Guarantee deposits from distributors | 293 | 369 | 424 | 544 |
| Liability for retirement plant costs — current | 137 | 148 | 94 | 27 |
| Total current liabilities | 3,537 | 3,215 | 2,417 | 10,227 |
| Long-term liabilities | | | | |
| Liability for retirement plan cost — noncurrent | 1,300 | 1,600 | 1,745 | 2,077 |
| Deferred income tax — noncurrent | 0 | 3,816 | 226 | 224 |
| Long-term debt | 0 | 0 | 4,071 | 0 |
| Long-term liabilities | 1,300 | 5,416 | 6,042 | 2,301 |
| Total liabilities | 4,837 | 8,631 | 8,459 | 12,528 |
| Shareholders' equity | | | | |
| Common shares[b] | 0 | 0 | 8,000 | 8,000 |
| New foreign investment | 458 | 458 | 0 | 0 |
| Revaluation and appraisal increment[c] | 645 | 9,543 | 2,018 | 2,018 |
| Retained earnings | 3,909 | 5,163 | 5,193 | 7,498 |
| Total shareholders' equity | 5,012 | 15,165 | 15,211 | 17,516 |
| Total liabilities & shareholders' equity | 9,849 | 23,795 | 23,670 | 30,043 |

[a]In 1993, accrued liabilities included in accounts payable.
[b]1980–1981: 2,500 shares @ Rp3 authorized, issued, and fully paid.
1982–1983: 8,000,000 shares, par value 1,000 rupees.
[c]Authorized write of assets on "going public." This does not represent new equity capital.

EXHIBIT 2

**P T SEPATU BATA (A)**
**Income Statements, 1980–1983**
(in million rupiah, except per share amounts)

| | *1980* | *1981* | *1982* | *1983* |
|---|---|---|---|---|
| Net sales | 18,069 | 21,493 | 23,408 | 29,203 |
| Cost of sales | 8,855 | 11,427 | 11,517 | 14,164 |
| Gross profit | 9,213 | 10,066 | 11,892 | 15,040 |
| Operating expenses | | | | |
| Selling and marketing | 2,273 | 2,787 | NA | NA |
| General and administration | 3,822 | 3,884 | NA | NA |
| Total operating expenses | 6,095 | 6,681 | 7,585 | 9,908 |
| Operating income | 3,118 | 3,384 | 4,307 | 5,132 |
| Other income | (1,344) | 16 | (443) | 926 |
| Total other income (expenses) | (1,344) | 16 | (443) | 926 |
| Income before corporate income tax | 2,984 | 3,401 | 4,263 | 6,059 |
| Corporate income tax | | | | |
| Current | 1,454 | 932 | 1,025 | 2,061 |
| Deferred | (1,800) | 367 | 442 | 93 |
| Total corporate income tax | 1,274 | 1,299 | 1,466 | 2,154 |
| Income before extraordinary item | 1,710 | 2,102 | 2,797 | 3,905 |
| Extraordinary gain on transfer of land rights, net of applicable corporate income taxes of Rp166,266 | 1,496 | 0 | 0 | 0 |
| Net income | 3,206 | 2,102 | 2,797 | 3,905 |
| Earnings per share | 401 | 263 | 350 | 488 |
| Earnings per share has been computed on the basis of weighted average number of shares outstanding: | 8 shares | 8 shares | 8 shares | 8 shares |
| Additions to property, plant, & equipment | 1,135 | 802 | 616 | 1,015 |
| Cash dividends | 1,300 | 953 | 2,750 | 1,600 |

Source: P T Sepatu Bata, Annual Reports, 1981–1983.

EXHIBIT 3

**P T SEPATU BATA (A)**
**Canadian Exchange Rate (midpoint)**

| *Year* | *Rupiahs per Canadian Dollar* |
|---|---|
| 1975 | 414 |
| 1976 | 427 |
| 1977 | 395 |
| 1978 | 554 |
| 1979 | 538 |
| 1980 | 540 |
| 1981 | 536 |
| 1982 | 561 |
| 1983 | 807 |
| 1984 | 831 |

Source: World Bank, *International Finance Statistics*, 1975–1988.

EXHIBIT 4

**P T SEPATU BATA (A)**
**Trend of Product Aggregates and Per Capita Income at 1983 Constant Market Prices, 1975–1984**

| *Year* | *Gross Domestic Product (in billion Rp)* | *National (in billion Rp)* | *Private Consumption Expenditure (in billion Rp)* | *Per Capita Income (in thousand Rp)* |
|---|---|---|---|---|
| 1975 | 46,370 | 39,618 | 24,639 | 303 |
| 1980 | 66,722 | 56,531 | 36,037 | 386 |
| 1981 | 71,553 | 61,911 | 39,698 | 413 |
| 1982 | 71,360 | 63,525 | 42,171 | 415 |
| 1983 | 73,697 | 65,230 | 44,739 | 417 |
| 1984 | 78,144 | 69,405 | 46,898 | 435 |

Source: CBS, *Statistical Year Book of Indonesia*, 1977–1985.

EXHIBIT 5

**P T SEPATU BATA (A)**
**Wholesale Price Indexes of Footwear, 1977–1984**

| *Year* | *Indonesia Indexes Prices* | *Bata Indexes Prices* | *Bata Average Price in Rupiahs* |
|---|---|---|---|
| 1977 | 42 | 31 | 1,237 |
| 1978 | 48 | 33 | 1,326 |
| 1979 | 62 | 46 | 1,864 |
| 1980 | 69 | 55 | 2,234 |
| 1981 | 76 | 64 | 2,603 |
| 1982 | 82 | 74 | 2,983 |
| 1983 | 90 | 90 | 3,640 |
| 1984 | 100 | 100 | 4,055 |

Sources: CBS, *Wholesale Price Indexes Indonesia, 1977–1985*; P T Sepatu Bata, Annual Reports, 1977–1984.

EXHIBIT 6

**P T SEPATU BATA (A)**
**Sales and Income, 1977–1983**

| *Year* | *Sales in Pairs (in thousands)* | *Sales (in million rupiah)* | *Net Income (in million rupiah)* |
|---|---|---|---|
| 1977 | 6,922 | 8,564 | 753 |
| 1978 | 7,243 | 9,603 | 725 |
| 1979 | 7,620 | 14,202 | 1,182 |
| 1980 | 8,485 | 18,957 | 1,710 |
| 1981 | 8,659 | 22,547 | 2,102 |
| 1982 | 8,233 | 24,559 | 2,797 |
| 1983 | 8,417 | 30,642 | 3,905 |

Source: P T Sepatu Bata, Annual Reports, 1977–1984.

EXHIBIT 7

## P T SEPATU BATA (A)
## Annual Survey of Large and Medium Manufacturing Establishments
## Industry Group: Manufacture of Footwear, 1975–1984

| *Year* | *Number of Establishments* | *Number of Persons Engaged* | *Employment Costs (in million Rp)* | *Average Wages (in thousand Rp)* | *Value of Gross Output (in million Rp)* |
|---|---|---|---|---|---|
| 1975 | 45 | 5,831 | 2,139 | 366 | 18,278 |
| 1980 | 57 | 7,495 | 3,294 | 439 | 31,252 |
| 1981 | 64 | 7,453 | 5,533 | 742 | 31,630 |
| 1982 | 56 | 6,305 | 6,003 | 952 | 33,650 |
| 1983 | 55 | 6,231 | 7,272 | 1,167 | 46,179 |
| 1984 | 61 | 6,772 | 8,756 | 1,293 | 56,880 |

Note: Manufacturing establishments are defined as one production unit engaged in economic activities, producing goods, located in a census building, keeping a business record concerning production and cost structure, with one or more persons assuming responsibility for the business risk.

Source: CBS, Industrial Statistics, *Survey of Manufacturing Industries Large and Medium*, vol 1, 1975–1984.

# SIFCO Industries, Inc (China)* 24

One afternoon in June 1989, Kevin O'Donnell, CEO of SIFCO Industries, Inc sat in his Cleveland, Ohio office contemplating SIFCO's joint venture project in China. Through numerous discussions over the past two-and-a-half years in both China and the United States, the three parties involved in the venture were ready to submit the formally signed joint venture contract, articles of association, and technology transfer agreement to the SIFCO board for approval. However, the June 4 occupation of Tiananmen Square by the Chinese army cast heavy clouds over this project, and Kevin O'Donnell was wondering whether the board would or should approve the project.

## SIFCO History

SIFCO was founded in Cleveland in 1913 by five men who were dedicated to applying relatively new scientific principles to improving physical properties of metals, specifically by the use of thermal cycles. While the art of heat-treating was ancient, the body of knowledge that would turn an art into a science was just beginning to accumulate. In 1916, this company merged with The Forest City Machine Company, a manufacturer of metal poles. Since the major manufacturing process for this product was forging, the merger added forging capability to the heat-treating company and the company was renamed the Steel Improvement and Forge Company (SIFCO).

---

*This case was prepared by Professor Liming Zhao, University of Alabama to serve as a basis for class discussion and is not intended to illustrate either effective or ineffective handling of an administrative situation. 

At the time SIFCO was formed, Cleveland was one of the centers of the rapidly growing automobile and steel industries, and the city became a leader in the volume of steel forgings produced. The economies and practices of the auto industry made it difficult for forging suppliers that depended on that industry for most of their business to earn a consistent profit. So SIFCO found applications for forged products in other industries. SIFCO served many industrial markets including oil and petrochemical, aerospace, nuclear power generation, transportation, ordnance, mining, and off-highway. SIFCO was a medium-size firm with annual sales of over US$60 million (Exhibit 1 highlights SIFCO's financial position).

Charles H Smith, Jr, son of the former president, became SIFCO's CEO in 1943 just after he completed his thesis at MIT on the forging of austenitic stainless steels for turbo-supercharger applications. He became Chairman of the Board in 1983 when Kevin O'Donnell was named President and CEO. An MBA graduate of Harvard Business School with years of experience in SIFCO, O'Donnell had also served in the Navy, Booz Allen, Atlas Alloys of Canada, and the Peace Corps in Korea and at the Washington, DC headquarters.

## Forging Technology

The forging process involved the use of closed-impression dies and forging hammers, forging machines, and forging presses to work hot steel into intricate shapes. Forging kneaded the hot metal, concentrating on the grain structure and fiber formation at points of greatest shock and stress (the basis of strength and toughness in forgings was the fiberlike structure inherent in the steel) to obtain maximum impact strength, toughness, and high fatigue resistance. The maximum refinement and improvement of the physical properties of metal were obtained only by the forging process.

The forging of hot metal began some 4,000 years ago based on a similar principle to that used today — the blow of a hammer to a billet of hot metal to form a tool or weapon. Over the years, technology had improved the power and precision of the hammer, but individual forgings were alike. A process developed in the 1850s by Elisha K Root and C E Billings at the Colt Arms Company in Connecticut proved to be a technological breakthrough in the art of forging; their innovation permitted the design of precision forging dies for making interchangeable parts at greater speed and eliminated a great deal of handwork (filing and grinding) to finish the parts.

Modern technologies, such as computer-aided design and computer-aided manufacturing, automatic temperature control, induction heating, and so on found great application in the forging industry. Modern forging was an incorporation of ancient ideas with the newest discoveries of space age metallurgy. Warm and cold forge technologies were developed and utilized to meet different requirements. Today's forged component offered greater strength, maximum weight/strength relationship, greater fatigue resistance, elimination of porosity, dimensional conformity, a refined crystalline structure, orientation of grain flow, faster and easier machining, lower scrap rates, and tremendous reliability.

## SIFCO Forge Group

The Forge Group was headed by Vice President and Group General Manager Edwin Schmidt, a graduate of Yale (BS) and the Wharton School of Finance and Commerce at the University of Pennsylvania (MBA).

The Forge Group had three divisions: Steel Improvement & Forge Division, Coldforge Division, and International Forging Sales. It manufactured hot, warm, and cold forgings for commercial and high-technology markets. The Forge Group had 11 sales offices in different states with general sales offices in Cleveland.

The Forge Group's die-forgings of complex shapes covered the range of carbon, alloy, high-temperature, and titanium metals. High-volume commercial forgings from 1 to 500 pounds and cold and warm forgings in low and medium carbon steels and alloys from 2 to 50 pounds were typical. Titanium weights ranged up to 90 pounds. The group provided complex forgings like airframe, engine component, crankshaft, landing gear, connecting rods, and other complex forgings and component assemblies. Some of the companies that specified SIFCO forgings included Alco, Armco, Avco Lycoming, Bell Helicopter, Boeing, Caterpillar, Chrysler, John Deere, Ford, General Motors, McDonnell Douglas, General Electric, International Harvester, Westinghouse, Pratt and Whitney, and Lockheed.

**International Operations**

SIFCO Forge Group's move into international business ventures and the transfer of forging technology and management to other countries began in 1951. The first program was in Canada and involved building and managing a plant for aircraft engine forgings. By 1990, SIFCO had business ties with Argentina, Brazil, India, Japan, France, Ireland, Korea, and England. These included an agreement to manage a government-owned facility; joint ventures partly owned by SIFCO; the transfer of managerial expertise, technology, and production assistance for a fixed fee; contracts for sales representation; and marketing orientation and development of products in the United States under licenses from abroad.

SIFCO's involvement in Argentina and Brazil was in the form of joint ventures and, in India, in the form of a technical assistance agreement. In each instance, the recipients not only became major concerns but also significant exporters. Charles H Smith, Jr once said:

> With steel improvement-related forge plants in both Argentina and Brazil, the company was asked to consider almost every new forging project proposed in any developing country. Unfortunately, few such projects met the basic criteria the company management considered essential for success. Even where these criteria were met, the company lacked the resources to invest in every developing country's quest for industrialization.

## China Project

In September 1986, through Kowin Development Corporation, a trading company based in Los Angeles, SIFCO learned that Shanghai Heavy Die Forging Plant (SHD), which was owned by Shanghai Mechanical & Electrical Industrial Investment Corporation (SMEIIC), had been seeking a foreign joint venture partner that could provide advanced forging technology and an export channel.

SIFCO's management viewed this as a good opportunity to enter China's market. Through the assistance of the Kowin Development Corporation, SIFCO and SMEIIC began correspondence. Within a few months, both parties had expressed a strong interest and in late 1986, SIFCO was invited to visit Shanghai.

After receiving SHD's invitation, SIFCO top management reviewed the strategic considerations that would affect any decision to enter China. Several issues were identified:

1. China had 25 percent of the world's population and was vastly underdeveloped. China represented the largest potential market in Asia for SIFCO Forge Group's products. Since forging parts had applications in a variety of industries, market demand for quality forgings in China would be great for a long time.
2. China had embarked on a grand modernization program in 1979 and had been developing rapidly. Forging was basic to the development of a country's infrastructure and its industries. SIFCO's forging technology represented a great improvement over what was current in China. And SIFCO had unique experience and capability in transferring forging technology to developing countries.
3. A major constraint in China's development plans was the hard currency to finance imports of badly needed foreign technology and capital equipment. Consequently, government policy encouraged investments with export or import substitution potential. SIFCO management expected strong demand for SIFCO forgings from Chinese manufacturers that were currently importing quality forgings from Japan, Germany, and other Western countries.
4. The manufacture of forging parts was highly labor- and overhead-intensive. With the lowest wage rates in the world, China could prove to be an excellent low-cost supply base for the world market. SIFCO had concentrated on the higher end of the U.S. forging market because of formidable competition from commercial forging manufacturers in Korea, Italy, Taiwan, and other countries. As part of an overall strategy, SIFCO could sell SIFCO-China joint venture products in U.S. commercial forging markets.
5. Since the goal was to establish a long-term relationship, a joint venture would be suitable. SIFCO could become a minority partner in a solid company. Management believed this was an opportunity for SIFCO to parlay its forging manufacturing and marketing expertise into significant increased earnings despite a flat U.S. forging market.

## China's Economic Outlook

China had a long-term target of quadrupling per capita national income between 1980 and 2000 and becoming a mid-level developed economy by 2050. Efforts to stabilize aggregate domestic demand and control imports, investment, inflation, and foreign exchange had dominated China's economic policy in recent years.

China's current economic reform began in 1978 to reduce inefficiencies in the economy, speed development, and raise consumer living standards (see Exhibit 2 for the key statistics for China's economy from 1970 to 1986). China was a relative newcomer to the international world of foreign direct investment, opening the country to such activity only in 1978. Beijing had subsequently put into place laws, regulations, incentives, and policies aimed at encouraging foreign investment. Beijing was interested in directing foreign investment to manufacturing rather than service industries, and into industries that were export-oriented and involved technologies new to China.

### The Joint Venture Law

China promulgated the Law of the People's Republic of China on Joint Ventures Using Chinese and Foreign Investment (see Exhibit 3) in July 1979 and Regulations for the Implementation of the Law of the People's Republic of China on Joint Venture Using Chinese and Foreign Investment in September 1983. This regulatory framework was intended to enable China to absorb capital and technology from abroad while conserving foreign exchange.

Several key features of the joint venture law and regulations were:

1. The law prescribed no upper limit to the proportion of foreign investment in a joint venture (Article 4). This was in contrast to the laws of most developing countries, which generally stipulated an upper limit of 49 percent. There was a lower limit of 25 percent, apparently to ensure the foreign participant would have sufficient commitment to the venture.
   Also in contrast to the laws of other developing countries, the Chinese law did not define preferred industries for joint ventures but preserved for the government the flexibility to direct investment funds through supplementary measures according to current needs.
2. The law provided for a tax holiday to cover the first two to three profit-making years (Article 7). This provision could take the form of either a reduction or an exemption and applied in particular to a joint venture "equipped with up-to-date technology by world standards."
3. The law was quite liberal with regard to marketing. The provisions of Article 9, which stated that the joint venture was encouraged to export while being permitted to distribute products within China, sought to balance China's desire to take advantage of a foreign participant's marketing network with the foreign partner's desire to penetrate the Chinese market.
4. The law seemed designed to protect China against exploitation and reflected China's experience with Soviet technical assistance in the late 1950s, which often involved outdated technologies. Article 5 provided that the "technology or equipment contributed by any foreign participant as investment must be truly advanced and appropriate to China's needs."
5. The regulation identified six categories of industries permitted for joint ventures (Article 3):
   a. Energy development building material, chemical, and metallurgical industries.
   b. Machine manufacturing, instrument, and meter industries; and offshore oil exploitation equipment manufacturing.
   c. Electronics and computer industries, and communication equipment manufacturing.
   d. Light, textile, foodstuffs, medicine, medical apparatus, and packing industries.
   e. Agriculture, animal husbandry, and agriculture.
   f. Tourism and service trades.
6. A joint venture had the right to hire and discharge its workers and staff.

China's State Council, the administrative body of the Chinese central government, issued policies to encourage foreign investment from foreign countries. The Shanghai municipal government issued special policies to give more favorable treatment to Sino-foreign joint venture firms with advanced technology, and a export-oriented business.

Under the joint venture law, a growing number of foreign firms had invested in joint ventures in China (see Exhibit 3 for a list of the major U.S. investments in China).

## Industrial Organization in Shanghai

Located at the mouth of the Yangtze River at the Pacific Ocean, Shanghai was the largest city in terms of both population and industrial output in China. The total population in the Shanghai metropolitan area was about 12 million. Historically, Shanghai had been China's leading technological and industrial base, providing a substantial percentage of industrial revenue to the nation and spearheading China's growing exports into foreign markets.

Shanghai was one of the three municipalities (Beijing and Tianjin being the other two) that were subordinated to the central government directly. Because of its strategic position in China's economic development, the Shanghai municipal government was delegated greater authority to do international business and approve joint venture projects. The governmental structure of Shanghai municipality included a party secretary, who set policy, and a mayor and seven deputy mayors, who carried out the administrative functions. One deputy mayor was in charge of all economic activity within the municipality.

Reporting to the mayor were a number of commissions and bureaus. Municipal commissions were generally higher than the bureaus in the hierarchy. The bureaus were responsible for all goods and services produced within Shanghai. All economic activity within Shanghai was effectively controlled at the municipal level.

There were six commissions in Shanghai, all making policies and plans and approving key projects. These six commissions were:

1. Planning Commission
2. Economic Commission
3. Foreign Investment Commission
4. Foreign Economic Relation and Trade Commission
5. Science and Technology Commission
6. Education Commission

There were 30 bureaus in Shanghai, 10 making industrial products and 20 providing services. The 10 industrial bureaus, which reported to the Economic Commission, were:

1. Chemical Industry (rubber, fertilizers, insecticides)
2. Electronic Industry (electronic element, device, instrument, computer)
3. Power Industry (power generation)
4. Petrochemical Industry (gasoline, oils)
5. Light Industry (bicycles, watches, shoes, sewing machines, flasks, arts and handicrafts)
6. Agricultural Machinery (tractors, diesel engines, farm implements)
7. Textile Industry (textiles and textile machinery)

8. Mechanical & Electrical Industry (machine tools, trucks, bearings, elevator, electrical devices)
9. Metallurgical Industry (iron, steel, rare metals)
10. Construction (and construction equipment)

Functional responsibility for the management of SHD belonged to the Shanghai Mechanical & Electrical Industry Bureau (SMEIB). There were 14 divisions in SMEIB overseeing the planning, technology, production, marketing, financing, personnel, import and export, and foreign investment associated with all facets of 80 plants including SHD. SMEIIC was in charge of forming joint ventures with foreign firms. This administrative structure was extremely hierarchical. However, many officials participated in several organizations (see Exhibit 4). These multiple roles provided a means for intra-organizational communication not inherent in the structure itself.

### Labor Practices

China did not have a free labor market. Workers were first recommended by the municipal office in charge of the plant needing additional workers. To achieve full employment, new workers often were assigned to a plant that did not need additional workers. Workers were trained by the factory at which they were employed, and plant discipline was maintained through social and incentive pressures. It was extremely rare for a worker, once hired, to be discharged.

Chinese workers in a forging plant earned an average wage of RMB240 (equivalent to US$60) per month for six eight-hour days. In addition to a bonus, the workers also received such benefits as rent for housing, free medical care and medication, a food allowance, children's educational allowance, a transportation subsidy, paid sick leave, 30 days' paid leave to visit a spouse (married) or parents (unmarried) if a worker lived in a different city from the spouse/parents. A cap on wages had been removed, and foreign-invested firms had freedom to set wages and offer differential wages. Some wages, however, were not set commensurate with productivity.

The total number of employees at a Chinese plant was far greater than at its U.S. counterpart because a Chinese plant had to operate its own cafeteria, nursery and kindergarten, cleaning fleet, security, intercity shipping, and other services.

## Shanghai's Heavy Die-Forging Plant

### Company Background

Located in Shanghai, China's largest city, SHD specialized in manufacturing general-purpose commercial forgings. As one of the key forging manufacturers in Shanghai, SHD directly reported to Shanghai Mechanical & Electrical Industrial Bureau (SMEIB). In creating a joint venture, SMEIIC represented SMEIB as the owner.

Both the Register of Shipping of China and the American Bureau of Shipping (ABS) issued documents indicating SHD was capable of producing marine forgings in accordance with the rules of the register and the bureau.

With more than 1,050 employees including about 100 engineers and technicians, the plant had annual sales of RMB 22 million yuan (about US$7 million), and the growth rate of earnings before taxes had been 6 percent for the past five years. SHD provided open forgings and certain closed die-forgings to domestic markets; export was rare.

### Industry Analysis

China's forging technology lagged about 10 years behind the world level. Most of the manufacturers in this industry used a hammer and hydropress to produce free forgings and die forgings with a quality below world standards. Mass production with mechanical presses was rare. Forging dies were made manually. High-quality forgings, particularly forgings made by press, had to be imported from abroad.

There were 15 forging plants or workshops in Shanghai under various bureaus, each producing for the needs of its respective bureau. There was little rationalization of production. Marketing across bureau lines, cities, or provinces was allowed. However, because of "protectionism," these kinds of sales needed greater efforts.

In 1984, the government established that, within four years, all forging firms in China would purchase materials and sell their forgings on the market freely. Competition was getting tense among the forging firms.

### Initiation of the Project

With the development of the open-door policy, Shanghai was given special permission to introduce foreign technology, absorb foreign capital, and export. On top of the Provisions of the State Council of the People's Republic of China for the Encouragement of Foreign Investment, Shanghai issued the Provisions of the Shanghai Municipality for the Encouragement of Foreign Investment in 1986, offering more favorable terms to foreign investors. SHD was one of the firms in Shanghai to be encouraged to acquire advanced technology and utilize foreign capital.

Z He (pronounced "Ha"), general manager of SMEIIC, said "I was the director of SHD for 10 years. I feel that SHD has the potential to be improved considerably and become competitive in the world market if more advanced technology is acquired."

Since late 1985, SHD had been actively looking for a joint venture partner that could provide capital and technology and was willing to sell joint venture products in the world market through its own marketing channel.

Once in a private discussion, a deputy director of SHD said: "If we can form a joint venture with a foreign partner according to the government regulations, we would enjoy more benefits like technology advancement, greater decision-making autonomy, a handsome salary and wage increase for all employees, better fringe benefits, more company cars. . . . You just name it!"[1]

## Merger Negotiations

### Initial Shanghai Round

After a couple of months of correspondence, SMEIIC invited SIFCO to visit. In December 1986, O'Donnell visited Shanghai and started a joint venture discussion with SMEIIC

[1]China discourages companies from owning company cars. Each Chinese company in Shanghai has a quota for the number of cars it can own. However, a foreign-Chinese joint venture can own more cars.

and SHD. The General Manager of SMEIIC was present at all the discussions. This visit ended with a memorandum of understanding. In this memo, both parties expressed the intent of forming a joint forging business venture in Shanghai and agreed to further explore the economic viability of the project. At the meeting, the Chinese side asked SIFCO to take the responsibility of selling forgings to the world market. During this visit, Mr Yu, Deputy Director of SMEIB, expressed his support for such a joint venture. Chen, the President of China Forging Industry Association, also voiced his support and discussed other cooperative possibilities with O'Donnell.

Later, O'Donnell recalled: "I think SHD demonstrated the capability of absorbing our technology. . . . I felt very comfortable dealing with SHD people. They were honest and sincere in venturing to reach an agreement."

In February 1987, a SIFCO Forge Group team headed by Ed Schmidt visited Shanghai to assess SHD's background and technological capability. The meetings further confirmed the technical and economic viability of the venture. Another memorandum of understanding was signed. SIFCO agreed in principle to transfer hammer forging technology to SHD and to sell the joint venture forgings to the U.S. market. The Chinese side agreed to provide land, building, labor, and cash. Schmidt later commented:

> SHD is ideally positioned for absorption of technical assistance and for rapid expansion to meet China's demand for forged product. With the basic core equipment of 6,000-pound to 20,000-pound closed die-forging steam hammers and up to 1,000-ton hydraulic presses for open die-forging already in place, we can plan a sharp increase in productive capacity through improved manufacturing methods and additions of selective forging and support equipment.

### Cleveland Round

In May 1987, the SMEIIC team headed by Mr He visited SIFCO in Cleveland. The purpose of the meeting was to discuss the major issues in a feasibility study for the joint venture. SIFCO hired a Chinese national, currently studying business in the United States, to be involved in the project.

During the meeting, the technology and export issues were discussed. The development plan was set, and SIFCO agreed to sell the forgings in the U.S. market — for a total of US$20 million in eight years starting from the third year after the venture was established. Differences continued around the following key issues:

1. **SIFCO's equity contribution.** The focus was on the estimation of SIFCO's technology value — US$2.06 million for technical know-how, technical assistance, and CAD/CAM hardware and software. SIFCO wanted to reinvest a substantial part of this amount in the venture as its equity contribution and use the remaining to cover training and technical assistance expenses. The Chinese kept questioning how SIFCO could put that value on its technology and insisted on a breakdown of the grand total.
2. **Financial data from SHD.** SIFCO provided SHD with all its financial data. However, SHD had not provided any data to show its profitability over the past five years. The only information the Chinese team gave was: "Believe us, we've been making money for the past 10 years." The SIFCO team asked: "How could we know we want to put money there without seeing your financial data?" At

last, the Chinese team told SIFCO it could not provide the information without getting permission from the Shanghai municipal government. The team promised to talk to the government and provide the financial data later somehow.

3. **Press technology.** SHD initially wanted SIFCO to provide press equipment and technology from the first year. SIFCO suggested it introduce press technology in the third or fourth year since China's market was not ready for press forging parts.

Both parties agreed to meet again soon, but then SIFCO did not hear anything from SHD for about two and a half months after the Chinese team left. So SIFCO telexed SMEIIC, saying: "Let us be honest with one another and in the spirit of cooperation and friendship that we have all displayed thus far, quickly decide if further JV study is worthwhile for SHD and SIFCO." Fifteen days later, SMEIIC telexed back, saying, "We wholeheartedly hope to keep on making arrangements for our joint venture; we are speeding up our work to send you the financial information." It took about three months for SMEIIC to report to the government and to get the go-ahead.

Before long, SIFCO received SHD's information related to the feasibility study, but the financial data was sparse. SHD also sent SIFCO its five-year projection of joint venture sales, cost of goods sold (COGS), earnings before taxes (EBT), and exports. SIFCO was surprised to find out that materials accounted for about 86 percent of COGS. SHD also included a request for the introduction of press equipment and technology in the first year to enable it to bid on potential orders from the Shanghai Volkswagen Automobile Company.

**Second Shanghai Round**

In November 1987, O'Donnell visited Shanghai again for further discussions. The terms of technology transfer and joint venture were discussed in full. O'Donnell faced between 8 and 12 people in all the meetings. The heated discussions were centered on profitability, equity contribution by each party, the value of SIFCO's technology, and work force considerations:

1. **Profitability of the joint venture.** When asked why the material cost was so high and EBT was so low in the projection, the SHD team said the highest market prices of materials were used so the projection was prudent and reliable and both sides would be happier when the actual profits exceeded the "conservative profitability projection." The team felt that by doing so it showed its sincerity and commitment. O'Donnell said: "I am your partner. But you treat me like your customer." When asked about the income statement, balance sheet, and other financial data, SHD said it could provide statistical data only as references. The SIFCO team said: "You never gave us your annual profit for the most recent five years. Our explanation is that the projection reflects your low profitability. We don't think SIFCO will invest under this situation.
2. **Equity contribution.** SIFCO wanted to have a smaller venture since it did not have that much money for the initial investment. SMEIIC insisted the whole existing plant and employees be included and SIFCO's equity contribution could not be below 25 percent, which is the minimum share the government set for foreign partners.

Neither side could reach agreement on these two issues. During the deadlock, the Chinese asked the accompanying Chinese student to explain the American business philosophy behind the projection. Then the Chinese promised to give SIFCO the financial data verbally since they could not get permission from the government agency concerned. He also said: "We started understanding him (O'Donnell). His questioning and argument showed his commitment to this joint venture. The American wouldn't put the money into water."

When negotiations resumed, the chief accountant of SHD provided the financial data, showing SHD's profitability was close to the top among all the forge shops in China. Then the past 11 months' average material cost was used as the average market price of materials in the projection. The projected profitability of the venture turned out to be very attractive.

3. **Value of SIFCO's technology.** SIFCO asked for US$2.06 million for its technology, of which US$860,000 would be an up-front payment. The remaining US$1.2 million would be paid equally in four years to cover the expense of SIFCO's technical assistance and training of engineers and managers. SIFCO estimated the total time needed would be about 2,400 worker-days in four years. The Chinese thought the figures were too high to accept.
4. **Work force.** To reduce initial capital investment requirements, both parties agreed to use SHD's existing building and facilities. However, SHD wanted the joint venture to take the existing work force of 1,050. SIFCO suggested a joint venture with a maximum work force of 450. O'Donnell questioned: "We are competing with Korea, Japan, the US, and Canada in the world market. Currently, SHD produces 180 pound forgings per day per person while the figure in SIFCO is more than triple that amount. What are we going to do with these people?" SHD insisted all employees be included, making a number of arguments:

   (a) Serious tension would be created among the existing employees if only part of the work force would be involved because of the great difference in wages and benefits.
   (b) SHD had the social responsibility to keep its employees.
   (c) Though the pound/person ratio was low in SHD, the projected cost of forging parts was only 60 percent of SIFCO's equivalents because of the low wages in China.

Mr Yu, Deputy Chief of SMEIB, met and entertained the SIFCO team. He seemed appreciative of this project and supportive of SMEIIC and SHD's positions.

The preliminary agreement reached from this negotiation included a two-phase investment plan suggested by SHD. In the first phase, SIFCO invested US$1.5 million and the Chinese side US$4.5 million. At the end of the second year, SIFCO would reinvest US$500,000 of the dividends it would earn and SHD would invest its remaining fixed assets of US$1.5 million. The equity of the joint venture would be in a ratio of 62.5 percent by SHD, 25 percent by SIFCO, and 12.5 percent by the China Investment and Development Bank. SHD would contribute buildings, land, and machinery. SIFCO would contribute cash and equipment. The bank would contribute cash.

Also, SIFCO agreed to transfer press technology together with hammer technology beginning the first year. SIFCO also agreed to act as the venture's export sales agent and be responsible for selling the forgings in the US market for US$20 million over eight years. SIFCO would receive advance commissions of US$100,000 per year for four years starting from the first year. However, the Chinese did not agree to the 10 percent commission rate. The preliminary agreement also stated that the duration of the joint venture contract would be 15 years with optional extensions at expiration.

Both parties agreed that the feasibility study would be completed by SHD with the assistance of SIFCO. SIFCO would list in detail the technology that it was to transfer. The commission rate was temporarily set at 10 percent. Prepared information would be exchanged on January 20, 1988. However, the Chinese still insisted the 1,050 employees be included and that SIFCO reduce its fees for technology transfer and the commission rate. The expected date for the discussion of the feasibility study and the pending issues was April 1989.

Back in Cleveland, SIFCO started working on the potential export of the venture's products. Some drawings of potential export products were sent to SHD and quotes were asked.

Early in 1988, SMEIIC informed SIFCO it had contacted a Hong Kong investment company, JF China Investment Ltd, which showed interest in the project. JF China's visits to Shanghai and the follow-up correspondence resulted in the understanding that SIFCO would provide technology and equipment as its equity share, SMEIIC would contribute SHD's existing equipment and building, and JF China would contribute cash. Both SIFCO and SMEIIC were happy with JF China's participation. The venture would not only solve the "two-phase investment" problem but also bring in some hard currency working capital. JF China also indicated it would like to be a "silent" partner, that is, not involved in management.

### The Third Shanghai Round

Before making another visit to Shanghai, SIFCO made careful preparations. First, O'Donnell contacted the Chinese Embassy in Washington and learned that the new Chinese government policy allowed the foreign-Chinese joint venture to determine the proper number of employees before business started. It was the responsibility of the Chinese supervising bureau of the Chinese partner (i.e., SMEIB) to assign new jobs to those not hired.

Second, SIFCO contacted potential customers for the forgings. It found that there was a good chance of selling the forgings at 65 percent of the prevailing U.S. market prices.

Also, the China Forging Industry Association invited SIFCO to give a seminar on contemporary forging technology at its annual meeting in Sichuan, China, in early May. SIFCO saw this as a good opportunity to gain more publicity in the Chinese forging industry and to contact more Chinese forging manufacturers. Though SIFCO had received a couple of invitations from Chinese firms to discuss creating a joint venture, it still believed SHD was the proper partner.

In late April, SIFCO's team visited Shanghai again. The negotiations were divided into two sessions and, in between, the SIFCO team attended the seminar in Sichuan. JF China was not present at the negotiations because of a scheduling problem. The tense and lengthy discussions revolved around the following issues:

1. **Value of SIFCO's technology.** SMEIIC and SHD still questioned the US$860,000 technology transfer fee and US$1.2 million expense. The Chinese said they were willing to pay SIFCO's experts' technical assistance and training on an actual expenditure basis. SIFCO argued that by paying this amount, all of SIFCO's commercial forging technologies including the ones developed during the term of the joint venture contract would be accessible by the venture, and a lot more costs, including opportunity cost and replacement cost, were involved in SIFCO's human resource costs. Additionally, SIFCO firmly stated that a technology transfer fee and expenses were the "keystone" for the joint venture deal.
2. **Work force.** Lengthy discussions occurred on this issue. At times, officials from SMEIB and the Foreign Economic Relation and Trade Commission participated in the meetings. SIFCO argued that the joint venture was not designed to be an employment vehicle for people but was to be a profit-making operation for its partners, who then employed the people. However, it was not until the negotiators met with Mr Ming, Vice Chairman of the Shanghai Economic Commission, who confirmed the government policy, that the Chinese relaxed a bit on this issue.
3. **Export price.** The Chinese argued that the export pricing was too low and insisted that SIFCO raise it to 75 to 80 percent of the prevailing US market prices. SIFCO tried to explain that

   (a) the higher the selling price, the more commission SIFCO would get;
   (b) it was the customer, not SIFCO, that decided the price; and
   (c) when the customer accepted the forgings, the price could be set higher than the entry price.

SIFCO's team was also told that foreign partners could bring their dividends out of China only at a hard currency ratio of RMB 3.72 if the venture had hard currency available. Otherwise the dividends could stay as an investment or be brought out at a soft currency ratio of RMB 6 to 1.

SIFCO and SMEIIC decided to start working on the design and manufacture of a flange for export in 1989.

A new memorandum of understanding contained the following agreement:

1. Technology transfer fee and expense were accepted. To save foreign exchange for the joint venture, up to US$220,000 of the expense would be paid in local currency RMB (renminbi).
2. The total number of employees should be substantially reduced. The exact number would be decided by the venture's start-up office.
3. Export price was set at 65 percent of the U.S. market price. It could be raised as the exports increased.
4. SMEIIC would appoint a general manager and SIFCO a deputy general manager.
5. To earn hard currency at the earliest possible date, both parties would work together diligently to make sample forgings for the U.S. oil market.
6. The commission rate was set at 8 percent of selling price.

### New Partner

JF China suddenly decided not to invest in the JV project in August 1988. The excuse was that JF China did not think its investment could be paid back as quickly as the feasibility study indicated. A new partner had to be found.

By the end of August, both SIFCO and SMEIIC had contacted Ek Chor Investment Co, Ltd, a subsidiary of Chia Tai Group of Companies headquartered in Thailand. Chia Tai had invested in 11 joint ventures in China. One of the joint ventures was Shanghai-Ek Chor Motorcycle Co, Ltd, which was importing quality forging parts from Japan. In September, three senior managers from Chia Tai's President's office visited SMEIIC and SHD. They disclosed that Chia Tai was considering investing in an automotive joint venture in China. In late October, Ek Chor's President and Vice President visited SMEIIC and SHD, and agreed to invest. Ek Chor wanted the venture to be the supplier of forging parts for the existing motorcycle and potential automotive subsidiaries in China. The three parties decided to discuss and finalize the arrangements in early December 1988.

### The Fourth Shanghai Round

The new agreement reached in Shanghai by the three parties added the following:

1. Chia Tai would invest US$1.5 million in cash. The equity share among SMEIIC, SIFCO, and Chia Tai would be 69.2 percent, 15.4 percent, and 15.4 percent, respectively.
2. The joint venture would give priority to the production of the forgings for Shanghai-Ek Chor Motorcycle Co, Ltd.
3. A controller would be appointed by Chia Tai.
4. The feasibility study, joint venture contract, article of association, and technology transfer agreement would be revised accordingly.
5. The Chinese partners and Chia Tai could earn commissions if they exported forgings through their own channels.

### Final Memo and the Signing of the Contract

In early March 1989, all the three partners gathered again to discuss the pending issues, particularly the work force. The final and binding memo signed included the following:

1. At the establishment of the joint venture, the total manning would be 850. Workers displaced by establishing this level would be the responsibility of the Chinese partner. The 850 workers would be under contract for employment for one year. At the end of that year, any additional workers who had been declared "surplus labor" (that is, in excess of the company's production needs) would be handled by the Chinese authority concerned.
2. Chia Tai's equity share was allowed to increase up to 30 percent in the future.
3. Official signing of the documents was set for May 1989.
   The official signing ceremony for the three documents was held on May 16, 1989 in Shanghai. It was reported that this was the first foreign-Chinese joint venture in the forging industry in China.

O'Donnell commented:

> This opportunity to enter the exciting Chinese market under the conditions we have been able to negotiate coordinates nicely with SIFCO's asset redeployment strategy. We are able to realize value for our 75 years of forging experience, both in up-front payments and through the continuing participation as an equity partner and sales agent in this newly created joint venture.

The *Plain Dealer* newspaper, PR Newswire, and Chinese local newspapers all included reports on this joint venture.

According to the agreement, the three documents were subject to the approval of the competent authorities, which would include the boards of directors for SIFCO and Chia Tai and government agencies (SMEIB and Shanghai Foreign Investment Commission) for SMEIIC. In addition, SIFCO had to obtain a U.S. export license for technology transfer to a communist country.

**Sudden Change**

On June 4, the Chinese army occupied Tiananmen Square. The whole world reacted. All media sources were full of news on China. European countries decided to impose economic sanctions against China. President Bush suspended arms and high-tech selling to China, and the U.S. State Department advised U.S. citizens not to travel to China. Exhibit 8 details U.S.-China venture policies before and after the Tiananmen Square incident. Many American firms backed out of China.

SIFCO's board meeting was scheduled for mid-July. There were so many questions to be answered and decisions to be made. SIFCO executives wondered what steps should be taken. There were many views of what was in the long-term interests of the people of China as well as of SIFCO.

EXHIBIT 1

## SIFCO INDUSTRIES, INC (CHINA)
## Selected Financial Data for 1983–1987

| | *1987* | *1986* | *1985* | *1984* | *1983* |
|---|---|---|---|---|---|
| Net sales | $63,112 | $61,323 | $59,255 | $56,008 | $54,959 |
| Operating income (loss) | 2,619 | 886 | (2,404) | (1,320) | 105 |
| Equity in net earnings (loss) of SIFCO, SA | — | — | 501 | 646 | (2,188) |
| Net gain on disposal of capital assets and investments | 815 | 1,403 | — | — | — |
| Income (loss) before income taxes | 3,434 | 2,289 | (1,903) | (674) | (2,083) |
| Provision (benefit) for income taxes | 1,374 | 505 | (1,048) | (229) | (536) |
| Income (loss) before cumulative effect of change in accounting method | 2,060 | 1,784 | (855) | (445) | (1,547) |
| Cumulative effect on prior years of change in accounting method | — | 736 | — | — | — |
| Net income (loss) | 2,060 | 2,520 | (855) | (445) | (1,547) |
| Net income (loss) per share before cumulative effect of change in accounting method | $0.95 | $0.83 | $(0.40) | $(0.21) | $(0.72) |
| Cumulative effect on prior years of change in accounting method | — | 0.34 | — | — | — |
| Net income (loss) per share | 0.95 | 1.17 | (0.40) | (0.21) | (0.72) |
| Cash dividends per share | 0.15 | 0.10 | 0.10 | 0.20 | 0.20 |
| Shareholders' equity | $29,693 | $27,898 | $25,512 | $27,561 | $28,583 |
| Shareholders' equity per share at year-end | $13.77 | $12.96 | $11.87 | $12.83 | $13.32 |
| Return on beginning shareholders' equity | 7.4% | 9.9% | (3.1%) | (1.6%) | (5.0%) |
| Long-term debt | $ 6,935 | $10,188 | $11,400 | $12,856 | $ 9,931 |
| Long-term debt-equity percent | 23.4% | 36.5% | 44.7% | 46.6% | 34.7% |
| Interest coverage | 4.5 | 3.6 | — | — | — |
| Working Capital | 12,171 | 14,471 | 10,519 | 11,203 | 12,945 |
| Current ratio | 1.8 | 2.3 | 1.8 | 2.0 | 2.5 |
| Net plant and equipment | $19,416 | $21,623 | $20,006 | $20,916 | $17,633 |
| Total assets | $55,369 | $54,655 | $54,806 | $55,853 | $50,319 |
| Shares outstanding at year-end | 2,157 | 2,152 | 2,150 | 2,148 | 2,146 |

### Stock Prices by Quarters

| | *1987* | | *1986* | |
|---|---|---|---|---|
| | *High* | *Low* | *High* | *Low* |
| First quarter | $8\frac{5}{8}$ | $6\frac{3}{4}$ | $5\frac{1}{4}$ | $4\frac{3}{8}$ |
| Second quarter | $11\frac{1}{8}$ | $7\frac{3}{8}$ | $7\frac{1}{8}$ | $4\frac{7}{8}$ |
| Third quarter | $9\frac{7}{8}$ | $8\frac{3}{8}$ | $7\frac{3}{4}$ | 6 |
| Fourth quarter | $9\frac{5}{8}$ | $8\frac{7}{8}$ | $7\frac{1}{2}$ | $5\frac{3}{4}$ |

EXHIBIT 2

**SIFCO INDUSTRIES, INC (CHINA)**
**China's Key Economic Statistics, 1970–1986 *(Estimates)*[a]**

| | *1970* | *1975* | *1980* | *1981* | *1982* | *1983* | *1984* | *1985* | *1986* |
|---|---|---|---|---|---|---|---|---|---|
| Industrial Production Index | | | | | | | | | |
| (1970 = 100) | 100 | 159 | 240 | 250 | 269 | 297 | 339 | 400 | 437 |
| Production | | | | | | | | | |
| Coal (MT millions)[b] | 327.4 | 473.0 | 620.0 | 620.0 | 666.0 | 715.0 | 789.0 | 830.0 | 870.0 |
| Crude oil (bpd millions) | 0.6 | 1.34 | 2.12 | 2.0 | 2.04 | 2.2 | 2.3 | 2.5 | 2.5 |
| Electric power (kWh billions) | 107.0 | 187.0 | 300.6 | 309.3 | 327.7 | 351.4 | 377.0 | 407.0 | 445.0 |
| Steel (MT millions) | 17.8 | 24.0 | 37.1 | 35.6 | 35.5 | 39.9 | 43.4 | 46.6 | 52.1 |
| Cotton (MT millions) | 2.0 | 2.4 | 2.7 | 3.0 | 3.6 | 4.6 | 6.2 | 4.14 | 3.34 |
| Cotton cloth (Meter billions) | 5.5 | 9.7 | 13.5 | 14.3 | 15.4 | 14.9 | 13.7 | 14.3 | 13.8 |
| Grain (MT millions) | 243.0 | 234.0 | 321.0 | 325.0 | 353.4 | 337.2 | 407.1 | 378.9 | 391.1 |
| GNP (1985 US$ billions) | 130.2 | 169.9 | 223.0 | 239.1 | 259.0 | 232.5 | 316.4 | 354.3 | 379.0 |
| Real GNP per capita | | | | | | | | | |
| Growth (yearly %) | 5.5 | 3.3 | 4.7 | 3.5 | 6.7 | 8.1 | 10.3 | 10.3 | 3.3 |
| Total foreign trade | | | | | | | | | |
| Current US$billions | 4.4 | 13.9 | 38.2 | 39.6 | 39.2 | 42.2 | 53.1 | 70.7 | 78.8 |
| Exports (fob $billions) | 2.2 | 7.1 | 18.9 | 21.6 | 22.4 | 23.7 | 27.6 | 31.3 | 30.9 |
| Imports (cif $billions) | 2.2 | 6.8 | 19.3 | 18.0 | 16.3 | 18.3 | 25.5 | 39.4 | 42.9 |
| U.S.-P.R.C. Trade[c] | | | | | | | | | |
| U.S. exports ($ millions)[d] | — | 303.0 | 3,754.0 | 3,603.0 | 2,912.0 | 2,173.0 | 3,004.0 | 3,856.0 | 3,106.0 |
| U.S. imports ($millions) | — | 170.0 | 1,161.0 | 2,062.0 | 2,502.0 | 2,477.0 | 3,381.0 | 4,224.0 | 5,240.0 |

EXHIBIT 2 (cont'd)

**U.S.-China Trade, January-September 1987**
*(in million US dollars)*

| | *September 1987* | *September 1986* | *August 1987* | *January–September 1987* | *January–September 1986* |
|---|---|---|---|---|---|
| U.S. exports | $ 304.0 | $ 216.5 | $ 278.2 | $ 2,373.3 | $ 2,421.7 |
| U.S. imports | 602.7 | 456.3 | 656.7 | 5,269.6 | 3,830.9 |
| Total | 906.7 | 672.8 | 934.9 | 7,642.9 | 6,252.6 |
| Balance | –$298.7 | –$239.8 | –$378.5 | –$2,896.3 | –$1,409.2 |

**Composition of Trade with China**
*(in million US dollars)*

| | *January–September 1987* | *January–September 1986* |
|---|---|---|
| U.S. Exports | | |
| Agricultural | $ 230.6 | $ 52.9 |
| Nonagricultural | 2,142.7 | 2,368.5 |
| U.S. Imports | | |
| Agricultural | 207.9 | 164.3 |
| Nonagricultural | 5,061.7 | 3,666.6 |

[a]Source: U.S. Central Intelligence Agency estimates as of September 1986.
[b]MT = metric tons.
[c]Source: U.S. Department of Commerce.
[d]Blank indicates data not available.

# Purba-Paschim Trading Company: A Small Business Considers Expansion to Bangladesh* 25

The Purba-Paschim Trading Corporation (PPTC), a small Minnesota-based private firm, was established in 1973 with personal equity from George Fruth and Richard Fisher. Until 1986, PPTC was engaged in importing seasonal garments and frozen fish from a number of South Asian countries, primarily Bangladesh, India, Sri Lanka, and Thailand to be sold to retailers located in the midwestern states of the U.S. market. Additionally, the company imported Italian wine to sell to several restaurant chains on a long-term contract basis.

Prior to 1985, company sales had increased about 10 percent per year, with peak sales reaching $13 million. Wine imports contributed 20 to 25 percent of the company's profit. However, with the increased competitive pressures for imported garments, especially those from Thailand, India, and Sri Lanka, it became evident that sales and profits were changing. Both Fruth and Fisher felt a need to reassess the changing situation and to develop a new strategy, given the emerging threats and opportunities facing PPTC.

Since Fruth was busy handling the Italian wine business, Fisher took the responsibility to study the current market for imported garments and to specifically identify the reasons that PPTC was now having difficulty obtaining favorable prices from the foreign manufacturers.

---

*This case was prepared by Hafiz G A Siddiqi, North South University, Bangladesh to serve as a basis for class discussion rather than to illustrate either effective or ineffective handling of an administrative situation. 

In his study, Fisher found that in 1986, PPTC had to buy merchandise from the manufacturers in Thailand, India, and Sri Lanka at higher average prices, which eventually reduced their 1986 profits from garment imports. PPTC was forced to pay higher prices because the local manufacturers of garments, particularly the larger firms, had gained sufficient international marketing expertise to begin exporting their own products without using a trading company.

Until the early 1980s, the local manufacturers in these less-developed countries preferred to market their products under some kind of joint venture arrangements with established foreign multinational companies. They did not have the capital, distribution channels, or knowledge of the market to sell their products internationally. Recently the situation had changed and most of the local manufacturers did not need any more help from foreign firms to market their merchandise.

Because the local manufacturers have developed their own marketing capability, the companies sell their total output, and thus the available sources of supply for a company like PPTC have been reduced. There are still some local firms who sell their merchandise to buyers like PPTC, although at higher prices. The price has gone up, not because of increased production costs, but because of increased demand. Fisher concluded, "Since PPTC is a relatively small buyer, we are likely to continue to lose ground against competition. This has already shown up in the reduction of our 1986 profit margin for garment imports from India, Thailand, and Sri Lanka."

Additionally, Fisher determined that if PPTC continued to depend on these countries for its garment imports, it would face another problem — quota restrictions. Recently, quota restrictions imposed by the U.S. government on the imports from nearly industrialized countries (NICs) and many less-developed countries (LDCs), including the three countries that were major sources of supply for PPTC, have been tightened.

For quite some time, the NICs and LDCs enjoyed unrestricted privileges to sell their garments in U.S. markets with reduced import duties. These privileges were granted by many of the industrialized nations to the poor countries with the intent of increasing the latter's share in world trade under the Generalized System of Preferences (GSP) proposed by the General Agreement on Tariffs and Trade (GATT).

The GSP granted by the United States was intended to help only the underdeveloped countries. Apart from the privilege of paying lower import duties during the initial stages, the United States had almost no restrictions on the quantity of garment imports from underdeveloped countries such as Bangladesh, India, Pakistan, and Sri Lanka. But as the number of countries clamoring for special treatment increased, the United States had to impose quotas for individual countries so that the benefits were equally available to all who were eligible. As a result, countries like India, Thailand, Sri Lanka, and others were assigned a quota, a fixed number of garments which they could individually export to the United States under GSP.

When Fisher had completed his description of the problems faced by PPTC, Fruth asked, "Why should the quota imposed by the U.S. government bother us? We can buy our merchandise in India and Sri Lanka and sell them here as we have been doing." Fisher responded:

> Although things vary from country to country, there is a typical pattern I can highlight. When the U.S. government assigns a quota to say, Sri Lanka, the Sri Lankan government or its designated

agency allocates to the eligible manufacturers or exporters a certain quantity or percentage of the country's total quota for the year. To be entitled to this allocation, a firm has to go through a very complex process. Foreign firms having wholly owned or joint venture arrangements usually receive allocation; however, in most cases, the amount is usually smaller than the company's capacity. Due to political and other contacts, there are some local firms who receive an allocation much higher than their capability to produce. These firms sell their quota at a premium price in the "officially unrecognized market." The general impact of this transaction is a substantial increase in the merchandise prices a company like PPTC has to pay to the local suppliers.

"That means we need to look for new sources of supply in the very near future. We will not be able to compete with the large and established local exporting firms who have larger quotas. And the prices we pay the small firms would also be higher because they can sell their quota to the large locals if we don't pay the higher prices," concluded Fruth.

"That's right," agreed Fisher. "As I see it we have two problems. First, the stronger bargaining power of the local manufacturers who have established their own marketing network, and second, the tightening of the quota restrictions imposed by the U.S. government. Our immediate problem is to identify what we're going to do to ensure PPTC's survival and growth."

Recently Fisher attended a seminar on U.S. trade relations with third world countries. In that seminar he learned that the Overseas Private Investment Corporation (OPIC) was created by the U.S. government to extend financial and other assistance to U.S. firms interested in investments in LDCs. He became convinced that PPTC should become involved in direct foreign investment in manufacturing the garments that they were currently importing into the United States. If PPTC could manufacture its products in one of the Third World countries, it could increase its margin and could in fact increase its sales by reducing prices since the demand for garments is highly price elastic.

Through initial rough calculations, Fisher found that if PPTC could establish one garment factory by investing approximately $3 million under a joint venture agreement with a local partner, the company could increase its present profit margin by 110 percent. Additionally, the joint venture should develop new opportunities for PPTC to expand its business.

Fisher thought it would be a good idea to find a country that is not subject to strict import quotas, where the labor is cheap, where there is no problem of procuring the necessary raw materials and other accessories to keep the plant operational, and most importantly, where adequate government support and protection would be available. Bangladesh appeared to be a country that met the needs Fisher had outlined.

During the eight weeks that Fisher collected information on Bangladesh, he met Abdur Razzaque, an attorney who specialized in international business law. Originally from Bangladesh and now a U.S. citizen, Razzaque is familiar with the quota problems for garment imports. He had handled two cases of international commercial disputes between U.S. and Sri Lankan firms that had plants at the Katunayake export processing zone in Sri Lanka.

While he was dealing with these cases, Razzaque studied conditions and regulations which usually apply in the export processing zones in South Korea, Taiwan, Malaysia, India, and Bangladesh. After reviewing the data provided by Fisher, he was convinced that it was a commercially viable opportunity for PPTC to establish a joint venture plant in the Chittagong export processing zone (CEPZ) in Bangladesh. Razzaque found it so attractive that he offered to provide one-third of the financing. He also expressed his willingness to use his contacts in Bangladesh to obtain government approval to establish the joint venture firm.

Fruth still had reservations and wanted to make certain that he and Fisher were thoroughly prepared before they met with Razzaque to discuss an investment in Bangladesh. Fisher agreed to develop a summary of everything he had learned about the opportunity (see Figure 1).

FIGURE 1

**MEMORANDUM**

**TO:** Mr George Fruth

**FROM:** Mr Richard Fisher

**SUBJECT:** Summary of Information Gathered for Evaluating Joint-Venture Production in Bangladesh

**INFORMATION FROM THE U.S. DEPARTMENT OF COMMERCE**

Since PPTC is already engaged in the import business, we have had frequent contacts with the U.S. Department of Commerce (DOC). I knew that the International Trade Administration (ITA) of the DOC would have some information on the investment opportunities in Bangladesh.

After talking with officials of ITA/DOC in Washington, I learned that the government of Bangladesh has recently enacted a number of laws to encourage and attract foreign investment in their country. In 1980, the government of Bangladesh passed the Foreign Private Investment (Promotion and Protection) Act, which established a legal framework for investment by guaranteeing protection against nationalization or expropriation, promising full indemnification, repatriation of investment, and fair treatment of all commercial claims. Additionally, the Bilateral Investment Treaty was signed in March 1986 between Bangladesh and the United States. It provided for unrestricted currency transfer, compensation for expropriation, dispute settlement procedures acceptable to the U.S. government, and the avoidance of double taxation. This bilateral agreement reduced both political and commercial risks for U.S. investors.

Further efforts have been made to encourage U.S. investment. The governments of the United States and Bangladesh have combined efforts to establish the Bangladesh–United States Business Council, located in Washington, D.C. The council acts as a chamber of commerce whose primary function is to gather and distribute information to American businesspeople who make inquiries concerning investment and other opportunities in Bangladesh.

In talking with the Business Council, I found confirmation for the opportunities in Bangladesh for PPTC. They suggested I contact James Novak, who has prepared a report on how U.S. investors could utilize the "excellent labor force" of Bangladesh. Novak worked as the representative of the Asia Foundation in Bangladesh from 1980 to 1984. I contacted the Asia Foundation office in San Francisco and gathered new insight from Novak. He suggested we consider establishing a factory in Bangladesh's CEPZ to take advantage of the special incentives the government of Bangladesh provides for U.S. investors.

## Introduction to Bangladesh

Bangladesh, previously called East Pakistan, emerged as an independent state in 1971. Located in the northeastern part of the Indian subcontinent, it is one of the most densely populated countries of the world with more than 105 million people in a land area the size of Wisconsin. It is also one of the poorest countries, with a gross domestic product (GDP) of less than $15 billion and per capita gross national product (GNP) of approximately $160. About 50 percent of its GDP is generated in the agriculture sector. The industrial and manufacturing sectors in Bangladesh are modest in size, accounting for only about 15 percent and 9 percent of GDP, respectively. Like most of the LDCs, efforts are made to strengthen the country's industrial base. To implement its economic development plans, it is highly dependent on foreign aid, particularly from the United States.

Development of import substitution and export-oriented industries are given high priority. The government's industrial policies are geared to the growth and development of export-oriented and import-substitution industries, which are considered essential for earning/saving scarce foreign exchange and the creation of new jobs.

In the past, Bangladesh had only three major exports: jute and jute goods, hides and skins, and tea. In an effort to reduce the dependence on the traditional exports, policy has shifted to accord higher priority to increasing exports of nontraditional items such as garments, shrimp, and leather goods. Industrial policies have recently been reformed under the guidance of the World Bank and the International Monetary Fund, the two major financing institutions for Bangladesh. The reforms include a more realistic exchange rate, import liberalization, and improved support for the private sector.

## Government Bureaucracy: Approval Procedures

As in other LDCs, there is an incredible amount of time wasted in obtaining approval for an investment proposal. The government has taken special steps to speed up the process and reduce bureaucratic red tape. In 1986, the investment approval system was liberalized and almost all restrictions on private investment were lifted. The revised industrial policy reserves only a few industries for the public sector. All other industries (125 of the total of 144) are now treated as free sectors which do not require prior approval if the investment is funded from the investor's own resources.

## Foreign Investment in Bangladesh

Because Bangladesh is a new and developing country, foreign investment is very low. As of 1984, total foreign investment was estimated to be as little as US$15.7 million, with an estimated annual average increase of US$4 million. According to the U.S. Department of Commerce, the government of Bangladesh recognizes that foreign investment could play a major role in the development of the country and has taken a number of important steps to improve the investment climate. As a result, foreign investors have started considering Bangladesh as a potential export platform.

If PPTC invests in Bangladesh, it would not be the first U.S. company to do so. Pfizer, Squibb, and Singer, among others, already have direct investments in Bangladesh. The United States ranks ninth in investment in Bangladesh, behind the United Kingdom, France, Hong Kong, South Korea, Singapore, the Netherlands, Canada, and Sweden.

## The Garment Industry in Bangladesh

The garment industry is relatively new in Bangladesh. Although initiated in the 1960s, it did not gain visibility until the late 1970s. When the United States and Western European countries imposed quotas on the imports of garments from Singapore, Hong Kong, Taiwan, and other major suppliers of garments, manufacturers looked for countries which had cheap labor but were not yet subject to quota restrictions. Bangladesh was such a country in the 1970s.

The country had abundant cheap and quality labor, but suffered from a high rate of unemployment. It was therefore natural for foreign investors to take advantage of the quota-free status of Bangladesh by setting up joint ventures in collaboration with Bangladeshi entrepreneurs. In most cases, the foreign partners had equity participation in hard currency and undertook the marketing responsibility. The local partners bore the primary responsibility for ensuring the needed supply of adequately trained workers who were able to perform the cutting, marking, and trimming activities.

Only labor from Bangladesh is used in manufacturing the garments. More than 80 percent of the garment factory workers are women. The employers prefer to hire female rather than male workers, which has created a cultural conflict in this Muslim-dominated society. Most of the country's factories are located in Dhaka, the capital city, and Chittagong, the port city.

The Bangladesh garment industry is totally dependent on imported raw materials. To manufacture export-quality garments, a company needs high-quality fabrics, threads, buttons, and other accessories, including packing materials. None is manufactured in Bangladesh; everything has to be imported. Despite this dependence, the garment industry has experienced phenomenal growth during the 1980s (see Exhibit 1).

The usual procedure is for a buyer, such as Sears or JC Penney's, to contact a garment manufacturer in Bangladesh to sign a contract for cutting, sewing, trimming, packaging, and shipping a series of orders at an agreed schedule. The buyer will provide the designs and detailed specifications for fabric, thread, buttons, and so on to the Bangladeshi firm. Additionally, the buyer will provide the sources (name of the countries and suppliers) from which the various components will have to be imported. If necessary, to procure the correct materials and components, the buyer helps the Bangladeshi firm to open back-to-back letters of credit against which the suppliers ship the materials to Bangladesh. The supplier is paid after the garments are manufactured, using the imported materials, and shipped to the original buyer. This kind of trade financing has been beneficial to Bangladesh.

## A Note on Export Processing Zones

An export processing zone (EPZ) is a legally demarcated geographical enclave in which an authorized firm can bring in imported inputs necessary for manufacturing or processing products exclusively for the purpose of exporting, without paying customs duties. The raw materials, components, accessories, packaging materials, plants, equipment, spare parts, and so on are imported to assemble, manufacture, or process the final products.

Although sometimes used interchangeably, an EPZ is quite different from a free trade zone. Although the former is exclusively for export promotion, the latter is used by both exporters and domestic importers. Usually strict application of customs regulations discourages a firm from engaging in the export business. On the other hand, almost all governments want to increase exports. One way to increase exports is to reduce customs barriers. By establishing EPZs, a government virtually removes many bottlenecks. Because the exporters do not have to pay taxes, their cost of production decreases. They can therefore sell the product at a lower price, which is likely to increase demand.

It should be noted that freedom from customs regulations is not the only incentive an EPZ provides. Within an EPZ, the host government generally develops required physical facilities and the necessary infrastructure such as readily available power and water supplies, a sewerage system, and telecommunications. In addition, most EPZs provide building facilities to house production, plant, equipment, and inventories. The EPZs are used mostly by the developing countries as a device to attract foreign investors. The EPZs offer to the investors from the United States, Western Europe, and Japan a wide range of support services as well as fiscal and financial incentives.

Fiscal incentives include tax holidays or reductions in corporate taxes and exemption from import duties, excise duties, and sales taxes, among others. The financial incentives include the availability of easy loans and credits, freedom from exchange controls, and easy repatriation of capital invested. The host government's objectives are to increase foreign exchange earnings, to create employment, and to gain access to international markets through the multinational corporations who establish factories in the EPZ.

The EPZs are more common in the LDCs. More than 30 developing countries have established EPZs. Within Asia, the governments of South Korea, India, Sri Lanka, Malaysia, Indonesia, Taiwan, China, and Bangladesh have authorized EPZs.

## Bangladesh Export Processing Zone at Chittagong

In 1982, the Bangladesh government created a new organization, the Bangladesh Export Processing Zone Authority (BEPZA), which would be responsible for developing and managing EPZs in Bangladesh. By 1988, BEPZA had established and developed one EPZ in the port city of Chittagong. The zone is located 2.41 kilometers from the principal seaport and 7.24 kilometers from the international airport.

Three types of investments can be made in the Chittagong (CEPZ):

**Type A:** 100-percent foreign-owned (including investments by Bangladesh nationals ordinarily residing abroad). The total investment in the project including the cost of construction, raw materials, and the working capital requirements are financed in foreign exchange from overseas.

**Type B:** Joint ventures between foreign partners and Bangladeshi entrepreneurs residing in Bangladesh. The total cost of capital machinery, spare parts, and raw materials may be provided by the foreign partners to be brought in from abroad. The Bangladeshi partners may contribute working capital in the local currency.

**Type C:** Owned 100-percent by Bangladeshi entrepreneurs residing in Bangladesh.

### Fiscal and Financial Incentives

A number of fiscal and financial incentives are offered to companies who locate in the CEPZ.

1. Zone enterprises are allowed a five-year tax holiday for all industries. Upon expiration of the initial five-year holiday, rebates of 50 percent on income tax on export sales are allowed.

2. Income tax exemption of oil salaries of foreign technicians for up to three years.
3. Income tax exemption on interest of borrowed capital from overseas.
4. Dividend income tax exemption for nonresident shareholders during the period of the tax holiday if the dividends are reinvested in the same project.

**Free Import and Export**

Import of capital machinery and spares, instruments, apparatuses and appliances, including testing quality control equipment and parts thereof, materials and equipment for the construction of building and factories in the zone, and imported items such as raw materials and packaging materials destined for re-export are freely allowed into the zone. Additionally, complete exemption from excise tax and export duties on goods produced is offered.

Other Privileges

1. Remittance of approved royalties and technical fees.
2. Employment of foreign technicians wherever required.
3. Exemption from national import policy restrictions.
4. No maximum or minimum ceiling on investment.
5. Freedom for sourcing raw materials, machinery, construction contractors, etc.
6. Freedom for appointing shipping and C&F agents, etc.
7. Availability of "one-window service" facility. The investors need to deal only with the BEPZA for all necessary correspondence.

**Performance of the Chittagong Export Processing Zone**

Exhibits 2 through 7 provide additional insights into the functioning of the CEPZ.

## Facilities at CEPZ

To facilitate the establishment of the export-oriented industrial units in the EPZ, the BEPZA developed the necessary infrastructure. The land is owned by the government, developed into factories and offices, and then handed over to the investors. The BEPZA constructs what they call "standard buildings" to house the factories for apparel and other industries approved by the government. Some companies construct their own factory buildings according to their own specifications. As of July 1988, eight local and foreign firms had constructed their own factory buildings and nine firms were renting "standard buildings" provided by the BEPZA.

After reading the information in the memo provided by Fisher, Fruth thought the opportunities for PPTC in Bangladesh appeared to be favorable. Perhaps it was time for the company to grow. He decided to review the material one more time before discussing it with Fisher. Their meeting with Razzaque tomorrow should be very interesting.

EXHIBIT 1

**PURBA-PASCHIM TRADING COMPANY**
**Exports of Garments from Bangladesh**
(in million taka)

| *Year* | *Value* |
|---|---|
| 1980–1981 | 120 |
| 1981–1982 | 171 |
| 1982–1983 | 348 |
| 1983–1984 | 983 |
| 1984–1985 | 1,209 |

Note: The Bangladesh currency is the taka (Tk). The current exchange rate is US$1=Tk32. During the last five years, the value of the taka depreciated by some 30 percent. One crore = ten million taka.

EXHIBIT 2

**PURBA-PASCHIM TRADING COMPANY**
**Industries Approved**
**March 1983–May 1987**

| *Type* | *Total Number of Industries* | *Total Investment Proposed (000 US$)* | *Total Number of Jobs to be Created* |
|---|---|---|---|
| A | 5 | 9,430 | 2,584 |
| B | 15 | 8,809 | 2,433 |
| C | 10 | 3,215 | 840 |

EXHIBIT 3

**PURBA-PASCHIM TRADING COMPANY**
**Industries Approved**
**June 1987–September 1988**

| *Type* | *Total Number of Industries* | *Total Investment Proposed (000 US$)* | *Total Number of Jobs to be Created* |
|---|---|---|---|
| A | 3 | 2,033 | 434 |
| B | 1 | 2,500 | 270 |
| C | 1 | 354 | 194 |

EXHIBIT 4

**PURBA-PASCHIM TRADING COMPANY**
**Descriptions of the Industries Approved**
**After June 1987**

Banla-Thai Nishikawa Ltd, a wholly owned Bangladeshi company, established at a cost of $1.54 million to manufacture imitation jewelry.

Tariq-Azim Textile Mills, a local-foreign joint venture textile manufacturing enterprise, set up at a cost of $2.5 million.

Youngones Corporation, a wholly foreign-owned ready-made garments manufacturing company, established at a cost of $3 million.

Young An Hat Co, a wholly foreign-owned company, set up at a cost of $0.6 million to manufacture headwear.

International AAB, a wholly foreign-owned electronics company, set up at a cost of $2.93 million.

EXHIBIT 5

**PURBA-PASCHIM TRADING COMPANY**
**Distribution of Industries**

| *Category* | *Number of Units Approved* | *Number of Units in Operation* |
|---|---|---|
| Garments | 8 | 6 |
| Textiles | 3 | 1 |
| Terrytowel | 9 | 6 |
| Steel chain | 1 | 1 |
| Electronics | 5 | 1 |
| Services | 2 | 2 |
| Acrylic sheet | 1 | — |
| Chemical and perfume | 2 | — |
| Footwear | 2 | — |
| Furniture | 1 | — |
| Imitation jewelry | 1 | — |
| Total | 35 | 17 |

EXHIBIT 6

**PURBA-PASCHIM TRADING COMPANY**
**Additional Information on the Units in Operation**

| *Type* | *Total Number of Units* | *Total Investment (000 US$)* | *Number of Jobs Created* |
|---|---|---|---|
| A | 6 | 10,330 | 2,297 |
| B | 7 | 5,500 | 977 |
| C | 4 | 1,458 | 76 |
| Total | 17 | 17,288 | 3,350 |

EXHIBIT 7

**PURBA-PASCHIM TRADING COMPANY**
**Export Performance of Chittagong EPZ Enterprises**

| *Year* | *Export Value (in 000 US$)* | *Export Value in Crore Taka* |
|---|---|---|
| 1983–1984 | 2,164 | 0.51 |
| 1984–1985 | 4,450 | 13.79 |
| 1985–1986 | 7,400 | 22.94 |
| 1986–1987 | 16,474 | 51.07 |
| 1987–1988 | 23,811 | 73.80 |

# DCM-Toyota Ltd (India)* 26

In the five years since the start of the joint venture between DCM Limited of India and the Toyota Motor Company of Japan to produce light commercial vehicles (LCVs), a great deal of progress has been made. The DCM-Toyota Ltd (DTL) plant in Surajpur is now building a world-class vehicle, one that Mr Awasthi, the company's executive director, believes is by far the best of its kind manufactured in India. The DTL LCV, called the "Dyna," is equipped with an engine that is more powerful, rugged, and fuel-efficient than its competitors. It has a sturdy construction, and its plush interior and exterior finish are superior to those of most Indian-built cars. The Dyna embodies the latest in LCV technology from Japan; in fact, certain components have even been strengthened for the harsh Indian driving conditions. The DTL plant is modern, well-engineered, and well-managed, and operates under the Toyota Production System. The employees are highly motivated, well-educated, and thoroughly trained. Even Toyota is impressed with the plant and with the high productivity of its Indian workers. And yet the company has been slow to make a profit. In fiscal year 1988, DTL lost Rs57,133,420 on Rs904,902,313 in total sales.[1] The company's performance continues to improve, however; it reported a modest profit of Rs3 million in the first quarter of 1989. The strong yen and stiff competition have made things difficult for DTL. In 1984,

---

* This case was written by Madhav S Shriram (DCM Shriram Industries, Inc), Alan G Robinson (University of Massachusetts at Amherst), and Dean M Schroeder (Valparaiso University) to serve as a basis for class discussion and is not intended to illustrate either effective or ineffective handling of an administrative situation. 

[1] The February 1989 exchange rate for Rupees (Rs) was approximately US$1 = Rs15.

when DTL was in the planning phase, the exchange rate was 21 yen to the rupee. In February 1989 the rupee bought only 8.25 yen. Critical LCV components imported from Japan now cost two and a half times more than planned. Three of DTL's competitors, which are also Indo-Japanese joint ventures, are suffering from the rapid rise in the yen as well. Eicher-Mitsubishi, for example, experienced a production cost increase, attributable entirely to the stronger yen, of Rs24,000 per vehicle from May to November 1988.

## Background

### DCM Ltd

DCM Ltd is the 14th-largest multiproduct manufacturing company in India. Its product line includes textiles, sugar, both industrial and potable alcohol, fertilizers, edible oils, business machines, cement, polyvinylchloride (PVC), and foundry products. In 1988 its sales were approximately 6.5 billion rupees and it employed 25,000 people.

DCM was founded in 1889 as Delhi Cloth Mills Ltd, largely through the efforts of Gopal Rai, the company's first secretary (i.e., top manager). The venture, which produced textiles, was so successful that it paid its first dividend to investors only six months later. When Gopal Rai's health failed in 1906, his younger brother, Madan Mohan Lal, took over as secretary. Shortly thereafter, the company began to falter, primarily because of the high prices it had to pay for raw cotton. The poor performance persisted until Shri Ram, son of Madan Mohan Lal, became actively involved in the company. It was Shri Ram who was the dominant figure in the growth of DCM into a successful conglomerate.

When he was in high school, Shri Ram got a job selling cloth as a shop assistant. Although it was then standard practice to stretch the cloth on the measuring table and shortchange customers by 2 inches per yard, Shri Ram gave his customers not only the full yard, but an extra 2 inches as well. The owner of the shop was furious when he found out, but soon realized that customers kept coming back and that his volume of business was growing quite rapidly. Shri Ram would later bring to DCM this philosophy of treating people fairly.

When Shri Ram first came to work at DCM, the firm was losing money. Shri Ram convinced his father to appoint him head of ginning, which had the worst record of all the departments. By introducing a system of worker incentives (a radical idea at that time in India), Shri Ram turned the department around in short order. The sudden increase in production and profits persuaded an initially reluctant Board of Directors to approve the company-wide implementation of these incentives. After this success, Shri Ram was able to talk the Board into giving him control of the other departments as well. Within three years of his joining the company, Shri Ram became the *de facto* secretary of DCM and his father a mere figurehead.

World War I brought the company an important break. The British, who had previously repressed the Indian textile industry in order to protect their domestic manufacturers, now encouraged it to produce as much as possible. Through the manufacture of canvas tents for troops, DCM grew rapidly and was able to lay down a financial base from which to continue its growth. In World War II DCM started to manufacture hurricane lamps and to diversify into agricultural products such as sugar and fertilizers. These moves were very natural for two reasons. First, the economy of India was largely based on agriculture (which, even in 1987, accounted for 80 percent of GNP). Second, the government, which wished to increase domestic production in order to reduce imports, was encouraging all companies to diversify as much as possible.

By the time India became independent from Great Britain in 1947, DCM had grown into one of the five largest business houses in India. Since Shri Ram's death in 1965, the firm has remained under the control of the Shriram family. In 1985 Bansi Dhar, a grandson of Shri Ram, was appointed chairman and managing director. Throughout all of DCM's divisions, the company still strives to deliver the high quality and extra value implicit in Shri Ram's 2 extra inches. For example, the company's two sugar plants adhere to the rigid international quality standards for crystal size, purity, opacity, evenness of grain, and speed of dissolution in water, rather than the much-less-stringent Indian standards.

### The Business Climate

India, a nation of over 800 million people, is the largest democracy in the world. It is an emerging nation with a wide gap between the rich and the poor. While the average Indian worker earns less than Rs15 ($1) per day, India boasts a world-class scientific community, excellent academic institutions (including five institutes of technology and the world-famous Tata Institute), as well as the ability to produce nuclear weapons and loft satellites into geosynchronous orbit. India has a tightly regulated and mixed economy. Although the private sector is very active, most of the core industries, such as mining and extraction (of coal, iron ore, and gold), steel, banking, electric power, airlines, shipping, railways, communications, and the postal service are nationalized. Some industries were taken over by the state owing to fears of exploitation by foreigners or monopolies, others because of their immense capital requirements or the desire to subsidize their products and services for the general public. By and large, these state-run industries are inefficient and poorly managed. For example, in 1989 the world price of steel was half of what it cost to produce it in India.

India's infrastructure can make industrial business operations quite challenging. The unreliability of electric power provides a good example. Because it is subject to frequent outages and disruptions, most medium-to-large firms have captive power generation plants to avoid the problems that an interruption in the power supply of even a fraction of a second can cause to equipment and instrumentation. An infrastructural issue of special concern to DTL is the quality of the Indian road system. Many of the roads were built shortly after independence from Britain and were designed to last for only five years. *India Today* recently called attention to the poor condition of these roads and to the poor management which compounds the problem:

> Though India ranks fourth in the world, after the U.S., Brazil, and the Soviet Union in road length, the quality of the road network would embarrass many small African countries. And the World Bank has categorized India as a country where both the road network and road building technology are obsolete . . .
>
> The fact that many officials connected with the road sector have been busy feathering their own nests has further added to the collapse of the system. The states' Public Works Departments (PWDs), which are responsible for both okaying road-building contracts and approving the work are notorious for corruption. . . . Senior officials estimate that often as much as half the money allocated for the construction of roads may disappear into the pockets of corrupt officials and private contractors. There have been instances of roads being built only on paper in remote areas — all the money having been creamed off.
>
> It has not helped matters that other officials connected with the road sector are equally corrupt. Overloaded trucks are a major cause of road deterioration, yet truckers defy the law with impunity

> by bribing the highway police. All-India Motor Transport Congress Secretary-General Chitaranjan Das points out that bribing the police is now such an established practice that even trucks which are not overloaded have to fork over money. The Income Department even accepts these payments as legitimate expenses incurred by truck operations.

Poor road conditions, in turn, inflict heavy damage on the nation's vehicles — an estimated Rs20 billion annually in excess wear and tear.

In 1947 India inherited a comprehensive system of licensing from the departing British. The system had been set up during World War II to ensure the efficient and equitable allocation of scarce resources such as power, coal, steel, cement, foreign exchange, petroleum products, and rail capacity. Although the system worked well initially, it gradually became more bureaucratic and complex. Nothing could be done until all the appropriate officials had approved and granted licenses. Typical business operations required clearances from the government for foreign exchange, power usage, raw materials, imports, and loans.

In 1980, however, Indira Gandhi was elected Prime Minister and began liberalizing the private sector. She also encouraged joint ventures with foreign companies, not only for technology transfer, but to open export markets as well. Licenses for joint ventures with foreign companies could now be obtained with greater speed and ease, and hundreds of foreign joint ventures were formed. In the motor vehicle industry they were begun with such companies as Toyota, Mitsubishi, Mazda, Nissan, Honda, and Suzuki.

In 1984 Mrs Gandhi was assassinated, and her son, Rajiv Gandhi, became the new Prime Minister. He continued to improve the Indian business climate: marginal income tax rates were reduced from as high as 97.75 percent down to 50 percent, quotas on imports of many capital goods and raw materials were abolished, and tariffs were lowered. These moves resulted in the rapid growth of exports and foreign investment in India. Industrial investment jumped 50 percent in the first year of the new policies. The stock market rose to over 250 percent above its 1980 level and hit new highs throughout fiscal 1986, and interest rates declined dramatically. New capital raised in the market by the private sector rose from almost none in 1980 to Rs10.6 billion in fiscal 1985, and again to Rs24.3 billion in fiscal 1987. Capital raised in the 1990 market is expected to set a new record. Other signs of increasing sophistication in the private financial markets include a rapidly growing number of institutional investors, and new opportunities for foreign investors through mutual fund portfolios of Indian stocks.

Although the business climate has improved considerably since 1980, many problems remain. Business leaders are calling for increased privatization of government-controlled firms in order to increase the quality and efficiency of the country's infrastructure as well as to help lower the national debt. Nevertheless, moves in these directions continue to meet with considerable resistance, since privatization is heresy to many powerful special interest groups in India. Another factor that may slow India's future growth is a projected shortage of electric power brought on by the increase in economic activity. Scheduled hydroelectric projects, which require long lead times under the best conditions, are being slowed by environmental concerns, as are new coal-burning power plants. Current government policy is shifting toward generating electric power with natural gas so as to make use of some recent major natural gas discoveries in India and to take advantage of the fact that its plants are cleaner and can be brought online quickly. Unfortunately, since there may not be enough capital available to make the needed improvements in the electric power infrastructure, continuing power shortages may slow industrial development.

## The LCV Market

The road system has absorbed most of the extra transportation capacity required by India's rapidly growing economy. In 1951 only 11 percent of Indian goods were transported by road; the rest were moved by rail or water. By 1986 this figure had grown to 50 percent; it is projected to reach 62 percent by the year 2001. Consequently, the demand for commercial vehicles has also been rising. Yet until 1980 there was a large gap in the product range of trucks available. The only trucks in the market were either small pickup trucks less than 1 ton in capacity, or full-sized trucks with a capacity of 7 tons or greater.[2] Very few LCVs, trucks with capacity ranging from 2 to 6 tons, were manufactured in India. The government projected a national market of 24,000 LCVs annually in 1985, which it expected to grow to 47,000 by 1991, the annual sales of LCVs since 1984 and the projections through 1991 made by DTL's marketing staff (see Exhibit 1).

Over the last decade, eight companies, four of them joint ventures with Japanese firms, have begun producing LCVs in India. The Indo-Japanese joint ventures include those of DCM and Toyota, Eicher Motors and Mitsubishi, Swaraj and Mazda, and Allwyn and Nissan (see Exhibit 2 for product volume and market share information for all eight firms). Five of them manufacture LCVs rated at 2 tons, the others produce 3.5-ton LCVs. The market for 2-ton trucks is dominated by two domestic companies, Bajaj and TELCO. Bajaj is known in India for its relatively small, three-wheeled delivery vehicles, while TELCO holds a hefty 75 percent of the full-size truck market. Mahindra, Standard, and Allwyn-Nissan (the only Indo-Japanese joint venture producing a 2-ton vehicle) all have relatively small market shares in the 2-ton market. All three of the 3.5-ton LCV manufacturers are Indo-Japanese joint ventures and produce very similar vehicles. DTL was the first of these companies to begin production; the other two were less than a year behind.

TELCO, the Tata Engineering and Locomotive Company, has been manufacturing large trucks in India since 1964; the LCV is the smallest vehicle it has ever produced. Most of TELCO's truck manufacturing technology is derived from commercial ties with Daimler-Benz of West Germany in the 1960s. Today TELCO is an entirely Indian company that relies exclusively on Indian design and engineering technology. TELCO produces two kinds of LCV: Models 407 and 608. The Model 608, a 3-tonner, has yet to be successfully launched into the market. It has been introduced several times but has been pulled back because of technical problems with the gearbox and other components. The Model 407, priced at Rs174,000, is much less expensive than the Indo-Japanese joint-venture LCVs, all of which are priced around Rs230,000. In addition, the 407 is simple and rugged in design. Although rated for loads of up to only 1.5 tons, it is in fact capable of carrying up to 4 tonnes. Its technology is older and commonplace. When a 407 breaks down, which happens quite frequently, it can be fixed in almost any village shop. The 407 gets relatively poor gas mileage of 8 to 10 km/liter, whereas all of the Indo-Japanese joint

---

[2]A ton, or metric ton, is equal to approximately 1.13 tons.

venture vehicles deliver approximately 12 km/liter. Its dominance of the LCV market is credited to its low cost, rugged construction, ease of repair, and to TELCO's name recognition — the company's full-sized trucks are the most common on India's highways.

Bajaj manufactures two-wheeled scooters and three-wheeled delivery vehicles. The market for scooters is very large because they are a primary mode of transportation for a large percentage of the population of India. Bajaj entered the 2-ton LCV market by purchasing the Matador line from the Firodia family. The Bajaj LCV comes in two standard configurations: a small bus or delivery van and a fixed-sided truck. The company's strategy is to pursue market share by maintaining the very low price of Rs100,000. Although the Matador has front-wheel drive and a fairly fuel efficient engine, DTL executives do not regard it as state-of-the-art and report that the vehicles often develop maintenance problems after about three years.

Mahindra manufactures four-wheel drive vehicles, including jeeps, which it supplies to the Indian armed forces. The military has also been a primary market for Mahindra's LCV. However, the company has been doing poorly in the civilian LCV market. It recently entered into a technical collaboration with Peugeot to produce an efficient diesel engine. It also purchased Allwyn-Nissan.

Allwyn-Nissan's vehicle is rated at 2 tons, which puts it in more direct competition with the TELCO 407 than with the products of the other Indo-Japanese joint ventures. Allwyn is a state-owned company; the joint venture was also run by the government, which provided most of its business. Sales have been reported to be very low. Rumor has it that workers are called in to manufacture trucks only after the company receives orders. To date, Allwyn-Nissan has not been much of a factor in the LCV market.

Standard is an automobile manufacturer based in Madras, in southern India. It sells primarily in the south and is not a major player in the LCV market. In fact, its LCV operation is now virtually shut down.

Eicher-Mitsubishi was the last to enter the field, beginning production in July 1986, and is so far the most successful of the four Indo-Japanese joint ventures. Eicher is one of the finest tractor manufacturers in India. By avoiding such expensive capital purchases as air-conditioning, conveyor belts, automation, and a modern new plant, great short-term savings and a much lower break-even point were made possible. Its 3.5-ton vehicle is almost identical to the DTL Dyna and, until recently, sold for the same price. (Unlike the Dyna, however, its trucks are not undercoated or painted electrostatically.) Much of the credit for Eicher-Mitsubishi's success is given to its Chairman and Managing Director, Mr Vikram Lal, who has been described as a human dynamo. Another factor is the company's dealership network; its trucks are sold through its tractor dealerships, which are well-established throughout India. Not surprisingly, the company makes many individual sales of trucks to farmers and independent truckers.

Swaraj-Mazda is a government-owned tractor manufacturer in the state of Punjab, a rich agricultural region of northern India. The company, which dominates the Punjab tractor market, intends to anchor its LCV market there as well. It began producing LCVs in October 1985. Although its truck is almost identical to the Dyna, DTL has nevertheless managed to be quite successful in Punjab, primarily because of an aggressive local DTL dealer.

## The DCM-Toyota Joint Venture

### History

In 1980 DCM Ltd proposed to Toyota a joint venture to manufacture LCVs in India. The two companies were well-matched in several respects. Both had similar backgrounds in textiles from which each had diversified, and each had a long tradition of high-quality manufacturing and providing excellent value to the customer.

Established in 1937, Toyota Motor Corporation is the largest automobile manufacturer in Japan and the second-largest in the world. Interestingly, its parent company, Toyoda Automatic Loom Works, once sold textile manufacturing machinery to Delhi Cloth Mills in 1930. In addition to 11 plants in Japan, the company has 30 plants in 15 other countries. It employs over 86,000 people and sells its vehicles in 140 countries. Non-Japanese sales account for almost half of its total production.

After the partners verified the high market potential with their own extensive surveys, DCM-Toyota Ltd (DTL) was incorporated on August 1, 1983 with its registered offices at the DCM building in New Delhi. Toyota took 26 percent of the equity and DCM 33 percent; the remaining 41 percent was raised in the Indian stock market, where it was oversubscribed seven-fold. The new company planned a plant to manufacture 15,000 LCVs per year, with a maximum annual capacity, with overtime, of 18,000 trucks. It was sited in Surajpur, a town of approximately 20,000 people, located about 35 kilometers southeast of New Delhi.[3] Because it was in an area targeted for economic development by the government, DTL benefited from some considerable tax breaks. All research and development costs are 100-percent deductible in perpetuity; 25 percent of DTL's profits are tax exempt for 7 years after plant startup; and 20 percent of the profits derived from the LCV business are exempt from taxes for 10 years after the first LCV is sold.

The new plant operates under the Toyota Production System (TPS). To learn it, foremen and managers from all levels in DTL were sent to Toyota City in Japan for training. During their absence the personnel department carefully selected workers from the local area who fitted desired profiles. TPS selection guidelines require all workers to have a high-school education or an ITT (technical school) diploma. They must be under 23 years of age, since older applicants are considered too inflexible and fixed in their thinking. Local villagers are preferred; at present they constitute some 120 of the total of 143 production workers. In addition to undergoing intelligence, aptitude, and dexterity tests, applicants must also undertake a complete medical examination, including psychological screening to assess whether each applicant is a "good person in heart and mind."

The workers are trained in the Toyota style, beginning with talks and video shows about Toyota. They are taught the aims and values of the TPS, which are rooted in the motto "good thinking, good product." They learn about Quality Circles, *kaizen* (continuous improvement), *muda* (waste), *poka-yoke* (mistake-proof devices), *kanban* (control cards), and all the other tools of the TPS, and also receive training on truck assembly and the DTL plant. The goal of this training is to instill a strong sense of responsibility for high quality in the workers, who are taught to stop the assembly line if any quality problems arise. Not only will no penalties be incurred for interrupting production, but stopping the line is

[3] A kilometer is approximately six-tenths of a mile.

encouraged since it exposes problems which can be solved once and for all. Because the TPS makes all workers responsible for quality control (QC), DTL keeps only a skeleton QC department of six people. Great care is taken to demonstrate to the workers their vital importance to the organization. To emphasize this, all personnel and guests eat together in DTL's one cafeteria.

The meticulous training has paid off. In the planning stage it was expected that the productivity of DTL's Indian workers would be only 20 to 35 percent of that of the workers in Toyota City. It soon became clear that this had been a gross underestimate; the Indian workers are 65 percent as productive as their Japanese counterparts and continue to improve. This figure is quite impressive since the Japanese plants are more highly automated than DTL's. Interestingly, DTL's target of zero defects before shipment is actually achieved on some days. As in Japan, the line and office workers are all strongly committed to the company; they frequently stay after hours (without pay) for quality circles or when additional production is needed. If the company needs extra workers on the line during peak periods, instead of the normal Indian practice of hiring temporaries, clerical staff are assigned there to help. Even Toyota executives are impressed by the productivity and high-quality output of the Surajpur plant.

**The Dyna Truck**

The DTL vehicle, the Dyna, comes in two basic models — the Dyna-1 and the Dyna-3. The Dyna-3 is a complete truck with a standard cab and deck. The Dyna-1, a mechanically complete truck without the cab or deck, is for customers who want to finish it for their own special purposes. Approximately 35 percent of the vehicles manufactured by DTL are Dyna-1 models. The Dyna-1 customer can either have DTL custom-finish the vehicle or can take it to a private body builder to be finished inexpensively with wood or other materials. The Dyna-1 trucks finished by DTL are sold mainly to government agencies or institutional buyers with special requirements. The cabs and decks are built in-house by DTL, and conform to Toyota's quality standards. These Special Purpose Vehicles (SPVs) can be delivery vehicles for soft-drink distributors, armored vehicles for the police and security forces, ambulances for emergency services, buses, or anything else a customer may want (see Exhibit 3 for Dyna production information for the last 21 months). SPV sales can be very seasonal for certain markets, such as soft-drink manufacturers who have high summer demand, and for whom it is very hard to build inventories because of planning uncertainty. For example, the factory of Campa Cola, the largest soft-drink manufacturer in northern India, was burned to the ground during demonstrations following Indira Gandhi's assassination. This led to a slump in demand for Dyna bottle carriers.

The capacity of the Dyna is 3.5 tons, but the truck is actually designed for up to 6 tons, and has been operated with loads as high as 10.5 tons. It is built for low-fuel-cost transport of goods, possibly perishable, which need to travel quickly. One advantage of a medium-size truck like the Dyna is that it can ply city streets 24 hours a day, whereas bigger trucks cannot because of laws against their daytime use in certain populated areas.

Experience quickly showed that the Dynas take a lot more punishment than was originally anticipated. They are often overloaded by 100 to 150 percent and driven at great speed over bad roads. The resulting burst tires, broken axles or leaf springs, bent frames, and completely stripped gears meant that, early in the venture, a lot of the parts needed to be upgraded. Also, the vehicles are frequently involved in high-speed accidents and are often dented owing to aggressive driving because many drivers are unaccustomed to the speeds and acceleration the Dyna can attain. The upgraded Dyna is a far more rugged vehicle than its Japanese counterpart. In fact, when riding with Indian drivers testing it under normal Indian road conditions, Japanese engineers never fail to express amazement at the punishment the Dyna can take.

**The Plant**

Of all the LCV producers, DTL has the most modern plant. Component parts feeding into the plant are either domestically produced or arrive from Japan in a completely knocked-down (CKD) state. The Japanese parts arrive by sea and are brought to the plant by road where they are held in a bonded area in the main plant building. No duties, levies, taxes, or payment for the parts are due until they are withdrawn from the bonded area.

As was mentioned earlier, the plant operates on the TPS, a pull system that was the original just-in-time (JIT) system. All operations are pulled on, ultimately, by the final assembly line; the other lines have only to keep small buffers of their finished products full. Instruction sheets fed in the beginning of each of the trim, deck, and chassis and final assembly lines ensure that they are all synchronized. All work-in-process movement is on dollies custom-designed for each specific operation. The plant has nine production lines: chassis and final assembly, frame assembly, hub and drum machining, axle assembly, engine assembly, and the welding, painting, trim, and deck lines (see Exhibit 4 for a diagram of the plant illustrating the process flow).

Chassis and final assembly is the leading line in the pull system; all the other lines eventually feed into it. After the frame is started on the line, the axles and suspension system are attached and the engine and gearbox are installed. Next come the cooling system and gear levers, the electrical harnesses, the fuel tank, and the wheels. Then the cab is mounted, the vehicle is trimmed, all fluids are poured in, the brakes and clutch are bled, and the engine is started. After this, the vehicle is thoroughly inspected and final adjustments are made to the wheels, brakes, and headlights.

Although frame assembly is the smallest line in the plant, it has the most powerful tools. Here the main members of the frame are hydraulically riveted and welded together.

The hub and drum machining line, along with the axle and engine assembly lines, is located in a building adjacent to the main assembly building (see Exhibit 4). Hubs and drums were manufactured in Japan until the end of 1988. Nowadays, the raw castings are made in India and machined by DTL with two advanced, five-axis, computer numerically controlled (CNC) machines. Their controlling computers must be housed in an enclosed, air-conditioned room with cables leading to the machines outside. Once completed, the hubs and drums are transported to the axle line.

The axle assembly line begins with each component being degreased and cleaned with steam and chemicals. The axle housings and reduction gears are then put on a special jig, where a worker installs the gears. Once the axle assembly is complete and thoroughly greased, it is hoisted into the axle painting station and painted against a backdrop curtain of water so that the unused paint is scrubbed out of the air.

The engine assembly line receives CKD engine parts from Japan coated in a special protective grease, which is removed by chemical treatment before the engine is assembled in a clean room. It is expected that the block, pistons, and rings will be manufactured in India before the end of 1989. Although many Indian companies produce these parts, at the moment few can attain the exacting quality standards required for the Dyna. LCVs in India have always been diesel-powered because of fuel costs; diesel sells at only Rs3.5 per liter as compared with petroleum gasoline at Rs10 per liter.

On the welding line, the sheet-metal components of the cab are set up in a jig and spot-welded together for alignment prior to the final welding and filling of all joints and crevasses. QC checks that no vital spots have been missed and that the welds are not defective.

The paint line is where cabs, decks, and frames are painted. Cabs and decks are first degreased and thoroughly cleaned by steam and various chemicals. Next, components are undercoated with phosphate to inhibit rust and to provide a porous surface for better paint adhesion. Then they are submerged in a dip tank filled with primer, which is deposited by electrolysis to ensure an even coat on all surfaces, including those parts which would be inaccessible to spray painting. After they have been dried in a paint oven, a heavy underbody coat for road protection is applied to both the cabs and decks, which are then leakproofed with a plastic paste, given a final coat of paint with electrostatic spray guns, and baked to harden the paint and plastic sealer. Finally, QC checks that the paint finish is of the desired quality.

The trim line is also jokingly known as the make-up line because of the cosmetic nature of much of its work. This work requires skill and dexterity since the parts are quite fragile as well as expensive, and many small operations must be performed. Since the results of this line are most of what the customer sees when buying and using the vehicle, the appearance and finish must be immaculate.

The deck line uses the basic fabricating operations of metal cutting and welding (no rivets are used). After fabrication, the decks flowing into the paint line are synchronized with the cabs to ensure they match in color. After painting, the decks are hoisted onto the truck and bolted into place.

**Suppliers**

At present, 25 percent by value of the component parts of DTL's vehicles are imported from Japan, either because, like the engine components and transmission gears, they require precision and high quality, or because, like the large frame and cab members, they must be stamped using dies and presses larger than those commonly available in India. DTL began with 42-percent local content, reached 75-percent local content by the end of 1988, and must attain 90-percent local content by the end of 1991, or face severe penalties. One of the problems DTL has encountered in its indigenization efforts is the need for more QC inspection personnel to monitor and control the quality of domestically produced components. Indigenization presents a major challenge for the following reasons:

Large, high-quality metal stampings and plastic-molded components are not readily available in India because of a shortage of presses and molding machines capable of handling the sizes of dies required.

The technology to bond rubber to metal, which is necessary for engine mounts, alternator mounts, and other critical components, is in its infancy in India.

The precision required for some parts to meet Japanese standards is not achievable in India, where much of the technology in use is very old.

DTL has one advantage over the other Indo-Japanese joint ventures: the company's Indian parent, DCM Ltd, operates a world-class foundry. Plans are in the works to have the engine blocks manufactured there. Pistons may be supplied by Shriram Pistons and Rings Ltd, another firm controlled by the Shriram family. DTL is also considering redesigning the dashboard to be manufactured in six parts instead of one. This would allow it to be produced domestically with smaller machines but raises concerns of increased assembly costs and lower quality.

Domestic suppliers can be divided into three classes: the large well-established suppliers; the Indo-Japanese joint venture suppliers; and the small, local, independent suppliers. The big manufacturers typically produce high-quality products, have excellent delivery, and are very responsive. Some of these companies, such as the tire suppliers, have affiliations with large international companies and operate in competitive markets. Others, such as Automotive Axles Ltd, which manufactures axle housings and gears, are near-monopolies because no other Indian companies can match their technology. The Indo-Japanese joint-venture suppliers fall into two categories:

1. Those established to serve DTL
2. Those established to serve the Indian government's joint venture with Suzuki to produce automobiles

The former deliver to DTL on a JIT basis and have excellent quality, though they tend to be high-priced. DCM and Toyota have established a collaboration, independent of DTL and located two kilometers from the Surajpur plant to supply wiper motors, starters, and alternators. The joint ventures set up to serve Suzuki do not always deliver reliably largely because DTL is such a small customer relative to Suzuki. The small, local manufacturers supply various special nuts, bolts, and small metal and plastic components. Delivery is usually not problematic, but quality can be. These suppliers make extensive use of DTL's Ancillary Development Department (ADD) to improve their quality.

Parts supplied by vendors are handled initially by the ADD, whose major tasks are to help indigenize the DTL vehicle, to integrate suppliers into the firm as JIT partners, and to provide suppliers with advice on techniques to improve their quality. Sometimes suppliers genuinely do not understand why higher quality is needed. For example, DTL had to work hard to persuade its bus-body builders that the vehicle needed to be watertight, should have no sharp edges, and should not rattle. One of them is quoted as saying, "This is a bus, not a car."

**DTL Marketing**

The DTL sales department has a staff of 20 in the head office and 5 salespeople stationed in regional offices around the country. It is divided into two groups: international/ institutional and domestic. Institutional customers include large companies and state and local governments. DTL is waiting for clearance to sell to the national government and armed forces, potentially a very large market. Helped by financial incentives from the government, DTL exports to Bangladesh, Nepal, Sri Lanka, Bhutan, Mauritius, and Pakistan, and is trying to gain business in countries in the Middle East.

Trucks are sold domestically through DTL's network of 53 main dealerships and 57 subdealers or branches. These are also supported by an additional 33 authorized service centers (see Exhibit 5 for the locations of all dealers, subdealers, branches, and service centers as marked on the map). Dealership status is granted only to those who can meet Toyota's rigorous standards, which require that facilities be staffed with factory-trained technicians with the knowledge and tools to do all required service and repairs to LCVs. Dealers also must maintain large inventories of spare parts. (Subdealers are those who are not yet fully qualified dealers.) The entire dealership network, established from scratch starting in 1985, includes some dealers who sell exclusively DTL products and some who sell other complementary products as well. DTL provides free training to service technicians and helps dealers import service equipment. The dealer's profit on a typical LCV sale is about Rs5,000. The normal procedure is for a dealer to get a customer order and forward it to the factory; delivery usually takes place within a month.

Until mid-1988 DTL competed on the basis of price with Eicher-Mitsubishi and Swaraj-Mazda, its two major rivals in the 3.5-ton LCV market. All three companies produce vehicles of similar sizes and capacities. Even though DTL executives viewed their vehicle as superior to the others in quality, engineering, and engine size, price was still used as the basis for competition. As a result, DTL held a slightly larger market share than either of the other two companies. In mid-1988 the marketing manager was transferred to another post in DCM and the marketing staff was restructured. A new strategy was adopted, which called for disengagement from the price wars and the marketing of the Dyna based on its superior quality. The Dyna is now priced about Rs10,000 higher than its competitors, and eight points of market share have been lost since last year. The strategy shift has resulted in one significant benefit: unlike its rivals, DTL is now profitable for the first time in its history. Vikram Lal, Chairman of Eicher-Mitsubishi, now the market leader in the 3.5-ton LCV class, is quoted as stating that his company would lose, "about Rs3 Crore (30 million) this year."

## The Future

Of the three Indo-Japanese joint ventures, DTL alone uses a JIT manufacturing system and conveyorized assembly lines. In addition, DTL has more modern painting facilities, with electrodeposition of primer and electrolytically deposited paint. While this gives DTL a competitive advantage in manufacturing technology and product quality, it is uncertain whether the added expense will be justified for three reasons. First, consumers are wary of the new technology in the Dyna trucks, particularly with the unfamiliar Toyota name on them. The new truck comes with a higher price tag than people expect and is built to much higher standards than consumers are accustomed to. The Dyna does not break down every few days, and problems common to older designs of LCVs like ruptured fuel lines and broken fan belts have, by and large, been eliminated. Tire wear is one of the major costs of truck ownership because tires are very expensive in India. Unlike the older truck designs, including TELCO's, the Dyna is designed to have its wheels aligned and tires balanced on computerized equipment, which greatly reduces tire wear. Quite apart from the generally high standards to which the entire vehicle is manufactured, this reduced tire wear alone makes the Dyna a less expensive vehicle to operate in the long run than the other LCVs. The second reason for concern is that service for the Dyna is not available in many parts of the country. India is vast, and the number of dealers capable of providing full service for the vehicle is relatively limited. The DTL dealership network is new, having been established from scratch only in the last four years, whereas competitors have been able to take advantage of long-standing truck or tractor dealership networks spread throughout India. Consequently, DTL has been less successful than the other LCV manufacturers in selling to individual buyers. The third concern for DTL is that its high standards make indigenization of components quite difficult. There are only a handful of suppliers in India capable of manufacturing certain necessary components to DTL's quality standards.

Despite these challenges, S G Awasthi, DTL's Executive Director, remains a steadfast supporter of his company's current strategy:

> The management policy adopted by DTL so far has paid rich dividends and this policy is likely to yield even richer dividends in the future. I am confident that the corporate strategy adopted by DTL would be a model for other automobile manufacturers in the years to come.

Vivek Bharat Ram, grandson of Shri Ram and the current Managing Director of DTL, shares his view of the company's future:

> The basic principle on which DTL has always operated is that of following the customer-first philosophy. This is the policy I intend to firmly adhere to in the future also.

DTL is committed to developing and implementing strategies which will offer the equivalent of Shri Ram's 2 extra inches to the LCV market.

EXHIBIT 1

## DCM-TOYOTA LTD (INDIA)
## LCV Sales and Demand Forecast, Past Trends, and Projections on April-March Basis

| *Class* | *1984–1985* | *1985–1986* | *1986–1987* | *1987–1988* | *1988–1989* | *1989–1990* | *1990–1991* |
|---|---|---|---|---|---|---|---|
| LCV (2T) | 23,409 | 22,881 | 23,918 | 30,569 | 30,651 | 32,000 | 34,000 |
| LCV (3.5T) | | 2,653 | 5,287 | 8,375 | 10,997 | 12,000 | 13,000 |

EXHIBIT 2

## DCM-TOYOTA LTD (INDIA)
## Sales and Market Share for Light Commercial Vehicles 1987–1988 and 1988–1989

| *Manufacturers* | *July–June 1987–1988* | *Market Share* | *July–June 1988–1989* | *Market Share* |
|---|---|---|---|---|
| LCVs (2-ton Class) | | | | |
| Bajaj | 12,663 | 42% | 9,513 | 40% |
| Mahindra | 5,276 | 17% | 3,567 | 15% |
| Standard | 1,689 | 6% | 857 | 4% |
| TELCO 407/608 | 8,680 | 29% | 8,013 | 34% |
| Allwyn-Nissan | 2,132 | 7% | 1,632 | 7% |
| Total | 30,440 | 100% | 23,582 | 100% |
| LCVs (3.5-ton Class) | | | | |
| DCM-Toyota | 3,417 | 37% | 2,439 | 29% |
| Eicher-Mitsubishi | 3,373 | 36% | 3,496 | 41% |
| Swaraj-Mazda | 2,498 | 27% | 2,529 | 30% |
| Total | 9,288 | 100% | 8,464 | 100% |

EXHIBIT 3

## DCM-TOYOTA LTD (INDIA)
## DCM-Toyota Limited Sales by Model during 1988–1989 (including exports)

| *Models* | *July–June 1987–1988* | *July–June 1988–1989* |
|---|---|---|
| Dyna-1 Models | | |
| Cowl and chassis | 297 | 191 |
| Bus | 193 | 141 |
| SPV (Special Purpose Vehicle) | 32 | 13 |
| Total | 522 | 345 |
| Dyna-3 Models | | |
| Cabin and chassis | 397 | 205 |
| Highside deck | 1,069 | 710 |
| Drop-side deck | 415 | 359 |
| Fixed-side deck | 917 | 772 |
| SPV | 230 | 164 |
| Total | 3,028 | 2,210 |
| Grand total | 3,550 | 2,555 |

EXHIBIT 4

**DCM-TOYOTA LTD (INDIA)**
**DTL's Surajpur Plant**

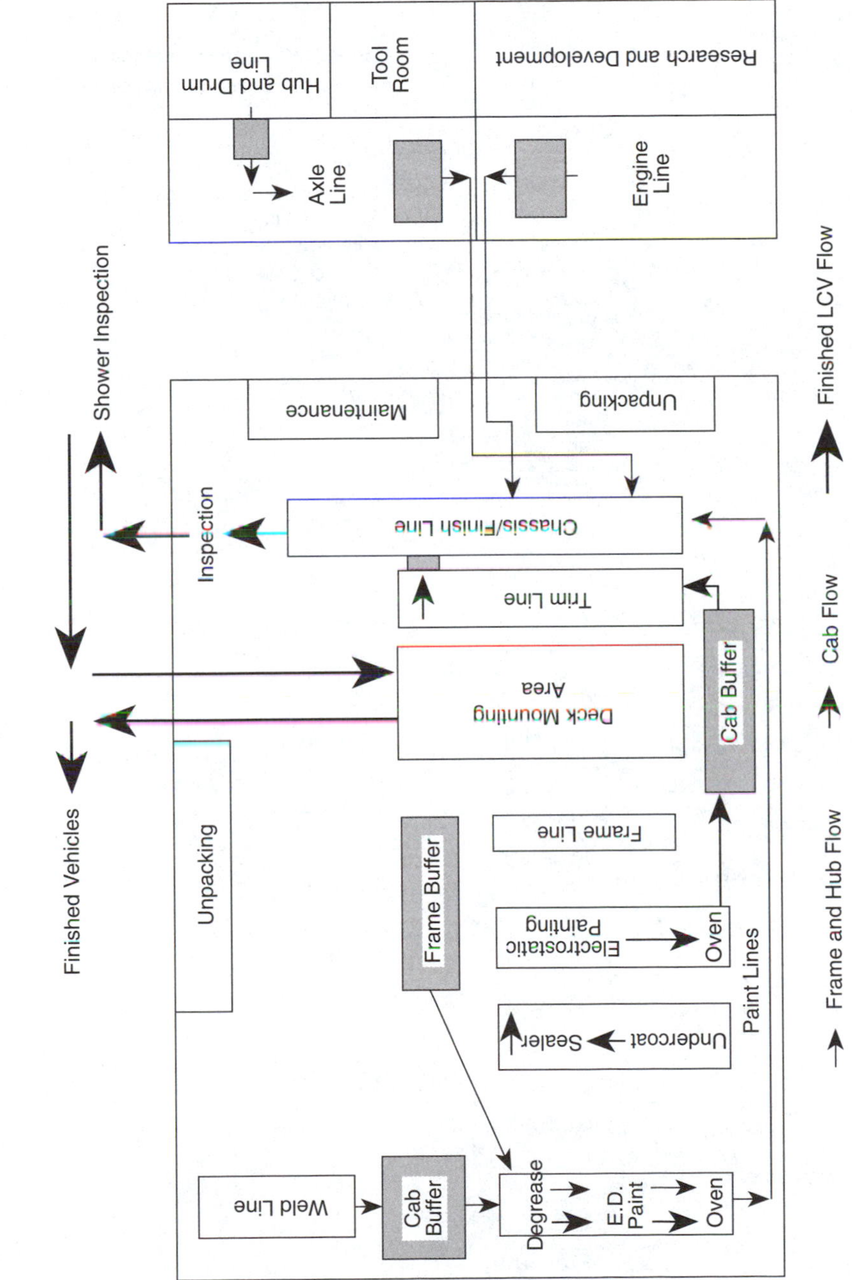

EXHIBIT 5

## DCM-TOYOTA LTD (INDIA)
## DTL Dealer Network

# Union Carbide Corporation: Industrial Plant Accident (Bhopal, India)* 27

In the middle of the night on December 3, 1984, J Mukund, Factory Manager of the Union Carbide (India) Limited (UCL) pesticide plant in Bhopal, was awakened by a telephone call from the night-shift supervisor informing him that an accident had occurred at the plant, causing a large amount of methyl isocyanate gas to leak out from the underground storage tanks. The lethal gas was causing havoc in the plant neighborhoods, injuring and killing untold numbers of people as they tried to escape the area. Within a short time, Mukund had driven to the plant and initiated damage control and emergency procedures. He telephoned the company headquarters in Bombay, which in turn notified divisional offices in Hong Kong and the parent company headquarters in Danbury, Connecticut. Within a few hours, news of the disaster had reached all key personnel in the company. The worst corporate crisis in history had just hit Union Carbide Corporation.

The morning of December 4, 1984 found death strewn over the stunned city of Bhopal. Bodies and animal carcasses lay on sidewalks, streets, and railway platforms, and in slum huts, bus stands, and waiting halls. Thousands of injured victims streamed into the city's hospitals. Doctors and other medical personnel struggled to cope with the chaotic rush, knowing neither the cause of the disaster nor appropriate treatment for the victims. Groping for anything that might help, they treated immediate symptoms by washing their

---

*This case was prepared by Professor Paul Shrivastava, Bucknell University to serve as a basis for classroom discussion rather than to illustrate effective or ineffective handling of an administrative situation. 

patients' eyes with water and then soothing their burning with eyedrops; they gave the victims aspirins, inhalers, muscle relaxants, and stomach remedies to provide temporary relief. Before the week was over, nearly 3,000 people had died. More than 300,000 others were affected by exposure to the deadly poison. About 2,000 animals died, and 7,000 more were severely injured. The worst industrial accident in history was over. But the industrial crisis that made the city of Bhopal international news had just begun.

The impact of the disaster on Union Carbide Corporation (UCC) was devastating. At the time of the accident in 1984, the corporation had sales revenues of $9.5 billion, a net income of $323 million, and total assets of $10.5 billion.[1] Three years later, the sales revenues had fallen to $6 billion, assets had shrunk to about $6.5 billion, and shareholders' equity fell from $4.9 billion to under $1 billion. This drastic reduction in size occurred without a single penny being paid in compensation to victims of the disaster.

During these turbulent three years, the company's financial survival was threatened more than once. First in 1985, a few months after the disaster, Carbide's stock price plunged from about $48 a share to about $33 a share. At the depressed price, speculators and arbitrageurs acquired large amounts of the company stock. On August 14, 1985, the GAF Corporation announced that it had acquired a significant stake in Carbide and would try to take it over. Samuel Heyman, Chairman of GAF, said he would sell off Carbide units that contributed about 40 percent of its revenues. With the money from those sales (estimated by GAF to be $4.5 billion), he would settle the Bhopal victims' claims. This immediately put the company in play in the takeover game. This was followed by frantic bidding and counterbidding wars between GAF and Union Carbide management.

Six months later, GAF gave up its takeover attempt, but only after Carbide management had been maneuvered into a radical financial restructuring. The restructuring involved selling off 25 percent of the most profitable assets of the company, closing several marginally profitable plants, and laying off about 4,000 people.

After more than four years of legal proceedings and acrimonious and contentious charges and countercharges, a settlement was reached in early February 1989 between the Government of India and UCL. The agreement called for UCL to pay $470 million. The agreement resolves all outstanding issues and claims by any and all parties against Union Carbide. The Supreme Court of India, in settling the claim, did not address the issue of who was to blame for the accident. Also as part of the settlement, the Indian Supreme Court ordered dismissal of all criminal charges and other civil suits in India against UCL.[2]

In the years since the accident, a great deal has happened and yet a great deal remains unchanged. Union Carbide Corporation went through the shock of a long, drawn-out hostile takeover battle which left the company severely battered, highly leveraged, and financially constrained. The accident also attracted worldwide attention to the broad scope of hazards associated with industrial accidents in general, and those in the Third World in particular. Although this accident was the most severe in history, it was by no means unique.

---

[1]All figures are in US dollars.

[2]Sanjay Hazarika, "Bhopal Payments Set at $470.0 Million for Union Carbide," *New York Times*, February 15, 1989: 1. See also "Union Carbide Agrees to Settle All Bhopal Litigation for $470.0 Million in Pact With India's Supreme Court," *Wall Street Journal*, February 15, 1989: A3.

Large-scale industrial accidents have created crises for corporations and the public regularly throughout this century. Since the beginning of this century, there have been 28 major industrial accidents in fixed facilities in the free world. These accidents do not include transportation accidents, such as airliner crashes or train derailments. These accidents occurred in both industrialized countries as well as developing countries. In the United States, the explosion of a ship with a cargo of ammonium nitrate caused the deaths of over 530 people in Texas City in 1947. In 1948, the explosion of confined dimethyl ether in Ludwigshafen, Germany killed nearly 250 people. In 1970, an accident at an underground railway construction site in Osaka, Japan, killed 92 people. In 1984, accidents in Mexico City and Cubatao, Brazil killed about 500 people each.

Major industrial accidents can occur anywhere — in industrialized as well as in developing countries, in small as well as in large organizations, in the public as well as in the private sectors. Accidents such as Bhopal, Chernobyl, and the NASA Challenger explosion have fundamentally changed the public's awareness of the technological hazards facing society. They have highlighted the very limited scope of our knowledge about these hazards and the extreme inadequacy of our ability and resources to cope with such major accidents.

Another sad realization to emerge out of the Bhopal case is that four years after the accident and despite an apparent settlement, the case is still mired in courts and there is no solution in sight for the victims. None of the victims have received a single penny in compensation for damages. While Union Carbide Corporation and the Government of India fight in the courts, the plight of the victims largely goes unnoticed. The survivors of those who died remain desperately poor and destitute with no alternative means of supporting themselves. Those who were partially or totally disabled suffer from a lack of adequate medical care and rehabilitation, loss of employment, and financial hardships. One thing is certain: many more will die before seeing justice done, and those who live long enough to see the courts resolve the case may not have much time left to make use of the compensation they eventually receive in any settlement.

## Issues for Analysis

The Bhopal case raises a number of important issues concerning public disclosure of potential hazards, appropriate technology transfers to developing countries, corporate responsibility and liability for overseas plant safety, and the role of host country governments in direct foreign investments. In addition, it highlights the importance of developing expeditious and equitable systems for resolving postaccident conflicts and compensation payment to victims:

1. What are the responsibilities of multinational corporations for their overseas operations, especially in developing countries, to ensure that these plants are operated safely with regard to workers, communities, and the environment? Can companies adopt a single uniform safety standard for all their plants around the world?
2. To what extent did Union Carbide Corporation (U.S.) and its Indian subsidiary exercise due care in this regard? What more could each of them have done to ensure plant safety?

3. How should environmental and safety concerns be incorporated in strategies for technology transfer to developing countries?
4. How can multinational corporations (MNCs) control the safety performance of their overseas operations?
5. To what extent can majority or other forms of ownership be used to ascertain the liability of various parties in case of major industrial accidents?
6. How do issues 3, 4, and 5 apply to the Bhopal case?
7. What should be the responsibility of government in ensuring plant safety? To what extent should government agencies be held responsible for losses to human lives and property? What should be done if such responsibility is poorly or inadequately discharged?
8. How do the issues raised in item 7 apply to the Government of India, the state government of Madhya Pradesh, and the local city government agencies in Bhopal?
9. What criteria should be used in determining compensation to victims? What kinds of compensation systems should be designed to ensure speedy and fair compensation? How much compensation can Union Carbide pay without going bankrupt?
10. Which country's courts should be responsible for handling cases involving multi-country accidents and liability disputes, and why? What role can the International Court of Justice play in this regard?
11. To what extent and under what circumstances are courts an appropriate forum for resolving international liability cases? What alternative forms of dispute resolution mechanisms can be recommended?
12. What corporate and business policies should firms adopt in order to minimize the occurrence of major accidents? How can they find a balance between the expense of being safe and cutting costs to be competitive?
13. What ethical issues does the Bhopal case raise? What ethical standards should be applied in making corporate policies regarding the case?
14. In light of Bhopal-type disasters, how should corporate responsibility toward environmental protection and worker and community safety change? What additional actions not warranted before Bhopal should corporations undertake voluntarily?

## Union Carbide Corporation

The organizational context of this accident may be understood by examining the position of the Bhopal plant in the overall business of Union Carbide Corporation (UCC). In 1984, UCC was the seventh largest chemical company in the United States, with total assets of $10.51 billion and sales approaching $10 billion. It owned or operated businesses in 40 countries and employed over 33,000 people worldwide. Its main product lines included dry cell batteries, chemicals, industrial gases, specialty alloys, and agricultural products.

The early 1970s were a turbulent period for the chemical industry and UCC. The highly cyclical chemical industry became even more volatile because of oil price fluctuations during the early 1970s. The oil embargo created an artificial shortage of petrochemicals and related products and sent their prices skyrocketing. In 1973 and 1974, UCC's sales grew at unprecedented rates of 21 percent and 35 percent, respectively. This created an upbeat mood at the company, and an aggressive program of growth and expansion was started. Capital expenditure increased annually until 1975. In 1975, the company got the first of a series of jolts. While its sales increased 6 percent in 1974, world recession triggered by the 1973 oil embargo reduced demand, resulting in a decline in sales and total employment. Inflation caused reductions in net earnings and led to cost-cutting measures and strategic reorientation. The company outlined three strategies: first, to strengthen its position in businesses with a good future and in areas where it had a strong market position; second, to withdraw from businesses which did not meet Carbide's criteria for financial performance; and third, to shift the business mix to include a greater proportion of performance products (e.g., Sevin and Temik pesticides). It also decided to diversify into related and unrelated businesses, and identified the areas of health, food products, environment, and energy as its future focus. The company estimated that about 60 percent of its business in 1975 was in growth categories, and it planned to allocate about 80 percent of its capital expenditure from 1975 to 1979 on these growth businesses. Specifically, pesticides and other agricultural products were considered as having high-growth potential, whereas old and mature chemical businesses were considered to be less desirable.

In 1976, Congress passed the Toxic Substances Control Act, placing more stringent requirements on the corporation's chemical businesses. UCC set up a new corporate-level health, safety, and environmental affairs department to ensure compliance with the new act and centralize internal administration.

The year 1977 saw a change in the top management of UCC. W S Sneath took over as chairman of the company, and Warren Anderson became the new President. Together they restructured UCC's business portfolio and started divesting some of its businesses. These decisions resulted in divestiture of over a billion dollars worth of assets over the next four years, including UCC's petrochemical business in Europe and the entire medical business in which the company had developed a number of new products.

In 1979, UCC once again benefited from the steep oil price hike by OPEC. Sales jumped 17 percent and earnings jumped 41 percent, and the total number of employees reached an all-time high of 115,763. In the 1980s, Union Carbide continued to refocus its portfolio of businesses away from chemicals and concentrated on industrial gases and batteries. It had divested almost three dozen business units and product ventures in the late 1970s to dilute its chemical operations in the United States. This was done in acknowledgment of increasing competition in the chemicals industry and lackluster financial performance of the company during the past decade.

In 1982, Warren Anderson took over as chairman while Alec Flamm became president. The early 1980s was a period of declining performance. Sales dropped, earnings declined, capital expenditures and working capital were reduced, maintenance expenditures were cut back, assets were stripped, and the employment level was curtailed (see Exhibits 1, 2, and 3).

## Union Carbide (India) Ltd

Union Carbide (India) Limited (UCIL) was incorporated in Calcutta under the name of Eveready Company (India) Ltd on June 20, 1934. Its name was changed to National Carbon Company (Ltd) and then to Union Carbide (India) Ltd in December 1959. The company's most important product is dry cells (batteries). In 1984, more than 50 percent of the company's revenues came from this product. But over the years, as its product lines in batteries, chemicals, and plastics matured, the company sought out new markets to maintain its growth.

The industries UCIL entered were typically technology- and capital-intensive. They catered to mass markets and required large-scale production and technically skilled labor. Most often, UCIL would enter industries still in their early stages of development and gain a dominant market position by using the superior technology of its parent company. One such industry was pesticides. In the 1960s, large-scale use of agricultural pesticides was promoted by the Indian government as part of its "green revolution" campaign to modernize agriculture. Pesticides quickly became popular among farmers, and their use tripled from 1956 to 1970.

The Agricultural Products Division was established in 1969. It developed carbaryl (Sevin) using methyl isocyanate (MIC) as the active agent for a range of pesticides. The Bhopal plant also began operating in 1969. It was located on the north side of Bhopal, about two miles from the railway station and bus stand — the hub of local commercial and transportation activities. Since the plant was initially used only for formulation (the mixing of different stable substances to create pesticides), it did not pose a grave danger to surrounding areas. In 1974, however, it was granted an industrial license to manufacture pesticides and began production of both Sevin and MIC in 1977. While these developments occurred inside the company, the pesticide industry underwent major changes. Many small manufacturers entered the industry as formulators. They were less capital-intensive and served small market niches.

The Bhopal plant was the key manufacturing facility of the Agricultural Products Division of the company. At the time of the accident in December 1984, Union Carbide (India) Ltd was the 21st largest company in India. Of UCIL shares, 50.9 percent were owned by Union Carbide Corporation, New York. The remaining shares were held by individuals and institutions in India.

The company manufactured a wide range of products including agricultural products, chemicals and plastics, marine products, battery products, and special metals and gases. It had five operating divisions. In addition, it owned majority interest in a joint venture: the Nepal Battery Company Limited.

UCIL was a well-respected company in India. It was considered a good business customer and a responsible and desirable employer. The company worked closely with local, state, and central government agencies to promote the government's family planning and other social programs. It thus developed strong contacts in the government. This excellent relationship with the government facilitated company-government interactions at many levels of operations. The company was easily able to get government permissions for dealing with a variety of operating issues. For example, the parent company was allowed to retain 51 percent of the stock in the Indian company, even after the revised Foreign Exchange Regulations Act (FERA) required foreign companies to hold less than 40 percent of a domestic (Indian) company's stock.[3] On another occasion, the company was able to get the Bhopal government's objection to its site overruled by the state government.[4]

[3]"City of Death," *India Today*, December 31, 1984: 2.

[4]Ward Morehouse and Arun Subramanyam, *The Bhopal Tragedy* (New York: Council on International and Public Affairs, 1986): 18, 32.

UCIL had 32.58 million outstanding shares. Of these, 16.58 million shares (50.89 percent) were held by Carbide Corporation, U.S.A., the holding company. The company had issued and subscribed a share capital of Rs325.83 million and accumulated reserves and surplus of Rs 293.89. In 1983, company revenues were Rs2100 million (US$1 = Rs12.8 rupees in 1984), excluding products used internally and valued at Rs 540 million. It reported profit before taxes of Rs148 million, and profit after taxes and Investment Allowance Reserves of Rs87 million. It declared a dividend of Rsl.50 per share. Net worth per share was Rs19.02, and earnings per share were Rs2.86. The company employed over 10,000 people, of whom nearly 1,000 earned incomes of over Rs3,000 per month, making the company one of the best-paying employers in India.[5]

### UCIL Management and Organization

UCIL was managed by an 11-member Board of Directors, with Keshub Mahindra, a well-known industrialist, as Chairman. The Vice Chairman was JB Law, who also served as the Chairman of Union Carbide Eastern, Inc, Hong Kong. VP Gokhale served as the Managing Director (Chief Executive) of the Company. He took this position on December 26, 1983 and was responsible for the overall management of the company. A mechanical engineer by training, Gokhale had been with the company since 1959. Each of the five operating divisions was headed by a vice president reporting to the managing director. Each division was a profit center, organized internally on a functional basis.

Management of the agricultural products division was characterized by frequent changes in top management. During the past 15 years, it had eight different division heads. Many of them came from the nonchemical businesses of the company. Discontinuity in top management created frequent changes in internal systems and procedures and uncertainty for managers. Many of the more talented managers, particularly those trained in the United States for operating the MIC plant in 1980, had left the company by 1984.[6]

### Operations

The company had 13 manufacturing facilities located in major Indian cities such as Bombay, Calcutta, Madras, Hyderabad, Bhopal, and Srinagar. Production technologies used in these facilities were modern and supplied by the parent corporation. For example, the Bhopal facility contained plants to manufacture methyl isocyanate and to formulate MIC-based pesticides. The company operated 20 sales offices and sold through a network of 3,000 dealers, who in turn sold to 249,000 retailers all over India. It had dominant market share in its main product (batteries) and was a significant competitor in other product lines, including pesticides, carbons, special metals, chemicals, and plastics. Differences in product lines, marketing philosophies, and operations made each division distinct and independent. For example, the battery division operated through a network of distributors and dealers and advertised intensively. The agricultural products division sent distributors to geographic areas where customers (private farmers) were concentrated. Promotion involved programs for farmers aimed at educating them about the usefulness of pesticides.

[5]Union Carbide Corporation and Union Carbide (India) Ltd, Annual Reports, 1983, 1984.
[6]Personal interviews with the author.

## Industrial Environment in Bhopal and India

Bhopal is the capital of the state of Madhya Pradesh and the most centrally located city in India. It has a good agricultural and forest base and two large lakes that ensure a steady supply of water to the city. The government controls the most important segment of the local economy. It is the largest employer, the largest producer, and the largest consumer. More than 90 percent of India's productive industrial resources are controlled directly or indirectly by agencies of the city, state, and central (federal) governments. Virtually all service organizations are nationalized, including banks, insurance companies, postal and telephone systems, radio and television stations, energy production and distribution, railways, airlines, intercity bus service, medical services, and education.

Urbanization and industrialization in Bhopal were not integrated with the rural development of its hinterlands. Agricultural production in rural areas was stagnant, while the state's population grew at a rate of more than two percent per year. These conditions forced the rural unemployed to seek work in urban areas, turning Bhopal into a rapidly growing urban area. Bhopal's population grew from 102,000 in 1961 to 385,000 in 1971, and to 670,000 in 1981 — a growth rate almost three times the average for the state and for the nation as a whole.

Migrants from rural areas were hardly equipped to deal with the difficulties of urban life. In 1971, almost two-thirds of the migrants were unemployed. Of these, half had not completed high school and 20 percent were totally illiterate. Bhopal's rapidly rising population, coupled with high land and construction costs, caused a severe housing shortage in the city. Government efforts to build housing resulted, for the most part, in the construction of expensive dwellings. Unable to afford housing, many migrants became squatters, illegally occupying land and creating slums and shanty towns. Most of these slums cropped up around industrial plants and other employment centers. Slum dwellers served as a pool of cheap labor for industrial plants, construction companies, and offices, as well as households seeking domestic help. By 1984, Bhopal had 156 slum colonies, housing nearly 20 percent of the city's population. Two of them — Jaya Prakash Nagar and Kenchi Chola — were located across the street from Union Carbide's plant, even though the area was not zoned for residential use.

In 1974, UCIL was granted an industrial license by the central government to manufacture, rather than simply formulate, pesticides. By 1977, UCIL had begun producing more sophisticated and dangerous pesticides in which carbaryl was the active agent. Component chemicals such as methyl isocyanate were imported from the parent company in relatively small quantities. Within a short period of time, however, the pesticides market became very competitive. Fifty different formulations and more than 200 manufacturers came into existence to serve small, regional market niches. Increased competition forced manufacturers to cut costs, improve productivity, take advantage of economies of scale, and resort to "backward integration," that is, to not only formulate the final products but to manufacture the raw materials and intermediate products as well.

While competitive pressures were mounting, the widespread use of pesticides declined. Agricultural production peaked in 1979, declined severely in 1980, and then recovered mildly over the next three years. Weather conditions and harvests during 1982 and 1983 were poor, causing farmers to cut costs temporarily by abandoning the use of pesticides. As a result of reduced demand, the pesticides industry became even more competitive in the early 1980s. The expansion and underutilization of production capacity, coupled with a decline in agricultural production, further fueled competition.

During this period of industry decline, UCIL decided to backward integrate into the domestic manufacture of MIC. Until this time, MIC was imported in small drums and did not need to be stored in great quantities. In 1979, the company expanded its Bhopal factory to include facilities that manufactured five pesticide components, including MIC. Using this strategy, UCIL hoped to exploit economies of scale and save on transportation costs. Manufacture of MIC required the establishment of a new hazardous plant and storage facility for MIC. More specifically, this arrangement required MIC to be stored in three large underground tanks with a capacity of about 60 tons each. This made the plant much more hazardous than it had been before.

Municipal authorities in Bhopal objected to the continued use of the UCIL plant at its original location. The city's development plan had earlier designated the plant site for commercial or light industrial use, but not for hazardous industries. With the addition of the MIC facility, this plant had clearly become a hazardous industry. However, at the behest of UCIL, the central and state government authorities overruled the city's objections and granted approval of the backward integration plan.

## The Accident and Its Possible Cause

At the core of any industrial crisis is a triggering event. In Bhopal, the triggering event was the leakage of a toxic gas, MIC, from storage tanks. Human, organizational, and technological failures in the plant paved the way for the crisis that ensued. The events leading to the accident are murky, which is not unusual when major accidents like the one in Bhopal occur. Moreover, the attributable causes of such accidents become highly contentious because of their impact in establishing culpability and payment of damages to the victims.

MIC is a highly toxic substance used for making carbaryl, the active agent in the pesticide Sevin. It is also very unstable and needs to be kept at low temperatures. UCIL manufactured MIC in batches and stored it in three large underground tanks until it was needed for processing. Two of the tanks were used for MIC that had met specifications, while the third stored MIC that had not met specifications and needed reprocessing.

### The Plant

A schematic layout of the storage tanks and various pipes and valves involved in the accident is shown in Exhibits 4 and 5. MIC was brought into storage tanks from the MIC refining still through a stainless steel pipe that branched off into each tank (see Exhibit 5). It was transferred out of storage by pressurizing a tank with high-purity nitrogen. Once out of storage, MIC passed through a safety valve to a relief-valve vent header, or pipe, common to all three tanks. This route led to the production reactor unit. Another common line took rejected MIC back to storage for reprocessing and contaminated MIC to the vent-gas scrubber for neutralizing. Excess nitrogen could be forced out of each tank through a process pipe that was regulated by a blow-down valve. Though they served different purposes, the relief-valve pipe and the process pipe were connected by another pipe called the jumper system. This jumper system was installed about a year before the accident to simplify maintenance.

Normal storage pressure, maintained with the aid of high-purity nitrogen, was one kilogram per square centimeter (kg/sq cm). Each storage tank was equipped with separate gauges to indicate temperature and pressure, one local and the other inside a remote control-room. Each tank also had a high-temperature alarm, a level indicator, and high- and low-level alarms.

The safety valve through which MIC passed on its way to the Sevin plant operated in conjunction with a mediating graphite rupture disk, which functioned like a pressure cooker: holding the gas in until it reached a certain pressure, then letting it out. The rupture disk could not be monitored from a remote location. Checking it required frequent manual inspection of a pressure indicator located between the disk and the safety valve.

The plant had several safety features. The vent-gas scrubber was a safety device designed to neutralize toxic exhausts from the MIC plant and storage system. Gases leaving the tank were routed to this scrubber, where they were scrubbed with a caustic soda solution and released either into the atmosphere at a height of 30 meters or routed to a flare. The gases could also be routed directly to the flare without going through the scrubber. The flare tower was used for burning normally vented gases from the MIC section and other units in the plant. Burning would detoxify the gases before venting them into the atmosphere. However, the flare was not designed to handle large quantities of MIC vapors. A few weeks before the accident, the scrubber was turned off to a standby position.

Two additional features of the plant were relevant for safety. The first was a refrigeration system used to keep MIC at low temperatures, particularly in the summer when the ambient air could reach temperatures as high as 120°F. However, the refrigeration system was shut down in June of 1984, and its coolant was drained for use in another part of the plant, thus making it impossible to switch on the refrigeration system during an emergency. The second important feature was a set of water-spray pipes that could be used to control escaping gases, overheated equipment, or fires.

## A Chronology of Events

The last batch of MIC manufactured before the accident was produced sometime between October 7 and October 22, 1984. At the end of the manufacturing cycle, one storage tank, called tank E610, contained about 42 tons of MIC, while the second tank, E611, contained about 20 tons. After the MIC production unit was shut down, parts of the plant were dismantled for maintenance. The flare tower was shut down so that a piece of corroded pipe could be replaced. On October 21, nitrogen pressure in tank E610 dropped from 1.25 kg/sq cm, which was about normal, to only 0.25 kg/sq cm. Because the first storage tank lacked sufficient pressure, any MIC needed in the manufacturing process was drawn from the other tank — E611. But on November 30, tank E611 also failed to pressurize because of a defective valve. Plant operators attempted to pressurize tank E610 but failed, so they temporarily abandoned it and, instead, repaired the pressure system in tank E611.

In the normal course of operation, water and MIC react with each other in small quantities in the plant's pipes, creating a plastic substance called trimer. Periodically, the pipes were washed with water to flush out all the trimer that had built up on pipe walls. Because the mixture of water and MIC was so volatile, the pipes were normally blocked off with a physical barrier, known as a slip blind, to prevent the water from going into the storage tank.

On the evening of December 2, the second-shift production superintendent ordered the MIC plant supervisor to flush out several pipes that led from the phosgene system through the MIC storage tanks to the scrubber. Although MIC unit operators were in charge of the flushing operation, insertion of the slip blind was the responsibility of the maintenance supervisor, a position that had been eliminated several days earlier. No worker had yet been given responsibility for inserting the slip blind. The flushing operation began at 9:30 pm. Because several bleeder lines, or overflow devices, downstream from the flushing were clogged, water began to accumulate in the pipes. Many of the valves in the plant were leaking, including one that was used to isolate the lines being flushed, so water rose past that valve and into the relief-valve pipe. When the operator noticed that no water was coming out of the bleeder lines, he shut off the flow, but the MIC plant supervisor ordered him to resume the process. The relief-valve pipe was about six meters off the ground, causing the water to flow downhill toward tank E610. First it flowed through the jumper system to the process pipe. From that pipe, which is normally open, the water flowed to the blow-down valve, which should have been closed. However, the blow-down valve is part of the system used to pressurize the tank with nitrogen, the same tank whose pressurization system had not been working for weeks. It is possible that this valve had been inadvertently left open or was not sealed properly.

With the blow-down valve open, about 500 kilograms of water flowed through another isolation valve, normally left open, and entered tank E610, where it began to react with the MIC being stored there. At 10:45 pm, a change of shift took place. At 11:00 pm, Suman Dey, the new control-room operator, noticed that the pressure in tank E610 was 0.70 kg/sq cm (10 psi), well within the operating range of 0.14 to 1.76 kg/sq cm (2–25 psi). Half an hour later, however, a field operator noticed a leak of MIC near the scrubber. Workers inspected the MIC structure and found MIC and dirty water coming out of a branch of the relief-valve pipe on the downstream side of the safety valve. They also found that another safety valve, called the process-safety valve, had been removed, and the open end of the relief-valve pipe had not been sealed for flushing. They informed the control room about this. By 12:15 am, Dey saw that the pressure in tank E610 had risen to between 1.76 and 2.11 kg/sq cm (25-30 psi) and was still rising. Within 15 minutes, it showed a reading beyond 3.9 kg/sq cm (55 psi), which was the top of the scale.

Dey ran to the tank. He heard a hissing sound from the safety valve downstream, indicating that it had popped. Local temperature and pressure gauges showed values beyond their maximums of 25°C (77°F) and 3.9 kg/sq cm (55 psi). Dey heard loud rumbling and screeching noises from the tank and felt heat radiating from it. He went back to the control room and tried to switch on the scrubber, which had been in a standby mode since the last MIC manufacturing run. But Dey's instruments indicated that the caustic soda, the neutralizing agent used in the scrubbers, was not circulating within the scrubber. In the meantime, field operators saw a cloud of gas gushing out of the stack.

Supervisors notified the plant superintendent, who arrived immediately, suspended operation of the MIC plant, and turned on the toxic-gas alarm to warn the community around the plant. A few minutes later the alarm was turned off, leaving only the in-plant siren to warn workers inside the plant. Operators turned on the firewater sprayers to douse the stack, the tank mound, and the relief-valve pipe to the scrubber. Because of low water pressure, the water spray did not reach the gases, which were being emitted at a height of 30 meters. The supervisors tried to turn on the refrigeration system to cool the tanks, but since the coolant from the system was drained, the refrigerator could not work. The safety valve remained open for two hours. A mixture of gases, foam, and liquid escaped at a temperature in excess of 200°C (close to 400°F) and a pressure of 12.65 kg/sq cm (180 psi).

Because the plant was so close to the slums, thousands of people were affected by exposure to this lethal mixture. Nearly 3,000 people died, although the exact number would never be fully determined. A few months after the accident, the Indian government officially put the death toll at 1,754. But various sources suggest a wide range of higher figures, and the best conclusion one can draw is that the death toll was probably close to 3,000. Thousands more were harmed in some way, many of whom experience illnesses that linger to this day. More than 2,000 animals were killed, and environmental damage was considerable. Bhopal was not equipped to handle an accident of this magnitude. Hospitals and dispensaries could not accommodate the flow of injured victims; likewise, government officials and registered mortuaries could not keep up with the certification and burial of the dead.

There are many reasons for discrepancies in death toll figures. There was no systematic method to certify and accurately count the dead as they were discovered or brought to government hospitals and cremation or burial grounds. For the first three days after the accident, all available medical personnel were engaged in caring for the injured. Few people were left to tend to the dead, register them, perform inquests and autopsies, issue death certificates, or arrange for systematic disposal of bodies.

Dead bodies piled up, one on top of another, in the only city morgue and in temporary tents set up outside of it. Many bodies were released to relatives for disposal without death certificates. Bodies were buried or cremated at unregistered facilities. Graves and funeral pyres registered as single burial units were made to accommodate many corpses because of worker and material shortages. Many people ran from Bhopal and died on roads outside the city and were buried or cremated by the roadside.

## The Long-term Health Effects

The long-term health consequences of exposure to MIC and other toxic gases remain largely unknown and are the subject of considerable controversy in scientific and medical circles. They are likely to be far more serious than originally anticipated.

The most serious permanent damage among the injured was to the respiratory tract. Many victims died of edema (fluid in the lungs). MIC also damaged mucus membranes, perforated lung tissue, inflamed lungs, and caused secondary lung infections. Many survivors could not be employed because they suffered from bronchitis, pneumonia, asthma, and fibrosis and were physically unable to work. Long-term epidemiological studies have been hampered by the unwillingness of various government agencies in charge of medical studies to share their data with outsiders. It was expected that this data would be produced in courts as medicolegal evidence. However, even four years after the accident, no comprehensive study of health effects of the disaster was available.

## Economic and Social Disruption

The accident did tremendous damage to the local economic and social structures. In addition to the shutdown of the UCIL plant, two mass evacuations (the first at the time of the accident, the second during a fear-ridden "scare" two weeks later) led to the closure of factories, shops, commercial establishments, business and government offices, and schools and colleges. These closures and labor scarcity resulting from death and injury, disrupted essential services and civil supplies. Establishments that remained open had few employees and few clients.

Estimates of business losses ranged from $8 million to $65 million. The closure of the Union Carbide plant alone eliminated 650 permanent jobs and approximately the same number of temporary jobs — jobs that were particularly important to the local economy because Union Carbide paid high wages. The plant shutdown also dismantled a $25 million investment in the city, which had provided secondary employment to about 1,500 persons. State and local governments lost untold thousands of dollars in taxes. The city, the nation, and the entire developing world suffered a loss of business potential because the accident damaged UCC's business image.

To make matters worse, relief efforts following the accident distorted prices and the availability of goods. At one point, almost 50 percent of the city's population was receiving free grain from the government. This caused grain prices to decline and labor prices to increase abnormally.

## Environmental Consequences

Damage to plant and animal life, while equally devastating, was not studied systematically because most available resources were deployed for mitigating human losses. Animal deaths probably exceeded 2,000 and included cows, buffaloes, goats, dogs, cats, and birds, although official government records put the figure at only 1,047. About 7,000 animals were given therapeutic care. Postmortems on farm animals suggested the possible presence of an undetected toxin, lending credence to the view that cyanide poisoning was involved. MIC exposure destroyed standing vegetation in surrounding areas. Of 48 plant species examined after the accident, 35 were affected to some degree and 13 appeared free from damage.

## Legal Proceedings

On hearing about the accident, Union Carbide called an emergency meeting of its top executives to develop a crisis management plan. It rushed some medical supplies and teams to Bhopal. Chairman Warren Anderson himself rushed to Bhopal to oversee relief and help to victims. Upon arrival, he was immediately arrested by the local police and confined at the Union Carbide Guest House. After a few hours and at the intervention of the central government, he was released and flown to New Delhi. He returned to the United States without making any headway on the relief mission. On the contrary, his visit and arrest served to create the ferociously adversarial mood that governed the subsequent relations between the company and the government of India.

Government agencies mounted a massive relief and rehabilitation effort to deal with the disaster. However, given their limited resources and the vast magnitude of the accident, the agencies were barely able to give first aid treatment to victims. The government made interim relief payments of $80 to $800 to help victims tide over their immediate financial needs. Once the immediate crisis subsided, however, relief efforts lost their intensity. Since then, government agencies have been criticized in the local press for their indifference and insensitivity to the plight of the victims.

## Consequences for Union Carbide Corporation

The accident threatened UCC's very survival. In its aftermath, the company was subject to worldwide humiliation. The day after the accident, the Bhopal plant was shut down and local managers were arrested on criminal charges. When UCC's Chairman, Warren Anderson, and UCIL's top management rushed to Bhopal, they too were arrested. The company's reputation came under intense attack by the news media worldwide.

The Bhopal accident triggered a series of sanctions and protests against Union Carbide all over the world. Public interest and activist groups initiated a variety of grassroots campaigns against the company. In Breziers, France, where Union Carbide used MIC made in the United States to make pesticides, the local community objected to reopening the plant after it was shut down following the Bhopal accident. In Rio de Janeiro, Brazil, the state government decreed that MIC could not be produced, stored, or transported within the state. In Scotland, despite a local unemployment rate of 26 percent, the city of Livingston rejected Union Carbide's proposal to set up a plant to manufacture toxic gases.

During this period of scrutiny and backlash, several accidents occurred at and deepened the company's crisis. On March 28, 1985, the chemical mesityl oxide leaked from the Institute, West Virginia plant, sickening eight people in a nearby shopping mall. Then, on August 11, 1985, another chemical, aldicarb oxyme, leaked from a storage tank at the same plant, injuring 135 people, 31 of whom were admitted to local hospitals. Two days later, another leak occurred at a sister plant in Charleston, West Virginia. Although no one was injured, the leak was highly publicized and spawned further investigations into company operations. Investigations also revealed that 28 major MIC gas leaks had occurred at the Institute, West Virginia plant during the five years preceding the Bhopal accident. One of them occurred just a month before the Bhopal leak, releasing 14,000 pounds of an MIC/chloroform mixture into the atmosphere.

## Legal Consequences

Soon after the accident, lawyers from the United States arrived in Bhopal, formed partnerships with Indian lawyers, and started arranging to represent victims in multimillion-dollar personal injury lawsuits against UCC (see Exhibit 6 for chronological development of the legal ramifications of the accident). UCC was not the only party taken to court.

Many victims also sued the Government of India, charging it with negligence in allowing the disaster to occur. Some lawsuits pointed out the delays, incompetence, and corruption involved in relief efforts. Others argued that the government was partly responsible because it had allowed UCL to locate and operate the hazardous facility and because it had legalized the slums around the plant early in 1984. Critics faulted the government for failing to act on the recommendation of its own labor department, which had urged a safety investigation at the plant, and for failing to prepare for the possibility of an emergency at the plant.

In March 1985, the Indian government passed a law conferring on itself sweeping powers to represent victims in the lawsuit and to manage all aspects of registering and processing legal claims. The following month it filed a lawsuit in the United States, charging UCC with liability in the deaths of 1,700 persons, the personal injury of 200,000 more persons, and property damages.

Union Carbide Corporation developed a multilayered defense strategy. First, it argued that the suits should be dismissed from U.S. courts because the accident happened in India, victims were mostly Indians, and most material evidence and witnesses were in India. It also suggested that Indian law and compensation standards should be applied in determining victim compensation in this case. The Government of India countered this argument saying that U.S. courts were an appropriate forum for the case because the parent company was a U.S. corporation. This claim was supported by private victim lawyers, who were interested in keeping the case in the United States where they could legally represent victims. The battle over the correct forum for trial of cases extended over several months. During this time, Carbide began negotiating an out-of-court settlement of the case with the Government of India and the private lawyers. The Government of India had bestowed on itself all rights to represent the victims. It did not accept the role of private lawyers in the case. These lawyers had also lost legitimacy in the eyes of the victims and the world media because of the insensitive way they had descended upon Bhopal to sign up clients after the accident. They had obtained clients by running newspaper advertisements with affidavit forms attached, which the victims could fill out and mail back to the lawyers' respective offices. Some of them never even met their clients or discussed with them the nature or extent of the damages. Their main interest was in the extremely lucrative attorney fees that were likely to result from the case if it were decided in an American court.

Judge J F K Keenan, the presiding judge in this case, attempted to balance the power of the opposing parties in order to keep them negotiating, but was not very successful. For example, in April 1985, the court ordered Union Carbide to pay immediately $5 million for interim relief, deductible from the final settlement amount. But the Government of India refused to accept the money, saying the corporation had imposed "onerous conditions" on its use. The court was unable to give away the money for seven months because the litigants could not agree on a plan for using it. This delay was embarrassing for all parties because, all the while, media reports detailed the woefully inadequate relief being provided to the victims.

Initial negotiations led to UCC's offer in August 1985 of about $200 million to be paid out over 30 years for a total and final settlement of the case. The government rejected the offer without explanation. Two detailed estimates of damage made public in 1985 suggested that the compensation to the victims should range from $1 billion to $2 billion.

In late March 1986, *The New York Times* reported that a tentative settlement of $350 million had been reached between Union Carbide and the private lawyers. The lawyers had a strong economic motive for settling the case early because if the case were moved to India, they would lose all their fees, which amounted to millions of dollars. But the Indian government's attorneys had not been involved in the negotiations, and they once again rejected the offer as absurdly low. Indeed, even if the agreement were sanctioned by the court, it would be virtually impossible to implement without the cooperation of the government, which was the only party with access to the information and administrative procedures needed to distribute the compensation money fairly.

In May 1986, Judge Keenan ruled on the forum issue, deciding to send the case to India for trial. In so doing, he imposed three conditions on UCC. First, the corporation had to submit itself to the jurisdiction of Indian courts. Second, UCC had to agree to satisfy any judgments rendered by Indian courts through due process. And third, the company had to agree to submit to discovery under U.S. law, which allowed more exploration of company-held information than Indian laws did. This last condition was appealed by UCC, which requested the court to make discovery under U.S. law a reciprocal condition and impose it on the Government of India too.

Union Carbide's second line of defense was to argue that it was not legally liable for the accident. It said that the parent company was not responsible for the accident because the plant in which it occurred was designed, constructed, owned, and operated by the Indian company Union Carbide (India) Ltd. It argued that the parent company had no control over its Indian subsidiary in matters of day-to-day operations. It suggested that the "corporate veil" between parent and subsidiary prevents it (the parent) from controlling the causes of the accident. Thus, it blamed the accident on the Indian company, which had total assets of only about $80 million. The Government of India argued against this position on the basis of Union Carbide's 51 percent ownership of its subsidiary and on the legal doctrine of strict liability. This doctrine says that as long as the source of damage or injury originates within a facility owned by a company, the company is strictly liable for the damages, regardless of whose fault led to the accident. The acceptability and applicability of this doctrine was contested by UCC.

Finally, the company argued that the accident was caused by sabotage. It said that a disgruntled employee had deliberately poured a large quantity of water into the MIC tank to cause the runaway reaction. However, UCC did not provide the identity of the saboteur. It argued that since the parent company was not in control of the day-to-day operations of the Indian subsidiary, it should not be held liable for the accident. This issue was being debated in courts in India even four years after the accident.

## Drive Toward a Settlement: The Unsettled Fate of Victims

As the case moved slowly through the court system in the United States, and then in India, the pressure on both parties to reach an out-of-court settlement increased. The Government of India wanted a settlement to prevent political backlash from the dissatisfied victims. UCC wanted a settlement to shake off the legal liability and protect its assets. The differences in their motives and objectives, and the backlash from the lawsuits kept them from reaching a settlement even four years after the accident.

The Board of Directors of Union Carbide Corporation decided to sell assets of the company and distribute to shareholders the net pretax sale proceeds above the net book value of the businesses. In 1985, the company divested about $2 billion worth of assets. In early 1986, it sold its battery division to Ralston Purina for $1.42 billion and announced intentions of selling its home and automotive products division for $800 million. It later sold its corporate headquarters building for $345 million and its agricultural chemicals business for $575 million.

These divestitures alarmed the Indian government. It asked the Bhopal court to bar the company from stripping assets, paying dividends, or buying back debt until a review ensured that these activities would not disadvantage the victims. The company was able to have the injunction lifted by agreeing to maintain at least $3 billion in assets, which could be used to settle the Bhopal claims.

In the Bhopal District Court, the Indian government had demanded $3 billion as compensation for damages. In April 1987, the district judge, M W Deo, suggested that the company make an interim relief payment of $4.6 million and urged the litigants to reach an agreement on the final amount of the settlement. In August 1987, the company agreed to distribute the $4.6 million interim aid and a few months later offered about $500 million as a final settlement amount. This money was to be paid over a 30-year period. The net present value of this amount was not different from the earlier offer made by the company. The offer was rejected by the government.

Frustrated by the unyielding positions of both sides and the increasing complexity of the litigation, Judge Deo ordered UCC to pay $270 million as interim aid to victims in December 1987. This money was to be placed with the Commissioner of Claims named by the Indian government. He suggested that this amount be distributed to victims as follows: $15,500 per death, $8,000 per severe injury, and lesser amounts for remaining victims.

UCC appealed this interim payment on the grounds that it amounted to "a judgment and decree without trial." The issue was moved up to the High Court in Jabalpur. The High Court Judge S K Seth in April 1988 upheld the order of the lower court but reduced the interim relief amount from $270 to $190 million. He also said that it was not necessary to hold a trial to determine damages to thousands of victims. He suggested that $7,800 should be paid to families of those killed or injured seriously, $3,900 be paid to those injured less seriously, and $1,050 to those with minor injuries.

One problem with implementing this order was the incomplete medicolegal documentation for determining which victims were injured seriously, less seriously, and in a minor way. A more serious problem, as previously stated, was that UCC refused to pay.

Unfortunately for the victims, even the Indian Supreme Court may not be the final arbiter of this case. Even after the Supreme Court rules on it, the judgment needs to be implemented in the United States. There is the possibility of the case being appealed in the United States. Even four years after the accident, the compensation issue was no closer to being resolved in the legal system. In the meantime, the victims who are poor and unable to work because of their medical conditions continue to die of their ailments and malnourishment.

In light of the agonizing plight of the victims, the issue of who is responsible becomes a crass legalistic exercise. UCC argues that the accident was caused by sabotage by a disgruntled employee. But it refuses to reveal the identity of the saboteur. It also claims that despite its 51 percent ownership of the Indian subsidiary, it did not control the Indian operation. Hence, it should not be held legally liable for damages. The Indian government argues that since the accident occurred at the company's premises, the company is liable for all damages accruing out of it. There are few legal doctrines and legal precedents available in deciding a case as complex as this one. Legal experts estimate that the case could continue in courts for many more years. Settling the case out of court is the legal, moral, and ethical challenge facing the company and the Indian government.

EXHIBIT 1

## UNION CARBIDE CORPORATION
## Selected Financial Data, 1980–1984

(dollar amounts in millions, except per share figures)

| | *1984*[a] | *1983*[b] | *1982*[c] | *1981* | *1980* |
|---|---|---|---|---|---|
| FROM THE INCOME STATEMENT | | | | | |
| Net sales | $9,508 | $9,001 | $9,061 | $10,168 | $9,994 |
| Cost of sales | 6,702 | 6,581 | 6,687 | 7,431 | 7,186 |
| Research & development expense | 265 | 245 | 240 | 207 | 166 |
| Selling, administrative & other expenses | 1,221 | 1,243 | 1,249 | 1,221 | 1,152 |
| Depreciation | 507 | 477 | 426 | 386 | 326 |
| Interest on long-term and short-term debt | 300 | 252 | 236 | 171 | 153 |
| Other income (expense) — net | 77 | 120 | 162 | 164 | 41 |
| Nonrecurring charge — closing of facilities | 0 | 241 | 0 | 0 | 0 |
| Income before provision for income taxes | 390 | 82 | 385 | 916 | 1,052 |
| Provision for income taxes | 227 | (10) | 58 | 258 | 360 |
| Income before extraordinary charge and cumulative effect of change in accounting principle | 341 | 79 | 310 | 649 | 673 |
| Extraordinary charge | (18) | 0 | 0 | 0 | 0 |
| Cumulative effect of change in accounting principle for ITC | 0 | 0 | 0 | 0 | 217 |
| Net income | 323 | 79 | 310 | 649 | 890 |
| Income per share before extraordinary charge and cumulative effect of change in accounting principle | 4.84 | 1.13 | 4.47 | 9.56 | 10.08 |
| Extraordinary charge per share | (0.25) | 0 | 0 | 0 | 0 |
| Cumulative effect per share of change in accounting principle for ITC | 0 | 0 | 0 | 0 | 3.28 |
| Net income per share | 4.59 | 1.13 | 4.47 | 9.56 | 13.36 |
| FROM THE BALANCE SHEET (at year end) | | | | | |
| Working capital | $1,548 | $1,483 | $1,747 | $2,147 | $2,124 |
| Total assets | 10,518 | 10,295 | 10,616 | 10,423 | 9,659 |
| Long-term debt | 2,362 | 2,387 | 2,428 | 2,101 | 1,859 |
| Total capitalization | 7,962 | 7,999 | 8,305 | 8,018 | 7,282 |
| UCC stockholders' equity | 4,924 | 4,929 | 5,159 | 5,263 | 4,776 |
| UCC stockholders' equity per share | 69.89 | 69.95 | 73.54 | 76.74 | 70.90 |
| OTHER DATA | | | | | |
| Funds from operations — sources | $964 | $708 | $715 | $1,172 | $1,211 |
| Dividends | 240 | 240 | 235 | 224 | 206 |
| Dividends per share | 3.40 | 3.40 | 3.40 | 3.30 | 3.10 |
| Shares outstanding (thousands at year end) | 70,450 | 70,465 | 70,153 | 68,582 | 67,367 |
| Market price per share — high | 65¼ | 73⅞ | 61 | 62⅛ | 52½ |
| Market price per share — low | 32¾ | 51 | 40⅛ | 45¼ | 35¼ |
| Capital expenditures | 670 | 761 | 1,179 | 1,186 | 1,129 |
| Number of employees (at year end) | 98,366 | 99,506 | 103,229 | 110,255 | 116,105 |

EXHIBIT 1 (cont'd)

## UNION CARBIDE CORPORATION
## Selected Financial Data, 1980–1984

(dollar amounts in millions, except per share figures)

| | *1984*[a] | *1983*[b] | *1982*[c] | *1981* | *1980* |
|---|---|---|---|---|---|
| SELECTED FINANCIAL RATIOS | | | | | |
| Total debt/total capitalization (at year end) | 33.7% | 34.0% | 33.9% | 30.3% | 29.9% |
| Net income/average UCC stockholders' equity | 6.6% | 1.6% | 6.0% | 12.9% | 15.3%[b] |
| Net income + minority share of income/average total capitalization | 4.5% | 1.4% | 4.3% | 9.1% | 10.6%[b] |
| Dividends/net income | 74.3% | 303.8% | 75.8% | 34.5% | 30.6%[b] |
| Dividends/funds from operations — sources | 24.9% | 33.9% | 32.9% | 19.1% | 17.0% |

[a] Amounts for 1982 and subsequent years reflect the adoption of Statement of Financial Accounting Standards No. 52.

[b] Net income in these ratios excludes the nonrecurring credit for the cumulative effect of the change in accounting principle for the investment in tax credit (ITC).

[c] Net income per share is based on weighted average number of shares outstanding during the year. *Funds from operations — sources* includes income before extraordinary charge and noncash charge (credits) to income before extraordinary charge. *Total debt* consists of short-term debt, long-term debt, and current installments of long-term debt. *Total capitalization* consists of total debt plus minority stockholders' equity in consolidated subsidiaries and UCC stockholders' equity.

EXHIBIT 2

## UNION CARBIDE CORPORATION
## Consolidated Statement of Income and Retained Earnings
## For the Year Ended December 31, 1982–1984

(dollar amounts in millions, except per share figures)

| | *1984* | *1983* | *1982* |
|---|---|---|---|
| Net sales | | | |
| Deductions (additions) | $9,508 | $9,001 | $9,061 |
| Cost of sales | 6,702 | 6,581 | 6,687 |
| Research & development | 265 | 245 | 240 |
| Selling, administrative, & other expenses | 1,221 | 1,243 | 1,249 |
| Depreciation | 507 | 477 | 426 |
| Interest on long-term & short-term debt | 300 | 252 | 236 |
| Other income — net | (77) | (120) | (162) |
| Nonrecurring charge — closing of facilities | 0 | 241 | 0 |
| Income before provision for income taxes | 590 | 82 | 385 |
| Provision for income taxes | 227 | (10) | 58 |
| Income of consolidated companies | 363 | 92 | 327 |
| Less: Minority stockholders' share of income | 39 | 32 | |
| Plus: UCC share of income of companies carried at equity | 17 | 19 | 19 |
| Income before extraordinary charge | 341 | 79 | 310 |
| Extraordinary charge | (18) | 0 | 0 |
| Net income | 323 | 79 | 310 |
| Retained earnings as of January 1 | 4,509 | 4,670 | 4,595 |
| Subtotal | 4,832 | 4,749 | 4,905 |
| Dividends declared | 240 | 240 | 235 |
| Retained earnings as of December 31 | $4,592 | $4,509 | $4,670 |
| Per share | | | |
| Income before extraordinary charge[a] | $4.84 | $1.13 | $4.47 |
| Extraordinary charge[a] | $(0.25) | 0 | 0 |
| Net income[a] | $4.59 | $1.13 | $4.47 |
| Dividends declared | $3.40 | $3.40 | $3.40 |

[a] Based on 70,478,524 shares (70,347,418 shares in 1983 and 69,305,609 shares in 1982), the weighted average number of shares outstanding during the year.

EXHIBIT 3

**UNION CARBIDE CORPORATION**
**Consolidated Balance Sheet**
**As of December 31, 1983 and 1984**
(millions of dollars)

| | *1984* | *1983* |
|---|---|---|
| Assets | | |
| Cash | $ 28 | $ 46 |
| Time deposits & short-term marketable securities | 68 | 72 |
| | 96 | 118 |
| Notes & accounts receivable | 1,512 | 1,460 |
| Inventories | | |
| Raw materials & supplies | 468 | 473 |
| Work in progress | 409 | 421 |
| Finished goods | 669 | 616 |
| | 1,546 | 1,510 |
| Prepaid expenses | 152 | 157 |
| Total current assets | 3,306 | 3,245 |
| Property, plant, & equipment | 11,131 | 10,708 |
| Less: Accumulated depreciation | 4,748 | 4,426 |
| Net fixed assets | 6,383 | 6,282 |
| Companies carried at equity | 288 | 300 |
| Other investments & advances | 139 | 121 |
| | 427 | 421 |
| Other assets | 402 | 347 |
| Total assets | $10,518 | $10,295 |
| Liabilities & stockholders' equity | | |
| Accounts payable | $ 470 | $ 492 |
| Short-term debt | 217 | 240 |
| Payments due within one year on long-term debt | 104 | 91 |
| Accrued income & other taxes | 124 | 114 |
| Other accrued liabilities | 843 | 825 |
| Total current liabilities | 1,758 | 1,762 |
| Long-term debt | 2,362 | 2,387 |
| Deferred credits | 1,119 | 865 |
| Minority stockholders' equity in consolidated subsidiaries | 355 | 352 |
| UCC stockholders' equity | | |
| Common stock | | |
| Authorized — 180,000 shares | | |
| Issue — 70,600,810 shares (70,567–283 shares in 1983) | 756 | 755 |
| Equity adjustment from foreign currency translation | (419) | (333) |
| Retained earnings | 4,592 | 4,509 |
| | 4,929 | 4,931 |
| Less: treasury stock, at cost — 150,579 shares (101,784 shares in 1983) | 5 | 2 |
| Total UCC stockholders' equity | 4,924 | 4,929 |
| Total liabilities and stockholders' equity | $10,518 | $10,295 |

EXHIBIT 4

**UNION CARBIDE CORPORATION**
**Schematic Layout of Common Headers of MIC Storage Tanks**

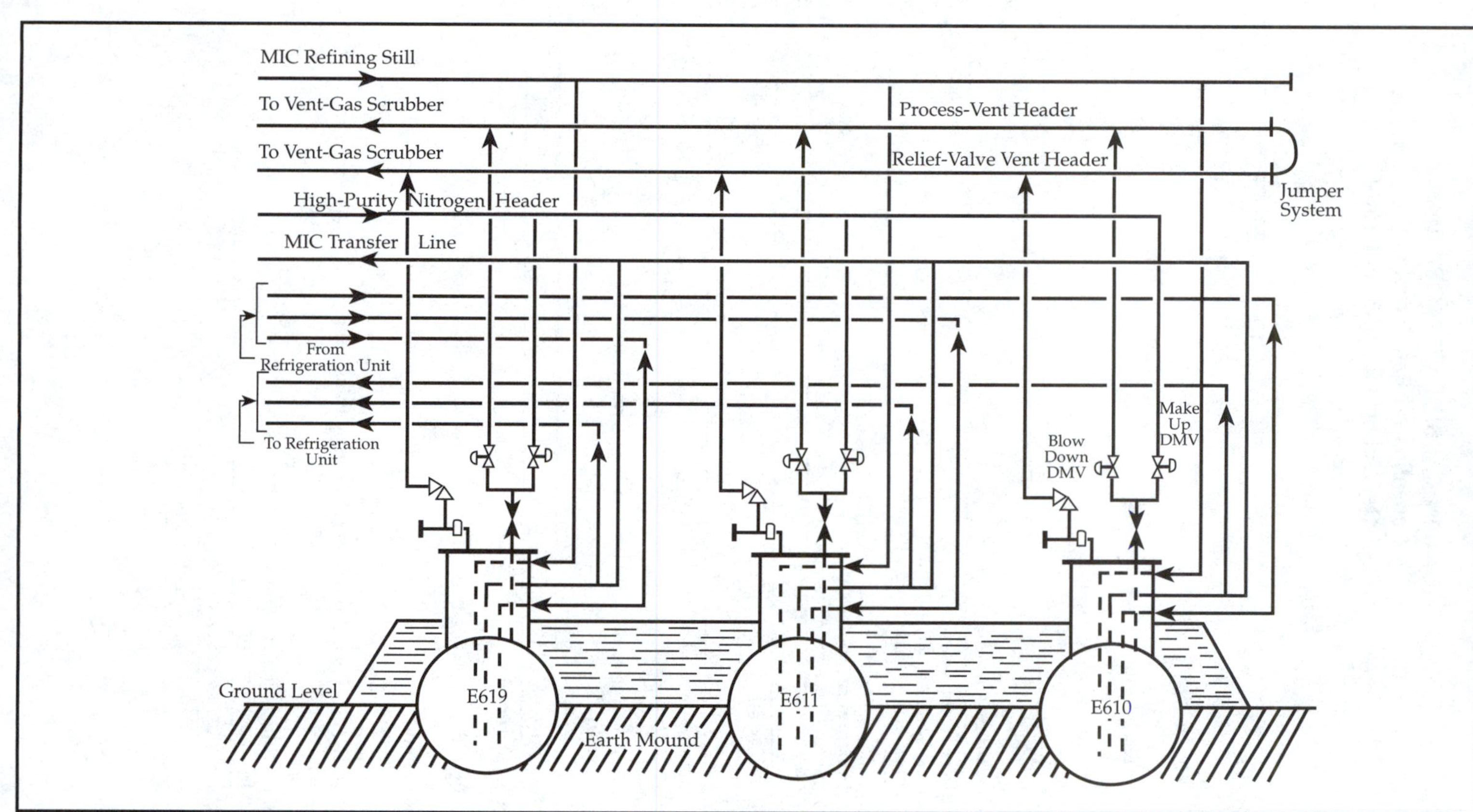


Source: Union Carbide (India) Ltd, *Operating Manual Part II: Methyl Isocyanate Unit* (Bhopal: Union Carbide (India) Ltd, February 1979).

EXHIBIT 5

**UNION CARBIDE CORPORATION**
**MIC Storage Tank**

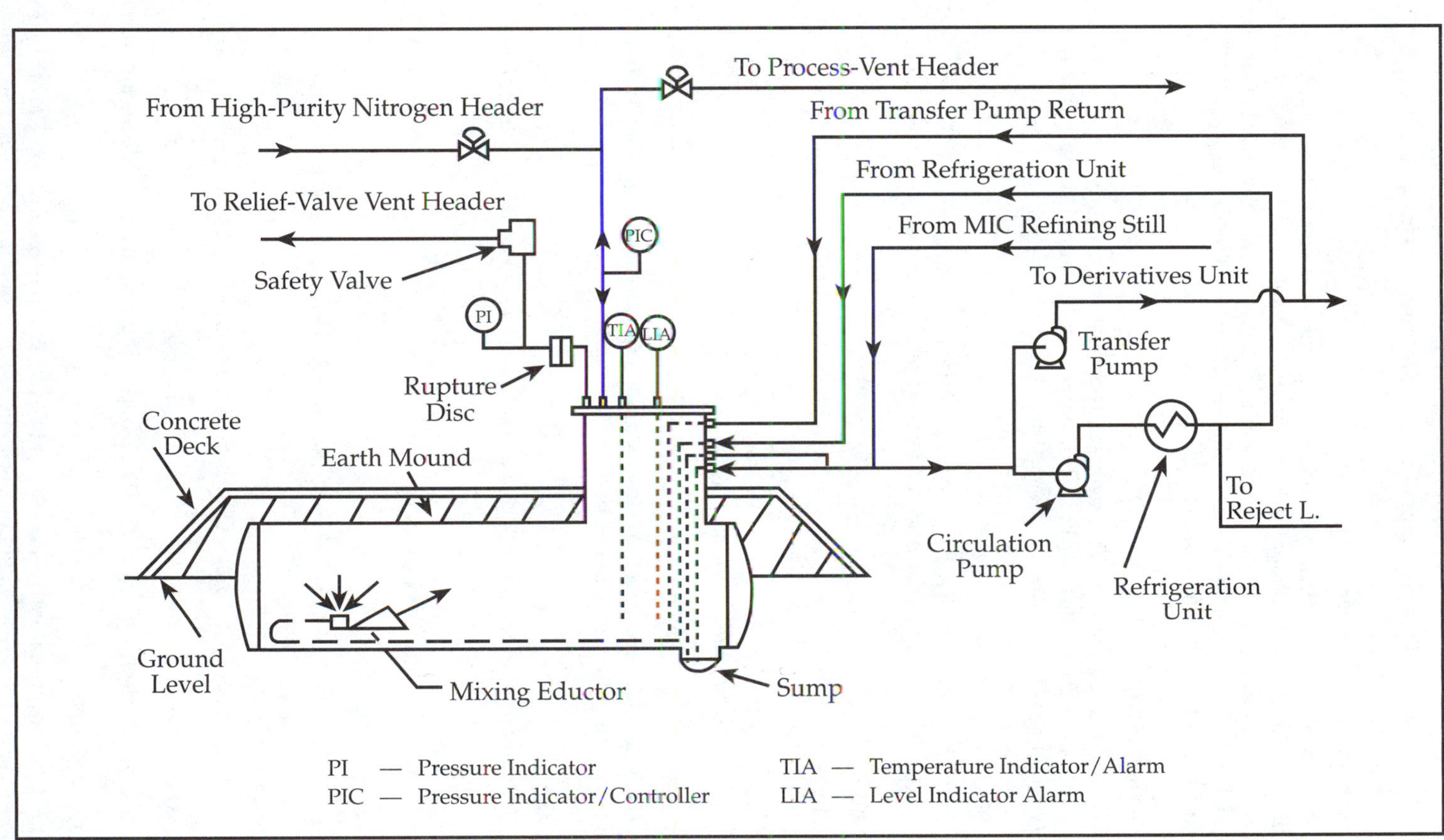


Source: Bhopal Methyl Isocyanate Incident Investigation, Team Report (Danbury, CT: Union Carbide Corporation, March 1985).

EXHIBIT 6

## UNION CARBIDE CORPORATION
## Developments in Lawsuits Against Union Carbide

**December 1984 and January 1985**

Over 45 suits filed against Union Carbide in various state and federal courts; 482 personal injury suits filed against UCIL in Bhopal; a $1 billion representative suit filed in Bhopal against UCIL and UCC; a suit in India's Supreme Court against UCIL and the government of India and Madhya Pradesh. Federal suits against UCC consolidated for pretrial proceedings in the Federal Court of the Southern District of New York under Judge J F K Keenan.

**March–April 1985**

The Bhopal Gas Leak Disaster (Processing of Claims) Ordinance, 1985 passed by Indian Parliament conferring on the government of India powers to secure claims arising out of the disaster. Government of India files *parens patriae* action against UCC.

**May 1985**

UCC offers $5 million for relief, to be deducted from payment of final settlement. It attaches stringent accounting requirements and demands detailed information on victims' health.

**July 1985**

UCC moves to dismiss cases against it on *forum non conveniens* grounds.

**Through 1985**

Out-of-court negotiations.

**March 1986**

Union Carbide and private victim lawyers reach a tentative settlement of $350 million for compensation. Government of India is not party to this settlement and rejects it as absurdly low.

**May 1986**

Judge Keenan rules on the forum issue sending the case to be tried in Indian courts.

**August 1986**

Government of India refiles case in Bhopal District Court.

**April 1987**

Judge Deo of the Bhopal Court revives the attempt to bring about a settlement.

**December 1987**

Bhopal Court orders UCC to pay to victims $270 million in interim payment. UCC appeals.

**April 1988**

Madhya Pradesh High Court upholds the Bhopal Court ruling but reduces amount to $190 million.

**February 14, 1989**

Supreme Court of India orders a settlement of the case whereby Union Carbide agrees to pay $470 million as full and final settlement of all claims arising out of the accident and subsequent litigation. The court also dismisses all criminal and civil charges then pending in India against the Company and its executives.

# PART THREE

## Appendices

# Appendix A
# The Case Method in Strategic Management*

"Because wisdom can't be told."

— *Charles I Gragg*
*(Harvard Business School, 1940)*

The case method is one of the most effective means of management education. Pioneered at the Harvard Business School, it is now widely used in schools of business throughout the world. The use of the case method is predicated upon the belief that tackling real business problems is the best way to develop practitioners. Unlike other pedagogical techniques, many of which may make you the recipient of large amounts of information but do not require its application, the case method requires you to be an active participant in learning activities that are the closest thing to a real life business situation in the classroom context.

It should go without saying that the case method requires students to do most of their studying before class, as contrasted with the lecture method, in which most of the studying occurs later, as class notes are reviewed. If you are going to understand fully the arguments and presentations of your fellow students in class, not to mention give a good presentation of your own, you must be prepared beforehand. In effect, you must place yourself in the role of the responsible manager in the case and make the decision and plan the action called for by the facts as you interpret them.

---

*This Appendix was adapted from a study guide prepared by Professor Luis Ma. R. Calingo at California State University, Fresno. The original study guide was prepared, and subsequently revised, using material from the sources listed in the References.

## Preparing the Case Study

When you prepare for class, plan on reading the case at least three times. Read the case through once, very quickly. The purpose of this reading is to make you familiar with the topic, the "cast of characters," the leading actor whose role you will play as you analyze the case, the general nature and quality of the evidence with which you must work, and some idea of the problem or problems that must be solved. You may wish to differentiate between facts and opinions expressed by the cast of characters. This quick reading is like the first approach to a new city, in which you quickly identify major roads, shopping areas, and office buildings. It is not until the second visit that you pay attention to the details of your own involvement with the city.

On your second reading, you should read the case in depth, at a much slower and more thoughtful rate. Take note of important facts in the prose passages, and carefully examine the exhibits in the case. It is generally true that the casewriter has put the exhibit there for a purpose. The exhibits contain information that will be useful to you in analyzing the situation. Ask yourself what that information is when you study each exhibit. By the end of the second reading of the case, you should be able to abstract from the case a statement of the problem(s) involved, the nature of the decision(s) facing the manager, and most of the major elements (constraints, opportunities and resources) which influence the actions the manager can take.

Finally, recheck the various important facts you have previously identified to make sure that your view of the situation is consistent with all the facts. It is at this point that you will prepare your analysis and recommendations using either the Strategic Management Audit format described in Appendix B or some specific analytical technique that you have learned in previous courses or in earlier sessions of the present course.

There is only one secret to good case learning and that is good preparation on the part of the students. The workload in a case method course is heavy, and you will find that you will need to spend a minimum of 3 to 4 hours preparing for every case session.

## The Use of Extra or Post-Case Data

You are encouraged to deal with the case as it is presented. You should put yourself in the position of the general manager involved in the situation and look at the situation through his or her own eyes. Part of the unique job of being a general manager is that many of your problems are dilemmas. There is no way to come out a winner on all counts. Although additional data might be interesting or useful, hindsight is *not* an effective way to learn about strategic management. *Therefore, you are strongly discouraged from acquiring or using extra or post-case data.* The only exception to this rule is the search for industry averages in conducting financial analyses (see Appendix C).

Some purists in the case method argue that a class should never be told what actually happened in a situation. Each person should leave the classroom situation with his or her plan for solving the problem, and none should be falsely legimitized. The outcome of a situation may not reflect what is, or is not, a good solution. You must remember that just because a company did something different from your recommendations and was successful or unsuccessful is not an indication of the value of your approach. It is, however, interesting and occasionally useful to know what actually occurred. Therefore, if warranted pedagogically, your instructor may tell you what really happened to a company since the time of the case.

## Participating in Class Discussions

Different instructors have different expectations about what should take place in class. The major differences surround the role of the individual student as contrasted to the role of groups of students, and there is no one best way. Each style has its purpose and its parallel circumstances in the real world.

It should be recognized that each student is "participating" in the class even while remaining silent. You should be listening to every other student's contribution to the discussion, constantly comparing what is being said with your own ideas and analysis. In the case method, it is far less important for you to take notes for later review than it is to listen actively to what is being said, and to plan your own next recitation. It is at this very point that the major difference between your learning knowledge (taking in information given to you by a lecturer), and your learning skill (practicing in decision-making and persuasion activities) becomes apparent. You should remember that you are engaged in learning just as much while you are actively listening and following the line of others' argument as you are when you are presenting your own ideas.

### Purely Individual Responsibility

Each student prepares the case analysis without any pre-class discussion with other students. The class consists of presentations of one student viewpoint after another. Depending upon the instructor's preferences, students may be asked to make fairly detailed complete statements of their arguments or they may be encouraged to offer shorter statements selected from their analyses at appropriate points in the development of the class discussion. As an example of the latter, the first student to talk might be asked to "give the relevant facts about the current situation and a forecast of the future environment." Other students might be asked to add to or suggest different interpretations of the situation.

On the one hand, eliciting complete individual arguments from each student often results in a series of statements which share many common points but which taken individually lack breadth. Further, there will likely be quite substantial differences among interpretations of some case facts. On the other hand, building a case analysis bit by bit from selected inputs from each student adds breadth and emphasizes the wide variety of ideas that can be identified in the case material. This second approach, however, may move too slowly to retain the interest of all students. Chances are that your instructor will use a combination of the two approaches. You should therefore feel comfortable whether you are asked to present your full analysis and conclusions or asked to probe deeply into the details of a part of your argument.

The eventual outcome of class discussions of individual efforts will usually be the development of consensus, or general agreement, about the relative merits of a limited number of alternative courses of action. Sometimes the class will develop a general preference for just one solution, even though several different solutions may have been suggested by other individuals. Most frequently this general agreement is reached because the discussion has helped the class discover ingenious ways to incorporate the "best" parts of several individual suggestions into a single preferred solution.

This teaching technique most closely parallels a real-world committee meeting of department heads of equal statuses — discussing a common problem on which each committee member has been supplied with the same background information. The skills in analysis, decision-making, oral presentation of your own position, and synthesis of a plan through compromise are all skills that are much in demand in the real world.

### Individual Input After Small Group Discussions

One very popular variant of the individual student responsibility model is for students to meet in small groups to discuss their individual analyses prior to the class where the instructor is present. This small group meeting allows the individual to "try out" ideas before exposing them to the larger class and the instructor.

Persons who tend to be quiet in larger group meetings often feel comfortable speaking out in small groups. In this method, no attempt is made to force a consensus within the small groups. Each individual is independently responsible for later presenting ideas in the full class. Often small groups retain their identities throughout the course; the same 3 to 5 persons may constitute a group for pre-class discussion of cases for weeks or months at a stretch. This continued contact is thought to encourage confidence on the part of shy participants and to take effective advantage of the differing strengths of various group members. For example, if a group contains a person with good accounting skills and another person with special sensitivity to personnel relations, each may learn much from the other in the pre-class discussions.

This variant has its parallel in the business world. Often large group meetings, such as annual general meetings, will occur after a subject has been discussed avidly by small groups in an organization.

### Group Oral Case Presentation

The instructor may expect that the pre-class discussion groups will reach a consensus within each group and nominate a spokesperson to present that viewpoint in class. This cuts down on the number of students who speak out in each class and often results in a longer time available to listen to each argument.

Another variation of this technique is the formal presentation, which is scheduled in advance. One group makes a formal presentation, usually 20 to 30 minutes in length, and the other groups take the role of a critical audience, putting forward questions, rebuttals, or alternative analyses. A typical ground rule for oral presentations is that all group members must be involved in the oral discussion. Although groups often divide the analysis work among group members, it is helpful if each group member also develops a preliminary analysis of the entire case to share and compare with group members.

The formal presentation most closely parallels business-world briefings of management by junior executives or, alternatively, the presentations made by consultants to the company's management.

## Preparing Written Analyses of Cases

Most instructors require students to submit written analyses of cases (known as WACs at the Harvard Business School). No matter what individual requirements regarding your WACs form and style may be set forth by your instructor, it is most important that your WAC makes clear what you recommend and why you recommend it. The ability to get these two ideas across clearly and in a few words has often been identified as one of the surest ways to succeed as a manager.

What action you recommend can easily be identified as the choice arrived at in Step 7 of the Strategic Management Audit presented in Appendix B. This can usually be stated in very few words — why you recommend the action you have selected as "best" in terms of the whole analytical plan you have carried out. How much of your reasoning needs to be repeated in the written report depends on a number of factors:

1. Whether your instructor has specified a maximum word limit for your report.[1] In general, references to case facts can be brief; most instructors are willing to assume that every reader of your WAC will have read the case carefully. Thus, your argument can focus on the inferences you have drawn from your combination of case facts. In contrast, where your argument is supported extensively by facts that are not in the case itself, you will need to introduce and qualify the facts.
2. The extent to which your objectives and/or your value systems differ from the expected norm of the class. For example, if you are writing a report about an American multinational corporation and you adopt the objective "maximizing profitability," you need to write little justification for your general standards. Most American firms can be reasonably assumed as operating according to such standards. However, if you believe that a firm such as the one in the case at hand "maximizes social welfare" or "promotes the equitable distribution of wealth," you should spend more time and words in justifying this less usual objective.
3. The extent to which your predictions of the future and/or your expected outcomes of actions are "conventional" or "unconventional" in your own culture. It may be difficult to sense whether this is so in writing a report; it is easier to do this in an oral presentation since you have a chance to respond to questions. However, the more unconventional your thinking, the more you should expect to have to explain yourself.

Although your instructor should make clear the requirements regarding your WACs form, the following are generally useful guidelines for writing a case analysis report:

1. Prepare a summary statement, no more than one page in length, that clearly states what you recommend and the 1 or 2 most important reasons why. This summary statement will become the first sheet of your report. Often in the business world, busy managers will refuse to read reports that are not accompanied by such summaries. Further, the busiest managers may not even read anything but the summaries of reports. Whether or not this is true for all cultures, the summary, clearly, is important. Although it will be presented as the first page of your WAC, you may in fact want to write it last, in order to be sure that it is as convincing as possible.

[1]The author normally prescribes a page limit of three single-spaced or five double-spaced typewritten pages. Exhibits such as tables and figures do not count toward this page limit.

2. The body of your report may well follow such an outline as the Strategic Management Audit format suggested in Appendix B, introducing ideas in the order shown below:

   a. Description of the organization's existing strategy
   b. Analysis of factors in the external environment and a forecast of changes in those factors
   c. Audit of the organization's resources and capabilities
   d. Identification of alternative actions that might be taken, with predicted consequences of each alternative
   e. Description in detail of the recommended action and its implementation

   Instructors differ in their preferences regarding the mention of case facts in the WAC. Some like a fairly detailed account of all the case facts that are later to be used in your argument. Others (like this author) prefer to assume that all readers of the WAC will have read the case. For those who prefer only a short introduction, references to case facts would appear only at those places in the report where they are especially pertinent to a point being made.
3. Many analyses involving mathematical comparisons and computation will be made much clearer by the use of tables, charts, and diagrams (generically referred to as "exhibits"). If you use only 1 or 2 exhibits in the WAC, it is best to insert them at the point in the text where you refer to the ideas they demonstrate. If there are many such exhibits, it is better to put them in an appendix at the end of the report, numbered in the order in which they are referred. Do not include tables or figures to which you do not refer in the text of your report. In fact, unless you have at least 1 to 2 sentences of conclusions or inferences that you have drawn from an exhibit, the table or figure should probably be left out.
4. If you need to add substantial material to the case, such as long quotations supporting your assumptions about the case, these may be included as appendices to your report. However, be sure that the point you are supporting warrants all the extra reading you are requiring your reader to do.
5. Depending on the length of your report you may need a short summary paragraph or two. Remember, however, that your first page is a summary in itself. If your WAC is no more than ten pages long, it will not need a final summary.

Throughout the WAC, whether there is a word limit or not, you should make sure that you include only those ideas which help you explain what you recommend and why. If you find that certain case facts are irrelevant to your decision, they should not be repeated in your report. If you have based your decision on a single-valued objective, you need not specify all the other objectives you might have developed. You should mention any truly supportable alternatives you considered and rejected since you can often show in this way very effectively why you chose as you did. But you should not try to include every conceivable alternative, including unrealistic ones, just out of a wish to appear "complete." To describe an alternative in 50 words, only to demolish it in 10 words, is often called "setting up a straw man:" creating an artificial adversary whose only importance is that he or she is easy to defeat.

The overall criterion for a written report should be your expected effect on your audience. Be as brief as possible given the level of understanding of your audience, but make the WAC long enough to persuade the reader that your appraisal of the case is effective. Whatever your specific recommendations, they must be supported by the evidence presented and the analysis made. There is no room for seat-of-the-pants decision-making in the case method.

All of case method learning is best done by experience — the major message of this Appendix. Analyze the case and participate in your class discussion. Receive feedback and try to analyze the case once more. Prepare a written analysis of the case. Receive feedback and try to analyze the case again. We have seen earlier that this is a good way to learn management skills. It is also true that one of the first skills you will learn is how to solve, with only limited or imperfect information, the messy, complex, yet interesting business problems that characterize the case method.

## References

Bednarz, Dan, and Donna J Wood. *Research in Teams: A Practical Guide to Group Policy Analysis.* Englewood Cliffs, NJ: Prentice–Hall, 1991.

Charan, Ram. "Classroom Techniques in Teaching by the Case Method." *Academy of Management Review* 1 (July 1976): 116–123.

Culliton, James W. *Handbook for Casewriting.* Makati, Philippines: Asian Institute of Management, 1973.

Dooley, A R, and W Skinner. "Casing Casemethod Methods." *Academy of Management Review,* 2 (April 1977): 277–289.

Easton, Geoff. *Learning from Case Studies.* 2nd ed. London: Prentice–Hall International, 1992.

Reynolds, John I. *Case Method in Management Development: Guide for Effective Use.* Management Development Series No. 17. Geneva: International Labour Organisation, 1980.

Ronstadt, Robert. *The Art of Case Analysis: A Guide to the Diagnosis of Business Situations.* 2nd ed. Dover, MA: Lord Publishing, 1980.

# Appendix B
# The Strategic Management Audit

## 1. PROFILE OF CURRENT STRATEGY

1.1. **Concept of Business.** How does the organization define its business?

1.1.1. What *customer functions* does it provide? Specify the breadth of the organization's product/service line, the way its product or service is positioned (e.g., a high-quality position), and whether the product/service definition is broad (representing a generic customer need) or narrow (subfunction).

1.1.2. What *customer segments* does it serve? Specify the breadth of market segments served and how the market is segmented (i.e., customer characteristics such as geographic location or product-related approaches such as product usage).

1.1.3. What is the *degree of vertical integration*? In which stages of the value chain (i.e., the sequence of stages from raw materials to finished products) does the company operate? (The more stages in the value chain the organization participates in, the more vertically integrated it is.)

1.1.4. With what *technology* does the organization perform its customer functions? (Several different technologies may provide the same function or satisfy the same customer needs. An organization may choose to employ all technologies, any single technology, or a combination of technologies. Employing multiple technologies can involve an increased investment and dilution of effort; however, complementary technologies provide the potential to share assets and result in economies.)

1.2. **Concept of Competition.** How does the organization compete within the boundaries of its business definition?
   1.2.1. What *weapons* does the organization employ in order to secure a sustainable competitive advantage in the marketplace (e.g., differentiation, cost leadership, focus, etc)?
   1.2.2. What is its *intended competitive position* in terms of market share, general image, and other key success factors in the industry (e.g., industry leader, challenger, follower or nicher)?

1.3. **Company Self-concept.** How does the organization define its self-concept?
   1.3.1. What are the organization's *performance goals and objectives* (e.g., profitability, growth, market share, social responsibility, etc)?
   1.3.2. What is the prevailing *corporate mentality and culture*? (Describe the organization's philosophy, top management style, risk-taking behavior, orientation toward its publics, and other internal factors that may influence strategic choice.)

## 2. ENVIRONMENTAL ANALYSIS

2.1. **Social, Economic, and Political Factors**
   2.1.1. Are there recent social, cultural, or demographic trends that will affect the organization?
   2.1.2. What national and international economic policies and events have a potential major impact on the organization?
   2.1.3. What present or forecasted economic conditions will have a potential major impact?
   2.1.4. To what extent does government regulation affect operations?

2.2. **Product and Technological Factors**
   2.2.1. What products and services are satisfying the market's needs? What improvements or innovations in the products/services are possible? Can complementary products be developed?
   2.2.2. What manufacturing processes are required to produce the product? What process innovations are possible?
   2.2.3. What ingredients or raw materials are required in the manufacturing process? What innovations in these inputs are possible?

2.3. **Industry and Competitive Factors**
   2.3.1. What is the level of jockeying for position among current industry competitors? (Who is the organization's competition? How intense is rivalry among competitors?)
   2.3.2. What is the bargaining power of the organization's suppliers? Can they substantially influence its costs?
   2.3.3. What is the bargaining power of the organization's customers? Can they substantially influence its prices?
   2.3.4. How significant is the threat of new entrants into the industry?

2.3.5. How significant is the threat of substitute products or services being introduced into the industry?

## 3. STRATEGIC FORECASTING

3.1. Which of the environmental forces identified earlier are likely to be important in the future?

3.2. What opportunities and threats will the organization face in the future?

## 4. INTERNAL ASSESSMENT

4.1. **Operational Dimension**

4.1.1. What are the critical requirements for success in the industry? What does it take to be a hero or a loser in the industry? (These are often expressed as required capabilities in the functional areas, such as marketing, production, finance, and research and development.)

4.1.2. What are the organization's capabilities in each of these critical success factors? What is it best at? Worst at?

4.1.3. Will the organization's capabilities increase or diminish as it matures or grows? In which areas?

4.1.4. What is the organization's ability to respond and adapt to new conditions in each functional area? (For example, can the organization adapt to competing on service? Competing on cost? Adding new products?)

4.2. **Financial Dimension**

4.2.1. How well is the organization performing in financial terms? (Evaluate the overall financial health of the firm. Calculate liquidity, activity, leverage, and profitability ratios. Then compare these ratios with industry norms,

The product life cycle and scenario development are two of the most commonly used tools in strategic forecasting. In forecasting the firm's environment, the strategist should monitor the following *driving forces* which create *discontinuities* via incentives or pressures for change (Porter, 1980):

1. Long-run changes in growth
2. Changes in buyer segments served
3. Buyers' learning
4. Reduction of uncertainty in the industry
5. Diffusion of proprietaries in the industry
6. Accumulation of experience
7. Expansion or contraction in scale
8. Changes in input costs and exchange rates
9. Product innovation
10. Marketing innovation
11. Process innovation
12. Structural changes in adjacent industries
13. Government policy change
14. Entries into and exits from the industry

past organization performance [if industry norms are not available], or absolute standards [if neither industry norms nor historical data are available.])

4.2.2. What is the organization's *maximum sustainable growth rate* in financial terms? How much in terms of *strategic funds* does this sustainable growth translate to? Given its existing financial condition, can it grow within the industry? Can it increase market share?

4.2.3. What is the organization's capacity to respond quickly to moves by others, or to mount an immediate offensive? (This is a function of organizational "slack" brought about by such factors as uncommitted cash reserves, reserve borrowing power and excess plant capacity.)

4.2.4. What is the organization's ability to sustain a protracted warfare, which may put pressure on earnings or cash flow? (This will also be determined by such considerations as cash reserves and lack of stock market pressure.)

4.3. **Management Dimension**

4.3.1. How does the organization measure up to the attributes of "excellent, well-managed" companies? (In *In Search of Excellence*, Thomas Peters and Robert Waterman identified these attributes as follows: a bias toward action, simple form, and lean staff; continued contact with customers; productivity improvement via people; autonomy to encourage entrepreneurship; stress on a key business value; emphasis on doing what it knows best, and simultaneous loose-tight controls.)

4.3.2. What kinds of managers comprise the organization's leadership, particularly the general manager (GM)? What are their backgrounds and experience? (Comment on the GM's willingness and ability to respond to environmental demands, leadership qualities, ability to motivate, and ability to coordinate particular functions or groups of functions.)

## 5. DEVELOPMENT OF STRATEGIC ALTERNATIVES

5.1. Can the organization's objectives be achieved by incremental changes (e.g., fine-tuning) of strategies presently being implemented?

5.2. What are the major feasible alternative strategies available to this organization?

5.2.1. How can the organization utilize its strengths to exploit the opportunities it faces?

5.2.2. How can the organization overcome its weaknesses to enable it to exploit its opportunities?

5.2.3. How can the organization utilize its strengths to ward off the threats it faces?

5.2.4. How can the organization overcome its weaknesses to enable it to ward off threats?

## 6. STRATEGY EVALUATION

Evaluate each alternative strategy, including the current strategy, in terms of the following criteria.

6.1. **Suitability**

6.1.1. Is the proposed strategy consistent with the foreseeable environmental opportunities and threats?

6.1.2. Does the strategy exploit or enhance a current competitive advantage, or does it create a new source of sustainable competitive advantage?

6.2. **Validity**

6.2.1. Are the main assumptions about key environmental trends and the outcomes of the strategy realistic?

6.2.2. Are the assumptions based on reliable and valid information?

6.3. **Consistency**

6.3.1. Are the basic elements of the strategy consistent with the objectives being pursued?

6.3.2. Are the basic elements of the strategy consistent with each other?

6.4. **Feasibility**

6.4.1. Is the strategy appropriate to the available resources?

6.4.2. Are the basic elements and premises of the strategy understandable and acceptable to the operating managers who will have the responsibility for implementation?

6.5. **Vulnerability**

6.5.1. To what extent are projected outcomes dependent on data or assumptions of dubious quality and origin?

6.5.2. Are the risks of failure acceptable? Are there adequate contingency plans for coping with these risks?

6.5.3. Can the decision be reversed in the future? How long will it take? What are the consequences?

6.6. **Potential Rewards**

6.6.1. Are the projected outcomes satisfactory in light of the provisional objectives for the business?

6.6.2. Are the adjustments to the objectives acceptable to the firm's "stakeholders?"

## 7. STRATEGIC CHOICE

7.1. Which of the strategic alternatives are you recommending for the organization and if it is a multibusiness firm, for each of its business units?

7.2. Justify your recommendation in terms of its ability to resolve both short- and long-term problems, create a sustainable competitive advantage, and achieve the organization's objectives.

## 8. STRATEGY IMPLEMENTATION

### 8.1. Functional Fits

8.1.1. What functional strategies and policies must the organization establish in order to best implement the strategy? (These should cover strategies for the manufacturing, marketing, financial, human resources, technology, and procurement areas.)

8.1.2. What functional strategies and policies is the organization actually pursuing?

### 8.2. Administrative Fits

8.2.1. What type of organizational structure, leadership, systems, and culture must the organization establish in order to best implement the strategy?

8.2.2. What type of structure, leadership, systems, and culture are actually in place?

### 8.3. Plan of Action

8.3.1. Of the changes required to achieve administrative and financial fits, which are most critical to the achievement of the chosen strategy? To what extent are they compatible with the organization's existing culture?

8.3.2. Prepare an action plan to implement the chosen strategy by adopting any or a feasible combination of the following generic approaches: (a) ignoring the culture, (b) managing around the current culture by changing the implementation plan, (c) attempting to change the culture to fit the strategy, and (d) changing the strategy to fit the culture.

8.3.3. Is the action plan feasible in light of available resources? Can *pro forma* budgets be prepared and agreed upon? Are priorities and timetables appropropriate to individual elements of the action plan?

8.3.4. Will new policies and procedures need to be developed?

### 8.4. Strategic Control

8.4.1. Are current control systems adequate to ensure conformance of organizational actions with the chosen strategy and action plan? Are appropriate performance standards and measures being used? Are reward systems capable of recognizing and rewarding good performance?

8.4.2. Is the current information system capable of checking systematically and continuously whether the premises on which the strategy is based are still valid?

8.4.3. Is the current information system capable of assessing whether the overall strategy should be changed in light of the results associated with the incremental actions to implement the overall strategy?

8.4.4. Is the current information system capable of monitoring a wide range of events that are likely to affect the course of its strategy, inside and outside the organization?

8.4.5. Does the organization have an agreed-upon mechanism for conducting a thorough, often rapid, reconsideration of the organization's strategy should a sudden, unexpected event occur?

# Appendix C
# Financial Analysis for Strategic Management*

## Introduction

The performance of financial analysis is imperative for the successful dissection of any policy-related case. The analysis provides insights into the past and present and helps predict the future condition of the organization given a certain set of assumptions. This appendix focuses on five major areas of financial analysis pertinent to analyzing business policy cases:

1. **Ratio analysis:** A tool used for evaluating a company's performance in relation to itself and its competitors.
2. **Working capital analysis:** A type of analysis used for evaluating the company's ability to meet short-term debt obligations and finance current operations.
3. **Capital budgeting:** A process by which proposals for capital investment are evaluated and selected.
4. **Mergers and acquisitions analysis:** A means of determining the value and method of payment.

---

*This note was initially prepared by Professors Manab Thakur and Amir Jassim of The Sid Craig School of Business at California State University, Fresno (CSUF), and was revised for this book by Professor Luis Ma. R. Calingo while on leave from CSUF. Reprinted with permission from Professors Thakur and Jassim.

5. ***Pro forma* financial statement analysis:** A comprehensive financial forecasting that, in most cases, needs to be made in order to justify your recommendations.

## Ratio Analysis

### Who Uses Ratio Analysis?

Users of ratio analysis can be divided into two groups: outsiders, such as private investors, corporate investors, bankers, and government agencies; and insiders, such as accountants, finance officers, and managers.

### How are Ratios Used in Evaluating Organizational Performance?

Ratios are used to compare an organization's performance with itself and/or with competitors of like size and structure. Primarily two methods are employed: *cross-sectional analysis*, an analysis of a company's performance with that of similar companies for a given time period, and *time-series analysis*, an analysis of a company's performance with itself and/or with companies of like size and structure covering successive time periods.

### What Kinds of Ratios are Used?

There are five major groups of ratios used for comparative analysis: profitability, liquidity, leverage, activity, and market. The data used in calculating ratios come primarily from the company's financial statements — the income statement (IS) and the balance sheet (BS).

### How are These Ratios Calculated?

1. Profitability ratios measure the overall effectiveness of management to generate a profit:

   a. Gross profit margin $= \dfrac{\text{Gross profit (IS)}}{\text{Total sales (IS)}}$

   b. Operating profit margin $= \dfrac{\text{Operating income (IS)}}{\text{Total sales (IS)}}$

   c. Net profit margin $= \dfrac{\text{Net income after taxes (IS)}}{\text{Total sales (IS)}}$

   d. Return on investment $= \dfrac{\text{Net income after taxes (IS)}}{\text{Total assets (BS)}}$

   e. Return on equity $= \dfrac{\text{Net income after taxes (IS)}}{\text{Stockholders' equity (BS)}}$

2. Liquidity ratios measure the ability of the company to meet its short-term debts:

   a. Current ratio $= \dfrac{\text{Current ratio (BS)}}{\text{Current liabilities (BS)}}$

   b. Quick ratio $= \dfrac{\text{Current assets (BS)} - \text{Inventories (BS)}}{\text{Current liabilities (BS)}}$

3. Activity ratios measure how efficiently the company's resources are being utilized; they focus on the generation of sales with a given asset base:

   a. Average collection period $= \dfrac{\text{Accounts receivables (BS)}}{\text{Average daily credit sales (IS)}}$

   b. Average payment period $= \dfrac{\text{Accounts payable (BS)}}{\text{Average daily credit purchases (IS)}}$

   c. Inventory turnover $= \dfrac{\text{Cost of goods sold (IS)}}{\text{Inventories (BS)}}$

   d. Total asset turnover $= \dfrac{\text{Sales (IS)}}{\text{Total assets (BS)}}$

   e. Fixed asset turnover $= \dfrac{\text{Sales (IS)}}{\text{Net fixed assets (BS)}}$

4. Leverage ratios measure the relative amount of long-term debt the company carries and its ability to service it:

   a. Debt to assets $= \dfrac{\text{Total liabilities (BS)}}{\text{Total assets (BS)}}$

   b. Long-term debt to equity $= \dfrac{\text{Long-term debt (BS)}}{\text{Stockholders' equity (BS)}}$

   c. Debt to capital $= \dfrac{\text{Long-term liabilities (BS)}}{\text{Long-term debt + Stockholders' equity (BS)}}$

   d. Short-term liabilities to total debt $= \dfrac{\text{Current liabilities}}{\text{Total liabilities (BS)}}$

   e. Times interest earned $= \dfrac{\text{Earnings before interest and taxes (IS)}}{\text{Interest (IS)}}$

5. Market ratios measure the performance of the common stock of a firm:

a. Earnings per share (EPS) $= \dfrac{\text{Net income available to common stockholders (IS)}}{\text{Number of common stock shares outstanding (BS)}}$

b. Dividend payout $= \dfrac{\text{Dividend per share of common share (BS)}}{\text{Earnings per share (BS)}}$

c. Dividend yield $= \dfrac{\text{Dividend per share of common stock (BS)}}{\text{Price per share (BS or WSJ)}}$

d. Price/earnings (PE) ratio $= \dfrac{\text{Price per share (BS or WSJ)}}{\text{Earnings per share (BS)}}$

e. Book value per share $= \dfrac{\text{Common stockholders equity (BS)}}{\text{Number of common stock shares outstanding (BS)}}$

f. Price to book value $= \dfrac{\text{Price per share (BS or WSJ)}}{\text{Book value per share (BS)}}$

## How Should These Ratios Be Interpreted?

It is important to remember that these ratios do not make much sense unless they are compared within the industry in which the company conducts its business. An industry is defined as a group of firms that produce products or services that can be considered close substitutes for one another. For example, an analysis of a case involving Sarsi will include a comparison of Sarsi's ratios with the averages of the soft drink industry. It is imperative to select the proper industry for making comparisons or the analysis will be misleading.

It is more difficult to perform a ratio analysis for a conglomerate. In this situation it is necessary to examine the relevant segment(s) of the business being reviewed and then compare the performance of each segment with the appropriate industry average. In other situations, it may be necessary to concentrate on the major product lines of the company to see where most of the revenues are being generated. Relevant industry averages are given by the Standard Industrial Classification Code (SIC), a three- or four-digit identification number assigned according to the primary type of business in which a firm engages. Classification descriptions are listed in the SIC Manual or similar guides produced by government statistical bodies.

Certain publications provide industry data and background information on publicly held corporations, mainly based in the United States or the United Kingdom. Among these references are the following:

1. **Moody's.** Data is provided by industry and include consolidated income statements, ratios' capital stock, and long-term debt.
2. **Standard & Poor's Corporation Records.** Same as Moody's, but includes one-page fact sheets for each company.
3. **Value Line Investment Survey.** Includes a wealth of editorial comments on corporations along with pertinent data on each.
4. **Industry Surveys.** Information is arranged by industry and includes comparisons of each company against the industry average.
5. **Annual Statement Studies by Robert Morris.** Prominent industry ratios are provided for comparison.

In addition, it is important to note the following:

1. Corporations listed in these sources have common stock that is publicly held and traded on the various stock exchanges. No information is given on privately held corporations.
2. Some company cases are "disguised." Naturally, there is no information for these organizations because names have been changed to protect the firm's identities. Nonetheless, it should be possible to find the related industry averages for comparative purposes.
3. Data on subsidiaries can be found if the parent company can be located. *Who Owns Whom* (Dun & Bradstreet) provides information.
4. In some cases, it may be difficult to extract ratios from the appropriate industry category because the library may not have the reference you seek. Therefore, it is always useful to consult with the reference librarian and to state specifically what is being sought.
5. The method used to compute a given ratio may vary. The formulas used by other sources do not always match up precisely with one's own. To make a proper comparison, the formula employed *must be identical.*

Because of these problems, Exhibit 1 provides rules of thumb for interpreting the ratios. Please note that these rules are for general guidance only.

Now, with an understanding of what some of the key ratios mean, calculate the ratios using Exhibits 2 and 3 and see if you arrive at the same results as Exhibit 4.

## Working Capital Analysis

By definition, working capital is the excess of current assets over current liabilities computed by subtracting current liabilities from current assets. It provides an index of financial soundness for current creditors and is one of the primary indicators of short-term-run solvency for a business. When a financial analysis is performed, a measurement of working capital should be considered in conjunction with the liquidity ratios. The current working-capital amount should be compared with the firm's past figures to determine if it is reasonable. Some caution should be exercised here since the relative size of the firm may be expanding or contracting.

Neither the balance sheet nor the income statement tells us anything about the transactions entered into during a given period to finance a firm's operations. For example, neither would show explicitly the sale of stock, a rollover of debt, or the purchase of land. A statement of changes in financial position focuses one's attention on changes in working capital and can provide information on items such as:

1. How funds provided by operations were used.
2. Where the funds used to invest in new plant and equipment came from.
3. How funds derived from a new bond issue or the sale of common stock were used.
4. How it was possible to continue payment of a regular dividend in the face of an operating loss.
5. The method of achieving debt repayment.
6. What funds were used to redeem the company's preferred stock.
7. How the increase in working capital was financed.
8. Why, despite record profits, the working-capital position is lower than last year's.

The balance sheet shows a variety of assets held by a company at a given time and the manner in which those assets are financed. The income statement gives the results of operations for a specific fiscal period. Since the generation of income will result in an increase in a variety of assets and the incurrence of expense will result in the consumption of assets and/or the creation of liabilities, it should be apparent that net income cannot be equated with an increase in liquidity. It is possible for a firm to be very profitable and still experience difficulty meeting debt obligations or lack of funds for future expansion. A business can successfully increase sales and at the same time dry up its liquidity position due to the investment of funds in assets that cannot be converted into cash fast enough to meet maturing obligations.

The statement of changes in financial position (see Exhibits 5 and 6) discloses the effect of earning activities on liquid resources. It focuses on such matters as what became of net income during the period, as well as what assets were acquired and how they were financed. It highlights clearly the distinction between net income and working capital provided by operations.

The significance of a change in liquidity, whether positive or negative, cannot be determined by the statement of changes in financial position alone. It should be linked to other variables in a firm's financial structure and operating results. For example, an increase in cash may have been gained by selling off assets whose earning power will be missed in the future, or the increase may have been caused by the incurrence of debt that has a high rate of interest expense and/or stringent repayment terms.

The statement of changes in financial position is also of great value to the analyst who wants to project operating results based on present and future productive capacity. In addition, the future potential for expansion and the sources from which this may be met can be forecasted. Using the financial statements as provided earlier, examine carefully how the statements are prepared.

## Capital Budgeting

A firm's earning power and value often rest on the effective use of its fixed assets (such as its building, plant, and equipment) as well as the proper use of its financial sources or funds. Fixed assets become obsolete or are abused from time to time and require attention. Since these assets primarily determine the potential of an organization, any decision for overhauling these earning assets has to be made with caution and prudence. Capital budgeting is a process that assists in evaluating the use of assets and funds and helps the firm in selecting the best alternatives with potentials for maximum return.

The capital-budgeting process involves three interrelated steps:

1. **Investment proposal generation.** Proposals could be generated by anyone in the company. Any proposal put forward must be scrutinized for its value-added contributions. Needless to say, the larger the capital outlays request, the more critical the scrutiny should be.

2. **Estimating relevant cash flows.** This is perhaps the most difficult task since the manager is not only examining the numbers but is also judging the feasibility of the project itself in terms of its cash usage. For example, cash outlay associated with the purchase of a new machine would include not only the purchase price but also the following:
   a. Machine transportation and installation costs
   b. Cost of training employees
   c. Cost of changing the administrative procedure (reporting forms may have to be redesigned, for example)
   d. If the new machine is replacing the existing one, then you should deduct the sales price of the existing machine from the cost of the new one and consider the tax implications as well. For instance:

      Old machine's book value = \$12,000
      Old machine's sale price = \$15,000
      Tax liability = \$3,000 × 0.34 = \$1,020

   (The firm is assumed to be in the 34 percent tax bracket and \$1,020 should be added to the cost of the new machine.)

   With the above explanation, consider now the illustration of cash outflow and cash inflow with the following illustration.

   The ABC Company is contemplating introduction of a product, and the life cycle of this product is estimated to be five years with a forecast of cash inflows to be:

| Year 1 | Year 2 | Year 3 | Year 4 | Year 5 |
|---|---|---|---|---|
| \$70,000 | 100,000 | 150,000 | 90,000 | 60,000 |

Cash outflows (labor, materials, promotion, etc but excluding the initial investment of \$100,000) are:

| Year 1 | Year 2 | Year 3 | Year 4 | Year 5 |
|---|---|---|---|---|
| \$40,000 | 60,000 | 90,000 | 60,000 | 40,000 |

The expected net cash flows from the new product are:

| | *Initial Investment* | *Year 1* | *Year 2* | *Year 3* | *Year 4* | *Year 5* |
|---|---|---|---|---|---|---|
| Cash in | | \$70,000 | 100,000 | 150,000 | 90,000 | 60,000 |
| Cash out | \$ 100,000 | 40,000 | 60,000 | 90,000 | 60,000 | 40,000 |
| Net C/F | –\$ 100,000 | 30,000 | 40,000 | 60,000 | 30,000 | 20,000 |

3. **Project selection.** Given the net cash flow figures as above, management now needs to decide whether to accept or reject the proposal. The following methods are usually used to arrive at a decision:

   a. The payback period is the number of years required to recover the initial investment. For the example cited above, $70,000 will be recovered in the first two years and when the third-year net of $60,000 is added, the payback period becomes 2.5 years. After two years and six months, the project proposal appears to be freestanding (remember, the initial investment was $100,000).
   This method, of course, is appealing because of its simplicity and emphasis on the liquidity of the project. However, it presents a problem when management is faced with more than one project with similar payback periods.

   b. The *net present value* (NPV) has to be computed for identical payback periods and, most importantly, for the consideration of the time value of money. NPV is calculated by subtracting the initial investment from the present value of the projects' cash inflows. For computation, one first ascertains the firm's cost of capital (i.e., at what rate of interest the company can borrow). Going back to the example in step 2 and assuming 12 percent as the cost of capital, the NPV of the project will be:

$$
\begin{aligned}
\text{NPV} &= CF_1(PVIF_{12,1}) + CF_2(PVIF_{12,2}) + CF_3(PVIF_{12,3}) \\
&\quad + CF_4(PVIF_{12,4}) + CF_5(PVIF_{12,5}) \\
&\quad - \text{initial investment} \\
&= 30{,}000(0.893) + 40{,}000(0.797) \\
&\quad + 60{,}000(0.712) + 30{,}000(0.636) \\
&\quad + 20{,}000(0.567) - 100{,}000 \\
&= 26{,}790 + 31{,}880 + 42{,}720 + 19{,}080 \\
&\quad + 11{,}340 - 100{,}000 \\
&= 31{,}810
\end{aligned}
$$

The company will add $31,810 to its value by accepting the project. If NPV comes to zero, it will mean that the project will cover only the cost of capital or break even. Alternatively, a negative NPV will denote a loss for the company. Consider another illustration where cash flow projection for ten years is $12,000 per year, the cost of capital is 11 percent, and the initial investment proposed is $80,000:

$$
\begin{aligned}
\text{NPV} &= \text{annual cash flow}(PVIFA_{i,n}) \\
&\quad - \text{initial investment} \\
&= 12{,}000(PVIFA_{11,10}) - 80{,}000 \\
&= 12{,}000(5.889) - 80{,}000 \\
&= 70{,}668 - 80{,}000 \\
&= -9{,}332
\end{aligned}
$$

The project will result in a net loss of $9,332. The major shortcoming of this method is that it assumes the cost of capital to be fixed for the duration of the project or investment period.

c. The internal rate of return (IRR) is the project's annual rate of return. If this rate of return is greater than or at least equal to the firm's cost of capital, the project may be accepted. For example, the project stipulates an initial investment of $40,000 with an expected annual cash flow of $7,000 for ten years. To find the IRR:

(1) Look at an annuity table (given at the back of any finance textbook) for the nearest discount factor of 5.714, which is derived from $40,000/$7,000.

(2) The nearest discount (interest) factor is 5,650, which corresponds to a discount rate of 12 percent (actually 5.714 lies between the factor of 5.650 for 12 percent and 5.889 for 11 percent. Through interpolation, one can find that 5.714, corresponds to an IRR of 11.73 percent).

Now what does this mean? By investing $40,000 now, the company will receive $7,000 per year for ten years. Thus, if invested in the proposed project, $40,000 will earn a rate of return of 11.73 percent. Whether this venture is worthwhile would greatly depend on the firm employing this capital somewhere else with a rate higher than an 11.73 percent rate of return.

Note that the process of calculating IRR by hand can be difficult when a project's annual cash flows are not equal. Nevertheless, the concept is of critical importance since it takes into account the time value of money and does not assume a fixed cost of capital during the life of investment.

**Points to Remember**

1. In evaluating investment projects, the company should use a weighted average to compute the cost of capital rather than the cost of a specific source of financing (debt, preferred stock, common stock, and/or retained earnings). The weighted average can be computed by multiplying the specific cost of each source of financing by its weight in the capital structure and adding the weighted values. To illustrate:

| *Source* (1) | *Amount* (2) | *After-Tax Cost* (3) | | *Weight* (4) | *Weighted Cost* (5) |
|---|---|---|---|---|---|
| Debt | $6 million | 0.08 | × | 30% | 0.024 |
| Preferred stocks | $2 million | 0.09 | × | 10% | 0.009 |
| Common stocks | $2 million | 0.12 | × | 10% | 0.012 |
| Retained earnings | $10 million | 0.11 | × | 50% | 0.055 |
| Total | $20 million | | | 100% | 0.100 |

WACC = 0.30(0.08) + 0.10(0.09) + 0.10(0.12) + 0.50(0.11) = 0.10

Columns 1 and 2 show the sources of capital and their respective amounts. Column 3 tells what the company is paying for these sources of capital. The weight of each source in column 4 is ascertained by the amount in each source divided by the total of column 2 (debt of $6 million/$20 million = 30 percent). The weighted cost is the amount one gets when the weight is multiplied by after-tax cost (30 percent × 0.08 – 0.024). The weighted cost of capital for this company from all sources comes to 10 percent, which means that in order to break even, the company must at least have a rate of return of 10 percent from the projects proposed. Since 10 percent is the minimum return wanted, any proposal for capital investment should be rejected if this rate of return is not achieved.

2. The element of risk can be incorporated into the capital-budgeting process by changing the required rate of return. The higher the project risk, the higher the required return should be. Risks in capital budgeting result from the uncertainty about the level of future cash inflows. One popular approach to deal with the risk associated with future cash flows is sensitivity, or "what if" analysis. Sensitivity analysis uses a number of likely values for a given variable (e.g., sales, cost of materials, cost of labor, tax rates) and assesses the impact on a project's future cash inflow, which could be done easily using spreadsheets.
3. Capital-budgeting projects can be classified as either independent or mutually exclusive. Independent projects do not compete with each other (e.g., selecting between a computer system and a site for a warehouse) and the organization should accept these projects as long as it has funds to finance them and these projects meet the company's accepted criteria. Mutually exclusive projects, on the other hand, serve the same purpose and thus compete with each other (e.g., selecting between two building sites). As suggested earlier, the organization should select the project that has the higher NPV or IRR.
4. Each firm faces capital rationing since no one has unlimited funds to adopt all possible projects. Hence the company should rank those projects based on their NPVs or IRRs and select the ones that will maximize the value of the company to the stakeholders and that are in line with the corporate strategic direction.

## Business Acquisitions

### What is a Business Combination?

Three types of business combinations can occur in the process of making an acquisition:

1. **Statutory merger.** Company A acquires company B; B goes out of business; A owns 100 percent of B's assets.
2. **Statutory consolidation.** Companies A and B transfer their assets to a newly formed company, C; A and B go out of business. C issues its stock to the old stockholders of A and B.
3. **Parent-subsidiary.** Company A acquires a majority (over 50%) of company B's outstanding voting stock. The combining companies retain their separate legal identities and separate accounting records even though they have become one economic entity.

### Purchase of Assets Versus Pooling of Interests

The terms *purchase of assets* and *pooling of interests* describe accounting methods that deal with statutory mergers and statutory consolidations and are not concerned with parent-subsidiary relationships. Under the pooling-of-interests method, the ownership interests of the combining companies are united and continue relatively unchanged. Since neither combining company is considered to have acquired the other, there is no purchase, no purchase price, and accordingly, no goodwill is created. The assets, liabilities, and stockholders' equity are carried forward to the combined entity at book values. In the United States, the Accounting Principles Board has set forth 12 conditions in APB Opinion No. 16 (19780) that must be met before the pooling-of-interests method is employed. The pooling-of-interests method is used if these 12 conditions are met:

1. Each of the combining companies is autonomous and has not been a subsidiary or division of another corporation within two years before the plan of combination is initiated.
2. The combination must be completed in accordance with a specific plan within one year after the plan is initiated.
3. The issuing corporation must offer and issue only common stock in exchange for substantially all (90 percent or more) of the outstanding voting stock for a combining company at the date the plan is consummated.
4. If the combining company holds shares in the issuing company, these shares must be converted into an equivalent number of shares of the combining company and also deducted from the outstanding shares to determine the number of shares assumed to be exchanged.
5. None of the combining companies can change the equity interest of the voting common stock in contemplation of effecting the combination within two years before initiation of the plan of combination or between the dates of initiation and consummation.
6. Each of the combining companies reacquires its own shares of voting common stock only for purposes other than the business combination.
7. The proportionate interest of each individual common stockholder in each of the combining companies remains the same as a result of the exchange of stock to effect the combination.
8. The voting rights in the combined corporation are to be immediately exercisable by the stockholders.
9. The combined corporation must not agree to retire or reacquire stock issued to effect the combination.
10. The combined corporation must not enter into financial arrangements for the benefit of the former stockholders of a combining company.
11. The combined corporation must not plan to dispose of a significant part of the assets of the combining companies within two years after the combination.

Under the purchase-of-assets method, the acquiring company receives control of the acquired assets and records them at their fair market value at the time of the business combination. Any excess of purchase price over the fair market value of the assets acquired is allocated to goodwill and is amortized over a maximum period of 40 years. This amortization expense, in turn, will reduce the reported earnings of the firm. One is able to perceive an incentive on the part of management to effectuate a pooling-of-interests transaction rather than a purchase of assets. In spite of this, cash purchases are more common due to the demands of stockholders who increasingly are not interested in just swapping stock.

In determining what price will be paid for a business acquisition, a number of factors should be determined, including earnings, dividends, and growth potential. We will divide our attention between a straight cash purchase and a stock-for-stock exchange in which the acquiring firm trades its own stock rather than pay cash for the acquired firm.

### Cash Purchases

Cash purchases can be viewed as a capital-budgeting decision. Instead of building a new plant or buying additional machinery, the purchaser has opted to acquire a business that has already established itself. For example, Pathumtani Industries, Inc wants to acquire Maharlika Amalgamated for $1 million. Maharlika has expected after-tax cash flows of $100,000 per year for the next five years and $150,000 per year for years 6 through 20. The synergistic benefits of combined production know-how and management expertise will add $10,000 per year to this after-tax cash flow. If Pathumtani Industries has a 10-percent required cost of capital (i.e., its total investment must generate at least a 10-percent return for it to stay in business), calculations show that the proposed purchase would have a positive net present value of $172,690. But how does one figure out how much to pay for Maharlika Amalgamated or, for that matter, any firm?

**Net present value method.** As discussed in the earlier section, the example just given illustrates one of the most widely used tools for determining if an investment will prove viable to a company. As the name suggests, the future earnings that will be generated by the investment in question are "discounted" back to the present via the present value method. Once this is accomplished, the initial investment amount is subtracted from this present value figure to arrive at a net present value, which is positive, zero, or negative. If this value is negative, the investment is viewed as providing a return below the required rate of return of the firm (this rate, occasionally referred to as the internal rate of return, is the rate used to compute the discounted cash flows generated by the investment). If this value is zero, the investment is said to be providing a return that meets the minimum requirement for serious consideration as a possible venture. Similarly, if the net present value is positive, the investment would appear to provide a better than satisfactory return to the firm over its useful life.

Now, let us look at our example again from an analytical standpoint:

1. Pathumtani Industries wants to buy Maharlika Amalgamated for $1,000,000 cash; the $1,000,000 initial cost is worth exactly $1,000,000 today in present value terms.
2. The investment in Maharlika will generate $100,000 per year in *after-tax* earnings for years 1 through 5 and $150,000 per year for years 6 through 20.
3. The combination of the two companies will produce an additional $10,000 per year in *after-tax* earnings for years 1 through 20.
4. Pathumtani Industries has a 10 percent required cost of capital.

With this information, we can create the following schematic:

| | *After-Tax Earnings Stream* | |
|---|---|---|
| *Year* | *1 through 5* | *6 through 20* |
| Earnings | $100,000 | $150,000 |
| | + | + |
| | $10,000 | $10,000 |

We must discount these figure earnings back to the present using Pathumtani's 10 percent required cost of capital figure. We then compare the present value of the earnings stream with the $1,000,000 initial cost to arrive at the net present value.

| | |
|---|---|
| Present value of earnings for years 1–5 | |
| $110,000 \times PVIFA_{10,5}$ | $ 417,010 |
| Present value of earnings for years 6–20 | |
| $160,000(PVIFA_{10,20} - PVIFA_{10,5})$ | |
| $160,000(8.514 – 3.791) | |
| $160,000 × 4.723 | 755,680 |
| Present value of earnings stream | $1,172,690 |
| Initial cash outlay | (1,000,000) |
| Net present value | $ 172,690 |

Our analysis shows that this business acquisition will have a positive net present value of $172,690. Unless Pathumtani Industries can come out with a better deal somewhere else, the purchase of Maharlika Amalgamated should prove to be a profitable investment.

**Determining the price to pay for an acquisition.** To begin, one may be tempted to look at the book value of the firm under consideration (by definition, book value = assets – liabilities). In reality, book value has become meaningless as a basis of valuation, except when it is significantly higher than the market value of the firm. In this case, we can compute the ratio of the book values of the two firms and use it as a basis of exchange. Usually this is not done unless the firm is being acquired for its liquidity and asset value rather than for its earning power. By and large, the fair market value of a firm's assets becomes the starting point for negotiations in setting the price for an acquisition. In addition, the firm's future earning potential may play an important part in this process, as was demonstrated by the net present value method.

### Stock-for-Stock Exchange

With a stock-for-stock exchange, a slightly different approach is used in determining the value of an acquisition. A ratio of exchange for the common stock of the two entities involved is employed:

$$\text{Price exchange ratio} = \frac{\begin{array}{c}\text{Market price}\\\text{per share for buyer}\end{array} \times \begin{array}{c}\text{No. shares offered by}\\\text{buyer per share of seller}\end{array}}{\text{Market price per share for seller}}$$

For example, Shaw Enterprises' stock is selling for $60 per share and it wishes to acquire company B, whose stock is selling for $30 per share. Shaw wishes to offer a half share of its stock for each share of B's; therefore, the ratio of exchange would be ($60 × 0.5)/$30 = 1.00. The stock of the two companies would be exactly even; that is,

2 shares of B for each share of Shaw. However, there is generally little incentive to swap on an even basis, so the acquiring firm usually must offer a price in excess of the current market price per share of the company it wishes to acquire. Instead of offering 0.5 shares of Shaw stock for each share of B, it might offer 0.6 shares at the current market value to persuade B's stockholders to make the swap. Under this arrangement, B's stockholders would receive 6 shares of Shaw for every 10 of their own instead of the original 5 shares.

In this case where a business acquires another business whose price-earnings ratio is lower than its own, there will likely be an increase in the acquirer's earnings per share. However, long-term considerations can influence the decision to buy a growth firm with a high price-earnings ratio. The long-term benefits should be evaluated in this instance and found to outweigh any short-term decrease in earnings per share.

In the case where a business acquires another business whose price-earnings ratio is lower than its own, there will likely be an increase in the acquirer's earnings per share. However, long-term considerations can influence the decision to buy a growth firm with a high price-earnings ratio. The long-term benefits should be evaluated in this instance and found to outweigh any short-term decrease in earnings per share.

In addition to the ideas already offered in establishing a price for an acquisition, there are other sources that may be able to provide some clue as to the worth of a firm. Look for a firm of comparable size in the same industry that has been bought recently and see what the purchaser had to pay. If no firm of comparable size can be found in the same industry, then try to locate a firm of comparable size in another industry. Another approach is to find a firm in the same industry regardless of size and compute the ratio of its purchase price to its book value. This ratio is then used to multiply the book value of the firm under consideration. This method is similar to the practice used in real estate for determining the value of a house in a given neighborhood. The real estate agent first finds out what other houses in that area have sold for and computes an average price per square foot. This figure is then multiplied by the square footage of the seller's house to arrive at an initial asking price.

**EBIT-EPS analysis.** Earnings before interest and taxes (EBIT), also known as operating profit, reveal how efficiently the firm is generating revenues and controlling expenses. When the EBIT is determined, expenses not related to operational matters, such as interest and taxes, are deducted to arrive at net income. Once net income is determined, it is simply divided by the number of common stock shares outstanding between EBIT. The subsequent EPS is affected by the level of EBIT, the size of the firm's interest expense, and the number of shares outstanding. The process of determining what mix of debt and equity to use when a firm is attempting to raise additional funds is known as EBIT-EPS analysis. It is this analysis that reveals the effects of financial leverage on earnings per share.

To illustrate an EBIT-EPS analysis of leverage, suppose that Summa Manufacturing Co wants to raise an additional $500,000 for expansion through one of three possible financing plans: (1) all debt will incur 15 percent interest, (2) all common stock will be priced at $50 per share, and (3) capitalization will be set at 50 percent debt and 50 percent stock. We will assume that with the expansion, sales will increase by $1,000,000, variable costs by $250,000, and fixed costs by $450,000. We will also assume a 14-percent tax rate and 100,000 shares of common stock initially outstanding. The following table shows the results of the three financing plans on earnings per share:

| | *Before Expansion* | *100% Debt* | *100% Common Stock* | *50% Debt + 50% Common Stock* |
|---|---|---|---|---|
| Sales | $2,000,000 | $3,000,000 | $3,000,000 | $3,000,000 |
| Variable costs | 500,000 | 750,000 | 750,000 | 750,000 |
| Fixed costs | 800,000 | 1,250,000 | 1,250,000 | 1,250,000 |
| EBIT | 700,000 | 1,000,000 | 1,000,000 | 1,000,000 |
| Interest | 100,000 | 175,000 | 100,000 | 137,500 |
| Earnings before taxes | 600,000 | 825,000 | 900,000 | 862,500 |
| Income taxes | 204,000 | 280,500 | 306,000 | 293,250 |
| Net income | $ 396,000 | $ 544,500 | $ 594,000 | $ 569,250 |
| Number of shares outstanding | 100,000 | 100,000 | 110,000 | 105,000 |
| Earnings per share | $3.96 | $5.45 | $5.40 | $5.42 |

The company should favor the combination that yields the highest earnings per share, thereby keeping its stockholders content. Notwithstanding, one must make the decision of financing with debt in light of the availability of credit. If Summa Manufacturing's debt-to-equity ratio is already high (60/40), it would be difficult to finance the expansion through the issuance of bonds. On the other hand, the company must also take into consideration the market demand for its common stock. Will a new issue of stock sell at $50 per share? If the market will pay only $45 per share, the firm will be forced to sell more stock than it had originally planned to finance the expansion. Consequently, as the number of shares outstanding increases, the corresponding earnings per share will decrease. The trick is, of course, to find the proper mix that everyone can live with.

You will recall here that since the new shareholders will have the right to vote, the current shareholders may not like this "crowding effect" and may prefer the company to issue debt rather than new stocks.

Further, the issuing of bonds has two specific advantages over the issuing of common stocks. First, interest payments on bonds are tax-deductible. Second, the bondholders, in general, do not have voting rights and therefore they are not in a position to exercise control over the corporation's affairs.

## Pro Forma Financial Statements

Recommendations will carry little weight unless their impact on the financial condition of the firm can be demonstrated. *Pro forma* financial statements represent the most comprehensive way of forecasting the results of future operations given a specific set of circumstances. Of major importance are the *pro forma* balance sheet, income statement, and cash budget. The *pro forma* income statement is a projection of anticipated sales, expenses, and income for given future cash flow requirements given the projected level of operations. The *pro forma* balance sheet is a projection of future asset, liability, and stockholder equity levels.

The following discussion is a summary illustration of how a forecast income statement, a cash budget, and a balance sheet are put together.

### The Importance of Sales Forecasting

The sales forecast is the most important link in constructing *pro forma* financial statements. Its accuracy is absolutely critical for determining production schedules and the subsequent costs to be incurred. When sales forecasting is attempted, the following factors should be considered:

1. Past pattern of sales
2. Estimates and opinions made by the sales force
3. Overall state of the economy
4. Competitors' present activity and possible reaction
5. Effects of target pricing
6. Advertising and sales promotion plans
7. Market research studies

### Creating Pro Forma Statements

Once the sales forecast is derived, plans are then formulated to estimate the related costs and cash flow for the specified level of sales. This is usually done through the use of schedules such as cash collections, purchases, and wages and commissions. Exhibit 7 provides an illustration of these schedules.

After these schedules are determined, the next step is to assemble a forecast income statement. Exhibit 8 illustrates this step.

The next step is to produce a forecast cash budget. As Exhibit 9 illustrates, cash receipts and disbursements are predicted on a monthly basis. The ability of the firm's management to foresee accurately what the cash requirements will be is crucial. An accurate forecast will ensure that adequate funds are available to provide for daily operational needs and to service all debt obligations as they come due.

The final step is the preparation of the *pro forma* balance sheet. Each account is projected in harmony with the *pro forma* income statement, cash budget, and supporting schedules. Exhibits 10 and 11 show the before-and-after results of anticipated operations.

An alternative to going through the process of tracing cash and accounting flows is to assume that the balance sheet accounts will maintain a given percentage of sales. We first estimate the new sales level and then apply the percentage relationships to arrive at the projected figures on our balance sheet. This is known as the percentage-of-sales method. It is a broad-brush approach that is not as meaningful as the *pro forma* approach described earlier.

### Cost-Volume-Profit Analysis

In addition to presenting *pro forma* financial statements to back up recommendations, it may be helpful to employ cost-volume-profit, or break-even, analysis, to lend more clarity to the argument. Using this technique, one is able to demonstrate the relationship of revenue, expenses, and net income as well as to predict what will happen to overall profit if a specific level of sales is achieved.

With the following information, we can derive the break-even point:

Using the equation: Net Income = Sales – Variable Expenses – Fixed Expenses

We get: Sales = Net Income + Variable Expenses + Fixed Expenses

Letting $x$ = the number of units to sell to break even, we get

$$\$.50x = 0 + \$.40x + \$6{,}000.00$$

(Note: To break even, our revenue should be exactly equal to our expenses, thereby yielding *zero net income*.) Solving for $x$, we get

$$\begin{aligned} \$.50 - \$.40x &= 0 + \$6{,}000 \\ \$.10x &= \$6{,}000 \\ x &= \$6{,}000/\$.10 \\ x &= 60{,}000 \text{ units} \end{aligned}$$

We must sell 60,000 units to break even. Our break-even dollar sales is simply 60,000 units × \$.50 sales price per unit = \$30,000. Using this equation, we can determine how many units need to be sold to obtain a given net income; conversely, we can also determine what our net income will be given the number of units sold.

For example, if we want to know how many units must be sold to generate \$75,000 in net income, we simply plug that figure into the equation:

$$x = \frac{\$6{,}000 + \$75{,}000}{\$.10} = \frac{\$81{,}000}{\$.10} = 810{,}000 \text{ units}$$

If, on the other hand, we sold 500,000 units, what would our net income be? Letting $I$ = net income, we substitute into the same equation and solve for $I$:

$$\begin{aligned} 500{,}000 &= \frac{\$6{,}000 + I}{\$.10} \\ \$.10 \times 500{,}000 &= \$6{,}000 + I \\ \$50{,}000 &= \$6{,}000 + I \\ \$50{,}000 - \$6{,}000 &= I \\ I &= \$44{,}000 \end{aligned}$$

By now it should be apparent that the form of the equation used in both cases is:

$$\text{Units sold} = \frac{\text{Fixed Expenses} + \text{Net Income}}{\text{Contribution Margin per Unit}}$$

Exhibit 12 illustrates the graphical application of the cost-volume-profit analysis.

In summary, you should attempt to present *pro forma* financial statements following your recommendations. In some instances, however, you may not be able to provide them due to lack of financial information contained in the case. Should this occur, it is suggested that you seriously consider presenting a financial impact statement. The impact statement in this instance would be a brief summary of the company's projected financial affairs given the student's set of recommendations.

EXHIBIT 1

## Ratio Interpretation and Its Rules of Thumb

| *Ratio* | *Interpretation* | *Rule of Thumb* |
|---|---|---|
| **1. Profitability Ratios** | | |
| a. Gross profit margin | Amount of gross profit generated per dollar of sales. | Industry average, when applicable. |
| b. Operating profit margin | Amount of profit from operations generated per dollar of sales. | Industry average, when applicable. |
| c. Net profit margin | Amount of after-tax profits per dollar of sales. | Industry average, when applicable. |
| d. Return on investment (ROI) | Rate of return on total assets employed. This is a measure of management's overall performance in generating a profit. | Should be equal to, or higher than market rate of return on Treasury bills during the time period in question. |
| e. Return on equity (ROE) | Rate of return on stockholders' investment in company. This is a measure of management's performance in generating a profit for the owners of the company. | Should be higher than ROI. |
| **2. Liquidity Ratios** | | |
| a. Current ratio | Ability to cover short-term debt as it comes due. | At least 2:1. A ratio above 4 would indicate that the company may not be using its short-term assets effectively. |
| b. Quick ratio | Expresses degree to which a company's current liabilities are covered by the most liquid current assets. | At least 1:1. |
| **3. Activity Ratios** | | |
| a. Average collection period | Average collection period for accounts receivable. | Equal to or less than credit period extended to customers by firm. |
| b. Average payment period | Average payment period for accounts payable. | Equal to credit period extended to the company by its creditors. |
| c. Inventory turnover | Indicates liquidity or activity of the company's inventory. | Industry average, when applicable. |
| d. Total asset turnover | Indicates how efficiently company is utilizing its assets to generate sales. | Industry average, when applicable. |

EXHIBIT 1 (cont'd)

**Ratio Interpretation and Its Rules of Thumb**

| *Ratio* | *Interpretation* | *Rule of Thumb* |
|---|---|---|
| e. Fixed asset turnover | Extent to which fixed assets are used in generating sales. | High value indicates productive use of fixed assets. |
| **4. Debt Ratios** | | |
| a. Debt to assets | Extent to which funds are provided by creditors. | Industry average, when applicable. |
| b. Long-term debt to equity | Extent to which funds are provided on a long-term basis by creditors versus owners. | Historical norm tends to be 40:60. |
| c. Debt to capital | Percentage of a firm's capitalization package that is made up of long-term debt. | Industry average, when applicable. |
| d. Short-term liabilities to total debt | Percentage of total debt borrowed from short-term creditors. | Industry average, when applicable. |
| e. Times interest earned | Extent to which earnings can decline without company becoming unable to meet its interest expense; provides a measure of the degree of security afforded to bondholders. | At least 2:1. |
| **5. Market Ratios** | | |
| a. Earnings per share | Net income per share available to common stockholders. | Industry average, when applicable. |
| b. Dividend payout | Percentage of net earnings paid out to common shareholders. | Growth companies generally have low payout ratios because they reinvest most of their earnings. |
| c. Dividend yield | Shows rate of return stockholders will receive from their investment in the short run. | Industry average, when applicable. |
| d. Price/earnings ratio | A measure of current price of stock to earnings per share. | High value indicates that company is growing and/or is a stable enterprise. |

EXHIBIT 1 (cont'd)

**Ratio Interpretation and Its Rules of Thumb**

| *Ratio* | *Interpretation* | *Rule of Thumb* |
|---|---|---|
| e. Book value per share | Indicates amount of common share available to stockholders if company's assets are sold at their book value and company's liabilities are paid off. | None exists. |
| f. Price to book value | Amount stockholders are willing to pay for each dollar of common stock book value. | None exists. |

EXHIBIT 2

## Comparative Balance Sheets, 1992–1995

(in millions)

| | *1992* | *1993* | *1994* | *1995* |
|---|---|---|---|---|
| Cash & equivalents | $ 45 | $ 38 | $ 41 | $ 62 |
| Accounts receivable, net | 350 | 289 | 410 | 455 |
| Prepaid expenses | 21 | 18 | 32 | 35 |
| Total inventories | 527 | 608 | 548 | 589 |
| Total current assets | 943 | 953 | 1,031 | 1,141 |
| Long-term investments | 95 | 121 | 134 | 149 |
| Plant and equipment | 2,334 | 2,609 | 2,915 | 3,241 |
| Accumulated depreciation | (1,124) | (1,292) | (1,384) | (1,521) |
| Net fixed assets | 1,210 | 1,317 | 1,531 | 1,720 |
| Other assets | 24 | 14 | 15 | 12 |
| Total noncurrent assets | 1,350 | 1,470 | 1,680 | 1,881 |
| Total assets | $2,272 | $2,405 | $2,711 | $3,022 |
| | | | | |
| Notes payable | 52 | 65 | 93 | 61 |
| Accounts payable | 96 | 101 | 114 | 106 |
| Income taxes payable | 47 | 42 | 71 | 79 |
| Other current liabilities | 112 | 126 | 131 | 148 |
| Total current liabilities | 307 | 334 | 409 | 394 |
| Long-term debt | 492 | 445 | 538 | 622 |
| Other liabilities | 114 | 123 | 129 | 127 |
| Total liabilities | 913 | 902 | 1,076 | 1,143 |
| Preferred stock | 25 | 25 | 25 | 25 |
| Common stock | 165 | 165 | 165 | 210 |
| Paid in capital | 150 | 150 | 150 | 185 |
| Retained earnings | 1,019 | 1,163 | 1,295 | 1,459 |
| Total stockholders' equity | 1,359 | 1,503 | 1,635 | 1,879 |
| Total liab.* & stockholders' equity | $2,272 | $2,405 | $2,711 | 3,022 |

*Liability.

EXHIBIT 3

## Comparative Income and Retained Earnings Statements

(millions except per share data, 1992–1995)

| | *1992* | *1993* | *1994* | *1995* |
|---|---|---|---|---|
| Net sales | $2,983 | $3,171 | $3,442 | $3,918 |
| Cost of goods sold | 2,312 | 2,413 | 2,737 | 3,107 |
| Gross profit | 671 | 758 | 705 | 811 |
| Selling, general & admin.* expenses | 214 | 232 | 241 | 258 |
| Depreciation and amortization | 134 | 168 | 92 | 137 |
| Operating income | 323 | 358 | 372 | 416 |
| Other income | 11 | 13 | 9 | 12 |
| Earnings before interest and taxes | 334 | 371 | 381 | 428 |
| Interest expense | 59 | 63 | 76 | 83 |
| Earnings before taxes | 275 | 308 | 305 | 345 |
| Income taxes | 89 | 92 | 98 | 103 |
| Net income after taxes | $ 186 | $ 216 | $ 207 | $ 242 |
| | | | | |
| Retained earnings, January 1 | 902 | 1,019 | 1,163 | 1,295 |
| Add: net income | 186 | 216 | 207 | 242 |
| Deduct: Common dividends | (65) | (68) | (71) | (74) |
| Preferred dividends | (4) | (4) | (4) | (4) |
| Retained earnings, December 31 | $1,019 | $1,163 | $1,295 | $1,459 |
| | | | | |
| Closing price on common stock | 47.25 | 54.625 | 52.50 | 56.25 |
| Common stock outstanding | 46.5 | 48.5 | 47.1 | 49.3 |
| Earnings per share | 3.91 | 1.46 | 4.31 | 4.83 |
| Dividends per share | 1.40 | 1.46 | 1.50 | 1.50 |

*Administrative.

## EXHIBIT 4

### Comparative Financial Ratios, 1992–1995

| | | *1992* | *1993* | *1994* | *1995* |
|---|---|---|---|---|---|
| **1.** | **Profitability Ratios** | | | | |
| a. | Gross profit margin | 22.5% | 23.9% | 20.5% | 20.7% |
| b. | Operating profit margin | 10.8% | 11.3% | 10.8% | 10.6% |
| c. | Net profit margin | 6.2% | 6.8% | 6.0% | 6.2% |
| d. | Return on investment | 8.2% | 9.0% | 7.6% | 8.0% |
| e. | Return on equity | 13.7% | 14.4% | 12.7% | 12.9% |
| **2.** | **Liquidity Ratios** | | | | |
| a. | Current ratio | 3.1 | 2.9 | 2.5 | 2.9 |
| b. | Quick ratio | 1.4 | 1.0 | 1.2 | 1.4 |
| **3.** | **Activity Ratios** | | | | |
| a. | Average collection period | 42.8 | 33.3 | 43.5 | 42.4 |
| b. | Average payment period* | 21.7 | 21.8 | 21.7 | 17.8 |
| c. | Inventory turnover | 4.39 | 3.97 | 4.99 | 5.28 |
| d. | Total asset turnover | 1.31 | 1.32 | 1.27 | 1.30 |
| e. | Fixed asset turnover | 2.47 | 2.41 | 2.25 | 2.28 |
| **4.** | **Debt Ratios** | | | | |
| a. | Debt to assets | 40.2% | 37.5% | 39.7% | 37.8% |
| b. | Long-term debt to equity | 36.2% | 29.6% | 32.9% | 33.1% |
| c. | Debt to capital | 26.6% | 22.8% | 24.8% | 24.9% |
| d. | Short-term liabilities to total debt | 33.6% | 37.0% | 38.0% | 34.5% |
| e. | Times interest earned | 5.66% | 5.89% | 5.01% | 5.16% |
| **5.** | **Market Ratios** | | | | |
| a. | Earnings per share (EPS) | $3.91 | $4.56 | $4.31 | $4.83 |
| b. | Dividend payout | 36 % | 32% | 35% | 31% |
| c. | Dividend yield | 3.0% | 2.7% | 2.9% | 2.5% |
| d. | Price/earnings (PE) ratio | 12.1 | 12.0 | 12.2 | 11.6 |
| e. | Book value per share | $28.69 | $31.78 | $34.18 | $37.61 |
| f. | Price to book value | 1.65 | 1.72 | 1.54 | 1.50 |

*Assumes that credit purchases equal 70 percent of cost of goods sold.

EXHIBIT 5

**Statement of Changes in Financial Position:
Sources and Uses of Funds**

| *Sources* | | *Uses* | |
|---|---|---|---|
| Earnings after taxes | $242 | Increase in cash and equivalents | $21 |
| Depreciation | 137 | Increase in accounts receivables, net | 45 |
| | | Increase in prepaid expenses | 3 |
| Decrease in other assets | 3 | Increase in inventories | 41 |
| Increase in income taxes payable | 8 | | |
| Increase in other current liabilities | 17 | Increase in long-term investments | 15 |
| Increase in long-term debt | 84 | Increase in plant and equipment | 326 |
| Increase in common stock | 45 | Decrease in notes payable | 32 |
| Increase in paid-up capital | 35 | Decrease in accounts payable | 8 |
| | | Decrease in other liabilities | 2 |
| | | Common stock dividends paid | 74 |
| | | Preferred stock dividends paid | 4 |
| Total sources of funds | $571 | Total use of funds | $571 |

EXHIBIT 6

**Statement of Changes in Net Working Capital**

| *Sources* | | *Uses* | |
|---|---|---|---|
| Earnings after taxes | $242 | Increase in long-term investments | $15 |
| Depreciation | 137 | Increase in plant and equipment | 326 |
| Decrease in other assets | 3 | Decrease in other liabilities | 2 |
| Increase in long-term debt | 84 | Common stock dividends | 74 |
| Increase in common stock | 45 | Preferred stock dividends | 4 |
| Increase in paid-up capital | 35 | Changes in net working capital | 125 |
| Total sources | $546 | Total uses | $546 |

EXHIBIT 7

## Supporting Sheet for Pro Forma Statements

| | *Nov '95* | *Dec '95* | *Jan '96* | *Feb '96* | *Mar '96* | *Total Jan–Mar 1996* |
|---|---|---|---|---|---|---|
| Forecast sales | $40,000 | $36,000 | $40,000 | $44,000 | $50,000 | $134,000 |
| Cash sales (0.30) | 12,000 | 10,800 | 12,000 | 13,200 | 15,000 | 40,200 |
| Collection of A/R | | | | | | |
| Lagged 1 mo (0.50) | | 20,000 | 18,000 | 20,000 | 22,000 | |
| Lagged 2 mo (0.50) | | | 8,000 | 7,200 | 8,000 | |
| Other cash receipts | | | 1,200 | 1,200 | 1,200 | |
| Total cash receipts | | | $39,200 | $41,600 | $46,200 | $125,800 |
| Purchases (0.6 @ sales) | 24,000 | 21,600 | 24,000 | 26,400 | 30,000 | |
| Cash purchases (0.20) | | 4,320 | 4,800 | 5,280 | 6,000 | |
| Payment of A/P | | | | | | |
| Lagged 1 mo (0.60) | | 14,400 | 12,960 | 14,400 | 15,840 | |
| Lagged 2 mo (0.20) | | | 4,800 | 4,320 | 4,800 | |
| Lease expense | | | 1,500 | 1,500 | 1,500 | |
| Wages and salaries | | | 4,200 | 4,350 | 5,250 | |
| Cash dividends | | | 2,500 | | | |
| Interest payment | | | | | 1,800 | |
| Commission (8% of current month's sales) | | | 3,200 | 3,520 | 4,000 | |
| Insurance | | | | | 900 | |
| Miscellaneous expenses (3% of sales) | | | 1,200 | 1,320 | 1,500 | |
| Fixed asset purchases | | | | 12,500 | | |
| Total cash disbursements | | | $35,160 | $47,190 | $41,590 | $123,940 |

EXHIBIT 8

**Pro Forma Income Statement**
**January 1 to March 31, 1996**

| | | |
|---|---|---|
| Sales | | $134,000 |
| Cost of goods sold | | 80,400 |
| Gross profit | | 53,600 |
| Operating expenses | | |
| Wages & salaries | $13,800 | |
| Sales commissions | 10,720 | |
| Lease expense | 4,500 | |
| Depreciation | 2,500 | |
| Insurance | 900 | |
| Miscellaneous expenses (4% of sales) | 5,360 | 37,780 |
| Operating profit | | 15,820 |
| Interest expense | | 1,800 |
| Profit before taxes | | 14,020 |
| Tax (0.25 × profit before taxes) | | 3,505 |
| Net profit after taxes | | $ 10,515 |
| Quarterly | | |
| Cash dividends (0.05 per share) | | 2,500 |
| Increase in retained earnings | | 8,015 |

EXHIBIT 9

**Pro Forma Cash Budget**
**January 1 to March 31, 1996**

| | *January* | *February* | *March* |
|---|---|---|---|
| Total cash receipts | $39,200 | $41,600 | $46,200 |
| Less: total cash disbursements | 35,160 | 47,190 | 41,590 |
| Net cash flow | 4,040 | (5,590) | 4,610 |
| Add: beginning cash balance | 8,500 | 12,540 | 6,950 |
| Ending cash balance | 12,540 | 6,950 | 11,560 |
| Less: minimum cash balance | 5,000 | 5,000 | 5,000 |
| Required borrowing | 0 | 0 | 0 |
| Excess cash balance | 7,540 | 1,950 | 6,560 |

EXHIBIT 10

**Balance Sheet**
**As of December 31, 1989**

| *Assets* | | *Liabilities & Owners' Equity* | |
|---|---|---|---|
| Cash | $ 8,500 | Accounts payable | $ 17,760 |
| Accounts receivable | 32,200 | Taxes payable | 3,100 |
| Inventories | 12,000 | Notes payable | 4,500 |
| Other current assets | 5,000 | Other current liabilities | 9,700 |
| Total current assets | $ 58,700 | Total current liabilities | $ 35,060 |
| | | Long-term debt | 40,000 |
| Fixed assets | $130,000 | | |
| Accum.* depreciation | (36,200) | Stockholders' equity | |
| Net fixed assets | 93,800 | Common stock (50,000, par $1) | 50,000 |
| | | Retained earnings | 27,440 |
| Total assets | $152,500 | Total liabilities and stockholders' equity | $152,500 |

* Accumulated.

EXHIBIT 11

**Pro Forma Balance Sheet**
**March 31, 1996**
**As of December 31, 1989**

| *Assets* | | *Liabilities & Owners' Equity* | |
|---|---|---|---|
| Cash[a] | $ 6,560 | Accounts payable[f] | $ 29,280 |
| Accounts receivable[b] | 43,800 | Taxes payable[g] | 3,390 |
| Inventories[c] | 20,000 | Notes payable | 4,500 |
| Other current assets | 6,400 | Other current liabilities | 9,700 |
| Total current assets | $ 81,400 | Total current liabilities | $ 46,870 |
| | | Long-term debt | 40,000 |
| Fixed assets[d] | $142,500 | Total liabilities | $ 86,870 |
| Accum. depreciation[e] | (38,700) | | |
| Net fixed assets | 103,800 | Stockholders' equity | |
| | | Common stock | $ 50,000 |
| | | Retained earnings[h] | 35,455 |
| | | Total stockholders' equity | $ 85,455 |
| | | Required new funds[i] | 12,885 |
| Total assets | $185,210 | Total liabilities and stockholders' equity | $185,210 |

[a] Cash: $9,910 from *pro forma* cash budget.
[b] Accounts receivable:

| | | | |
|---|---|---|---|
| February sales | 44,000 x 0.20 | = | 8,800 |
| March sales | 50,000 x 0.70 | = | 35,000 |
| | | | 43,800 |

[c] Inventories represent about 40 percent of sales. Inventories consist of $4,000 or 20 percent in raw material and goods in process and $16,000 in finished goods.
[d] Fixed assets consist of $130,000 balance on December 31 and $12,500 bought on February of next year.
[e] Accumulated depreciation is $36,200 as of December 31, 1996, and $2,500 depreciation for the next three months from the pro forma income statement.
[f] Accounts payable ($5,280 from February purchases, 26,400 × 0.20, and $24,000 from March purchases, 30,000 x 0.80).
[g] Taxes payable assumed to equal next quarter taxes of $3,390 from the pro forma income statement.
[h] Retained earnings increased by $8,015 from the *pro forma* income statement.
[i] This comprises the required new funds necessary to balance the company's balance sheet. The company has to plan to raise these funds by borrowing or issuing new common stocks to support the forecast sales of $134,000 for the next quarter.

EXHIBIT 12

**Cost-Volume-Profit Relationships**

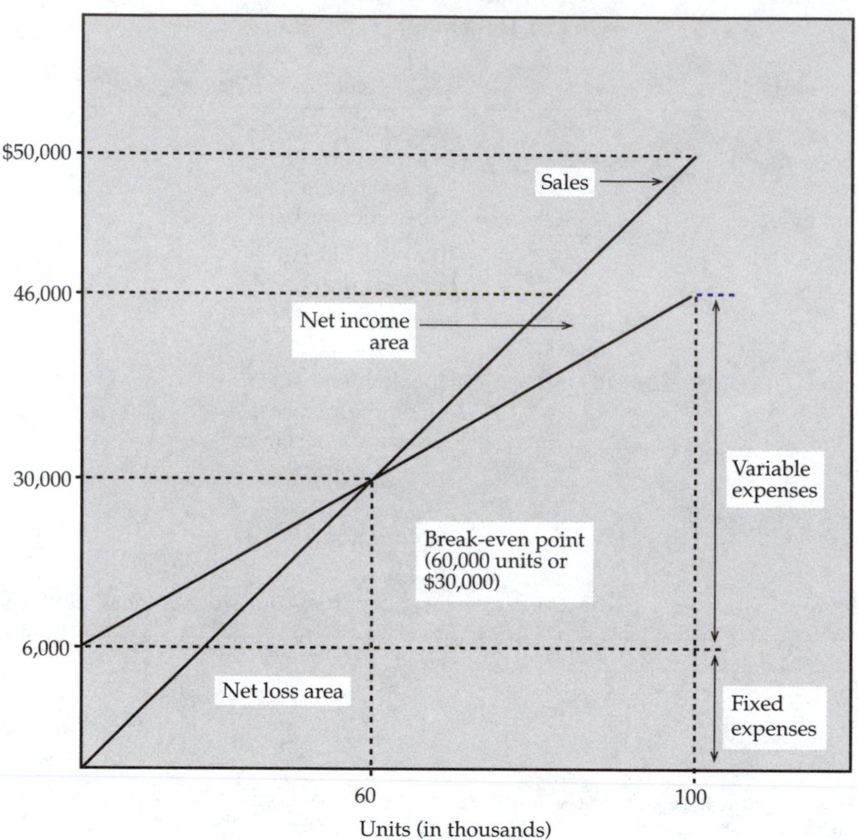


Note: Not drawn to scale.

# Appendix D
# Asian Economic and News Management

## Information to be Used with Cases Whose Decision Year is 1995

**Top News Stories of 1994:** Japanese Prime Minister Morihiro Hosokawa resigns; Japanese Prime Minister Tsutomu Hata and his minority government replaced by coalition government of Social Democratic Party leader Tomiichi Murayama; Singapore's caning of American Michael Fay; North Korean–U.S. standoff on North Korean nuclear weapons program; North Korean President Kim Il-sung dies, son Kim Jong-il takes over; Israel completes military withdrawal from the Palestinian autonomous area of the Gaza Strip; Palestinian autonomy in the Gaza Strip; Jordan–Israel peace declaration; Over 100 states sign Final Act of the Uruguay round of GATT.

**Summary of Economic and Social Indicators, 1994**

| *Indicators* | *Bangladesh* | *China* | *Hong Kong* | *India* | *Indonesia* | *South Korea* | *Malaysia* | *Philippines* | *Singapore* | *Thailand* |
|---|---|---|---|---|---|---|---|---|---|---|
| BANK RATES | | | | | | | | | | |
| Average prime lending rate (%) | — | — | 8.50% | 10.35% | 21.00% | 11.50% | 7.20% | 13.00% | 7.00% | 12.25% |
| Time deposit rate, 12 mos (% pa) | 8.60% | — | 4.75% | 11.00% | 12.99% | 9.50% | — | 11.00% | 3.54% | 9.25% |
| CURRENCY EXCHANGE RATE | Taka | Yuan Renmimbi | Dollar | Rupee | Rupiah | Won | Ringgit | Peso | Dollar | Baht |
| Worth of US$1 in foreign currency | 40.21 | 8.62 | 7.73 | 31.37 | 2,164.20 | 803.44 | 2.62 | 26.42 | 1.53 | 25.15 |
| STOCK MARKET INDICES | — | Shanghai Composite | Hang Seng | E Times All-India | JSE Composite | Composite | NST Indl. | Comm. & Indl | ST Indl. | Book Club |
| Stock Index | — | 640 | 7,789 | 1,881 | 454 | 1,033 | 911 | 2,603 | 2,102 | 1,279 |
| Average P/E ratio | — | — | 13.0 | 36.2 | 27.4 | 38.6 | 22.2 | 28.6 | 27.1 | 24.2 |
| ECONOMIC INDICATORS (amounts in US$) | | | | | | | | | | |
| GDP growth | 4.5% | 11.4% | 5.5% | 4.2% | 6.7% | 7.7% | 8.1% | 5.1% | 10.2% | 7.4% |
| Per-capita GDP (PPP) | 1,230 | 2,428 | 20,050 | 1,210 | 2,970 | 8,950 | 8,050 | 2,480 | 16,720 | 5,890 |
| Inflation rate | 3.7% | 27.4% | 7.9% | 9.0% | 9.2% | 5.7% | 3.7% | 7.8% | 4.0% | 5.8% |
| Exports for 12 months (in $ billions) | 2.5 | 110.0 | 141.0 | 23.5 | 37.0 | 91.2 | 48.4 | 12.4 | 88.8 | 41.2 |
| SOCIAL INDICATORS | | | | | | | | | | |
| Population (million) | 120.7 | 1,196.5 | 6.1 | 911.0 | 193.4 | 44.6 | 19.4 | 66.2 | 3.1 | 59.8 |
| Population growth rate (%) | 2.2% | 1.2% | 1.8% | 2.1% | 1.7% | 0.9% | 2.6% | 2.3% | 2.0% | 1.5% |
| Literacy rate (%) | 36.6% | 80.0% | 90.0% | 52.1% | 84.4% | 93.8% | 80.0% | 93.5% | 91.6% | 93.8% |

## Information to be Used with Cases Whose Decision Year is 1994

**Top News Stories of 1993:** Chinese National People's Congress elects Jiang Zemin as the country's president; UN-supervised elections in Cambodia; Prince Sihanouk elected King of Cambodia; Benazir Bhutto sworn in as Prime Minister of Pakistan; Israel–PLO peace accord; Uruguay round of GATT negotiations successfully concluded hours before the deadline with an agreement between the U.S. and the E.C. over the audiovisual, agricultural, and services sectors.

**Summary of Economic and Social Indicators, 1993**

| *Indicators* | *Bangladesh* | *China* | *Hong Kong* | *India* | *Indonesia* | *South Korea* | *Malaysia* | *Philippines* | *Singapore* | *Thailand* |
|---|---|---|---|---|---|---|---|---|---|---|
| BANK RATES | | | | | | | | | | |
| Average prime lending rate (%) | — | — | 6.50% | 9.75% | 19.00% | 8.50% | 8.65% | 18.00% | 5.75% | 12.25% |
| Time deposit rate, 12 mos (% pa) | 8.29% | — | 3.80% | 12.00% | 14.20% | 8.50% | 6.97% | 10.10% | 2.84% | 7.00% |
| CURRENCY EXCHANGE RATE | Taka | Yuan Renmimbi | Dollar | Rupee | Rupiah | Won | Ringgit | Peso | Dollar | Baht |
| Worth of US$1 in foreign currency | 39.57 | 5.76 | 7.74 | 30.49 | 2,089.30 | 802.67 | 2.57 | 27.12 | 1.62 | 25.32 |
| STOCK MARKET INDICES | — | — | Hang Seng | E Times All-India | JSE Composite | Composite | NST Indl. | Comm. & Indl. | ST Indl. | Book Club |
| Stock Index | — | — | 9,294 | 1,557 | 522 | 822 | 1,024 | 3,627 | 2,152 | 1,377 |
| Average P/E ratio | — | — | 18.7 | 43.9 | 27.6 | 21.9 | 30.6 | 26.2 | 21.4 | 24.5 |
| ECONOMIC INDICATORS (amounts in US$) | | | | | | | | | | |
| GDP growth, real | 3.6% | — | 5.5% | 5.3% | 7.3% | 8.4% | 8.5% | 4.3% | 10.1% | .. |
| Per-capita GDP (PPP) | 1,206 | 2,413 | 19,446 | 1,198 | 2,891 | 8,694 | 7,992 | 2,440 | 16,647 | 5,665 |
| Savings as a % of GDP | 3.0% | 39.0% | 32.0% | 19.0% | 36.0% | 36.0% | 30.0% | 19.0% | 47.0% | 32.0% |
| Inflation rate | 5.4% | 10.5% | 9.0% | 5.9% | 9.8% | 5.4% | 3.7% | 8.1% | 2.4% | 3.6% |
| Exports for 12 months (in $ billions) | 1.9 | 88.8 | 128.0 | 19.5 | 33.9 | 79.0 | 43.5 | 10.7 | 72.0 | 33.2 |
| SOCIAL INDICATORS | | | | | | | | | | |
| Population (million) | 124.6 | 1,187.2 | 5.9 | 890.8 | 189.5 | 44.2 | 19.0 | 64.6 | 3.1 | 59.2 |
| Population growth rate (%) | 2.7% | 1.4% | 1.0% | 2.1% | 1.8% | 0.9% | 2.6% | 2.3% | 2.0% | 1.5% |
| Literacy rate (%) | 35.3% | 73.3% | 88.1% | 52.1% | 81.5% | 96.0% | 78.5% | 93.5% | 91.0% | 93.0% |
| Infant mortality rate | 105.6 | 30.5 | 6.8 | 80.0 | 56.0 | 10.6 | 12.6 | 42.2 | 5.8 | 36.4 |
| Per-capita calorie intake | 2,021 | 2,639 | 2,853 | 2,229 | 2,750 | 2,852 | 2,774 | 2,375 | 3,198 | 2,316 |

## Information to be Used with Cases Whose Decision Year is 1993

**Top News Stories of 1992:** ASEAN Free Trade Area comes into being; Fidel Ramos wins Philippine presidential elections; UN Conference on Environment and Development opens in Rio de Janeiro; Chris Patten arrives as the 28th Governor of Hong Kong; U.S., Canada, and Mexico agree to establish the North American Free Trade Agreement (NAFTA); China and South Korea establishes diplomatic relations; 14th Chinese Communist Party congress opens with a speech by Jiang Zemin calling for a "socialist market economy"; Kim Young-sam wins South Korean presidential election; India's Ayodhya mosque razed by Hindu militants.

**Summary of Economic and Social Indicators, 1992**

| *Indicators* | *Bangladesh* | *China* | *Hong Kong* | *India* | *Indonesia* | *South Korea* | *Malaysia* | *Philippines* | *Singapore* | *Thailand* |
|---|---|---|---|---|---|---|---|---|---|---|
| BANK RATES | | | | | | | | | | |
| Average prime lending rate (%) | — | — | 6.50% | 18.50% | 24.00% | 10.00% | 9.50% | 23.00% | 5.88% | 13.00% |
| Time deposit rate, 12 mos (% pa) | 10.29% | — | 4.60% | 9.00% | 18.93% | 10.00% | 8.03% | 12.80% | 3.34% | 8.50% |
| CURRENCY EXCHANGE RATE | Taka | Yuan Renmimbi | Dollar | Rupee | Rupiah | Won | Ringgit | Peso | Dollar | Baht |
| Worth of US$1 in foreign currency | 38.95 | 5.51 | 7.74 | 25.92 | 2,029.90 | 780.65 | 2.55 | 25.51 | 1.63 | 25.40 |
| STOCK MARKET INDICES | | | Hang Seng | E Times All-India | JSE Composite | Composite | NST Indl. | Comm. & Indl. | ST Indl. | Book Club |
| Stock Index | — | — | 5,268 | 1,226 | 280 | 623 | 638 | 1,835 | 1,443 | 860 |
| ECONOMIC INDICATORS (amounts in US$) | | | | | | | | | | |
| GDP growth, real | 4.5% | 15.1% | 5.8% | 3.7% | 7.3% | 5.8% | 8.3% | 2.1% | 10.1% | 8.2% |
| Per-capita GDP (PPP) | 208 | 325 | 14,102 | 310 | 605 | 6,489 | 2,475 | 725 | 13,600 | 1,605 |
| Inflation rate | 7.4% | 5.0% | 9.5% | 12.8% | 8.7% | 5.7% | 5.0% | 14.9% | 2.4% | 4.7% |
| Exports for 12 months (in $ billions) | 1.7 | 71.9 | 104.2 | 19.3 | 29.4 | 74.0 | 34.7 | 8.2 | 58.8 | 30.4 |
| SOCIAL INDICATORS | | | | | | | | | | |
| Population (million) | 117.7 | 1,168.7 | 5.8 | 873.0 | 184.7 | 43.6 | 18.1 | 62.7 | 3.1 | 57.7 |
| Population growth rate (%) | 2.7% | 1.4% | 0.9% | 2.1% | 1.8% | 0.9% | 2.6% | 2.3% | 1.1% | 1.4% |
| Literacy rate (%) | 35.3% | 73.3% | 88.1% | 52.1% | 85.0% | 96.0% | 78.5% | 93.5% | 90.7% | 93.0% |
| Infant mortality rate | 108.0 | 31.0 | 7.0 | 82.0 | 58.0 | 11.0 | 13.0 | 44.0 | 6.0 | 37.0 |
| Per-capita calorie intake | 2,019 | 2,727 | 3,144 | 2,395 | 2,753 | 3,285 | 2,889 | 2,257 | 3,114 | 2,434 |

## Information to be Used with Cases Whose Decision Year is 1992

**Top News Stories of 1991:** In Singapore, four Pakistani hijackers seize an airplane and demand the release of a number of prisoners held in Pakistan; Rajiv Gandhi, former Indian Prime Minister, assassinated; Khaleda Zia becomes Bangladesh's first woman Prime Minister; Singapore holds general election; Philippine government announces that the U.S. would be given one year to withdraw its armed forces from the Philippines; North Korea becomes member of the United Nations; A hundred people reported killed by Indonesian forces in East Timor after protests against Indonesian rule; U.S. and Vietnam opens talks intended to lead to the restoration of full diplomatic ties; China agrees to sign the Nuclear Non-Proliferation Treaty.

**Summary of Economic and Social Indicators, 1991**

| *Indicators* | *Bangladesh* | *China* | *Hong Kong* | *India* | *Indonesia* | *South Korea* | *Malaysia* | *Philippines* | *Singapore* | *Thailand* |
|---|---|---|---|---|---|---|---|---|---|---|
| BANK RATES | | | | | | | | | | |
| Average prime lending rate (%) | — | — | 8.50% | 16.50% | 27.00% | 10.00% | 8.95% | 26.00% | 8.00% | 15.25% |
| Time deposit rate, 12 mos (% pa) | 11.88% | — | 7.00% | 9.00% | 22.76% | 10.00% | 7.41% | 15.40% | 5.06% | 10.50% |
| CURRENCY EXCHANGE RATE | Taka | Yuan Renmimbi | Dollar | Rupee | Rupiah | Won | Ringgit | Peso | Dollar | Baht |
| Worth of US$1 in foreign currency | 36.60 | 5.32 | 7.77 | 22.74 | 1,950.30 | 733.35 | 2.75 | 27.48 | 1.73 | 25.52 |
| STOCK MARKET INDICES | | | Hang Seng | E Times All-India | JSE Composite | Composite | NST Indl. | Comm. & Indl. | ST Indl. | Book Club |
| Stock Index | — | — | 4,190 | 897 | .. | 620 | 3,290 | 1,623 | 1,431 | 687 |
| ECONOMIC INDICATORS (amounts in US$) | | | | | | | | | | |
| GDP growth (PPP) | 6.2% | 5.0% | 2.4% | 4.5% | 7.0% | 8.6% | 10.0% | 3.0% | 8.3% | 10.0% |
| Per-capita GDP (PPP) | 179 | 325 | 12,069 | 350 | 555 | 5,569 | 2,305 | 727 | 11,810 | 1,418 |
| Inflation rate | 9.3% | 2.1% | 11.3% | 13.6% | 9.1% | 11.0% | 4.5% | 14.9% | 3.4% | 6.0% |
| Exports for 12 months (in $ billions) | 1.5 | 62.1 | 82.0 | 19.3 | 26.8 | 68.0 | 34.7 | 8.2 | 52.2 | 20.3 |
| SOCIAL INDICATORS | | | | | | | | | | |
| Population (million) | 115.6 | 1,152.5 | 5.7 | 845.7 | 182.0 | 43.2 | 18.1 | 63.0 | 3.0 | 56.3 |
| Population growth rate (%) | 2.7% | 1.4% | 0.9% | 2.1% | 1.8% | 0.9% | 2.3% | 2.3% | 1.1% | 1.4% |
| Literacy rate (%) | 33.1% | 72.6% | 88.1% | 52.1% | 85.0% | 92.7% | 72.6% | 89.8% | 90.1% | 91.0% |
| Infant mortality rate | — | 31.0 | 6.0 | 88.0 | 65.0 | 21.0 | 13.0 | 40.0 | 7.0 | 24.0 |

## Information to be Used with Cases Whose Decision Year is 1991

**Top News Stories of 1990:** Singapore statesman Lee Kuan Yew resigns as Prime Minister; Opposition National League for Democracy wins Myanmar's first multi-party elections in 30 years; Iraqi troops invade and occupy Kuwait; UN peace plan to end civil war in Cambodia; Japanese Emperor Akihito enthroned; Burmese military regime bans the National League for Democracy; Nepal celebrates the end of autocratic rule; Soviet government formally dismissed; Start of civil war in the former Yugoslavia; Asia's first privately funded satellite, AsiaSat 1, is launched.

**Summary of Economic and Social Indicators, 1990**

| *Indicators* | *Bangladesh* | *China* | *Hong Kong* | *India* | *Indonesia* | *South Korea* | *Malaysia* | *Philippines* | *Singapore* | *Thailand* |
|---|---|---|---|---|---|---|---|---|---|---|
| BANK RATES | | | | | | | | | | |
| Average prime lending rate (%) | — | — | 10.00% | 16.50% | 23.50% | 10.00% | 7.50% | 30.00% | 8.00% | 17.00% |
| Time deposit rate, 12 mos (% pa) | 12.13% | — | 8.20% | 9.00% | 18.53% | 10.00% | 6.57% | 17.30% | 5.51% | 13.75% |
| CURRENCY EXCHANGE RATE | Taka | Yuan Renmimbi | Dollar | Rupee | Rupiah | Won | Ringgit | Peso | Dollar | Baht |
| Worth of US$1 in foreign currency | 34.57 | 4.78 | 7.79 | 17.50 | 1,842.80 | 707.76 | 2.70 | 24.31 | 1.81 | 25.59 |
| STOCK MARKET INDICES | | | Hang Seng | E Times All-India | JSE Composite | Composite | NST Indl. | Comm. & Indl. | ST Indl. | Book Club |
| Stock Index | — | — | 3,179 | 591 | .. | 735 | 2,853 | 849 | 1,180 | 632 |
| ECONOMIC INDICATORS (amounts in US$) | | | | | | | | | | |
| GDP growth, real | 6.6% | 5.1% | 3.4% | 4.9% | 7.2% | 9.5% | 9.7% | 3.0% | 8.8% | 11.6% |
| Per-capita GDP (PPP) | 179 | 305 | 10,939 | 320 | 520 | 4,968 | 2,050 | 727 | 10,521 | 1,194 |
| Inflation rate | 8.0% | 4.1% | 10.1% | 10.0% | 6.4% | 9.2% | 2.8% | 12.5% | 3.5% | 5.8% |
| Exports for 12 months (in $ billions) | 1.3 | 57.0 | 73.7 | 16.8 | 21.9 | 63.0 | 24.9 | 7.8 | 45.8 | 20.3 |
| SOCIAL INDICATORS | | | | | | | | | | |
| Population (million) | 110.4 | 1,136.1 | 5.9 | 836.3 | 184.3 | 43.0 | 18.0 | 61.9 | 2.7 | 56.7 |
| Population growth rate (%) | 2.6% | 11.0% | 0.7% | 1.8% | 1.3% | 0.8% | 1.6% | 2.0% | 2.2% | 1.3% |
| Literacy rate (%) | 29.2% | 65.5% | 88.0% | 40.8% | 67.3% | .. | 69.4% | 83.3% | 89.1% | 88.0% |
| Infant mortality rate | 116.2 | 30.3 | 7.0 | 95.4 | 65.6 | 23.5 | 22.6 | 42.7 | 7.0 | 28.8 |
| Per-capita calorie intake | 1,925 | 2,632 | 2,899 | 2,104 | 2,670 | 2,878 | 2,686 | 2,255 | 2,892 | 2,287 |

## Information to be Used with Cases Whose Decision Year is 1990

**Top News Stories of 1989:** Exxon Valdez worst oil spill in U.S. territory; Death of Japanese Emperor Hirohito; Vietnam's withdrawal from Cambodia; 400–800 fatalities and 5,000 injured in Tiananmen Square incident; End of 41-year communist insurgency in Peninsular Malaysia and Thailand; Dismantling of the Berlin Wall and start of breakup of communism in Eastern Europe; U.S. invasion of Panama; U.S. savings and loan crisis; Coup attempt against Philippine President Aquino defeated following U.S. intervention; Myanmar's ruling junta SLORC places Aung San Suu Kyi under house arrest.

**Summary of Economic and Social Indicators, 1989**

| *Indicators* | *Bangladesh* | *China* | *Hong Kong* | *India* | *Indonesia* | *South Korea* | *Malaysia* | *Philippines* | *Singapore* | *Thailand* |
|---|---|---|---|---|---|---|---|---|---|---|
| BANK RATES | | | | | | | | | | |
| Average prime lending rate (%) | — | — | 10.00% | 16.50% | 20.50% | 10.00% | 7.00% | 24.00% | 6.75% | 13.00% |
| Time deposit rate, 12 mos (% pa) | 13.25% | — | 8.00% | 9.00% | 18.58% | 10.00% | 5.08% | 14.50% | 4.42% | 9.88% |
| CURRENCY EXCHANGE RATE | Taka | Yuan Renmimbi | Dollar | Rupee | Rupiah | Won | Ringgit | Peso | Dollar | Baht |
| Worth of US$1 in foreign currency | 32.27 | 3.77 | 7.80 | 16.23 | 1,770.10 | 671.46 | 2.71 | 21.74 | 1.95 | 25.70 |
| STOCK MARKET INDICES | — | — | Hang Seng | E Times All-India | JSE Composite | Composite | NST Indl. | Comm. & Indl. | ST Indl. | Book Club |
| Stock Index | — | — | 2,763 | 407 | .. | 845 | 2,722 | 1,740 | 1,449 | 696 |
| ECONOMIC INDICATORS (amounts in US$) | | | | | | | | | | |
| GDP growth, real | 2.5% | 3.6% | 2.6% | 6.6% | 7.5% | 6.4% | 9.2% | 6.2% | 9.4% | 12.2% |
| Per-capita GDP | 175 | 355 | 9,643 | 320 | 520 | 3,910 | 1,820 | 650 | 9,455 | 995 |
| Inflation rate | 12.0% | 21.4% | 10.1% | 9.1% | 8.0% | 7.1% | 2.4% | 8.1% | 3.6% | 4.0% |
| Exports for 12 months (in $ billions) | 1.1 | 40.1 | 72.9 | 14.0 | 17.2 | 60.9 | 20.1 | 7.6 | 33.0 | 19.9 |
| SOCIAL INDICATORS | | | | | | | | | | |
| Population (million) | 109.6 | 1,110.3 | 5.8 | 817.4 | 177.0 | 42.5 | 17.5 | 60.5 | 2.7 | 55.6 |
| Population growth rate (%) | 2.0% | 1.3% | 1.2% | 2.0% | 2.3% | 1.0% | 2.8% | 2.4% | 1.9% | 1.9% |
| Literacy rate (%) | 29.2% | 65.5% | 88.0% | 40.8% | 67.3% | .. | 69.4% | 83.3% | 88.4% | 88.0% |
| Infant mortality rate | 118.0 | 31.0 | 8.0 | 98.0 | 84.0 | 27.0 | 24.0 | 44.0 | 6.6 | 38.0 |
| Per-capita calorie intake | 2,040 | 2,640 | 2,860 | 2,230 | 2,610 | 2,830 | 2,670 | 2,340 | 3,120 | 2,280 |

## Information to be Used with Cases Whose Decision Year is 1989

**Top News Stories of 1988:** Palestinian Intifada ("cast off the yoke of the past") uprising in the Gaza Strip and the West Bank; Soviet withdrawal from Afghanistan; Iran-Contra Affair indictments; U.S. Navy involvement in Iran-Iraq War; Drastic changes in the USSR's political system; Ceasefire in the Iran-Iraq War; Popularization of the fax machine in business communications; Benazir Bhutto becomes the first woman premier of a Muslim nation; Burma's military crushes pro-democracy demonstrations and seizes power; Toh Tai Woo and Lee Teng-hui are inaugurated presidents of South Korea and Taiwan respectively.

**Summary of Economic and Social Indicators, 1988**

| *Indicators* | *Bangladesh* | *China* | *Hong Kong* | *India* | *Indonesia* | *South Korea* | *Malaysia* | *Philippines* | *Singapore* | *Thailand* |
|---|---|---|---|---|---|---|---|---|---|---|
| BANK RATES | | | | | | | | | | |
| Average prime lending rate (%) | 16.00% | — | 10.00% | 16.50% | 24.50% | 11.00% | 7.25% | 17.00% | 5.96% | 12.50% |
| Time deposit rate 12 mos (% pa) | 13.25% | — | 5.40 | 9.00% | 18.49% | 10.00% | 4.24% | 11.90% | 3.56% | 8.63% |
| CURRENCY EXCHANGE RATE | Taka | Yuan Renmimbi | Dollar | Rupee | Rupiah | Won | Ringgit | Peso | Dollar | Baht |
| Worth of US$1 in foreign currency | 31.73 | 3.72 | 7.81 | 13.92 | 1,685.10 | 731.47 | 2.62 | 21.09 | 2.01 | 25.29 |
| STOCK MARKET INDICES | — | — | Hang Seng | E Times All-India | JSE Composite | Composite | NST Indl. | Comm. & Indl. | ST Indl. | Book Club |
| Stock Index | — | — | 2,666 | 362 | — | 911 | 1,759 | 898 | 1,001 | 339 |
| ECONOMIC INDICATORS (amounts in US$) | | | | | | | | | | |
| GDP growth, real | 2.9% | 11.3% | 8.0% | 9.9% | 5.8% | 11.3% | 8.9% | 6.8% | 11.3% | 13.3% |
| Per-capita GDP (PPP) | 160 | 280 | 8,227 | 270 | 500 | 2,800 | 1,800 | 650 | 7,550 | 881 |
| Inflation rate | 11.4% | 18.2% | 8.1% | 8.8% | 8.0% | 5.5% | 2.5% | 8.8% | 3.6% | 4.3% |
| Exports for 12 months (in $ billions) | 1.1 | 34.1 | 53.3 | 12.1 | 17.2 | 53.7 | 20.3 | 6.8 | 33.0 | 11.9 |
| SOCIAL INDICATORS | | | | | | | | | | |
| Population (million) | 104.5 | 1,086.3 | 5.7 | 812.6 | 174.9 | 42.8 | 16.9 | 58.7 | 2.1 | 54.5 |
| Population growth rate (%) | 1.9% | 1.4% | — | 1.9% | 2.8% | — | 2.4% | 2.4% | 1.5% | 1.8% |
| Literacy rate (%) | — | — | — | — | — | — | — | — | 87.7% | .. |
| Infant mortality rate | 118.0 | 31.0 | 11.0 | 97.0 | 68.0 | 24.0 | 23.0 | 44.0 | 6.9 | 30.0 |
| Calorie supply per capita | 1,925 | 2,632 | — | 2,104 | 2,670 | 2,878 | 2,686 | 2,255 | — | 2,288 |

## Information to be Used with Cases Whose Decision Year is 1988

**Top News Stories of 1987:** Beijing stock market opens; Iran–Contra affair; Oil tankers in Persian Gulf become targets of Iranian and Iraqi missiles and warplanes; Record 508-point drop in the Dow Jones Industrial Average during Black Monday; Michael Gorbachev's policy of *glastnost* ("openness"); U.S.-USSR treaty agreeing to eliminate all medium- and short-range nuclear missiles; Filipinos approve new constitution; Indian troops surround Sikh terrorists and rebels in the Golden Temple in Amritsar; Korean People Power forces Chun Doo Hwan to agree to direct presidential elections.

**Summary of Economic and Social Indicators, 1987**

| *Indicators* | *Bangladesh* | *China* | *Hong Kong* | *India* | *Indonesia* | *South Korea* | *Malaysia* | *Philippines* | *Singapore* | *Thailand* |
|---|---|---|---|---|---|---|---|---|---|---|
| BANK RATES | | | | | | | | | | |
| Average prime lending rate (%) | 16.00% | — | 6.60% | 16.50% | 21.67% | — | 8.19% | 13.34% | 6.10% | 15.00% |
| Time deposit rate, 12 mos (% pa) | 13.25% | — | 4.20% | 8.50% | 17.50% | 10.00% | 4.50% | 10.00% | 3.47% | 7.25% |
| CURRENCY EXCHANGE RATE | Taka | Yuan Renmimbi | Dollar | Rupee | Rupiah | Won | Ringgit | Peso | Dollar | Baht |
| Worth of US$1 in foreign currency | 30.95 | 3.72 | 7.80 | 12.96 | 1,643.80 | 822.57 | 2.52 | 20.57 | 2.11 | 25.72 |
| STOCK MARKET INDICES | | | Hang Seng | E Times All-India | | Composite Index | NST Indl. | Comm. & Indl. | ST Indl. | Book Club |
| Stock Index | — | — | — | 352 | — | — | — | 890 | — | — |
| Average P/E ratio | | — | — | — | — | — | — | — | — | — |
| ECONOMIC INDICATORS (amounts in US$) | | | | | | | | | | |
| GDP growth, real | 4.2% | 10.2% | 13.00% | 4.8% | 4.9% | 11.5% | 5.4% | 4.3% | 8.9% | 9.5% |
| Per-capita GDP, nominal | 170 | 278 | .. | 326 | 445 | — | 1,935 | 600 | 7,648 | 887 |
| Savings as a % of GDP | 3.2% | 36.1% | 33.00% | 19.6% | 32.9% | 36.6% | 37.3% | 17.5% | 40.0% | 24.8% |
| Inflation rate | 9.5% | 8.8% | 5.50% | 11.3% | 9.3% | 3.1% | 0.9% | 3.8% | 0.5% | 2.6% |
| Exports for 12 months (in $ billions) | 1.1 | 39.5 | 48.5 | 11.3 | 17.1 | 47.3 | 17.9 | 5.6 | 28.7 | 11.7 |
| SOCIAL INDICATORS | | | | | | | | | | |
| Population (million) | 102.6 | 1,080.7 | 5.6 | 781.4 | 170.2 | — | 16.5 | 57.4 | 2.6 | 53.6 |
| Population growth rate (%) | 1.9% | 1.4% | .. | 2.0% | 1.9% | — | 2.6% | 2.4% | 0.8% | 1.8% |
| Infant mortality rate | — | 38.0 | 7.0 | 93.0 | 75.0 | — | 17.0 | 53.0 | 8.0 | 40.0 |

## Information to be Used with Cases Whose Decision Year is 1987

**Top News Stories of 1986:** U.S. space shuttle Challenger blows apart 74 seconds after blast-off; People Power Revolution in the Philippines sends Ferdinand Marcos into exile; Benazir Bhutto returns to Pakistan from self-imposed exile in England; Chernobyl nuclear power plant accident; Malaysian parliamentary elections give Mahathir Mohammad's National Front coalition landslide victory; U.S. government revelation of Iran-Contra Affair; OPEC production cutback decision leads to US$18 oil price per barrel; Japan abandons 10-year-old policy of limiting military expenditures to no more than 1% of GNP.

### Summary of Economic and Social Indicators, 1986

| *Indicators* | *Bangladesh* | *China* | *Hong Kong* | *India* | *Indonesia* | *South Korea* | *Malaysia* | *Philippines* | *Singapore* | *Thailand* |
|---|---|---|---|---|---|---|---|---|---|---|
| BANK RATES | | | | | | | | | | |
| Average prime lending rate (%) | 14.00% | — | 7.10% | 16.50% | 21.49% | 10.00% | 10.80% | 17.53% | 6.82% | 17.00% |
| Time deposit rate, 12 mos (% pa) | 14.00% | — | 4.30% | 8.50% | 15.72% | 10.00% | 7.42% | 11.50% | 4.25% | 9.50% |
| CURRENCY EXCHANGE RATE | Taka | Yuan Renmimbi | Dollar | Rupee | Rupiah | Won | Ringgit | Peso | Dollar | Baht |
| Worth of US$1 in foreign currency | 30.41 | 3.45 | 7.80 | 12.61 | 1,282.60 | 881.45 | 2.58 | 20.39 | 2.18 | 26.30 |
| STOCK MARKET INDICES | | | Hang Seng | E Times All-India | | Composite | NST Indl. | Comm. & Indl. | ST Indl. | Book Club |
| Stock Index | — | — | — | 384 | — | 299 | — | 417 | — | — |
| Average P/E ratio | — | — | — | — | — | — | — | — | — | — |
| ECONOMIC INDICATORS (amounts in US$) | | | | | | | | | | |
| GDP growth, real | 4.3% | 7.7% | 10.80% | 4.9% | 5.9% | 11.6% | 1.2% | 3.4% | 4.8% | 5.5% |
| Per-capita GDP, nominal | 151 | 257 | — | 304 | 479 | 2,572 | 1,711 | 549 | 6,777 | 793 |
| Savings as a % of GDP | 3.0% | 34.6% | 28.60% | 18.5% | 27.3% | 34.0% | 32.1% | 16.5% | 39.3% | 21.6% |
| Inflation rate | 11.0% | 7.0% | 2.90% | 8.7% | 5.8% | 2.7% | 0.7% | 0.8% | –1.4% | 1.8% |
| Exports for 12 months (in $ billions) | 0.9 | 31.4 | 35.4 | 9.4 | 16.1 | 34.7 | 13.8 | 4.8 | 22.5 | 8.9 |
| SOCIAL INDICATORS | | | | | | | | | | |
| Population (million) | 100.6 | 1,065.3 | 5.5 | 766.1 | 166.9 | 41.2 | 16.1 | 56.0 | 2.6 | 52.6 |
| Population growth rate (%) | 2.0% | 1.4% | 1.3% | 2.0% | 2.2% | 0.9% | 2.7% | 2.4% | 1.6% | 1.9% |
| Infant mortality rate | 120.0 | 39.0 | 11.0 | 86.0 | 87.0 | 33.0 | 35.0 | 53.0 | 18.0 | 51.0 |

## Information to be Used with Cases Whose Decision Year is 1986

**Top News Stories of 1985:** Ronald Reagan starts second term as U.S. president; East-West relations thaw under new Soviet leader Mikhail Gorbachev; Coca-Cola Company introduces New Coke; TWA Boeing 727 hijacking by Shiite terrorists; A H Robins Company files for bankruptcy as a result of lawsuits arising from harmful effects of the Dalkon Shield; Palestinian terrorists seize Italian cruise ship Achille Lauro; French secret agents sink The Rainbow Warrior in Auckland harbor; Texas jury orders Texaco, Inc to pay US$10.53 billion to Pennzoil Company for interfering in Pennzoil's 1984 takeover deal with Getty Oil Company; Scientists discover a hole in the earth's ozone layer.

Sources: *Asiaweek; The Economist Book of Vital World Statistics: A Complete Guide to the World in Figures* (London: Hutchinson, 1990); *Human Development Report* (London: Oxford University Press, 1994); *International Financial Statistics* (Washington: International Monetary Fund, 1990); *Key Indicators of Developing Asian and Pacific Countries* (Manila: Asian Development Bank, 1995); *Social Indicators of Development* (Baltimore and London: The Johns Hopkins University Press for the World Bank, 1988–) *Whitaker's Almanack* (London: J. Whitaker, 1988–); *World Tables 1995* (Baltimore and London: The Johns Hopkins University Press for the World Bank, 1995).

**Summary of Economic and Social Indicators, 1985**

| *Indicators* | *Bangladesh* | *China* | *Hong Kong* | *India* | *Indonesia* | *South Korea* | *Malaysia* | *Philippines* | *Singapore* | *Thailand* |
|---|---|---|---|---|---|---|---|---|---|---|
| BANK RATES | | | | | | | | | | |
| Average prime lending rate (%) | 12.00% | — | 8.20% | 16.50% | — | 10.00% | 11.54% | 28.61% | 7.93% | 19.00% |
| Time deposit rate, 12 mos (% pa) | 14.00% | — | 4.50% | 8.00% | 18.47% | 10.00% | 9.27% | 19.80% | 5.57% | 13.00% |
| CURRENCY EXCHANGE RATE | Taka | Yuan Renmimbi | Dollar | Rupee | Rupiah | Won | Ringgit | Peso | Dollar | Baht |
| Worth of US$1 in foreign currency | 28.00 | 2.94 | 7.79 | 12.37 | 1,110.60 | 870.02 | 2.48 | 18.61 | 2.20 | 27.16 |
| STOCK MARKET INDICES | | | Hang Seng | E Times All-India | | Composite | NST Indl. | Comm. & Indl. | ST Indl. | Book Club |
| Stock Index | — | — | — | 315 | — | 183 | — | 260 | — | — |
| ECONOMIC INDICATORS (amounts in US$) | | | | | | | | | | |
| GDP growth, real | 4.8% | 12.7% | –0.1% | 6.6% | 2.5% | 6.9% | –1.0% | –4.3% | –1.6% | 3.5% |
| Per-capita GDP, nominal | 151 | 270 | — | 283 | 534 | 2,278 | 1,992 | 602 | 7,595 | 742 |
| Savings as a % of GDP | 2.3% | 33.6% | 27.3% | 21.0% | 29.8% | 30.7% | 32.7% | 16.2% | 40.6% | 20.6% |
| Inflation rate | 10.7% | 11.9% | 3.2% | 5.6% | 4.7% | 2.5% | 0.3% | 23.2% | 0.5% | 2.5% |
| Exports for 12 months (in $ billions) | 1.0 | 27.6 | 30.19 | 9.1 | 18.6 | 30.3 | 15.4 | 4.6 | 22.8 | 7.1 |
| SOCIAL INDICATORS | | | | | | | | | | |
| Population (million) | 98.7 | 1,050.4 | 5.46 | 750.9 | 163.4 | 40.8 | 15.7 | 54.7 | 2.6 | 51.7 |
| Population growth rate (%) | 2.0% | 1.1% | 1.1% | 2.0% | 2.2% | 0.7% | 3.2% | 2.5% | 1.6% | 1.9% |
| Literacy rate, males (%) | 39.7% | 83.1% | — | 54.8% | 77.5% | — | 79.6% | 83.9% | 91.6% | 92.3% |
| Infant mortality rate | 119.0 | 38.0 | — | — | — | — | — | — | — | — |
| Per-capita calorie intake | 1,953 | 2,596 | 2,724 | 2,179 | 2,578 | 2,822 | 2,688 | 2,182 | 2,929 | 2,286 |

# Appendix E
# Researching Strategic Management Topics

The research process, like any process, is one that requires strategic preparation, careful execution, and revision based on feedback from results (not unlike the formulation of a corporate strategic plan).

Although strategic management as a concept dates back to the late 1970s, it has not yet been fully regarded as a true subject heading utilized in indexes and abstracts to literature. Many print indexes still require the researcher to look under "strategic planning" or "corporate planning." However, research in strategic management is currently ubiquitous. A search at UMI Proquest's CD-ROM database *ABI/Inform* listed 5,888 entries under "strategic planning" from January 1994 to March 1995 alone. This list could go on and on; we have not even begun to look at related keywords (e.g., "corporate planning," "competitive advantage," "mission statements," "strategic business units") or Internet resources yet!

If you wish to refine research strategies to manage optimally information retrieval, there are some key strategies to follow. Clearly, the information is available, and it is now a question of focusing on specific subtopics linked with strategic management in order to improve your search results. A researcher may begin within the indexes and abstracts of business literature to look for implementation of strategic management in all possible industry and services areas. Two of the most useful of these indexes/abstracts are *ABI/Inform*, as mentioned previously, and *Business Periodicals Index*, published by Wilson Co. Both are available in CD-ROM format, as well as through on-line access via DIALOG and WILSONLINE. DIALOG offers *One Search* or the capability to search simultaneously many management-oriented databases, such as Management Contents, ABI/Inform,

PAIS International, Harvard Business Review, Delphes European Business, and EIU: Business International. This is a boon to researchers, especially from an international perspective. It is not, however, free of charge. While many libraries will typically hold many CD-ROMs that are generally available to the public, on-line access rarely is, and is usually on a fee-for-service basis. Always consult your local public or academic library professional for the types and costs of resources available.

Many publishers specialize in strategic management and related areas, among them *John Wiley & Sons* (605 Third Ave., New York, NY 10158, U.S.A.; 800-225-5945; http://www.wiley.com) and *Business One Irwin* (1818 Ridge Rd., Homewood, IL 60430, U.S.A.; 800-634-3961; http://www.irwin.com). This list is not inclusive, merely representative of publishers currently producing numerous titles related to strategic management. Catalogs are readily available from publishers so that you can keep abreast of the most recent trends and purchase volumes directly if you so desire.

The Internet is a rich source of information on strategic management. In addition to numerous library on-line catalogs that may be searched for their holdings on strategic management topics, there are specific discussion lists associated with strategic management or management issues in the Asia-Pacific region. One of the best of these is EASTASIA (East Asia Discussion Forum), maintained at the University of South Carolina, U.S.A. Researchers may subscribe using the following standard message to the LISTSERV@UNIVSCVM.SCAROLINA.EDU, with no entry in the subject field, "SUBSCRIBE EASTASIA firstname lastname." Another list is SEASIA-L (Southeast Asia Discussion List), maintained at Michigan State University, U.S.A. Researchers can join this group by sending the message "SUBSCRIBE SEASIA-L firstname lastname" to LISTSERV@MSU.EDU.

In addition, researchers can subscribe to the various Usenet "newsgroups" (discussion groups and news services). For example, the addresses of the newsgroups relating to various Asian countries are as follows:

| | |
|---|---|
| Bangladesh | news:soc.culture.bangladesh |
| Cambodia | news:soc.culture.cambodia |
| China | news:soc.culture.china |
| Hong Kong | news:soc.culture.hongkong |
| India | news:soc.culture.indian |
| Indonesia | news:soc.culture.indonesia |
| Japan | news:soc.culture.japan |
| Korea | news:soc.culture.korean |
| Laos | news:soc.culture.laos |
| Malaysia | news:soc.culture.malaysia |
| Myanmar | news:soc.culture.burma |
| Pakistan | news:soc.culture.pakistan |
| Philippines | news:soc.culture.filipino |
| Singapore | news:soc.culture.singapore |
| Sri Lanka | news:soc.culture.sri-lanka |
| Taiwan | news:soc.culture.taiwan |
| Thailand | news:soc.culture.thai |
| Vietnam | news:soc.culture.vietnamese |

Other pathways on the Internet, either using Gopher Jewels (a subject collection of Internet files) by keyword, or PEG (a peripatetic, eclectic gopher) using Veronica to search the "virtual reference desk," will lead the researcher to files detailing books, articles, projects, and a variety of files on strategic management. The list is seemingly endless, although Internet browsing, or "surfing," often leads the surfer around in circles, and you can find yourself accessing a file today that disappears tomorrow. This will change as the Internet becomes more organized, and is catalogued or indexed by information professionals seeking to make access more efficient. In the meantime, enjoy the ride and expect many technical delays.

Researchers now have a wealth of information available to them. As is often the case, an information professional can be the best guide through the forest to the specific trees that will yield the information the researcher is seeking. Always check with your business or other subject-specialist librarian for the sources that can give you the best results.

Increasingly, Internet tools which greatly aid information seekers have been developed. Most useful is the graphical universe of networked information, the World Wide Web (WWW), and the numerous "browsers" (e.g., Netscape), which have been created to search it. Some of the information sources researchers can freely access on the WWW are the following:

1. **The CIA World Factbook** containing encyclopedic information on various countries. Address: http://www.odci.gov/cia/publications/95fact/index.html
2. **Asia, Inc.** magazine. Address: http://www.asia-inc.com
3. **Wall Street Journal** headlines and top stories. Address: http://www.wsj.com/wallstreet/headlines/topstories
4. **Business Week** magazine. Address: http://www.enews.com/magazines/bw
5. **Business Times, Singapore newspaper**. Address: http://www. asia1.com.sg/biztimes/
6. **Asian stock market closings** updated at the end of each market day by Lippo Securities. Address: http://www.asia-inc.com/lippo/index.html
7. **Currency conversions** for more than 40 countries. Address: http:/www.dna.lth.se/cgi-bin/kurt/rates
8. **U.S. State Department travel warnings** containing travel tips for various countries. Address: http://www.stolaf.edu/network/travel-advisories.html
9. **Government Sources of Business and Economic Information on the Internet** listing hundreds of U.S. government databases accessible through Internet. Address: ftp://una.hh.lib.umich.edu/inetdirsstacks/govdocs:tsangaustin

A more complete listing of Internet resources for the Asian Manager or Business Researcher was featured in the September 1995 issue of *Asia, Inc*, (8/F Kinwick Centre, 32 Hollywood Road Central, Hong Kong, 852-2581-8088) and can be accessed at http://www.asia-inc.com/aid/index.html.

Searchers with access to Netscape, Mosaic, Lynx, or other "browser" interfaces can make direct queries to multiple data collections about their specific areas of interest, retrieving ranked results which can usually be downloaded or printed in a full-text format, often with accompanying graphics. In addition to these search engines, "lists" or "guides" by subject area abound on WWW "Home Pages."